From Coastal Wilderness to Fruited Plain is an account of the making of a large part of the American landscape following European settlement. Drawing upon land survey records and early travelers' accounts, Dr Whitney reconstructs the 'virgin' forests and grasslands of the northeastern and central United States during the presettlement period. He then documents successively the clearance and fragmentation of the region's woodlands, the harvest of the forest and its game, the plowing of prairies, and the draining of wetlands.

The native American, the trapper, the farmer, and the lumberman all benefited from the land and its resources, and the degree to which their activities altered the soil, climate, flora, fauna and water cycles of the region to form the present-day managed agro- and urban ecosystems is evaluated. This well-illustrated and referenced book should be of interest to all those concerned about the sustainability of ecosystems, and the imprint of the past on the contemporary landscape.

FROM COASTAL WILDERNESS TO FRUITED PLAIN

FROM COASTAL WILDERNESS
TO FRUITED PLAIN

A History of Environmental Change in
Temperate North America
1500 to the Present

GORDON G. WHITNEY

CAMBRIDGE
UNIVERSITY PRESS

Published by the Press Syndicate of the University of Cambridge
The Pitt Building, Trumpington Street, Cambridge CB2 1RP
40 West 20th Street, New York, NY 10011-4211, USA
10 Stamford Road, Oakleigh, Melbourne 3166, Australia

© Cambridge University Press 1994

First published 1994

Printed in Great Britain at the University Press, Cambridge

A catalogue record for this book is available from the British Library

Library of Congress cataloguing in publication data

Whitney, Gordon Graham.
From coastal wilderness to fruited plain: a history of environmental change in temperate North
America, 1500 to the present / Gordon G. Whitney.
p.   cm.
Includes bibliographical references (p.   ) and index.
ISBN 0-521-39452-X
1. Landscape changes–United States–History.   2. Man–Influence on nature–United States.
3. Biotic communities–United States–History.   I. Title.
GF503.W53   1994
333.73'13'0973–dc20   93–29701   CIP

ISBN 0 521 39452 X hardback

Contents

Figures

Tables

Acknowledgements

The idea that North America has a cultural history that is worth studying is not a new one. The fact that it also has an interesting ecological history has only recently been discovered. Witness the current spate of articles on the ecological consequences of Columbus' discovery of the New World. I first came to the realization that a detailed study of the northeastern United States might be a worthwhile endeavor when I taught a freshman studies course on 'Man and the Land in America' in 1978. If nothing else, the course convinced me that the ecological ramifications of European settlement of the New World had not been fully explored. Research over the last ten to fifteen years on the consequences has been an enjoyable experience. It has taken me to a wide variety of source materials, a host of institutions and a number of interesting individuals.

Much of the serious work was initiated during a sabbatical leave I spent at Yale in the School of Forestry and Environmental Studies. The Forestry School's periodical and book holdings in the resource sciences are incomparable. They provided a comprehensive background for the study. A year spent at the Harvard Forest as a Bullard Fellow allowed me to initiate the writing. I thank the late John Torrey, David Foster, and the late Ernie Gould for providing a hospitable environment for formulating many of the ideas expressed in the book.

A number of individuals assisted in the production of the book. I am indebted to Joe Miller, the director of Yale's School of Forestry and Environmental Studies library, and Marcia Brightman and Barbara Flye, librarians at the Harvard Forest, for obtaining otherwise inaccessible articles. Monica Mattmuller and Walter Völlenkle translated several German references for me. Andy Baker, Christopher Collier, George Peterken, and Oliver Rackham kindly shared their knowledge of eighteenth and nineteenth century agricultural practices, the history of New England, and English woodland practices respectively. Andy and George reviewed the chapters in their specialties. Barbara Flye, Francis Phillips, and Dorothy Smith typed the tables. William Jordan III, Charlie King, Paul Nelson, George Parker, Tom Siccama, and Ron Vasile provided access to a number of the prints employed in the photographic essay. Marcheterre Fluet duplicated several of the prints. The editorial staff at Cambridge University Press, particularly Karin Fancett and Tracey Sanderson, deserve a note of thanks for their meticulous review of the manuscript.

My graduate advisor F. Herbert Bormann initially piqued my interest in the field of historical ecology. He kindly provided office space during my stay at Yale and alternately chided and encouraged me to complete the project. I owe a special debt of gratitude to my sister Loralyn for reviewing the entire manuscript and suggesting a number of stylistic changes which improved the fluency of the manuscript.

Finally I thank my mother and my late father for their faith and encouragement and their support in a variety of ways throughout the long course of this study. I dedicate the book to them.

Conversion of English to metric units

English	Metric
inch =	2.540 centimeters
foot =	0.3048 meter
pole or rod =	5.0292 meters
chain (surveyor's) =	20.1168 meters
mile =	1.6093 kilometers
acre =	0.4047 hectare
board foot (bd ft) =	0.002359 cubic meter
1000 board feet =	2.3598 cubic meters
cord =	3.624 metric cords or steres
US bushel =	0.352 hectoliter
pound =	0.4536 kilogram
short (US) ton =	0.9072 metric ton

Note: 'Billion' throughout is the American billion (thousand million).

US State abbreviations

Conn.	Connecticut	Mo.	Missouri
Del.	Delaware	N.H.	New Hampshire
Ill.	Illinois	N.J.	New Jersey
Ind.	Indiana	N.Y.	New York
Iowa	Iowa	Ohio	Ohio
Ky.	Kentucky	Pa.	Pennsylvania
Mass.	Massachusetts	R.I.	Rhode Island
Md.	Maryland	Vt.	Vermont
Maine	Maine	Wis.	Wisconsin
Mich.	Michigan	W. Va.	West Virginia
Minn.	Minnesota		

Note: U.P. Mich. is the Upper Peninsula of Michigan; L.P. Mich. is the Lower Peninsula of Michigan, D.C. is the District of Columbia.

Common and scientific names of trees mentioned in the text

Common name[a]	Scientific name[b]
Alder	*Alnus* spp.
Ash, black	*Fraxinus nigra*
blue	*Fraxinus quadrangulata*
prickly	*Zanthoxylum americanum*
white	*Fraxinus americana*
Aspen, bigtooth	*Populus grandidentata*
quaking	*Populus tremuloides*
Basswood, American	*Tilia americana*
Beech, American	*Fagus grandifolia*
Birch, black	*Betula lenta*
gray	*Betula populifolia*
paper (white)	*Betula papyrifera*
yellow	*Betula alleghaniensis*
Blackgum (gum)	*Nyssa sylvatica*
Buckeye	*Aesculus* spp.
Butternut	*Juglans cinerea*
Cedar, Atlantic white	*Chamaecyparis thyoides*
eastern red	*Juniperus virginiana*
northern white	*Thuja occidentalis*
Cherry, black	*Prunus serotina*
choke	*Prunus virginiana*
pin	*Prunus pensylvanica*
sweet	*Prunus avium*
Chestnut, American	*Castanea dentata*
Coffeetree, Kentucky	*Gymnocladus dioicus*
Cottonwood, eastern	*Populus deltoides*
Dogwood, flowering	*Cornus florida*
Elm, American	*Ulmus americana*
red (slippery)	*Ulmus rubra*
Fir, balsam	*Abies balsamea*
Hackberry	*Celtis occidentalis*
Hemlock, eastern	*Tsuga canadensis*

Hickory, bitternut	*Carya cordiformis*
mockernut	*Carya tomentosa*
pignut	*Carya glabra*
shagbark	*Carya ovata*
shellbark	*Carya laciniosa*
Honeylocust	*Gleditsia triacanthos*
Hop hornbeam, eastern	*Ostrya virginiana*
Locust, black	*Robinia pseudoacacia*
Magnolia, cucumber	*Magnolia acuminata*
Maple, red	*Acer rubrum*
silver	*Acer saccharinum*
sugar	*Acer saccharum*
Oak, black	*Quercus velutina*
blackjack	*Quercus marilandica*
bur	*Quercus macrocarpa*
chestnut	*Quercus prinus*
chinquapin	*Quercus muehlenbergii*
northern red (red)	*Quercus rubra*
pin	*Quercus palustris*
post	*Quercus stellata*
scarlet	*Quercus coccinea*
scrub	*Quercus ilicifolia* in states along the East Coast; *Quercus ellipsoidalis* (Hill's oak) or a hybrid complex of oaks containing genes from *Q. coccinea*, *Q. rubra*, and *Q. velutina* in the Upper Midwest
shingle	*Quercus imbricaria*
white	*Quercus alba*
Pawpaw	*Asimina triloba*
Pecan	*Carya illinoensis*
Persimmon	*Diospyros virginiana*
Pine, eastern white	*Pinus strobus*
jack	*Pinus banksiana*
pitch	*Pinus rigida*
red	*Pinus resinosa*
Plum, wild	*Prunus americana*
Poplar	*Populus* spp., name also applied to yellow-poplar (tuliptree) in the South
Sassafras	*Sassafras albidum*

Spruce, black	*Picea mariana*
red	*Picea rubens*
white	*Picea glauca*
Sweetgum	*Liquidambar styraciflua*
Sycamore	*Platanus occidentalis*
Tamarack	*Larix laricina*
Tuliptree	*Liriodendron tulipifera*
Tupelo, black	*Nyssa sylvatica*
Walnut, black	*Juglans nigra*
white	*Juglans cinerea*

[a] Names in parentheses are other common names of species.

[b] Scientific names of trees follow Little (1979).

Photographic essay illustrating the character and the demise of the presettlement vegetation of the Northeast and the Midwest

Plate 1 (opposite) Magnificent stands of old-growth white pine, like those shown in this 1912 photograph of the Cathedral Pines, in Cornwall, Connecticut, were the mainstay of the early lumber industry. George Nichols Collection. Courtesy Yale School of Forestry and Environmental Studies.

Plate 2 (above) Large old-growth white pine and hemlock, Pisgah tract, Ashuelot, New Hampshire, 1915. Ecological studies suggest that many of these large (40 inch diameter) pines date back to a hurricane and fire in the mid-1600s. This stand was destroyed by the hurricane of 1938. Courtesy Harvard Forest.

Plate 3 Old-growth beech–hemlock forest with shrub layer of mountain laurel and hobblebush, North Colebrook, Connecticut, 1912. The Colebrook forest was the last extensive tract of old-growth forest in the state of Connecticut. It was photographed by the well-known Yale ecologist, George Nichols, prior to its cutting in 1912. George Nichols Collection. Courtesy Yale School of Forestry and Environmental Studies.

Plate 4 Virgin hemlock forest with birch in background and hobblebush and mountain laurel in understory, North Colebrook, Connecticut, 1912. George Nichols Collection. Courtesy Yale School of Forestry and Environmental Studies.

Plate 5 Large ($3\frac{1}{2}$ foot diameter) yellow birch, North Colebrook, Connecticut, 1912. George Nichols Collection. Courtesy Yale School of Forestry and Environmental Studies.

Plate 6 Few individuals living today have ever seen mature chestnut in the forest like this 2 foot diameter tree in the North Colebrook tract. The chestnut blight eliminated the chestnut as a canopy species in the 1920s. George Nichols Collection. Courtesy Yale School of Forestry and Environmental Studies.

Plate 7 Red spruce was the dominant species of the spruce–fir forests of the higher elevations of northern New England. Spruce attained a diameter of 28 inches and a height of 95 feet as in the case of this virgin stand of red spruce on the upper slopes of the White Mountains, New Hampshire. Courtesy US Forest Service.

Plate 8 Sugar maple is a characteristic species of the northern hardwoods and beech–maple forest types. It reached its best development in the Upper Great Lakes region as shown in this S. V. Streator photograph of an old-growth sugar maple forest near Petoskey, Michigan. Courtesy Forest History Society.

Plate 9 White oak was a dominant species of the presettlement oak–hickory forests of southern Pennsylvania and the lower Midwest. It was particularly common on the western slopes of the Appalachians as this photograph of the Allegheny Plateau in West Virginia suggests. Leo Klikoff Collection. Courtesy Ohio Biological Survey.

Plate 10 The deep, fertile soils of the lower Wabash River Valley once supported a magnificent hardwood forest. Robert Ridgway, a well-known ornithologist, photographed the forest in the late nineteenth century before it was cleared. Ridgway is shown in this 1875 photograph of a giant sycamore near Mt Carmel, Illinois. The sycamore was 15 feet in diameter, 168 feet high, with a 134 foot spread at the top.
Ridgway Collection. Courtesy Chicago Academy of Sciences Archives.

Plate 11 A diverse assemblage of trees characterized the presettlement forests of the lower Wabash River Valley. This 1888 Ridgway photograph shows a large tuliptree and a beech tree near Vincennes, Indiana. Courtesy Purdue University Archives.

Plate 12 Oak savannas bordered many of the Midwest's tallgrass prairies. Ha Ha Tonka Savanna Natural Area, a restored post oak savanna in Missouri, preserves the character of the early savannas. Courtesy of the Missouri Department of Natural Resources.

Plate 13 Tallgrass prairie, like this late summer photograph of big bluestem in the Avoca Prairie of Wisconsin, once covered much of the Midwest. Courtesy of the University of Wisconsin Arboretum.

Plate 14 The tallgrass prairie contained a number of forbs as well as grasses. The large-leaved forb in this photograph of the restored Henry Greene Prairie at the University of Wisconsin is prairie dock (*Silphium terebinthinaceum*). Courtesy of the University of Wisconsin Arboretum.

Plate 15 The careless cutting of the forests and the attendant fires prompted the rise of the early conservation movement. Conservationists could point to 'areas of desolation' like this burned-over slope in the White Mountains of New Hampshire. Courtesy US Forest Service.

1

Introduction

Both history and ecology may be defined as the study of organisms
in all their relations, living together, the differences between plant,
animal, and human ecology or history being primarily a matter of
emphasis.

J. C. Malin. 1950. 'Ecology and history.'

Ecology becomes a more complex but far more interesting science
when human aspirations are regarded as an integral part of the
landscape.

Rene Dubos. 1980. *The Wooing of Earth.*

Ecology has invariably been defined as the study of the organism and its environment. The reciprocal relationship of the organism and its environment is
expressed in the ecological terms action and reaction. The influence or action
of the environment on the organism and the effects or reaction of the organism
on its environment constitute the focus of ecology (Weaver and Clements
1929). In the economy of nature, one organism looms well above the rest. That
organism, needless to say, is *Homo sapiens.* As the noted ecologist Paul Sears
(1956a) pointed out, man has always been and continues to be 'a part of the
web of life and the living landscape.' Quite predictably, two of the more
important themes in the history of western thought, (1) the influence of the
environment on human culture and (2) man's modification of the earth's surface (Glacken 1967; Goudie 1981), are variants of the organism–environment
or action–reaction concept.

The study of landscapes is a good beginning for the study of man's role in
changing the face of the earth, because 'men must live on and off the land as
the first condition of their survival' (Homans [1941] 1975, 12). Consequently
the landscape reflects the technological innovations, the economic constraints,

1

and the cultural aspirations of its human inhabitants, all of which are superimposed upon its natural features. Like a palimpsest or a surface which has been written on many times after previous inscriptions have been partially erased, it represents a blend of the past and the present, of the human environment and the natural environment. The landscape is a historical document, a cumulative record of man's impact on the natural world (Nash 1970).

The study of landscapes is necessarily a synthetic discipline. Historians, geographers, and ecologists have all at times intentionally or unintentionally stepped within its bounds. Historians have traditionally emphasized the temporal dimensions of the landscape while geographers have commented upon its spatial relationships (Sauer 1938). All have stressed the advantages of a landscape level approach to their respective disciplines (Homans [1941] 1975; Forman and Godron 1986; Williams 1989).

Placing the appropriate emphasis on either side of the organism/environment or society/environment relationship has always been a difficult balancing act. Many historians and geographers initially stressed the degree to which the environment shaped human culture. At its worst, this form of investigation degenerated into a form of environmental determinism. Nature disciplined and shaped society to the point that history became a saga of accommodation to the environment. Notable examples of this school of thought include Frederick Jackson Turner's ([1893] 1961) analysis of the impact of the frontier on America's history and Walter Prescott Webb's (1931) study of technological adaptations to a grassland environment (White 1985).

The realization that society could also significantly alter its environment was relatively slow in coming. Most investigators credit George Perkins Marsh with the idea that man could gain a mastery over the natural world (Olwig 1980). As Marsh noted in a letter describing his seminal work *Man and Nature* 'whereas [others] think that the earth made man, man in fact made the earth' (Lowenthal 1953). Emphasis on the other side of the society/environment equation eventually culminated in today's 'cultural determinism' (Coones 1985; White 1985). Nature became a passive object, a *tabula rasa*, upon which society inscribed its larger goals. The natural landscape gave rise to the cultural landscape. It was humanized to the point it became a collection of artifacts - of houses, fences, and roads – reflecting society's values and material culture (Meinig 1979; Jackson 1984).

There are several dangers inherent in the strictly culturally oriented approach. First, it is inappropriate to lump all landscapes under the same heading. Eastern North America, for instance, contains a continuum of landscapes – ranging from the almost wholy humanized landscape of New York City to the natural or semi-natural landscape of the Adirondacks or the Boundary

Waters Canoe Wilderness Area. Second, human activities can never really be divorced from natural laws and processes (Coones 1985). Natural laws are operative in the more humanized environments. Frequently their action is exacerbated by human activities. Note the high incidence of soil erosion, flood control problems, and the cycling of toxic wastes in urban areas.

Both ecology, the study of the organism's environment or home, and economics, the management of the home, are derived from the same Greek work, 'oikos.' Unfortunately, for many, the similiarity often ends there. As the well-known ecologist Aldo Leopold once noted: 'One of the anomalies of modern ecology is that it is the creation of two groups, each of which seems barely aware of the existence of the other. The one studies the human community almost as if it were a separate entity, and calls its findings sociology, economics, and history. The other studies the plant and animal community, [and] comfortably relegates the hodge-podge of politics to "the liberal arts." The inevitable fusion of these two lines of thought will, perhaps, constitute the outstanding advance of the present century' (Meine 1988, 360). Some of the more recent studies of society/environment relationships highlight the advantages of analyzing natural processes within a cultural context. Stephen Pyne's (1982) history of the use of fire by various cultures in North America and Alfred Crosby, Jr.'s (1972, 1986) review of the exchange of pathogens between the New and the Old World are two of the more notable examples.

Historians and geographers have naturally tended to emphasize the human dimensions of the man-environment relationship (Malin 1950). The recognition that *Homo sapiens* is a major agent of environmental change is a basic tenet of the new field of environmental history (White 1985; Worster 1988). Nineteenth century historians typically extolled the advance of civilization across the American landscape. Humankind improved upon nature as wasteland was transformed into a garden. Contemporary historians have emphasized the more deleterious aspects of the settlement process (Rakestraw 1972). Many post-Earth Day, environmental histories have concentrated almost exclusively on the ecological degradation or the 'destructive exploitation' (Sauer 1938) of the New World's resources (e.g., Worster 1979; Merchant 1989). Where does the reality lie? Most human activities have beneficial as well as deleterious effects. Too great an emphasis on the negative aspects runs the risk of creating a relatively biased view of history. Deciding exactly what is beneficial or deleterious for a given ecosystem alone is a question which requires a great deal of scientific thought. From a more positive viewpoint, the rise of an ecologically oriented history has encouraged a greater awareness of ecological processes (e.g., Cronon 1983; Opie 1983). Historians discussing ecological issues are more likely to define their issues in a sound ecological manner. This may involve offering 'some definition of what healthy ecosystems are and what constitutes their decline' (White 1985).

The great conservationist, Aldo Leopold ([1949] 1968, 205), once called for 'an ecological interpretation of history.' What is really needed, however, is an examination of history from the viewpoint of nature. America's plant and animal communities are as much a product of past events as they are an illustration of contemporary processes. The ecologist who overlooks the past is likely to misinterpret the present (Hamburg and Sanford 1986). European ecologists have made great strides in the field of historical ecology (Rackham 1980; Birks *et al.* 1988; Ellenberg 1988). Part of their success may be due to the fact that they never had the luxury of dealing with an environment unaffected by human activity. Seven thousand years of human history have left an indelible imprint upon the European landscape (Behre 1988). As a result, it is not surprising that the cultural landscape, the landscape formed by years of human activity, is a rather popular topic of research in Europe. Unfortunately American ecologists have been relatively slow to follow the lead of their European counterparts. There are a variety of factors responsible for their reticence. Part of it may be due to an attempt to simplify the complexities of the real world. Classical ecological thought in America has always emphasized the climatic or the edaphic control of the landscape. As the dean of America's plant ecologists, Frederic Clements (1936) once noted 'most ecological studies are carried out in settled regions where disturbance is the ruling process ... In all such instances it is exceedingly difficult or entirely impossible to strike a balance between stability and change, and it becomes imperative to turn to regions much less disturbed by man, where climatic control is still paramount.' Human activities have long represented an aberration which tends to obscure the more important plant/environment relationships. America's plant ecologists have traditionally shown a strong tendency to avoid such messy problems. They have preferred instead 'to study the plant and animal associations of mountaintops and jungles rather than those of dooryards and gardens, to think of plant and animal communities as they must have been in some blissfully innocent era before the advent of man' (Anderson 1956). Ecologists are still interested in minimizing mankind's disturbing influences (Christensen 1989), although they are less likely to do so under the rubric of climatic control.

The historian's reliance on anecdotal and often subjective materials has also discouraged many scientists' entry into the field of historical ecology. Ecology is increasingly a quantitative field of study. Few historical records meet the more rigorous ecologist's demand for quantification or statistically verifiable change. The uncontrolled nature of many 'historical experiments' also makes it difficult to assign causality to a specific factor. The decline of a given species, for instance, may be related to climatic change or it may be due to human pressure or a combination of natural and anthropogenic causes (Brush 1986). Coincidence does not assure causality. Despite the above-mentioned caveats, reliance upon the historical approach has filled in many of the blanks in the scientific record and in the process created a greater awareness of both the rate and the extent of environmental change (Catchpole and Moodie 1978; Hooke and Kain 1982). The recent upsurge of interest in long-term ecological research has only highlighted the value of good historical records extending back over the last 10–300 years.

Over 100 years ago, George Perkins Marsh ([1864] 1965, 13) stated in his pioneering work, *Man and Nature*, '[the reaction of man on nature] has not ... so far as I know, been made [a] matter of special observation, or of historical research by any scientific inquirer.' Marsh's ([1864] 1965, 14–15) contention that there had been little systematic observation on the subject, that the existing data were scattered, and that many of the ideas put forward were largely a matter of speculation is still true today (Williams 1989).

The present study represents an attempt to scientifically assess the character and the extent of the changes occasioned by European colonization of a segment of the North American landscape. By focusing on both the living, e.g., biotic, and the nonliving, e.g., abiotic, features of the landscape, it endeavors to create an integrated picture of the land use history of the northeastern and the midwestern portions of the United States. Man's role as a geomorphological agent of change is emphasized as well as his impact upon the fauna and the flora of the area. Since one's use of the environment is often conditioned by one's perception of the land, the role of the environment in the formation of America's land use patterns is also explored.

From the standpoint of man's interaction with the land, a study of the northeastern quarter of the United States from 1500 to the present offers several distinct advantages. Climatically and culturally the area is a relatively homogeneous entity. A humid to subhumid climate characterizes most of the area (Hunt 1974; Trewartha and Horn 1980). Many of the soils were amenable to the small grain and cattle farming tradition imported from northwestern Europe in the early 1600s (Carrier 1923; Sauer [1976] 1981).

For the Northeast and the Midwest, the time span from 1500 to the present was a period of very rapid and far-reaching change. As the eighteenth century French-born 'American farmer', Crèvecoeur (1925, 141) noted, the Americans had 'done the most in the least time of any people.' Forest clearance, a process which took centuries in western Europe (Darby 1956; Glacken 1967, 290), was condensed to decades in America. The conversion of 'an immense wilderness into a fruited plain' (Dwight [1822] 1969, 4:365) was a unique experience which few of the more discerning observers overlooked. Alexis de Tocqueville ([1835] 1966, 1:291), the French visitor, inquired 'in what part of human history can be found anything similar to what is passing before our eyes in North America?' To the more romantically inclined, it was the collision of a primeval, untouched land with an advanced civilization (Tocqueville [1835] 1966, 1:291), 'a struggle between civilized man and barbarous, uncultivated nature' (Marsh [1848] 1973), in which 'all the resources of European mechanical invention were brought to bear against nature' (Sears [1935] 1959, 66).

Few areas on the earth's surface have experienced as extensive and dramatic a change in their fauna and flora as the mid-latitude forests and grasslands of eastern North America (Haggett 1979, 229–230; Klopatek *et al.* 1979). One English emigrant (Collins [1830] 1971, 35) conveniently summarized the changes as follows: 'the wild animals, in many places, have almost disappeared; and thousands of square miles of prairie, abounding with all kinds of indigenous plants, have been exchanged for cultivated fields.' The later shift from an agrarian society to an industralized, urban-based society in the nineteenth and twentieth centuries only compounded the earlier modifications.

Many of the changes coincided with an increased interest in the sciences and an awareness of man's ability to alter the environment (Glacken 1967, 471–497). The New World represented a vast natural laboratory for testing the prevalent European theories on man's modification of the earth's surface. The effects of clearing, drainage, cropping practices, etc., on the climate, the fertility of the soil, and the health of the inhabitants were only a few of the questions that concerned many of Europe's statesmen and scientists (Chinard 1945; Glacken 1967, 358, 685). Fortunately, for our purposes, the rapid advance of science in the eighteenth and nineteenth centuries made it possible to quantify and document many of the changes. In the eighteenth century, for instance, Linneaus' binomial system of nomenclature replaced the more cumbersome polynomial system of nomenclature. America's flora and fauna could be described on a more scientific basis (Benson 1979). The increased use of thermometers and other scientific instruments (Kincer 1933; Brown 1943; Chinard 1945) also provided a better measure of the change. Naturalists were closer to converting their armchair speculation into hard facts.

If European colonization placed an indelible mark on North America's landscape, the encounter with the New World also altered the colonists' perception of nature. Europe's Romantics may have been the first individuals to extol the virtues of a wilderness environment. It was the more pragmatically minded Americans, however, who set aside large areas of their landscape in the form of parks and forests for the preservation of nature (Nash 1973; Runte 1979; Faegri 1988). Perhaps as Roderick Nash (1970) and others have implied there is a connection 'between where men live and what they think.' The ensuing chapters provide a more detailed exploration of the reciprocal relationship of society and the New World's resources – of the human activities which generated the cultural landscape and the environment which in turn shaped America's perception and use of the land.

2

Reconstructing the past

Trees and stones will teach you that which you can never learn
from masters.

St Bernard of Clairvaux. Cited in Fritts (1976),
Tree Rings and Climate, p. ii.

The basic goal of the historical ecologist is to document the environmental
changes of the past and to determine the factors responsible for their occurrence. Deciphering the available evidence or disentangling the complex web
of natural and anthropogenic forces is not as easy as it might appear initially.
Several cautionary notes are worth emphasizing. (1) Few ecological or environmental issues are of an explicitly qualitative nature. Most involve questions
relating to the frequency of an event or the abundance of a species in the past
and are therefore of a more quantitative nature. The recent debate among ecologists over the Indians' use of fire and its effects on the presettlement forest of
the East is a case in point (Forman and Russell 1983; Myers and Peroni 1983).
Few would disagree with the idea that the Indians occasionally set fires. It's
certainly easy enough to cite isolated accounts of the Indians' use of fires.
Documenting the intentional, systematic, and widespread use of fire by
Indians, however, is a much more formidable task. Resolving the issue
requires a knowledge of both the frequency and the extent of Indian-set fires in
the past. (2) Many environmental changes are rather complex issues which
involve the interaction of a variety of forces. As a result, logical cause and
effect scenarios can be constructed *ad infinitum*. Changes in the climatic
regime occasioned by deforestation were frequent topics of conversation or,
more appropriately, speculation in the eighteenth and nineteenth centuries.
The Vermont historian, Samuel Williams (1794, 57–65), for instance, noted
that clearing exposed the ground to the sun's influence. Clearing also allowed

8

the entry of warm winds (Volney [1804] 1968, 219), hastened snowmelt, and reduced the snow's chilling influences (Holyoke 1793, 69; Watson 1866). The result was a warmer, drier climate. Others argued, with equal justification, that clearing had a cooling effect. Deforestation favored the entry of the colder winds that carried off the 'warm vapours' arising from the ground (Barker 1958, 20). All of the scenarios may have been true to a limited extent. The real issue, however, lies in ascertaining their relative importance in a quantitative manner. (3) The simultaneous occurrence of two events does not necessarily imply a cause and effect relationship. Environmental changes have frequently been attributed to human activities because the two events coincided. Historians (Cronon 1983, 9) have termed this error the *post hoc ergo propter hoc* fallacy, i.e., the after this, because of this, fallacy. One of the more notable examples is the old adage that rainfall follows the plow. At least part of its popularity during the settlement of the Great Plains in the latter half of the nineteenth century was due to a period of above average rainfall (Webb 1931, 375–378; Brown 1948, 488–489). Unfortunately in the case of the rain follows the plow adage, the coincidences were buttressed by a good deal of scientific speculation (Emmons 1971).

'How to' books, outlining the techniques of the historical ecologist are practically nonexistent. Apropos the Old World, the British have produced several excellent guides to analyzing change in the physical (Hooke and Kain 1982) and the biological (Sheail 1980) components of the landscape. North America possesses some of the best documentary evidence of environmental and land use change in the world (Clawson and Stewart 1965, 81). Unfortunately the evidence is spread across a wide variety of printed and manuscript materials and is difficult to locate. Unearthing the appropriate records often involves sifting through a large amount of material of little use. Freidel (1974), Jakle (1980), Grim (1982), Prucha (1987), Stephens (1991), and Trimble and Cooke (1991) have reviewed many of the research aids and source materials available to the historian and the historical geographer. They at least provide a starting point for the historical ecologist, albeit a somewhat diffuse one. The present section represents an attempt to specifically address the above-mentioned problems by (1) reviewing the available source materials in the field of historical ecology and by (2) commenting upon their use and limitations.

Knowing where and how to look for information is probably one of the more important keys to success in the field of historical ecology. The sources fall into two basic categories: printed and manuscript materials and information preserved in the landscape. Table 2.1 outlines the available documentary and field evidence. The sources, of course, differ with respect to their temporal applicability.

Table 2.1. *Sources of information in historical ecology*

A. Documentary evidence
    1. Written materials
        a. travelers' and settlers' accounts
        b. gazetteers
        c. local histories
        d. emigrant guides
        e. legal documents
        f. scientific literature
    2. Graphical materials
        a. maps
        b. photographs
    3. Statistical series
        (land use data bases, census data, climatological data, etc.)
    4. Manuscript materials
        (especially land survey records, farm account books, etc.)
B. Field evidence
    1. Studies of old-growth forests or primary forests
        a. disturbance histories
        b. stand structure
        c. tree form
    2. Archaeological evidence
    3. Pollen analysis and lake sediment studies

A. Documentary evidence

1. Written materials

*Travelers' and settlers' accounts, gazetteers, local histories,
and emigrant guides*

A mastery of the written evidence should precede any ecologist's investigation of past events. Fortunately a number of individuals recorded their impressions of the early American landscape in a variety of printed and manuscript forms. Travelers' narratives, settlers' accounts, emigrant guides, gazetteers, and local histories represent some of the more prominent printed documents. Consult Vail (1949), Hubach (1961), Coad (1972), Freidel (1974), Jakle (1977), Cole (1984), and Downs (1987) for lists and reviews of the more important travel narratives. Freidel (1974) and Bidwell and Falconer ([1925] 1941) also have lists of the major gazetteers and emigrant guides. Each type of document has its strengths and weaknesses. Travel accounts and gazetteers provide a cross-sectional view of the landscapes of the past by focusing on differences from place to place. Settlers' accounts and local histories are more likely to compare the landscapes of the past with the landscapes of the present. The do-it-your-self emigrant guides are particularly valuable because they provide a view of the earliest phases of the settlement process.

The impressions of the early travelers were often tempered by a variety of factors, any one of which could lead to a disparity between reality and the written record (Jakle 1977; Williams 1981; Russell 1983). The worst followed a very conventional and stylized format. References to allegory and classical mythology and pastoral and biblical imagery fill many of the early accounts of New England (Carroll 1973, 25). The best provided a qualitative impression of the landscape.

Biases, of an intentional or an unintentional nature, frequently infected accounts. They deserve at least a cursory treatment because they can distort our perception of the early landscape. Promotional tracts like the relations or voyages of the early seventeenth century inevitably emphasized the more positive aspects of the landscape. Frequent references to mulberries, grapes, sassafras, raspberries, hurtleberries, pot herbs, and strawberries (Brereton [1602] 1906; Pring [1625] 1906; Levett [1628] 1893; Higgeson [1630] 1806) are more a commentary on the agricultural and medicinal commodities in vogue in England in the 1600s than a report of the New World's flora (Carroll 1973, 42–44; Thirsk 1984). The tendency of many early Pilgrim narratives to accentuate the positive likewise limits their utility. Bradford and Winslow's ([1622] 1865) description of Cape Cod – a wooded duneland covered with rich black earth – contrasts dramatically with Captain John Smith's ([1616] 1963) more realistic appraisal of the same area – a headland of high hills of sand, over-growne with shrubbie pines, hurts [*Vaccinium* and *Gaylussacia*], and such trash. Bradford and Winslow's glowing description led at least one historian (Dexter 1865, 10) to conclude that Cape Cod's current 'barrenness and desolation' was due to deforestation. Thoreau more wisely attributed the so-called changes to exaggeration on the part of the Pilgrims. The exaggeration probably reflected the Pilgrims' heartfelt thanks at having reached land. The trees never had been that large nor the soils that deep and fertile (Thoreau 1914, 306–311).

Commercial ventures concerned with the sale of land also spawned their share of overly optimistic reports. Few of the promotional tracts of the eighteenth and nineteenth centuries exceeded the blatant propaganda of the large Midwestern land companies (Dexter 1981). All identified their land in terms of superlatives, each of course possessing the most accessible, the most fertile, and the most salubrious land on the face of the earth. Manasseh Cutler, an eighteenth century clergyman, botanist, and official in the Ohio Land Company, for instance, described the rugged hill country of southeastern Ohio as a land of 'deep rich soil, producing in abundance, wheat, rye, Indian corn, buckwheat, oats, barley, flax, hemp, tobacco, indigo, silk, wine, cotton, and rice.' It was a land of 'innumerable herds of deer, elk, buffalo, and bear' and if it lacked its biblical share of milk and honey, it abounded in wine (from native grapes) and sugar (from sugar maple trees) (Cutler [1787] 1888).

The biases were often of an unintentional nature. Many of the travelers followed major travel routes along rivers, canals, and national roads, and pikes. Their accounts were likely to be biased by what they saw along the way. Caleb Atwater (1838, 87), one of Ohio's early naturalists, commented that a European traveling along the Ohio River might conclude that the state of Ohio was one unbroken forest when, in reality, much of the interior had been cleared.

Descriptions were also influenced by the background, the training, the culture, and the interests of the commentator. Visitors accustomed to the relatively open landscapes of Europe were likely to overestimate the amount of woodland (Dwight [1822] 1969, 4:150–151; Brown 1943, 22). Europeans, on the other hand, were more likely to report what Americans took for granted (Jakle 1977, 17). The British, the Swedes, and the Germans produced some of the best descriptions of the structure or physiognomy of America's early forests, its early agroecosystems, and its ruderal flora. Individuals who made a living from the land, e.g., surveyors, farmers, etc., contributed disproportionately to the more valuable accounts.

With respect to the overall utility of the reports, one must also separate the unique from the ordinary and hearsay from first-hand information (Russell 1983). Many travelers included accounts of the devastation of forests by winds and the destruction of prairies by fire. It is not always clear whether the events were included because they typified the commonplace or because they represented the unique, the exceptional, or to use the appropriate romantic terminology, 'the sublime.' Second-hand information and outright plagiarism, in the case of the emigrant guides, are other problems. Elias Pym Fordham (1906, 70–71), a nineteenth century immigrant from England, criticized many an early writer on the West for going to a tavern keeper, pumping him for information, and then publishing the purposely distorted information. Fordham concluded, 'No dependence can be placed on any representation but that of an intelligent, honest man long resident in the country and who is personally well disposed toward you.' His conclusion should be amended to read 'an intelligent, inquisitive, scientifically literate, honest man.'

Legal documents

Legal documents provide another point of access to the early American landscape. Often legislative enactments mirrored the dominant ecological concerns of the age (Sears 1942). Bounties on wolves and regulations on the cutting of trees and the use of fire on the towns' commons figured prominently in the early colonial records (Kawashima and Tone 1983). Drainage laws, game control legislation, and laws regarding the spread of weeds, pests, and diseases dominated the nineteenth century period while flood control and water conservation legislation fill the records of the twentieth century (Sears 1942). The legacy of many of these legislative enactments is still evident in the forests and parks and flood and water control districts which cover much of eastern North America (Kelly 1974b).

Scientific literature

Ecologists or their forerunners, the early naturalists, contributed relatively little to our understanding of the American landscape until the later part of the eighteenth century. Most were preoccupied with cataloguing the native flora and fauna (Stearns 1970; Greene 1984). By the time the tide of settlement crossed the Appalachians in the period from 1780 to 1820, however, much of the preparatory groundwork, i.e., floras and faunas, had already been lain. Naturalists like Daniel Drake, Samuel P. Hildreth, and Jared Kirtland in Ohio and Increase Lapham in Wisconsin were very cognizant of the ecological changes accompanying settlement and frequently recorded their impressions in the scientific journals of the day. By the 1890s ecology had finally established itself as a formal discipline (Brewer 1960). Ecologists scrambled into the field to record 'the original appearance of the country before the march of civilization ... destroyed primeval conditions' (Harshberger 1911, 1). By the 1920s many ecologists were utilizing quantitative measures of plant abundance in permanently established plots. Their papers are now historical documents and have frequently been used to assess changes in the abundances of various species, e.g., Brewer (1980), Whitney (1984), Barton and Schmelz (1987). Meisel's (1924–1926) *Bibliography of American Natural History: The Pioneer Century, 1769–1865* provides an entrée into the early natural history literature. Compilations of many of the early ecological studies are available for various regions of the study area, e.g., Braun ([1950] 1967) and Nowacki and Trianosky (1993) – the East; Egler (1959) – the Northeast; Heerwagen (1971) – the Midwest; Miller (1932) – Ohio; House (1941–1942) – New York; Darlington (1945) – Michigan; Greene and Curtis (1955) – Wisconsin; Risser (1984) – Illinois; and Roberts and Stuckey (1974) – Ohio. Ecologists interested in documenting the changing flora of the Northeast may find the lists of early local floras cited in Britton (1890) and Day (1899–1900) useful.

Historical ecologists may also wish to consult the applied science literature. Ecology has always had a close working relationship with the more applied disciplines of forestry and agriculture (Egerton 1985). Early agricultural periodicals like the *New England Farmer*, the *Cultivator*, and the *Prairie Farmer* are full of references to the agricultural practices of the past. Most have been reproduced on microfilm for the American Periodical Series. The various nineteenth century state board and department of agriculture reports and the agricultural reports of the US Commissioner of Patents also contain a large number of papers related to agricultural topics of an ecological nature (Edwards 1939). The bibliography section of Bidwell and Falconer's classic ([1925] 1941) *History of Agriculture in the Northern United States, 1620–1860* is still one of the better starting points for an introduction to the agricultural literature. Forestry was rather late in coming to North America. By the twentieth century, however, the US Forest Service was producing a flood of documents and many states had state forestry commissions, which issued annual reports on the status of their forests. Kinch (1983) has very ably reviewed the relevant forestry literature. Bibliographies on the history of agriculture and the history of forestry and conservation in North America can be found in Rehder (1911–1918), Munns (1940), Bowers (1969), Schlebecker (1969), Bowers and Hoehn (1973), Fahl (1977), and Harvey (1979). More recent works are likely to appear in the Agricultural History Society's journal, *Agricultural History*, and the Forest History Society's journal, *Forest and Conservation History*. Historical ecologists may also find abstracting journals like *America: History and Life*, *Forestry Abstracts*, and the *Bibliography of Agriculture* useful.

2. Graphical materials

Maps

Maps are among the more useful forms of information because they allow one to quantify the changing spatial relationships of the landscape, particularly with respect to woodland coverage and vegetation types. In many portions of the United States it is possible to find a series of maps, depicting the extent of woodland coverage from the presettlement period to the present. The plat or township maps of the early federal land surveys have frequently been followed up with the ubiquitous county atlases of the nineteenth century (Stephenson 1967; Conzen 1984), and the county-wide land economic and forest survey inventories of the 1930s and 1940s (Curtis 1959; Mladenoff and Howell 1980; Whitney and Somerlot 1985; Whitney 1987). J. T. Curtis' (1956) early analysis of the changing woodland coverage of Cadiz Township, Green County, Wisconsin, is still one of the classic studies of landscape change in the Midwest. The reader might wish to consult Küchler and McCormick ([1965] 1971), Gordon (1969), Barnett (1979), and Hawes (1933) to determine the areas which have been mapped by vegetation type in Wisconsin, Ohio, Michigan, and Connecticut respectively.

Photographs

Many of the natural plant communities of the East were destroyed well before the advent of daguerreotypes and photographs in the early to middle nineteenth century. As a result, photographs of the changing landscape in the East have not enjoyed the popularity or success they experienced in the West (Gibbens and Heady 1964; Hastings and Turner 1965). Photographs taken at fixed points, however, have documented the effects of deforestation (Voss 1972) , natural plant succession (Cooper 1928; Stephens and Waggoner 1980), urbanization (Trefethen 1976; Vale and Vale 1983), and the cessation of grazing (Dunwiddie 1992).

Aerial photographs, at a scale suitable for identifying major vegetation types (1:20 000), extend back over the past 50 years. Many are stored in the Cartographic Archives Division of the National Archives and Records Service (Taylor and Spurr 1973). They have proven useful in documenting short-term changes in the woody vegetation of small natural areas (Annala, DuBois, and Kapustka 1983; McClain 1983) and in illuminating the changing land use patterns of larger political tracts (MacConnell 1975). The recent development of satellite imagery and geographic information systems has made it easier to process information over larger and larger areas. Iverson and Risser (1987) and Iverson (1988), for instance, have utilized the early federal land survey records, aerial photography, and satellite imagery to compile a record of landscape change in Illinois over the past 160 years.

3. Statistical series

The northeastern United States is particularly rich in long-term land use data bases, most of which have been critically reviewed by Clawson and Stewart (1965). The earliest records are associated with the efforts of the colonies and the states to record the status of the land for tax purposes (Wolcott 1832). Each of the various types of land, e.g., woodland, unimproved, unimprovable, pasture, tillage, upland mowing, and meadow, etc., as in the case of the eighteenth century Massachusetts tax valuation returns, had its own special tax rate. Valuation returns and state census figures formed the basis of much of Raup and Carlson's classic (1941) study of the history of land use in the Harvard Forest. Many of the early colonial or state census returns are available in manuscript form in the appropriate state archives (Massachusetts and New York, for example) or in rare cases have been published (Pruitt 1978).

The Census of the United States is the oldest, continuous source of information on the land use and resource utilization patterns of the past. Although the federal census dates back to 1790, the Sixth Census of 1840 was really the first to collect detailed data on the output of agricultural and forest products on a county by county basis (Defebaugh 1906, 1:489; Bidwell and Falconer [1925] 1941, 467; Williams 1980). The Seventh Census of 1850 represented a radical departure from the earlier census-taking techniques (Lathrop 1948). The creation of manuscript census schedules with their emphasis on the amount of improved and unimproved land, the crops, and the animals of individual farm units permits an even more detailed view of the farm and forest landscape of the nineteenth century (Lathrop 1948; Conzen 1969; Whitney and Somerlot 1985). Many of the manuscript returns for the agricultural schedules for the 1850–1880 censuses are available in state libraries, state archives, and historical societies. Caution should be exercised in the interpretation of the terms 'farms', 'improved land' and 'unimproved land' as their exact definition often differed from one census period to the next (Harper 1918a; Black 1950, 54–65). The normal ten year interval between censuses was shortened to five years with the creation of the first stand-alone Census of Agriculture in 1925. The output of America's forests never received as much attention as the yield of her farms, although there are some figures in the Census of Manufactures. Steer (1948) has summarized much of the information on lumber production on a state by state basis. Charles Sprague Sargent's monumental (1884) *Report on the Forests of North America* in the Tenth Census of the United States contains some of the best information on the use and status of America's forests in the nineteenth century.

Detailed information on the nature and status of America's forests awaited the passage of the McSweeney–McNary Forest Research Act of 1928. The Act authorized periodic reports, usually on a state by state basis, of the nation's timber resources under the Nationwide Forest Service Survey program (Clawson and Stewart 1965, 63). Forest conditions are periodically monitored on a series of fixed- and variable-radius plots (Beltz *et al.* 1992). The updated continuous forest inventories (CFIs) are an excellent source of information on the current composition and areal extent of America's forests (Hahn and Hansen 1985; Whitney 1987). The CFI data, for instance, has been utilized to construct tree species distribution maps, showing the dominance, or growing stock volume, of major tree taxa across the eastern United States on a county by county (Beltz *et al.* 1992) or a contoured basis (Delcourt, Delcourt, and Webb 1984).

Long-term data bases relating to temperature, precipitation, and water flow are critical to understanding the vagaries of climate and its impact on human activities, e.g., agriculture and water supply problems. Colonial diaries contain some of the earliest information on the occurrence of storms, floods, droughts, and killing frosts. Historians have converted these qualitative descriptions of the weather into quantitative data by means of content analysis (Baron 1982). Content analysis has been used to construct long-term growing season, temperature, precipitation and cloud-cover indices for the New England area (Baron and Gordon 1985). Reliable instrumental temperature readings generally extend back to the mid-eighteenth century (Brown 1940; Baron 1989). The early nineteenth century records of US Army Surgeons at various military posts and later the work of the Army's Signal Service represent the first attempt of the federal government to establish a meterological network (Kincer 1941; Baron 1989). Many of these long-term climatological data bases have been published (Miller 1927; Baron *et al.* 1980; Baker, Watson, and Skaggs 1985). Since 1891 the US Weather Bureau and its successor, the National Oceanic and Atmospheric Administration (NOAA), have been responsible for collecting information on the climatic characteristics of the United States (Kincer 1941). NOAA's monthly publication *Climatological Data* is one of the best known and widely used sources of weather information (Haines 1977). Water supply or streamflow records begin in the mid-nineteenth century and have been carried up to the present time by a number of local and state agencies and the US Geological Survey (Benson 1962; Patric and Gould 1976). Changes in precipitation and temperature are often mirrored in variations in the annual growth rings of trees. Tree ring widths provide a proxy measure of climatic change and have extended our shorter instrumentally based chronologies in the East back three centuries (Brubaker and Cook 1983; Blasing and Duvick 1984). Long-term climate chronologies have been constructed to address questions related to the impact of climatic stress on agriculture and out-migration in Maine in the nineteenth century (Smith *et al.* 1981), the occurrence of drought and streamflow patterns in the East over the past two and a half centuries (Cook and Jacoby 1977, 1983), and climatological factors associated with the occurrence of major forest fires in the Great Lakes region (Lorimer and Gough 1988).

4. Manuscript materials

Much of the best information pertaining to the American landscape, particularly that relating to the early land survey records, is still in manuscript form. Determining their exact location, their disposition and their suitability for various projects can be a rather time-consuming process. The Library of Congress' ongoing *National Union Catalog of Manuscript Collections* (NUCMC) is the standard guide to manuscript collections open to researchers in the United States. It describes the holdings of various depositories down to the collection level. Collections are usually identified by family or personal names, e.g., John Greig papers. Indices published at three to five year intervals allow the accessing of the collections by personal names, places, subjects, and historical periods. One can look under the subject heading 'surveying,' for instance, to find papers relating to the early land surveys, e.g., survey notes of the New York Military tract in the John Greig papers collection at Cornell University. There are also several large computerized data bases, like the OCLC (Online Computer Library Center) catalog, which contain information on the manuscript holdings of their member institutions. In a very limited number of cases, manuscript materials have been collated by discipline or subject area. Notable examples include Davis' (1977b) *North American Forest History: A Guide to Archives and Manuscripts in the United States and Canada*, and Lurie's (1953) 'Some manuscript resources in the history of nineteenth century American natural science.'

The National Archives is the official repository of the federal government's records. It maintains a diverse array of materials of interest to the historical ecologist, e.g., public land records, maps and aerial photographs – to name only a few. Evans (1971) and Ehrenberg (1975) provide reviews of its holdings. Manuscripts related to state records, e.g., land survey and census records, are typically stored in state archives, libraries, and historical societies. Many have produced detailed guides and finding aids to their manuscript collections. The guides have been reproduced in microfiche in the *National Inventory of Documentary Sources in the United States* (1983–). Good guides to manuscript records at the county and township level, proprietors' records for instance, are much more difficult to obtain, although the Historical Records Survey of the Works Progress Administration made a start in this direction in the 1930s and 1940s (Freidel 1974, 98).

Land surveys

No discussion of manuscript source materials would be complete without at least a brief review of the early colonial, state, and federal land survey records. North America is one of the few areas on the surface of the earth which possesses detailed land survey records describing the nature of its vegetation prior to major alterations by European settlement (Barber 1976). The use of early land survey records, however, is not without its pitfalls. A brief discussion of their use and limitations follows. Land ownership has always been an integral part of the average American's way of life. Soon after their settlement, the New England colonies mandated the formal recording of land ownership. The earliest land conveyances in New England in the seventeenth century generally noted only the type (pineland, upland, meadow, etc.), the acreage, and the adjoining properties of the land in question (Stilgoe 1976). As a result their utility has been limited to broader generalizations about the vegetation and its relation to the landscape (Whitney and Davis 1986). The next two centuries, however, witnessed the development of survey procedures that were more detailed and sophisticated. The survey procedures have been reviewed by Clewley ([1910] 1976), Stewart (1935), Pattison ([1957] 1970), Ernst ([1958] 1979), Love (1970), Stilgoe (1976), and White (1984).

The metes and bounds surveys which appear increasingly in the colonial records towards the end of the seventeenth century tied the property boundaries to specific features of the landscape. Trees figured prominently in many metes and bounds descriptions as the following 1735 property deed from Scarborough, York County, Massachusetts (now Maine), demonstrates:

... beginning at the Foot of the Gulley below his House and running three hundred and twenty Pole North Five Degrees West to Red Oak marked AB, then running Eighty three Pole East Five Degrees North to a Spruce Tree markd AB then running South three hundred and twenty Pole to a Pitch Pine markd then running Fifty three Poles West and by South which makes up the one hundred & thirty four Acres ...

(Pattison [1957] 1970, 80).

Although there were often governmental pressures to conform to a systematic or rectangular system of survey (Clewley [1910] 1976, 26; Love 1970, 68, 200), the property boundaries in many metes and bounds surveys were often very irregular. This was particularly true of the warrant and patent system of land allotment utilized by Pennsylvania, the southern colonies and the Virginia Military District of southwestern Ohio. Typically the holder of a warrant for a certain acreage of unimproved land specified the area he wanted surveyed (Love 1970). Asymmetric or serpentine shapes in many of the resulting patents or deeds reflected the attempt of the early warrantee to engross the better land (Crowl 1937, 29; Love 1970, 82).

The rectangular system of survey, which prevailed in many of the towns of New England and the townships of western New York late in the eighteenth century (Clewley [1910] 1976, 26), was far superior to the indiscriminate system of survey employed by Pennsylvania and the southern colonies. The rectangular system eventually formed the basis of the federal land survey system mandated by the Ordinance of 1785. Since much of the Midwestern portion of the United States was subdivided according to the principles of the Ordinance of 1785 and its successors, a more detailed description of the federal government's rectangular survey system follows. Public lands typically were divided into six mile square townships composed of thirty-six one mile square lots or sections (Fig. 2.1). Posts were erected at mile and half mile intervals along the survey lines. Neighboring trees were blazed and inscribed with numbers to mark the location

Open Spruce Pine

Sec 6   Sec 5   the River   Sec 4   Sec 3   Sec 2

A 7388   Branch   A 74472   A 72017   A 68842   A 66431

Beaver Pond   Navigable for Canoes   Light sandy

Grass   the

Sec 7   Sec 8   Sec 9   Sec 10   Sec 11

A 630.29

Burnt Land   Open   Marsh

Barren Sandy plain

Sec 18   Sec 17   Sec 16   Sec 15   Sec 14

A 64709   open

Sec 19   Sec 20   Sec 21   Sec 22   Sec 23

A 65783   Cranberry Marsh   Spruce Pine Thicket

Marsh

Some rolling   Aspen Oak Birch and W & Y Pine

Sec 30   Sec 29   Sec 28   Sec 27   Sec 26

A 66733   W & Y Pine   W & Y Pine & Burnt Pine

Indian land Claim

Sec 31   Sec 32   Sec 33   Sec 34   Sec 35

A 66830

Gently rolling good 2nd rate W & Y Pine   Beech & flat

Old Cor   Old Cor   Old Cor

Marsh

By Whom Surveyed.	Date of Contract.	Amount of Surveys			When Surveyed.	When Charged in the Surr Genl's acct	
		M.	Chs	Lks			
... Burt	April 20, 1852	6	03	25	2nd Quar 1852	Ft Rpt 3125	The above
		3	01	00	2nd Quar 1852	do	Principal
... Burt	April 20, 1852	60	60	68	2nd Quar 1852	correct	of the survey
...nk	Nov 14 1836	3	00	00	2nd Quar 1837		Surveyor

Total number of Acres 23481.80

Resurveys finished for prs Genl Land office

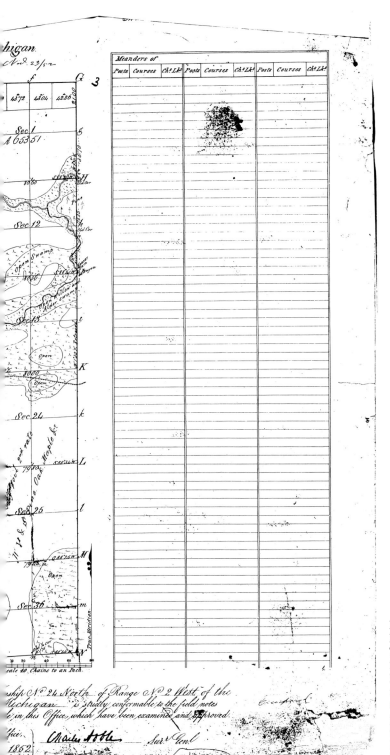

Fig. 2.1 1852 General Land Office plat map of Township 24N, Range 2W, Roscommon County, Michigan. Note reference to vegetation and burnt areas. Stippled areas are predominately wetlands. Courtesy of US Bureau of Land Management, public information.

of the section and the quarter section posts. Data on the species, estimated diameter, compass direction or bearing and distance from the section or quarter section posts to blazed and marked witness trees known as bearing trees were entered in the surveyor's field book. Surveyors also noted trees occurring on the survey line, i.e., station or line trees, and summarized the vegetation (both overstory and understory), the quality of the soil and the occurrence of windstorms on the mile long section lines (Whitney 1986; Hutchison 1988). Detailed township maps or plats showing the location of the survey lines, streams, rivers, ponds, lakes, swamps and prairies accompanied the surveyor's report (Fig. 2.1).

Few people are aware of the wealth of land survey records available to the historical ecologist. In the case of New England some surveys have been published as town or proprietors' records (Jewett 1889; Leach 1958, 276–281) or have appeared in lists of deeds (Richardson *et al.* 1903-1910). Other surveys for New England and the Mid-Atlantic states have been maintained in manuscript form at the appropriate state (state historical society, state archives, state library, secretary of state's office) or local office (town or county clerk's office, note Goodlett 1954; Winer 1955, 99; McIntosh 1962; Siccama 1971; Table 2.2). Record copies of the federal land surveys, better known as the General Land Office (GLO) surveys after 1812, are available on microfilm at the National Archives (for the states of Ohio, Indiana, Illinois, Iowa, and Missouri) and the Bureau of Land Management (for Minnesota, Wisconsin, and Michigan) in Washington, D.C. (Harrison 1954; Pattison 1956; Ronald E. Grim, letter to author, 1981). All of the states in the Midwest also maintain originals or copies of the township plats and the field notes of the federal surveyors for their respective areas (Table 2.2). Although the GLO materials have received the most attention, records of the private land companies are also worth viewing. Occasionally they surpass the GLO records in terms of their quality and their detail (Fig. 2.2).

The uses of the early land surveys are as varied as their sources (Stearns 1974). First and foremost they provide a qualitative and a quantitative picture of the presettlement forest. A number of investigators have used the quantitative information to produce maps of the original vegetation at both the state and the local (county) level (e.g., Kenoyer 1930; Brewer, Hodler, and Raup 1984). Marschner and Perejda's (1946) map of Michigan, Smith's (1954) map of New York, Kucera's (1961) map of Missouri, Lindsey, Crankshaw, and Quadir's (1965) map of Indiana, Gordon's (1966) map of Ohio, Marschner's (1974) map of Minnesota, and Finley's (1976) map of Wisconsin are representative of the larger projects. Our best estimates of the species composition, the size-class structure, and the density of the presettlement forest are based on the GLO records. Because the GLO section and quarter section points are still

Table 2.2. *Sources of early land survey records*

State	Depository	Location
New England		
Maine	Maine State Archives (Land Office)	Augusta
New Hampshire	Secretary of State's Office	Concord
Vermont	Secretary of State's Office[a]	Montpelier
Connecticut, Massachusetts, Rhode Island	The early land survey records for southern New England are dispersed across a wide range of governmental agencies. Try the town records and proprietors' records stored in the town clerks' offices or the state library (Conn.), and the town (Conn., R.I.) and county (Mass.) deed registries	
Mid-Atlantic		
New York	New York State Archives[b], Holland Land Company Manuscript Preservation Project	Albany, State University of New York at Fredonia
New Jersey	Scattered sources, see Russell (1981) and Loeb (1987)	
Pennsylvania	Pennsylvania Historical and Museum Commission (Division of Land Records)[c]	Harrisburg
Midwest		
Ohio[d]	Auditor of State's Office (Land Office)	Columbus
Indiana[d]	Indiana State Library	Indianapolis
Illinois[d]	Illinois State Archives	Springfield
Michigan	Department of Natural Resources (Land Division)	Lansing
Wisconsin	Department of Natural Resources (Division of Trust Lands and Investments)	Madison
Minnesota	Secretary of State's Office	St Paul
Missouri[d]	State Archives	Jefferson City
Iowa[d]	Secretary of State's Office	Des Moines

[a] For a catalog of the holdings, see F.H. Dewart (ed.) 1918. State Papers of Vermont, Vol. 1, Index to the Papers of the Surveyors-General. Rutland, Vt.: Tuttle Company.

[b] For a catalog of the holdings, see D.E. Mix 1859. Catalogue of maps and surveys, in the Office of the Secretary of State, State Engineer and Surveyor and Comptroller and the New York State Library. Albany: C. Van Benthuysen.

[c] A detailed listing of the holdings can be found in Munger (1991).

[d] Copies of the plats and field notes of the General Land Office surveys for the states of Ohio, Indiana, Illinois, Iowa, and Missouri can also be obtained at the National Archives (Washington, D.C.). The plats and field notes of the remainder of the public land states are in the custody of the Bureau of Land Management.

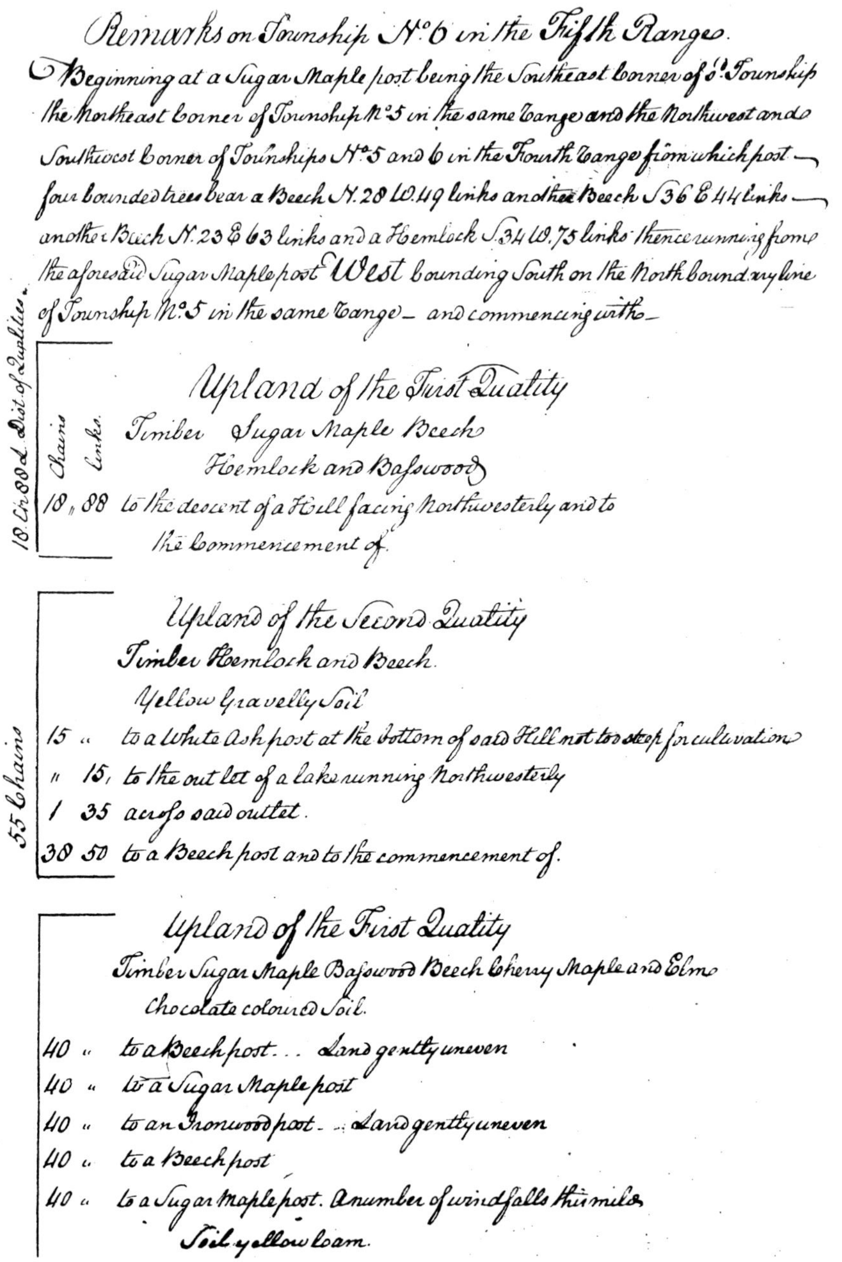

Remarks on Township N.º 6 in the Fifth Range.

*Beginning at a Sugar Maple post being the Southeast corner of s.ᵈ Township the Northeast corner of Township N.º 5 in the same Range and the Northwest and Southwest corner of Townships N.º 5 and 6 in the Fourth Range from which post four bounded trees bear a Beech N. 28 10.119 links and the Beech S 36 E 44 links another Beech N. 23 S 63 links and a Hemlock S. 34 10.75 links thence running from the aforesaid Sugar Maple post WEST bounding South on the North bound ary line of Township N.º 5 in the same Range _ and commencing with_*

Upland of the First Quality

Timber   Sugar Maple Beech
Hemlock and Bassowood

18, 88   to the descent of a Hill facing Northwesterly and to the Commencement of.

Upland of the Second Quality

Timber Hemlock and Beech.
Yellow Gravelly Soil

15	"	to a White Ash post at the bottom of said Hill not too steep for cultivation
"	15,	to the out let of a lake running Northwesterly
1	35	across said outlet.
30	50	to a Beech post and to the commencement of.

Upland of the First Quality

Timber Sugar Maple Bassowood Beech Cherry Maple and Elm
Chocolate coloured Soil.

40	"	to a Beech post … Land gently uneven
40	"	to a Sugar Maple post
40	"	to an Ironwood post … Land gently uneven
40	"	to a Beech post
40	"	to a Sugar Maple post. A number of windfalls this mile.
		Soil yellow loam.

(Left margin annotations: *18 Ch 88 L. Dist. of Qualities.* / *Chains* / *links* / *55 Chains*)

Fig. 2.2 Section of field notes of 1798 survey of Township no. 6 in the Fifth Range, Holland Land Company, western New York. Courtesy of the Holland Land Company Manuscript Preservation Project, State University of New York at Fredonia.

marked on most US Geological Survey topographic maps, it is possible to tie the bearing trees at those points to specific soil associations or physiographic positions, to in effect reestablish vegetation–site conditions in the presettlement forest (Shanks 1953; Lindsey 1961; Crankshaw, Quadir, and Lindsey 1965; Whitney 1982; Whitney and Steiger 1985; Whitney 1986). The GLO records have also been used to determine the incidence and the extent of catastrophic events, i.e., fire and windthrow, in the presettlement forest (Lorimer 1977; Canham and Loucks 1984; Whitney 1986). Shifts in the species composition of the forest have long been a concern to many ecologists. In this sense the early land survey records provide valuable baseline data for documenting change from the presettlement period to the present, e.g., Siccama (1971), Whitney and Somerlot (1985), Whitney (1987).

Use of the land survey records requires discretion. There are a variety of shortcomings or irregularities which can creep into the records and minimize their utility. Some of the more important considerations are as follows:

(1) Fraud. Stewart (1935) and Bourdo (1955, 83) have documented the more flagrant cases of fraud. Most involved the creation of spurious or fictitious records, of the description of lines and corners that never were established. Although the early GLO records should be scrutinized for the occurrence of fraud, it is wise to point out that the more obvious cases of malpractice were corrected with a resurvey of the lines at a later date (Bourdo 1955, 87). The validity of the survey records can be checked by matching the survey's section line descriptions (most contained information on the occurrence of streams and topographic features) against their counterparts on modern US Geological Survey topographic maps. Most are considered reliable (Hutchison 1988).

(2) Date of survey. Much of the Midwestern portion of the United States was surveyed prior to European settlement. As a result the bearing or witness trees recorded in the GLO surveys reflect the nature of the forest prior to widespread European disturbance. Where the two events coincided, i.e., settlement and survey, references to fields, roads, and other cultural features in the surveyors' field notes provide some indication of the degree to which the landscape had already been altered by human activity (Walters and Mansberger 1983). It is more difficult to determine the extent of European influences in the case of the early colonial land surveys. The subdivision and survey of many of New England's townships, for instance, frequently extended over a period of several decades. The opportunity for manipulating the unsurveyed lands certainly existed, although there were stringent regulations against exploiting the town's undivided commons

(Geller 1974). Counts of the number of exotic trees in the record, apple for instance, is one of the more obvious ways of assessing the human impact.

(3) Misidentification of trees in surveys. The uncertain state of the taxonomy and the fact that surveyors were not trained botanists might suggest misidentifications were common in the early surveys. The wide variety of trees employed in many of the surveys, however, indicates a more than passing familiarity with the tree species (Lutz 1930a; Crowl 1937; Winer 1955, 92; McIntosh 1962). Comparisons of the trees reported in the surveys and bearing trees still existing in the Midwest today suggest that the surveyors were accurate in their identifications (Kilburn 1958, 34). The use of common names also complicates the interpretation of the record. Although it is generally easy to determine their Linnean taxonomic equivalents in the federal surveys in the Midwest, the equivalents are not always as apparent in the earlier colonial records. Both Winer (1955, 73–86) and Ogden (1961) have commented upon the imprecise nature of the colloquial names of the colonial period. Many conifers were simply known as pine while hickory fell under the heading of walnut. The frequent use of collective or generic terms like oak, pine, poplar, and maple also limits the utility of the early survey records.

(4) Sampling biases. Often the size of the allotment and thus the sampling intensity varied in the colonial surveys. As a result certain vegetation types are over-represented while others are under-represented. Winer (1955, 96) has even attributed the general lack of interest in metes and bounds surveys 'to their irregular pattern and inconsistent use of trees.' Winer's (1955, 104) study of the proprietors' records of several towns in northwestern Connecticut showed that the proportion of nontree bounds, i.e., stakes and stones, varied significantly from one survey or land division to the next. McIntosh (1962) noted that high elevation sites were under-represented in his study of the survey records of the Catskills. An analysis of the eighteenth century proprietors' records of the town of Petersham, Massachusetts, highlights some of the sampling biases associated with the early colonial surveys (Table 2.3). Surveys associated with roads on the uplands inevitably contain a high proportion of xeric or dry site species (oak, pitch pine, and chestnut) while the fifth division survey, consisting of the leftover wet meadow and swampland, had more than its share of hemlock, tamarack, and spruce. Jeremy Belknap (1813, 3:58) noted dry, level, well-drained pitch pine lands were the preferred sites for roads.

(5) Bias in the selection of trees. Bias in the selection of bearing or witness trees is probably one of the more perplexing issues facing the investigator. Were bearing trees selected on the basis of their relative abundance in the

Table 2.3. *Effect of time and type of survey on trees reported in early metes and bounds surveys of Petersham, Massachusetts. Values represent percentage of total number of trees reported in given survey*

Survey	Species												
	White oak	Black oak	Red oak	Oak	White pine	Pitch pine	Pine	Chestnut	Maple	Black birch	Beech	Hemlock	Other species
1st–4th divisions of land (34 trees) 1733–1753	17	9	7	2	8	2	12	11	8	4	4	5	11
5th division (63 trees) 1770	6	5	–	3	11	2	3	2	13	–	3	29	24
Road surveys (207 trees) 1739–1755	27	13	7	5	6	8	6	12	4	1	1	5	6

Source: Proprietors' Records, Town Clerk's Office, Petersham, Massachusetts.

forest and their proximity to the section and quarter section posts? Or, as some have suggested, were they chosen on the basis of their conspicuous and enduring nature (Grimm 1981, 22–33), their low economic value (Lutz 1930a), or the ease with which they could be inscribed (Bourdo 1955, 89)? The instructions often differed from one surveyor general's office to the next. Some stated that the bearing trees should be 'alive and healthy and not less than 5 inches diameter'. Another noted that the surveyor should select 'those which are the soundest and most thrifty in appearance, and of the size and kinds of trees which experience teaches will be the most permanent and lasting' (Bourdo 1956). The general instructions of 1831 and 1850 stated that the trees chosen should be those nearest the corner (Dodds *et al.* 1943; Bourdo 1955, 120). Several tests have been developed to assess the degree of bias (Bourdo 1956; Hushen *et al.* 1966; Delcourt and Delcourt 1977). All are based on species' comparisons of the mean distances of the corner posts to the bearing trees. Any bias in the selection of bearing trees should result in a lower mean distance for the preferred species as evidenced by the chi-squared test. The test, however, is limited to the more abundant size classes of the more common tree species of a given vegetation type (Bourdo 1956). The dubious underlying assumption that tree species are always randomly distributed in the field has also led some investigators to question the validity of the chi-squared test of the mean distance (Grimm 1984).

Lacking any certified test for bias, many investigators have emphasized the internal consistency of the data, i.e., they have compared one surveyor's results with anothers in the same general area (Crowl 1937, 38–39; Russell 1981) or they have checked their witness tree counts against the written descriptions of the vegetation in books and on the accompanying section line descriptions (Beatley 1959, 67; Siccama 1971; Lorimer 1977; Russell 1981; Whitney 1986). The frequency of citation of the more abundant species has generally paralleled the written descriptions. It is impossible to definitively resolve the issue of bias. Biases may have existed, but it is unlikely that they obscured real differences in the abundances of the more common species (Winer 1955, 109). Bourdo's (1956) conclusion that species preferences were not important 'because the choice of species adjacent to a corner post was limited' is probably the best summary of the bias issue to date.

The early land survey records can only be exploited to their fullest by one who is familiar with their detail and idiosyncrasies (Hutchison 1988). Since surveying regulations varied from one time period or surveying district to the next, it is imperative that the investigator familiarize him or herself with the appropriate instructions for the area and time period in question (Kilburn 1958, 35; Grimm 1981, 6). The regulations issued by the Surveyors General and their respective Deputy Surveyors have been reprinted in White (1984). Inappropriate use of the records has occasionally led to erroneous conclusions. Both Bourdo (1955, 118) and Grimm (1981, 45–46), for instance, have criticized Cottam (1949) and Cottam and Curtis' (1949) use of the GLO records for the determination of the density and the basal area of the presettlement forests. The random pairs method of Cottam and Curtis (1949) assumes that the two bearing trees are adjacent or nearest neighbors when in reality the requirement of adjacency in the GLO instructions refers to the bearing trees and the corner post, not the several bearing trees (Bourdo 1955, 120). Use of the technique consistently underestimates the true density and basal area of the presettlement forest (Bourdo 1955, 120–121; Grimm 1981, 46).

In conclusion, the early land survey records are still our best source of information on the nature of the presettlement forest. The federal land survey notes provide a systematic glimpse of the vegetation prior to European settlement. At their worst they indicate the presence of certain tree species. At their best they 'constitute an unbiased sample of the vegetation as it existed in presettlement times' (Curtis 1959, 64).

B. Field evidence

1. Studies of old-growth forests or primary forests

Roderick Nash's (1970) statement that the landscape is a historical document emphasizes the importance of scientific studies of the landscape. Fortunately ecologists have made great strides in the last ten to thirty years in deciphering the historical records of limited segments of America's landscape, more specifically long-lived woody plant communities. Much of the early work of the twentieth century focused on describing small remnants of America's presettlement plant communities. The work was intended to (1) record the nature of America's primeval forests before they disappeared and to (2) provide information on the processes operative in natural plant communities 'where disturbing influences have been kept to a minimum' (Lutz 1930b). The resulting knowledge could then be applied to the management of natural forest stands (Lutz 1930b). The federal government (Federal Committee on Research Natural Areas 1968; US Department of the Interior, Heritage Conservation and Recreation Service 1980) and various state and public agencies have also issued lists of unique natural areas (note Fig. 2.3). Compilations of studies of these areas can be found in the scientific literature section.

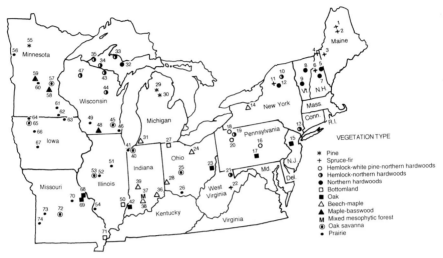

Fig. 2.3 Outstanding natural areas (remnant prairies, savannas, and old-growth forests) of the northeastern and midwestern United States. Key to sites is as follows: 1. Big Reed Pond Preserve, 2. Wassataquoik Lake, 3. Elephant Mountain, 4. Norton Pool, 5. Mt Pond, WMNF, 6. Nancy Brook, WMNF, 7. The Bowl Research Natural Area, WMNF, 8. Lords Hill SNA, 9. Gifford Woods SNA, 10. Ampersand Mountain, Adirondack Park, 11. and 12. Five Ponds Wilderness , Adirondack Park, 13. Mianus River George, 14. Hart's Wood, 15. William L. Hutcheson Memorial Forest, 16. Snyder-Middleswarth NA, 17. Frank Masland State Forest NA, 18. Hearts Content Scenic Area, ANF, 19. Tionesta Scenic and Research Natural Areas, ANF, 20. Cook Forest SP, 21. Cathedral SP, 22. Gaudineer Scenic Area, MNF, 23. Dysart Woods, 24. Crall Woods, 25. W. Pearl King Prairie Grove, 26. Lynx Prairie, 27. Goll Woods SNP, 28. Hueston Woods SNP, 29. Hartwick Pines SP, 30. Roscommon Red Pines NA, 31. Warren Woods NA, 32. Dukes Research Natural Area, HNF, 33. Huron Mountain Club Nature Research Area, 34. Sylvania Recreation Area, ONF, 35. Porcupine Mountains Wilderness SP, 36. Officer's Woods, 37. Donaldson's Woods NP, Spring Mill SP, 38. Pioneer Mothers' Memorial Forest, WNF, 39. Hoot Woods, 40. Woodlake Savanna, 41. Hoosier Prairie NP, 42. Hemmer Woods NP, 43. Bose Lake Research Natural Area, NNF, 44. Jung Hemlock–Beech Forest SSA, 45. Eagle Oak Opening SSA, 46. Chiwaukee Prairie SSA, 47. Flambeau River Hemlock–Hardwood Forest SSA, 48. Abraham's Woods SSA, 49. Avoca River Bottom Prairie SSA, 50. Beall Woods NP, 51. Weston Cemetery Prairie NP, 52. Reavis NP, 53. Sand Prairie–Scrub Oak NP, 54. Fults Hill Prairie NP, 55. Itasca Wilderness Sanctuary, Itasca SP, 56. Bluestem Prairie SNA, 57. Helen Allison Savanna SNA, 58. Wolsfeld Woods SNA, 59. Partch Woods SNA, 60. Roscoe Prairie SNA, 61. Dodge County Prairie SNA, 62. Wild Indigo SNA, 63. Hayden Prairie, 64. Cayler Prairie, 65. Clay County Conservation Board Savanna, 66. Kaslow Prairie, 67. Sheeder Prairie, 68. George A. Hamilton Forest NA, 69. Wegener Woods, 70. Tucker Prairie, 71. Big Oak Tree NA, Big Oak Tree SP, 72. Ha Ha Tonka NA Savanna, Ha Ha Tonka SP, 73. Taberville Prairie NA, 74. Golden Prairie. Abbreviations are as follows: NF = National Forest, e.g., ANF (Allegheny), HNF (Hiawatha), MNF (Monongahela), NNF (Nicolet), ONF (Ottawa), WMNF (White Mountain), WNF (Wayne-Hoosier); NA = Natural Area; NP = Nature Preserve; SNA = State Natural Area (in Vt.), Scientific and Natural Area (in Minn.); SNP = State Nature Preserve; SP = State Park; SSA = State Scientific Area. Sites selected from the National Park Service's Registry of Natural Landmarks, various state nature preserve, natural area, and scientific area directories, and articles in the *Natural Areas Journal*.

Although studies of remnant forest stands have often provided valuable baseline data for resurveys of the same area at a later date, extrapolations from remnant stands to the nature of the 'climatic climax' or the virgin forest is hazardous at best (Davis 1965). To what degree, for instance, were the stands representative of the presettlement forest? In many cases the remnants probably represent a biased sample of the forest communities of the pre-European era. The better sites, i.e., the level bottomlands and stream terraces, were converted to cropland while the forests were confined to the agriculturally marginal sites (Griggs 1914; Shanks 1953; Auclair 1976; Bowen 1981, 19). The scientific and natural areas that were set aside late in the nineteenth century and early in the twentieth century probably fit the conservationist's concept of pristine, old-growth forests (Barnes 1989). They mirrored a romanticized version of the presettlement forest, an uninterrupted expanse of massive, old-growth trees. It would have been difficult to justify the preservation of immature stands like those arising after a natural catastrophe (Lorimer 1985a). Land use practices and management policies, i.e., the elimination of fire, overgrazing by deer, and the introduction of pathogens, have also altered the status of many reserves (Bourdo 1955; Wright 1974; Bowen 1981; Ahlgren and Ahlgren 1984; Barnes 1989). It is difficult to determine to what degree they depart from their pre-European state. Finally the argument can be advanced that the size of most of the reserves is simply too small to encompass the entire range of variability that existed in the presettlement forest. It is impossible to duplicate the mosaic of mature and immature forests and xeric and mesic plant communities that reflected the natural disturbance regime and the site to site variability of the presettlement forest. A few potentially biased samples of old-growth forests do not do justice to the diversity of the presettlement landscape.

Disturbance histories

Few historians are aware of the fact that the forest represents a storehouse of information, a unique repository of past events which have impinged upon the life of the forest. The information comes in a variety of forms, most of which are included under the heading 'reconstructing the forest's disturbance history' (Lorimer 1985a). Although much of the disturbance ecology literature deals with natural disturbances, e.g., fires and windthrows, there is also a growing body of information on the impact of fire, cutting, grazing, and other anthropogenic disturbances on the forest's structure. Fires, both the catastrophic stand-destroying type and the low-intensity surface or ground fire, are among the more important determinants of forest structure. Severe fires have often resulted in the establishment of relatively even-aged stands of shade-intolerant species. By coring trees in even-aged stands and determining their date of origin, Miron Heinselman (1973) was able to compile a series of maps showing the occurrence of fire at various points in time over the past 400 hundred years in the 400 000 hectare (ha) Boundary Waters Canoe Area of northern Minnesota. Heinselman's study demonstrated that European settlement initially increased the incidence of fire. The amount of area burned annually, however, dropped substantially with the implementation of an active fire suppression program in the twentieth century. Surface fires rarely kill the older or the fire resistant trees. They do however leave fire scars on the trunks of the more decay resistant survivors, like red pine. By noting the location of fire scars with respect to the annual growth of the tree or the tree's rings, it is possible to construct a detailed fire chronology of a region (Arno and Sneck 1977). Most of the existing studies again have illustrated the degree to which settlement has altered the natural fire regime (Frissell 1973; Simard and Blank 1982; Henderson and Long 1984).

If charcoal and fire scars are indicative of fires, tip-up mounds and pit/mound topography reflect the occurrence of severe windstorms. Mounds, created by the uprooting of trees, can be dated on the basis of their profile structure, their height, damage to neighboring trees and the age of trees growing upon the mounds (Stephens 1956; Henry and Swan 1974; Oliver and Stephens 1977; Zeide 1981). Disturbances which open up the forest canopy also leave a record of their occurrence in the accelerated growth rate of the surviving trees (Lorimer and Frelich 1989). A number of investigators (Stephens 1955; Henry and Swan 1974; Oliver and Stephens 1977) have combined the study of windthrow mounds with a detailed analysis of living stems, downed stems, and rotting wood fragments, to give us a detailed picture of short-term (200–300 year) forest change. The so-called historical–developmental approach to forest history has been used to determine the response of central New England's forests to natural (Henry and Swan 1974) and anthropogenic (Oliver and Stephens 1977) disturbances. Unfortunately, the very time-consuming nature of the historical–developmental approach limits its utility to rather small plots (<0.5 ha). Species differences in the decomposition of dead wood fragments also introduce a bias as one extends the history further back in time (Henry and Swan 1974; Stephenson 1987).

Stand structure

Counts of the number of stems by size class, i.e., size-class structure or diameter distribution determinations, have often proven useful in deciphering the history of forest stands. Deviations from the theoretically expected inverse J-shaped distribution (Schmelz and Lindsey 1965) or the rotated sigmoid curve (Goff and West 1975) have been attributed to selective logging (Johnson and

Bell 1975), the introduction of pathogens (Leak 1964), grazing (Whitney and Somerlot 1985), coppicing (Russell 1979), and the cessation of surface fires (Johnson and Risser 1975). Due to confusion about the appropriate form of the diameter distribution curve under equilibrium or nondisturbance conditions and the weak relationship of size and age, however, direct age determinations are often preferable to size-class distributions (Lorimer 1985a).

Tree form

The growth form of a tree frequently provides clues as to its origin. Open-grown trees generally have large, spreading crowns which cover most of the stem, while their forest-grown counterparts have narrow crowns which are restricted to the upper part of the stem (Kramer and Kozlowski 1979, 621). Many of the large, spreading, open-grown oaks seen in woods throughout the Northeast and the Midwest today are relics of wooded pastures or open, fire-maintained savannas (Cottam 1949; Whitney and Davis 1986). Frequently a few older, spreading 'wolf' trees will be completely surrounded by forest-grown trees which invaded the area following the cessation of fires or grazing. In the case of conifers, open-growing conditions favor the development of large branches near the base of the stem. Open-grown, old-field white pine can frequently be separated from forest-grown white pine on the basis of branch size (Lutz and McComb 1935) and crown form. 'Cabbage pines' are a characteristic feature of old-field sites throughout the Northeast. The cabbage-like appearance of the pine is due to the high incidence of the white pine weevil in open sites. Weeviling kills the leading shoot and encourages the growth of a number of lateral branches, giving the pine a bushy appearance. The even-aged coppice hardwood stand is another forest form that can be attributed to land use. Stands dominated by multiple-stemmed hardwood sprout clumps usually denote a history of repeated cutting at frequent intervals. Although they are rare today, stands of sprout hardwoods once covered much of southern New England.

2. Archaeological evidence

Although North America does not have a long archeological record relative to European colonization, it does possess a number of relics and artifacts which can provide valuable clues to the past. Much of the information falls under the heading of 'above-ground or landscape archaeology' (Schlereth 1980). Items as simple as a stone wall can be useful in reconstructing the past. In New England thick stone walls were constructed by erecting two parallel rows of large boulders. The intervening trough served as a repository for the stones that were later unearthed in the adjoining cultivated field. Thick stone walls

and the presence of a homogeneous Ap or plow horizon are indicative of land
that was formerly tilled. Narrow walls composed of a single row of boulders,
by way of contrast, mark land that was formerly pastured or grazed (Spurr
1956). Vestiges of former land use patterns also survive in the vegetation of
the region. Exotics like lilacs, false spiraea, daylilies, perwinkle, live-forever,
and lily-of-the-valley mark the location of many an abandoned homestead.
Stone walls and exotics are only a small part of the material culture evidence
of the past (Schlereth 1980; Fogle, Mahan, and Weeks 1987).

3. Pollen analysis and lake sediment studies

The sporadic availability of manuscript materials and published information
often makes it impossible to obtain a continuous record of environmental
change. The pollen and spores preserved in a stratigraphic sequence in sedimentary deposits can fill many of the lacunae in the documentary record. In
Europe, in fact, pollen is the major source of information on human-mediated
change over the last 5000 years (Birks *et al.* 1988; Roberts 1989).

Most of the air-borne pollen produced by plants is destroyed by oxidation
and soil microbes (King, Klippel, and Duffield 1975). Pollen and spores find
their best preservation in anoxic, waterlogged lake sediments, peat deposits,
and soils with low pH values. Mor humus soils are often employed as sample
sites because aggregates of humic material trap the pollen in place and the
acidic nature of the soil discourages subsequent mixing by earthworms
(Bradshaw 1988). Each of the deposits has its assets and liabilities. The pollen
preserved in closed-canopy sites, e.g., small, wet, peat-filled hollows and acid,
mor humus soil profiles, provides a detailed picture of vegetation change at the
stand level. Although a number of investigators have expressed concern about
the differential preservation of pollen and the problem of dating events
(Andersen 1986; Bradshaw 1988), the spatially precise nature of most closed-
canopy site studies argues for their expanded use. Most of the pollen comes
from within 20 to 30 m of the sample site. As a result, hollow and mor humus
studies often pick up (1) phenomena in the immediate vicinity of the soil core,
e.g., changes in forest structure due to localized windthrow or pathogen attack
(Jacobson and Bradshaw 1981) and (2) taxa that are poorly represented in
other pollen studies due to their limited powers of dispersal (Bradshaw 1988).

The analysis of pollen in peats suffers from many of the same problems associated with soils. There is the issue, for instance, of attaching a precise time scale
to events in the pollen record. Chronological control is usually based upon a few
radiocarbon or lead-210 dates or stratigraphic markers, e.g., the ragweed
(*Ambrosia*) rise or the chestnut decline. It is assumed the peat accumulation rates
are constant between the dated intervals. Depending on the climatic regime, peat

can form rapidly, stop growing, and then restart again. The result is an uneven record of peat accumulation and a hiatus in the pollen record (Turner and Peglar 1988). Peat deposits over lake sediments represent a special problem. The pollen record of lakes is often unduly influenced by the water-borne input of pollen from inflowing streams. This may lead to a bias in favor of taxa growing along the edge of the stream, e.g., alder (Birks and Birks 1980, 181–183; Jacobson and Bradshaw 1981). The expansion of peat over the lake basin can block the influx of the stream's pollen, leading to a change in the source area of the pollen and an apparent change in the pollen spectra (Pennington 1979).

Most published pollen studies in North America are based upon sediments from moderate-sized lake basins. They normally collect pollen from within a 20 to 30 km radius of the sample site (Bradshaw 1988). Like peat deposits, lake sediments develop in an orderly fashion. Faunal mixing of the sediments and sediment redeposition during spring and autumn overturns of the lake's water column, however, can blur the lake's stratigraphic sequence (Edwards 1979; Birks and Birks 1980, 183–187). Davis (1974) for instance, demonstrated that benthic fauna can redistribute the pollen vertically up to 15 cm in small lakes. The use of varved or annually laminated sediments circumvents many of the above-mentioned problems. Varved sediments usually result from seasonal variations in the supply of inorganic or organic (diatoms and algae) sediments or changes in the solubility of iron and inorganic carbon (O'Sullivan 1983). Benthic fauna can destroy the varves. Meromictic lakes are lakes that are so deep and sheltered from the wind that their top and bottom waters never mix. Anoxic conditions in meromictic lakes prevent the buildup of a bottom fauna and the attendant destruction of the varves. Varved sediments are ideal for the analysis of pollen because they provide a precise time scale for dating events in the pollen record (Turner and Peglar 1988). Unfortunately lakes with varved sediments are relatively uncommon.

The analysis of short sedimentary cores covering the postsettlement era is a relatively recent development in the field of paleoecology. Our understanding of the pollen record of the historic period awaited a number of methodological refinements. First there was the problem of attaching a precise time scale to events in the pollen record. Radiocarbon analysis (for events occurring more than 200 years ago), lead-210 analysis (for events occurring 10 to 150 years ago), and the use of stratigraphic markers (the chestnut decline) resolved much of the dating problem (Saarnisto 1988). Research into the biological and the physical processes affecting the production and the dispersal of pollen has also enhanced our understanding of the recent pollen record. The pollen percentage values employed in most pollen diagrams cannot be translated directly into plant abundances (Grimm 1988). Species which produce copious quantities of light, wind-dispersed pollen grains, e.g., pine, are over-represented while insect-pollinated species with heavy grains are under-represented, e.g., maple (Prentice 1988). In the case of a few problem species like poplar (*Populus* spp.), poor preservation of the pollen in lake sediments can even create a blind spot in the pollen record (Webb 1974; Schwartz 1989). The pollen source area or the area from which the pollen is derived also varies by species and the spatial distribution of the species about the collecting basin. Jackson (1990), for instance, found that most of the large, poorly dispersed *Tsuga* (hemlock) and *Picea* (spruce) pollen deposited in a series of small ponds in the northeastern United States came from within 500 m of the shore while much of the *Quercus* (oak), *Pinus* (pine) and *Betula* (birch) pollen came from a source more than 1000 m away. A number of equations have been developed to correct the representation biases and convert the pollen percentage values into tree abundances. It should be pointed out, however, that the equations, like the extended R-value method of Prentice, are applicable to a given region, a given time period, and/or a given sized basin. Pollen–tree correction factors based on modern tree and pollen frequency relationships are not always applicable to presettlement conditions (Schwartz 1989). Intensive land use, e.g., coppicing and forest clearance, can complicate the calibration by causing shifts in the representation of different species in a genus or by altering the amount of pollen produced and the size of the area from which the pollen is derived (Prentice 1986; Schwartz 1989).

Our ability to reconstruct the vegetation changes of the last 400 years has also been hampered by a number of other problems. Many pollen types can only be identified to the genus or the family level, e.g., the genus *Quercus* – the oaks. Some of the more important indicators of human activity, the cereals, for instance, are poorly dispersed and thus under-represented in the pollen record. The weeds associated with the cereals are more likely to be represented in the record than the self-fertilizing cereals. This creates difficulties because, unlike Europe (Behre 1981), we have a poor understanding of the indicator significance of many of North America's weedy species. To what degree, for instance, were plantain (*Plantago*), dock (*Rumex*), ragweed (*Ambrosia*), and knotweed (*Polygonum aviculare*) associated with specific crops, habitats, or agricultural practices?

A few isolated pollen studies really cannot do justice to the regional idiosyncrasies of the postsettlement history of the Northeast and the Midwest. Ideally a network of pollen sites judiciously placed across the landscape would provide the best picture of the regional patterns of change accompanying settlement. Unfortunately, the time-consuming nature of most pollen analytical studies has prevented the buildup of a large data base. Webb's (1973) analysis of the modern and presettlement pollen assemblages of 23 short cores distributed throughout the Lower Peninsula of Michigan represents one of the few attempts to place the change in a broader geographic context.

Pollen is not the only source of information on the past preserved in lake sediments. The stratigraphic analysis of lake sediments and their associated charcoal, chemicals, and fossil organisms, especially diatoms and cladocerans, has provided a better picture of many of the environmental changes accompanying settlement. Winter and Wright (1977), Engstrom and Wright (1984), Patterson and Backman (1988), and Mannion (1989), have prepared reviews of the sedimentary record of accelerated erosion and fires following settlement and the more recent history of lake eutrophication and acidification. Patterson and Backman's (1988) analysis of the fire history of the Northeast and the Midwest is particularly instructive in this regard because it shows how several pieces of information, in this case the pollen record and the charcoal record, can be linked together to create a more complete picture of the vegetation changes following settlement (Fig. 2.4).

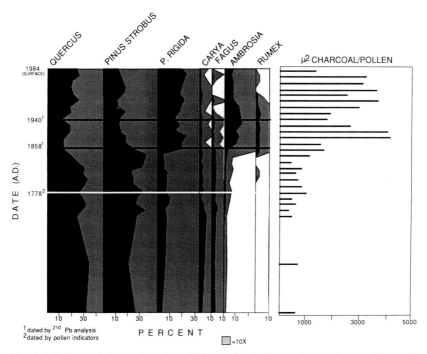

Fig. 2.4 Pollen and charcoal profile of Charge Pond, Carver, Massachusetts. Note fall of white pine (*Pinus strobus*) and rise of pitch pine (*P. rigida*) coincides with increasing incidence of fires and charcoal. (From Patterson and Backman 1988.) Reprinted by permission of Kluwer Academic Publishers.

Summary

The preceding discussion has dwelt at length on the limitations inherent in both the written and the scientific record for analyzing changes in the landscape. Each has its strengths and weaknesses. Weaknesses can be overcome by combining several lines of evidence. The pollen record, for instance, can provide detail that the written record lacks and vice versa. One form of evidence can be checked against another for consistency. The historical ecologist should be willing to bring all the available sources of information to bear on the problem at hand.

Skeptics might argue that the historical ecologist can never attain the degree of certainty required by scientists because of the imperfect or incomplete nature of the record (Christensen 1989). Such an attitude, however, overlooks the fact that the existing landscape is also a product of the past. Omitting a historical perspective in one's interpretation of the present is just as hazardous as reconstructing the past on a limited amount of evidence (Hamburg and Sanford 1986). The ecologist can rarely divorce him or herself from the human dimensions of North America's landscape. As the great American essayist Ralph Waldo Emerson ([1836] 1950) once noted: 'All the facts in natural history, taken by themselves, have no value, but are barren, like a single sex. But marry it to human history, and it is full of life.'

3

Nature imposes ...

The student of natural history is interested in the conditions and forces which determine climate, topography, soils, drainage, and plant covering, together with the dependent fauna; the student of human history is concerned with the progress which man makes under the conditions thus provided by nature. The two interests are often antagonistic but always intimately related, and the history of the one practically begins where that of the other ends.

Bohumil Shimek. 1911. 'The pioneer and the forest.'

In a society which is increasingly divorced from its natural environment, it is easy to overlook the fact that all human actions take place in a physical context. Soil, climate, and relief set limits on human activities and 'modes de vie' (East 1965). As a result, it is salutary to examine the landforms and climatic regimes which have shaped the biota and the human history of the Northeast and the Midwest.

Landforms

Physical geographers (Fenneman 1938) have subdivided the northeastern United States into a series of relatively homogeneous landform units known as physiographic provinces (Fig. 3.1). Recent developments in the fields of plate tectonics and continental drift have increased our understanding of the factors underlying their formation. Although the details are still a matter of debate, the broader picture which emerges is one of a stable continental interior and a marginal area repeatedly subjected to collisions with other land masses and attendant mountain-building episodes. A review of their origin follows.

The Superior Uplands of northern Michigan, Wisconsin, and Minnesota and the Adirondack Mountains of northern New York contain some of the oldest

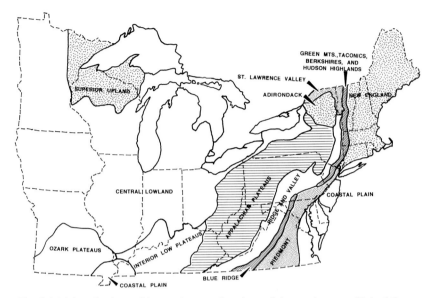

Fig. 3.1 Major physiographic provinces and regions of the northeastern United States. (Modified from Fenneman 1931.)

rocks in North America. Both are southern extensions of the continent's ancient nucleus of crystalline Precambrian rocks known as the Canadian Shield. They represent the beveled roots of ancient mountain systems. The relatively subdued relief of the Superior Uplands reflects the gentle downwarping and upfolding of the earth's crust in that region. Recent updoming of the Precambrian basement rocks has produced the much more rugged terrain of the Adirondacks.

The north–south trending Appalachian Mountains occupy the eastern edge of the North American land mass. They represent a 2500 km fold-and-thrust mountain system. As the term fold-and-thrust implies, the Appalachians are a thick pile of sediments, much of which has been compressed, metamorphosed, faulted, intruded, folded, and crumpled in a complex manner over the last 500 million years (Skinner and Porter 1987, 436). Three major episodes of compression and mountain building – the Taconian, the Acadian, and the Alleghenian – affected the Appalachians. Precambrian igneous and metamorphic rocks form the core of the Blue Ridge Mountains, the New Jersey Highlands, the Hudson Highlands, the Berkshire Mountains, and the Green Mountains. They date to the Taconian Revolution of the early Paleozoic era when collision with a land mass to the east forced blocks of crystalline Precambrian basement rocks to the surface (Raymo and Raymo 1989).

During each phase of mountain-building, the mountains shed sediments to the interior of the continent. Coarse-textured sediments near the base of the mountains graded into clays and lime to the west. Compression and deformation of these sediments during later mountain-building episodes created the anticlines (uparching folds) and synclines (downarching folds) of the Ridge and Valley Province. Erosion left the more resistant strata, chiefly the conglomerates and the sandstones, standing as ridges while the less resistant strata, the limestones, the dolostones, and the claystones, form the valley floors. Intense pressure and deformation also converted the buried plant remains of the deltaic deposits into the high-grade coal of northeastern Pennsylvania's famed anthracite fields.

Lessening pressures left the flat-lying, sedimentary Paleozoic strata of the Appalachian Plateaus to the west intact. The Appalachian Plateaus Province reaches its greatest relief in the Catskill and the Pocono Mountains, exhumed deltaic deposits composed of resistant conglomerates and sandstones which refused to fold. The Allegheny Front, a 500 to 3000 foot escarpment, marks the eastern edge of the province while isolated outliers and promontories of more resistant Mississippian and Pennsylvanian aged rocks, known as 'knobs,' form the western edge of the plateaus in Kentucky and Ohio (Hunt 1974, 262). The Appalachian Plateaus are significant for a variety of reasons. The plateaus and the Adirondacks to the north formed a major barrier to the east–west transport of goods in the early nineteenth century (Billington 1974, 91). The Mississippian, Pennsylvanian, and Permian strata of the plateaus also contain some of the major bituminous coal producing beds of the world.

Current theory suggests the Piedmont and most of New England represent accreted terrane or fragments of continents, islands, or volcanic island arcs, which were welded to the edge of North America by plate movement during the Paleozoic (Raymo and Raymo 1989). Metamorphic rocks, like schist and gneiss, and intrusive igneous rocks, like granite, form most of the bedrock of the Piedmont and the New England states. The more resistant forms of these rocks make up the highest summits of New England, e.g., the White Mountains, Mount Monadnock, and Mount Katahdin (Denny 1982). Pockets of sedimentary rock fill the numerous block-fault basins of New England and the Piedmont. The red Triassic sedimentary rocks of the Connecticut Valley, the Newark Basin, and the Gettysburg Basin date back to a period of crustal stretching approximately 200 million years ago.

The topography of much of the midwestern portion of the United States is relatively subdued. Nearly level to gently undulating Precambrian rocks form the basement of the Central Lowland Province and the Interior Low Plateaus Province. Near Cincinnati the Precambrian basement rises to form a dome or arch. From the exposed Superior Uplands of northern Wisconsin, the Precambrian sinks in southern Illinois and Michigan to form major depositional basins which were innundated by shallow Paleozoic seas. The youngest sediments of these seas, including many coal measures of Mississippian and Pennsylvanian age, are preserved in the centers of the basins while older carbonates of Ordovician and Devonian age frequently outcrop along the edges of the basins. The resistant Silurian-age Niagara Dolomite, for instance, forms the famous Niagara Escarpment which curves around the Door Peninsula in Wisconsin to the Bruce Peninsula in Ontario and eventually to Niagara Falls on the United States – Canadian border. Likewise in the unglaciated Interior Low Plateaus section of southern Indiana, the more resistant Mississippian siltstones and sandstones form uplands and escarpments, juxtaposed against the limestones and shales of the adjacent lowlands (Schneider 1966).

From a chronological point of view, the Coastal Plain Province represents the youngest province in the East. It is composed of Cretaceous and younger sediments deposited on the edge of the crystalline Piedmont and New England's lowlands. Low topographic relief and alternating tracts of marshes and sand hills characterize the coastal plain of Maryland, southern New Jersey, Long Island, and Cape Cod. Some of the best harbors and sheltered anchorages on the east coast are found on the Coastal Plain. North of Cape Cod, the Coastal Plain continues as a series of submerged platforms or banks. The shallow banks support a prolific growth of phytoplankton and tremendous schools of fish (Hunt 1974, 216–217).

Surficial geology

Few events altered the North American landscape as dramatically as the recent ice age. From source areas east and west of Hudson Bay, the Laurentian ice sheet spread south until it covered all of New England, most of New York, northern Pennsylvania, and the Midwest. Generally the lobes of the glacier followed the lines of least resistance, penetrating the low-lying basins of what are currently the Great Lakes and then moving up onto the uplands. In the east their advance was stopped by the more resistant uplands of the Appalachian Plateau (Muller 1963). In the Central Lowlands of the Midwest they penetrated to the 38th parallel and almost reached the Mississippi Embayment of the southern Coastal Plain (Fig. 3.2).

The Laurentide ice sheet left its imprint upon the landscape, creating landforms and soils unique to each region of the Northeast and the Midwest. The following discussion represents a relatively broad-brushed approach to the surficial geology of the region. Glaciers act through their ability to both (1)

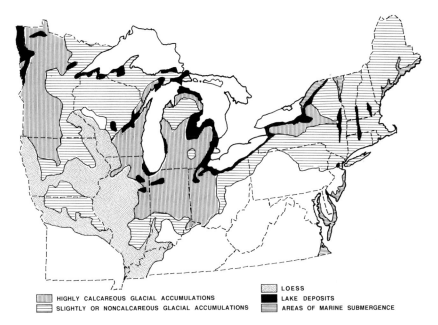

LOESS
HIGHLY CALCAREOUS GLACIAL ACCUMULATIONS   LAKE DEPOSITS
SLIGHTLY OR NONCALCAREOUS GLACIAL ACCUMULATIONS   AREAS OF MARINE SUBMERGENCE

Fig. 3.2 Surficial geology of the northeastern United States, showing the distribution of parent materials of soils. Unshaded regions are areas of consolidated rocks, south of the glacial border. Based on information in Jenny (1941), Goldthwait, White, and Forsyth (1961), Farrand (1982), Hobbs and Goebel (1982), Richmond (1983a, 1983b), Richmond and Fullerton (1984), and Thompson and Borns (1985).

destroy old landforms through erosion and (2) create new landforms through deposition.

The less resistant sedimentary rocks were particularly susceptible to erosion. Many lake basins, from the smaller lakes of northern Minnesota to the Great Lakes, owe their origin to the ice age. The ice, for instance, severely scoured the weak Paleozoic shales underlying the pre-Pleistocene river valleys of what are today Lakes Michigan, Ontario, Huron, and Erie. Hundreds of feet of sedimentary rock sandwiched between more resistant outcrops of basalt were also removed from the Lake Superior trough or syncline (Paull and Paull 1977, 77). In Illinois it has been estimated that an average of 100 feet of sedimentary rock was ground to sand, silt, and clay and redeposited elsewhere (Willman and Frye 1970). On the more resistant crystalline rocks of New England, the movement of the ice streamlined the tops of major obstacles, creating large roches moutonnées with steep, plucked, lee-side slopes.

Although the glaciers sculpted the land through their erosional activities, they are even better known for their depositional landforms. Often this took the form of a thin or discontinuous veneer of sediments or drift. Flint (1930) estimated an average thickness of 1.5 to 3 m for till in Connecticut, while Stewart and MacClintock (1969) cited a value of less than 7 m for Vermont. By way of contrast Willman and Frye (1970) suggested an average thickness of greater than 30 m for Illinois, while Mickelson *et al.* (1983) placed the total thickness of Pleistocene sediments in the Great Lakes region at greater than 50 m. It is not surprising that outcrops of bedrock are extremely common in New England while in the Midwest thick deposits of drift obscure most of the bedrock. Stated differently, bedrock largely controls the topography of New England and the Mid-Atlantic states, while the Midwest is more a depositional landscape.

Large quantities of soil and bedrock were incorporated in the glaciers and then spread over the land as glacial drift. Many of the preglacial valleys of the Midwest were filled, creating the flat till plains of Ohio, Indiana, Illinois, and Iowa. Till refers to poorly sorted, nonstratified drift deposited directly by the ice. The low relief of the till plains is occasionally broken by long, curving, parallel bands of morainal ridges, 15–30 m high. The morainal ridges represent thicker accumulations of till associated with stillstands of the ice margin or glacial readvances. The flowing ice also produced streamlined mounds of glacial till known as drumlins. Due to the finer textured nature of their compact till and consequently their high water-holding capacity, many of southern New England's drumlins mark the location of high-quality pastures and orchards (Millington 1930; Winer 1955, 16).

Till very closely reflects the lithology of the bedrock lying immediately up-ice (Mickelson *et al.* 1983). Tills differ according to their age and source area. Goldthwait, Goldthwait, and Goldthwait (1951) and Goldsmith (1982), for instance, have emphasized the boulder-making character of New England's more resistant crystalline rocks. Outcrops of granite and gneiss produced boulders that ended up in moraines or at the base of slopes beneath ledges. New England's prominent boulder-studded fields prompted one wag to state that stone walls were 'the first and fairest harvest' of many New England soils (Winer 1955, 16). As a general rule, the acidic, crystalline rocks of the Adirondacks and New England yielded tills that were thin, sandy, and gravelly (Mickelson *et al.* 1983).

The less resistant sedimentary rocks of the Central Lowlands were ground into finer textured tills. Sandstone produced sandy tills while fine-grained sandstone and siltstone formed loams (Denny and Lyford 1963). Much of the older Late Wisconsin till south of the Great Lakes in Ohio, Indiana, Illinois, and Pennsylvania has a loamy texture due to its derivation from older glacial deposits and weathered coarse-textured bedrock or regolith. Fine-textured lake sediments were reworked to a clayey till. Tills of the last (Woodfordian) re-advance of the glaciers out of the Lake Erie and southern Lake Michigan basins are typically more clayey (Mickelson *et al.* 1983). The source area of the till also affected the till's nutrient status and the fertility of the soils derived from the till. Tills derived from sandstones and crystalline rocks typically have a low calcium carbonate content while tills from carbonate rocks and Quaternary lake sediments are more calcareous (Denny and Lyford 1963; Mickelson *et al.* 1983; Fig. 3.2). In upstate New York the percentage of carbonate materials incorporated in the till decreases progressively to the south with increasing distance from the mid-Paleozoic carbonate outcrops parallel-ing the southern shore of Lake Ontario (Denny and Lyford 1963).

Much of the drift was sorted by wind and water. On relatively level terrain shifting meltwater streams removed the fine silts and clays from the glacial debris, resulting in the formation of broad aprons of water-washed sands and gravels or outwash plains in front of the ice margin. Meltwater confined to nar-row river valleys often built up coarse-textured outwash deposits known as valley trains. Ice-contact stratified drift deposits are coarse-textured deposits formed in intimate association with the melting ice. They are generally not as well sorted as outwash deposits and often exhibit collapse features where the confining or the supporting ice melted away. Long linear ice-contact features and valley trains are characteristic of the river valleys of New England and the Appalachian Plateau while extensive areas of outwash plains typify the lower relief areas of the Midwest, e.g., the Anoka sand plains of central Minnesota and the Kankakee outwash plain of northern Indiana. Much of Cape Cod, Nantucket, Martha's Vineyard, and Long Island consists of outwash plains, although in this case the plains were formed on the relatively level coastal plain (Flint 1971, 580; Oldale 1982).

Coarse-textured meltwater deposits were particularly common in inter-lobate areas. Glaciers moving out of the Huron–Erie basins and the Michigan basin created the coarse-textured outwash deposits of southwestern Michigan. Ice in the Michigan basin and the Saginaw basin generated a similar area to the north on the High Plains of Michigan's Lower Peninsula (Burgis 1977; Lineback *et al.* 1983).

Wind also reworked the glacial sediments, creating the deep, silt-rich loess deposits of western Indiana, western Illinois, southern Iowa, and northern Missouri (Ruhe 1983). The very cohesive nature of the loess is responsible for the steep slopes of the loess hills of western Iowa and the loess bluffs on the eastern side of the Mississippi and Illinois River Valleys.

Glacial sediments deposited in water, either of a marine or a lacustrine nature, represent another legacy of the ice age. The melting ice released large quantities of water which drowned northern New England's coastline and sent marine waters into Vermont's Champlain basin. The slow rebound of the earth's surface following the removal of the ice eventually spilled the marine waters off the continent's edge (Stewart and MacClintock 1969, 183–184). Many of these areas today are blanketed by marine deposits of silts and clays (Stewart and MacClintock 1969; Thompson 1982).

Lake sediments are even more variable and difficult to interpret than marine sediments. Many of the lakes were temporary proglacial lakes formed when meltwater was trapped between morainal ridges or heights of land and the retreating ice. Others, like glacial Lake Maumee, glacial Lake Chicago, and glacial Lake Whittlesey, were predecessors of the modern Great Lakes. Finer particles were frequently transported into the interior of the lake basins, forming large bodies of silt and clay. Much of the Lake Plains section of northwestern Ohio, for instance, is underlain by very heavy clays laid down by a forerunner of Lake Erie. The clays and the level nature of the terrain impeded drainage and encouraged the buildup of large quantities of organic matter. The high organic content and the calcareous nature of the soils of the Lake Plains section makes this one of the more productive farming areas of the United States today (Noble and Korsok 1975, 52–57). The clay deposits of a number of proglacial lakes were often overlain by coarse-textured deltaic deposits derived from tributary streams. The sand plains of the Connecticut and the Hudson River Valleys for the most part represent deltaic deposits of glacial Lakes Hitchcock and Albany respectively (Jahns and Willard 1942; Dineen 1975). The smaller basins of many proglacial lakes were also frequently filled with coarse-textured deltaic deposits. When the lake shoaled, the finer suspended sediments were swept out of the basin by lake currents. Many of the small sand plains of eastern Massachusetts can be traced to glaciolacustrine sediments deposited in these ephemeral lakes (Stone 1982). Lake currents and wind also reworked the coarser sediments of the lakes, creating coarse-textured strand lines or beach ridges, bars, and sand dunes (Forsyth 1959; Calkin 1969). Notable examples are the sandy beds of proglacial Lake Wisconsin in south-central Wisconsin (Paull and Paull 1977, 105) and the sandy oak openings areas of the Lake Erie basin in northwestern Ohio (Forsyth 1970).

Lakes are a prominent feature of the glaciated sections of North America. Some are glacial, erosion-scoured depressions. Others, known as kettlehole basins, formed when stagnant blocks of ice melted out of outwash plains or moraines. Lakes and swamps have long been associated with the immature topography of recently glaciated areas. Due to the limited amount of time since glaciation, the drainage network of these regions is poorly developed (Paull and Paull 1977, 78).

Time is an important variable in another sense. Many soil-forming processes take long periods of time. Water percolating through the soil slowly removes the carbonates and other nutrients in solution. Across the Midwest the substrate left by the most recent period of glaciation, the Wisconsin, is still relatively fresh and unweathered. South of the glacial border, however, the upland soils have experienced a longer period of weathering. In Illinois the Shelbyville Moraine separates the younger Wisconsin-age drift of northeastern Illinois from the older Illinoian-age drift of southern Illinois. Southern Illinois is a region of heavily weathered clay-pan soils. Over time the finer clay particles of the surface layers have been translocated to the lower levels of the soil where they accumulate to form a clay-pan. The impermeable clay-pan in turn creates a 'perched' water table which restricts the growth of roots. The loss of nutrients and the shallow rooting zone has significantly reduced the productivity of the clay-pan soils. Yields of corn per acre under good farming practices are typically 20 to 40 bushels less on the clay-pan soils of southern Illinois as opposed to the younger, less weathered soils of northeastern Illinois (Fenton 1978a, 100–104).

Climate

Climate has often been viewed as a major determinant of soils and vegetation (Marbut 1935; Clements 1936). It thus sets the ground rules for the development of the flora and the fauna of a given area. Two major climate-related questions were of concern to the early colonists: (1) how did the climate of the New World compare with that of the Old World and (2) what were the regional patterns of climatic variation within the New World.

To interpret the early European colonists' reactions to the New World, one must also develop an understanding or at least an appreciation of northwestern Europe's climatic regime. Climate is largely controlled by air masses – large, relatively homogeneous portions of the earth's atmosphere which remain over an area long enough to acquire the temperature and the humidity of the region. Northwestern Europe is dominated by moist, oceanic or maritime masses of air. The evaporation of large quantities of water from the ocean's surface creates a very humid mass of air while the ocean's ability to store heat over a great depth and water's high specific heat (the large amount of energy required to raise the temperature of the water) moderates any rapid changes in temperature (Trewartha and Horn 1980, 26). Since the ocean warms and cools very slowly, it minimizes the seasonal extremes of temperature. The northerly flow of warm tropical water in the Gulf Stream and the North Atlantic Drift also warms Europe's maritime air masses.

The flow of air in Europe is largely from west to east. During the winter months, the westerly flow of air over the warm waters of the offshore North Atlantic Drift moderates northwestern Europe's temperatures. The eighteenth century Swedish naturalist Peter Kalm (Sauer [1976] 1981, 22–23) summarized the natural consequences of northwestern Europe's mild oceanic winter climate very effectively when he wrote:

The air in England is much softer than in Sweden. Its inhabitants in part have to thank their more southerly position for this; in part they owe it to the sea that is all about them … There are entire winters when [cattle] … are not driven in at all but seek their feed throughout the year in pasture and field. … These farmers know little of the burden of providing feed in winter, such as we experience. … The ground … is so little affected by frost that they plow all winter long. There is scarcely a month in the year in which something is not being planted. … Although snow falls occasionally in winter, it ususaly remains no longer than three days.

Summers are also cool and wet. Prolonged hot spells are rare. Both the mild winter temperatures and the cool, wet summers are congenial to the year-round growth of a number of important cool-season forage grasses and forbs, notably the bluegrasses, the fescues, the bentgrasses, the rye-grasses and several of the true clovers (*Trifolium pratense* and *T. repens*) (Tansley 1953, 488). The same cool, wet summers which encouraged the growth of a number of important forage species and root crops, e.g., turnips and beets, however, were not as favorable to species which required sunnier weather. Wheat, for instance, found its best growth in the drier, sunnier sections of southeastern England (Sauer [1976] 1981, 32). As the American geographer Carl Sauer ([1976] 1981, 39) expressed it, northwesten Europe has a climate 'more favorable to the growth of leaf and stalk than for the ripening of seed.'

Eastern North America, by way of contrast, has a much more continental climate. Compared to water, soil is a very poor conductor of heat. As a result most of the energy absorbed by the earth's surface is concentrated in the upper few feet of the soil. The surface layer warms up rapidly and transfers or reradiates its energy to the atmosphere. Air masses developing over continents are often characterized by extremes of temperature and moisture. During the winter season, eastern North America is often dominated by extremely cold, often dry masses of continental air, which form over north-central Canada. A warmer, more humid mass of air, originating in the Gulf of Mexico, the maritime tropical air mass, prevails in the region during the summer months. The overall effect is to produce a very dramatic seasonal change in temperatures. The changes were often discomfiting to the early European colonists. As Cadwallader Colden (1851) wrote, the weather is much 'colder in Winter than those parts of Europe, which ly under the same parallels of Latitude.' Francis

Higgeson ([1630] 1806) expressed the thoughts of many an early inhabitant of New England when he stated 'In the summer time, in the midst of July and August, it is a good deale hotter than in Old England: And in winter, January and February are much colder.' Eastern North America within the short space of two or three months of time partook of the climate of Sweden, England, and Italy (Collin 1793).

Summer temperatures throughout much of the East approximate those of the tropics. Europeans noted that the higher summer temperatures hastened the ripening and the maturity of smaller grains (Budd [1685] 1966). Long, warm, humid summers also made the region a very productive area for the growth of tropical or subtropical crop species. Many of the annuals domesticated by the American Indians, e.g., corn, beans, squash, and pumpkins, originated in the tropics of the New World. Since most tropical species are susceptible to frost damage (Jenkins 1941), the length of the growing or the frost-free season was an important determinant of the Indian's agricultural patterns (Kroeber 1939; Yarnell 1964). Fortunately all but the more northern or high-altitude areas of the Northeast and the Midwest have a climate suitable for the growth of corn.

It was obvious to the early colonists, accustomed to a mild maritime climate, that the winters were 'both sharper and longer in New England than Old' (Winslow [1624] 1844, 368). New England's winters were also accompanied by 'deep snows and bitter frosts' (Josselyn [1675] 1833, 248). Fortunately the bitter cold was mitigated by an abundant supply of wood (Wood [1634] 1977, 28) which provided 'good living for those that love good fires' (Higgeson [1630] 1806). The problem of providing an adequate supply of fodder for the livestock during the winter was not as easily surmounted (Smith [1631] 1833, 37; Josselyn [1675] 1833, 338). If the summers were hotter and the winters colder, North America did have one obvious advantage over Europe – the air was 'sweet and clear' (Penn [1683] 1912, 226). Only infrequently was New England 'troubled with mists, or unwholesome fog, or cold weather from the sea' (Wood [1634] 1977, 27).

The climate of the Northeast and the Midwest is not as uniform as the cursory discussion above might suggest. There are a number of regional differences related to altitude, proximity to major bodies of water, and other factors. The coastal areas of New England and the Mid-Atlantic states, for instance, have a subcontinental climate. Temperature extremes are not as pronounced as those in the interior. Occasionally maritime polar air masses penetrate the coast from the east, bringing cold, misting rain to the region. Regional climatic effects are also apparent in the areas immediately to the south and east of the Great Lakes. The lakes moderate temperature extremes and warm and humidify the cold polar air masses as they move across the lakes from west to east.

When the air hits the cooler uplands to the south and the east, precipitation results. The growing season immediately adjacent to the lakes is somewhat longer, and locally heavy snowfalls dominate the windward shores of the lakes, creating a snowbelt effect.

Precipitation is another variable which imparts a distinctive regional aspect to the climatic regime. Much of the precipitation of the eastern United States is the result of the interaction of contrasting air masses (cyclonic or frontal precipitation) or the local updraft of warmer, humid air (convectional precipitation). With cyclonic precipitation, the more dense air of the continental polar air mass forces the warm, moist air of the maritime tropical air mass aloft or the warm air overrides the cooler air. In either case the warm air is cooled as it rises. The moisture in the air changes from its vapor to its liquid state and precipitation results. Cyclonic precipitation is typical of much of the region in the autumn, winter, and spring months of the year. Convectional precipitation dominates the summer season.

Rainfall generally decreases from the East Coast to the interior. Low periods of precipitation are particularly pronounced in a wedge-shaped region extending across the central portion of the Midwest (Fig. 3.3). The area lies to the north of a zone of high winter precipitation and to the south of a zone of high snowfall. Much of the precipitation, particularly to the west, is concentrated in the growing season in the spring and the summer (Trewartha and Horn 1980, 306). During certain years, however, the region is characterized by abnormally high summer temperatures, below average cloud cover, and severe summer droughts. The rainfall deficits coincide with the strong summer flow of dry continental air eastward from the base of the Rocky Mountains (Borchert 1950). The air initially starts over the Pacific as a moist maritime polar mass of air. As it moves up over the western mountains, however, it is cooled and loses much of its moisture in the form of precipitation. By the time it reaches the Midwest, it is a relatively dry mass of air with clear skies. At infrequent intervals the strong westerly flow of dry continental air displaces the moist maritime tropical air which normally dominates the region in the summer (Borchert 1950). Severe droughts associated with this influx of dry continental air are largely confined to areas which were dominated by grasslands and oak openings in the presettlement period.

During normal periods, the lower precipitation of the subhumid Midwest makes it an extremely productive area. From an agricultural standpoint, few areas on the surface of the earth are as well endowed physically (Trewartha 1941). The high precipitation of the East has leached many of the more important nutrients from the soil. Leaching is not as intense in the drier Midwest and more of the water that enters the soil is lost to evapotranspiration. As a result,

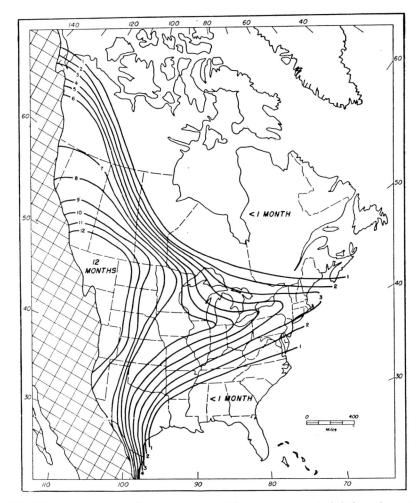

Fig. 3.3 Average number of months per year with a mean transport of air from the eastern base of the Rocky Mountains. Dry air from the west is associated with an increasing incidence of summer drought. From Borchert (1950). Reprinted by permission of the Association of American Geographers.

the Midwest's soils are often rich in soluble nutrients. The seasonal distribution of the precipitation also makes the Midwest ideal for the production of a variety of crop species. Corn makes its best growth where the moisture is well distributed throughout the growing season as in the case of the Corn Belt states of Iowa, Illinois, Indiana, and Ohio (Jenkins 1941). In the wheat-growing regions of Minnesota and the Dakotas, the rain is concentrated in the early part of the growing season. Water is particularly critical in May and June, during the early stalk forming period of growth. A timely decrease in the precipitation later in July and August minimizes vegetative growth and lodging and favors the ripening of the wheat grain (Salmon 1941; Trewartha 1941).

4

The forest primeval

This is the forest primeval. The murming pines and the hemlocks,
Bearded with moss, and in garments green, indistinct in the twi-
light ...
>
> Henry Wadsworth Longfellow. [1847] 1893. 'Evangeline.'

But when we apply some simple historical methods and find out
what the pre-colonial forest actually was, we find it was by no
means in equilibrium ... In fact, the more we learn about it the more
evident it becomes that the old forest was not far different from
what we have now. There is every reason to believe that it was
nearly as variable over the landscape as it is now, and we believe
its species composition has changed very little.
>
> Hugh M. Raup. 1957. 'Vegetational adjustment to the
> instability of the site.'

Structure of the forest

From the tropical rain forests of Yucatan to the taiga of the north, forests were
the dominant feature of North America's presettlement landscape. In the
words of the more civilized Europeans, it was 'the leafy continent' (Hedrick
1933, 19), 'one immense uninterrupted forest' (Baird 1832, 131), 'an ocean of
woods' (Pownall [1776] 1949, 30). Later interpretations suggested 'a squirrel
might have leaped from bough to bough for a thousand miles and never have
seen a flicker of sunshine on the ground' (Adams 1931, 4) or 'a savage might
skulk from the Hudson to Lake Erie without once exposing himself to the glare
of the sun' (Hedrick 1933, 5). To the early observer on the ground, the tops of
the trees were 'so close to one another for many miles together, that there
[was] no seeing which way the clouds drive, nor which way the wind sets: and
it seem[ed] almost as if the sun had never shone on the ground, since the creation' (Bartram 1751, 37).

Due to the idiosyncrasies of topography and past climatic events, North America also possessed a very rich arboreal flora (Billings 1970, 62–69). As the early Massachusetts arboriculturist, George Emerson (1846, 17) pointed out, there were more trees in the state of Massachusetts than in any country of Europe. To the more scientifically inclined of the eighteenth and nineteenth centuries, the diversity and the grandeur of North America's trees (Bradbury 1817, 288–289) added up to only one thing – 'the greatest [forest] upon the earth' (Williams 1794, 66).

Unfortunately, most of the early colonists were too preoccupied with making a living to give us their impressions of the early landscape. Then, too, the few pictures of the forest which have filtered down through the past two to three hundred years must be interpreted in light of the biases of the writers. The prevailing approaches to nature or the ruling paradigms of the age also left their imprint on our concept of 'the forest primeval' (Bowden 1992). Most of our images of the presettlement forest reflect one or more of the following approaches: (1) the romantic, (2) the literary, (3) the utilitarian, and (4) the ecological. It is important to understand these approaches to nature because they can produce a biased or at least a stylized impression of the presettlement forest.

The romantic ideal emphasized America's more pristine and primitive aspects (Nash 1973, 44–66). The forest primeval was a world undefiled by man's hands, a world that directly reflected the hands of its Creator. It was the abode of the noble savage and paradisiacal simplicity (Todd 1962). America's forests were 'as ancient as the world itself (Charlevoix [1761] 1966, 1:245). Her woods were populated with 'venerable trees, hoary with age, and torn with tempests' (Smyth [1784] 1968, 1:36–37). 'Preadamite trees' were scattered about the forest floor 'like the ancient monuments of Egypt, Greece and Rome' (Beltrami [1828] 1962, 33). America's dark and foreboding forests bore the impress of the sublime (Latrobe [1836] 1970, 1:41) and incidentally supported the pen of many a European Romantic.

Although closely allied to the romantic, the literary approach was more a product of native American writers. The primeval forest provided an appropriate backdrop for the advance of civilization. An epic story required a dramatic stage. Writers like Longfellow, Hawthorne, Cooper, and Parkman created the endless, the wild and often foreboding forests through which solitary pioneers like Cooper's Bumpo threaded their unerring way or the soldiers of France and England clashed for the control of a continent. The primeval forest also gave America's writers the opportunity of extolling the virtues of their landscape. America lacked many of Europe's cherished cultural antiquities. Its 'natural' antiquities, e.g., its primeval forests, however, were the equal of any of the cul-

tural antiquities, e.g., the castles and ruins, so beloved by the European roman-
ticists (Runte 1979, 5–9; Novak 1980, 59).

To the more practically minded, America's forests have always been a
source of wealth. Naturally their descriptions tended to emphasize the economically more important species. New England's forests, for instance,
'abounded with the finest oaks of all kinds' (Trumbull [1818] 1898, 1:19).
There were also extensive groves of white pine, while white wood
(*Liriodendron tulipifera*), an excellent wood for boards and clapboards, was
'the natural growth of the country' (Trumbull [1818] 1898, 1:19). Many of the
popular county histories of the nineteenth century likewise suggest an expanse
of black cherry and black walnut in the central hardwood forests of the
Midwest. Given the strong emphasis on commercial species in the popular literature, it is not surprising that many foresters and botanists also came to an
erroneous conclusion as to the abundance of the more valuable species in the
presettlement forest. Contrary to popular, and often scientific, opinion (Hawes
1923; Andrews 1948), 'vast unbroken seas of white pine' did not extend from
Maine through Michigan. Extensive stands of high-quality white oak, black
cherry, and black walnut were not synonymous with the Midwest's rich central hardwood forests (Den Uyl 1955).

The primeval forest has long played a central role in the development of
ecological thought and theory. For many years traditional ecological theory
suggested that the growth of the forest eventually culminated in a community
in complete harmony with its environment. Frederick Clements (1936), one of
America's most influential plant ecologists, felt that climate was the overrid-
ing factor that determined the nature of that final plant community. A given
climatic regime eventually produced a stable, self-replicating forest community, the climatic climax, in equilibrium with its environment. As the older
trees in the canopy succumbed to disease or old age, they were succeeded by
their shade tolerant progeny. The replication of the climax forest was a gradual
process which involved 'but little break in the "boundless contiguity of shade"
... Trees [fell] singly, not by square roods' (Marsh [1864] 1965, 30) in the climax forest and they were soon replicated in kind. It was easy for the ecologist
to equate the forest primeval with the climax forest. Both seemingly represented a stable equilibrium, free of mankind's disturbing influence. Both eventually became a biological datum plane, against which mankind's destructive
influences could be measured (Raup 1967).

Not all of America's ecologists, of course, agreed with Clement's concept
of the harmonious, self-perpetuating primeval forest. Some, like the Harvard
Forest's Hugh Raup (1964), had the temerity to suggest that succession rarely
progressed to the hypothesized climax stage. The presettlement forest was

beset by a variety of factors, e.g., fire, windthrow, disease, and insects, which precluded the development of the climax forest over large areas. Until very recently, most ecologists ignored Raup's suggestions and proceeded to reconstruct the presettlement forest on the basis of the few existing forest remnants or on their knowledge of the more shade tolerant species of the area, which should theoretically have dominated the primeval forest. They attempted to fit reality into their preconceived notions of the primeval forest or, as Margaret Davis (1965) noted: 'We do not know what the virgin vegetation of the pioneer days was like because all the ecologists were so busy looking for a nonexistent climax that they forgot to record what was actually growing there.' A more detailed examination of the early descriptions of the presettlement forest – its structure, its dynamics, and its composition – is warranted. Hopefully we can separate the fictitious from the real and, in the process, develop an appreciation for the factors responsible for the forest's development.

Francis Parkman's ([1865–1892] 1983) epic seven volume series *France and England in North America* gave a historical legitimacy to many of the more popular concepts of the forest primeval. His sketch of the forests of the New World is worth citing as is the natural historian Wilson Flagg's (1872) portrayal of New England's early forests. Parkman's and Flagg's descriptions will serve as a point of departure for our analysis of the structure of the presettlement forest. Parkman ([1894] 1983, 1:1322) constructed a verbal picture of the primeval forest based on his visit to a virgin forest on the upper reaches of the Pemigewasset River in northern New Hampshire. The water and the ancient forest formed a cave of verdure where

…the noonday sun pierces with keen rays athwart the torrent, and the mossed arms of fallen pines cast wavering shadows on the illumined foam; pools of liquid crystal turned emerald in the reflected green of impending woods; rocks on whose rugged front the gleam of sunlit waters dances in quivering light; ancient trees hurled headlong by the storm to dam the raging stream with their forlorn and savage ruin; or the stern depths of immemorial forests, dim and silent as a cavern, columned with innumerable trunks, each like an Atlas upholding its world of leaves, and sweating perpetual moisture down its dark and channelled rind; some strong in youth, some grisly with decrepit age, nightmares of strange distortion, gnarled and knotted with wens and goitres; roots intertwined beneath like serpents petrified in an agony of contorted strife; green and glistening mosses carpeting the rough ground, mantling the rocks, turning pulpy stumps to mounds of verdure, and swathing fallen trunks as bent in the impotence of rottenness, they lie outstretched over knoll and hollow, like mouldering reptiles of the primeval world, while around, and on and through them, springs the young growth that battens on their decay, – the forest devouring its own dead.

Flagg's (1872, 5) description of the forest primeval also emphasizes many of the same points although it is not as colorful as Parkman's.

One of the conditions most remarkable in a primitive forest is the universal dampness of the ground. The second growth of timber, especially if the surface were entirely cleared, stands upon a drier foundation. This greater dryness is caused by the absence of those vast accumulations of vegetable debris that rested on the ground before it was disturbed. A greater evaporation also takes place under the second growth, because the trees are of inferior size and stand more widely apart. Another character of a primitive forest is the crowded assemblage of trees and their undergrowth, causing great difficulty in traversing it. Innumerable straggling vines, many of them covered with thorns, like the green-brier, intercept our way. Immense trunks of trees, prostrated by hurricanes, lie in our path, and beds of moss of extreme thickness cover a great part of the surface, saturated with moisture. The trees are also covered with mosses, generated by the shade and dampness ...

The more prominent features of these accounts include an emphasis on :

(1) the large size and age of the trees, implying a continuity with the past;
(2) considerable quantities of coarse woody debris and decayed organic matter, humus, on the forest floor;
(3) an abundance of epiphytes covering the trees and mosses on the forest floor;
(4) the relatively dense nature of the forest – a 'crowded assemblage of trees and their undergrowth' (Flagg 1872, 5), 'with young seedlings in millions spring[ing up] every summer ... crowding, choking, and killing each other, perishing by their very abundance ...' (Parkman [1892] 1983, 2:359).

For many individuals the primeval forest has long been synonymous with trees of an exceedingly great magnitude and age. America's forests were generally depicted as taller and denser than their managed European counterparts (Mittleberger [1756] 1898, 73; Cooper 1794, 104–112; Stuart 1833, 1: 272–273). Canopy height varied considerably, depending upon site conditions and species composition. The average height of the dominant trees of 22 old-growth stands in the eastern deciduous forest in the Midwest was 97 ft or 30 m (Auten 1941). At the upper end of the spectrum, the hemlock–white pine–northern hardwood forests of the Northeast had an average canopy height of 80 ft (24 m) with an emergent layer of white pine up to 150 ft or 46 m (Johnson 1819, 46). Stands of large white pines were particularly impressive to foreign visitors. The English farmer William Strickland (1971, 145), for instance, described one small tract of original pineland in the Hudson River Valley as consisting of trees of a 'wonderful magnitude, ... standing so thick on the ground that though there is no underwood and they have no branches for many feet in height, they admit not of view in any direction above a few hundred yards.' The trees were 'from four to six feet in diameter [and] frequently not as many yards asunder' (Strickland 1971, 146).

The larger trees in the forest invariably caught the attention of the more botanically minded observers. White pine was recognizably the tallest tree, often growing up to 150 to 180 ft (46–55 m) and occasionally 200 ft (61 m) in height (Belknap 1813, 3:56; Thompson 1842, 216), while sycamore (up to 15 ft (4.6 m) diameter), tuliptree (5–6 ft (1.5–1.8 m) diameter), and cottonwood possessed the largest diameters (Michaux [1805] 1904, 229–230; Nuttall [1821] 1905, 90; Nuttall 1951, 63). Travelers and naturalists stated that oaks 4 ft in diameter and tuliptrees 4–5 ft in diameter were common in the Ohio River Valley (Atwater 1818, 229; Baily 1856, 214). Limited areas in the Midwest contained 'tulip trees with trunks straight as an arrow, eighty or more feet in height and five or six feet in diameter' (Schweinitz 1927, 233). The lower Ohio and Wabash River Valleys supported some of the largest hardwoods on the continent (Telford 1927). Robert Ridgway's (1872) description of the original forests of the lower Wabash River Valley provides a detailed picture of the structure of the magnificent, hardwood forests of the region.

The [Wabash] river flows for the greater part between dense walls of forest ... If the forest is viewed from a high bluff, it presents the appearance of a compact, level sea of green, apparently almost endless, but bounded by the line of wooded bluffs three to seven miles back from the river; the tree-tops swaying with the passing breeze, and the general level broken by occasional giant trees which rear their massive heads so as to overlook the surrounding miles of forest. The approximate height above the ground beneath of the average tree-top level is about one hundred and thirty feet – the lowest estimate after a series of careful measurements – while the occasional, and by no means infrequent, 'monarchs' which often tower apparently for one-third their height above the tree-top line, attain an altitude of more than one hundred and eighty feet, or approach two hundred feet.

Going into these primitive woods, we find symmetrical, solid trunks of six feet and upwards in diameter, and fifty feet, or more, long to be not uncommon, in half a dozen or more species; while now and then we happen on one of those old sycamores, for which the rich alluvial bottoms of the western rivers are so famous, with a trunk thirty or even forty, possibly fifty or sixty, feet in circumference, while perhaps a hundred feet overhead stretch out its great white arms, each as large as the biggest trunks themselves of most eastern forests, and whose massive head is one of those which lifts itself so high above the surrounding tree-tops. The tall, shaft-like trunks of pecans, sweet gums or ashes, occasionally break on the sight through the dense undergrowth, or stand clear and upright in unobstructed view in the rich wet woods, and rise straight as an arrow for eighty or ninety, perhaps over a hundred, feet before the first branches are thrown out.

Although the above descriptions certainly suggest magnificent specimen trees existed, it would be hazardous to conclude that all of the landscape was dominated by massive, old-age trees. The nature and the vicissitudes of the presettlement forest were of special interest to the Swedish botanist Peter

Kalm. Kalm's ([1772] 1972, 210) description of the woods of eastern Pennsylvania leaves little doubt as to the very transitory nature of many trees in the old-growth forest.

> The woods of these parts consist of all sorts of trees, but chiefly of oak and hiccory. These woods have certainly never been cut down, and have always grown without hindrance. It might therefore be expected that there are trees of an uncommon great age to found in them; but it happens otherwise, and there are very few trees three hundred years old. Most of them are only two hundred years old; and this convinced me that trees have the same quality as animals, and die after they are arrived at a certain age. Thus we find great woods here, but when the trees in them have stood an hundred and fifty or an hundred and eighty years, they are either rotting within, or losing their crown, or their wood becomes quite soft, or their roots are no longer able to draw in sufficient nourishment, or they die from some other cause. Therefore when storms blow, which sometimes happens here, the trees are broke off either just above the root, or in the middle, or at the summit. Several trees are likewise torn out with their roots by the power of the winds. The storms thus cause great devastations in these forests. Everywhere you see trees thrown down by the winds after they are too much weakened by one or the other of the above-mentioned causes to be able to resist their fury. Fire likewise breaks out often in the woods, and burns the trees half way from the root so that a violent gust of wind easily throws them down.

Destructive insect outbreaks also took their toll on the forest. One competent observer, John Winthrop, Jr. (1882), an early governor of Connecticut and a charter member of the Royal Academy of Science, attributed the scarcity of large, old oak trees in southern New England's early forests to massive outbreaks of defoliators. Although many of the dominant tree species of the eastern United States have a maximum lifespan of three to five centuries (Harlow, Harrar, and White 1979), few trees survived the vagaries of their early years.

Estimates of the total amount of wood produced on a per acre or a per hectare basis (2.47 acres = 1 ha) provide a more reliable measure of the biomass or weight of the presettlement forest. Unfortunately both the accuracy of the estimates and the units employed (cords, board feet, and metric tons) vary considerably from one study to the next, making it difficult to compare the studies. The potential of the forest as a source of fuel encouraged the early use of the cord as a measure of forest biomass, a cord being a stack of wood 4 by 4 by 8 feet. Samuel Williams' (1794, 72–72) estimate of 50 to 200 cords per acre for a virgin forest in Vermont was probably the first attempt to quantify the biomass of the New World's forests. Lumbering interests employed the board foot (bd ft) as a measure of forest biomass, the bd ft being a piece of rough, green lumber 1 inch thick, 1 foot wide, and 1 foot long. The major disadvantage of the bd ft measure is the fact that it neglects the unmerchantable materials, i.e., the cull trees, the smaller trees, the branches, and the smaller portions of the trunk. It is more a relative than an absolute measure of the total volume of the stand. Averages of 7700 bd ft/acre for Maine's original forests (Coolidge 1963, 773), 8000 bd ft/acre for Illinois' forests (Miller 1923, 297), 13 000 bd ft/acre for Ohio's forests (Chapman 1944), and 17 500 bd ft/acre for Pennsylvania's forests (Illick 1923) suggest a wide range of values for virgin stands in the Northeast and the Midwest. The low volume of the mixed spruce–fir and northern hardwood forests of Maine and the upland oak and hickory forests of Illinois are immediately apparent. Averages for the hemlock–white pine type (common in northern Pennsylvania) and the bottomland forests of the lower Wabash River Valley in southern Indiana were much higher. Small selected tracts of the hemlock–white pine type and the mixed forests of the Wabash yielded up to 100 000 bd ft/acre and 25 000 bd ft/acre respectively (Roth 1898a; Hawes 1923; Telford 1927). A number of investigators (Hawes 1923; Illick 1923) have assumed that these few high-volume stands were representative of the presettlement forest as a whole. It would be inappropriate, however, to extrapolate from these sites to larger regions, and to assume, for instance, as Hawes (1923) did, that all of the Connecticut River Valley was covered with massive stands of pine and hemlock.

Absolute basal area values, i.e., the cross-sectional area of all trees at a height of 4.5 feet (1.3 m) above the ground, have been utilized extensively by ecologists as a proxy measure of the biomass of the few remaining old-growth stands. Actual measurements of the living biomass of the forest awaited the development of dimension analysis techniques in the mid-twentieth century (Whittaker and Marks 1975). Due to the time-consuming and laborious nature of the techniques, however, very few old-growth stands have been measured in their entirety. Recent work (Crow 1978) suggests a strong positive relationship between total above-ground biomass and stand basal area × stand height. Fitting the easily acquired measurements of stand basal area and stand height into the appropriate regression equation yields a crude estimate of the biomass of the few remaining old-growth stands.

Table 4.1 represents a compilation of the basal area and biomass values of the more thoroughly researched old-growth stands in the Northeast and the Midwest. Basal area values range from a low of 20.6 m^2/ha in the storm-damaged Hutcheson Memorial Forest to a high of 70.0 to 90.0 m^2/ha in the Hartwick tract of Michigan and the former Pisgah Forest tract of southern New Hampshire. Most of the values reported for the deciduous forests hover about 30.0 m^2/ha, a value Held and Winstead (1975) have suggested is representative of mesic old-growth or 'climax' forest systems in the eastern United States. Mixed hemlock–white pine–northern hardwood stands consistently overrun this value and approach the maximum basal area value of 70.0–90.0

Table 4.1. *Density, basal area, height (Ht), and biomass values of representative old-growth forests grouped by forest type*

Name of woods	Location	Density no. stems > 10 cm (unless otherwise noted)	Basal area (m²/ha)	Ht (m)	Biomass (t/ha)	Sources
Beech–sugar maple						
Hueston	SW Ohio	325	32.0			Runkle, Vankat, and Snyder 1984
Schmidt	C Ohio		32.7			Gilbert and Riemenschneider 1980
Hoot	S Ind.	198	28.1	> 37		Petty and Lindsey 1961; Abrell and Jackson 1977
Jackson	S Ind.	269	25.7			Jackson and Allen 1969
Potzger	S Ind.	300	26.8			Jackson and Allen 1969
Shenk	Ind.	258 (> 12 cm)	23.9			McCune and Menges 1986
Warren	S Mich.	311	39.6	34	378[a]	Brewer and Merritt 1978; Woods 1979
Mixed mesophytic						
Lilley–Cornett	E Ky.	315 (> 12 cm)	30.0		235 (17)[b]	Martin 1975; Muller and Liu 1991
Rock Creek	E Ky.	329	23.3			Cameron and Winstead 1978
Dysart	SE Ohio		54.0			Lafer and Wistendahl 1970
Cox	S Ind.	324	27.1			Lindsey, Schmelz, and Nichols 1969
Donaldson	S Ind.	277	30.4		370 (16)[b]	Schmelz, Barton, and Lindsey 1975; MacMillan 1981; Barton and Schmelz 1987; Muller and Liu 1991
Beall	S Ill.	282	45.8			Lindsey 1962

Table 4.1 (*cont.*)

Name of woods	Location	Density no. stems > 10 cm (unless otherwise noted)	Basal area (m²/ha)	Ht (m)	Biomass (t/ha)	Sources
Northern hardwoods						
The Bowl	C N.H.	566	28.2	20	260 (42)[b]	Leak 1973; Martin 1977; Carboneau 1986; Gore and Patterson 1986
Mt Pond	N N.H.	450	37.6			Carboneau 1986
Dukes Expt. Forest	U.P. Mich.	283	34.4		325	Mroz et al. 1985
McCormick Expt. Forest	U.P. Mich.	344	43.2		284	Mroz et al. 1985
Sugar maple–basswood						
Douglas	Mo.	627	44.0			Kucera and McDermott 1955
Long Lake	Wis.	728	38.5			Eggler 1938
Minnetonka	S Minn.	352	38.4	27.1	303[a]	Daubenmire 1936
Northfield	S Minn.	528	42.9	23.8	298[a]	Daubenmire 1936
Oak–hickory						
Bonayer	Ky.		31.8			Bougher and Winstead 1974
Davis–Purdue	C Ind.	320	31.0			Parker, Leopold, and Eichenberger 1985
Hutcheson Memorial Forest	N.J.	348	20.6	30	240 (21)[b]	Reiners and Reiners 1965; Lang and Forman 1978
Weaver	S Ill.		30.0			Weaver and Ashby 1971
Former prairie groves						
Baber	C Ill.	279	26.9			Newman and Ebinger 1985
Brownfield	C Ill.	483 (>6 cm)	31.6			Miceli et al. 1977

Funk Forest	C Ill.	202	28.5			Cox, Miller, and Hostetler 1972
Trelease	C Ill.	572 (>6 cm)	26.0			Pelz and Rolfe 1977
White and red pine						
Baraga County	U.P. Mich.	419	46.0			Bourdo 1961
Roscommon	L.P. Mich.	398	52.4			Lindsey 1955
Five Ponds, Adirondacks	N N.Y.	419	44.5			Roman 1980
Hemlock–northern hardwoods						
Gifford	C Vt.	385	47.2	32	418[a]	Bormann and Buell 1964
E Tionesta	NW Pa.		32.4			Hough 1936
Huron Mts	U.P. Mich.		59.6			Willis and Coffman 1975
Drummond	N Wis.		65			Stearns 1951
Laona	N Wis.		57			Stearns 1951
Tenderfoot Lake	N Wis.		62			Stearns 1951
Hemlock–white pine–northern hardwoods						
Heart's Content	NW Pa.	358	44.0	34, pine to > 40 m	440[a]	Morey 1936; Whitney 1984, unpub. data
Hartwick Pines	L.P. Mich.		72.6	36	681	Rose 1984
Hemlock–white pine						
Pisgah	S N.H.	300–400	70.0–90.0	35	735[a]	Hawes 1923; Foster 1988a
Heart's Content	NW Pa.	413	46.7	34, pine to > 40 m	437[a]	Morey 1936; Whitney 1984, unpub. data
Cook Forest	NW Pa.	323	63.9			Morey 1936
Spruce–northern hardwood						
Five Ponds, Adirondacks	N N.Y.	535	34.7			Roman 1980

Table 4.1 (*cont.*)

Name of woods	Location	Density no. stems > 10 cm (unless otherwise noted)	Basal area (m²/ha)	Ht (m)	Biomass (t/ha)	Sources
Spruce–fir						
Basin Ponds	Maine		59.0			Foster and Reiners 1983
Bernard Mt	Maine		45.0			Foster and Reiners 1983
N Traveler Mt	Maine		41.0			Foster and Reiners 1983
Gibbs Brook	N.N.H.	1124	44.0			Foster and Reiners 1983
Nancy Brook	N.N.H.	1035	44.8		248[a]	Oosting and Billings 1951; Carboneau 1986
			(34.6 in 1986)			
Norton Pool	N.N.H.	469	22.8			Carboneau 1986
(Spruce flat)						
Pittsburg Township	N.N.H.	895	38.1			Chittenden 1904
(Spruce slope)						
Pittsburg Township	N.N.H.	744	40.7			Chittenden 1904
McComb Tract	N.Y.	913	27.0			McCarthy and Belyea 1920

[a] Estimate of biomass based on equation developed by Crow (1978).

[b] The first value is the above-ground living biomass, while the value in parentheses is the biomass of the dead woody debris; i.e. the downed logs and branches.

m^2/ha reported by Goff and Zedler (1968), Rose (1984), and Foster (1988a). Assuming an average stand height of 30–35 m and applying Crow's (1978) technique yields a biomass estimate of approximately 560–820 t/ha for these same stands. The extremely high biomass values of the mixed conifer–hardwood or hemlock–white pine stands probably represent a maximum for forests in the eastern United States. The high values may reflect a very effective utilization of the site's resources, i.e., light and moisture, by these highly stratified stands. The sun-adapted white pine forms an emergent layer over the more shade tolerant hemlock, beech, and sugar maple (Kelty 1984). Alternatively the high values could be more a function of the unique biological properties of the species, i.e., their great longevity and their ability to produce photosynthate under a wide range of conditions.

The amount of coarse woody debris or downed trees in the presettlement forest is difficult to determine with any degree of accuracy. Theoretically the natural senescence of older trees in the primary forest would suggest a high input of woody debris to the forest floor (Harmon *et al.* 1986). Thoreau ([1864] 1972, 151) bemoaned the loss of New England's presettlement forest with its 'countless fallen and decaying trees' and 'its wild, damp and shaggy look,' but his conception of the primary forest may have been inaccurate. Contrary to popular opinion (Carroll 1973, 34), relatively few observers commented upon the amount of dead and decaying wood on the forest floor. The lack of comments may have been due to cultural conditioning and the observers' backgrounds. Most Europeans had a finely tuned sense of the scarcity of wood and an attendant emphasis on the value of dead wood (Kalm [1772] 1972, 348). To the wood-conscious European, America's forests possessed 'an incredible quantity of fallen timber' (Amphlett 1819, 82). Americans were accustomed to an abundance of wood and more prone to overlook the occasional log on the forest floor.

Most of the historic observations on large accumulations of coarse woody debris appear to be concentrated in the hemlock–white pine–northern hardwoods forest type (Bartram 1751, 28; Schoepf [1788] 1968, 1:168; Castiglioni [1790] 1983, 31; Maximilian 1843, 39; Strickland 1971, 146). Of particular note was the Great Swamp of northeastern Pennsylvania where 'thousands of rotten and rotting trunks cover[ed] the ground,' forming a thick rich mold which sucked up moisture like a sponge (Schoepf [1788] 1968, 1:168). The scarcity of fire in the moist hemlock–white pine–northern hardwoods type, the large amount of living biomass leading to a high woody debris input rate, the slow decay rate of the conifers, and low temperatures (Harmon *et al.* 1986) were probably the leading factors responsible for the large quantities of coarse woody debris in the hemlock–white pine–northern hardwoods type. Hemlock, for instance, has been known to persist in a recognizable form for up to 200 years (Stephens 1955; Hole 1975). The rapid decay rate of most hardwoods precludes the accumulation of large quantities of coarse woody debris in the deciduous forest (Gore and Patterson 1986). The few available studies of old-growth hardwood stands in the east (Table 4.1) suggest a maximum of 15–30 tons of dead wood per hectare in the central hardwoods forest region and up to 40–50 t/ha in the cooler, hemlock–northern hardwod forest region (MacMillan 1981; Gore and Patterson 1986; Muller and Liu 1991).

An abundance of mosses and lichens draping the trees and covering the ground is a conspicuous feature of Parkman's and Flagg's descriptions of the forest primeval. Emerson (1846, 61) likewise commented upon the luxuriant growth of crustose, fruticose, and foliose lichens covering many an old white pine in the depths of New England's forests. In actuality the moisture-loving, epiphytic mosses, hepatics, and lichens were probably limited to the cooler, more humid forest types of the north. As the early Moravian naturalist and missionary John Heckewelder (1958, 375) noted, considerable 'moss on the branches and treetops [was] a sure sign of an area of cold.' Summer vacations in the north woods influenced many a New Englander's perception of the forest primeval (Parkman [1885] 1983, 1:1322) and probably contributed to Longfellow's allusion to murmuring pines and hemlocks 'bearded with moss.'

Many species of lichens in Europe have been shown to require continuity of mature timber for survival (Rose and James 1974; Rose 1976). Their restriction to old, continuously wooded sites may be due to the high humidity maintained beneath the canopy of the undisturbed forest (Tubbs 1986, 150) or to the lichens' limited powers of dispersal (Hawksworth and Hill 1984, 139–140). Cutting and exposure to a drier atmosphere apparently is lethal to the more moisture sensitive species (Rose and Wolseley 1984). A few of the European species, e.g., *Lobaria pulmonaria*, *Haematomma elatinum*, *Catillaria atropurpurea*, and *Dimerella lutea*, also occur in North America and appear to be indicative of ancient or old-growth forests in the New World (Hawksworth and Hill 1984, 139–140; Selva 1988).

The density of the undergrowth of the presettlement forest, as the historians S. and E. Buck (1939, 9) pointed out, is 'a matter of some dispute.' A few areas, particularly those dominated by mountain laurel, were described as impenetrable (Lutz 1930a). Other areas were correspondingly rather open – open enough for the growth of a large amount of herbage (Doddridge [1824] 1912, 51; Teas 1916, 252). Pea vines, buffalo clover, and grass were particularly abundant in the more open oak–hickory forests of the Mid-Atlantic states and the Midwest (Kalm [1772] 1972, 176; Morris 1785; Hildreth 1848, 485; Baily 1856, 214; Hutchins 1878; McInteer 1952). Most observers attributed the lack of underwood to burning by Indians (Wood [1634] 1977, 38; Hildreth 1848, 485) or in the case of the denser forests to shade (Ashe 1808, 20; Fearon 1819, 218).

The nature of the presettlement forest is not entirely an academic question. To many the primeval forest or, to use the ecological term, the 'climax' forest has always represented a forest in equilibrium with its environment. It formed a productive, biologically balanced whole, capable of perpetuating itself indefinitely. Who could fault the magnificent primeval forests which contained up to 300 to 600 t/ha and produced 20 000 to 100 000 bd ft per acre? The degraded second-growth forests of the nineteenth and twentieth centuries with their 100 t/ha (Crow 1978) and 890 bd ft per acre (Illick 1923) paled into insignificance beside them. The virgin climax forest represented a balanced system that many foresters attempted to emulate (Lutz 1930b), a forest that in its areal extent, its variety, and its utility 'will never again be seen by man' (Jennings 1958; Raup 1967). Unfortunately, it was destroyed so thoroughly that it is difficult to believe it ever existed (Mayr 1890b).

Attempts to assess the validity of the above-noted climax model of the primeval forest awaited the latter half of the twentieth century. Spurred on by the early studies of Hugh Raup (1964, 1967) and faced by an accumulating amount of evidence in the field of 'disturbance' ecology, many ecologists altered their concept of the forest primeval. Like the pendulum which swings from one extreme to another, contemporary ecological thought has shifted to the view that truely age-old primeval forests were rare even in the presettlement period and that 'most of the forests seen by the first settlers in America were in their first generation after one or another kind of major disturbance' (Raup 1967). Both the climax model and the disturbance model contain elements of reality. The real problem lies in determining the geographical extent of the disturbances, their frequency, and their severity.

Much of the available evidence suggests a very strong regional pattern of catastrophic disturbance in the forests of the Northeast and the Midwest (Runkle 1990). Meteorological records provide a starting point for the analysis of severe storm events. Due to the inherent human interest in tornadoes and hurricanes, particularly among meteorologists and the insurance sector, our knowledge of the regional occurrence of tornadoes and hurricanes is well developed. Relatively complete data extend back to the 1950s for tornadoes (Thom 1963) and to the late nineteenth century for hurricanes (Neumann *et al.* 1981). Ludlum (1963, 1970) has compiled information on the occurrence of tornadoes and hurricanes for the pre-1870 period from a variety of historical sources.

The devastating effects of hurricanes or tropical cyclones are largely a coastal phenomena. The Mid-Atlantic states have traditionally been considered outside the hurricane belt (Dunn and Miller 1960, 275). Hurricanes, however, are much more a fact of life in New England. Plymouth was barely fifteen years old when the hurricane of 1635 struck and 'blew downe many hundered thowsands of trees, turning up the stronger by the roots, and breaking the hiegher pine trees of in the midle, and ye tall yonge oaks & walnut trees of good biggnes were wound like a withe' (Bradford 1856, 337–338). Although existing records indicate that five to ten hurricanes hit New England each century (Foster 1988a), it would be hazardous to suggest that universal destruction was the fate of all of New England's forests. A number of factors mitigated the effects of the hurricanes. First, not all of New England was equally affected by the hurricanes. Second, the worst effects of the hurricanes were limited to the more exposed sites and stands. D. M. Smith (1946) has plotted up the storm tracks and the maximum estimated areas of severe storm damage of New England's seven major hurricanes from 1620 to 1950. Only portions of southern New England (Fig. 4.1) have been subject to two or more hurricanes during the last three centuries. The hurricane of 1938 virtually leveled over 240 000 ha of central New England's forests along a north–south swath 100 km wide (NETSA 1943). Even here, however, stands on the more sheltered sites to the lee of the wind, in this case stands on west to north facing slopes, suffered minor damage (Clapp 1938; Smith 1946; Fetherston 1987). Stands less than 30 years old, particularly young hardwood stands, were also fairly immune to the effects of the hurricane. Physiographic and vegetational features moderated the effects of the hurricane, creating a very complex, landscape level pattern of damage (Foster 1988a, 1988b).

Tornadoes represent another major disturbing influence in the life of the forest. Due to unique topographical and meteorological conditions, the central portion of the United States experiences the highest incidence of tornadoes of any region on the surface of the earth (Flora 1973, 23). Although the north–south band of the 'tornado alley' from Texas to Nebraska has received the most attention, another major belt of tornado activity extends east across central Indiana (Kelly *et al.* 1978). By determining the mean number of tornadoes per year (Kelly *et al.* 1978), and the average area of ground path contact for each tornado (see Howe 1974), one can determine the average percentage of the area under consideration destroyed each year. Its inverse is the rotation period or the average number of years required for tornadoes to destroy a tract equal to the area in question. Figure 4.2 suggests a range of values with a minimum rotation period of approximately 1200 to 1300 years in central Indiana to a maximum value greater than 10 000 years for most of the Northeast.

The widespread incidence of pit and mound topography in many forests in eastern North America is evidence of the occurrence of catastrophic wind-

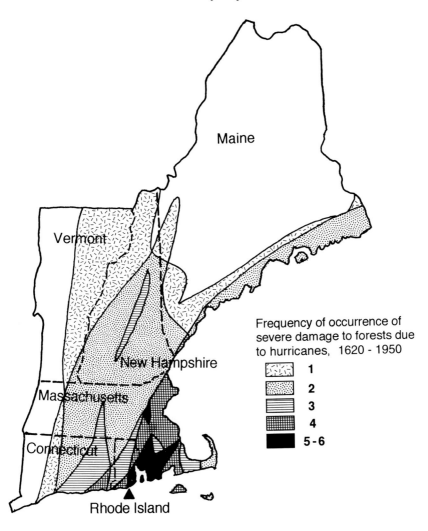

Fig. 4.1 Frequency of occurrence of major hurricanes in New England, 1620–1950. Based on maps showing severe damage of hurricanes to forests in Smith (1946).

throw in the past (Stephens 1956; Schaetzl *et al.* 1989). The pit and mound topography created by windthrows can persist for several centuries (Stephens 1956; Stone 1975) or under optimal conditions more than 1000 years (Schaetzl and Follmer 1990). It is interesting to note that one of the earliest attempts to estimate the frequency of tornadoes in the United States was based on the occurrence of pit and mound topography in western Indiana over 100 years ago. John Campbell (1886), an early surveyor, used his own knowledge of the

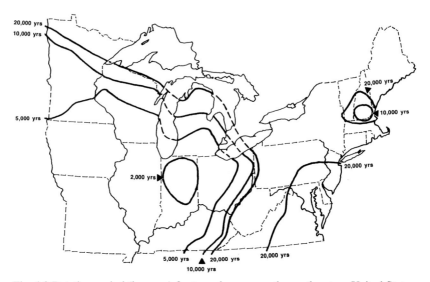

Fig. 4.2 Rotation period (in years) for tornadoes across the northeastern United States. Based on data in Howe (1974) and Kelly *et al.* (1978).

location of windthrow mounds and the childhood reminiscences of others to reconstruct the location of a tornado track in Parke County. The so-called 'Indian graves' covered approximately one-tenth of the surface area of the forests. Since the mounds lasted at least 300 years as determined by a count of the rings of a tree growing on one of the mounds, one can conclude that the maximum percentage of the area affected annually was 0.10/300 or 0.033%. This yields a rotation period of approximately 3000 years, i.e., 1/0.00033. Tornadoes destroyed an area equal to the size of the area in question every 3000 years, a value well below their perceived frequency of occurrence in John Campbell's day. Campbell resolved the issue by noting that uprooting also required a period of protracted rain and was limited to the less root firm species, all of which had to be in full leaf.

   Few areas in contemporary ecology have received more attention than the role of fire in the destruction and the perpetuation of forest ecosystems (Mooney *et al.* 1981; Pyne 1982). Charcoal fragments in lake sediments indicate that fires have been common for thousands of years throughout the Northeast and the Midwest (Swain 1973, 1978; Cwynar 1978; Winkler 1985; Clark 1988; Patterson and Backman 1988). In the humid Northeast, however, high fire frequencies have probably been limited to the more fire prone sites, e.g., exposed ridgetops (Russell 1979, 66), areas of coarse-textured soils associated with deltaic, outwash, shoreline, and windblown deposits of sand, and recent blowdowns and other sites with high fuel loadings (Patterson *et al.* 1985). Close interval sampling of pollen and charcoal in several small sedimentary basins in the Northeast suggests that fires occurred at intervals of 800 to 1400 years in the hemlock–northern hardwoods type and 100 to 200 years in the coastal birch and spruce type (Patterson and Backman 1988). Citings of fires are infrequent in the early land survey records of the Northeast (Lutz 1930a; McIntosh 1962; Siccama 1971). Occasionally one unearths references to 'barren or burnt hills' (western Pennsylvania; Burges 1965, 5), to 'burnt [pine] plains' (Plattsburgh, New York; Cook, Smith, and Stone 1952), and to 'fallen timber hills' kept in a vine and shrub covered state by subsequent fires (western Pennsylvania; Porter 1880). Again, however, the limited frequency of their occurrence suggests their impact was fairly localized. The famed grass, oak, and hazel covered glades of the Allegheny Mountains of southwestern Pennsylvania (Fithian 1934, 107), the scrub oak barrens and the pitch pine plains of coastal New England, New Jersey, and Long Island (Englebright 1980; Forman and Boerner 1981; Backman 1984; Winkler 1985), and the oak barrens of the karst limestone regions of southern Indiana and western Kentucky (Keith 1983) were all unique fire maintained or fire dependent communities.

Fire played a much more pervasive role in the climatically drier regions to the west (Patterson and Backman 1988). Throughout southern Wisconsin, for instance, mature forests composed of the more fire sensitive, shade tolerant species like sugar maple and basswood were limited to protected sites, e.g., deeply dissected terrain or the leeward side of marshes, rivers, lakes, and other major fire barriers (Ellarson 1949; Zicker 1955; Kline and Cottam 1979). Hemlock occupied a similar position in northern Wisconsin. Its western boundary roughly coincided with that of the Chippewa River (Goder 1955). References to 'the usual burnt and fallen black [jack] pines' on the poorer sites (Garrison 1881, 189) and the ubiquitous, fire dependent aspen and birch forest type on the better sites (Houghton 1958, 262) saturate the early travel literature of Minnesota. Detailed studies of the charcoal and pollen associated with varved sediments substantiate many of these observations. Fires were extremely common in the aspen and paper birch forests of northern Minnesota, occurring on the average at 70–80 year intervals (Swain 1980). Fire return intervals greater than 140 years in northern Wisconsin favored the development of a forest composed of the more fire sensitive species, e.g., hemlock, yellow birch, and sugar maple (Swain 1978).

The development of the federal land survey system in 1785 encouraged a more systematic analysis of the land and its accompanying vegetation. Surveyor General Tiffin in 1815 instructed his deputy surveyors to record the kinds of vegetation and any 'uncommon, natural, or artificial' phenomena they encountered along their transect or survey lines (White 1984a, 249). The 1833 instructions required note of all 'tracks of tornados or hurricanes, commonly called "windfall," or "fallen timber" ' as well as descriptions of the face of the country, soil, timber, etc. (White 1984a, 300). Often the surveyor specified the exact point at which he entered and left windfalls and burnt areas on his mile long north–south, east–west section lines. By summing the length of the burns and the windfalls on the section lines and dividing by the total length of the section lines surveyed, it is possible to determine the area affected on a percentage basis. Dividing by the estimated number of years the burn or windfall remained conspicious (generally 15–30 years) yields the percentage area affected on a yearly basis or its inverse, the rotation period. Table 4.2 is a compilation of the few existing studies where the survey data were detailed enough to permit the determination of rotation periods. Values for windthrow are highest in central Indiana, although even here they are relatively infrequent. The 855 year rotation estimate for central Indiana as based on the survey data is less than the 1000–2000 year estimate based on meteorological data (Fig. 4.2). The difference probably reflects the addition of 'thunderstorm downbursts' to the survey data. Generally associated with thunderstorms, downbursts are rapidly moving downward currents of air which spread out in a starburst pattern when they hit the ground. Although downbursts have frequently been included in the government's *Storm Data* record, they have not been recorded on a systematic basis (Fujita 1981). The large size of many of the blowdowns (up to 1 mile wide, see Dorney 1983) in Canham and Loucks' (1984) study of catastrophic windstorms in early Wisconsin and the low frequency of tornadoes in the same area today suggests that thunderstorm downbursts were responsible for most of the catastrophic windthrow in Wisconsin's presettlement forests.

If the occasional windfall characterized the hardwood forests of the Midwest, fires dominated the more flammable, resinous pine forests of the coarser textured soils. In the Lower Peninsula of Michigan, for instance, rotation periods for stand initiating fires were as low as 80 years for jack pine and 100 to 200 years for white and red pine (Table 4.2). Rotation periods for hemlock and hardwood stands on similar substrates were considerably longer (Table 4.2). Fires were not as likely in the cool, moist microclimate of the hemlock–hardwood community (Backman 1984).

Forest clearance and the manipulation of the remaining stands has significantly altered the structure of most forests, converting heterogeneous areas into relatively homogeneous tracts of second and third-growth forests. Changes in the composition, the fuel loading, and the vertical profile of the

Table 4.2. Estimate of natural rotation or return periods for various forms of disturbance based on land surveys records or mean stand age

Forest type	Location	Fire		Wind		Sources
		% area affected by fire/yr	Rotation period (years)	% area affected by wind/yr	Rotation period (years)	
Northeastern United States						
Hemlock–hardwoods–spruce–fir	N Maine	0.12[a]	800	0.086[b]	1150	Lorimer 1977
Hemlock–white pine–northern hardwoods	NW Pa.	0.04[c]	2500	0.05–0.10[bc]	1000–2000	Whitney 1990
Beech–maple–hemlock	W N.Y.	–	–	0.05[c]	2000	Seischab 1990
Beech–maple–basswood–oak	C N.Y.	0.007–0.039[c]	2600–14000	0.011[c]	9000	Marks, Gardescu, and Seischab 1992
Midwestern United States						
Hemlock–white pine–northern hardwoods	Wis.	–	–	0.08[c]	1210	Canham and Loucks 1984
Beech–maple	C Ind.	–	–	0.12[c]	855	Whitney unpub. data
Jack pine	Mich.	1.20[c]	80	0.007[c]	12500	Whitney 1986
Red and white pine	Mich.	0.80[c]	130	0.060[c]	1600	Whitney 1986

Table 4.2 (*cont.*)

| Forest type | Location | Fire | | Wind | | Sources |
		% area affected by fire/yr	Rotation period (years)	% area affected by wind/yr	Rotation period (years)	
Hemlock–white pine–northern hardwoods	Mich.	0.07[c]	1400	0.080[c]	1200	Whitney 1986
Swamp conifer	Mich.	0.03[c]	3000	0.070[c]	1300	Whitney 1986
Prairie and oak savanna	Wis.	–	16	–	–	Dorney 1981
Canada						
Spruce–feather moss	Quebec	–	130[d]	–	–	Cogbill 1985
Jack pine	Quebec	–	70[d]	–	–	Cogbill 1985
Aspen–birch	Quebec	–	70[d]	–	–	Cogbill 1985

[a] Estimate assumes post-fire birch–aspen type visible for 75 years after a fire.
[b] Estimate assumes windfalls on survey lines evident for 30 years.
[c] Estimate assumes disturbance noted on survey lines evident for 15 years. The higher estimate for fire in central N.Y. assumes that half of open woods and brushy areas noted in the surveys were due to fire.
[d] Estimate based on mean stand age, see Cogbill (1985).

forest accompanying these modifications have also altered the forest's susceptibility to natural disturbances, *vide* Goodlett (1954). In a few cases extensive
areas of old-growth forests have been left intact, so that ecologists have been
able to monitor the effects of natural disturbances on primary forests over a
range of site conditions. Their studies have given us a better appreciation of
the varied response of the virgin forest to catastrophic disturbances. Work on a
series of old-growth hemlock–white pine–northern hardwood plots in the 2000
ha Pisgah tract in southern New Hampshire by the Harvard Forest has documented a history of periodic disturbance by several major windstorms and one
fire (Henry and Swan 1974; Foster 1988a). Major pulses of tree establishment
were tied to the hurricanes of 1635 and 1938 and an extensive fire in 1650.
Cline and Spurr (1942) and Foster (1988a) noted that the frequent occurrence
of winds and fires on the more exposed ridge tops of the Pisgah tract maintained a unique assemblage of pioneer species, e.g., white pine, paper birch,
and oak, on these sites.

The Tionesta Scenic and Research Natural Area, a 1670 ha tract in the
Allegheny National Forest in northwestern Pennsylvania, is probably the
largest remaining example of the virgin hemlock–northern hardwood type in
the Northeast. Research by the United States Forest Service indicates that the
area has been subject to three major windstorms over the past 185 years. One
hundred hectares were blown down in 1808. One hundred and fifty hectares
were destroyed in 1870 and 320 ha devastated in the unique tornado outbreak
of 1985, the most severe in Pennsylvania's history (Olenderski 1985). The
total area affected was approximately 570 ha, yielding an average of 3.1
ha/year and a rotation period of approximately 540 years. Most of the second-
growth stands of sugar maple, red maple, beech, and black cherry, which
cover approximately 25% of the area today, date to these disturbances
(Bjorkbom and Larson 1977). Unfortunately it is difficult to tell if the rotation
period of a limited area like the Tionesta tract is representative of
Pennsylvania's forests as a whole or if it is unduly influenced by the idiosyn-
cratic occurrence of extreme events like the 1985 tornado outbreak.

The Upper Peninsula of Michigan contains some of the largest remaining
tracts of primary forest in the Midwest. Notable among these are the 2500 ha
Huron Mountain Club tract, the 14 500 ha Porcupine Mountain Wilderness
State Park and the 6000 ha Sylvania Wilderness Area of the Ottawa National
Forest. Frelich and Lorimer (1991) analyzed the radial growth patterns of the
canopy trees of seventy 0.5 ha plots randomly distributed across these tracts.
They equated rapid growth in the sapling stage or a release from suppression
with a disturbance in the immediate vicinity of the cored tree. The resulting
disturbance chronology suggested that major disturbances which destroyed

> 60% of the canopy were rare events in the hemlock–hardwood forests of the region. Disturbances of this magnitude had a rotation period of > 1500 years. Small gaps or episodes of light disturbances which removed < 20% of the canopy accounted for the entry of most of the trees into the canopy (Frelich and Lorimer 1991).

Miron Heinselman's (1973) study of the fire history of the 215 000 ha Boundary Waters Canoe Area of northern Minnesota exemplifies the important role fire played in the presettlement forests of the Upper Great Lakes region. Relying upon historical evidence, fire-scarred trees, and dates of stand origin, Heinselman was able to construct a detailed picture of the fire history of the area. Heinselman's estimate of a natural fire rotation period of 100 years for the area as a whole is indicative of the state of flux of the vegetation in the Boundary Waters Canoe Area. Red and white pine stands on islands or to the east of natural fire barriers burned less frequently, experiencing a rotation period of 150 to 250 years, while jack pine stands burned at 50 to 100 year intervals. The high incidence of fire probably reflected the dry climatic regime of the area, the flammable nature of much of the vegetation, especially the conifers, and the high fuel loading of the area associated with the region's thin soils and the susceptibility of the vegetation to breakage and uprooting (Heinselman 1973).

At this point, it is difficult if not impossible to construct a detailed map of the incidence of disturbance in the presettlement forest. The requisite information is either too crude or too sketchy. The studies, to date, however, allow one to rough in the broader outlines of the map. Fires apparently dominated much of the birch, aspen, pine, and oak forests of the upper Midwest and isolated areas in the Northeast, while hurricanes, occurring at a frequency of one every 100 to 150 years, kept much of southern New England in a state of flux. Over the remainder of the area, however, it was probably the death of an occasional tree in the canopy that determined the dynamics of the stand (Runkle 1982; Lorimer 1989; Schaetzl *et al.* 1989). Marsh ([1864] 1965, 30) was apparently correct, at least for northern New England, when he stated that 'trees fall singly, not by square roods.' If the primeval forest 'did not consist of stagnant stands of immense trees stretching with little change over vast areas' (Cline and Spurr 1942), neither was it an amalgamation of pioneer species recovering from one form of disturbance or another.

Composition of the forest

Although primary or old-growth forests covered most of North America as recently as 100 to 300 years ago, we still have surprisingly little information about their composition. Early travel accounts are often vague as to the relative abundance of the tree species or to the regions involved. A number of ecologists (Braun [1950] 1967; Küchler 1964) have constructed maps of the natural or the presettlement vegetation of the eastern United States, drawing fine lines between what were frequently gradual changes in the composition of the forest. Often the designated vegetation types were largely theoretical constructs, statements of the 'potential natural' vegetation or the vegetation in the absence of disturbing influences (Heinselman 1975). Figure 4.3 represents an attempt to depict the character of the vegetation at the time of the earliest land surveys. All of the data were extracted from the land survey literature or from manuscript sources. Although the use of data from the surveys is not without its pitfalls (note discussion of limitations in chapter 2), the surveys still constitute one of the few quantitative sources of information on the composition of America's early forests. Most of the areas were surveyed prior to extensive European settlement or disturbance.

A number of investigators have utilized the early land survey records to construct state or county maps of the major vegetation types before settlement. Unfortunately the strong community emphasis of these maps has often obscured the more subtle response of individual species to site conditions. The 'isotree' maps shown in Fig. 4.3 provide a better picture of the abundance of the more important species of the presettlement era. The solid lines connect points with similar levels of percentage abundances in the survey data. Each of the plotted points is based on a sample of 100 or more witness, bearing, or line trees, 100 being the minimum size recommended by Bourdo (1955, 144) as providing a consistent percentage over the area under consideration. Most of the points in Fig. 4.3 are based on a sample of several hundred to several thousand trees spread over a township or a county. In several cases the county data was broken into smaller, more homogeneous units. In many ways the 'isotree' maps compliment the 'isopoll' maps developed by palynologists to show the regional distribution of modern pollen types (Bernabo and Webb 1977). A brief review of the maps, supplemented with a running commentary of early travelers' observations, follows.

The geographer Carl Sauer (1941) once commented on the similarity of the vegetation of the New World and the Old World by stating that it would have been impossible for the early colonists to have crossed an ocean anywhere in the world and have found as little that was unfamiliar on the opposite side. Certainly the abundance of oaks in New and Old England lends credence to Sauer's statement (Fig. 4.3a). Forests of oaks, particularly white oak, stretched in a broad band across southern New England, north up the Hudson River Valley to within 20 miles of Albany (Colden, 1851), then south and west

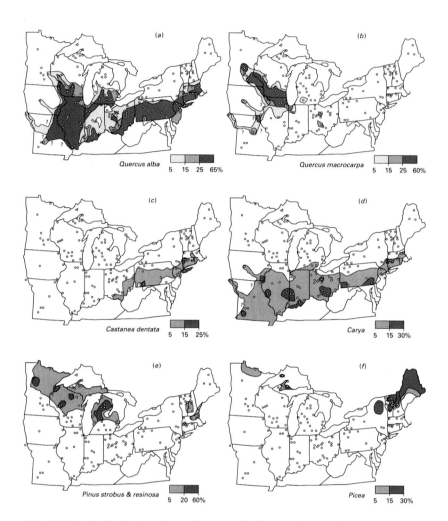

Fig. 4.3 Maps depicting abundance of tree species in presettlement forests, expressed in contoured values of percentage of trees noted in early land surveys. Much of the birch in northern Minnesota and Wisconsin (Fig. 4.3j) is *Betula papyrifera*. Survey sites shown in Fig. 4.3o and sources of information are as follows (Twp. = Township): (1)–(3) various regions in N Maine, Lorimer (1977), (4) Woodstock, N.H., 1792 manu-script map of town lots in Woodstock, N.H., New Hampshire Historical Society, (5) Campton, N.H., Hamburg (1984), (6) Lebanon, N.H., Torbert (1935), (7) Henniker, N.H., Clark (1970, 218), (8)–(15) various regions of N Vt., Siccama (1971), (16) Williamstown, Mass., Saterson (1977), (17) Petersham, Mass., Proprietors' Records, Town Clerk's office, Petersham, (18) Concord, Mass., Whitney and Davis (1986), (19) Manchester, Mass., Jewett (1889), (20) Salisbury, Conn., Warner (1932), (21)-(23) Norfolk, Goshen, and Canaan, Conn., Winer (1955), (24) Woodstock, Conn., Proprietors' Records, Connecticut State Library, (25) Greenwich, Conn., Niering and

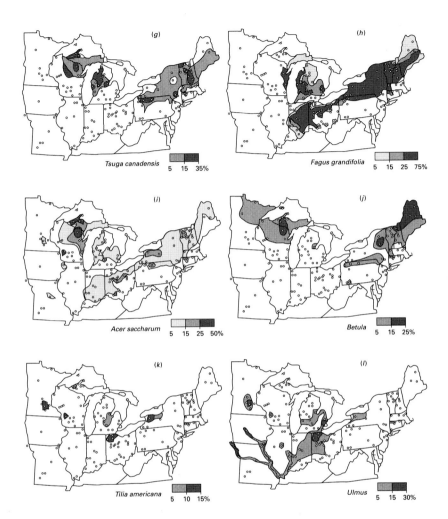

Fig. 4.3 *cont.*
Egler (1981), (26) NW N.Y., field notes of McCombs Purchase, tracts 1–3, printed in *Annual Report of the State Engineer and Surveyor of the State of New York for the fiscal year ending September 30, 1903*. Albany: Oliver A. Quale, State Printer, (27) Adirondacks, maps and field notes of Totten and Crossfield Purchase, N.Y. State Archives, (28) Catskills, McIntosh (1962), (29) Hudson River Valley, Hurley and Rochester Patents, McIntosh (1962), (30) Oyster Bay, Loeb (1987), (31) survey of township lines in N Genesee, S Orleans Counties, *in* Description of Genesee lands according to the situation in 1798 by J. Ellicott, microfilm reel 115, Holland Land Company Papers, Reed Library, State University of New York at Fredonia, (32) Military Tract, Marks, Gardescu, and Seischab (1992), (33) southern and western boundary of Chautauqua County, Commissioners on the Boundary Line between the State of New York and the State of Pennsylvania (1886), (34) part of S Cattaraugus

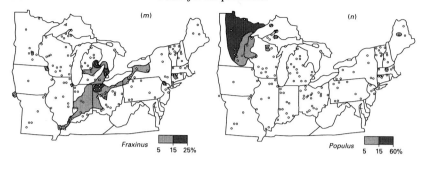

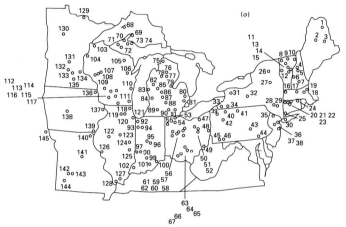

Fig. 4.3 *cont.*

County, Gordon (1940), (35)–(38) Wantage Twp., Sussex County; Elizabeth Town, Essex County; Middlesex County; Shrewsbury Twp., Monmouth County, Loeb (1987), (39) Crawford County, survey map of Donation Lands, Crawford County Historical Society, (40) Allegheny National Forest, Whitney (1990), (41) Potter County, Goodlett (1954), (42) Clarion County, Holland Land Company surveys and surveyors' notes, Huidekoper Collection, Crawford County Historical Society, (43) West Hanover Twp., Dauphin County, warrantee twp. map, Pennsylvania State Archives, (44) northern Lancaster County, Lemon ([1972] 1976, 243), (45) northwestern Dunbar Twp., Fayette County, warrantee twp. map, Pennsylvania State Archives, (46) southeastern Dunbar Twp., Fayette County, warrantee twp. map, Pennsylvania State Archives, (47) Brecksville Twp., Cuyahoga County, Williams (1949), (48) Township 12, Range 3 of the Seven Ranges, manuscript map showing survey of twp. by Isaac Sherman in 1786, map collection, Pussey Library, Harvard University, (49) Townships 2 and 3, Range 7, Washington County, Seven Ranges Survey township plat maps, Land Office, State Auditor's Office, Columbus, Ohio, (50)–(52) N Wayne and Ashland Counties, S Wayne and N Holmes Counties, S Holmes County, Whitney (1982), (53) 2 twps. in oak openings region, Fulton and Henry Counties, Congress Lands Survey plat maps, Land Office, State Auditor's Office, Columbus, (54) Bartlow and Richfield Twps., Henry County and Henry, Jackson, and Milton Twps., Wood County, Shanks (1938, 104–105), (55) 3 twps. in Black Swamp, Paulding County, Congress Lands Survey plat maps, Land Office, State Auditor's Office, Columbus (56)–(57) regions bordering

Sandusky Plains and Sandusky Plains, Crawford, Marion, and Wyandot Counties, Whitney and Steiger (1985), (58) Delaware County, Ogden (1965), (59) Bowles Creek, Perry, and Rush Creek Twps., Logan County, Diller (1932), (60) Harrison, Lake , Liberty, and Washington Twps., Logan County, Diller (1932), (61) Auglaize County, Gysel (1944), (62) Shelby County, Shanks (1953), (63) Darby, Deer Creek, Perry, Scioto, and Wayne Twps., Pickaway County, Shupe (1930), (64) Ross County, Crowl (1937), (65) E Vinton County, Beatley (1959, 109), (66)–(67) Brush Creek Twp., White Oak Twp., Highland County, Norris (1948, 99), (68) Isle Royale, Janke, McKaig, and Raymond (1978), (69)–(70) Tier 58N in Ranges 27–29, Keweenaw County, 6 twps. about Misery Bay, Ontonagon and Houghton Counties, Bourdo (1955), (71) N Ontonagon County, Detwyler (1966), (72) 8 twps. on headwaters of east branch of the Ontonagon River, S Ontonagon County, Lawrence (1954), (73) 4 twps. in central Baraga County, Bourdo (1955), (74) 3 twps. in NW Marquette County, Bourdo (1955), (75) 3 twps. in Cheboygan County, Kilburn (1958), (76)–(77) Crawford County, Roscommon County, Whitney (1987), (78) selected sections in 16 twps. of Missaukee County, Elliott (1953), (79) 7 twps. in Bay County, Jones and Kapp (1972), (80)–(81) St Clair County, Macomb County, Young (1952), (82)–(87) 4 S twps. of Lake County, Oceana County, Ottawa County, Mecosta County, Montcalm County, Ionia County, manuscript, Lawrence Brewer, 'A study of the vegetational tension zone in Michigan using pre- and postsettlement tree surveys', (88) Eaton County, Dodge (1987), (89) Kalamazoo County, Kenoyer (1930), (90) Jackson County, Hartesveldt (1951), (91) Washtenaw County, Merk (1951), (92)–(94) Lake County, Newton County, Jasper County, Rohr and Potzger (1950), (95) Hendricks County, Potzger and Potzger (1950), (96) Marion and Johnson Counties, Blewett and Potzger (1950), (97)–(98) floodplains and terraces of Wabash River, Vigo County, uplands, Vigo County, Donselman (1975), (99) Lawrence County, Potzger and Potzger (1950), (100) Clark, Floyd, Jefferson, Scott, and Switzerland Counties, Ross (1950), (101) Harrison and Washington Counties, Keith (1983), (102) 1 twp. (T3S, R13W), Gibson County, Potzger, Potzger, and McCormick (1956), (103) Brule River basin, Douglas County, Fassett (1944), (104) uplands of Crex meadows, W Burnett County, Vogl (1964), (105) 1 twp. (T35N, R14E), Forest County, Stearns (1949), (106) twp. in E Shawano County, Ward (1956b), (107)–(109) northern forest region, oak–pine barrens region, oak openings region, Eau Claire County, Barnes (1974), (110) twp. in S Sheboygen County, Ward (1956b), (111) oak openings of W Racine County, Goder (1957), (112) S Kickapoo River watershed, Kline and Cottam (1979), (113) Aldo Leopold Memorial Reserve, Sauk County, Liegel (1982), (114) Columbia County, Tans (1976), (115) parts of 7 twps., Dane County, Cottam (1949), (116) Iowa County, Stroessner and Habeck (1966), (117) Beloit Twp., Rock County, Ward (1956a), (118) Lake County, Moran (1978), (119) DeKalb County, Moran (1980), (120) Kane County, Kilburn (1959), (121) lake plain of glacial Lake Chicago, Cook County, Hanson (1981), (122)–(123) Mason County, McLean County, Rodgers and Anderson (1979), (124) Douglas County, Ebinger (1986), (125) Coles County, Ebinger (1987), (126) upland forest, lower Illinois River Valley, Zawacki, Hausfater, and Meyers (1969), (127) Williamson County, Anderson and Anderson (1975), (128) unglaciated S Illinois, Leitner and Jackson (1981), (129) Kabetogama Peninsula, Voyageur's National Park, Ferris (1980, 21), (130) Itasca State Park, Spurr (1954), (131)–(135) N oak–aspen area, W aspen area, Big Woods area, E oak area, S oak area, Grimm (1984), (136)–(139) Allamakee County, Jackson County, Lee County, selected twps. on the Des Moines River, Dick-Peddie (1955, 24–25, 54), (140)–(141) Clark County, Boone County, Howell and Kucera (1956), (142)–(143) barrens and oak–hickory forests, lower Pomme de Terre River basin, McMillan (1976), (144) Dade County, Howell and Kucera (1956), (145) Nemaha County, Pappas, Toews, and Fischer (1982).

across the limestone valley and ridge section of southern Pennsylvania
(Schoepf [1788] 1968, 1:308) to the low, dry oak and chestnut-covered hills
and ridges of western Pennsylvania (Hutchins 1778, 1) and southeastern Ohio
(Gibbons 1983, 112). In many cases white oak was so abundant, it almost constituted a monoculture. The well-known botanist F. A. Michaux (1818, 2:18)
stated that western Pennsylvania was dominated by 'large forests, nine tenths
of which consisted of White Oaks.' White oak was also common on the drier,
more rugged terrain of southern Indiana and the Ozark Plateau. Hickory (Fig.
4.3d) and chestnut (Fig. 4.3c) were frequent associates of the oaks. Chestnut
reached its greatest abundance in the oak–chestnut forests of the southern
Appalachians (Michaux 1819, 3:9). Its range, however, extended north to
southern New England and west to the acid sandstone outliers of the
Allegheny Plateau of central Ohio (Norris 1948, 58–60) and the dry beach
ridges south of Lake Erie (Ives 1947, 17). Surveyors rarely separated the hickories into species. The hickory category as a result contains a heterogeneous
mix of species. It includes a number of taxa characteristic of the drier upland
areas of the east, e.g., shagbark hickory, mockernut hickory, and pignut hickory, as well as a few species, e.g., big shellbark hickory and pecan, associated
with the bottomlands and moister areas of the Midwest (Dobbins 1937, 57,
72).

Estimates of the abundance of white pine and some of the other commercially important species in the presettlement forest have varied widely. A number of investigators, undoubtedly influenced by tales of the amount of pine
extracted from the region (Andrews 1948), have assumed that pine was the
dominant species of the Northeast (Recknagel 1923). In reality large concentrations or pure stands of white pine were probably limited to areas of light,
sandy soils along the rivers and upland areas subject to frequent blowdowns
(Fisher 1921; Spurr and Cline 1942). William Wood ([1634] 1977, 40), for
instance, cited the occurrence of 'stately high-grown [pine, presumably white
pine] trees ten miles together' on at least one of New England's rivers while
Peter Kalm ([1772] 1972, 326) noted white pine was abundant in the Hudson
River Valley north of Albany. On the coarser textured soils, particularly the
deltaic and wind-blown sands, white pine graded into pitch pine. Excellent
examples of the pitch pine type could be found on the pine plains of the lower
Connecticut River Valley (Judd 1905, 295; Hawes 1906b) and the pine bush
between Albany and Schenectady, New York (Huey 1975, 7–8). White pine
was also a component of the mixed conifer–hardwood forests of central and
northern New England. Regionally, however, white pine never represented
more than 5 to 15% of the witness trees recorded in the early land surveys of
the Northeast (Fig. 4.3e).

Extensive stands of white and frequently red pine were much more common in the Midwest where together they often comprised more than a quarter to a half of the bearing trees reported. Coarse-textured soils associated with outwash deposits in interlobate areas, e.g., the High Plains region of lower Michigan, and postglacial beaches and shorelines, e.g., the Saginaw basin, favored the occurrence of many of the great pineries of the Lake States (Whitney 1986). Filbert Roth's early (1898b) map of the pineries of northern Wisconsin, for instance, shows a very strong correspondence with Thwaites (1956) map of the sandy outwash deposits of the same area. The map of the presettlement pineries can almost be superimposed on the outwash deposits.

Of the remaining conifers, only spruce and hemlock were abundant enough to warrant more than a passing comment. Red spruce was the characteristic tree of the Adirondacks and the higher elevations of northern New England (Fig. 4.3f). It dominated the spruce flats of the lower elevations of the Adirondacks and often formed over 60% of the stand on the spruce slope community above 2400 feet (730 m) in the Adirondacks and the White Mountains (Hosmer and Bruce 1901, 18; Chittenden 1904). The role of hemlock in the presettlement forest is a particularly intriguing question. Due to its ability to endure shade, many ecologists have portrayed it as the climax species par excellence. Large sections of the Northeast have accordingly been mapped as variants of the climax hemlock–northern hardwoods or hemlock–white pine–northern hardwoods forest type (Nichols 1935; Braun [1950] 1967; Westveld *et al.* 1956). Figure 4.3g suggests that hemlock's importance in the presettlement forest was overexaggerated. Outside of a few areas – the 'Greenwoods' of northwestern Connecticut (Winer 1955, 71–77), portions of the Connecticut River Valley, the Catskills, and the 'Black Forest' of northern Pennsylvania (Bishop 1923), hemlock rarely constituted more than 15% of the recorded trees. In the Upper Great Lakes region high concentrations of hemlock were often confined to the finer, heavier textured soils (Bourdo 1955, 33, 51; Goder 1955, 51; Whitney 1986). Fire, as noted earlier, appears to have been a major determinant of the western extension of hemlock's range in Wisconsin (Goder 1955, 89). The southern boundary of hemlock's range across central Wisconsin and lower Michigan follows a major climatic break and a floristic discontinuity known as a tension zone (Potzger 1948; Curtis 1959). Areas to the north of the zone are characterized by higher rainfall, greater snowfall, less evapotranspiration, and cooler temperatures and a stronger flow of cool, moist air masses (Goder 1955, 89–90; Curtis 1959).

Ecologists have frequently suggested that beech's predominance in many remnant stands in the Midwest may be an artifact of high grading (Cain 1935; Gordon 1969, 35). According to this scenario the selective removal of the other, more commercially valuable, species converted many forests of mixed hardwoods to beech. The overwhelming representation of beech in the early land surveys (Fig. 4.3h) belies this hypothesis. Throughout northern Pennsylvania, upstate New York, and northern New England, beech made up over 20% and occasionally over 40% of the trees reported in the surveys (McIntosh 1962; Siccama 1971). As the early surveyor, Richard Smith (1906, 54) noted while working in upstate New York in 1769, 'Beech is the Master Wood [here] as Oak is in Pennsylvania.' Forests of beech also spread across much of the Midwest, reaching their best expression on the deeper, finer (clay to silt) textured tills derived from lake sediments (Quick 1923; Whitney 1982; Dodge 1989). Beech was 'the principal kind of timber' (Rupp 1836, 269) in Indiana where one observer (Chamberlain 1849, 16) estimated that beech in conjunction with the oaks 'constituted not less than two-thirds of the whole number of forest trees.'

Sugar maple was a frequent associate of beech, forming the well-known beech–maple community of the lower Great Lakes region (Fig. 4.3i). In contrast to the more moisture-loving beech, sugar maple occupied the slightly elevated, better-drained sites of the Till Plains region of Ohio (Gilbert and Riemenschneider 1980; Whitney 1982). It was particularly abundant in the fertile Genesee region of upstate New York (Campbell [1793] 1937, 211) and in the Upper Peninsula of Michigan. Yellow birch is the third species in a triumvirate of species (beech–sugar maple–yellow birch) that have long been recognized as the dominants of the northern hardwoods community. One should not infer, however, that all of the species were equally abundant in the presettlement forest. Over much of its range, yellow birch accounted for less than 15% of the trees recorded in the surveys (Fig. 4.3j).

Soil moisture was probably the most important determinant of the character of the species composition of the presettlement forest. In at least one species, however, the nutrient status of the soil also appears to have been a limiting factor. Basswood is considered a relatively calcium demanding species (Ashby 1959). It is interesting to note that high concentrations of basswood, i.e., greater than 10% of the trees reported in the early surveys, were associated with some of the more calcareous sites – the high lime till of upstate New York's Genesee region, the maple–basswood region of southern Minnesota and the high lime, glacial lakebed sediments of northwestern Ohio (Fig. 4.3k). F. A. Michaux (1819, 3:102) stated that in some areas of the rich Genesee region basswood constituted 'two thirds and sometimes the whole of the forests.'

Lowlands supported a very distinctive type of forest. Clay deposited in several of the high, ice-dammed, late-glacial predecessors of Lake Erie and Lake Huron created the extremely water retentive soils of the Lake Plains sections of Ohio and Michigan. Surveyors and early accounts described much of the region as an 'interminable morass' (Hubbard 1881), an area of marshes and timbered swamps unfit for cultivation (Tiffin 1834). Most of the low-lying plains, like the infamous Black Swamp of northwestern Ohio, were centers of the elm–ash swamp forest type (Fig. 4.3 l and m). The elm and ash were replaced by forests of white cedar, tamarack, and black spruce, the conifer bog-swamp community, to the north (Curtis 1959, 221–242; Whitney 1986).

Comparatively shade intolerant species like white birch and aspen (*Populus tremuloides* and *P. grandidentata*) have long been considered indicators of disturbed site conditions (Lorimer 1980; Ahlgren and Ahlgren 1984, 171–179). Their prevalence in the presettlement forests of northern Wisconsin and Minnesota (Fig. 4.3j and n) underscores the high incidence of fire in the past in this area.

Presettlement grasslands or prairie

Contrary to popular opinion and the views expressed at the beginning of this chapter, eastern North America was not an uninterrupted expanse of woods at the time of European settlement. Europeans encountered outliers of the continental interior's vast plain of grasslands along the east coast (Fig. 4.4). The outliers were termed 'plains,' a word more closely allied with the nature of the vegetation, than a feature of the topography. Plains were open areas free of trees (Johnson 1805). Daniel Denton ([1670] 1966, 6) described one of the better known plains, the Hempstead Plains of New York, as follows: 'Towards the middle of Long-Island lyeth a plain, sixteen miles long and four broad, upon which plain grows very fine grass, that makes exceeding good hay, and is very good pasture for sheep or other cattel.' Other open areas like the Montauk Downs of western Long Island apparently took their name from the grass-covered Downs of Sussex, England (Taylor 1923). Both the Hempstead Plains and the Montauk Downs formed open grasslands that were probably dominated by little bluestem (*Schizachyrium scoparium*) when the Europeans arrived (Mitchill 1807, 165; Taylor 1923; Svenson 1936).

Natural breaks or glades in the forest were also a characteristic feature of the more rugged interior sections of the East and the Midwest, i.e., the Allegheny Mountains of western Pennsylvania, the knobs of southern Indiana and the Ozark Mountains of Missouri. Although the term glades was generally applied to small openings in the woods (Schroeder 1983), several of Pennsylvania's historic glades covered a considerable area (Losensky 1961, 26). The Ohio naturalist S. P. Hildreth (1843) described the famed glades region of southwestern Pennsylvania in 1788 as 'an elevated platteau, which in many points

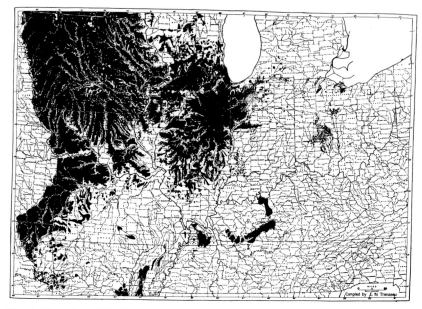

Fig. 4.4 Location of the Prairie Peninsula as shown by Transeau (1935). Reprinted by permission of the Ecological Society of America.

bears a strong resemblance to the prairies of the west. The soil is dark colored, thinly coated with trees, and covered with coarse grass.' Most investigators have attributed the occurrence of glades to shallow soil overlying relatively resistant bedrock (Bourne 1820; Nelson and Ladd 1983). The soils were often saturated with water in the autumn, the winter, and the spring. Due to their low water-holding capacity, however, very xeric, stressful conditions prevailed for the trees during the summer months (Kucera and Martin 1957; Aldrich, Bacone, and Hutchison 1981; Bacone, Casebere, and Hutchison 1982).

The French were the first Europeans to encounter the great open plains of the Midwest. They applied the term 'prairie,' meaning meadow land, to the grasslands of the Mississippi River Valley (Gleason 1909). The English later adopted the French term 'prairie' and applied it liberally to all tracts of land naturally devoid of trees (Oliver [1843] 1966, 22). The term encompassed a wide range of treeless areas including sedge meadows, marshes, and bogs or 'cranberry prairies' (Gleason 1917; Sears 1926). Plant geographers designated the eastward bulge of grassland (Fig. 4.4), the 'Prairie Peninsula' (Transeau 1935; Stuckey 1981). In reality the area more nearly resembled an archipelago (Sears 1981). Outliers of the main body of grasslands in Iowa, Illinois, western Minnesota, and Missouri (Table 4.3) could be found far to the east in Ohio

Table 4.3. *Extent of prairies and savannas during the presettlement and postsettlement periods*

State	Extent (million ha)	% total area of state	Amount remaining (ha)	% of original	Sources
Prairies					
Illinois	8.5	59	1000	0.01	Schwegman 1983
Indiana	1.3	15	150	0.01	Betz 1978; Runkle and Roosa 1989
Iowa	12.0	85	1200	0.02	Smith 1981
Michigan	n.d.	n.d.	n.d.	n.d.	
Minnesota	7.3	35	30300	0.40	Wendt 1984
Missouri	4.8	26	30000	0.60	Schroeder 1983
Ohio	0.2	2	n.d.	n.d.	Cusick and Troutman 1978
Wisconsin	0.8	6	n.d.	n.d.	Curtis 1959
Total	34.9				
Savannas and barrens					
Illinois	n.d.	n.d.	530	n.d.	
Indiana	0.5	5	620	0.12	Nuzzo 1986
Iowa	n.d.	n.d.	20	n.d.	Nuzzo 1986
Michigan	0.2[a]	1	150	0.07	Nuzzo 1986
Minnesota	2.2	10	500	0.02	Nuzzo 1986
Missouri	5.3	30	310	< 0.01	Nuzzo 1986
Ohio	0.2	2	< 20	< 0.01	Nuzzo 1986
Wisconsin	2.9[b]	16–20	470	0.02	Curtis 1959; Nuzzo 1986
Total	11.0–13.0		~2600	0.02	Nuzzo 1986

[a] Probably an underestimate.
[b] Includes 0.7 million hectares brush prairie or oak barrens.
Note: n.d. = no data available.

(Dobbins 1937, 105–127; Whitney and Steiger 1985) and Michigan (Veatch 1927; Butler 1947–1949).

Broad expanses of grassland were 'an anomaly in the economy of nature' (Stuart 1833, 406) to the early Europeans more familiar with the deciduous forests of the Atlantic seaboard. The grasslands of the presettlement period remain an enigma to many contemporary investigators. As one prominent ecologist, Henry Gleason (1909) noted, prairies were converted into cornfields long before the development of the field of ecology and any formalized scientific studies. Questions still remain as to their origin, their species composition, their structure, their dynamics and their relationship to the surrounding woodlands. To the historian and the scientist alike, these are the unsolved problems of the prairie (Gleason 1909).

Historians have attempted to outline the early settler's response to the prairie (Angle 1968; Jakle 1977; Williams 1981). Unfortunately European reactions were often conditioned by literary conventions. As in the case of forests, an emphasis on the picturesque, the romantic, and the sublime colored many impressions of the prairie in the first half of the nineteenth century. Most observers described the prairie in very general terms. The prairie was an 'immense flower garden' (Curtis 1852, 221), 'a heaving sea of tall herbs and plants' (Gerhard 1857, 241), 'a boundless landscape of tall grasses waving in the breeze' (Flagg [1838] 1906, 214). The season of the year and the inconveniences of traveling also influenced the observer's reaction to the prairie. Charles Dickens ([1842] 189?, 185) considered one prairie near St. Louis to be 'oppressive in its barren monotony' in the early spring. 'The grass was not yet high; there were bare black patches on the ground [presumably burned]; and the few wild flowers that the eye could see, were poor and scanty.' To naturalists like Lewis Beck (1823, 9), the Grand Prairie in central Illinois was little more than 'a dreary uninhabited waste.' Travel across the extensive 'wastes' of the prairie was almost impossible during the summer months when swarms of green-headed flies (probably horseflies, deerflies, and mosquitoes) attacked the weary traveler (Beck 1823, 81; Oliver [1843] 1966, 97; Short 1845; Vestal 1939; McManis 1964, 59).

Unlike the early land survey records of forested areas, the General Land Office survey field notes are surprisingly devoid of information on the nature of the early tallgrass prairie. Sketchy references to 'wet, grassy prairies,' 'rich dry prairies,' or 'prairies of good quality, high grass' dominate the early surveyors' section line descriptions (Whitney and Steiger 1985). Occasionally a surveyor would note some of the more conspicious forbs and shrubs, e.g., redroot (*Ceanothus americanus*), rosin (*Silphium terebinthinaceum*), hazel (*Corylus americana*), indigo (*Baptisia* sp.), and sunflowers (*Helianthus* spp.), encountered on the prairie (Moran 1978, 1980, 45). The different species of grasses, however, were rarely delineated. It was not until 1833 that the Surveyor General of Ohio, Indiana, and Michigan required the surveyor to record 'the kind of grass or other herbage' the prairies produced (White 1984a, 299, 370).

A few remnants of the prairie persisted down to the twentieth century. Many investigators (Clements 1920, 308; Sampson 1921; Curtis and Greene 1949) acknowledged that even these had probably been altered by years of grazing, haymaking, drainage, chance meterological events, and a change in the fire regime of the prairie.

Ecologists attempting to reconstruct the nature of the presettlement tall-grass prairie were forced to rely upon early nineteenth century herbarium specimens (Reihmer 1939). Most of the existing studies (Weaver and Fitzpatrick 1934; Curtis and Greene 1949) suggest the prairie contained 200 to 300 species of plants as opposed to over 2000 species for the eastern decidu-ous forest (Bazzaz and Parrish 1982). The Compositae, the Gramineae, and the Leguminosae were particularly well represented in the flora (Allen 1870; Curtis and Greene 1949).

Grasses formed the matrix of the prairie. On the drier, upland sites they were very short (Dablon 1900). In the moister areas or the sloughs the grasses often ranged up to 5 to 6 feet (1.5 to 1.8 m) or more in height (Dablon 1900; Weaver 1954, 11–12). Early accounts (Bebb 1860; Parsons 1920, 260) and reminiscences of the settlers (Hilgard 1915; Sampson 1921) indicate that big bluestem (*Andropogon gerardii*), colloquially known as bluejoint (Gleason 1917), and Indian grass (*Sorghastrum nutans*) covered large segments of the open tallgrass prairie. *Spartina pectinata* (prairie cordgrass), *Calamagrostis canadensis* (also known as bluejoint) and *Panicum virgatum* (switchgrass) probably dominated the wetter areas (Sampson 1921).

Forbs were responsible for much of the patterning and color of the prairie. Two of the more informative accounts of the composition and the structure of the original prairie are reproduced below. The first is an early description of Illinois' prairies by the botanist C. W. Short (1845).

[The] leading feature [of Illinois' prairies] is rather the unbounded profusion with which a few species occur in certain localities, than the mixed variety of many different species occuring any where. Thus from some elevated position in a large prairie the eye takes in at one glance thousands of acres literally empurpled with the flowering spikes of several species of *Liatris* [blazing star] ... In other situations, where a depressed or flattened surface and clayey soil favor the continuance of moisture, a few species of yellow-flowered *Coreopsis* occur in such profuse abundance as to tinge the entire sur-face with a golden burnish ... This peculiarity of an aggregation of individuals of one or more species, to something like an exclusive monoply of certain localities, obtains even in regard to those plants which are the rarest and least frequently met with; for when-ever one specimen was found there generally occurred many more in the same immedi-ate neighborhood.

Eugene Hilgard, the well-known soil scientist, likewise emphasized the patchwork or mosaic-like nature of the early prairies of southern Illinois. A section of his 1915 manuscript on the prairies of Illinois before the coming of the railroads is reproduced below. A [?] indicates that the modern-day equivalent of the scientific name given in the manuscript is difficult to ascertain.

In open spaces and the general open prairie the tall *Andropogon*s cover large areas almost alone, but usually interspersed with tall-growing flowers, especially composites of many kinds. Among these the three *Silphium*s (*S. perfoliatum, terebinthinaceum, and laciniatum*) were especially prominent, and with them a number of sunflowers of other genera, notably *Helianthus grosseserratus, doronicoides,* and *mollis,* also *Heliopsis helianthoides, Verbesina helianthoides,* and in the draws several *Bidens, Rudbeckia laciniata, Bidens bipinnata* and *Coreopsis grandiflora.* Where the grasses were lower there were glaring patches of *Rudbeckia hirta, Echinacea purpurea, Coreopsis aristata* [?], and others. Large purple patches were also formed sometimes in the tall *Andropogon,* sometimes solidly, by *Vernonia praealata* [?], and with it usually various *Eupatorium*s, notably *E. purpureum, altissimum, rugosum, Aster novae-angliae, Ambrosia trifida*; numerous species of *Solidago,* among which *S. canadensis, speciosa, rigida* and *altissima,* sometimes formed almost solid masses several acres in extent, especially the first named. *Cacalia tuberosa, Polymnia canadensis, Erigeron canadensis, Agastache nepetoides* were also abundant among the sunflowers, and *Physostegia virginiana, Petalostemum purpureum, Liatris scariosa,* various *Asclepias* – *A. purpurascens, incarnata, glaberrima* [?], *tuberosa* – and roses (*R. rubifolia* [?], *rubiginosa* [?]) added to the color. *Apocynum cannabinum, Campanula americana, Laportea canadensis* were also in evidence. It may be said that most of the species growing on the prairies had a tendency to grow in more or less compact patches, so as frequently to remind one of a varicolored quilt.

The changing seasonal aspect of the prairies attracted the attention of a number of observers.

The first coat of grass is mingled with small flowers; the violet [*Viola pedatifida*], the bloom of the strawberry [*Fragaria virginiana*], and others of the most minute and delicate texture. As the grass increases in size, these disappear, and others, taller and more gaudy, display their brilliant colors upon the green surface, and still later a larger and coarser succession rises with the rising tide of verdure

(Hall 1837, 75).

The height of the flowers always exceeded that of the grasses. The dimunitive phlox (*Phlox pilosa*), the baptisias and the shooting stars (*Dodecatheon meadia*) of spring gave way to the prairie clovers (*Petalostemum* spp.) and the coneflowers (*Echinacea pallida* and *Ratibida pinnata*) of summer and the taller composites of the autumn, notably the *Silphium*s and the sunflowers (Anonymous 1857).

The wetter segments of the prairie were dotted with thickets or 'roughs' of hazel, sumac, dogwood, plum, and willow (Short 1845). Streams or 'sloughs' protected the woody shrubs from fire. The temporary cessation of fire also encouraged the growth of a number of ligneous species, e.g., plums and crabapples, on the edges of the prairie (Thomas [1819] 1970, 207).

Forests defined the shape and the extent of the tallgrass prairie. In Missouri one had only to travel a few miles to encounter a change from timber to prairie and vice versa (Schroeder 1983). Few overlooked the intricate pattern created by the interplay of the forest and the prairie. As John Peck (1837, 8) wrote in his *Gazetteer of Illinois*: '... south of the national road leading from Terre Haute [Indiana] to the Mississippi, the prairies [of Illinois] are comparatively small, varying in size from those of several miles in width to those which contain only a few acres. [To the north] they widen and extend on the more elevated ground between the water courses to a vast distance, and are frequently from six to twelve miles in width. Their borders are by no means uniform. Long points of timber project into the prairies, and line the banks of streams, and points of prairie project into the the timber between these streams. In many instances are copses and groves of timber, from one hundred to two thousand acres, in the midst of prairies, like islands in the ocean ....' Timber was generally confined to the ridges, i.e., the moraines, and the water courses (Jones 1838, 34; Caird 1859, 49).

Detached bodies of trees known as prairie groves represent a particularly interesting chapter in the geography and the changing distribution of the forest and the prairie. Many of the remnant prairie groves are dominated by a number of wind and bird-dispersed species, e.g., sugar maple, hackberry, and elm, and are believed to be of a rather recent vintage, i.e., the last 400 to 600 years (Vestal and Heermans 1945). Most of the prairie groves were bounded on the west by water courses which preserved them from the action of fire (Short 1845; Caton 1876). Some scientists attribute the formation of the groves to the cooler and wetter conditions of the Little Ice Age. Streams which are intermittent now may have been more effective fire breaks during the Little Ice Age, which started approximately 800 years BP and ended in the nineteenth century (King and Johnson 1977). The formation of the prairie groves may have been part of a broader advance of trees onto the prairie (McComb and Loomis 1944; Howell and Kucera 1956; Wood 1976).

Although many were impressed by the uniformity of the prairies, the more competent observers recognized at least three different types of prairies: wet prairies, dry prairies, and bushy prairies (Flint [1828] 1970, 1:40). The wet prairies were characterized by extensive areas of standing water in the winter and the spring. They were incapable of being drained and uniformly regarded as 'unsuitable for improvement' or 'unfit for cultivation' (Bradley 1906; Meyer 1956). Most of Ohio's (Sears 1926; Dobbins 1937, 120), northeastern Illinois' (Dana 1819, 134), and north central Iowa's grasslands (Hewes 1951) fell under the heading of wet prairies. In contrast, a number of surveyors (Dana 1819, 32–34; Meyer 1956) and naturalists (Atwater 1827) recognized the agricultural potential of the dry prairies at a very early date. Dry prairies were more characteristic of Michigan's (Gordon 1959) and Wisconsin's rolling uplands. Segments of the Midwest's prairies contained a number of small trees and shrubs. Fire probably kept the hazel, the oak, and the sassafras sprouts under control and maintained the dominance of the grasses (Curtis 1959, 300). The result was a brushy prairie. Scientists typically recognize a wider range of prairies today (Betz 1978; White and Madany 1981; Wendt 1984). Modern systems of classification reflect the very diverse nature of the prairies' substrate, e.g., black silt–loam prairies, sand prairies, dolomite prairies, and gravel or loess hill prairies.

Few questions occasioned as much debate and speculation as the origin of the prairies. Most of the theories focused on one of three major factors – fire, climate, and soil (Transeau 1935). The fire hypothesis was popular with many of the early settlers who noted that the appearance of trees on the prairie coincided with settlement and the cessation of fires (Wells 1819; Caton 1876; Reynolds 1887, 231–232). The grass of the prairie represented a finely divided fuel which dried readily and was very combustible (Anderson 1983). Fires were as much a consequence as they were a cause of the prairie (Gleason 1912). They could maintain but did not always initiate a prairie. Geologists often favored the substrate hypothesis, pointing out what they perceived to be a close relationship between the occurrence of prairie and the nature of the soil (Lesquereux 1865; Whitney 1876). Prairies, however, embraced a wide range of soil types and topographic conditions (Shirreff [1835] 1971, 244). All of the above-mentioned theories failed because they attempted to account for the different types of prairies under a simple, all-encompassing principle. The reality was much more complex. The climate set the broader pattern. The Prairie Peninsula is characterized by a strong flow of dry continental air from the west (Fig. 3.3). Summer precipitation is often erratic. Extended droughts are more common than in areas immediately to the north and the south of the Prairie Peninsula (Borchert 1950). Within this climatic regime, soils and fires often tipped the balance in favor of the grasses (Gray 1878; Sampson 1921). They created an environment inhospitable for the growth of treees. Certain areas were simply too dry by virtue of their exposure or their coarse-textured soils. Over much of the Midwest, however, the story was more complex. The last continental ice sheet left large segments of the Midwest covered with level or slightly concave surfaces and clayey soils. Water accumulated on the level surfaces over the impervious subsoils during the winter and spring months and inhibited the normal development of the roots of the trees. Evapotranspiration and the flow of dry western winds dried out the prairie in the summer and subjected the trees to moisture stress (Whitney and Steiger 1985). The prairie was alternately too wet and too dry for the growth of trees (Newberry 1860; Englemann 1863; Whitford 1970). Fires ignited in the dry grass exacerbated the situation and may have indefinitely maintained the grasses on the coarser textured soils.

Savannas or openings

The distinction between the forest and the prairie was not always a clearcut affair (Collot 1909). Segments of each were often intermixed forming a complex mosaic. Terms like savanna, openings, scrub woodlands, and barrens emphasized the mixed character and physiognomy of the prairie–forest border (Baird 1832, 204). Most of these communities had a very transitory existence. They were maintained by fire and disappeared when the fires ceased. Most were gone within 20 to 40 years of settlement (Hubbard 1887, 67; Nuzzo 1986). Ecologists initially either overlooked them or considered them a variant of forests or grasslands (Brewer, Hodler, and Raup 1984). As a result, few appreciated their significance in the presettlement period. Work by Stout (1946), Cottam (1949), and Curtis (1959) eventually led to the 'rediscovery' of the oak savanna in Wisconsin. Our knowledge of the nature of the field layer of the savanna is limited to the observations of a few early naturalists (Packard 1988a). There is still a debate over the extent to which the savanna approximated a prairie with trees or the degree to which it supported its own distinctive flora. An increasing amount of evidence suggests that the savanna contained a number of animal-dispersed species (*Smilacina, Polygonatum,* and *Corylus*) as well as species that are common on the edge of woodlands today (Packard 1988b; Betz and Lamp 1992). The isolated trees of the openings probably attracted a number of birds and mammals that defecated seeds or buried nuts on the ground underneath the trees. Comprehensive discussions of the Midwest's original oak savannas and barrens can be found in Grimm (1981), Anderson (1983), and Nuzzo (1986).

Europeans developed a number of terms to describe the continuum between the forests and the prairies. Openings, a term used here interchangeably with savannas, represented breaks in the forest which were relatively destitute of trees (Dwight [1822] 1969, 4:36). Curtis (1959, 330) arbitrarily fixed the upper limits of the openings at 50% canopy coverage, a value which translated into a density of 2.5 to 47 trees per hectare (Anderson and Anderson 1975). As settlers penetrated the Midwest, they applied the term oak openings to very open groves of oak with an understory of grass and herbs (Blois [1838] 1975, 24; Peters 1970, 1972, 1978). Their structure and physiognomy varied depending upon the species of oak involved. The bur oak openings of Michigan and Wisconsin often bore a striking resemblance to orchards (Hoffman [1835] 1966 1: 183; Shirreff [1835] 1971, 218; Scott [1843] 1960, 181; Fox 1856;

Lanman 1871, 11). James Fenimore Cooper's (1860, 10–11) novel, *The Oak Openings*, provides a good description of the bur oak openings of Kalamazoo, Michigan, in 1812.

The country was what is termed 'rolling,' from some fancied resemblance to the surface of the ocean, when it is just undulating with a long 'groundswell.' Although wooded, it was not, as the American forest is wont to grow, with tall straight trees towering toward the light, but with intervals between the low oaks that were scattered profusely over the view, and with much of that air of negligence that one is apt to see in grounds, where art is made to assume the character of nature. The trees, with very few exceptions, were what is called the 'burr-oak,' a small variety of a very extensive genus; and the spaces between them, always irregular, and often of singular beauty, have obtained the name of 'openings,' the two terms combined giving their appellation to this particular species of native forest, under the name of 'Oak Openings.'

These woods, so peculiar to certain districts of country, are not altogether without some variety, though possessing a general character of sameness. The trees were of very uniform size, being little taller than pear-trees, which they resemble a good deal in form; and having trunks that rarely attain two feet in diameter. The variety is produced by their distribution. In places they stand with a regularity resembling that of an orchard; then, again, they are more scattered and less formal, while wide breadths of the land are occasionally seen in which they stand in copses, with vacant spaces, that bear no small affinity to artificial lawns, being covered with verdure. The grasses are supposed to be owing to the fires lighted periodically by the Indians in order to clear their hunting-grounds.

By way of contrast, many observers emphasized the more stately, park-like character of the white oak openings (Fox 1856; Hubbard 1928, 443). The white oaks were large and of a brittle and torn appearance (Gordon 1959).

Although government reports (Wilson 1868, 8–11) and travelers' accounts (Peters 1970, 1978) often stressed the luxurious nature of the grasses, it is obvious that the openings also contained a number of small oak 'grubs' (Hubbard 1847a). Fires prevented the maturation of the oak sprouts and maintained the open, grassland character of the openings (Muir 1916, 181–184; Whitford 1976).

Oaks were the characteristic species of the drought prone openings (Table 4.4). White and black oak dominated the shallow limestone openings of western New York (Maude 1826, 123) and the interlobate outwash sand and gravel openings of Michigan (Hubbard 1847a). Black oak was particularly common on the coarser textured soils of the fossilized sand bars of the Great Lakes region (Hehr 1970, 54; Betz 1978) and the outwash and wind-blown sands of the Illinois (Rodgers and Anderson 1979) and Wisconsin Rivers (Tans 1976). The drought resistant bur oak reached its highest abundance in the Midwest (Fig. 4.3b). Open-grown bur oak bordered many of the richer, more calcareous

Table 4.4. *Species composition of oak openings and barrens. Values represent percentage of trees recorded in early land surveys*

	Oak savanna or openings							Oak barrens
				Wisconsin (Columbia County)				
	New York (Erie and Genesee Counties)	Ohio (Marion, Wyandot, and Crawford Counties)	Illinois (Lake County)	Black oak sav.	Bur oak sav.	Wisconsin (Eau Claire County)	Missouri (Benton and Hickory Counties)	Indiana (Harrison County)
White oak	34	24	32	21	18	16	5	32
Bur oak		28	47	20	64	35	2	–
Black oak[a]	44	15	14	57	17	39	19	29
Post oak							58	
Blackjack oak							5	
Shingle oak		4						
Chinquapin oak							3	
Hickory	4	24	3			3	5	25
Aspen	11		1					
Other	8	5	3	2		7	4	14
No. of trees	156	683	?	313	438	?	227	392

[a] Includes some *Q. ellipsoidalis*, in Wisconsin.

Sources: New York (unpublished data, Holland Land Co. Survey, N.Y. State Archives); Ohio (Whitney and Steiger 1985); Illinois (Moran 1978); Wisconsin, Columbia Co. (Tans 1976); Wisconsin, Eau Claire Co. (Barnes 1974); Missouri (McMillan 1976); Indiana (Keith 1983).

prairies of northern Illinois, Indiana, Ohio, and southern Wisconsin (Potzger and Keller 1952; Whitney and Steiger 1985), while post oak and blackjack oak dominated the oak savannas of the western Ozarks (Table 4.4; Howell and Kucera 1956; McMillan 1976).

The exact extent of the openings is problematical. We still lack good estimates of the area formerly in openings in several key states (Table 4.3). One of the more knowledgeable land surveyors of Michigan, Bela Hubbard (1847a), stated that 'somewhat more than half of the [lower] peninsula [of Michigan] consist[ed] of openings and plains.' Oak savannas and barrens probably covered some 11 to 13 million hectares at the time of settlement (Nuzzo 1986), an area roughly one-third the size of the Midwest's presettlement grasslands (Table 4.3).

Barrens were 'tracts of land ... covered with low shrubs [especially hazel (Gleason 1922)] and brushwood' (Blaney [1824] 1916, 278). The term was originally applied to the limestone barrens of Kentucky (Peck 1837, 9) and southern Indiana (Keith 1983). It was later expanded to include the hardpan post oak barrens of southern Illinois (Dana 1819, 140; Engelmann 1865; Vestal 1936) and southern Indiana (Aldrich and Homoya 1984), and the sandy black and Hill's oak barrens of lower Michigan and southern Wisconsin (Finley 1951, 210; Lindsey 1961; Nuzzo 1986). In northern Wisconsin and Michigan, the oak barrens graded into jack pine barrens (Curtis 1959, 339–341). Most of the oak woodlands bordering Minnesota's prairies also fell into the barrens category – 'dense thicket[s] of scrub oak and brush resembling chapparal' (Grimm 1981, 165).

Fires and drought were the major factors responsible for the maintenance of the openings and the barrens (Curtis 1959, 334; Whitford and Whitford 1971; Whitney and Steiger 1985). The openings and the barrens bordering the grasslands were particularly susceptible to fires generated in the flammable matrix of the prairie. Fires also had a free reign on the limestone barrens due to the scarcity of effective fire breaks in the form of surface streams (Keith 1983). The various tree species of the openings and barrens differed with respect to their resistance to fire. The larger bur oak with their thick bark survived most of the fires. In contrast, the thin-barked black and Hill's oak were always susceptible to fire. Annual fires in the grass kept the black oaks in a diminutive, shrub-like condition (Curtis 1959, 336–337). A few trees managed to escape the fire 'by having the good fortune to grow on a bare spot at the door of a fox or badger den, or between straggling grass-types wide apart on the poorest sandy soil' (Muir 1916, 183). Shading also reduced the herbage and the fuel load under the larger trees and may have permitted the continued existence of the older, more fire sensitive oaks in the savanna (Anderson and Brown 1983).

The buildup of leaf litter in the barrens over the course of several fire-free years sustained a much more intense fire. The result was the more shrub-like, multiple sprout appearance of the oak barrens (Thor and Nichols 1974; Henderson and Long 1984).

The disappearance of the openings and the barrens coincided with settlement. Savannas were unstable plant communities which ceased to exist when the disturbance regime which sustained them was eliminated. As Charles Sprague Sargent (1884, 354) noted in his classic *Report on the Forests of North America*, the Midwest's oak openings were rapidly losing 'their open, park-like character [due to] the appearance of a young growth [predominately black oak and maple (Ames 1881; Beal 1904)] which has sprung up among the old trees.' The cessation of fires permitted the maturation of the black oak grubs and an influx of the more fire sensitive species (Auclair and Cottam 1971). Black oak and white oak significantly increased their representation and density in a number of bur oak openings in southern and western Wisconsin (Cottam 1949; Ward 1956a; Barnes 1974). Scientists have documented the changing character of two oak openings, one in Wisconsin (Cottam 1949) and one in Missouri (Etter 1953), by means of detailed size-class and age structure analyses. A few spreading, open-grown bur and white oak are still the largest trees in the predominately white and black oak forests of Stewarts Woods, Wisconsin (Cottam 1949). Etter (1953) found that open-grown blackjack oak and hickory played a similar role in the shingle oak–black oak–pignut hickory woods of Wildwood, Missouri. Pasturage has maintained the open, park-like character of a few of the old oak openings. Unfortunately heavy grazing has also destroyed much of the herbage and ground layer of the remaining openings (Curtis 1959, 351). High-quality, oak savannas today account for less than 0.02% of their presettlement extent (Nuzzo 1986).

5

Preservers of the ecological balance wheel

> I am convinced that Indians were indeed conservators. They were
> America's first ecologists ... [They] preserved an ecological bal-
> ance wheel.
>> W. Jacobs. 1978. 'The great despoilation: Environmental themes
>> in American frontier history.'

> The conventional or traditional concept of the state of nature must
> be abandoned – that mythical, idealized condition, in which natural
> forces, biological and physical, were supposed to exist in a state of
> virtual equilibrium, undisturbed by man. The role of aboriginal
> man within the ecosystem must be recognized as a major ecologi-
> cal fact.
>> J. C. Malin. 1953. 'Soil, animal, and plant relations of the
>> grassland, historically reconsidered.'

Research on the modification of North America's plant communities by aboriginal populations has had a long and varied history. The concept of the
Indian silently gliding through the forest leaving nothing but the imprint of his
moccasined foot is a prevailing theme in much of the literature of the western
world. Historians and ecologists have likewise emphasized the generally
benign influence of America's earliest inhabitants (Sears [1935] 1959, 4;
White 1984b). Indians have variously been depicted as America's 'first ecologists' (Jacobs 1980, 60) and her earliest conservationists (Johnson 1952).
Native Americans established a symbiosis with nature (Vecsey 1980, 8). They
carefully husbanded her fauna, her flora, and her resources (Hughes 1977). A
very strong philosophical or attitudinal argument runs through much of the literature. Indians were conservers because their religious beliefs fostered a concern for the earth. As Roderick Nash (1972, 75) observed 'even with a power
saw in his hand there is reason to suspect that the pre-Columbian Indian would

have been environmentally responsible.' Aside from the rhetoric and philosophical observations, White (1984b) has suggested that the current popularity
of the 'noble savage' concept among historians and environmentalists implies
a condemnation of the European American's attitude towards the land.
Kirkpatrick Sale's (1990) recent book *The Conquest of Paradise* epitomizes
the dichotomy of the pristine, ecologically balanced landscape of the Indian
and the exploited, environmentally disrupted landscape of the European
American. Unfortunately, few investigators have attempted to piece together
the documentary and the scientific evidence regarding the Indian's impact.
The following represents an attempt to analyze the Indian's role as an agent of
change within an ecological framework.

Conventional wisdom suggests that the native American's impact was limited for a number of reasons. (1) The low density of the Indian population precluded major modifications of the environment. Few Indian populations actually reached the carrying capacity of the environment, i.e., they rarely attained
the maximum number of individuals the environment could theoretically support (Hughes 1983, 95–96). Population pressures on the land's resources were
minimal. (2) The native American husbanded the land and its resources
because he lacked both the technology and the market oriented incentives of
the European. (3) The hunting and gathering based subsistence economy of the
Indian also minimized the native American's impact. Unlike the European, the
Indian had no domestic animals. Overgrazing, the creation of pastures, and the
production of hay were not major concerns of the native American (Thomas
1976; Jacobs 1980, 189; Cronon 1983, 139). Not all investigators, of course,
have concurred with the above statements. There have been a few notable
dissenters to the view that the Indians 'touch [upon the land] was almost
unbelievably light' (Jacobs 1980, 61).

Size of native American populations

The total size or the density of the Indian population is an item of more than
passing interest. Anthropologists, like A. L. Kroeber (1939) for instance, have
utilized the size of the population to determine the total acreage under cultivation or the area directly affected by the Indians. Most of the early estimates of
Indian populations in the Northeast are based on historical citations of the number of warriors per tribe and the average family size (Cook 1976). Multiplying
the two yields the total post-contact population size. Extrapolating from the
post- to the pre-contact situation, however, is fraught with a number of difficulties. Many of the coastal populations of New England, for example, experienced a major series of epidemics associated with the advent of European

pathogens in the early 1600s. The epidemics of 1616–1619 and 1633 resulted in massive die-offs and the precipitous decline of the coastal populations (Cook 1973). As Alfred W. Crosby (1972) thoroughly documented and Calvin Martin (1974) stated 'all of the microscopic parasites of humans, which had been collected together from all parts of the known world into Europe' were deposited on America's shores. Few of the native Americans possessed a natural immunity to European diseases like smallpox and the plague (Cook 1973). Estimates of the mortality vary widely, ranging up to 95% of the total population. Most investigators, however, now believe that the early estimates of the mortality were conservative and should be revised upward (Snow 1980, 34). Seventeenth century North America in Francis Jennings' (1975, 15) telling phrase was much more a 'widowed land' than a virgin land. The result has been a significant upward readjustment of the pre-epidemic populations.

With the exception of some of the Iroquoian language groups, estimates of the size of the tribes in the Midwest or the interior are more difficult to obtain. Tribal disruption and dismemberment accompanying the Iroquois or beaver wars of the seventeenth century reduced large segments of the Ohio Valley and the Great Lakes region to a virtual no man's land (Mason 1981, 10). Most of the existing eighteenth century estimates reflect the debilitating effects of wars and epidemics. Table 5.1 represents a compilitation of the pre-epidemic population sizes and densities of the more eastern tribes. The densities vary by over two orders of magnitude. The very high densities of southern New England's offshore islands, i.e., Martha's Vineyard, Nantucket, and Block Island, can probably be attributed to the marine resources of the region and intensive corn cultivation (Cook 1976, 45). A heavy reliance on corn likewise made Huronia in southern Ontario and the Iroquois' homeland in western New York some of the more densely populated areas in the Great Lakes region (Mason 1981, 37). Densities were considerably lower in the hunting and gathering based subsistence economies north of the 120 to 130 day frost-free, corn cultivation line (Bennett 1955).

Impact of agricultural practices

Corn cultivation, of course, entailed major alterations of the land. Some might insist that the Indians lacked the technology or the means of clearing large areas of a heavily wooded landscape. Girdling and fire provided an efficient mechanism of clearing the forest. With the Iroquois, deforestation often preceded the initial cultivation of the field by one or more years. The larger trees were girdled with stone hatchets in the spring. The following spring the underbrush was burned off (Loskiel 1794, 1:54; Parker 1910, 21). By piling brush

Table 5.1. *Estimates of size and density of pre-Columbian Indian populations*

Tribe (location)	Population size	Density (no. per mile²)[a]	Sources
Eastern Abenaki (Maine)	11900	0.5	Snow 1980
Western Abenaki (Champlain drainage)	4200	0.6	Snow 1980
Pennacook (New Hampshire)	12000	1.0–3.5	Cook 1976
Massachusetts (E Massachusetts)	4500	4.0	Cook 1976
Wampanog (SE Massachusetts)	5000	4.0	Cook 1976
Nauset (Cape Cod)	2140	5.5	Cook 1976
Wampanog related tribe on Martha's Vineyard	3500	35.0	Cook 1976
Wampanog related tribe on Nantucket	2500	50.0	Cook 1976
Narragansett (Rhode Island)	7500	7.5	Cook 1976
Natives of Block Island	300	30.0	Cook 1976
Mohegan and Pequot (E Connecticut)	3500	7.0	Cook 1976
Nipmuck and Connecticut Valley bands	5300	10.0	Cook 1976
Wappinger Confederacy (E New York and W Connecticut)	13200	4.2	Cook 1976
Mahican (upper Hudson River)	5000	?	Cook 1976
Natives of Long Island	7500	5.4	Cook 1976
Munsee Delaware (Lower Hudson and upper Delaware Rivers)	27000	3.6	Snow 1980
Mohawk (Mohawk River)	10000	2.6	Snow 1980
Hurons (Ontario)	20000	60.0	Heidenreich 1978

[a] To convert to number per km² multiply by 0.39.

around the larger trees and then applying fire to different parts of the stem and the branches, the tree could be divided into smaller pieces for eventual use as firewood (Loskiel 1794, 1:55).

Attempts to determine the total amount of land under cultivation have generally been based on estimates of the size of the population, the yield of corn and per capita food requirements. Most investigators feel an acre of corn could support anywhere from one to five individuals (Willoughby 1906; Kroeber 1939, 146; Bennett 1955; Thomas 1976; Mason 1981, 39). Martin Pring ([1625] 1906), the early English explorer, stated that each Indian family cultivated an acre of ground. Utilizing the lower figure of one acre of corn per person and the low population estimates of the 1930s, A. L. Kroeber (1939) came to the conclusion that the eastern Indians tilled less than 1% and probably less than 0.5% of the land. The total acreage under cultivation represented a minute speck on the landscape (Kroeber 1939, 142).

It should be pointed out that Kroeber's technique yields only a minimum estimate of the area affected at any given point in time. Continued cropping eventually depleted the fertility of the soil and forced the Indians to clear new areas for cultivation. There is a limited amount of evidence that the Indians used a short-term fallow on some of the poorer sites. Champlain noted the occurrence of a number of fallow fields on sandy Cape Cod in 1605. When the Indians wished to bring the old fields into cultivation, they set fire to the weeds and worked over the soil with wooden spades (Champlain [1905] 1968, 88). John Winthrop, Jr. (1863) also noted that the Narragansetts, living on Rhode Island's light sandy soils, 'have every one 2 fields which after the first 2 years they lett one field rest each yeare, & that keeps their ground continually in hart.' A long-term fallow or a slash-and-burn system appears to have been the norm on most sites in the Northeast. Sites were cropped from 8 (Wood [1634] 1977, 35) to 30 years (Pratt 1976, 15–16) with the finer textured, more fertile soils maintaining an acceptable level of output for longer periods of time (Pratt 1976, 7).

Some tribes developed a very elaborate and ecologically sound system of maintaining the long-term productivity of the soil. Heidenrich (1971, 180–185), for instance, has attributed the extended periods of cropping of the Hurons to (1) increasing nitrification and the release of nutrients associated with the annual burning of brush and weeds, (2) increasing nitrogen fixation resulting from the intercropping of beans and corn and (3) the advantages of minimum tillage, i.e., without the use of a plow, soil disturbance, erosion, and leaching was kept to a minimum. Coastal tribes may have utilized fish as fertilizers to maintain the soil's fertility, although documentary evidence of their use of fertilizers is somewhat ambiguous (Rostlund 1957; Ceci 1975).

The use of a short or a long-term fallow meant that the area exploited was considerably more than the area under cultivation at any given point in time. As a crude first approximation, the land under cultivation can be multiplied by a factor of 2 to 5. The factor of 2 to 5 is based on two assumptions: (1) the land was cropped for approximately 10 years (the most frequently cited figure in the literature) and (2) it required 20 to 50 years to restore the natural fertility of the soil (Heidenrich 1971, 188; Thomas 1976). The second assumption, the 20 to 50 year recovery period, is somewhat more problematic as it is based on the supposition that the amount of time it takes to revegetate the site is equivalent to the time it takes to build up the organic matter or nutrient reserves of the soil (Heidenrich 1971, 187–188). Unfortunately there is very little scientific evidence to either substantiate or disprove the equivalency of the two events.

The area in the immediate vicinity of the village was also deforested for a variety of other reasons. Loskiel (1794, 1:55) noted that the Delaware and the Iroquois kept a constant fire burning in their houses, consuming more wood than was absolutely necessary. Undoubtedly some of the fuelwood was a byproduct of the forest clearance process associated with cultivation. Day (1953) and Pratt (1976, 11), however, believed that the Indians shifted to cutting live wood as the readily available supplies of dead wood were exhausted. Prodigious quantities of wood were also used in the construction of stockades, palisades, and long houses. Archaeologists have attempted to determine the amount of wood utilized for construction purposes. Pratt (1976, 12), for instance, estimated that 7 to 15 acres had to be cleared to supply the wood for several stockaded Iroquois villages while Heidenrich (1971, 152–153) came to the conclusion that a large Huron village of 1000 individuals required 46 acres of woodland. Given the Indian's great dependence upon wood, it is not surprising that the progressive depletion of the wood and the retreat of the forest forced the relocation of many a village (Lifitau 1724). As Loskiel (1794, 1:56) stated 'from these and other causes, firewood at last begins to be scarce, and necessity obliges them to seek other dwelling-places, as the Indians can not bear the trouble of fetching firewood from any distant parts.' Whole villages were frequently relocated from one site to another, eventually giving rise to the 'Old Town' designation so characteristic of many early maps of Pennsylvania and Maine (Wallace and Hunter 1981, 36).

Many Indian activities were localized on certain portions of the landscape. As a result their impact was concentrated and magnified. The crude implements of the Indians limited cultivation to the coarser textured, more friable, easily worked soils (Stoltman and Baerreis 1983, 261). In New York, for example, the pattern of Indian settlement followed the coarser textured, outwash soils of the streams and valleys (Olson 1968). Corn plantations were frequently situated on low rich soils adjacent to lakes, rivers, and brooks (Loskiel 1794, 1:52–53).

Early explorers' accounts suggest that the cumulative impact of the Indians was substantial in the more densely populated areas. One of the earliest descriptions of the New England coast, produced in 1524 by Verrazano

([1905] 1968, 13–21), contains numerous references to a populated, agriculturally oriented countryside and open plains 25 or 30 leagues in extent in the interior of Rhode Island. Both Champlain ([1905] 1968, 80) and John Smith ([1616] 1963, 6) likewise noted a great deal of cleared land planted with Indian corn and gardens along the Massachusetts coast in the early 1600s. Francis Higgeson, the early Puritan divine, in what may have been an exaggeration, extolled the large amount of ground already cleared by the Indians in northeastern Massachusetts. 'I am told that about three miles from us a man may stand on a little hilly place and see diverse thousands of acres of ground as good as need to be, and not a tree, in the same' (Higgeson [1630] 1806). Land along the Taunton River in southeastern Massachusetts was also described by Bradford and Winslow ([1622] 1865, 103) as being for the most part cleared. 'Thousands of men have lived there, which dyed in a great plague not long since; and pitty it was and is to see, so many goodly fieldes, & so well seated, without men to dresse and manure the same.' Abandoned Indian fields minimized the laborious process of clearing the forest and were among the first sites selected by the Europeans for plantations (Carrier 1923, 38–40). Bradford and Winslow's ([1622] 1865, 64–65) comment that the Pilgrims decided to establish their plantation at Plymouth 'on high ground where there is a great deale of land cleared, and hath beene planted with corne three or four yeares agoe' exemplifies the value attatched to cleared land.

There are also accounts of extensive areas of cleared land in the interior. An Onondaga town in New York in 1677, for instance, had cleared corn fields extending for at least two miles (Greenhalgh 1853). Bela Hubbard (1881), an early government surveyor, likewise reported that Indian clearings stretched for several miles along the Shiawassee River in southern Michigan. The Ottawas are said to have cleared an area of approximately 15 miles by 1 mile for their major village at Arbre Croche, Michigan, in the eighteenth century (Blackbird 1887, 10). Reports of punitive expeditions against the Indians frequently include estimates of the number of acres or bushels of corn destroyed, e.g., note references to expeditions against the Iroquois in Parker (1910, 18–20), but these may have been inflated. Heidenreich's (1971, 198–199) detailed analysis of the Huron culture in southern Ontario represents one of the few attempts to actually determine the area affected by a corn-based system. Heidenreich concluded that the Hurons used about a quarter of the total land in Huronia. Most of the area was devoted to long-term fallows. As opposed to being an underpopulated area, Huronia was approaching a population maximum. A number of anthropologists believe similar population pressures characterized a variety of other agriculturally based systems in the East (Stoltman and Baerreis 1983, 261). It is not surprising that many of the early European accounts of Huronia emphasized the comparatively open nature of the countryside – a land full of 'open fields, [and] very beautiful broad meadows bearing much excellent hay' (Sagard-Theodat 1939, 90).

The long-term influence of the Indian on the flora was apparent to even the casual observer. By altering the light and the nutrient status of large areas and by disturbing the soil, the Indian created a very heterogeneous or patchy environment. Deforestation probably released a flush of nutrients in the fields surrounding the village while decaying stumps produced pockets of organically rich soil. Garbage dumps and middens containing animal bones and wood ashes built up the calcium, phosphorus, and magnesium levels of the soil in the immediate vicinity of the village (Dietz 1956; Heidenreich 1978). Soil compaction characterized the more heavily utilized portions of the village and the spaces between the corn hills (Delabarre and Wilder 1920). Sauer (1947) has depicted the overall effect as spheres or zones of decreasing influence extending outward from the center of the village. By altering the environment, the Indian, either intentionally or unintentionally, became an agent of selection (Sauer 1947). Charred or carbonized plant remains from archaeological sites have yielded a host of weedy plant species or ruderals (Table 5.2), formerly thought to have been introduced by Europeans. High nitrogen demanding species like the amaranths or the pigweeds found a hospitable habitat in refuse dumps (Anderson [1952] 1971, 150). Other species, goosefoot (*Chenopodium* spp.), purslane (*Portulaca oleracea*), and Jerusalem artichoke (*Helianthus tuberosus*), for example, were part of what Yarnell (1964, 103) has termed the 'early eastern agricultural complex,' weedy food plants that may have grown as volunteers on garden plots (Yarnell 1976, 269; Stoltman and Baerreis 1983). Pre-Columbian pollen and seeds of the potherb purslane, for instance, have been found in lake sediments and there are a number of seventeenth century references to its occurrence in Indian corn fields (Byrne and McAndrews 1975). Frequent cultivation, trampling, compaction, and light would have favored weedy, prostrate annuals like purslane. Abandonment of the worn-out corn fields encouraged the entry of a new suite of opportunistic perennials (Delcourt *et al.* 1986). Indian hemp (*Apocynum cannabinum*), strawberries, raspberries, blackberries, hazel, sumac, and Indian grass (*Sorghastrum nutans*) figure prominently in many of the early accounts of Indian old fields (Williams [1643] 1810, 221; Blackbird 1887, 11; Cook 1887, 10; Smith 1906, 61; Heckewelder 1958, 337). The grasses and short-lived perennials were eventually replaced by a variety of shade intolerant old-field tree species – junipers, black cherry (Blackbird 1887, 128; Hedrick 1948, 134–135), red cedar and tuliptree (Chapman *et al.* 1982), aspen (Smith 1906, 61), ash (Cook 1887, 10), and honeylocust and black locust (Heckewelder 1888, 83). Even-aged stands

Table 5.2. *Carbonized remains of weedy plant species found at*
pre-Columbian Indian sites

Common name	Scientific name
Amaranth	*Amaranthus graecizans* and *retroflexus*
Bedstraw	*Galium* sp.
Carpetweed	*Mollugo verticillata*
Charlock	*Brassica kaber*
Chickweed	*Cerastium* sp.
Goosefoot	*Chenopodium* spp., e.g., *hybridum*
Jerusalem artichoke	*Helianthus tuberosus*
Knotweed	*Polygonum* sp., e.g., *aviculare*
Nettles	*Urtica* spp.
Pokeweed	*Phytolacca americana*
Purslane	*Portulaca oleracea*
Three-seeded mercury	*Acalypha* sp.
Wild sunflower	*Helianthus annuus*

Sources: Kaplan (1973); Chapman, Stewart, and Yarnell (1974); Byrne and McAndrews (1975); Powell (1981); Crabtree (1983); Jacobson, Petersen, and Putnam (1988).

of white pine have been traced to abandoned Indian sites throughout New England, New York, and southern Ontario (Bowman 1979). Many were associated with the coarse-textured outwash soils of terraces along rivers (Gordon 1940, 15). The Algonquin term for the pine tree, 'Coos', was frequently applied to intervals or terraces along the Connecticut River, suggesting a former Indian occupancy (Huden 1962, 59). In several cases, cooperative research efforts between archaeologists and palynologists have allowed us to piece together a fairly detailed picture of the impact of Indian occupancy on the surrounding vegetation (Finlayson and Byrne 1975; McAndrews, 1976; Burden, McAndrews, and Norris 1986; Delcourt *et al.* 1986). By analyzing the pollen sequence of varved sediments in Crawford Lake in southern Ontario, John McAndrews (1988) and his colleagues were able to document the clearance of the original forests of beech and sugar maple, the cultivation of maize by the Iroquois in the fourteenth to seventeenth centuries, and the subsequent occupancy of the abandoned site by oak and white pine.

Unintentional changes in the vegetation often followed the Indian's modification of the environment. Food gathering and the collection of plants for medicinal purposes constituted a more direct and purposeful exploitation of the landscape's floral resources. The Indians harvested and utilized a wide range of native plant species (Arnason, Hebda, and Johns 1981).

Unfortunately their impact is largely conjectural. Digging for edible roots and bulbs probably disturbed the soil and stimulated the vegetative reproduction of pieces that had been missed (Sauer 1947). Food gathering may also have almost exterminated at least one species, the Pomme de Prairie (*Psoralea esculenta*), a prairie legume prized for its fleshy taproot (Curtis 1959, 463).

The very sporadic distribution of certain plant species and their association with old Indian sites provides circumstantial evidence for the introduction of plants by the Indians. Gilmore (1930), Moseley (1930), Hedrick (1933, 27), Day (1953), Curtis (1959, 463), and Yarnell (1964, 90–92) have reviewed the evidence for the introduction of a number of useful food and medicinal species like Canada plum (*Prunus nigra*), sweet flag (*Acorus calamus*), and the lotus (*Nelumbo lutea*). From an ethnobotanical standpoint, Kentucky coffeetree (*Gymnocladus dioicus*) is one of the more interesting species. Its association with Indian sites in New York and Wisconsin has variously been attributed to the use of its seed as a beverage (Hedrick 1933, 27) and as dice in a traveling game of chance (Curtis 1959, 463).

The direct and the indirect effects of the Indian on the wildlife are more difficult to evaluate. Certainly Indian activities like clearing and cultivation created a very heterogeneous environment, a mosaic of vegetation types of varying ages. The juxtaposition of open fields and woods favored species associated with edge habitats. Quail, turkeys, ruffed grouse, and deer were the major beneficiaries (Thompson and Smith 1971). Deer were almost universally the preferred game species in the East (Witthoft 1953). They reached their highest abundance in edge or ecotonal habitats (Kay 1979). Communal deer drives, stalking, snares, and deadfalls tended to reduce their numbers, although their cumulative impact is difficult to ascertain. Fenton's (1978b) estimate of a total yearly kill of 11 000 deer for the Iroquois hunters is relatively small when compared with the average annual New York State harvest of 80 000 deer in the 1970s. Some anthropologists, however, feel that game depletion may have characterized the more densely populated Iroquoian areas (Mason 1981, 37) and could have been responsible for the Iroquois' early shift to an agriculturally based subsistence pattern (Ritchie and Funk 1973, 365). The historic period witnessed an increase in large game (deer and buffalo) in areas where tribal boundaries were disputed and hunting decreased due to hostilities (Hickerson 1965; Jakle 1967).

Native Americans' use of fire

Most investigators agree that fire was one of the more significant and effective tools employed by the native American. With fire he could alter an area out of all proportion to his numbers. For the past 150 years, however, the frequency and the extent of its use has been hotly debated. Indians have been depicted as (1) aboriginal pyromaniacs (Raup 1937) intent upon converting most of the forest of the East into one vast prairie (Shaler 1891, 186; Maxwell 1910), (2) responsible wildlife managers who used fire sparingly as a management tool (Hughes 1983, 55–56), and (3) interested observers who only infrequently and accidentally 'augmented the number of natural fires' (Russell 1983). Fires were purportedly used by the Indians to clear land for cultivation, to facilitate travel and hunting, and to improve game habitat. Criticism of the 'Indian burning hypothesis' has centered on the observations that (1) there is very little ethnographic evidence for the Indians' purposeful use of fire, (2) the existing accounts of Indian-set fires are unreliable or unspecific in location and extent, and (3) most of the fires attributed to the Indians had natural causes, i.e., lightning, etc. (Russell 1979, 8; 1983; Russell and Forman 1984). A more detailed analysis of each of the above points follows.

Lightning is one of the more obvious and frequently cited causes of fire. Although it constitutes an important fire ignition source, it also generally supplies a fire retardant in the form of rain. Wet lightning rarely ignites forest fuels (Ahlgren and Ahlgren 1984, 47). Dry lightning, i.e. lightning which occurs without any precipitation reaching the ground, on the other hand, frequently results in forest fires. Dry lightning ignited fires, however, are largely limited to the West and the Florida panhandle (Ahlgren and Ahlgren 1984, 47). The fire regime or the fire climate of the Northeast and the Midwest, for the most part, is characterized by a very low incidence of lightning ignited fires (Schroeder and Buck 1970). The incidence of dry lightning fires is simply too low to account for the importance of fires in the prehistoric period (Curtis 1959, 461).

The purposeful use of fire by the American Indians is a question which has fascinated anthropologists and geographers for a number of years (Stewart 1951, 1963; Sauer 1956). Despite Russell's (1983) claim to the contrary, there is a good deal of historical, ethnological, and paleoecological evidence supporting the Indian's purposeful use of fire (Mellars 1976; Patterson and Sassaman 1988). Driver and Massey's (1957) massive ethnographic monograph on North America's Indians indicates the use of fire was widespread throughout the Northeast and the Midwest. Native Americans had a sophisticated knowledge of the use of fire (Patterson and Sassaman 1988). Fire was employed to drive game and to clear and fertilize agricultural land (Driver and Massey 1957, 188, 191, 225–226). Many reliable seventeenth and eighteenth century observers who worked and lived among the Indians stated that the Indians intentionally used fire for a variety of purposes. Roger Williams, the early New England divine, even justified the Indians' occupation of the land on the basis of their attempt to improve the land with fire. Williams (1963, 2:47) noted that the Indians 'burnt up all the underwoods in the Countrey, once or twice a yeare and therefore as Noble men in England possessed great Parkes, and [as] the King, great Forrests in England onely for their game ...' Deer were the Indian's cows and the burnt open woods, his pastures (Dwight [1822] 1969, 4:38–39; Bakeless [1950] 1961, 309). John Heckewelder (1958, 366), a Moravian missionary, observed that the Indians burn 'immense tracts of land' to make the country 'more open to hunt in' and to produce a 'greater abundance of grass for the deer to feed on.' The burning of woods and prairies was so common in the Midwest in the autumn that the peculiar kind of haziness and the red sky accompanying it was known as Indian summer (Foot 1836; Heckewelder 1958, 366).

Historical evidence for the Indians' use of fire is more problematic. Many of the references are based on second-hand information or are simply inferences or items which have been pirated from undetermined sources. Once the dross is eliminated, however, there still remain a number of reliable, first-hand accounts of the Indian's use of fire. Table 5.3 is a compilation of some of the better references. Many of the accounts, particularly those by reputable naturalists or scientists in the Midwest, e.g., Samuel Hildreth, are beyond reproach. The eighteenth century French botanist, Andre Michaux (1889), who traveled extensively throughout eastern North America, stated 'one does not have any idea in Europe of the considerable extent of woods which are burnt annually in America by the savages and the European inhabitants themselves.' After analyzing over 600 historical accounts relating to prairie fires in central North America, Moore (1972) came to the conclusion that Indians were a major source of ignition. Naturally caused lightning fires accounted for less than 0.5% of the total number of prairie fires reported. H. J. Lutz (1931), a long-time student of the use of fire by America's Indians, came to essentially the same conclusion when he stated 'the literature abounds with what appears to be well authenticated statements of responsible individuals to the effect that the Indians commonly did employ fire in the forest to achieve various ends.'

Legislative and legal evidence also lends credence to the Indian burning hypothesis. Upon hearing 'that great damage hath hapned to seuerall persons in the outskirt plantations by Indians kindling fires in the woods,' the court of the Massachusetts Bay in 1679 summarily subjected the Indian inhabitants of the colony to the same stringent laws that governed the Europeans' use of fire (Shurtleff 1854, 5:230–231). Occasionally Indian-set fires were viewed in a more positive light. The regrowth of bushes and brambles following the cessation of Indian burning was of concern to many of the early colonists of the

Table 5.3. Historic references to the use of fire by Indians

Location/Date	Vegetation type	Tribe	Time and extent of fire	Purpose	Sources
Massachusetts 1629–1633	oak–hickory	n.s.	November	suppress underwood and improve hunting	Wood [1634] 1977, 30, 38
Massachusetts 1620s–1630s	oak–chestnut, hickory	n.s.	spring and autumn in all places where they come	eliminate under-weeds and improve travel	Morton [1632] 1967, 172
Massachusetts 1630s	oak	n.s.	–	facilitate hunting deer and bear	Johnson [1654] 1910, 85
Massachusetts and Rhode Island 1640s	n.s.	n.s.	burnt all underwoods in country once or twice a year	destroy vermin, eliminate weeds and produce game parks for hunting	Williams 1963, 97
New York ~1655	pine, oak–hickory	n.s.	burn woods, plains and meadows in autumn and where missed in April	facilitate hunting (reduces noise) and improve growth of grass	Van der Donck [1656] 1968, 20–21
New York 1632	n.s.	n.s.	winter	facilitate hunting	DeVries [1655] 1857
New Jersey and Pennsylvania 1654–1656	oak	Delaware	spring	ring hunt	Lindestrom [1925] 1979, 213–215

Location and date	Vegetation	Tribe	Fire description	Purpose	Reference
New York and Pennsylvania 1769	beech, maple chestnut, oak–hickory	Iroquois Delaware?	burnt sections of uplands along Susquehanna and Delaware Rivers	n.s.	Smith 1906, 69, 72
New York	n.s.	Iroquois	n.s.	to drive deer	Morgan [1901] 1954, 1: 336
New York 1749	pine	n.s.	burnt yearly	due to carelessness of Indians who make great fires while hunting	Kalm [1772] 1972, 361
Pennsylvania and Ohio late 1700s	n.s.	Delaware Iroquois	spring and sometimes autumn, fires run for many miles	accidental origin or to produce fresh herbage, ring hunts	Loskiel 1794, 55
W Pennsylvania 1772	oak, walnut	Mingo?	n.s.	facilitate hunting	McClure 1899, 58–59
NW Pennsylvania 1780s	oak, northern hardwoods	Seneca	n.s.	to kill poisonous snakes	Tome [1854] 1928, 35
Ohio 1755–1759	tall-grass prairie	Ottawa	fire ran through whole prairie, 50 miles by 25 miles	ring hunt for deer	Smith [1799] 1907, 86–87
Ohio 1788	oak, poplar, hickory, chestnut	n.s.	yearly autumn, fires on hills bordering the Ohio River	to produce pastures and hunting grounds for deer and buffalo	Hildreth 1848, 484–485

Table 5.3 (*cont.*)

Location/Date	Vegetation type	Tribe	Time and extent of fire	Purpose	Sources
Ohio 1780s	woods	n.s.	burn yearly	to produce good pasture for deer and improve hunting	Barker 1958, 63
S Ontario 1798	deciduous woods	Delaware	burn immense tracts of land in spring	to produce herbage for deer and facilitate hunting	Heckewelder 1958, 366
Kentucky and Midwest 1802	barrens and savannas	n.s.	flames occupy extent of several miles	to make game more visible	Michaux [1805] 1904, 221
N Ohio 1823	savanna	Wyandotts?	every autumn burn leaves and grass in circle of 15–20 miles	ring hunt	Finley [1857] 1971, 384
Midwest 1766–1768	tallgrass prairie	n.s.	autumn	ring hunt for buffalo	Carver 1778, 287–289
Michigan late 1700s, early 1800s	prairies and savannas	n.s.	annual fires once covered much of southern Michigan	facilitate hunting and promote growth of grass	Pierce 1826
Ontario Lake Superior region 1840s	boreal forest, pine, etc.	n.s.	n.s.	due to carelessness, allow campfires to escape	Agassiz and Cabot 1850, 73

Location/Date	Vegetation	Tribe	Description	Purpose	Reference
Wisconsin 1820s	prairies and woods	Winnebago	fire brush once a year so vast regions they traverse are burned	drive game	Beltrami [1828] 1962, 176–177 203
Minnesota 1830s	prairies	n.s.	all prairies watered by Mississippi and Missouri are work of Indians	to assure animal food	Nicollet 1976, 56–67
Minnesota 1835	prairies	n.s.	annually fire whole of country	to prevent buffalo from wandering, also due to carelessness; occasionally set for amusement	Featherstonhaugh [1847] 1962, 411
Michigan, Indiana 1679	prairies	Miami	annually burn in autumn	to drive buffalo	Hennepin [1698] 1903, 145–147
N Indiana early 1800s	prairies and woods	Potawatomi	much of prairies and timbered land annually burned in autumn	n.s.	Robinson [1835] 1936, 54
Illinois 1720s	prairies	n.s.	n.s.	ring hunt for buffalo	Charlevoix [1761] 1966, 1: 203–204
Illinois 1750	prairies and savanna	n.s.	fire in autumn, fire spreads everywhere except wet lowlands	n.s.	Vivier 1900, 207

Table 5.3 (*cont.*)

Location/Date	Vegetation type	Tribe	Time and extent of fire	Purpose	Sources
Illinois early 1800s	prairie	n.s.	grass fired in autumn, flame spreads over all country	to drive game	Ernst 1904
Illinois early 1800s	prairie	n.s.	customarily set fire to grass in autumn or winter	to dislodge game	Blaine 1918, 74
Missouri early 1800s	woods	n.s.	n.s.	facilitate travel and hunting	Wells 1818
Missouri 1832–1834	forest	n.s.	n.s.	to escape enemies	Maximilian 1843, 124

Note: n.s. means not stated or given.

Connecticut River Valley and Long Island because it destroyed valuable herbage. The inhabitants of Northhampton, Massachusetts, even petitioned the General Court for a plantation at Squakeag (Northfield) in 1671 on the grounds that the Indians had deserted the place and that for want of inhabitants to burn the meadows and woods, the pesky underwood had increased (Judd 1905, 98). On Long Island the cessation of Indian-set fires and the regrowth of the underwood prompted the Governor to order every inhabitant in 1672 to turn out for four days of brush cutting (Wood 1828, 4).

Given the fact that the Indians considered fire a useful management tool, the next obvious question is the degree to which they employed it. In other words, what was the frequency, the extent, and the severity of the Indian-set fires? The majority of the fires were probably surface fires, light fires which burned the surface litter and left the larger, thicker barked, more fire resistant trees unharmed. As the Dutch observer Adriaen Van der Donck ([1656] 1968, 20–21) noted:

The Indians have a yearly custom ... of burning the woods, plains and meadows in the fall of the year, when the leaves have fallen and when the grass and vegetable substances are dry. Notwithstanding the apparent danger of the entire destruction of the woodlands by the burning, still the green trees do not suffer. The outside bark is scorched three or four feet high, which does them no injury, for the trees are not killed. It however sometimes happens that in the thick pine woods, wherein the fallen trees lie across each other, and have become dry, that the blaze ascends and strikes the tops of the trees, setting the same on fire, which is immediately increased by the resinous knots and leaves, which promote the blaze, and is passed by the wind from tree to tree ...

The more serious crown fires, as Van der Donck implied, were limited to sites with a dense fuel load of downed wood and an overstory of resinous, flammable pine.

By stimulating the growth of grasses, forbs, and certain shrubs, light surface fires increased the amount of available browse and eventually the number of deer the environment could support. Deer were also attracted to the more nutritious and palatable food supplies produced by the burn. Concentrating the deer on the burned sites facilitated the Indians' hunting by minimizing the amount of time, energy, and effort required in harvesting the deer (Mellars 1976).

Most of the early accounts (Morton [1632] 1967, 172) suggest the Indians fired the woods in the spring and the autumn 'when the grass is withered and the leaves dried' (Wood [1634] 1977, 38). Grasses and leaves dried rapidly and supplied the finer fuels required for the ignition process (Patterson and Sassaman 1988). Although a portion of the woods was burned each year, there is little solid evidence to suggest that the same sites were repeatedly subjected to fires on an annual or a biannual basis (Dwight [1822] 1969, 4:40). The pattern of frequent burning may have been more a response to fire's relatively transient effects. The amount of browse and herbage resulting from burning declines substantially two to five years after the fire (Mellars 1976). A series of years without burning would have converted many of the open deer pastures into closed or bushy forests.

Determining the actual extent of the fires is a more formidable task. The opinions expressed range from very localized burns (Russell 1983) to the annual conflagration of most of southern New England (Bromley 1935). Thomas Morton's ([1632] 1967, 172) comment that Indian-set fires spread themselves 'against, as with the winde; burning continually night and day, untill a shower of raine falls to quench' them implies that fires were fairly extensive. At least two factors, however, would have worked against large-scale burns. The first is that not all of the sites were equally flammable. As Timothy Dwight ([1822] 1969, 4:38) expressed it:

The Indians annually, and sometimes oftener, burned such parts of the North American forests as they found sufficiently dry. In every such case the fuel consists chiefly of the fallen leaves, which are rarely dry enough for an extensive combustion except on uplands, and on these only when covered with a dry soil. Of this nature were always the oak and yellow pine grounds, which were therefore usually subjected to an annual conflagration. The beech and maple grounds were commonly too wet to be burned.

The more barren pitch pine [probably Dwight's yellow pine] plains were set on fire every year by the Indians (Winthrop [1756] 1968). The swamps, the floodplains, and the moister beech and maple lands on the other hand were simply too wet to burn (Morton [1632] 1967, 172; Wood [1634] 1977, 38). The second factor was that fires were limited to the more densely populated or well-traveled areas of the Northeast and the Midwest. Day (1953) summarized an intensive review of the Indian's pyromaniac propensities by stating 'it seems that there is no evidence in the early authorities for the wholesale conflagration of southern New England ... but only burning in those places where the Indians inhabit' (see also Wood [1634] 1977, 38). Paleoecological evidence also suggests that there were a number of strong regional contrasts in the use of fire related to density and land use patterns (Patterson and Sassaman 1988). Pollen analysis and charcoal counts of lake sediments indicate that fires were relatively common on the more densely populated coastal sites of Massachusetts and Long Island. Fires were virtually nonexistent in the sparsely populated Berkshire Mountains of western Massachusetts and in inland Maine (Patterson and Sassaman 1988). References to burnt woodlands or barren burnt plains in the early surveyors' notes of the Midwest have also been associated with major Indian trails and villages (Whitney 1982). The occurrence of a disjunct oak savanna near several major historic Potawatomi and Winnebago Indian villages in northeastern Wisconsin was attributed to the use of fire by Indians (Dorney and Dorney 1989). Indian encampments and Indian-set fires may also have been responsible for the maintenance of pine on several small, isolated pockets of outwash along the southern shore of Lake Superior (Loope 1991).

Among the more important effects of Indian-set fires was the role they played in selectively altering the species composition of the forest. Both Bromley (1935) and Niering and Godwin (1962) have agreed that the more fire sensitive species had a very restricted distribution in the presettlement forests of southern New England. Seedlings of hemlock and white pine are very sensitive to surface fires and were probably limited to swamps, low moist sandy areas, and shallow ridges during the presettlement period. During drier episodes, fires even penetrated the swamps. An early eighteenth century map depicting the timber resources of the Piscataqua River in New Hampshire carries the caption 'large swamp of white pine burnt by the Indians' (note fig. 3 in Candee (1970)). On many sites throughout the Northeast and the Midwest, fires at infrequent intervals retarded the invasion of the more shade tolerant species dependent upon advance regeneration (Brown 1960). Hemlock, for instance, has such a superficial root system that even the larger size classes are susceptible to surface fires. There are a number of accounts of fire having eliminated hemlock from stands for an extended period of time. Both Nichols (1913) and Winer (1955, 128–129), for instance, have described segments of mature hemlock–hardwood stands in northwestern Connecticut in which hemlock was practically absent. Both of the segments had experienced fires 100 years before the initiation of the studies. Unfortunately, we have very little information on the frequency of surface fires at a given point or location in the past. It is extremely difficult to detect their presence in the pollen and the charcoal record (Mellars 1976). Major influxes of charcoal into lake sediments, as in the case of Patterson and Sassaman's (1988) study, reflect the occurrence of major crown as opposed to surface fires. Buell, Buell, and Small's (1954) count of the fire scars on an old white oak in Mettlers Woods in New Jersey suggests light surface fires occurred at 10 to 15 year intervals prior to settlement. Fires of this frequency would certainly have eliminated the more fire sensitive species.

Indian-set fires assured the maintenance of a number of plant communities. Pitch pine is one of the more fire resistant species of the Northeast. Its dominance on the sandy plains of Concord, Massachusetts, during the presettlement period was probably due to Indian-set fires (Whitney and Davis 1986). Conversion of the area to white pine followed the cessation of fires in the nineteenth and the twentieth centuries. Oak's dominance in many of the hardwood forests of southern New England has likewise been attributed to a high incidence of fire (Brown 1960). Most oaks have a thick insulating bark, resist decay once they have been injured by fire, and resprout following severe fires (Buttrick 1912; Komarek 1983). Given the above characteristics, it is not surprising that fires generally increase the representation of oak in the forest (Brown 1960; Swan 1970).

Fires at frequent intervals over an extended period of time can alter the forest's physiognomy as well as its composition. Many of the earliest accounts of the East Coast emphasized the relatively open or park-like nature of the forests (Morton [1632] 1967, 172). The woods were 'thin of timber in many places, like our Parkes in England' (Johnson [1654] 1910, 85) or 'open and without underwood, fit either to go or ride in' (Bradford and Winslow [1622] 1865, 11). Likewise, the early explorer Rosier ([1605] 1887, 143) described part of the coast of Maine in these terms, 'surely it did all resemble a stately Parke, wherein appeare some old trees with high withered tops, and others flourishing with living greene boughs.' The seventeenth century usage of parks refers to privately owned areas of grassland and scattered trees enclosed by a fence and intended for the keeping of deer (Rackham 1976, 142–146). Gawen Lawrie's (Smith [1765] 1877, 179) 1684 statement that 'the trees [in east New Jersey] grow generally not thick, but some places ten, in some fifteen, in some twenty-five or thirty upon an acre' provides even greater detail as to the density of the woods. Woods of that density today would be considered savannas or at least relatively open woodlands, savannas having anywhere from 1 to 17 trees per acre (Tans 1976). The herbaceous vegetation reflected the relatively open nature of the woods. Both Wood ([1634] 1977, 33) in New England and Budd ([1685] 1966, 8) in Pennsylvania referred to the 'good fodder' and coarse grass to be got amongst the thin or open woods. 'Even the most woody places ...' supported 'greene grassie ground' (Brereton [1602] 1906, 335). It should be pointed out that the above descriptions are confined to the coastal sections of New England and the Mid-Atlantic states. It would be hazardous to assume that open, park-like forests were the norm throughout the Northeast and the Midwest (Raup 1937) as some have implied (Williams 1989, 45). There are, however, numerous references to open woods, filled with great quantities of pea vine (*Amphicarpa bracteata*), buffalo clover (*Trifolium reflexum*), and sedges and grasses in the early surveyors' and travelers' accounts of the Ohio River Valley (Cooper 1794, 32; Imlay 1797, 233; Caldwell 1897; McInteer 1952). All of the above herbs are species which are intolerant of heavy shade and species which increase following fires (Buell and Cantlon 1953; Swan 1970). The early Ohio country naturalist Samuel Hildreth (1848, 485) summarized the effects of Indian-set fires very cogently when he stated:

The yearly autumnal fires of the Indians, during a long period of time, had destroyed all the shrubs and under growth of woody plants, affording the finest hunting grounds; and in their place had sprung up the buffalo clover, and the wild pea vine with various other indigenous plants and grapes, supplying the most luxuriant and unbounded pastures to the herds of deer and buffalo, which tenanted the thousand hills on the borders of the Ohio.

Barrens, areas of brushy timber or stunted growths of trees, have also been attributed to Indian-set fires. Those noted by the early land surveyors in southeastern Ohio were invariably associated with major Indian villages and trails (Gordon 1969, 62–63). Michaux ([1805] 1904, 221) likewise commented that the barrens of Kentucky as well as the savannas of the Midwest were regularly burned by the Indians. The early settlers of Lancaster County, Pennsylvania, found large sections of land burnt over by the Indians. They called the areas 'grubenland' on the basis of the large number of oak saplings or 'grubs' which dominated the region (Fletcher 1950, 4; Mast 1957). Lancaster County was the site of several major villages of the Susquehannocks (Jennings 1978) and the Shawnee (Callender 1978). Both the grubenland of Lancaster County and the barrens of southeastern Ohio and Kentucky reverted to woodland following the cessation of the fires (Dicken 1935; McInteer 1946; Mast 1957; Gordon 1969, 62–63).

Many investigators believe the Indians' crowning achievement was the creation of the open savannas and prairies of the Midwest. Anthropologists (Carter 1950; Stewart 1951, 1956; Sauer 1956) and ecologists (Curtis 1959, 461–462; Komarek 1965; Dorney 1981) alike have tied the open parklands and grasslands of the Midwest to the Indians' use of fire. Suffice it to say, there is not unanimous agreement on the factors responsible for the occurrence of prairies and savannas. A variety of causative mechanisms have been proposed and are reviewed in chapter 4. It is probably safe to say, however, that Indian-set fires were at least a contributing, if not a major, factor in the maintenance of the prairies and the oak openings of the Midwest.

Since fire was one of the more important game management tools of the American Indian, it is not surprising that it had a positive impact on a number of game species. Bromley (1945) described the situation as primarily 'a symbiotic relationship among the plant associations, the Indian, and his game animals.' Fires favored the acorn-bearing oaks and their dependents, the turkeys. Fires also maintained the blueberry barrens of the Northeast, the prime habitat of the heath hen (Bromley 1945). High densities of important game species like the deer were preferentially associated with the mosaic of open woodlands, closed forests, and edge habitats generated by Indian-set fires (Kay 1979). Investigators (Jakle 1967; Thompson and Smith 1971) have also tied the occurrence of the bison in the eastern woodlands to grassland enclaves maintained by Indian-set fires. Game animals and fires may occasionally have acted synergistically to create a more open type of vegetation. By concentrating their browse on the resurging woody plant growth following a severe fire, deer, for instance, can maintain a relatively open environment. At least one investigator (Niering 1981) believes that the glades of southwestern Pennsylvania, those broad, elevated expanses of grassland, frequently noted by early travelers, owed their existence to just such a set of circumstances.

The cumulative impact of the Indian's activities was substantial. The popular concept that the Indian played a relatively inconspicious role in nature's economy is not borne out by the facts (Denevan 1992). In the more densely populated regions, he significantly altered the face of the landscape. His villages, his cornfields, and his open woods filled the East Coast, the riverine valleys of the interior, and the shores of the Great Lakes. The effects, however, were still localized. Large segments of the interior, i.e., northern New England, the Allegheny Plateau region of Pennsylvania and New York, and the High Plains region of Michigan, were almost devoid of Indian activity. In retrospect, perhaps the alterations should not be all that surprising. Anthropologists have long recognized the ability of aboriginal cultures to modify their environment (White 1984b). Robert Heizer (1955) summarized the anthropologist's viewpoint very succinctly when he stated, '... at any given point in time or space where man has occupied a region he has materially affected the soil, the fauna, the flora, and even the climate, through the intermediary of that one distinctive human possession which we call culture.' America's cultural landscape took root when the first Indian set foot on North America's shores.

6

European precedents

A history of man and the land can never ignore its human dimensions without peril, and ironically the chief obstacle to an environmentally informed history may now reside less in an ignorance of the natural world than in an ignorance of the nature of past human endeavors.

W. S. Cooter. 1978. 'Ecological dimensions of
medieval agrarian systems.'

The study of landscapes is a study of the societies which both fashion and reflect those landscapes. Societies, of course, are not created out of thin air. They evolve and give rise to new cultures with time. To appreciate the seventeenth century colonist's response to the American landscape, one must understand the cultures and the landscapes which produced the colonist. Societies have a certain inertia. The persistence of English values and customs in early New England represented an attempt to recreate a familiar society and its accompanying landscape (Powell 1963; Breen 1980; Allen 1981). Often the colonists' actions were misinterpreted because they deviated from known 'American' practices. Viewed in the light of their prior European experience, however, the actions simply represented a continuation of old and familiar ways. Understanding European society is valuable in other respects. In the seventeenth century, England and New England were very different countries. England was a very densely populated country, according to the standards of the day. New England, on the other hand, was a *vacuum Domicilium*, a sparsely populated land with an abundance of wood for building materials and fuel and an ample supply of water, game, and other resources. One of the major goals of this book is to highlight the response of the two societies to their respective environments. England represented one end of a population/resources continuum, while New England formed the other extreme. How did a European culture conditioned to scarcity or at least a low level of resources react to a resource-rich environment? Did the New World dramatically alter the European's view and ultimately his use of the land and its resources? In order to evaluate the changing patterns of resource utilization, one must first be familiar with the precedents. A study of England's landscape and society in the seventeenth century provides an appropriate point of departure.

Scholars (Powell 1963; Breen 1980; Allen 1981) studying the transfer of local English customs to the New World have emphasized the diversity of the English landscape and its associated social structures. The contrast between the pastoral western Highland Zone and the arable eastern Lowland Zone (Thirsk 1967, 5), the woodland and the open countryside or champion (Homans [1941] 1975, 13), and the Planned Countryside of the Midlands with its open fields and clustered villages and the Ancient Countryside of Essex and Herefordshire with its winding lanes, small woods, and isolated farmsteads (Rackham 1985, 69) was very real. One should not overlook the fact, however, that all of the inhabitants were faced with the same problem of making a living from the land. The similarities, i.e., the need to maintain the cattle, the fertility of the soil, and the supply of wood, far outweighed the differences.

John Norden (1618, 27–39), the acclaimed seventeenth century surveyor, divided the English countryside into four major categories: 'Wood, Meddow, Pasture, and Arable.' Although the areal extent of each of the categories varied from one region to the next, all were critical ingredients of life in the seventeenth century. Since English society revolved about the use of wood and timber, a review of the status and management of England's woodlands is critical to understanding the early seventeenth century landscape. An analysis of the Domesday Book suggests that by the middle of the eleventh century, England was one of the least wooded countries in Europe. Woodlands covered less than 15% of the land. Most of the woods were less than 100 acres in size. In the more agriculturally oriented portions of the Midlands, woodland coverage rarely exceeded 10% and over 50% of the villages were devoid of woodlands (Rackham 1980, 111–127). Three to five hundred years later the woodland areas were reduced to less than 10% of the land's surface area (King [1696] 1936, 35; Rackham 1980, 134). Given the open nature of the English countryside, it is not surprising that the New World, 'full of woods and thickets,' presented 'a wild and savage hue' to the early English colonists (Bradford [1856] 1981, 70).

Use of timber and wood

Archaeologists and palynologists have traced the progressive decline of England's forests in the pollen record. Although it is often difficult to separate anthropogenically induced change from climatically driven change, an increasing amount of evidence suggests that *Homo sapiens*, was responsible for much of the forest's decline and alteration (Godwin 1975; Behre 1988). Some believe that *Homo sapiens'* impact can even be traced back to the hunter–gatherer societies of the Mesolithic period 7000 years ago (Simmons 1988). The high frequency of charcoal in many Mesolithic deposits has been cited as evidence of the controlled use of fire by Mesolithic folk. Fire, and the clearings which followed, would have favored edible nut-bearing species like hazel and would have increased the amount of deer browse (Simmons 1988).

The pollen record is even clearer in the case of the advent of agriculture and the start of the Neolithic period approximately 5000 years ago. The initiation of the Neolithic period roughly coincided with the elm decline and the formation of a number of heaths and blanket mires (Godwin 1975; Birks 1986). There is strong circumstantial evidence linking forest clearance with the expansion of mires (Moore 1975); and fire, mowing, and grazing with the rise and maintenance of heaths (Moore 1986a; Behre 1988). It is more difficult to explain the sudden and almost synchronous decline of elm across much of Europe, although human activities appear to have been involved (Moore 1986b). In many cases, episodes of forest clearance alternated with the reappearance of the forest. The forests which returned, however, differed significantly from their predecessors. The elm and lime of the undisturbed, primary woodlands of lowland England gave way to the ash, birch, beech, and shrubs of the secondary woodlands (Turner 1962; Godwin 1975; Moore 1977; Peterken 1981a, 178–184; Thorley 1981; Greig 1982). The woodlands of England assumed an artifical or a semi-natural state several thousand years ago (Peterken 1981a).

By the sixteenth and seventeenth centuries, 'the great decay of [England's] timber and woods' (Nisbet 1906) had become a very public concern. Pamphleteers decried 'the general destruction and waste of wood' (Sharp 1975). Parliament enacted a wide range of laws to deal with 'the scarcity of woods,' e.g., An Act for the Assize of Fuel 1553, 7 Edward VI, c.8., (James 1981, 118–128). Two of the better known scholars of the period suggested that England faced a critical shortage of wood (Bridenbaugh 1967, 64), a veritable 'timber famine' (Bindoff 1950, 11). No less a personage than John Winthrop, the first governor of the Massachusetts Bay Colony, listed 'the common scarcitie of woode and tymber' as one of the seven major grievances requiring action by parliament (Winthrop 1929).

Before examining any of these issues in detail, it is important to note that timber and wood were two distinct entities in the seventeenth century. Timber refers to the trunks of larger trees suitable for beams, planks, and masts, while wood encompasses the smaller material used in fencing, light construction, firewood, and charcoal burning (Rackham 1980, 3). As timber and wood were required for a variety of activities, both will be examined with respect to their availability and their purported scarcity in the seventeenth century.

Robert Albion's ([1926] 1965) classic work, *Forests and Sea Power*, popularized the importance of ship timber to the English Navy. The 'decay of [England's] wooden walls' was also a subject that John Evelyn covered at length in his famous *Silva: or, a Discourse of Forest-Trees*. Evelyn's *Silva*, incidentally, was commissioned by the Royal Navy. Although native-grown oak was an important ingredient of England's naval superiority, complaints of a shortage of oak stemmed more from the parsimonious habits of the Navy and the economically inaccessible nature of much of the timber than from a lack of suitable trees (Rackham 1980, 154). Due to transport problems, the supply of naval timber was limited to areas within 15 to 20 miles of navigable water (Hammersley 1957; Flinn 1959).

Wood or charcoal was also a basic raw material of the iron and glass industries. J. U. Nef (1932, 2:325–326) has argued that the increasing scarcity of fuelwood and the high price of charcoal forced many iron manufacturers to turn to coal. There is little evidence, however, that iron manufacturers were forced to shut down due to a shortage of wood (Flinn 1959). The gradual shift to coal was due more to its lower price, the labor cost of producing coal being less than the labor cost of manufacturing charcoal (Flinn 1959). Complaints of iron-works destroying woods often reflected the frustrations of other wood users and their inability to compete with iron manufacturers for wood (Hammersley 1957). Due to their insistence on maintaining a long-term supply of fuelwood from coppicewoods, iron manufacturers preserved more woods than they eliminated (Rackham 1980, 153; James 1981, 122–123).

Probably more wood was used in domestic heating than in any other activity (Rackham 1976, 73; James 1981, 119). The demand for firewood expanded dramatically in the rapidly growing urban areas of the seventeenth century and placed a premium on the economically accessible supplies of firewood. Exceptionally severe winters proved to be particularly distressing to the urban poor (Flinn 1959). Due to the difficulty of transporting a bulky commodity like wood, local deficiencies in one area often coincided with surpluses in a neighboring area. 'Wood was ... too expensive to be sold readily at a distance but often too cheap for sale close at hand' (Hammersley 1957, 157). Oliver Rackham (1980, 153, 161–170), reviewing the available evidence on the spiraling cost of wood and timber in sixteenth and seventeenth century England, came to the conclusion that the timber famine was an illusion. Most of the 'catastrophic' rise in price was attributed to the normal course of inflation. In the case of the critical urban fuelwood market, increased shipments of coal probably kept the price of wood down (Rackham 1980, 166–168).

If wood and timber supplies were adequate, they still did not represent resources which could be used with abandon. Peter Kalm's eyewitness accounts of eighteenth century England give one some idea of the close utilization and care of the island's woodland resources. He noted that trees were cut down 'close to the ground so that no part of the trunk shall be wasted ... the roots ... are dug up, cut into small pieces and stacked to be dried. The twigs are also carefully gathered, cut up ... and tied up into bundles.' '[When a tree is cut down] they even collect the sawdust, dry it and use it for fuel' (Dahllöf 1966). The barely adequate supply of wood also encouraged a careful division of the existing resources between competing demands. An emphasis on sustained yield and multiple-use management, i.e., the use of woodlands for developing timber and fuelwood supplies and the use of wood-pastures for the production of forage and fuelwood, was more than a slogan to seventeenth century England. Silvicultural practices were designed to satisfy a variety of needs on a sustained yield basis. The traditional coppice-with-standards management system applied to woodlands, for instance, produced both fuelwood and timber. Coppicing relied on the ability of many underwood species, notably ash, oak, hazel, maple, elm, and lime, to resprout from their stumps or their root systems once they had been cut. Cutting at short intervals of 5 to 30 years generated an endless succession of fuel and fencing material from the permanent base of the tree, i.e., the stool. Standards were the larger timber trees scattered among the stools. Generally oaks or occasionally ashes and limes, they were allowed to persist through several underwood cutting cycles (Rackham 1976, 72–83; 1980, 137–150; Peterken 1981a, 18–23).

Wood-pastures were open, savanna-like areas managed for the production of trees and the generation of forage for deer, sheep, and cattle. Some occupied common lands, i.e., 'wooded commons.' Others served as enclosures for nobles' deer, i.e., 'parks,' or in the case of the legal term 'forests,' housed the king's deer (Rackham 1976, 135–169). Since it was important to preserve both the few remaining trees as well as the grasses, the trees were seldom felled. Instead they were pollarded or cut at 6 to 15 feet above the ground. Pollarding prevented the animals from grazing the new sprouts and insured an indefinite supply of poles (Rackham 1976, 22; Harding and Rose 1986).

In England common rights represented a rigidly defined code of conduct designed to minimize conflict over increasingly scarce resources (Hoskins 1968). The use of trees on the common land, for instance, was carefully apportioned between the lord of the manor and the commoners. Although the lord of the manor generally owned the timber, the commoners frequently had the right or 'bote' to cut wood for specific purposes, i.e., firebote, hedgebote, house-bote, cartbote, or wood for fuel and fencing and timber for buildings and equipment (Rackham 1980, 174). Even the trees in the hedgerows were enumerated with care and subdivided down to the last scrap of ligneous material. The hedgerow timber and the base of the pollard – the bolling – was the property of the lord while the wood from the regrowth of the pollard was reserved for the tenant (Rackham 1976, 169–170, 1977). As the medieval historian H. S. Bennett (1937, 59–60) noted 'the commoners knew what they could knock off, pull down or pick up off the ground – by hook or by crook' from the undivided common land or waste. Trees were a community resource to be carefully apportioned among the inhabitants of the community. Numerous regulations prevented excessive cutting or the overzealous exploitation of the wood on the part of any given individual. Self-aggrandizement or taking more than one's share of the resources was discouraged (Bennett 1937, 84; Hoskins 1968, 160; Rackham 1976, 138). For the most part, it was not a question of conservation in the modern sense of the word. Legislation was motivated by the more practical concern of carefully defining and regulating every individual's use of a valuable community resource (Glacken [1967] 1976, 329). 'The commons was a ... treasure-house ... and it was jealously guarded as such' (Hoskins 1968). Many of New England's early regulations concerning the use of wood reflect a similar concern for a publically owned resource (Powell 1963; Kawashima 1992). England's timber legislation also represented an attempt to minimize conflict between competing demands. The Act of 1543, requiring the maintenance of at least 12 timber trees or standards per acre, the Act of 1559, prohibiting the cutting of larger trees near navigable water, and the Act of 1581, prohibiting the use of trees for iron-works in certain locales, were designed to preserve ship-timber and domestic fuelwood respectively (Flinn 1959). Conservation was a practical, utilitarian affair, rather than a respect for the aesthetic or the ecological qualities of the woodlands per se.

Agrarian practices

The close regulation of the land's resources was even more important in the case of food production. Seventeenth century Europe contained a variety of distinctive farming traditions, each associated with a specific region and a unique physical environment. Livestock and small grain or cereal crops, however, were the mainstays of the mixed farming systems characteristic of much of seventeenth century Europe. The mixed farming tradition will form the core of the following discussion. For a more detailed analysis of the other farming systems, the pastoral tradition of the highlands, for instance, the reader should refer to Thirsk's (1967) comprehensive *Agrarian History of England and Wales*.

The deep, rich soils and the drier climate of southern and eastern England supported a cereal grain and grass economy (Thirsk 1967, 2), much of which was based upon the common-field system. The system integrated the production of grasses and fodder for livestock with the production of cereal grains for human consumption. The livestock, in turn, represented a source of energy and fertilizer as well as a supply of cheese, milk, mutton, and beef. Their usefulness as a source of energy for tillage and a source of manure for fertilizers kept the system functioning and the land 'in heart' (fertile).

Meadows, tillage, and pastureland were the major components of the mixed farming system. Sustainable agriculture required an appropriate mix of all three types of land. Many of the animals were stall-fed during the winter months and required large quantities of fodder. Livestock feed in the form of oats, barley, legumes, and straw, supplied some of the necessary fodder. Meadows, however, were the major source of winter provender. Although they constituted only 8 to 15% of the land in a typical manor in the Midlands (Thirsk 1957, 61–62), small meadow lots were valued above all other forms of land. Generally the meadows were subdivided into strips or lots which cumulatively might total 6 acres for the average husbandman (Franklin 1953, 74). An acre of meadowland was worth two to four times as much as an acre of the best arable land (Franklin 1953, 45; Ault 1965, 33) or woodland (Rackham 1980, 170).

The meadows represented the more fertile wetlands. Because meadowlands were highly valued, most of England's alluvial woodlands were converted to open meadows at an early date (Orwin and Orwin 1967, 57). As a result, England is particularly deficient in ancient alluvial woodlands today. Black poplar (*Populus nigra*), a species characteristic of riverside meadows and floodplains, is currently one of the rarer trees in England (Rackham 1976, 37; 1986, 208). Streamside habitats were especially favorable to the growth of grasses. The reliable supply of moisture insured a sustained yield of grasses throughout the growing season. Most meadows were harvested for hay in July and then opened for the grazing of the regrowth, also known as the aftermath, in August. Winter flooding brought 'fatnesse' or dissolved and particulate nutrients to the alluvial meadows (Kerridge 1968, 251), restoring the nutrients lost in the hay. Studies of the few remaining meadows in England (Baker 1937; Duffey *et al.* 1974, 89) suggest that they were dominated by a number of species characteristic of continental meadows, e.g., oat-grass (*Arrhenatherum elatius*) and meadow brome (*Bromus commutatus*). The grasses of the meadow tolerated cutting but declined under sustained grazing.

During most of the year, the livestock foraged upon the common waste, i.e., the nonarable or the uncultivated land of the manor. Outside the occasional marling or manuring of the land and the sowing of seeds from the hayloft, little attempt was made to improve the common pastureland of the seventeenth century (Fussell 1964). The grazing as Joan Thirsk (1967, 183) phrased it 'was as nature made it and the stock ate and fertilized it.' Fortunately, nature did a very effective job. England's oceanic climate has always provided the constant supply of moisture which many grasses require for their best growth. The frequent occurrence of precipitation during the spring and summer months coupled with the mild open winters promoted a long growing season (Tansley and Proctor 1968, 153; Sauer [1976] 1981). The best pastures have always been associated with oceanic climates and heavy, clay soils which are superior at retaining their moisture. Perennial rye-grass (*Lolium perenne*), orchard grass (*Dactylis glomerata*), timothy (*Phleum pratense*), meadow grass (*Poa pratensis*), red clover (*Trifolium pratense*), white clover (*Trifolium repens*), ribwort plantain (*Plantago lanceolata*), wild carrot (*Daucus carota*), and dandelion (*Taraxacum officinale*) were only a few of the 'grasses' and forage species which profited from England's climate and filled her grasslands and pastures (Franklin 1953, 91; Fussell 1964). Most are palatable, nutritious species adapted to pasture culture (Franklin 1953, 33–34; Ellenberg 1988, 597). Meadow grass, perennial rye-grass, and white clover are species which are noted for their resistance to the ill-effects of trampling (Bates 1935, 1937). Because their regenerative tissue or their growing points are at or below ground level, many grasses can also tolerate a heavy regime of grazing. Grazing stimulates the production of lateral shoots or new buds and new tillers, eventually resulting in the formation of a solid turf of grass. It diverts energy from flowering and seed production to vegetative growth (Tansley 1953, 488). The geographer Carl Sauer ([1976] 1981) has labeled the meadow and pasture grasses of northwestern Europe 'one of the most important contributions of this region to the outside world.' Their resistance to frequent cutting or grazing and trampling makes many of these same species, e.g., *Poa pratensis*, better known as Kentucky bluegrass in North America, and *Lolium perenne*, major components of our present-day lawns.

Maintaining adequate pasture for the livestock was extremely important, important enough to warrant a major shift in the farming system as the land available for pasture decreased. Joan Thirsk has very convincingly argued that population growth and the conversion of much of the waste to tillage placed an increasing pressure on the remaining grasslands. Eventually the pressure resulted in the development of the common-field system of land ownership and farming with its elaborate set of bylaws regulating the activities of the livestock and the planting of the crops (Thirsk 1964). In the more densely pop-ulated regions of England, rights to the use of the pasture were carefully apportioned among the tenants. To avoid overgrazing, each tenant was restricted as to the number of beasts he could pasture on the common land. Generally the number of beasts allowed, i.e., the stint or the gate, was related to the size of the tenant's holding (Hoskins 1968).

Under the normal three-course rotation system typical of the period, a spring grain was followed by a winter grain. Then the land was allowed to lie fallow for a year until the sequence was repeated again. The volunteer growth of grasses, legumes, and weeds on the fallow land as well as the aftermath in the cut meadows, the strips of grassland scattered throughout the plowland, and the stubble following the harvest represented an important source of food for the livestock. The fact that in the thirteenth century the grass and weeds of the fallow were said to feed two sheep per acre gives one some idea of the value and the rapid revegetation of the fallow fields in England's moist, oceanic climate (Franklin 1953, 75). Access to all potential supplies of food for the livestock was carefully controlled by the bylaws of the common-field system. Thirsk (1964) concluded that the development of the common-field system, in fact, allowed a more efficient use of the forage on the arable fields and the meadows. In the common-field system, a given field was generally devoted to one grain. The tenant's holdings were scattered across a number of fields, each with its own crop. The crops planted on a given field were regu-lated so that the grain on the individual holdings matured at same time and the field could be opened for grazing once the harvest was completed. Activities were coordinated to maximize the livestock's access to all of the available for-age, both on and off the arable fields.

The end result of the common-field approach to farming was a sustainable and an almost symbiotic system of agriculture. The forage of the arable fields supported the livestock, while the manure from the livestock kept the fields in heart. Each of the crop fields was manured prior to planting. The manure pro-duced by the cattle in the winter was mixed with straw and carted to the field for the spring grain. Sheep produced some of the best manure (Ault 1965) and were a major source of fertilizer for the more demanding winter grain (Thirsk 1967, 105). They were grazed on the poorer pastures by day and then folded at night on the land soon to be plowed for the winter grain. The agricultural his-torian, Eric Kerridge (1973, 20–21), observed that sheep were the muck-spreaders, the package fertilizer manufacturers, distributors, and spreaders that helped fat the ground.

There have been a number of analyses of the common-field system in terms of its nutrient balance and ultimately its sustainability (Cooter 1978; Loomis

1978). At least one investigator has depicted the common-field system as ushering in a short-term burst of productivity followed by a steady decline in productivity. 'Fertility was drained from the uncropped hinterlands [in the form of manure] to sustain the arable' (Cooter 1978). The result was the progressive impoverishment of the pasture and lower yields of hay and grasses.

In actuality, the common-field system functioned, and functioned effectively, for hundreds of years. There is very little historical evidence of soil exhaustion or a steadily declining yield (Bennett 1937, 78). The system worked because low nutrient losses or outputs were balanced by low nutrient inputs. Crop yields probably averaged 9 to 15 bushels of wheat per acre, a relatively low value by modern standards (Thirsk 1967, 651). As a result, the amount of nitrogen exported from the system in the form of grain probably totaled less than 20 kilograms per hectare (2.47 acres) annually (Loomis 1978). Manure was one of the critical nitrogen inputs to the system. Due to the limited number of livestock, however, it was always in short supply. The manure produced by the several (6 to 9) cows and horses and the 20 to 30 sheep the average husbandman owned (Thirsk 1967, 91) had to be spread across 20 to 30 acres of plowland (Bennett 1937, 78–79). Any deficiencies in the nitrogen budget due to losses associated with erosion, leaching, and crop removal were balanced by nitrogen inputs from the rain and dust (estimated at 8 to 12 kg/ha) and the seed (4 kg/ha), and by biological nitrogen fixation by free-living bacteria (2 to 5 kg/ha), leguminous crops (20 to 40 kg/ha), and weeds (2 to 10 kg/ha, Loomis 1978). Pulses (peas and beans) were grown as crops on the arable while native legumes (vetches and tares) frequently volunteered or were deliberately sown as hitch crops on the fallow (Kerridge 1968, 46, 93; Lane 1980). Low inputs of manure, straw, weeds, and stubble stabilized the organic matter in the soil and ultimately led to a low but steady yield of crops (Loomis 1978).

7

Assault upon the forest. Part I. The farmer

...when the steel axe of the white man rang out in the startled air
[the American forest's] doom was sealed. In the settlement and the
civilization of the country, bread more than timber or beauty was
wanted; ... the early settlers ... regarded God's trees as only a larger
kind of pernicious weed ... [They] waged interminable forest wars;
chips flew thick and fast; trees in their beauty fell crashing by millions, smashed to confusion, and the smoke of their burning has
been rising to heaven more than two hundred years.
>   John Muir. 1897. 'The American forest.'

We have these farms, these citizens, these railroads, and this civilization to show for it, and they are worth what they cost.
>   Eugene Davenport. Dean of the College of Agriculture at Illinois,
>   1915. Quoted in Twining (1964).

The transformation of North America from an 'immense wilderness' to a 'fruitful field' (Dwight [1822] 1969, 4:365) was one of the more significant, yet little
publicized events of American history. Forest clearance was a major American
enterprise as vast numbers of trees were swept off the landscape in the seventeenth through the nineteenth centuries. Popular opinion suggests there were
basically two scenarios: (1) the settler or farmer, patiently chopping his way out
of the dark woods and into the sunlight over the decades and (2) the timber
baron, slashing and burning his way across the landscape, feeding timber into
the maw of an expanding nation (Tessendorf 1972). One should not, however,
overlook the less dramatic and often incidental factors which contributed to the
destruction of the forests. Cutting for industrial fuelwood and domestic heating
consumed large quantities of wood. Grazing livestock also exacted their toll on
the forest, so much so that Charles Sprague Sargent (1882) listed them as one of
the great enemies of the forest in the nineteenth century.

Techniques of forest clearance

Most of the early founders of the nation, including Ben Franklin, considered agriculture 'the great Business of the Continent' (Cox *et al.* 1985, 51). Agriculture required the elimination of the forest. Clearing the brush and the trees was the first task of the new settler. The amount of work required varied with the nature of the terrain and the encumbering vegetation. Due to its spreading, superficial root system, beech was universally considered a difficult species to clear (Michaux [1805] 1904, 214; Gordon 1832, 28; Williams 1843; Washington 1925, 442; Schweinitz 1927, 233). John Lorain (1814), a distinguished pioneer farmer in Pennsylvania, preferred clearing hemlock and white pine to hardwoods because 'the roots [were] more easily broken by a plow, suckers [did] not spring up as much, [there was] not as much brush to grub out because of the dense shade, and the timber [was] more readily burnt, being softer and more inflammable ...'

Fortunately, the settler had a variety of techniques and traditions to draw upon for the process of forest clearance. There was the old English tradition of laboriously and very thoroughly assarting or grubbing up a few acres of woods at a time (Darby 1951). The trees were cut, the roots were exhumed, and the land was plowed prior to planting. Many accounts (Eliot [1760] 1934, 7–8; Schoepf [1788] 1968, 2:264; Chinard 1945; Carroll 1973) suggest that the earliest colonists followed a similar procedure in New England and the Mid-Atlantic states. Small patches of land were cleared with infinite care, 'stubbing all Staddle' (Eliot [1760] 1934, 7), or pulling the small trees out by the roots, cutting the larger trees, and extracting their roots. The price of clearing land in this laborious fashion was often exhorbitant as a bill of £50 sterling for clearing one acre in Hartford, Connecticut, in 1638 attests (Blois [1838] 1975, 27–28). The value gained by improving or clearing the land seldom warranted the expense of rooting up the stumps (Cooper 1794, 118). The English visitor William Brown, for instance, cited a cost of $60 for extracting the 200–300 stumps per acre in northeastern Ohio in the early 1800s. Improved land was valued at $15 per acre in the same area (Tessendorf 1972). It was much easier to let the normal process of decay complete the job. Most of the hardwood stumps left in the field decayed or could easily be removed within ten years (Weld [1807] 1968, 232; Shirreff [1835] 1971, 370–384; Chinard 1945, 487). The smaller stumps and the less resistant hardwoods, i.e., aspen and birch, decayed within five years (Evans 1852, 684; Guillet 1963, 326). White pine, with its resin filled heartwood, remained solid for over 50 years. As the New Hamsphire historian Jeremy Belknap (1813, 3:81) expressed it 'no man ever cut down a pine, and lived to see the stump rotten.'

The Germans in Pennsylvania, the English in New England, and the wealthier or 'strong-handed' individuals in general preferred the compromise cut and burn method. The trees were cut at 2 to 3 feet above the ground, allowed to dry for several months to two years, and then burned. The fallen trunks and the material left after the first burn was cut into easily transportable 12 to 20 foot lengths, assembled into piles and burned again to eliminate the remaining debris (Belknap 1813, 3:97–98; Dwight [1821] 1969, 2:325–326; Bidwell and Falconer [1925] 1941, 77; Chinard 1945, 484–486; Fletcher 1950, 64–65). 'Flames consumed what the iron was unable to destroy' (Chastellux [1786] 1963, 1:80).

Land could be brought into production even more quickly by girdling the trees, i.e., removing a wide ring or circle of bark. Girdling saved the time and expense of cutting and burning the trees during the very critical early years of the farm-making process. Danhof (1941) cites an average cost of $5 to $8 per acre for girdling as opposed to $10 per acre for cutting and burning in the nineteenth century. With the shade eliminated, the land could be sown to corn, rye, wheat, grass, or clover. It took three to four years for most of the twigs and the branches to fall off the standing trees (Old Seventy 1840; Harvey [1841] 1925; Loomis 1855). The trunks remained upright for varying lengths of time, depending upon the soil and the species. Hemlock stood for eight or nine years, oak four to five years, and maple three to four years (La Rochefoucauld-Liancourt 1799, 1:164). Eventually the downed timber had to be cut or burnt into pieces, piled, and disposed of in the final conflagration of a 'log rolling' episode to which the farmer invited his neighbors (Old Seventy 1840; Fletcher 1950, 64). Where clearance for pasture was the prime consideration, as in the case of large sections of New England, the trunks were allowed to rot on the ground, fertilizing the pasture in the process (Belknap 1813, 3:98). The total time span from the girdling of the trees to the disappearance of the logs was commonly estimated as 15 to 20 years (Bidwell and Falconer [1925] 1941, 266). Girdling was severely criticized on the grounds falling limbs made it dangerous to animals and fences, it was uncouth and disgusting, and the fallen timber made it difficult to mow and necessitated frequent clearing (Belknap 1813, 2:97; Dwight [1821] 1969, 2:83–84; Chinard 1945, 484). Over the long run, the costs of clearcutting versus girdling were probably similar. Girdling simply deferred the task of disposing of the fallen timber to a more propitious time (Williams 1989, 115).

For many a New England farmer, clearing away the forest was only the beginning of the process of converting forest to plowland. Boulders had to be removed from the stony soils and placed in walls, heaps, or pits (Shaler 1896). It is said that it required one generation to clear the land of trees and another generation to remove the stones and level the 'cradle-knolls' or tip-up mounds of the trees (Towle 1886).

Foreign observers often described the effects of forest clearance in very graphic terms. By night, the traveler was 'lighted on his way with the blaze of huge piles, that crackling and roaring in the wind, irradiat[ed] the heavans; and by day the strike of the axe, or the crash of falling timber [could] be heard everywhere' (Griffiths 1835, 33). The four or five large heaps of logs produced per acre often burned incessantly for a week during the firing process (Schweinitz 1927, 238). Travelers had 'to suffer from smoke and heat' while hot ashes often scorched the feet of their horses (Heckewelder 1958, 360). The result was luxuriant crops set amidst an unsightly waste of half-burnt stumps and blackened trunks (Tudor 1834, 1:217–218; Griffiths 1835, 34).

The cumulative effect of all the cutting and burning was a very open countryside. Americans, as many English observers liked to point out, had an 'unconquerable aversion to trees' (Weld [1807] 1968, 1:39). Neglecting the precepts of the more fashionable English landscape architects of the time, i.e., Humphry Repton or Capability Brown, they cleared all the trees before them (Johnson 1819, 57). Few were left for shade or ornamental purposes. Unfortunately, the visiting critics failed to realize that the tall spindly, forest-grown trees left after the cutting were neither particularly ornamental nor windfirm. If they were not cut down, they either died in the fire following the cutting or they succumbed to windthrow or drought (Trail [1846] 1929, 205–206; Chinard 1945, 486).

The ecological impacts of forest clearance, particularly the use of fire, were vigorously debated. During dry periods, fires often escaped to the surrounding woods (Beardsley 1852, 37; Wood 1880). From a short-term perspective, burning speeded up the rate of mineralization, releasing the nutrients contained in the organic matter. The resulting nutrient pulse stimulated the growth of the first crops, the grains and the grasses (Lorain 1825, 335–336). Over the long-term, however, many believed that the destruction of the humus or the organic matter impoverished the soil (Coxe 1794, 450–457; Lorain 1825, 335–336). A considerable amount (probably 50–90%) of the nitrogen contained in the above-ground biomass and the forest floor was likely volatilized and lost during the burning process (Bormann 1982, 109; Wang 1984, 187–193). On marginal, sandy, nutrient-poor sites where the nitrogen reserves of the soil were relatively low (< 100 g/m^2) and as much as 40% of the nitrogen may have been contained in the living biomass and the forest floor (Wang 1984, 76), the flush of nutrients and crops was rather short-lived. On a majority of sites, however, the large quantities of nitrogen stored in the organic matter in the mineral soil (360–760 g/m^2) (Bormann, Likens, and Melillo 1977;

Cole and Rapp 1981, 393) probably buffered the system against any short-term declines in crop productivity.

Value and use of trees on the frontier

A number of important questions related to the forest clearance process remain unanswered. Economists and historians, for instance, have long tried to evaluate the utility of the forest to the pioneer (Turner 1920; Muntz 1959, 50–53; White 1979). Were trees simply an obstacle to be disposed of as quickly as possible, a pernicious kind of weed as John Muir suggested, or were they a potential source of income as a number of historians (Gates 1969, 1972; White 1979; Williams 1983) have implied? A related issue is the amount of waste the clearance process generated. Conservationists have typically focused on the utter waste and carnage of the clearing while historians and geographers have implied that much of the wood was put to use (Cox *et al.* 1985, 36; Williams 1989, 56).

Unfortunately, the early settler rarely took the time to write about the more prosaic matters of establishing a farm on the frontier. Fortunately a perusal of the historical evidence, however fragmentary and ancedotal, can still shed light on the value and use of America's original forests.

Information on the quality of the soil and the potential productivity of the land was always of value to the prospective settler as well as the speculator. Through trial and error, Europeans gradually developed a practical lore for determining the value of the land for agricultural purposes. Trees were among the more obvious products of the soil. Since the dominant trees of each tract of land were generally believed to be determined by the soil, the soil was 'best known and always described by the European Settlers from its peculiar Vegetation, as Oak land, Birch, Beech, or Chestnut Land; Pine-Barren, Maple Swamps, etc. As these different Species of Wood predominate[d] on each Place, the Soil [was] pronounced to be of Mould, loomy and moist, stony or sandy, light or stiff' (Pownall [1776] 1949, 24, 64). To the intelligent cultivator, trees were an infallible indicator of the fertility of the land, superior even to chemical analyses of the soil (Browne 1832, 325). Large land companies and speculators often advertised the value of the land on the basis of the trees it supported (Michaux [1805] 1904, 228; Ellis 1879, 27). The English traveler Thomas Ashe (1808, 90) stated that the occurrence of sugar maple, black cherry, and sassafras on a tract of land could raise its selling price. States like Kentucky and Pennsylvania used trees to determine the market value and the tax rate of their lands (Michaux [1805] 1904, 228–230; Hilgard 1914, 314). Corrupt land speculators were even known to falsify the trees marking the boundaries of the early land surveys to mislead the buyer (Plummer 1975).

Trees were not the only or even the best means of assessing the potential productivity of the land, some argued. There were a number of problems associated with the perceived indicator status of the tress. Soils could vary while the timber remained the same (Munroe [1804] 1849, 1173) or a species' indicator status could change from one region to the next (Cooper [1810] 1897, 34–35). There was also the problem of the very dynamic or changing nature of the vegetation. Disturbances and fortuitous events could alter the pattern of forest growth (Peters 1808), making it difficult to tie a particular species to a particular soil type. In light of the above problems, it is not surprising that some of the more intelligent observers like Joseph Ellicott (1795), the head surveyor of the Holland Land Company in western New York, came to the conclusion that 'no certain rule can be laid down in respect to the quality of the land by the timber.' An analysis of some of the major tree–soil classification schemes of the eighteenth and nineteenth centuries, their rationale, their use by the early settlers, and their validity follows.

Settlers' guides and travelers' accounts furnish an introduction to the major soil classification schemes of the period. Lands were commonly divided into three to five classes or qualities on the basis of their vegetation (Table 7.1). Given a knowledge of the agricultural limitations of the time, few would probably fault the systems of classification represented in Table 7.1. Dark, stone-free loams were generally considered the best soils (Wyckoff 1981). Walnut, sugar maple, basswood, cherry, hackberry, buckeye, pawpaw, honeylocust, blue ash, and coffeetree were the species associated with these soils, the rich alluvial soils of bottomlands or the loamy, calcareous soils of uplands (Hilgard 1914, 514–515). Given the limited use of manures and artificial fertilizers throughout much of the eighteenth and nineteenth centuries, it is not surprising that settlers placed a premium on calcareous soils and bottomlands with their influx of fertilizing elements during overflow periods. Species associated with the poorest sites (class 3 or lower) are likewise easy to interpret. Many occur on sites which were dry and infertile initially, e.g., pitch pine on outwash sands, or they occupy sites which have lost most of their nutrients through long periods of leaching, e.g., blackjack oak and post oak on the clay-pan soils of southern Illinois. Others (pitch pine, chestnut, chestnut oak, and red cedar) commonly dominate mountainous terrain too rugged to cultivate. The low-ranked spruce, fir, and hemlock are more characteristic of colder soils, i.e., areas with a short growing season. Evergreens such as hemlock also produce a forest-floor layer that is relatively recalcitrant to decomposition and the release of nutrients (Carlyle 1986). This may have contributed to the poor reputation and low productivity of many hemlock sites (Belknap 1813, 3:95–97).

Table 7.1. *Eighteenth and nineteenth century ratings of soil quality based on vegetation growing on site*

Region	Soil quality				Sources
	1st rate (best land)	2nd	3rd	4th (worst land)	
New England	chestnut, walnut	beech, white oak	balsam fir, hemlock, pitch pine	whortleberries (blueberries and huckleberries), marsh and shrubs on poorest land	Douglass 1760, 2: 216; Morse 1792, 143
N Pennsylvania and W New York	elm, walnut, sycamore, ash, lynn or basswood, cherry, cucumber	black oak, white oak, white pine	sassafras, chestnut, laurel, scrub, black and white oak, pitch pine, red maple	barrens are unfit fit for cultivation	Ellicott 1795
Ohio	walnut, sugar maple, ash, buckeye, locust, cherry, spicebush	black oak, white oak, hickory dogwood	beech, elm, red maple		Smith [1799] 1907; Howe 1908, 1: 87

Table 7.1(*cont.*)

Region	Soil quality				Sources
	1st rate (best land)	2nd	3rd	4th (worst land)	
Kentucky	sugar maple, elm, ash, beech, pawpaw, locust, cherry, walnut, buckeye	oak, hickory, dogwood	black oak, red oak, some hickory, gum	blackjack oak and conifers on broken, hilly land	Imlay 1797, 278
Kentucky and Tennessee	cherry, white walnut, buckeye, white and blue ash, hackberry, elm, coffeetree, shingle oak, honeylocust, pawpaw	chestnut, red oak, black oak, sassafras, persimmon, sweet gum, gum	black oak, chestnut oak, red oak, red cedar and pine on dry mountains		Michaux [1805] 1904, 228–230
Illinois	black walnut, hickory, pawpaw, sugar maple, hackberry	various oaks, hickory, sweetgum	oak, especially post oak and blackjack oak		Short 1845, 196–197

The most useful accounts of the period are those which specifically match crops, soils, and different types of vegetation (Table 7.2). Although they are not as common as the rating approach, they provide a more detailed picture of the pioneer's knowledge of crop requirements and species–site relationships. It is important to emphasize the fact that a number of factors entered into the settler's assessment of the soil. The texture, the fertility, the durability, the temperature, and the moisture of the soil – all were components of the evaluation process. Settlers commonly knew that finer textured soils were associated with grasses (note Belknap's and Gordon's evaluations). Clay-rich soils were often characterized by impeded drainage. A reliable supply of moisture favored the more moisture-loving beech and sugar maple on these soils and the continued growth of grasses throughout the drier, mid to late summer period. By the same token, however, cold, wet, clay soils were unsuitable for the growth of small grains because they shortened the growing season. Due to the high specific heat of water, large amounts of radiant energy had to be absorbed in the spring before the soil temperature was suitable for the growth of small grains. Winter wheat also suffered from frost heaving on the finer textured soils (Russell 1857, 29–30).

Fertility was another important consideration. Corn was the crop of the rich dales and bottomlands while wheat found a niche on the lighter, less fertile soils of the oak and hickory uplands (Russell 1857, 20–29; Campbell [1793] 1937, 223). Bottomlands dominated by walnut, sugar maple, and cherry were almost universally recommended for the production of the more demanding species like corn (Morris 1785; Gordon 1832, 28; Gibbons 1983). The deposition of particulate materials and nutrients during the overflow period each spring kept the bottomlands and intervales fertile. High levels of nitrogen, however, also contributed to the excessive vegetative growth and lodging of wheat planted on the richer bottomland soils (Eliot [1760] 1934, 205; Baily 1856, 212; Gibbons 1983). Wheat performed better on the drier, warmer, somewhat less fertile soils of the uplands (O'Reilly 1838, 44–45; Hubbard 1847a; Fleischmann 1849, 36–37; Baily 1856, 212). Oaks, particularly white oak, and wheat were almost synonymous with the light, warm soils of western Pennsylvania, Ohio, and the Genesee region of western New York. Rye, buckwheat, and, to a lesser extent, oats were consigned to the lower end of the nutrient gradient, i.e., the nutrient impoverished, pitch pine sands (Druckerman 1926; Sauer 1941, [1976] 1981). Farming was totally out of the question in the case of the acidic outwash soils of the jack pine plains of the Upper Great Lakes region (Mayr 1890a, 207).

The ease of bringing the land into production was another important consideration in the overall evaluation of the land. Broken, stone-filled land, a habitat

Table 7.2. *Nineteenth century appraisals of agricultural potential of land associated with various forest types. Arranged according to increasing agricultural value and fertility from left to right*

Region (and source)	Dominant vegetation of site					
	Pitch pine	White pine	Spruce and hemlock	Beech and sugar maple	Oak	Mixed hardwoods
New Hampshire (Belknap 1813, 3: 95–97)	dry and sandy, soon worn out	light and dry	generally cold, moist soil, poor for grain, suitable for grass	warm, rich loam, easy to cultivate, good for grain and grass	white oak – hard and stony, good for corn, difficult to establish grass	black and yellow birch, white ash, elm, alder – good deep, moist rich soil, easy to cultivate, good for grain and grass
New York (Cooper [1810] 1897, 34)	thin, sandy		birch and spruce – poor, land last taken up	alder – good grassland	poplar – good wheat land	basswood, bitternut, sugar maple, white ash, elm, beech – good soil for grass and grain; walnut found only in strong, durable land
New York (Munro [1804] 1849, 1173)				beech – clayey, wet and cold	oak – durable, but harder to till and not as productive as maple	sugar maple and basswood – durable, best land for grass and probably for grain

Western Pennsylvania (Gordon 1832, 28)	pine lands – not favorable to any grains	beech, maple, black ash – good grassland	white oak – best adapted to small grains	hickory, walnut, cherry, sugar maple – best for Indian corn
Ohio (Anonymous 1811)			white oak and bitternut hickory – thin, sandy soil; not very durable unless mixed with shellbark hickory and poplar where soil is much better	black walnut, blue ash, red elm – rich soil; with spicebush – very productive of almost all kinds of crops
Lower Michigan (Hubbard 1847a, 1847b, 1928)		elm–ash – cold, wet, clayey subsoil soil near surface; however, rarely suffers drought; adapted to meadow	white oak, black oak and bur oak openings – dry, porous sands and gravels, easily brought into cultivation; good wheat land, well adapted to grain and root crops	sugar maple, beech, tuliptree black walnut, white ash, elm, white pine – deep, gravelly loam; soils more durable than openings; better for grains, good wheat land

frequently dominated by chestnut oak and hemlock, was obviously avoided (Wyckoff 1981). Although they were often among the more fertile sites, wetlands and swamps also rated relatively low in the surveyors' assessments due to the difficulty and the expense of draining land in the first half of the nineteenth century (Howe 1908, 1:87; Kelly 1974a, 1975a; Wyckoff 1981). The fertile swamps of the Lake Plains sections of Ohio and Michigan, for instance, were long considered interminable morasses, 'unfit for cultivation' (US Congress 1860; Bingham 1945, 34–35). By the twentieth century, however, many of these same 'third class' lands had been drained and turned into 'the garden soils of the Midwest' (Howe 1908, 1:87). On the more positive side, site conditions could hasten the settlement process. The coarse-textured soils of the oak openings of Michigan, for instance, were preferred over the more durable soils of the timberlands due 'to the ease with which they could be brought into crops' (Hubbard 1847a). Settlers with limited capital often selected the sandier soils of the uplands due to the ease of clearing the open woodlands on the lighter soils (Bingham 1945, 29; Kelly 1970).

The federal land survey records and land entry tract books constitute the best source of information on the early evaluation of the land and its vegetation. Surveyors of the federal lands in the Midwest were required to note the kinds of timber and the quality of the soil, whether first, second, or third rate, on each mile-long section line they ran (White 1984a, 249, 299, 369, 466). Entry tract books, also maintained by the federal government, record the date at which the land was first purchased. Some researchers consider entry tracts a more realistic appraisal of the value of the land because they focus on what people did as opposed to what they wrote (McManis 1964, 62).

Unfortunately, few investigators have utilized the early survey records to their fullest extent. Clarke and Finnegan (1984) employed the somewhat more cursory colonial survey records of Essex County, Ontario, to determine the tree species associated with good and poor lands. Wyckoff (1981) tabulated the trees associated with four categories of land in the early Holland Land Company surveys of western New York (Table 7.3). Kiefer's (1969) study of Rush County, Indiana, is one of the more thorough analyses of the evaluation and settlement of a forested landscape. Kiefer found that the better drained soils of the rolling uplands, i.e., the first-rate sugar maple land, were the first areas settled in the county. Occupation of the poorly drained, level, beech, elm, and ash lands lagged behind the rest of the county. Natural drainage conditions dictated the value of the land. The wetter land was avoided because the soil warmed up later in the spring, standing water and flooding were threats to the crops, and the incidence of malaria was higher than on the better drained sites (Kiefer 1969, 34).

Table 7.3. *Association of trees and quality of land along the Holland Land Company's early survey lines in western New York*

| Tree species | Percentage of observations by quality | | | | Total number of observations |
	1st quality	2nd quality	3rd quality	Swamp	
Sugar maple	68	31	1	t	761
Beech	44	52	4	t	568
Hemlock	6	81	9	4	460
Black ash	2	16	0	81	243
Oak	28	64	8	1	133
Elm	42	51	1	5	113
Pine	26	63	10	1	86
Basswood	63	37	0	0	80
Ash	42	28	0	30	40
Chestnut	16	65	19	0	37
Bitternut	92	8	0	0	24
Alder	0	17	0	83	24
Hickory	45	45	10	0	11
Tamarack	0	0	0	100	10
Birch	11	89	0	0	9
Walnut	86	14	0	0	7
Poplar	83	17	0	0	6
Sycamore	100	0	0	0	6
Cedar	0	0	0	100	5

Note: t indicates trace, present but < 1%.
Source: Slightly modified from Wyckoff (1981).

In spite of varied critiques of the use of trees as indicators, most observers believed that differentiating soils on the basis of tree growth was justified (Belknap 1813, 3:97). Trees were not the last word in evaluating the soil's potential fertility. They responded to a number of other factors unrelated to the nutrient status of the soil. Eventually they were superseded by chemical determinations of the soil's fertility. It is surprising, however, to note how well the folk wisdom of the nineteenth century, built up over a long period of trial and error, mirrors the more sophisticated, scientifically based knowledge of vegetation–site relationships in the twentieth century.

In addition to their usefulness as soil-quality indicators, trees provided settlers with a raw material that could be adapted to a variety of uses. As the French entrepreneur and statesman Talleyrand (1942, 141) noted while touring the United States, 'the natural products of the land are to be considered not only as a sign and means of judging the quality of the land, they must also be envisaged as an intrinsic wealth ... There is no raw material applicable to so many uses and having such an extensive consumption as wood.'

One of the more obvious uses of wood was for timber in frame construction and building materials. In the latter half of the eighteenth century and the early nineteenth century, the spread of sawmills paralleled or followed shortly behind the advance of the agricultural frontier (Defebaugh 1907, 2:307–312; Dinsdale 1963, 33; Williams 1980). The term timber, however, was applicable to only a small number of tree species. Due to its strong and durable, yet easily worked nature, white pine was the preferred species for most buildings, i.e., for timber frame construction, for panels, for clapboards, for doors, windows, sashes, and molding (Michaux 1819, 3:240–243). South of the white pine region, white oak and tuliptree were popular building materials (Michaux 1819, 1:20–21). The author of *American Husbandry* stated 'timber is of no slight value to the new settlers, as it yields a certain price and is a commodity regularly exported ...' (Carman [1755] 1939, 43–44). He elaborated on the well-to-do settler who established his own sawmill and paid for most of the expense of clearing through the sale of boards, planks, shingles, and staves (Carman [1755] 1939, 80–81). John Heckewelder (1958, 345) likewise commented upon the flow of lumber, boards, shingles, and ship-timber down the Susquehanna River in the 1790s, a flow of wood products which made possible the up-river transport of necessary store goods. In the mixed hardwood–white pine forests of lower Michigan, the occasional pine was often worth more to the settler than the cost of the land that produced it (Hubbard 1847b). Not all woods, however, were composed of oak and white pine. Nor were they equally close to a major artery of transportation, i.e., a river with access to an urban market. Rarely could timber repay the heavy expense of overland transport (Evans [1753] 1939, 103). The local demand for timber was easily satisfied early in the nineteenth century and the capacity of the mills was rather low – typically less than 2000 board feet per day (Pickering 1832, 158).

It is extremely difficult to ascertain the amount of cut wood which was converted to lumber on the frontier. Ohio was still largely a forested frontier state in 1820. Responses to a questionnaire sent out by Governor Ethan A. Brown concerning early manufacturers in the state suggest that the actual amount of lumber cut was relatively low. William Utter's (1942) summary of the returns from 18 representative counties in the state indicates an annual output of 22 570 000 bd ft of lumber. Assuming the average acre of virgin forest in Ohio contained 13 000 bd ft (Chapman 1944, 82), this represents a cut of approximately 1700 acres or less than 3 square miles out of a total area of approximately 10 000 square miles. Forest clearance in Ohio averaged 1% of the land surface area of the state per year for the first 50 years of the state's existence (Hough 1884). The area potentially cleared on a yearly basis, 100 square miles, suggests only a small percentage of the wood cut was converted to building material.

The last half of the nineteenth century witnessed an upsurge in the commercial exploitation of the more valuable hardwoods of the agriculturally oriented Midwest. The expansion of the railroad system in the 1850s through the 1870s gave a big boost to the region's hardwood lumber trade (US Forest Service 1920, 44). Ohio and Indiana were the major centers of the hardwood lumber industry, ranking either fourth or fifth among the states in the production of all types of lumber from 1850 to 1890 (Kellogg 1906). Black walnut and to a lesser extent oak, ash, and tuliptree on the farmer's back forty brought a very high price in the urban timber markets of the East (US Forest Service 1920, 44; Kiefer 1969, 38–39). Hardwoods supplied the raw materials for the furniture, the transportation (ships and wagons), the cooperage, and the implement industries.

The deforestation of North America converted large quantities of trees into fuel. The amount involved was probably substantial, although it is difficult to believe the assertions of some investigators (Williams 1982) that the majority of the wood was converted to domestic fuel. Due to its bulky nature, fuelwood was a marketable commodity only near urban areas or convenient waterways. Farmers in the immediate vicinity of urban areas like Utica, New York, commonly spent the winters cutting fuelwood. The wood chopped off one acre paid the cost of clearing four acres of land (Collins [1830] 1971, 171). Drawing upon information contained in the federal censuses of 1840 and 1880, the historian Paul Gates (1972) estimated that the average Maine farmer produced 5 cords of wood in 1839 and 12 cords of wood in 1879. It is unlikely that the 5 to 12 cords contributed unduly to deforestation in Maine given the fact that Maine's virgin forests averaged 20 to 30 cords per acre and the fact that much of the wood undoubtedly came from second-growth woodlands maintained as coppicewoods.

Staves for barrels, charcoal for industrial purposes, bark for tanning and ties for railroads represented other potential sources of revenue for the farmer clearing his land (Deane 1797, 54; Utter 1942, 236–238; Olson 1971; Gates 1972; White 1979, 29–30). Most of these industries, at least during the early phases of their development, were enterprises undertaken by rural communities. They required little in the way of equipment and could be carried out in the farmer's spare time (Hedrick 1933, 138–144; Coyne 1940, 12; Fletcher 1950, 328–329; Hergert 1983). The use of wood in the above industries, however, was limited by the special nature of the wood required or, in the case of charcoal, by local demand. Due to the occurrence of tyloses, which plugged its pores, white oak was the preferred species for staves for tight casks, i.e., casks holding liquids. Staves of white oak were among the major commodities shipped east on the early Erie Canal (Bidwell and Falconer [1925] 1941, 182). Red oak was employed for dry casks or slack cooperage (Douglass 1760, 59, 67). The use of bark in the tanning industry was largely limited to species with high (6–14%) tannin concentrations, i.e., hemlock, black oak, and chestnut oak (Brown 1919, 64; Hergert 1983). Before 1890 white oak accounted for most of the wood used in railroad ties (Olson 1971, 17).

One should not overlook the more obvious use of wood for building materials, fuel, fences, and a variety of other items on the farm. The log cabin, a standard feature of the frontier in the eighteenth and the nineteenth centuries, typically required about 80 logs in addition to wood for the roof (Youngquist and Fleischer 1977, 28). Wood also kept the farmer's house warm in the winter. The use of wood for fuel will be considered in greater detail in the next chapter. Fences were a basic ingredient of any successful farm operation. Occasionally the early settler resorted to makeshift fences thrown together out of cut branches, trunks, dead trees, and stumps (Fletcher 1950, 86; Youngquist and Fleischer 1977, 28). Most settlers, however, preferred the Virginia rail or zigzag fence (Williams 1989, 69–71). Straight timber of the appropriate species was almost universally set aside for rails during the process of clearing (Cooper 1794, 117; Flint [1828] 1970, 1:359; Marshall 1845, 18). Due to their durability, red cedar, chestnut, black locust, and to a lesser extent black walnut and oak were the preferred species selected for making rails (Fessenden 1835, 214–215). Contemporaries (Schaff 1905, 84) have criticized the early settlers for their profligate use of black cherry and walnut rails. They overlook the fact that walnut and cherry were among the more easily split woods and the fact that much of the wood would have gone up in smoke if it had not been converted to rails (Schweinitz 1927, 241).

The timber selected for fencing material was cut into 10 to 11 foot logs and split into 4 inch diameter rails (Holditch 1818, 64). The Virginia rail fence required large amounts of wood – 100 rails for every 6 rods (Woods [1822] 1968, 29) or approximately 800 rails to fence one acre (Fletcher 1950, 66, 85). It, however, had the advantage of being easy to construct, repair, and move. It avoided the laborious and costly work of digging holes and mortising posts and rails (Youngquist and Fleischer 1977, 30) and it lasted longer than the post-and-rail fence which rotted where it was buried in the ground (Williams 1989, 71). Its biggest disadvantage was the fact that it required considerably more wood for its construction than the post-and-rail fence (Williams 1989, 72). As wood became scarce, the Virginia rail fence of the frontier gave way to the less wood-demanding post-and-rail fence of settled areas (Cooper 1794, 118; Michaux [1805] 1904, 134; Fletcher 1950, 86).

Two wood-related products stand out in particular as sources of income for the frontier farmer. One, potash, was a valuable byproduct of forest clearance. The other, maple sugar, often resulted in the destruction of segments of the forest. Potash, a potassium-based alkali, was the most important industrial chemical of the Northeast in the late eighteenth and early nineteenth centuries. It was a basic ingredient in the production of flint glass, soft soap, and gunpowder and in the bleaching of linens and the scouring of wool (Kreps 1930; Roberts 1972). Hardwood ashes which generally contain about 5% potash (K_2CO_3) by weight, and stove ashes which range from 10 to 15% potash by weight (due to more complete combustion) were the raw materials of the potash industry (Office of Forest Investigations 1919, 32). Softwoods like hemlock and pine are much lower in their potassium salts. Their ashes were not even considered worth collecting (Mitchel 1748; Cooper [1810] 1897, 23).

Although there had long been a European demand for North America's potash, production was relatively low at first due to the large amount of capital required to establish a potashery. Technological developments in the mid-eighteenth century brought the costs of production within the means of the more ambitious farmer and local merchant (Roberts 1972). Ashes collected from the field were often stored in small log sheds to prevent the leaching of the mobile potassium by rainwater (Pickering 1832, 159). During the processing the ashes were placed in wooden barrels with a false bottom and leached with water to produce a potassium lye. The lye was boiled down in a cast-iron vessel to produce a dark colored residue known as crude potash or 'black salts.' The remaining organic impurities were then burned off by subjecting the salts to intense heat in a thick-walled, cast-iron vessel known as a 'potash kettle.' The result was the enriched American potash (potassium carbonate) of commerce. Further refining produced pearlash, a product with a purity of 70–95% K_2CO_3. Occasionally slacked lime ($Ca(OH)_2$) was added to the leaching tubs to form the more caustic form of potash, potassium hydroxide (KOH) (Miller 1980; Multhauf 1981; Roberts 1983).

In newly settled regions potash represented a valuable cash crop for the more impecunious settler. A farmer could take up his axe when the autumn work was done and generate money for store goods and taxes (Cheney 1971). Merchants and commercial enterprises known as potasheries paid 6 to 8 cents for a bushel of ashes (Imlay 1797, 129; Seaver 1918, 28). Given an average yield of 60 to 150 bushels of ashes per acre of forest (Imlay 1797, 129; Marshall 1845, 20; Lincklaen 1897, 71), a farmer could clear $4 to $12 for each acre of woods he cut. The more enterprising settlers rented potash kettles to produce commercial potash, worth $80 to $200 per ton (Kreps 1930; Brady 1964). As it generally took about ten acres to provide ashes for a ton of potash

(Lincklaen 1897, 71; Hedrick 1933, 110; Fletcher 1950, 65), the income generated per acre was much higher when the farmer produced his own potash. Normally potash was a byproduct of forest clearance. On only a few occasions was the price high enough to justify cutting trees solely for their potash content (Kreps 1930; Roberts 1983).

Since forest clearance generated large amounts of ashes and it was difficult to manhandle a heavy barrel of potash, potash production was largely limited to frontier regions with a water route to market. As a leading American economist, Tench Coxe (1814), noted 'it is considered that potashes and pearlashes nearly compensate the settler for the expense of clearing the portion of a new farm assigned for cultivation in all situations convenient for boat navigation.' Northern Vermont with its access to Montreal via Lake Champlain and the Richelieu and Saint Lawrence Rivers was the major center of potash production in the United States during the first quarter of the nineteenth century (Blowe 1820, 237; White 1979, 47–52). With the opening of the Erie Canal in 1825 the center of production shifted to New York and later to the southern shores of Lake Ontario and Lake Erie (note fig. 3 showing potash and pearlash production by county in 1840 in Williams (1980)). Potash was one of the major goods shipped east during the first 20 years of the Erie Canal (Bidwell and Falconer [1925] 1941, 182). Production dropped precipitously in the 1850s, however, with the import of cheap synthetic alkalis from England (Roberts 1983) and the development of alternative sources of potassium carbonate, i.e., sugar beets (Kreps 1930).

It is difficult to determine the actual amount or the percentage of wood converted to potash. One can produce a crude estimate of the importance of the industry by analyzing New York's state census returns for 1835 and 1845 (New York Secretary of State 1836, 1846). The state censuses provide the acreage of improved, i.e., cleared land, and the value of the produce of the state's asheries in dollars on a county basis for 1835 and 1845. Assuming a value of approximately $150 per ton of potash, an upper estimate for the period (Brady 1964), one can determine the number of tons of potash produced in 1835 and 1845. Taking the average of the two years and multiplying by ten yields an estimate of the potash produced for the ten year period. Multiplying by ten (the average number of acres required to produce a ton of ash) provides an estimate of the number of acres of woodland impacted during the interval. The data from two representative counties in upstate New York, Wayne County and Allegany County, suggests that 20 to 34% of the area cleared from 1835 to 1845 was utilized for the production of potash. At the height of the potash craze, potash production was a major ingredient of the forest–farm economy and the process of forest clearance (White 1979, 51).

Maple sugar was another potential cash crop of the early settler (Imlay [1797] 1849). Although other species of maples were occasionally employed in the manufacture of sugar, sugar maple (*Acer saccharum*) was the preferred species due to the high sugar content of its sap (Snow 1964). The real boom era for maple sugar was the post-Revolutionary War period. From 1790 to 1820 maple sugar represented a cheap alternative to expensive cane sugar imported from the West Indies. A number of influential Americans, including Tench Coxe (1814), the physician Benjamin Rush (1793), and Judge William Cooper (1792), publicized the value and the potential of the native sugar industry. Locally produced sugar was touted because it eliminated America's dependence on the slave colonies of the West Indies. It would improve America's balance of trade. It represented a source of income for the settler and it could be used to attract settlers (Butterfield 1958). Rush (1793) even provided a detailed, if somewhat overoptimistic, calculation of the profits to be derived from the sugar industry. Sugar maple, he noted, often occurred at a density of 30 to 50 trees per acre. An open-grown tree yielded 7 pounds of sugar in a season. A family attending to a 'sugar orchard' of 200 trees could produce 1400 pounds of sugar. Subtracting 200 pounds of sugar for the family's personal use, left a total of 1200 pounds for sale at 6.7 cents a pound or a profit of $80. Rush failed to mention the fact that trees growing in the woods produce closer to 3 pounds per season (La Rochefoucauld-Liancourt 1799, 125). Even the more ambitious settlers tapped only 100 to 150 trees. The total yield was closer to 300 to 400 pounds of sugar a season as opposed to Rush's 1200 pounds (Williams 1809, 2:363; Coxe 1814; Fletcher 1950, 333; Crèvecoeur 1964, 136). The sugar craze encouraged a number of entrepreneurs from Holland to purchase large tracts of sugar maple lands in upstate New York with the goal of producing a million and a half pounds of sugar per year. Unfortunately, the enterprise collapsed when their wooden, gravity feed collecting trough system failed to function properly (Evans 1924, 14–19, 63–66).

Sugar maple was a source, albeit not a large source, of income that could be bartered for store goods in many a new settlement (Coxe 1794, 452–453). Williams (1809, 2:363) estimated that two-thirds of all the families in Vermont were involved in the manufacture of maple sugar at the turn of the century. On the Ohio River, sugar tree lands were commonly fenced off. Trees were rented at 6 cents to neighbors and townsmen while landlords prohibited tenants from cutting sugar trees (Heckewelder 1958, 337).

The introduction of cane sugar from Louisiana in 1810 to 1820 forced the maple sugar industry into a decline (Flint [1828] 1970, 1:65–66; Fletcher 1950, 332). Sugar maples were increasingly cleared away for other more valuable 'improvements' (Pease and Niles 1819, 254; Macauley 1829, 1:536; Sauer 1920, 121). Although the on-farm consumption of maple sugar remained strong (Butterfield 1958) and the total amount of maple sugar produced in the United States peaked in 1860 (Brown 1919, 380), the per capita production of maple sugar dropped steadily after 1840 (Bidwell and Falconer [1925] 1941, 505).

It is difficult to determine the long-term impact of the maple sugar industry on the early frontier. During the early phases of the industry, the crude practice of extracting syrup by notching a tree with an axe killed many a sugar maple (Belknap 1813, 3:85; Crèvecoeur 1925, 98). The English visitor, Thomas Ashe (1808, 225), who rarely had a kind word for Americans, felt that sugar camps in the Midwest were hastening the sugar maple 'to dissolution and decline.' In contrast, the more responsible sugaring techniques of the prudent farmer preserved the sugar maple. Northern hardwood stands dominated by old sugar maples are a characteristic feature of many a sugarbush in northern New England today (C. Cogbill, pers. comm. 1989).

As the above review suggests, wood was used in a host of activities in the early forest–farm economy. Potash, maple sugar, and other wood-related cash crops often maintained the settler until his fields came into production. The monetary returns in most cases, however, were limited. In upstate New York the $5 gained per acre from the sale of ashes paled before the $20 gained per acre on the same farm from the sale of wheat (Warden 1819, 3:251–252). Wood products alone rarely formed the basis of a profitable farm operation. In terms of the ultimate fate of the wood, the liquidation of the forests entailed more waste than use. Most nineteenth century observers argued that the vast majority of the wood rotted or went up in smoke outside the home (Priest 1802, 36; Holditch 1818, 64; Johnson 1819, 56–57; Woods [1822] 1968, 42; Pickering 1832, 159; Niemcewicz 1965, 242; Hutslar 1971; Tessendorf 1972). Former chief of the Forest Service W. B. Greeley (1925) estimated that the timber cut on three-quarters of all the land cleared for agricultural purposes was wasted. The major factor responsible for the waste was the lack of a market and an effective transportation network. As America's first forester, Bernhard Fernow (1899, 45), noted in 1899, ' Timber being a great obstacle to the settlement of the land, and the market for it until recently being confined and limited, a large amount had to be wasted and disposed of in the log pile, where the flames made quick work of the scrub as well as of the finest walnut trees.' To the farmer it was the creation of improved land out of waste land.

Although the wood may have been of little value and clearing itself was a very laborious and time-consuming activity, forest clearance could generate wealth in another form. As the Vermont historian, Samuel Williams (1809,

2:353) argued it represented an opportunity to accumulate capital. Williams noted:

When he [the early settler] comes to apply his labor to his own land, the produce of it becomes extremely profitable. The first crop of wheat will fully pay him for all the expense he has been at, in clearing up, sowing, and fencing his land, eight or ten times the original cost ... In this way, the profits attending labor on a new settlement, are the greatest that ever can take place in agriculture; the laborer constantly receiving double wages. He receives high wages in the produce of his corn or wheat; and he receives much higher wages of another kind, in the annual addition of a new tract of cultivated land to his farm.

To a certain extent, the rise in the value of the land was part of the normal process of the filling in of the frontier. Local demand or relatives wishing to settle in the area bid up the price of the unclaimed land (Talleyrand 1942, 154). Probably most of the increase in the value of the land was due to forest clearance. There was always a demand for improved land and operating farms among those who were less inclined to bear the rigors of the first few years of settlement. In the late eighteenth century, uncultivated land could rise two to three times in value during the course of ten years while the value of improved, i.e., cleared, and often cultivated, land increased 5 to 20 times (Talleyrand 1942, 154). Many farmers, in fact, made a profession out of clearing new land, selling the improvements at a good price, and then purchasing new unimproved land to the west (Danhof 1969, 101). To many a twentieth century conservationist, forest clearance fell under the heading of waste and despoilation. To economists like Stuart Bruchey (1965, 23), deforestation created the capital which fueled America's economic growth.

Rate and extent of forest clearance

The clearing of the woodlands has generally been portrayed as an operation which took centuries in Europe (Darby 1956). In North America forest clearance was a much more rapid process, often the work of a generation or two. There were, however, a number of variations on the general theme of clearing and the rapid, monotonic decline of the forests. Occasionally forest clearance extended over one or two centuries or it never reached completion. It occurred on a variety of scales – from the farmer clearing his back forty to the larger continent-wide pattern of deforestation. What factors influenced the overall rate and extent of clearance through time? Did the pattern of forest clearance differ from one geographical region to another? A more detailed analysis of a few selected sites provides a chronological picture of the pattern of clearance (see Fig. 7.1).

(a)

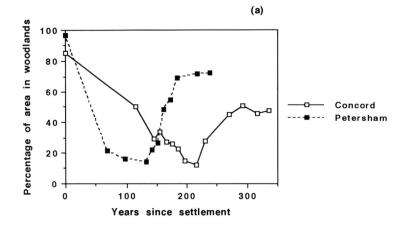

(b)

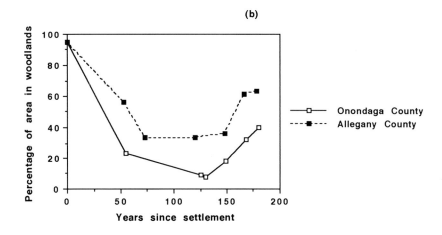

(c)

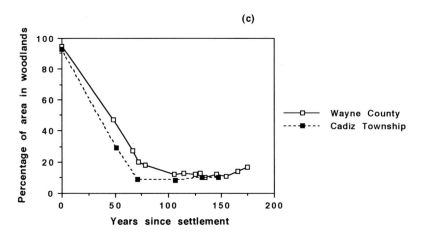

The earliest phases of forest clearance on the East Coast were extremely slow. In Concord, Massachusetts, for instance, deforestation proceeded at a rate of 0.4% or less of the land each year. It required at least 100 years to clear 50% of the land. Studies of several other Massachusetts towns (Greven 1970, 67; Jedry 1979, 62) have also indicated that much of the land remained unbroken forest for the first few generations. Over 61% of Andover, Massachusetts, fell into the category of unimproved, i.e., largely wooded land, after the first 118 years of its existence (Greven 1970, 176–177). For coastal Chebacco, Massachusetts, the figure was approximately 60% unimproved land after 100 years (Jedrey 1979, 62). Even as late as 1767, many of the counties of Rhode Island were still comparatively well wooded (Fig. 7.2). A similar rate of clearance of about 0.5% a year appears to have held for southeastern Pennsylvania in the early eighteenth century (Lemon [1972] 1976, 168). Part of the low rate of deforestation can be attributed to the early New Englanders' hesitancy to distribute the land and the large size of the early land grants (Greven 1970, 49, 58–65). Grants of 150 acres per individual were not unusual for the early inhabitants of eastern Massachusetts (Lockridge 1968; Greven 1970, 59). Given the fact that the average farmer was limited in the amount of land he could effectively cultivate, much of the land went unused until it was apportioned among the farmer's sons and grandsons (Greven 1970, 66–67). The typical farmer had 6 to 8 acres in tillage (Jedry 1979, 63). Six to eight acres of corn could be tended by one individual and produced enough food to feed a family of five to seven individuals for a year (Perkins 1980, 46). The lack of a market probably discouraged production in excess of the family's needs. The upsurge (of 0.8% to 1.3% per year) in the rate of clearance in Concord, and Petersham, Massachusetts, after 1750 (115 years and 17 years following settlement respectively in Fig. 7.1) suggests a new set of forces at work. Both of the upsurges in land clearance occurred at a period of time when the human population had roughly stabilized, but the number of cattle and the area in pasture expanded significantly (Raup and Carlson 1941, 25; Kimenaker 1983;

Fig. 7.1 Changing woodland coverage of selected townships and counties. Regions with approximate date of settlement and sources of information are as follows: (a) Concord, Mass., 1635 (Whitney and Davis 1986; Parmenter, 1929), Petersham, Mass., 1733 (Cook 1917; Raup and Carlson 1941; MacConnell and Niedzwiedz 1974; 1801 Valuation lists of towns, Mass. State Archives; 1831 Valuation of Mass., Massachusetts State Library); (b) Onondaga County, New York, 1800 (Hough 1857; Nyland, Zipperer and Hill 1986), Allegany County, New York, 1802 (Hough 1857; Hough 1878, 435; Recknagel 1923; USDA Forest Service 1954; Ferguson and Mayer 1970; Considine and Frieswyk 1982); (c) Wayne County, Ohio, 1806 (Whitney and Somerlot 1985), Cadiz Township, Green County, Wisconsin, 1832 (Guntenspergen 1983).

Gordon 1986). The increased interest in cattle during the late colonial period was associated with the expanding West Indian market for beef (Egnal 1975). By the late eighteenth century the hill towns of central Massachusetts, like Petersham, were supplying beef to the meat-packing industry of the Connecticut River Valley (Pruitt 1984). On poorer, stone-filled sites forests were often converted directly into pastures. The large number of rocks scattered about the fields and the second-growth woods of Petersham suggest that most of Petersham was never tilled (Raup and Carlson 1941, 26–27).

The interval between subsistence farming and a more market oriented economy was briefer in the Midwest (Danhof 1969, 150). The early establishment of a transportation network, including canals and railroads, linked the Midwest with the rapidly expanding urban markets of the East (Gates 1960, 165). Technological innovations in the form of reapers, improved plows, and cultivators in the mid-1800s also expanded the area a farmer could cultivate and harvest (Gates 1960, 287, 293). Although the maximum extent of clearance was similar in the East and the Midwest (Fig. 7.1), deforestation proceeded at a more rapid rate in the Midwest (1.0 to 1.3% per year). Within 70 to 80 years most of the land in the Midwest had already been 'cleaned up,' reflecting a rapid integration into the larger commercial market.

A regional perspective

State maps showing the forested areas on a county by county basis provide a broad regional overview of the pattern of forest clearance (Fig. 7.2). Three areas, Rhode Island (a region representative of the earliest phase of settlement on the East Coast), Ohio (a representative example of the agricultural heartland), and Michigan (an area typical of the more timber oriented Upper Great Lakes region), were selected for a more detailed analysis of the clearance process. The large amount of woodland acreage (>50%) remaining in Rhode Island in the 1760s, over 130 years after the first settlement, is evidence of the slow rate of clearance during the precommercial period. New England's industrious farmers responded to the more market oriented economy of the nineteenth century by clearing more of their land. By 1875 the forest had been reduced to 32% of the surface area of the state.

Ohio presents a very different picture. Little more than half a century was required for the clearance of approximately 50% of Ohio's woodlands. Most of the initial clearance was concentrated in a broad band which ran diagonally across the state from the northeast to the southwest. The rugged terrain of the Appalachian Plateau, inhibited clearance to the southeast, while the poorly drained Lake Erie plain (a region long known as the Black Swamp) delayed the development of the northwest corner of the state (Kaatz 1955). By the

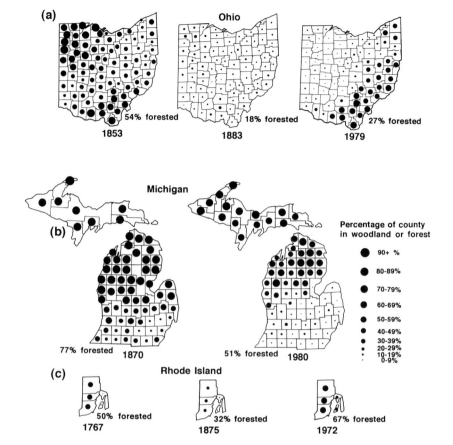

Fig. 7.2 Changing woodland coverage of (a) Ohio, (b) Michigan, and (c) Rhode Island by county. Sources of information are as follows: Ohio (Leue 1886; Dennis and Birch 1982), Michigan (method of Harper (1918a) applied to data in US Census Office (1872a, 1872b); Spencer 1983), Rhode Island (Defebaugh 1907, 2: 293; Peters and Bowers 1977).

twentieth century, the formerly forested Lake Plain section was the richest agricultural region in Ohio and the least wooded.

Compared to Ohio, settlement and deforestation in Michigan proceeded slowly. The climate of the Upper Peninsula of Michigan, the 'fag end of the world' as Lahonton expressed it (Fritzell 1983), was marginal at best for most agricultural pursuits. The Lower Peninsula likewise suffered from a bad press. The federal government's Tiffin Report of 1815 described much of southern Michigan as low wet marshes and swamps, interspersed with poor, barren, sandy land and scrubby oaks (Tiffin 1834). Settlement and forest clearance progressed the most rapidly on the oak openings of Michigan's southern tier of counties due to the ease with which the openings could be brought into production (Hubbard 1847b). Large-scale agricultural clearance never really reached the sterile High Plains section of northern lower Michigan. In Michigan, as in Ohio, the fertile, yet poorly drained Lake–Border Plains region was the last area to experience extensive woodland clearance.

Effects of forest clearance

The conversion of much of the eastern half of the continent to a productive agricultural landscape resulted in the breakup and the fragmentation of North America's woodlands. Under the federal land survey system, characteristic of much of the Midwest, land was sold in rectangular 40 to 640 acre (quarter quarter-section to full section) tracts (Rohrbough 1968; Johnson 1976). The straight boundaries and the dispersed nature of many woodlands in the Midwest today reflect the operation of the early land survey system. As forest clearance proceeded, the remaining forests were increasingly confined to agriculturally marginal areas, e.g., steep slopes, stony lands, and poorly drained soils (Curtis 1956; Guest and Stevens 1967; Auclair 1976; Marks and Smith 1989). While a number of researchers have documented the formation of isolated forest habitat islands set amidst a sea of arable land (Guest and Stevens 1967; Auclair 1976; Rodgers and Anderson 1979; Dorney and Stearns 1980; Hill 1985; Whitney and Somerlot 1985), few have delineated the patterns as thoroughly or speculated on the results as provocatively as the Wisconsin plant ecologist, John T. Curtis (1956). Utilizing data from the early land survey records, the Wisconsin Land Economic Survey, and aerial photographs, Curtis mapped the changing configuration of the forests of Cadiz Township, Green County, Wisconsin, from 1831 to 1950 (Fig. 7.3). The decreasing size and the increasing edge to area ratio of the forest habitat islands is evident in Table 7.4.

The fragmentation of the forest had a number of implications for the species composition of the remaining woodlots. Light surface fires were a characteristic feature of the oak-dominated forest regions of New England, southern New York, New Jersey, southern Pennsylvania, southern Michigan, and southern Wisconsin during the presettlement period (Komarek 1983; Lorimer 1985b; Patterson and Sassaman 1988). Saplings of white oak are relatively resistant to light surface fires and a number of investigators (Rogers 1959; Anderson and Adams 1978; Merritt 1979; Lorimer 1985b) believe that ground fires at periodic intervals may have been responsible for white oak's dominance throughout the area. The creation of a mixed farm–forest landscape initiated a new fire regime. The interpolation of farmland between the remnant forest stands and

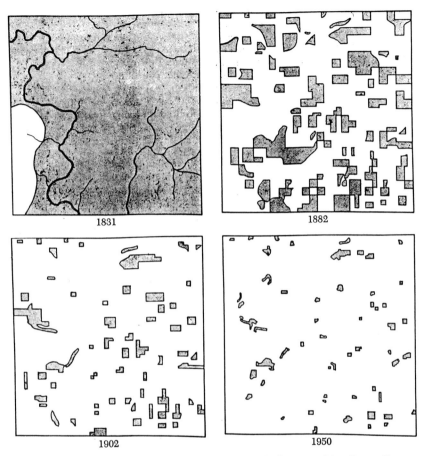

Fig. 7.3 The loss of woodlands (shaded areas) in Cadiz Township, Green County, Wisconsin, from the presettlement period (1831) to 1950. Township is six miles on a side. Reprinted from Curtis (1956) by permission of the University of Chicago Press. © 1956. The University of Chicago.

the conscious suppression of fire by farmers reduced the incidence and the spread of fire (Curtis 1956). In many woodlots a decrease in the ground fires permitted the buildup of a seedling and sapling layer composed of the more fire sensitive species, e.g., the maples and the cherries (Dodge and Harman 1985). The seedling establishment of oak was inhibited under the dense shrub and sapling layers of sugar maple (Carvell and Tryon 1961). Oak still dominates the larger size classes of many of the relatively undisturbed old-growth woodlots of the Midwest and the Northeast. Its poor representation in the smaller size classes of the same woodlots (Dix 1957; McClain and Ebinger

Table 7.4. *Details of forest fragmentation from presettlement period (1831)
to the present in Cadiz Township, Green County, Wisconsin*

	1831	1882	1902	1935	1950	1978
Total forest area in hectares	8724	2583	841	419	318	473
Percentage of initial forest area		30	10	5	4	5
Number of forest islands	1	70	61	57	55	84
Average island size in hectares	8724	36.9	13.8	7.4	5.8	5.6
Total perimeter of islands (km)	–	156.9	97.0	74.8	63.1	94
Edge/area ratio (m/ha of forest)	–	61	115	179	198	199

Sources: Curtis (1956); Burgess and Sharpe (1981); Dunn *et al.* (1991).

1968; Lafer and Wistendahl 1970; Schmelz, Barton, and Lindsey 1975), however, probably reflects the implementation of a new fire-free regime (Monk 1961; Anderson and Adams 1978; Merritt 1979; Whitney and Somerlot 1985; Pallardy, Nigh, and Garrett 1988). Sharpe *et al.*'s (1987) study of the changing composition of the woods of Cadiz Township, Green County, Wisconsin, over the last 150 years exemplifies many of these changes (see Table 7.5).

Curtis (1956) further hypothesized that the fragmentation of the forest should favor species characteristic of edge habitats. Subsequent research (Wales 1972; Levenson 1981; Ranney, Bruner, and Levenson 1981; Whitney and Runkle 1981; McCune, Cloonan, and Armentano 1988) has substantiated Curtis' hypothesis. The edges of woods with their high light intensity and their xeric environment characteristically support a flora of the more light demanding yet drought tolerant tree species (Jacquart, Armentano, and Spingarn 1992), e.g., hawthorn, oaks, hickories, aspen, ash, basswood, sweet cherry, and sassafras. The interiors of the same woods are often dominated by shade tolerant species, e.g., beech and sugar maple. Whitney and Runkle (1981) found that the species differences in the edge and the interior plots of an old-growth beech–sugar maple woodlot in Ohio were greater than the species differences between plots in the old-growth woodlot and an adjacent second-growth stand. Several investigators have noted that forests in Wisconsin must be at least 2 to 8 ha in size to contain a fair representation of interior species (Levenson 1976; Mudrak 1978; Guntenspergen 1983).

Curtis (1956) believed that chance events could lead to the loss of a species in a woodlot and that the isolation of the woodlot would inhibit the reinvasion

Table 7.5. Changing composition of woods in several agriculturally oriented counties of the Midwest from the pre- to the postsettlement period. Tabulated values are percentages of stems greater than 8 cm in diameter or in the case of Cadiz Township, importance values based on both density and basal area. Dates are dates of surveys; dash indicates that species was not noted or was present in small amounts in survey. Heavy cutting and pasturing resulted in an increase of black cherry, elm, shagbark hickory and hop hornbeam in Ohio's woods. Grazing and the cessation of fires are probably responsible for the white oak, cherry and hickory invasion of Beloit's bur oak openings and the increase in sugar maple, basswood and ash in Cadiz Township.

	Wayne County, Ohio		Auglaize County, Ohio		Beloit Township Rock County, Wisconsin		Cadiz Township Green County, Wisconsin (E of Pecatonica River)	
	1806	1940	1798–1832	1940	1834	1956	1833	1984
Red maple	6.7	6.5	<1.0	<2.0	–	–	–	–
Sugar maple	4.2	6.0	8.9	9.5	–	–	3.4	28.2
Chestnut	2.1	0.1	–	–	–	–	–	–
Hickory	11.1	8.9	7.2[a]	22.8[a]	–	30[a]	–	–
Hackberry	–	–	–	–	–	–	0.4	2.4
Dogwood	3.7	3.6	–	–	–	–	–	–
Beech	8.7	10.6	38.6	3.8	–	–	–	–
White ash	4.4	7.4	9.6	7.7	–	–	2.2	10.4
Black ash	–	–	4.2	2.6	–	–	–	–
Black walnut	0.4	<0.5	1.6	2.1	–	–	–	–
Blackgum	1.8	<2.0	–	–	–	–	–	–
Hop hornbeam	2.6	4.7	<1.0	2.5	–	–	–	–
Black cherry	1.3	7.6	–	–	–	12	1.0	3.6
White oak	36.1	10.5	7.4	5.2	12	34	34.0	4.6
Bur oak	–	–	1.0	<2.0	68	<1	10.6	1.6

Table 7.5(cont.)

	Wayne County, Ohio		Auglaize County, Ohio		Beloit Township Rock County, Wisconsin		Cadiz Township Green County, Wisconsin (E of Pecatonica River)	
	1806	1940	1798–1832	1940	1834	1956	1833	1984
Red oak	1.3	3.1	3.9	4.5	–	–	16.7	5.4
Black oak	5.9	3.4	1.3	<2.0	20	24	4.2	<0.1
Basswood	–	–	2.5	4.0	–	–	6.9	11.4
Elm	4.2	12.9	6.7	20.7[b]	–	–	13.2	14.6

[a] Predominantly shagbark hickory.
[b] Predominantly American elm.
Sources: Wayne County (Whitney and Somerlot 1985); Auglaize County (Gysel 1944); Beloit Township (Ward 1956a); Cadiz Township (Sharpe et al. 1987).

of the species from other forest habitat islands. Recent work by Middleton and Merriam (1983) suggests that Curtis may have underestimated the persistence or the mobility of many plant species. Their study of farm woodlots in Ontario failed to document any consistent response of the plant taxa to the fragmentation of the forest. They concluded that most woodland species have evolved efficient mechanisms for medium-distance dispersal. There is also evidence, however, that some species may be limited by their powers of dispersal. In southern Wisconsin, for instance, forest fragmentation and the lack of a seed source has prevented the normal progression of forests of red oak to forests of the more shade tolerant sugar maple and basswood (Auclair and Cottam 1971). A number of investigators (Nyland, Zipperer, and Hill 1986; Marks and Smith 1989) have demonstrated striking differences in the tree species composition of residual forests, i.e., primary woodlands, and forests that have developed on former agricultural sites, i.e., secondary woodlands, in upstate New York. The primary woodlands contained a much higher abundance of basswood, hemlock, and nut-bearing species like beech, oak, and hickory, suggesting that these species were relatively slow to invade secondary or old-field sites. The same differences also extend to the herb and the shrub strata of primary and secondary woodlands in eastern North America (Marks and Smith 1989). Whitney and Foster (1988), for instance, found that a number of species, notably hobblebush (*Viburnum lantanoides*) and striped maple (*Acer pensylvanicum*), had a much higher frequency of occurrence in old-growth forests in central New England as opposed to second-growth forests established on old-field sites. Cope (1936) likewise noted the preference of hobblebush and several herbaceous species for old-growth hemlock–hardwood sites in northern Pennsylvania. Canada yew (*Taxus canadensis*), Indian cucumber root (*Medeola virginiana*), leatherwood (*Dirca palustris*), and a number of orchids appear to be preferentially associated with old-growth forests in the Lake States (Tyrrell and Crow 1989). Some of the differences in the last two studies, however, may be due to the heavy cutting history of second-growth sites. Cutting has been shown to eliminate some of the more sensitive old-growth species like Canada yew and hobblebush (Jensen 1943). The North American old-growth studies are reminiscent of Peterken's (1974) classic work on the 'indicator species' of ancient woodlands in England. Peterken (1981b) and Peterken and Game (1981) attributed *Mercurialis perennis* and *Anemone nemorosa*'s association with relict woodlands to their limited powers of long-distance dispersal and their slow rate of vegetative spread. Many ant-dispersed (myrmecochorous) species fall into the category of slow colonists and are poorly represented in secondary woods in continental Europe (Dzwonko and Loster 1992). Ants are likewise responsible for the dispersal of many of North America's early spring wildflowers, e.g., wild ginger (*Asarum canadense*), spring beauty (*Claytonia virginica*), Dutchman's breeches and squirrel corn (*Dicentra* spp.), trout lily (*Erythronium* spp.), bloodroot (*Sanguinaria canadensis*), trillium (*Trillium* spp.) and bellwort (*Uvularia* spp.) (Thompson 1981). The impoverished vernal flora of many secondary woods in the Midwest compared to neighboring primary woods (DeMars and Runkle 1992) may be due to the low density of ants in secondary woods (Woods 1984) or to the limited dispersal capabilities of the ants.

Fencerows or hedgerows in many ways represent the extreme expression of the forest edge habitat or 'woodland edges without the woods' (Pollard, Hooper, and Moore 1974). Although they are disappearing at an alarming rate (Vance 1976; Whitney and Somerlot 1985), hedgerows still represent an important component of the more agriculturally oriented landscapes of the eastern United States. The average square mile of farmland in Ohio and Illinois in the 1930s and 1940s contained more than ten miles of fencerow habitat or >6000 m/km^2 (Sears 1947; Vance 1976), while similar figures for southern Wisconsin ranged from 1000 to 3000 m/km^2 (Sharpe *et al.* 1986). One study of a major dairy and cash grain county in Ohio, Wayne County, revealed that fencerows still constitute about 3% of the tree covered area of the county (Whitney and Somerlot 1985).

Three different types of hedgerows have been defined according to their mode of origin: planted, spontaneous, and remnant (Forman and Baudry 1984). Remnant hedgerows, i.e., rows of trees and shrubs left standing after the process of forest clearing, have never been common in the United States. Due to the abundance of wood, Americans rarely resorted to the use of planted hedgerows during the colonial period. Most found the planting and upkeep of live hedges 'too troublesome' (Schoepf [1788] 1968, 1:132). During the early nineteenth century there was some experimentation with the use of the English thorn (*Crataegus oxycantha*) and the American hawthorn (*Crataegus crusgalli*) near the larger urban areas (Shirreff [1835] 1971, 24, 43, 58). The opening of the Midwest's sparsely wooded grasslands also stimulated a massive osage orange (*Malcura pomifera*) planting craze in the 1850s to the 1870s (Powell 1914, 3–4; Steavenson, Gearhart, and Curtis 1943; Smith and Perino 1981). Wire fencing, however, soon supplanted the use of the more labor-intensive osage orange hedges (Steavenson, Gearhart, and Curtis 1943). Trees were also deliberately planted as windbreaks and shelterbelts about isolated farmsteads in the Midwest (Heilbron 1931).

The vast majority of America's hedgerows have always been of spontaneous origin. As befits their edge environment, fencerows have typically been dominated by a number of rapidly growing, shade intolerant tree species

Table 7.6. *Dominant fencerow tree species in order of abundance*

New Jersey (Forman and Baudry 1984)	Massachusetts (McChesney 1974)[a]	New York (Petrides 1942)
Black cherry	White ash	Choke cherry
Sassafras	Red oak	American elm
White ash	Sugar maple	Hawthorn
Choke cherry	Bitternut hickory	Black cherry
Pin oak	Black cherry	Shagbark hickory
Red cedar	Birch	Pin cherry
	Red maple	
SW Ohio (Dambach 1948)	NW Ohio (Allen 1941)	NE Ohio (Whitney and Somerlot 1985)
Hackberry	Hawthorn	Black cherry
American elm	Prickly-ash	White ash
Black cherry	Elm	Pin oak
Bitternut hickory	Wild plum	Hickory
Shagbark hickory	Hickory	Sweet cherry
Honeylocust	Honeylocust	American elm
	Ash	

Iowa
(Best and Hill 1983)[b]
Hackberry
Honeylocust
Cherry
Black locust
American elm

[a] Predominantly along stone walls.
[b] Not necessarily in order of abundance.

(Table 7.6). Most of the woody plant species in hedgerows, however, represent a unique subset of the more shade intolerant trees. They are predominantly bird-dispersed species (Whitney and Somerlot 1985). Fences serve as perch sites for the birds and seed deposition sites or recruitment foci for bird-dispersed species, e.g., black cherry (McDonnell and Stiles 1983). It is not surprising that the species composition of fencerows often differs signi-ficantly from that of the surrounding woodlands (Whitney and Somerlot 1985).

New England's 'fencerows,' or more appropriately stonewalls, are probably an exception to the bird-dispersed norm (Table 7.6). Sugar maples were intentionally planted for the production of maple sugar or syrup along many a roadside stonewall in New England during the nineteenth century (E. Gould, pers. comm., 1986). In the minds of many individuals, New England is still synonymous with stonewalls and sugar maples. Stonewalls in open fields were also heavily utilized by small mammals as nesting, hiding, and seed cache sites

(Sinclair, Getz, and Bock 1967; McChesney 1974). Small mammals are probably responsible for the higher incidence of heavy seeded oaks and hickories in New England's 'fencerows' today.

Grazing out the woods

In addition to the obvious methods of deforestation by clearing and burning, there were also a number of subtle, long-term processes at work that resulted in the elimination of the forest. Livestock grazing was one of the more serious threats. Wood-pasture management started with the burning practices of the native Americans. Burning thinned the forest and provided herbage and browse for white-tailed deer, the Indians' livestock (Williams 1963, 2:47). The much more intensive approach of the Europeans, however, really 'put the livestock industry on a business basis' (Altpeter 1937, 22). Livestock husbandry formed the mainstay of New England's agriculture during the colonial period (Russell 1976). John Winthrop ([1866] 1896) even listed 'the possibility of breeding of kine wch grows to a greater bulke of body in [New England] than with us' and the ease of raising 'swine wch breed in great numbers by reason of the abundance of acornes, groundnutts' as two of the major reasons for the Puritans' relocation to New England. Profit, as one early colonist expressed it, revolved about an increase of improved land and an increase in livestock (Smith [1765] 1877, 187). Few species found the New World's woods as inviting as the domesticated pig. Early livestock husbandry in New England, in fact, displayed many of the characteristics of an earlier era in English and European history – the medieval period of swine and woodlands (Carroll 1973, 62; Rackham 1980, 155). Domesticated pigs are descended from the wild pig or boar, a denizen of Europe's woodlands (Bennett 1970; Grigson 1982). Although pigs are omnivores and will eat almost anything, they throve on the abundant supply of beech-nuts, acorns, ground nuts, tubers, wild peas, and vetches in the East Coast's forests (Plantagenet [1648] 1898, 2:26; Van der Donck [1656] 1968, 41–42; Montanus [1671] 1851, 118; Pond 1976, 64). They multiplied rapidly, having two large litters a year (Bennett 1970; Jones 1983, 123), required a minimum of care, and gave a good account of themselves in their encounters with bears, wolves, and rattlesnakes (Bidwell and Falconer [1925] 1941, 31, 111).

   The free-running forest-pig industry reached its zenith in the Midwest in the first half of the nineteenth century. Cheap corn, abundant mast, and free range made Ohio, Indiana, Kentucky, and Illinois the centers of the swine industry (Bidwell and Falconer [1925] 1941, 430). F. A. Michaux ([1805] 1904, 246) noted of Kentucky in 1802:

Of all domestic animals, hogs are the most numerous; they are kept by all the inhabitants, several of them feed a hundred and fifty or two hundred. These animals never leave the woods, where they always find a sufficiency of food, especially in autumn and winter. They grow extremely wild, and generally go in herds. ... They stray sometimes in the forests, and do not make their appearance again for several months; they accustom them, notwithstanding, to return every now and then to the plantation, by throwing them Indian corn once or twice a week.

After two years of free range, the swine were collected, fattened on corn and packed off to hog marketing centers like Cincinnati (Hall 1837, 145; Bidwell and Falconer [1925] 1941, 436; Jones 1983, 122). Until the passage of restrictive range laws in the 1830s and 1840s, razorbacks were about as common as 'grains of sand on the sea-shore' in the forests of the Midwest (Dickens [1842] 189?, 197).

The impact of droves of foraging hogs on the forest can only be surmised. Swine were very adaptable creatures. Normally they foraged upon the thin-shelled, more palatable mast species, i.e., beech-nuts and white oak acorns, and on herbs with fleshy nonpoisonous corms, tubers, and roots, e.g., *Apios tuberosa* and *Claytonia virginica* (Gleason 1923; Bratton 1974). Poisonous plants like mayapple (*Podophyllum peltatum*) or oaks with bitter acorns, i.e. black oak, were normally avoided (Deane 1797, 228; Sargent 1884, 493; Bratton 1974). Rooting about the forest floor coincidentally destroyed many herbaceous species like *Allium tricoccum*, the wild leak (Gleason 1923). At the same time, it also altered seedbed conditions, favoring the establishment of tuliptree and other species requiring an exposed mineral seedbed (Merz 1981, 16). A number of investigators (Sargent 1884, 493; Elliott 1953; Smith 1976) think that the depredations of hogs may have resulted in a decline in the abundance of beech and white oak throughout the Northeast and the Midwest. Farmers occasionally attributed the inability of many an oak wood to regenerate to the destruction of acorns and young trees by hogs (Leue 1886, 102). During the more extreme winters when the ground was covered with a thick coating of ice or snow, swine often resorted to peeling the nutritious mucilagenous bark of slippery elm. It is not surprising that the razorback hogs were also known as 'elm-peelers' in Indiana (Kiefer 1969, 94–95).

Sheep were among the first grazing animals imported to the New World (Wentworth 1948, 38). They were difficult to establish, however, because they suffered from exposure during the colder winters and they were subject to attack by wolves (Bidwell and Falconer [1925] 1941, 28). As a result, large-scale, commercial wool-growing activities were confined to the more protected peninsulas and offshore islands like Martha's Vineyard and Nantucket (Bidwell and Falconer [1925] 1941, 110). The island of Nantucket developed a thriving sheep industry soon after it was settled in 1659 (Wentworth 1948, 42–43). Unlike the mainland, most of the land in Nantucket was held in common for the purpose of grazing sheep. By 1773, fifteen thousand sheep had reduced Nantucket to one vast sheep pasture (Russell 1976, 156). Long-standing tradition aside (Macy [1880] 1972, 23–26), it is unlikely that Nantucket was well-wooded in the period immediately preceding settlement. Strong winds, damage from salt spray, and a dense population of native Americans probably limited the woody growth on the island for the most part to thickets of scrub oak, pitch pine, and red cedar (Jones 1935; Rice 1946). Groves of beech, tupelo, maple, and hickory may have been present on the more protected sites (Dunwiddie 1990). Forest clearance and the addition of thousands of hungry sheep to the island's ecosystem did little for the growth of woody plants. As the Secretary of the Massachusetts State Board of Agriculture, Henry Colman (1841, 392) stated: 'On the island of Nantucket, where no wood is grown, and where the impression prevails generally, that none can be grown, the sheep which run at large over the island, mutton-heads as they are, if they could speak, would at once solve the mystery. On the island of Tuckernut near by, and equally exposed, I saw a flourishing growth of young oaks of seven years old, which as well as I could learn ... the Nantucket sheep had not seen, unless it were across the water.' Sheep-grazing was prohibited late in the nineteenth century. Many botanists and historians commented upon the dramatic change in the vegetation occasioned by the cessation of grazing (Godfrey 1882, 36–37; Redfield 1886). Photographs taken at the turn of the century and today document the invasion of Nantucket's open sandplain grasslands and heathlands by a variety of shrubs (bayberry, arrowood, etc.) and trees (scrub oak, black cherry, and red cedar) (Dunwiddie 1989, 1990, 1992).

Cattle constituted another major threat to the integrity of the forest. Trees were deliberately cut for fodder during the early years of many settlements when grass and hay were scarce (Deane 1797, 34; Johnson 1819, 75). Cattle, for instance, were kept throughout the winter on twigs cut from the more palatable species, i.e., sugar maple, basswood, and tuliptree (Munro [1804] 1849, 1182; Maude 1826, 53; Reynolds 1938, 77). Crèvecoeur (1964, 182), in fact, maintained that cattle came running from all directions as soon as a sugar maple was cut in the winter. Cattle were also commonly turned loose in the woods during the summer to forage upon wild grasses, legumes, pea vines, and shrubs (Latrobe [1836] 1970, 1:138; Peck 1837, 7; Evans 1852, 686; Acrelius 1876, 153–154; Tocqueville [1960] 1971, 367). Grazing cattle in the woods had its inconveniences and hazards. Not all of the plants were equally palatable or even safe for the cattle to graze. Livestock generally avoided the mints, the arum family, the mustard family, mayapple, milkweeds, bracken fern, and most sedges (Diller 1937). Alkaloids in the foliage and roots of Dutchman's breeches (*Dicentra cucullaria*) are known to have poisoned cattle (Korling and Petty 1977, 20). Cattle grazing in the woods of the Midwest were often attracted to white snakeroot (*Eupatorium rugosum*), a species which remains green during late summer droughts. Unfortunately, the leaves of white snakeroot also contain tremetol, a fat-soluble substance which attacks the nervous system. Cattle eating the tender leaves either developed a malady known as trembles or passed the lethal poison on in their milk to their owner's families. Trembles or milk-sickness plagued many early settlements in the Midwest (Daniels 1988).

Like their Indian predecessors, Europeans soon found that light surface fires increased the amount of herbage. A number of towns in southern New England formed special committees to supervise the annual burning of the outlying woods (Field [1819] 1892, 13; Temple [1889] 1905, 20; Sheldon 1895, 1:378; Judd 1905, 98; Goodrich 1954, 6). Burning commonly increased the supply of forage. Light surface fires destroyed the smothering leaf litter and encouraged the growth of the grasses (Dahllöf 1966). It represented an effective means of improving pasture conditions in the woods and was widely employed in the Mid-Atlantic states as well as southern New England (Schoepf [1788] 1968, 1:160; Sargent 1884, 493; Crèvecoeur 1964, 342; Niemcewicz 1965, 217–218). The Pennsylvania conservationist, J. T. Rothrock (1894a) decried the use of fire in Pennsylvania's more rugged, forested terrain as late as 1894. Although light surface fires left the larger trees intact, they eliminated the saplings of the less resistant species, white pine and beech for instance (Rothrock 1894a). Over an extended period of time, they created a relatively open landscape (Dwight [1822] 1969, 4:40).

The use of woods as pasture was generally a transistory affair in North America. Unlike England, little attention was given to pollarding the trees and the long-term maintenance of the woods. Day and Den Uyl (1932), Diller (1937), Den Uyl, Diller, and Day (1938), and Den Uyl (1961) have very graphically described the various stages through which a grazed woodland passes on its way to an open pasture. A density of one cow for every two acres is sufficient to eliminate most of the trees less than 4 to 6 inches in diameter and to create an obvious browse line in the first five to ten years of grazing. As George Perkins Marsh noted ([1864] 1965, 274), 'a few seasons suffice for the total extirpation of the "underbrush", including the young trees on which alone the reproduction of the forest depends.' Within 20 to 40 years a complete cover of sod is established. Soil compaction, poor aeration, a decrease in the infiltration of water into the soil, and competition with grasses for water seriously stress the remaining trees. Continued grazing eventually culminates in open park-like conditions with a few widely spaced stagheaded trees.

The above scenario outlined by Den Uyl and Marsh, of course, only occurred where a large number of cattle were pastured on a limited area of woodland for an extended period of time. With the exception of a few areas near cities where great quantities of cattle were common (Lemon [1972] 1976, 164), livestock were rarely numerous enough in the colonial period to seriously damage the woods (Muntz 1959, 64). By the early nineteenth century, however, concern was increasingly expressed about the impact of cattle running at large on New England's commons (Lincoln 1814; Welles 1831). Cattle, as Marsh noted, attacked the woods at their weakest point – their regeneration. Cattle were particularly fond of the succulent growth of sprouts on recently cutover lands or coppicewoods. In coastal Massachusetts a few cattle running in the woods were enough to keep the natural growth in check and, in some towns, to totally destroy the woods (Lincoln 1814).

Overgrazing reached its peak in many farm woodlots in the Midwest in the late nineteenth and early twentieth centuries. The passage of many fence or herd laws late in the nineteenth century compelled farmers to confine their formerly free-ranging livestock. The result was increased grazing pressure on the remaining farm woodlots (Cawley 1960, 4; Jackson 1972, 64). The farm economy of the Corn Belt emphasized the production of feedstock grain, forage, and livestock. Most of the land was arable and a large percentage of the arable was devoted to corn and forage. The limited amount of land devoted to improved pastures encouraged many farmers to utilize their woodlands as pastures (Day and Den Uyl 1932). Woodlands in the 1910 census, for instance, typically accounted for 30 to 50% of all the pastureland in the Midwest (Table 7.7). Grazing pressure on the few remaining woodlands was intense. Data from the 1910 census again indicate that 66 to 82% of the area in farm woodlands in the Midwest was grazed. Farmers realized that the yield of forage from grazed woodlands was very low (Diller 1937; Ahlgren *et al.* 1946). But they still overstocked the woodlands with up to one cow per acre, a value well in excess of the 3.5 acres required per cow on the better farm pastures (Day 1930). Woodlands provided space for exercise and the green forage required as a conditioner or a supplement to the normal diet of feed grain and prepared rations.

Under sustained grazing, deterioration of the remaining woodlots was inevitable. In the richer agricultural areas of Ohio and Indiana, their status was summed up in the phrase 'approaching extinction' (Day 1934; Diller 1935). In 1932 Day and Den Uyl placed 50% of the total acreage of grazed farmwoods in the Corn Belt section of Indiana in the heavily degraded open park category. Surveys of a number of Ohio's Corn Belt counties, likewise, indicated that fairly open park-like conditions dominated 15 to 30% of the area in farm woodlots (Conway 1940; Root 1941; Tonti 1941; Gysel 1944).

Table 7.7. *Percentage of farm woodland grazed in 1909, 1924, and 1982.*
Values in parentheses for 1909 represent woodland pasture as a percentage
of the total area in pasture

	1909[a]	1924	1982
Maine	36 (52)	39	11
New Hampshire	52 (65)	59	12
Vermont	61 (42)	67	22
Massachusetts	45 (52)	43	14
Rhode Island	32 (46)	35	15
Connecticut	50 (46)	49	16
New York	54 (32)	53	21
New Jersey	19 (23)	14	14
Pennsylvania	38 (37)	39	19
Ohio	69 (29)	66	29
Indiana	72 (43)	69	30
Illinois	81 (34)	72	40
Michigan	82 (45)	73	19
Wisconsin	77 (53)	78	36
Minnesota	74 (44)	75	47
Iowa	– (25)	89	64
Missouri	49 (41)	64	56

[a] Note that the 1909 values for percentage of farm woodland grazed are probably conservative as the grazed woodland or woodland pasture category for the 1909 tabulation was defined as grass-covered areas with scattered timber. The 1909 definition did not include woods in the early stages of conversion to pastures, i.e., without grass in the herb layer.
Sources: Data from Goldenweiser and Ball (1918) and US Bureau of the Census (1932, 1984).

Fortunately, by the time the Ohio surveys were completed in the 1940s, the wood-pasture tradition was on the way out. A variety of factors contributed to the decline. Many states passed laws compensating farmers for suspending grazing in their woods (Day and Den Uyl 1932; Whitney and Somerlot 1985). New Deal bureaucrats typically believed overproduction was the main farm problem of the 1930s. New Deal programs, e.g., the Agricultural Adjustment Act and the Soil Conservation and Domestic Allotment Act, encouraged the conversion of cropland to hay and permanent pastures (Day 1934; Diller 1937; Schlebecker 1975, 238–242). By increasing the area in improved pastures, New Deal programs reduced the pressure on farm woodlots. The decline of the wood-pasture tradition was not an overnight affair (see fig. 1 in Whitney and Somerlot 1985). It occurred gradually over a long period of time and is still a common practice in Iowa and Missouri (Table 7.7). Over most of the Northeast and the Midwest, however, grazing has been discontinued. Farm woodlots are once again regenerating successfully and are much healthier today than they have been for years.

Given the low level of grazing today, it is easy to overlook the impact of past grazing practices on the structure of the current woodlots. Many of today's woods were either (1) initiated under a heavy grazing regime, e.g., old-field stands of white pine in New England, or (2) are in the later stages of recovery following the cessation of grazing, e.g., numerous farm woodlots in the Midwest. Grazing altered the course of succession. By modifying the characteristics of the seedbed and the makeup of the seedling and the sapling populations, it altered the future composition of the woods. Grazing often accompanied the gradual abandonment of New England's pastures in the nineteenth and early twentieth centuries. Many observers (Fisher 1918; Hawley 1924; Stickel and Hawley 1924; Behre *et al.* 1929; Bromley 1935; Egler 1940) have attributed the abundant old-field stands of red cedar in southern New England, white pine in central New England, and spruce in northern New England to grazing. Heavy grazing created the open, weak sod seedbeds favored by the slow-growing white pine (Fisher 1918). It also retarded the growth of the more palatable, aggressive hardwoods, thereby favoring the slower growing conifers (Stickel and Hawley 1924; Behre *et al.*, 1929; Bromley 1935; Egler 1940).

The effect of grazing on the hardwood forests of the Midwest was a more complex affair. Again browsing eliminated the palatable species, e.g., sugar maple, leaving the less palatable hop hornbeam, blue beech (*Carpinus caroliniana*), and hawthorn (*Crataegus* spp.) (Day and Den Uyl 1932; McMaster 1941). Species which sprouted repeatedly, e.g., red elm and shagbark hickory, could also persist under a moderately heavy grazing regime (Cheney 1942, 295). The frequent occurrence of red elm and large hop hornbeam in many farm woodlots throughout the Midwest today is largely a legacy of the wood-pasture tradition of the last 80 years (Cawley 1960, 36–39).

The decline of the wood-pasture tradition and the cessation of grazing set the stage for the rise of a new group of species. Their germination and establishment was closely tied to seedbed conditions and the past history of the stand (Dambach 1944; Whitney and Somerlot 1985). In lightly grazed woodlots, abundant leaf litter provided a favorable medium for the establishment of sugar maple. Sugar maple dominates the intermediate size classes of many of these stands today. The grass sod of the heavily grazed, open, park-like woodlands, however, prevented the establishment of sugar maple and the larger seeded oaks, hickories, and beech. Few of the larger seeds could work their way down to the mineral soil. Lacking a protective cover of leaves, they were also subject to dessication (Olson and Boyce 1971; Whitney and Somerlot

1985). In contrast, black cherry, white ash, hop hornbeam, and elm seeded in freely on the grass sod and are well represented in the intermediate size classes of many farm woodlots in the Midwest today (Den Uyl 1961; Apsley, Leopold, and Parker 1985; Dodge and Harman 1985; Whitney and Somerlot 1985; note also Table 7.5).

Livestock also altered the nature of the herbaceous vegetation. Grazing, trampling, soil compaction, dessication, and the dislocation of the normal nutrient cycling regime took their toll on the native flora (Leaf 1958; Cawley 1960). Studies by Lutz (1930c), Diller (1937), Marks (1942), Dambach (1944), and Steinbrenner (1951) have detailed the sensitivity of the native species to various grazing regimes. Not all species, however, decreased. Some found the drier, more open environment of the grazed woodlot favorable to their increase. Enchanter's nightshade (*Circaea quadrisulcata*) and richweed (*Pilea pumila*), for example, were native, nitrophyllous species which thrived on the dung-enriched soils of the grazed woodlot. Other species like clover and many of the grasses were exotics whose seeds were spread in the dung of the livestock (Lutz 1930c). Woodlots that were heavily grazed eventually ended up with a trampling and grazing resistant flora dominated by grasses, sedges, rosette plants, and thorny dicots (Cawley 1960, 38). Dambach (1944) found that ten years of protection from grazing was sufficient to restore much of the herbacous flora of a grazed sugar maple woodlot with isolated patches of grass. The re-establishment of the woodland flora was a much slower affair in the case of open, park-like woods with a heavy grass sod.

8
Assault upon the forest.
Part II. The lumber industry

> To describe the progress of the lumbering industry during the last
> hundred years is to write of a class of sturdy people who have car-
> ried the first germs of civilization into the deepest wilderness of our
> vast forests, and who have furnished one of the most essential
> materials for the building up of our civilization and development in
> all parts of the country. But it also means the recording of a
> destruction and deterioration of natural resources such as perhaps
> nowhere else been witnessed in so short a span of time.
>
> Bernhard E. Fernow. 1895. 'American lumber.'

Wood and its byproducts have always been a basic ingredient of North
America's commerce. As Thoreau ([1862] 1980) once noted 'In wildness is
the preservation of the world. The cities import it at any price. Men plow and
sail for it. From the forest and wilderness come the tonics and barks which
brace mankind.' Wood was New England's first crop. Clapboards were
included in the first boat-load of goods shipped from Plymouth to the Old
World in 1622 (Forman 1970). Shipments of large masts of white pine helped
maintain the naval supremacy of the English fleet during the colonial period
(Albion [1926] 1965; Malone 1964, 47). Although Baltic fir (better known as
Pinus sylvestris or Scots pine) was utilized extensively for the smaller masts,
only New England's white pine could satisfy the Royal Navy's demand for the
larger (> 30 inch) masts of the ships of the line (Albion [1926] 1965, 4, 28–32;
Carlton 1939; Malone 1964, 55–56). From the viewpoint of shipping tonnage,
timber and timber products topped the list of New England's exports throughout the seventeenth century (Carroll 1975).

Forests also figured prominently in the economy of new settlements.
Throughout the Northeast, sawmills were often the first manufacturing plant
established in a town (Dinsdale 1963, 33). By 1700 every New England town

had at least one sawmill (Forman 1970). In upstate New York, sawmills were generally constructed within 10 to 15 years of the formation of a new settlement (Fox 1902; Defebaugh 1907, 2:307–312).

Expansion of industry after the Civil War

The commercial importance and particularly the magnitude of these early wood-related trades, however, should not be overemphasized. The sawmills were typically small-scale, family affairs oriented to local markets (Douglass 1760, 2:55; Fox 1902; Dinsdale 1963, 49). Even the much publicized mast trade barely dented New England's forests of white pine. Joseph Malone (1964, 53), for instance, has shown that at the most only 4500 masts were shipped to the Royal Navy from 1694 to 1775. Large-scale commercial exploitation of North America's forests awaited the second half of the nineteenth century (Fernow 1895). At least four factors facilitated the dramatic expansion of the lumber industry after the Civil War.

(1) The increasing demand for lumber. The rise of the lumber industry coincided with the rapid growth of urban areas in the East and the settlement of the treeless prairies in the West. The conversion of timber to dwellings represented one of the larger and the more effective housing programs in human history (Rector 1953, 43). Census figures suggest that approximately ten million dwellings were constructed in the United States between 1860 and 1900 (Wilhelm 1953, 4).

(2) Untapped sources of wood. The first step in any pattern of forest exploitation is obviously finding a forest to exploit (Lower 1938, 28). By 1860, settlement had engulfed most of the Northeast and the lower Midwest and was moving into the Upper Great Lakes region (see fig. 9 in Marschner (1959) for settlement isochrons). The Northeast, however, still possessed a number of sparsely populated areas which were marginal from an agricultural standpoint. Either the climate or the topography limited the realization of a strong, agriculturally based economy (Dinsdale 1965). Brewer's (1874) and Greeley's maps (Fig. 8.1) of the woodlands of the United States give one a crude impression of the extent and the location of these areas in the late 1800s. Forests still dominated the colder regions of northern Maine, the mountainous areas of northern New Hampshire and the Adirondacks, the rugged High Plateau region of northern Pennsylvania and the northern half of the Great Lakes region.

(3) The development of an effective transportation network. Timber was useless unless it could be transported to market on a low-cost basis. The mar-

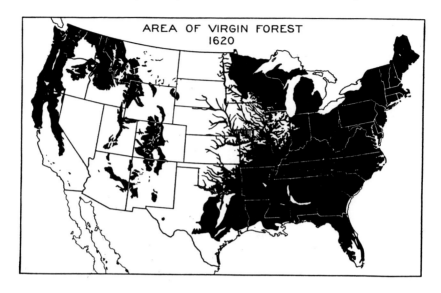

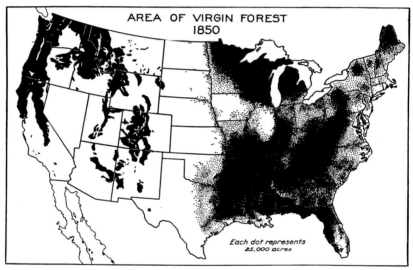

Fig. 8.1 Extent of uncut 'virgin' forest in 1620, 1850, and 1920. Areas of forests are based on estimates by states. Each dot represents 25 000 acres. Dots are not all correctly located. The Black Swamp region of northwestern Ohio, for instance, was almost a solid forest in 1850. Reprinted with permission of publisher from W. B. Greeley (1925), *Economic Geography* 1: 4–5.

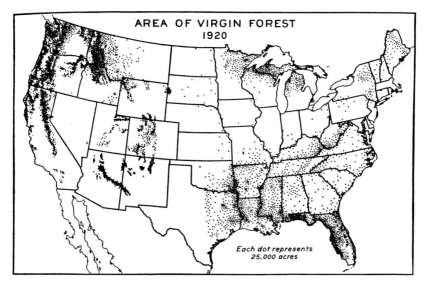

AREA OF VIRGIN FOREST
1920

Each dot represents
25,000 acres

ket value of a bulky, inexpensive commodity like timber was eaten up
quickly by transportation costs when it was carried overland. During most
of the nineteenth century, rivers and streams were the major avenues of
transport. Rafting, and later log driving, provided a low-cost mechanism of
uniting the supply and the demand (Rector 1953). Rivers like the
Penobscot, the Kennebec, the Androscoggin, and the Connecticut in New
England, and the Hudson, the Delaware, and the Susquehanna in the Mid-
Atlantic states, linked the inland forests of the East with the urban centers
on the coast. The Allegheny, the Ohio, and the Mississippi River and its
tribuitaries, i.e., the Wisconsin, the Chippewa, etc., kept the Midwest supplied with wood. Often the flow of lumber was altered by the creation of
artificial waterways. The opening of the Erie Canal in 1825, for instance,
eventually resulted in the marketing of pine from the Great Lakes region in
Albany while the completion of the Illinois–Michigan Canal in 1847
encouraged an influx of Michigan pine to the prairies (Rohe 1984; Cox *et
al.*, 1985, 104, 118). The dramatic expansion of logging railroads in the
1880s represented another landmark of the lumbering and transportation
industries in the nineteenth century (Maybee [1960] 1976, 4; Dunbar and
May 1980, 399–400).

(4) A technology capable of generating large quantities of lumber and finished
wood products. The adoption of a number of technological advances
(Table 8.1) also figured prominently in the expansion of the lumber industry. First there was the shift from water to steam as the major source of
power, a shift which liberated the sawmill from its dependence on falling

Table 8.1. *Timeline of technological advances in America's lumber and woodworking industries*

Date of general adoption	Harvest in the woods (logs cut per day)	Transport to the mill	Milling output (bd ft/day)	Woodworking
1600		log rafts (mid-17th century)	hand-powered pit saw (100–200) water-powered sash saw (1000–3000)	
1700	American felling axe (70 logs)			
1800				
1810		log driving		
1820				
1830				Woodworth planing machine
1840		major boom companies organized	water-powered muley saw (5000–8000)	
1850	double-bitted axe		steam-powered gang saw (40 000+)	gang edger
1860		Peavy for log driving artificial icing of roads	steam-powered circular saw (40 000+)	veneer lathe
1870	crosscut saw (160 logs)	logging railroads with powerful, geared locomotives high wheels for summer hauling		
1880			steam-powered band saw (50 000)	
1890			use of hot pond for winter sawing	
1900				
1910		Lombard log hauler		
1920	bucksaw for pulpwood	crawler tractors		
1930				
1940	chainsaw			
1950		skidders		
1960		feller-bunchers		
1970				

Sources: Wood (1935, 161–162); Larson (1949, 349–353); Hochschild (1962); Dinsdale (1963, 83, 90); Rosenberg (1975); Cox (1983); Fleischer (1983); Hart (1983); Rector (1983); Cox *et al.* (1985, 64–67); Williams (1989, 167–170, 201–216).

water (Dinsdale 1965). The later phases of the lumber industry in the nineteenth century were also characterized by a move to year-round operations. Big wheels and railroads provided a reliable supply of logs to the mills on a year-round basis while log ponds heated with hot water or exhaust steam kept the mills operating in the winter. The cumulative result of the above-mentioned activities was a dramatic increase in the output of inexpensive lumber. The mill which produced several thousand board feet a day in the 1840s had a capacity of 50 000 to 300 000 board feet a day in the 1890s (Hotchkiss 1898, 660).

Technological advances were expensive to adopt. They required large amounts of capital. Lumbering was part of the encompassing drive to big business at the end of the nineteenth century. By the 1880s and 1890s, large firms characterized much of the lumber industry, firms like Knapp, Stout and Company with 2000 employees and 115 000 acres of pineland in Wisconsin (Merk 1916, 74; Fries 1951, 126–127), and the Goodyear Lumber Company with 2400 employees, 75 miles of railroad track and 80 000 acres of hemlock and hardwoods in Pennsylvania (Righter 1898).

Americans have always been ambivalent about the disposal and exploitation of their forests. The quote at the beginning of the chapter exemplifies the attitude of many Americans who were proud of the economic contributions of the lumber industry yet, at the same time, expressed reservations about its effect on the forest. By 1860 lumber production was the second largest manufacturing industry in the United States, ranking second only to the cotton industry in the value added by manufacture (Cox *et al.* 1985, 111). In a more limited locale, like the state of Michigan in 1870, it accounted for one-third of the total employment and 40% of the value added by manufacture (Benson 1976, 2). The lumber industry also provided the raw materials which allowed the rapid settlement of the prairies (Larson 1949, 407). As the early educator and natural resource manager, Samuel T. Dana (Dana, Allison, and Cunningham 1960, 18) expressed it, forests were among 'the most potent factors' in the economic life of the country. 'They provided a cheap and ample supply of raw materials that was essential for the construction of homes, factories, and other buildings; and they offered welcome opportunity for the useful employment of labor and capital.'

Some individuals viewed the activities of the large lumber concerns with satisfaction and equanimity. Others saw the destruction of the forest as shortsighted, wanton, and stupid (Anonymous 1882), a saga of forest riches to forest rags (Illick 1923). The Canadian historian A. R. Lower (1938, 26) expressed this attitude incisively when he stated, 'The sack of the largest and wealthiest of medieval cities could have been but a bagatell compared with the sack of the North American forest and no medieval ravisher could have been more fierce and unscrupulous than the lumberman.'

The scenario of forest devastation presented by the early forest conservationists emphasized three major points: (1) the destruction of the forests was thorough and complete, (2) lumbering reduced the forests to wastelands or unproductive second and third-growth forests, composed of inferior 'weed' trees, and (3) the destruction of the old-growth forest precipitated a timber famine. An evaluation of the validity of each of the above statements follows.

Pattern of lumbering

In this section we evaluate the validity of the first statement: (1) the destruction of the forests was thorough and complete. In most of the major lumbering areas exploitation of the forest's resources went through a series of stages or phases (Curtis 1956). The earliest phases of the extractive process were selective with respect to the area and the size and the species of trees cut. Only the later stages approached the full-scale pattern of utilization described by the early conscrvationists.

Phase I. Highly selective white pine era

As long as the supplies of lumber exceeded the demand, the price of lumber remained low. Only larger trees of the best species with their lower cost of handling per unit value and their higher sale value, warranted the expense of transport to a distant market. Throughout most of the seventeenth, eighteenth, and nineteenth centuries, white pine (*Pinus strobus*) was the preferred species. The terms 'white pine' and 'lumber' were synonymous. It was known as the loftiest and most valuable of America's productions (Michaux 1819, 3:161), the 'most important building wood in the history of the world' (Maxwell 1915). The march of the lumbermen across the eastern half of the continent, from Maine in the late 1700s to New York and Pennsylvania in the mid-1800s to Michigan, Wisconsin, and Minnesota in the last half of the nineteenth century, was depicted as a quest for pine (Curtis 1956). White pine has a number of obvious advantages. It is soft, easily worked and sawed, and lightweight. It takes paint and is not prone to warp (Hudgins 1961, 61). Like many other conifers, e.g., hemlock, spruce, and fir, it floats and thus was a good candidate for rafts and log driving. It was recognized as a valuable commodity at a very early date. Many of the early proprietors of the towns of southern New England subdivided their limited holdings or areas of pine into small lots to insure an equitable distribution of the white pine timber (Winer 1955, 54, 110).

The earliest cutting focused on the best white pine. Best in this case meant the 'cork' or pumpkin pine - the pine associated with large, mature, old-growth trees with a small crown (Beal 1888). Mature trees were preferred because their naturally pruned trunks were relatively free of knots and they produced the soft, easily worked, early springwood dominated layers of annual growth so prized for finish grades of lumber. Mature trees probably ceased producing large quantities of supportive late-wood cells with their thick cell walls because their height growth had ceased and they had already developed a strong stem. They continued, however, to manufacture the thin walled, early-wood cells so essential to their water conducting system (Smith 1986, 73). Unfortunately, cork pines were scarce. David Ward, the great lumberman and timber cruiser for pine in Michigan, believed cork pine originally represented only 1% of all the pine in Michigan (Ward 1912, 86). An increasing demand for pine and a market for the coarser grades of lumber eventually made it profitable to harvest more of the 'bull sapling,' the 'sapling,' and the Norway pines which were neglected in the earliest harvests (Hotchkiss 1898, 378). Bull sapling pines were tall, thrifty white pines with a large crown. Their wood was harder and heavier than that of the cork or pumpkin pine (Jack and Conners 1883). Sapling pine was probably the most abundant form of white pine. Although it frequently produced a good 12 to 18 inch diameter sawlog (Jack and Conners 1883), the knots in its wood lowered its market value (Beal 1888). Norway pine was the lumberman's term for red pine (*Pinus resinosa*). As prices rose and the smaller logs and the poorer grades of pine became marketable, the lumbermen frequently went to the same area for a second, third, or fourth cut of the remaining sapling pines and the Norway pines (Hotchkiss 1898, 378).

How prevalent was white pine in the 'untouched' presettlement forests of North America? Much of our early knowledge of white pine is based upon observations which stressed the size and the stumpage, in short, the commercial importance of the species. There are reliable reports of white pine 6 to 7 feet in diameter and up to 250 feet in height (Spalding and Fernow 1899, 12). A 270 foot white pine was cut in 1770–1771 on the site of the present Dartmouth College campus in the upper Connecticut River Valley (McClure 1811, 56). Although the better white pine probably contained on the average approximately 1000 board feet per tree (Lorimer 1977), single trees occasionally scaled up to 5000 to 7000 board feet (Sparhawk and Brush 1929).

The reports of the early pine timber cruisers or 'land-lookers' contain some of the best estimates of the amount of pine in the presettlement forest (Fig. 8.2). Twenty-five to fifty trees to the acre, from 16 inches to 3 feet in diameter, was generally considered thick for pine in Michigan (Maybee [1960] 1976,

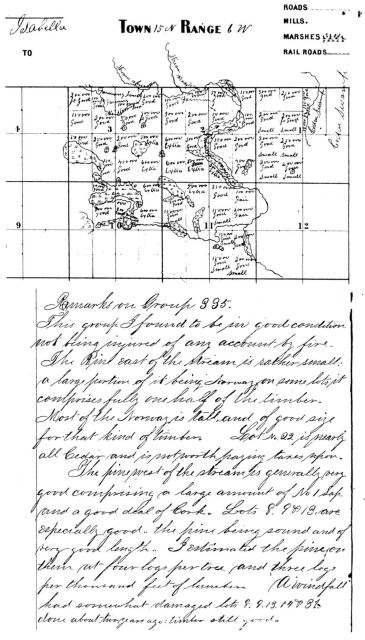

Fig. 8.2 1866 report of S. Hastings on survey of pine in the northeast corner of Township 15N, Range 6W, Isabella County, Michigan. Numbers are estimates of board feet of pine per 40 acre lot based on counts of trees, their quality, and their size. Michigan Pine Land Association Papers, file 1865–66. Courtesy of the Burton Historical Collection, Detroit Public Library.

17). Densities of merchantable pine, however, could go as high as one hundred per acre in the pineries or pine districts of northern lower Michigan (Whitney 1986) or as low as one to ten trees per acre in the mixed pine and hardwood forests of Wisconsin and southern Michigan (Hubbard 1847b; Dopp 1913). Similarly, single acres could scale out at 100 000 board feet (Hotchkiss 1898, 727). The value per acre decreased as larger areas were considered. A stand of 25 000 board feet per acre, for instance, was considered good for a 40 acre tract while whole townships or counties occasionally averaged 10 000 board feet per acre (Spalding and Fernow 1899, 20).

Although much of the Northeast and the Upper Great Lakes region has been termed the hemlock–white pine–northern hardwoods region (Braun [1950] 1967), white pine was not uniformly distributed throughout the region. Pure stands of white pine were generally limited to the rockier areas or the coarse-textured soils of outwash plains, ice-contact features, old beach ridges, deltaic areas, dunes, and shorelines. The Northeast was predominantly the land of mixed pine and hardwood forests. Stands of pure white pine occupied tracts of a few hundred acres (Michaux 1819, 3:165; Pinchot and Graves 1896, 21). White pine reached its best expression in the Upper Great Lakes region (Fig. 8.3). The High Plains region of northern lower Michigan was part of a super pine belt. Its position between two lobes of the melting Laurentide ice sheet

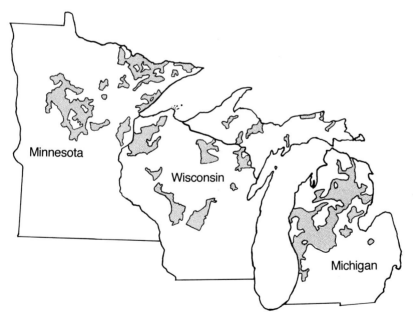

Fig. 8.3 Location of Great Lakes pine forests in the presettlement period. Based on Küchler (1964).

Table 8.2. *Amount of white pine harvested by state up to 1900*

	Billion board feet white pine produced
Michigan	162
Wisconsin	86
Minnesota	67[a]
New York	35
Pennsylvania	32
Maine	28
Total	410

[a] Estimate for Minnesota is amount harvested up to 1930.
Sources: Hotchkiss (1898, 638); Spalding and Fernow (1899, 19); Steer (1948); Larson (1949, 402); Coolidge (1963, 49–50, 91).

12 000 to 14 000 years ago was responsible for the occurrence of the large quantities of ice-contact and glacial outwash sands and gravels, white pine's preferred substrate (Whitney 1986). Data on the harvest of white pine throughout the seventeenth to nineteenth centuries provides a crude estimate of white pine's abundance in various sections of the country (Table 8.2). The pre-eminence of Michigan and, to a lesser degree, Wisconsin is immediately apparent.

The first phase of the logging industry was selective not only with respect to the species, but also the area harvested. Large white pine logs could be moved cheaply by water. Land transportation, however, was another matter. The usual distance for hauling logs from the forest to the nearest navigable stream or river was one to four or occasionally up to six miles (Righter 1898; Fox 1902, Rector 1953, 190). Timber greater than five to ten miles from the stream bank would not pay the cost of hauling (Pringle 1884). The use of splash dams with their accumulated head of water extended the transport of logs to the smaller streams. Up until the 1880s, however, logging was largely a water-dependent phenomenon. Sargent's (1884) 1881 map of the cutting history of Wisconsin's forests very clearly demonstrates the degree to which water transport influenced the cutting of pine. Most of northern Wisconsin was still relatively unscathed in Sargent's map. All of the major rivers of Wisconsin, however, are outlined with a narrow, approximately ten-mile-wide band, of harvested pine.

Phase II. Diversification of logging activities with an emphasis on the secondary species

The depletion of the readily accessible white pine towards the end of the nineteenth century left the lumberman with two options: exploit the remaining species or move to new territory in the South and the Pacific Northwest. Many selected the former. The secondary species were inferior to white pine for a variety of reasons. Hemlock, for instance, produced a relatively brittle, coarse, knotty, tough and splintery wood. It was considered a veritable pariah among woods in the early nineteenth century (Hotchkiss 1898, 378; Wilhelm 1953, 9–10). Its only redeeming feature was the fact that it held nails well (Bryant 1871, 184). Hemlock assumed a new importance, however, with the depletion of the white pine. By 1885 the best hemlock lumber was marketable in Pennsylvania and by 1900 even the poorer grades were used in the manufacture of boxes and in rough construction (Clepper 1934).

The secondary species which the lumber industry turned to varied in importance from one section of the country to the next. They lent a strong regional flavor to the post-white-pine lumbering era and often led to the development of new wood products industries. Maine, Pennsylvania, and Michigan were selected for a more detailed analysis of phase II of the lumbering industry because they exemplify the diversity and the major trends of the era.

Maine

Red spruce has long been an important component of the forests of northern Maine. It was not until the 1840s, however, that lumbermen turned their attention to spruce. By the 1890s red spruce had replaced white pine as the major species cut for lumber (Wood 1935, 23; Coolidge 1963, 50, 65; see also Fig. 8.4). Although red spruce was utilized intensively as a substitute for pine, it soon found its greatest value in the wood pulp industry. Plant cells or cellulose 'fibers' have long formed the basic ingredient and raw material of the American paper industry. Until the nineteenth century, most of the pulp used for making paper was obtained from cotton and linen rags. The increasing scarcity of rags in the nineteenth century prompted an increased interest in the use of wood as a substitute for cloth. The result was the development of a number of innovative techniques for the manufacture of wood pulp, techniques like mechanical grinding and the chemical digestion of the nonfibrous parts of the wood (Fulling 1956; Smith 1970). Maine's woods were ripe for the rapid expansion of the pulp and paper industry which emerged in the United States in the 1870s and the 1880s. Maine still contained large quantities of high-quality wood suitable for the paper industry. Initially the industry relied on aspen obtained from farmers (Smith 1972, 235). Unfortunately, the fibers of hardwoods are generally too short to make a strong paper. Red spruce represented a more viable alternative. It was available in large quantities in central and northern Maine and its long fibers (tracheids in the terminology of plant anatomists) matted down well to form a strong, tough paper (Buttrick 1916).

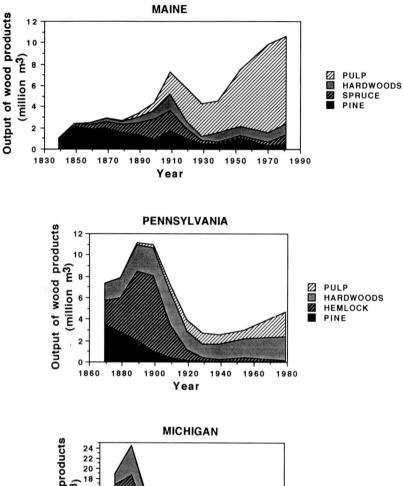

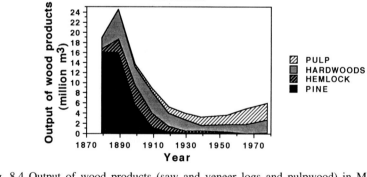

Fig. 8.4 Output of wood products (saw and veneer logs and pulpwood) in Maine, Pennsylvania, and Michigan from 1839 (1869) to 1979. Sources of information: Reynolds and Pierson 1940; Steer 1948; Ferguson 1958; Hair 1958; Coolidge 1963, 88; Ferguson and Kingsley 1972; Powell and Considine 1982; Nevel, Lammert, and Widmann 1985; Whitney 1987. Determination of output in cubic meters followed conversion factors outlined in Nevel, Lammert, and Widmann, 1985, 25).

The rise of the pulp industry altered the forest products industry and the history of Maine in a number of important respects. By 1890 the state of Maine led the nation in the production of wood pulp (Nevel, Lammert, and Widmann 1985) and by 1919 the production of pulpwood on a volume basis surpassed the output of the lumber industry (Fig. 8.4). Wood pulp was well on its way to becoming Maine's largest industry. Intense competition and overexpansion of the pulp and paper industry at the end of the nineteenth century led to the consolidation of a number of small firms and the formation of the giant International Paper Company in 1898 and the Great Northern Paper Company in 1899 (Smith 1972, 247–258).

With appropriate supervision, the spruce and fir forests of Maine can be managed to produce pulpwood at short intervals on a sustained basis. Both International Paper and Great Northern moved rapidly to acquire large tracts of land to assure a continual supply of raw materials for their expensive mills. The arrival of several other large paper corporations, notably Diamond International, Georgia Pacific, and the Scott Paper Company, from the West and the South in the 1960s and the 1970s augmented the development of Maine's industrial forests (Ireland 1982, 29). Much of northern Maine today is owned by a few large paper companies (Ferguson and Kingsley 1972; Ireland 1982, 118). The Great Northern Paper Company alone holds over 2.1 million acres (850 000 ha) in the northern part of the state (DeCoster 1983).

In the early days of lumbering in Maine, only the larger white pine and red spruce were cut from the woods. Many have characterized this as an 'ecologically benign system of exploiting the forest', a system which allowed the logger to return to the forest several decades later for another cut (Ireland 1982, 32). With the rise of pulp operations, the smaller red spruce were cut. Later balsam fir and, in many areas, hardwoods were added to the list of pulp species (Oosting and Reed 1944). Cutting practices in northern Maine today largely follow the dictates of the pulpwood industry. The development of mechanized harvesting systems, i.e., skidders and feller-bunchers, and lower product requirements in the last few decades have encouraged an interest in even-aged silvicultural management (Ferguson and Kingsley 1972; Ireland 1982, 33). Clearcutting, or at least cutting all the softwoods to a minimum diameter limit, is the prevailing form of management of the spruce–fir region of northern Maine today (Wallach 1980).

Throughout much of the United States, the cutting of the old-growth forests forced a shift to woodworking industries dependent upon second-growth timber and stumpage. Maine was one of the few states to make the transistion from 'big' woods to 'small' woods successfully. The pulp and paper industry has long had a vested interest in maintaining Maine's second and subsequent-growth forests. They had their woods and they cut them, too (Smith 1972, 410).

Pennsylvania

If northern Maine was the home of the spruce, northern Pennsylvania was the land of the hemlock. Most lumbermen agreed that initially hemlock was much more abundant than pine in Pennsylvania (Pringle 1884). It was particularly common in northern Pennsylvania (Rothrock 1894a). Foresters noted that the region possessed 'the largest block of hemlock in the world' (Defebaugh 1907, 2:621; French 1922). Although hemlock was frequently mixed with hardwoods, it occasionally occurred in almost pure stands. The 80 000 acres owned by the F. H. and C. W. Goodyear Company in 1897, for instance, contained an average of 15 000 board feet of hemlock and 2000 board feet of hardwoods per acre (Taber 1971, 524). The better tracts of hemlock yielded 25 000 board feet to the acre (Defebaugh 1907, 2:573). Dense stands of hemlocks gave part of northern Pennsylvania the appellation the 'Black Forest' (Taber 1972, 425, 463).

Although hemlock was rapidly integrated into Pennsylvania's lumber market as a replacement for white pine in the 1880s and 1890s (Fig. 8.4), it gained its earliest notoriety in the tanbark trade. Tanbark was a major ingredient of the leather industry and hemlock and, to a lesser extent oak, were the major sources of tanbark in the nineteenth century. The tannins extracted from the bark of hemlock acted on the proteins in hides to produce strong, flexible, resistant leather (Fulling 1956). From 1880 to the exhaustion of hemlock early in the twentieth century, Pennsylvania was the center of the hemlock tanbark industry and the leather industry (Riley 1935, 51, 78). The tannins extracted from the bark of hemlock were particularly suitable for the production of heavy shoe sole, belt, and harness leathers (Onthank 1917, 8, 19–24). Pennsylvania's old-growth forests of hemlock supplied approximately one-half (565 000 cords of bark) of the hemlock employed in the leather industry in 1900 (Houghton 1902, 725).

Tanning started out as a small cottage-industry devoted to processing farmers, hides for local consumption. By the middle of the nineteenth century, however, the increasing demand for shoes, harnesses, saddles, and belting for the nation's factories had transformed the leather business into the nation's fifth largest industry (Ellsworth 1975, 12). Like the wood pulp industry, competition eventually led to the consolidation of many of the tanneries and the formation of large combines like the US Leather Company. In 1901, the US Leather Company controlled 75% of Pennsylvania's lumber stumpage. By 1910 its successor, the Central Leather Company, was one of the ten largest firms in the United States (Taber 1974, 1090–1091).

The large sole leather factories of northern Pennsylvania required enormous quantities of hemlock bark (Fig. 8.5). At the end of the century the larger operations were utilizing 10 000 cords of hemlock bark a year (Walsh 1896). At 10 cords per acre (Walsh 1896) and four trees per cord (Pringle 1884) that translated to an annual cut of 1000 acres (400 ha) of hemlock or 40 000 trees. Since the tanning of each hide required 12 times its weight in bark, it was obviously advantageous for the tanneries to be located close to the source of the bark. The high cost of transporting bark to the tannery limited most barking operations in the Adirondack Mountains of New York State to an area within 10 miles of the tannery (McMartin 1992, 12, 48–50).

The sole leather industry was another case where America's old-growth forests furnished the raw materials for a major extractive industry. By 1870 the large supply of hemlock in the Catskill Mountains in New York had been liquidated (Haring 1931, 91; Ellsworth 1975, 76–78) and the major center of activity shifted to the High Allegheny Plateau region of southern New York

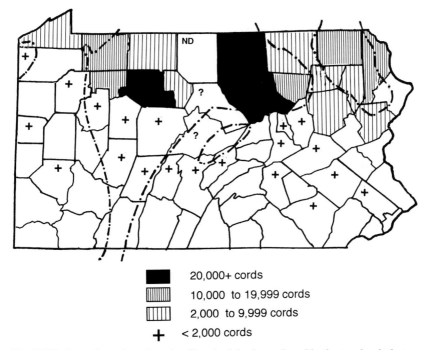

■ 20,000+ cords
▥ 10,000 to 19,999 cords
▨ 2,000 to 9,999 cords
+ < 2,000 cords

Fig. 8.5 Estimated number of cords of hemlock bark employed in the tanning industry in Pennsylvania by county in 1881. Data from Hough (1882, 88–95). ND indicates no data available for county. ? indicates figure on bark use available only for combined category of hemlock and oak. Dash and dot line shows location of hemlock forests in state according to Sargent (1884, 506–510).

and northern Pennsylvania. Armed with axes and spuds, instruments for removing the bark, large armies of men moved from ravine to ravine, methodically eliminating the hemlock (Haring 1931, 100). Unfortunately, hemlock regenerates very slowly following its removal (Riley 1935, 108). Pennsylvania's 'inexhaustible' supplies of hemlock lasted into the 1920s and the demise of the large hemlock-based tanning industry followed shortly thereafter. Changing market demands, the development of new tanning agents, and a scarcity of hemlock contributed to the decline of the industry (Fulling 1956; Taber 1974, 1091; Hergert 1983).

The second phase of the lumber industry witnessed an expansion in the area logged as well as an increase in the number of marketable species. Much of the change was due to the advent of the logging railroad which made it feasible to harvest the poorer grades of logs as well as the timberlands distant from driveable streams (Maybee [1960] 1976, 38). Logging railroads opened up a number of the more rugged areas of the Northeast. Their introduction signaled the demise of the old-growth forests of the High Allegheny Plateau region of northern Pennsylvania as well as the virgin forests of the White Mountains of New Hampshire (Hitchcock 1874, 576; Defebaugh 1907, 2:609).

Logging railroads were extremely expensive items. Only the wholesale use of the forest's resources justified their construction. As a result, a period of clearcutting and intensive exploitation often followed the construction of the railroad. In northern Pennsylvania the logging railroad period constituted 'the highest degree of forest utilization that the world has ever seen in any commercial lumbering area' (Marquis 1975). Every species and almost every part of the tree was utilized – from pine butts and limbs to waste slabs and sawdust (Righter 1898). The Kaul and Hall mill at Saint Marys, Pennsylvania, was typical of many of the cutting operations of the late nineteenth century. It specialized in processing hemlock logs. A stave company in the same town cut Kaul and Hall's hardwoods, while a kindling wood company used the waste from the Kaul and Hall mill. A chemical plant converted the smaller hardwoods into methanol (wood alcohol) and acetate of lime (calcium acetate) (Taber 1974, 1003–1004).

Prior to the rise of the petrochemical industry in the 1920s, all of our industrially important organic chemicals, notably acetone and methanol, were distilled from wood (Baker 1983a). Heavy resin-free species like sugar maple and beech made the best chemical wood (Brown 1917). An established railroad network, an abundance of hardwoods, and a copious supply of fuel in the form of coal and natural gas made northern Pennsylvania the center of the chemical wood distillation industry (Hale 1906; Taber 1975). Pennsylvania accounted for over 60% of the value of all the products of the wood distillation industry in 1900 (Munroe and Michatard 1902).

Michigan

The commercial exploitation of Michigan's forests in the post-pine era followed a very different scenario than the pattern which developed in Maine and Pennsylvania. Michigan shifted from an emphasis on softwoods to a concentration on hardwoods. The forests of the northern half of the Lower Peninsula and the Upper Penninsula contained large numbers of beech, birch, sugar maple, elm, and basswood trees. Most of the forests were relatively untouched except for the removal of an occasional pine. Starting in the late 1800s, a number of factors combined to push the availability and the use of hardwoods up. The appearance of the logging railroad made it possible to transport the heavy, unfloatable hardwoods to the mill. Woodworking techniques, saws, and planing blades were developed to deal specifically with the dense hardwoods. Kiln drying stabilized the dimensions of sawn hardwood lumber, eliminating much of the warping and cracking which had plagued the earlier hardwood industry (Sandberg 1983). By 1910, Michigan's mills were turning out large quantities of hardwoods for flooring, interior finish, cabinet work, and furniture. Sugar maple was the major timber species of the state (Fig. 8.4). Michigan mills alone produced about half of the total sugar maple lumber output of the country (Maxwell 1912, 7, 14).

Phase III. Mop-up operations and the portable mill

By 1910 lumbering throughout much of the northeastern and midwestern United States was a desultory mop-up operation of the few, small, remaining old-growth stands and a culling of the second and third-growth areas for their more valuable products. Small, portable steam and later internal-combustion-powered mills permitted the cutting of the smaller, more isolated tracts of softwoods (Nichols 1913; Cheyney 1916; Egler 1940; Schmidt 1962) and the extraction of the better hardwoods from farm woodlots.

The early twentieth century also witnessed an increasing emphasis on a wider variety of forest products. Many of these products, e.g., bowls, pails, boxes, spools, staves, shingles, mine props, railroad ties, and posts and poles, were derived from the smaller trees of the second-growth forests. New England's white birch was converted into spools (Milliken 1983) while the durable tamarack and white cedar of the northern bogs, the chestnut and oak of southern New England's sprout hardwood forests, and the white oak of the Midwest's farm woodlots went into railroad ties, posts, and poles (Hotchkiss 1898, 371; Hawley and Hawes 1912, 365; Olson 1971, 14–22). Paul Sears ([1935] 1959, 36) succinctly summarized many of these activities when he noted 'Following on the heels of the main lumbering activity were numerous industries which utilized second growth timber, stumpage, etc. Stave and hoop mills, bending works, wagon and handle factories, may be mentioned among these transient industries which shifted west in a slow afterwave.'

The cumulative impact of many of these apparently innocuous activities was often substantial. As an example, America's railroads were cutting 620 000 acres (250 000 ha) of timber in 1910 to produce the 124 million crossties required for the construction of new, and the repair of old, railroad tracks (Olson 1971, 12). This translated into a total output of 4 billion (4 000 000 000) board feet (assuming a conversion factor of 1000 bd ft for 30 ties, see Brown 1919, 279) or a value equivalent to approximately 10% of the lumber produced that year (Hair 1958). Sherry Olson (1971, 14) observed that the railroads' demand for wood during this period of time was insatiable.

Even 'small-time' wood products industries had a major impact on the landscape where their activities were confined to a limited area. Over 140 000 acres (55 000 ha) of forests (an area > 200 square miles) were cut per year in Pennsylvania in the 1890s for mine props (Rothrock and Shunk 1896, 346). The oak forests in the vicinity of northeastern Pennsylvania's anthracite mines were repeatedly clearcut at short intervals.

Fires often followed the cutting and converted the forests of mixed red, black, white, and chestnut oak to barrens of stunted scrub oak, pitch pine, and a variety of ericaceous shrubs (Burnham, Ferree, and Cunningham 1947; Ineson and Ferree 1948; Donahue 1954). Scrub oak (*Quercus ilicifolia*) was particularly adaptable to this type of a cutting and fire regime since it sprouts rapidly after a fire, bears acorns at an early age (< 10 years), and is a shade intolerant species (Hawley 1933). The cutover, burned-out scrub oak barrens of the anthracite region were long considered a 'problem area' (Wible 1951) and a 'menace to the prosperity of the Commonwealth' of Pennsylvania (Rothrock and Shunk 1896, 34).

Impact of lumbering

We now come to the second concern of early forest conservationists: (2) lumbering reduced the forests to wastelands or unproductive second and third-growth forests, composed of inferior 'weed' trees. By 1910, the great period of land clearance for agriculture had essentially ended. Lumbering had surpassed agriculture as the major factor responsible for the disappearance of America's old-growth forests in 1880 (Greeley *et al.* 1923). Even lumbering, however, was well past its peak in the eastern United States. The US Forest Service could sit back and analyze the results of the last 300 years of settlement and assess the nation's remaining timber supply. The Forest Service's evaluation is interesting because (1) it provides an estimate of the amount of virgin forest lost to various activities and (2) it provides an outline of the status of America's forests at the start of the twentieth century (Table 8.3). Agriculture represented the greatest drain upon the forest, accounting for over 40% of the formerly forested land in the Northeast and the Midwest. Even this figure, however, is a conservative estimate of the loss because some of the farm land had already been abandoned and was included in the forest land figures for 1908. Thirty percent of the region's original forests had been cutover or burned and a third of that was not regenerating adequately. Only a fraction of the merchantable timber category, the quarter of the original forest left, could still be considered virgin forest as much of it had been selectively logged. The larger trees and the more valuable species were missing.

The cumulative result of North America's assault upon the forest was a dramatic decrease in the area of untouched old-growth or virgin forest. By 1920, the Northeast and the Midwest had lost 96% of their old-growth timber (Reynolds and Pierson 1923). Although it is difficult to make definitive statements as to the amount of virgin, old-growth timber left today, the best available estimates (Table 8.4) suggest a total of approximately 6000 acres (2400 ha) for Maine (Wommack 1986), 14 000 acres (5700 ha) for Pennsylvania (Smith 1989), probably 50 000 to 150 000 acres (20 000 to 60 000 ha) for New York (Ketchledge 1965), and less than 1000 acres (400 ha) for Ohio (Fleischman 1985). Maine and Pennsylvania have less than 0.06% of their original forests left. The loss was even greater in the case of the rich, agricultural heartland of the Midwest. The untouched central hardwood forests of Ohio and Indiana have dwindled to approximately 0.005% of their presettlement extent. The harvest of eastern North America's old-growth forests was complete and thorough. A statement in an old historical gazetteer succinctly summarized the status of the region's old-growth forests 'after three successive attacks on the primitive forests there was little left to encourage the lumbermen' (Gordon 1937, 79).

The rapid liquidation of the East's old-growth forests at the turn of the century left an indelible imprint on America's early conservationists. As Gifford Pinchot (1937) expressed it 'The American Colossus was fiercely at work turning natural resources into money.' 'A perfect orgy of forest destruction' had begun (Pinchot 1937) and by the time it was complete, it was difficult to believe any productive forests had ever existed in the East (Mayr 1890b). Henry Shoemaker's (1914, xv–xvi) reaction to the devastation of the hemlock forests of northern Pennsylvania was typical of the response of many early conservationists. He returned in 1907 to an area he had visited in his youth and wrote, 'Miles of slashings, fire-swept wastes, emptiness, desolation and ruin met the eye on every side; the lumbermen had done their work. ... Gone were

Table 8.3. *Status of forest land in 1908, showing loss of timber supply due to agricultural clearing, cutting, etc., in formerly forested eastern states. Values in parentheses are percentages of forest land*

| | Farmland 1910 | Forestland 1908 | | | | Miscellaneous | |
	Cropland and pasture (ha)	Cutover land restocking (ha)	Cutover land not restocking (ha)	Merchantable timber (ha)	Forests as % total land	urban, etc. (ha)	Total (ha)
Connecticut	409	463 (65.2)	4 (0.6)	243 (34.2)	56.8	130	1249
Indiana	5981	1247 (59.6)	162 (7.7)	682 (32.6)	22.5	1226	9298
Maine	1069	1822 (28.9)	162 (2.6)	4325 (68.5)	81.4	368	7746
Massachusetts	469	405 (30.0)	148 (11.0)	798 (59.0)	64.8	263	2083
Michigan	4655	1214 (12.1)	4327 (43.3)	4453 (44.6)	67.1	245	14894
New Hampshire	431	627 (35.3)	154 (8.7)	997 (56.0)	76.0	131	2340
New Jersey	616	425 (50.8)	210 (25.1)	202 (24.1)	43.0	493	1946
New York	5681	2391 (41.6)	916 (16.1)	2432 (42.3)	46.5	927	12347
Ohio	7098	1054 (45.9)	271 (11.8)	972 (42.3)	21.8	1161	10556
Pennsylvania	4438	3478 (58.9)	404 (6.8)	2024 (34.3)	50.8	1272	11616
Rhode Island	65	87 (56.5)	4 (2.6)	63 (40.9)	55.8	57	276
Vermont	1039	691 (46.1)	– –	809 (53.9)	63.4	–	2364
Totals	31951	13904 (36.0)	6762 (17.5)	18000 (46.5)	50.4	6273	76715

Sources: Greeley (1909); Kellog (1909); Goldenweiser and Ball (1918).

Table 8.4. *Best estimates of remaining old-growth forests in selected states of the Northeast and the Midwest*

	Old-growth forests(ha)	% existing forested land	% originally forested land	Sources
Maine	2400	0.04	0.03	Wommack 1986
New York	20000–60000	0.54	0.36	Ketchledge 1965
Pennsylvania	5700	0.08	0.05	Smith 1989
Ohio	400	0.01	< 0.01	Fleischman 1985
Indiana[a]	600	0.04	< 0.01	Parker 1989
Illinois[a]	2000	0.13	0.03	Parker 1989

[a] Data available only for mesic, old-growth, deciduous forests.

the hemlocks, beeches, maples and pines ... The hand of man had changed the face of nature from green to brown.' America's forests faced a bleak future. It seems appropriate to inquire whether the concerns of the early conservationists were justified. To what extent had the species composition, the structure, and the productivity of America's forests been altered? Just how accurate, widespread, or long lasting was the scenario of forest devastation outlined by the denudiacs (a derogatory term applied to the early conservationists)?

Response of species to cutting

The effects of cutting were far reaching. Cutting opened up the canopy, creating a new microclimate and a habitat with an increased availability of light and nutrients (Barrett, Farnsworth, and Rutherford 1962; Marquis 1972; Bormann and Likens 1979). Many species responded positively to the new environment. Others were reduced in numbers. Cutting the forest to a small diameter limit or clearcutting favored the rapidly growing, generally short-lived, shade intolerant species which reproduced aggressively outside the forest. These were the extensive reproducers of Frothingham (1915), e.g., the aspens, most of the birches, and the cherries. Because they produced large numbers of light, wind-dispersed seeds or seeds with a long viability, they were capable of exploiting the site's disturbed conditions. Another group of species, the more shade tolerant, intensive reproducers increased in numbers when the forest was selectively cut. Most of these species exhibited at least a moderate degree of mobility and an ability to respond to large gaps in the canopy *inside* woods (Hill 1895; Zon 1914; Frothingham 1915; Forcier 1975). Sugar maple is probably the best example of an intensive reproducer in the northern hardwood forest region while balsam fir fills a similar niche in the spruce–fir region. Both species produce large numbers of wind-dispersed seeds. Their shade tolerant seedlings frequently carpet the forest floor and can persist in a suppressed condition in the understory for long periods of time (Hett and Loucks 1968; Bourdo 1983). Partial destruction of the canopy simply stimulates the rapid growth of the sugar maple and fir seedlings, eventually sending them into the canopy.

Finally, a third group of species, putatively considered old-growth or 'climax' tree species, e.g., beech, hemlock, and red spruce, generally declined following cutting. The slow but steady growth of their seedlings and saplings in the understory gave them the opportunity to utilize the naturally occurring gaps in the canopy of the old-growth forest (Westveld 1953; Kelty 1986; Canham 1988). Many shade tolerant trees or saplings probably went through several release–suppression cycles before they reached the overstory (Runkle 1982). The human-imposed disturbance regime of the nineteenth and twentieth centuries attacked these species at their weakest link – the prolonged, suppressed sapling stage. Cutting, fires, exposure, and the dense, even-aged, second-growth stands which followed the initial harvest destroyed many of these saplings or at least prevented the buildup of a new layer of advance regeneration (Westveld 1953; Barrett, Ketchledge, and Satterlund 1961, 134–136; Whitney 1990). Unlike other species, notably the maples and the oaks, few of their saplings were capable of sprouting following injury. The low production and the restricted dispersal of beech's heavy seed appears to have hindered its reestablishment (Maxwell 1912; Forcier 1975). Young hemlocks have long been known to be sensitive to direct sunlight (Hix and Barnes 1984). Throughout the drier portions of hemlock's range, the selective removal of white pine and other associates often triggered the inevitable decline of hemlock (Sargent 1884, 510; Pinchot and Graves 1896, 22; Eyre and Zillgitt 1953). A single stroke of the axe (Cooper [1810] 1897) or exposure following a break in the canopy was enough to kill it. It was common knowledge that hemlock could not endure civilization (Clepper 1934).

A diversity of opinion exists on the amount of long-term change engendered by European settlement. Some investigators, like Hugh Raup (1964), have argued that the history of the human use of the forests is similar to that of the natural disturbance regime. Forests are very resilient. The forests of the twentieth century bear a striking resemblance to their presettlement counterparts. Others (Bray 1930; Spurr and Cline 1942) have depicted the change as one of major proportions. The more valuable species decreased in number while the inferior weed species increased. Many of the early discussions of post-European change in the species composition of the forests were hindered by a lack of quantiative information on the nature of the presettlement forest. Fortunately, we now have a wider variety of techniques and a larger data base for assessing the magnitude of these changes.

On a local scale there are a number of comparisons of old-growth or virgin woodlands with neighboring areas of cutover woodlands (Woollett and Sigler 1928; Zon and Scholz 1929; Potzger and Friesner 1934; Noble *et al.* 1977; Whitney and Runkle 1981; Hix and Barnes 1984; Albert and Barnes 1987; Abrams and Scott 1989). Silviculturalists have long had a professional interest in the effects of logging on the regeneration of the forest. Their studies, generally based on a before and after analysis of permanently established plots (Belyea 1924; Zasada 1952; Leak and Wilson 1958; Barrctt, Farnsworth, and Rutherford 1962), provide added insight into the issue of post-logging changes in the composition of the forest.

The pollen preserved in lake sediments and bogs also reflects the changing composition of the forest. Although it is difficult to tie pollen percentage values to absolute measures of tree abundance, one can detect changes in the relative abundance of the various arboreal species. Cutting appears to have decreased the representation of the more sensitive 'climax' species, e.g., beech, hemlock, and red spruce throughout the Northeast and the Midwest (Webb 1973; Swain 1978; Davis 1985; Engstrom, Swain, and Kingston 1985; Overpeck 1985; Anderson *et al.* 1986; Gajewski 1987; Gajewski, Swain, and Peterson 1987). Hemlock maintained its presettlement importance only in areas which escaped major episodes of logging (Bradshaw and Webb 1985). White pine also suffered a general postsettlement decline in abundance (Bradbury *et al.* 1975; Swain 1978; Gajewski, Swain, and Peterson 1987), although the causative factors may have been more complex than simply selective logging. The decline is particularly well marked in sediment cores from the Midwest (Webb 1973; Davis 1977a). Birch and aspen (the extensive reproducers) and, in some areas, oak were the major species which increased their representation in the pollen spectra following cutting (Webb 1973; Swain 1978; Davis 1985; Gajewski, Swain, and Peterson 1987).

A comparison of the early land survey records and more recent forest survey data provides the best means of assessing changes in the forest's composition. Survey data frequently furnishes information on species which are poorly preserved in the pollen record. Unlike the old-growth and second-growth stand comparisons, the results are applicable to a wide area. A compilation (Table 8.5) of some of the more reliable data in the Northeast highlights many of the changes, particularly the decline of hemlock and beech and the rise of the maples. The precipitous decline of beech throughout much of the Northeast can probably be attributed to the introduction of beech bark disease as well as past cutting practices and beech's low mobility. For many species the time since the last major human disturbance has not been long enough for them to regain their former ascendancy. Hemlock, for instance, is a very slow-growing

Table 8.5. *Pre- to postsettlement changes in the species composition (percentage values of trees reported by species) of woodlands in several heavily logged areas in the Northeast. Dates are dates of surveys. Dash indicates that the species was not noted or was present in small amounts in survey. An n.s. denotes that the species was noted but its abundance was not specified.*

Species	N Maine		N Vermont, Chittenden County		New York, Catskills		Pennsylvania, Allegheny National Forest	
	1793–1827	1982	1763–1802	1962	1749–1800	1960	1793–1819	1973
Red maple	2.9	4.1	15.8	23.8	1.2	7.0	4.7	27.3
Sugar maple	5.4	6.5	} 5.1	} 16.2	12.8	23.2	5.3	13.3
Birch	16.4	6.4	n.s.	–	7.3	10.7	6.3	8.5
Chestnut	–	–	40.4	4.7	0.5	–	2.8	–
Beech	12.9	4.5	3.3	2.3	49.5	12.8	43.4	6.0
Ash	2.7	1.3	6.3	12.0	0.4	3.7	0.8	2.1
Pine[a]	0.5	0.4	0.4	2.6	0.5	n.s.	3.1	0.4
Aspen	0.1	7.1			<0.2	n.s.	0.1	4.9
White oak	–	–	} 2.8	} 5.6	<0.1	<0.1	4.1	2.0
Red oak	–	<0.1			0.1	12.3	0.6	2.3
Chestnut oak	–	–	–	–	0.1	5.2	0.4	0.2
Black cherry	–	<0.5	n.s.	n.s.	0.9	n.s.	0.8	22.6
Fir	20.5	25.1	0.2	1.4	0.4	n.s.	–	–
Spruce[b]	19.0	24.4	5.6	1.9	0.2	n.s.	–	–
White cedar	14.8	18.2	1.0	1.2	–	–	–	–
Hemlock	2.4	1.3	7.3	11.0	20.3	9.5	19.9	5.8

[a] Predominantly white pine.
[b] Predominantly red spruce.
Sources: Maine (Lorimer 1977; Powell 1985); Vermont (Siccama 1971); New York (McIntosh 1962, 1972); Pennsylvania (Whitney 1990).

species which has still not recovered from heavy exploitation at the turn of the century. It appears to be infiltrating many hardwood stands in the Northeast, however, and in another century or two may form a large part of the overstory of the stands (Spurr 1956; Kudish 1971, 195).

Often it was not the cutting of the overstory per se which disrupted the normal equilibrium of the forest but the cutting at short intervals and the destruction of the advance growth that altered the composition of the forest. Many foresters in Maine's spruce–fir region, for instance, believe that clearcutting at short intervals favored balsam fir over red spruce (Westveld 1931; Coolidge 1963, 9; Hart 1963). Fir has been described as a very aggressive species while spruce is more persistent (Westveld 1930). The larger seed, the more frequent seed years, the greater ease of establishment, and the higher growth rate of fir relative to spruce increased fir's representation in young second-growth stands (Oosting and Reed 1944; Hart 1963). Red spruce's tolerance and greater longevity, however, eventually allowed it to dominate the older forests (Smith 1986, 501–502). Cutting forests at short intervals for pulpwood has reduced the maturity of the spruce–fir forests across much of northern Maine (Wallach 1980). The result has been an increase in fir. The forest commissioner of Maine cited a ratio of 7 to 1 for the volume of spruce to the volume of fir in 1902 (Zon 1914). By 1972 the spruce:fir volume ratio had shifted to a more equitable 54:51 (Ferguson and Kingsley 1972). The low value for the density of fir in the 1982 survey of northern Maine in Table 8.5 is somewhat anomalous as it reflects a high rate of fir mortality over the past 15 years due to insect outbreaks of epidemic proportions (Powell 1985).

Hemlock and beech suffered a similar fate in the Allegheny Plateau region of northern Pennsylvania. Here the stands were clearcut at short intervals for the chemical wood industry. Most of the advance growth was either intentionally cut back to the ground or unintentionally broken during the harvest. Reproduction is rather limited for the first 40–50 years of growth of most second-growth stands due to the dense nature of the canopy and the lack of mature seed-bearing trees. Cutting the immature second-growth stands for chemical wood before they established a seedling layer favored those species which sprouted vigorously from the stumps (Whitney 1990). Black cherry increased its representation after each cutting. The result was a wholesale conversion of the hemlock–hardwood forests of the presettlement period to the cherry and maple dominated Allegheny hardwood forests of today (Table 8.5). Northern Pennsylvania is the source of much of the nation's commercial supply of high-grade black cherry furniture and veneer.

Of all the contingencies accompanying lumbering, none was more destructive than fire. Foresters at the turn of the century unanimously agreed that fire was the worst enemy of the forest (Pinchot and Graves 1896, 33). Estimates of the amount of timber lost to fire run as high as 20% of Michigan's original 380 billion board feet of sawtimber and 15% of Wisconsin's merchantable pine (Roth 1898a). The worst effect of fire, however, was its impact upon the future status of the stand. Normally the smaller trees or the defective trees left by the lumbermen reseeded the cutover area. Fires soon destroyed most of these 'seed' trees as well as their fire sensitive seedlings (Maxwell 1912, 9).

Three factors combined to create some of the worst forest fires in history. The first was an abundant supply of fuel. Lumbering generated a large amount of waste material. Tops and branches were strewn over the ground, forming extensive areas of woody debris know as slashings (Sargent 1882; Merk 1916, 101). Many trees were debarked to improve the quality of their pulp (Fox 1902) or to reduce friction when moving them along the ground (Wood 1935, 88). In the early phases of the tanbark industry, the trunks of the low-value hemlock were often left to decay in the woods (Pringle 1884). Bark and tree trunks added to the quantity of combustible material.

The high incidence of cutting in conifer stands also increased the probability and the intensity of fires. Solid bodies of conifers produced the most slash since a large percentage of the trees were merchantable. Conifer slash also lasts longer than hardwood slash (Scholtz 1930) and is more susceptible to fire. The needles and limbs of conifers contain large quantities of flammable resins (Mutch 1970). Hemlock's heavy crown and fine spray dries off quickly when propped up off the ground and forms a particularly fire prone environment (Putnam 1882; Pinchot and Graves 1896). Fires originating in hemlock slashings often burned for days (Marquis 1975). In contrast, fires were less frequent in forests dominated by deciduous species (Gordon 1937) and in lightly cutover forests (Zon 1928, 46). Virgin forests also had a lower incidence of serious conflagrations (Sargent 1884, 550).

An increase in the number of ignition sources accompanied the fuel buildup and exacerbated the fire situation. Charles Sprague Sargent (1884, 491) tabulated the causes of forest fires across the United States in 1880 in his *Report on the Forests of North America*. Sargent attributed most of the fires to a variety of human activities which often accompanied or followed lumbering. Forty-two percent of the fires in the Northeast and the Midwest were due to land clearing operations. Settlers often picked the driest periods to burn the woody debris left on the cutover land. The fire frequently escaped to the neighboring woods. Hunters accounted for another 19% of the fires. In the East (Pennsylvania, New Hampshire, Massachusetts, and New Jersey), sparks from railroads were the primary cause of fires (Sargent 1884, 491; Chittenden 1904, 89–90).

Forest fire records attest to the significance of the fire problem. Information on the occurrence of fires in the nineteenth century is fragmentary. There are estimates of the extent of the more dramatic fires like the fires of 1825 in Maine which burned 832 000 acres (330 000 ha or more than 4% of the state, Fobes 1948) and the Great Fires of 1871 which covered 2 000 000 acres (800 000 ha) in Michigan, over 5% of the state, and 1 300 000 acres (520 000 ha) in Wisconsin (Dana 1939). Historians believe that fires in the last quarter of the nineteenth century averaged about 500 000 acres (200 000 ha) per year in Wisconsin (Kleinmaier 1973) and another 500 000 acres in Michigan (Mitchell and Robson 1950).

Fires scars on some of the fire resistant tree species provide a detailed picture of the fire regime which followed the logging. Fires followed each other in rapid succession. In northern lower Michigan, for instance, many sites were burned over at least two to three times with an average interval of nine years between fires (Kittredge and Chittenden 1929; Kilburn 1958, 77–80). A determination of the age of stems or the period of stand initiation on one burnt-over area on the Allegheny Plateau in northern Pennsylvania indicated the occurrence of four fires in the first quarter of the twentieth century (Hough 1955).

The twentieth century witnessed the proliferation of a number of state agencies and later cooperative federal and state projects designed to deal with the fire problem (Pyne 1982, 233; Williams 1984). They developed more detailed record keeping schemes on a state by state basis. Table 8.6 shows the area burned expressed as a percentage of the total forested area for the states of Maine, Michigan, and Pennsylvania. Dividing the total forested area by the average area burned each year yields the rotation period or the time it took to burn over an area equal to the area in question. The destruction of the conifer forests of Michigan and, to a lesser degree, Pennsylvania clearly initiated a series of destructive fires which carried over into the first two to three decades of the twentieth century. Maine, on the other hand, was one of the first states to embark upon an ambitious program of fire control and forest protection. An interest in pulpwood production and sustained yield forestry undoubtedly contributed to Maine's early implementation of an effective forest fire control program (Wilkins 1978). Pennsylvania and Michigan were affected by a 'cut and get out' attitude which thwarted the early development of an effective fire control policy. The exponential decrease in the area burned in all three states is related to improved efficiency in detecting and reporting fires, improved access to the fires, and improved fire-fighting techniques and equipment (Wilkins 1978, 144–145; Fahey and Reiners 1981). Fire rotation periods now are probably much greater than those of the presettlement period.

Table 8.6. *Percentage of forested area burned annually in Maine, Pennsylvania, and Michigan for various time periods, and resulting fire rotation periods*

Period	Maine	Pennsylvania	Michigan
1880–1890			2.50 (40)
1903–1910	0.40 (250)[a]		
1911–1920	0.16 (620)	2.12 (50)[b]	1.11 (90)
1921–1930	0.17 (590)	1.41 (70)	1.24 (80)
1931–1940	0.15 (670)	0.53 (190)	0.42 (240)
1941–1950	0.21 (480)	0.27 (370)	0.12 (830)
1951–1960	0.05 (2000)	0.20 (500)	0.04 (2500)
1961–1970	0.02 (5000)	0.11 (910)	0.05 (2000)

[a] Values in parentheses are rotation periods, i.e., number of years it takes to burn over an area equal to the forested area of the state in question.
[b] Percentage of area burned in Pennsylvania is for period of 1913 to 1920.
Sources: Maine (Fahey and Reiners 1981); Pennsylvania (Wirt 1936; USDA Forest Service 1950–1971; Cobb 1958); Michigan (Mitchell and Robson 1950; USDA Forest Service 1950–1971; Michigan Department of Conservation 1951–1960).

Fires have long been an integral part of the natural environment. Relatively few species, however, could tolerate the increased frequency of fires occasioned by human activity. White pine's thin bark during the first 30 to 50 years of its existence makes it susceptible to even light surface fires (Pinchot and Graves 1896, 33). Hemlock is another species which is very vulnerable to fire. One or two fires can virtually eliminate hemlock from an area for a long period of time (Nichols 1913; Winer 1955, 128–129; Detwyler 1966, 90). Much of hemlock's postsettlement decline in the Upper Great Lakes region has been attributed to fire (Kilburn 1958, 76; Detwyler 1966, 71–72).

A few species responded positively to the fire prone conditions of the early twentieth century and significantly increased their representation in the post-logging forests. Usually these were species which sprouted vigorously from dormant or adventitious buds after a fire, e.g., aspen, paper birch, pin cherry, and scrub oak (*Quercus ellipsoidalis* and *Q. ilicifolia*), or species that released their seed from serotinous cones opened by the fire, e.g., jack pine. Species that produced seed at an early age such as jack pine and scrub oak (*Q. ilicifolia*) also increased their representation. Every area contained a suite of these opportunistic species. Aspen and pin cherry followed fires on the Allegheny Plateau of northern Pennsylvania (Hough and Forbes 1943). Impenetrable thickets of scrub oak (*Q. ilicifolia*) covered many of the burnt-over ridges and summits of eastern Pennsylvania (McIntyre 1932). Repeated fires also favored the extension of the shrubby pitch pine barrens of southern New Jersey (Lutz 1934; Little 1946). Paper birch was the primary beneficiary of fires in northern New England and northern New York. Extensive stands of paper birch still mark the location of areas devastated by fires in the past (Dana 1909; Fobes 1948).

Michigan was the site of some of the greatest conflagrations of the nineteenth and early twentieth centuries. Michigan also possesses some of the best documented examples of the response of the vegetation to the new human-initiated disturbance regime (Elliott 1953; Kilburn 1958; Harman and Nutter 1973; Whitney 1987). Fires in the High Plains region of north-central Michigan converted large areas of white and red pine to aspen and scrub oak (*Q. ellipsoidalis*) (Fig. 8.6). During the presettlement period, oak was relegated to a subordinate position in the understory of the pine forests where it persisted as a few dispersed, slow-growing seedlings or seedling sprouts. Cutting, and the frequent fires which followed, eliminated both the few remaining seed trees of pine and the newly established pine seedlings. The oaks responded to the fires by resprouting. When released from competition with the pine, the oaks seeded in the more open areas, eventually converting

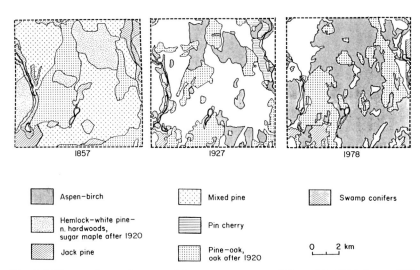

Fig. 8.6 Changes in areal extent of forest cover types of Township 28N, Range 2W (originally a red–white–jack pine area), Crawford County, Michigan. Unshaded areas are largely grasslands and open shrublands. Information based on 1857 presettlement GLO field survey notes and township plat maps, 1927 Michigan Land Economic Survey map of Crawford County, and 1978 Michigan Resource Inventory System cover type maps of townships. From Whitney (1987).

much of the mixed pine and pine and oak types to pure oak. As Maissurow (1935) noted, the disappearance of the pine 'was brought about by a disturbed balance between the seed-bearing capacity of the forest and [the] frequency or destructiveness of forest fires.' The demise of the Great Lakes pine forest was not unique to the High Plains region. It occurred throughout Michigan (Table 8.7), Wisconsin and the remainder of the Great Lakes region. Understory plants commonly associated with forests of conifers still mark the location of many a former white pine and hemlock stand in the Upper Great Lakes region (Grigal and Ohmann 1975; Overlease and Overlease 1976).

Human activities also altered the configuration of the vegetation by creating a number of new disturbance mediated plant communities (Fig. 8.7). Due to its relatively shade intolerant nature, aspen was a minor and temporary constituent of windthrows and other disturbed sites in the presettlement forests of Michigan. It frequently represented less than 5% of the bearing trees recorded by the early land surveyors throughout Michigan and Wisconsin (Table 8.8). Like the phoenix, however, aspen grew out of the ashes of the Great Lakes' forests. Fire created the bare mineral soil required for aspen's establishment. It also encouraged sprouting and the development of an invasive network of aspen roots (Graham, Harrison, and Westell 1963; Ahlgren and Ahlgren 1984). Despised for a number of years as a worthless species, aspen and its associate jack pine, today are the premier species of the new industrial pulpwood forests of the Upper Great Lakes region (Whitney 1987).

The last 350 years have witnessed a major change in the composition of America's forests. The list of species is the same and often the boundaries between the major forest types are the same. The proportional representation

Table 8.7. *Pre- and postsettlement extent of various forest types in Michigan*

Forest type	Presettlement (million ha)	1935 (million ha)	1955 (million ha)	1980 (million ha)
Pine	4.0	0.4	0.6	0.7
Spruce–fir	1.8	0.6	0.3	0.3
Coniferous swamp[a]	1.4	0.5	0.6	0.7
Northern hardwoods	3.6	1.9	1.9	2.5
Oak–hickory	2.0	0.5	0.7	0.7
Lowland hardwoods[b]	1.2	0.3	0.4	0.5
Aspen–paper birch	–	2.0	1.9	1.5
Scrub or poorly stocked forests	0.2	1.4	1.2	0.1

[a] Predominantly spruce–white cedar–tamarack.
[b] Predominantly elm–ash–red maple.
Sources: Findell *et al.* (1960); Spencer (1983).

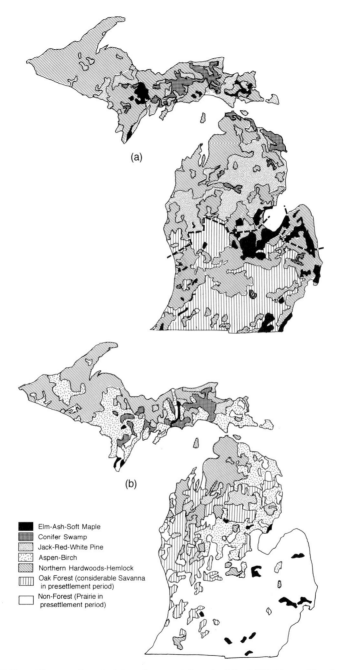

Fig. 8.7 Presettlement forests (a) and current forests (b) of Michigan. Hemlock was uncommon in the northern hardwoods–hemlock forest type south of the dashed line in (a). The northern hardwoods–hemlock type is largely composed of sugar maple and birch today. Slightly modified from Stearns and Guntenspergen (1987).

Table 8.8. *Pre- and postsettlement changes in the species composition (percentage values of trees reported by species) of several forested areas in the Upper Great Lakes region. Dates are dates of surveys. Dash indicates that species was not noted or was present in small amounts in survey. Birch, pine, and spruce categories refer to trees that were identified only to genus in early survey*

Species	Crawford County, Michigan[a]		SE Eau Claire County, Wisconsin		Isle Royale, Michigan	
	1836–1859	1980	1850	1973	1847–1848	1974
Red maple	0.6	1.7	10.4	17.3	–	–
Sugar maple	3.3	3.0	–	–	–	–
Birch	1.5					
Paper birch	0.1	0.7	8.0	7.7	13.3	44.3
Yellow birch	0.2	–	2.8	–	–	–
Beech	7.6	1.9	–	–	–	–
Pine	11.2					
Jack pine	12.3	13.6	0.7	6.0	–	–
Red pine	37.9	12.2	9.0	0.5	–	–
White pine	11.5	2.7	43.6	6.7	–	–
Aspen	1.0	12.4	3.8	22.7	5.9	15.3
White oak	1.9	5.9	13.2	7.2	–	–
Red oak	–	–	6.9	30.7	–	–
Scrub oak	1.2	37.9	–	–	–	–
Balsam fir	0.2	0.2	–	–	44.4	9.6
Tamarack	1.9	0.3	–	–	2.0	–
Spruce	0.5	–	–	–	19.6	23.3
White cedar	2.0	0.2	–	–	10.8	3.4
Hemlock	5.1	1.0	–	–	–	–

[a] Percentages for Crawford County based on medium and large trees, i.e., those with a d.b.h. > 28 cm.
Sources: Crawford County (Whitney 1987); Eau Claire County (Barnes 1974); Isle Royale (Janke, McKaig, and Raymond 1978).

of the species, however, has changed (Detwyler 1966, 187; Smith 1976). A comparison of the presettlement tree species abundance maps presented in chapter 4 (Fig. 4.3) and recent Forest Service timber volume distribution maps showing growing stock on a county by county basis (Beltz *et al.* 1992) highlights the broader patterns of change. Hemlock and beech have decreased and have a much spottier distribution in the Midwest today. Sugar maple has increased in the Northeast. Aspen has expanded dramatically in the Upper Great Lakes region while white pine's center of distribution has shifted to the Northeast. One might plausibly argue that the forest has always been a dynamic entity, changing its composition in response to natural disasters and shifts in climate. The question then becomes one of the magnitude of the change. Were the changes accompanying European settlement different from those associated with natural disturbances? Quantitative analyses of the fossil pollen deposited in lake sediments over the last 10 000 years at a variety of sites spread across eastern North America provides a partial answer (Jacobson and Grimm 1986; Jacobson, Webb, and Grimm 1987). They suggest that the last 100 years have witnessed more vegetation change than any other century in the Holocene.

Effects of cutting on structure and productivity of forests

Human activities dramatically altered the structure of eastern North America's forests. Since many of the activities, i.e., lumbering, fires, etc., were roughly synchronized across the Northeast and the Midwest, they left an indelible imprint upon the age distribution of the succeeding forests. Vermeule (1900, 19–20) noted the increasing age of forests across northern New Jersey as cutting on a 20 year cycle for charcoal ceased in the 1850s. Many forest stands in the Northeast date to the last major episode of lumbering in the late 1800s and the early 1900s and are now approaching maturity (Marquis 1975; Whitney 1990). A large share of Michigan's forests also date to the implementation of an active fire control program and the cessation of fires in the 1920–1939 period (Spencer 1983).

The long-term effect of cutting and fires on the productivity of the forest is more difficult to evaluate. Forest historians hold differing opinions regarding the amount of long-term change occasioned by settlement. Photographs of cutover areas taken early in the twentieth century certainly justified the use of the term 'areas of desolation and devastation' (Rothrock 1915). Logging and repeated fires kept about a fifth of the forested land in the Northeast and the Midwest in the early 1900s in a poorly stocked or relatively open condition (Table 8.3). With the exception of a few problem areas, however, the revegetation of the cutover sites was rapid once the forests were protected from fires. From a functional viewpoint, the forests returned to their predisturbance condition. Dry sites with coarse-textured soils, e.g., outwash plains, and mountainous terrain with shallow soils, constituted two major problem areas. Dry sand plains have long been equated with areas which are particularly susceptible to degradation by fires. According to conventional wisdom, fires destroyed much of the humus and organic matter built up on these sites over the years. The loss of organic material reduced the limited water-holding capacity and the nutrient supply of the soil and ultimately the productivity of the site (Lovejoy 1921; Donahue 1935; Daniel, Helms, and Baker 1979, 236).

Recent evidence suggests that the effects of fire on coarse-textured soils were either superficial or transitory. The loss of organic matter was largely confined to the superficial litter and humus layers of the soil (Kilburn 1958, 228). With respect to the effect of fire on the moisture-holding capacity of the soil, the literature is more confusing. The presence of charcoal, for instance, can actually increase the moisture-holding capacity of sandy soils (Wells *et al.* 1979). Perhaps the most telling argument against the permanent impoverishment of sandy sites by fire is the rapidity with which forests rebuild the organic matter of the site. In Wisconsin, for instance, Wilde (1964) found that the growth of pine plantations over a 40 to 50 year period restored the organic matter and the nutrient content of the soil.

Soils with thick organic layers overlying bedrock, i.e., soils currently classified as borofolists, represented another problem area. Borofolists are common in the more rugged areas of the Northeast. Fires have long been considered the scourge of the Adirondacks and the northern Appalachian Mountains due to the combustible nature of the borofolists and the potential for erosion following fires. References to denuded hills and 'piles of bare rock, stripped of [their] vegetation' occur repeatedly throughout C. S. Sargent's (1885) report on the forests and watersheds of the Adirondacks. Unfortunately it is difficult to obtain any hard data on the extent or the severity of the problem. One study of the Adirondacks (Diebold 1941) indicated that the average depth of the forest floor in the spruce–fir forest type was 2 inches in burned areas as opposed to 14 inches in unburned areas. Approximately 30 000 acres (12 000 ha) or approximately one-tenth of the area above the 2500 foot contour in the park were categorized as having nearly all of the humus layer destroyed with moderate to severe erosion of the remaining mineral soil. Bare mineral soil undoubtedly favored the establishment of the paper birch stands so common throughout the High Peaks region of the Adirondacks today. The bare, rocky terrain that characterizes many of northern New England's subalpine summits, e.g., Mt Chocoura, Mt Monadnock, and Mt Cardigan in New Hampshire, and Cadillac Mountain in Maine, has also been attributed to postsettlement fires (Fobes 1948, 1953; Baldwin 1977). Although the creation of at least one of these bare summits has been documented historically (Bormann and Likens 1979, 188–189), it would be hazardous to associate all of the open summits with fire. The earliest available descriptions of many of these sites suggests that they have always had open expanses of rock (Whitney and Moeller 1982).

Timber famine

As noted earlier in the chapter, conservationists expressed several major concerns about the wholesale destruction of the forest. We now discuss the validity of their third major point, (3) the destruction of the old-growth forest precipitated a timber famine. The depletion of the old-growth timber resources of the Northeast and the Midwest fostered a concern for an approaching timber famine. Many individuals feared that the country's huge wood reservoir was almost empty (Starr 1865). From C. S. Sargent's first report on the forests of the United States in 1884 to the numerous Forest Service studies of the 1920s and 1930s, figures were produced showing the approaching exhaustion of America's timber (Dietz 1947). The liquidation of America's virgin forests was of special concern to the US Forest Service. Virgin forests were the major source of America's timber and they were being mined at an alarming rate (Greeley *et al.* 1923; Greeley 1925). US Forest Service personnel like Chief Forester William B. Greeley 'stoked the fires of concern about depletion' by compiling maps (Fig. 8.1) showing the disappearance of America's virgin forests (Williams 1984). Many individuals forecast a dramatic rise in the price of lumber and associated forest products. The prosperity of the nation was at stake (Pinchot 1919).

Fortunately, the predicted timber famine never materialized. A variety of factors stayed the onslaught of the timber famine. Competition forced the adoption of more efficient techniques of harvesting the wood's resources (Fries 1951, 34–35). Cutting close to the ground and the use of band saws insured that more of the tree was converted into lumber. The use of smaller, less desirable species prolonged the nation's supply of timber (Dietz 1947).

Many of the early estimates of the nation's wood supply were also misleading because they treated timber as a finite resource. Old-growth forests certainly could be depleted or destroyed by fire and cutting. Given appropriate protection or growing conditions, however, forests can also regenerate. They represent a renewable resource. The growth rate or the net annual addition of wood of a young regenerating forest, in fact, is often greater than that of a mature, old-growth forest (Smith 1986, 38–39). The US Forest Service's early estimates of the annual growth of the nation's wood supply appear to have been low due to the crude methods employed and an inability to foresee the productive potential of the regenerating forests (Clawson 1979; Williams 1984).

The exploitation of new, untapped sources of timber also provided a much needed reprieve. As the timber supply of the Northeast and the Midwest approached exhaustion, the lumber industry shifted its base of operations to the South and the Pacific Northwest (Greeley 1925; Reynolds and Pierson 1925). Even the depletion of the old-growth timber in these areas, however, never really initiated a timber famine. By the 1920s, brick, stone, iron, cement, and steel had replaced wood throughout much of the building industry (Sharp 1949). The effect of the increasing use of wood substitutes can be seen in the steady decrease in the per capita consumption of lumber after 1906 (Fig. 8.8). The wooden era of the nineteenth century had given way to the iron, brick, and cement era of the twentieth century (Hotchkiss 1898).

More efficient ways of utilizing the wood's resources, an unanticipated rise in the productive capacity of America's second-growth forests, and the development of effective substitutes for lumber averted the wholesale dislocation of the economic system. The real price of lumber rose steadily throughout most of the nineteenth and the twentieth centuries (Clawson 1979). It would be hazardous to suggest, however, that the passing of the old growth created anything resembling an economic crisis.

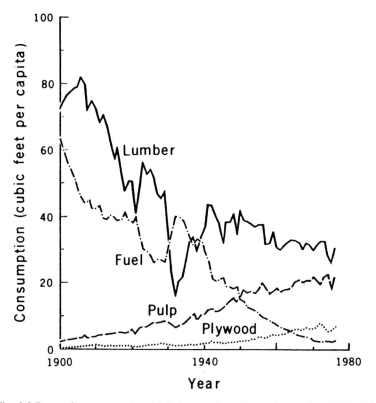

Fig. 8.8 Per capita consumption of timber products, by major product, United States, 1900 to 1976. Reprinted from Clawson, M. (1979), Forests in the long sweep of American history, *Science* 204: 1168–1174, by permission of the American Association for the Advancement of Science. Copyright 1981 by the AAAS.

9

Assault upon the forest. Part III. Fuelwood

Here is good living for those that love good fires.
Francis Higgeson. [1630] 1806. 'New England's Plantation.'

Firewood

In an era where fossil fuels supply most of life's necessities, it is easy to overlook the fact that America once operated on a wood-based energy economy
(Fig. 9.1). Wood was an indispensable fact of life. It supplied heat for homes,
energy for industries, and fuel for much of the transportation system. North
America's temperate climate necessitated the use of fires for seven months of
the year (Franklin [1744] 1960). Fortunately, as the early New England divine,
Francis Higgeson ([1630] 1806) noted, North America's forests also provided
a 'good living for those that love good fires ... here we have plenty of fire to
warme us, and that a great deal cheaper than they sel billets and faggots in
London: Nay, all Europe is not able to afford to make so great fires as New-
England.' Many of the early colonial fireplaces were extremely large – up to
ten feet wide and four feet deep (Fletcher 1950, 380). The profligate use of
large, 6 to 7 foot long, logs in the fireplace was disgusting to the wood-conscious European visitors (More 1961; Niemcewicz 1965, 250). Large fireplaces saved on the cutting and splitting of logs (Webster 1817), but were very
inefficient in the conversion of wood to useful heat energy. Estimates of the
amount of wood used in the eighteenth century vary widely, ranging from 20
to 60 cords per family, a cord of wood being a stack of wood 4 feet by 8 feet by
4 feet (Webster 1817; Carroll 1970, 401; Youngquist and Fleischer 1977, 20).
Most estimates, however, indicate a fairly extravagant consumption of wood
by today's standards. New England's ministers were commonly allotted 30 to
60 cords of wood a year (Temple [1889] 1905, 21; Judd 1905, 99). The historian Sylvester Judd (1905, 100) noted that Hadley, Massachusetts, consumed

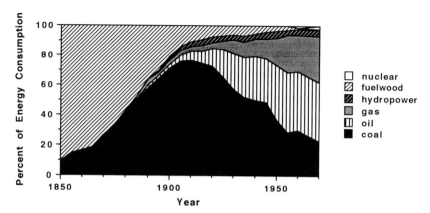

Fig. 9.1 Energy sources in the United States as percentages of total energy consumption, 1850–1970. Based on data in Schurr and Netschert (1960, 36–39) and McMullan, Morgan, and Murray (1976, 3).

3000 cords of wood or 30 cords per family in 1765. The smaller and more efficient fireplaces of the early nineteenth century brought the consumption down to a more manageable 10 to 20 cords per family (Pease and Niles 1819, 97; Madison 1833; Carroll 1970, 401). Converted into an area basis, every fireplace required the maintenance of 10 to 20 acres of woods (Deane 1797, 125; Rose 1821; Drown and Drown 1824, 253; Quercus 1833). This is in line with the fact that an acre of wood typically produces about 0.5 to 1.0 cord of wood a year (Beattie, Thompson, and Levine 1983, 41). The average farmer spent a good share of the winter (30 to 50 days) cutting, hauling, and splitting firewood for personal use and sale in nearby urban areas (Gates 1972; Smith 1988).

On a national basis, the consumption of fuelwood was impressive. As Timothy Dwight ([1821] 1969, 1:75) noted 'An Englishman who sees the various fires of his own country sustained by peat and coal only, can not easily form a conception of the quantity of wood, or, if you please, of forest, which is necessary for this purpose.' Peter Kalm ([1772] 1972, 229) likewise, in the mid-eighteenth century expressed concern about the fate of America's forests given the fact that wood was 'really squandered away in immense quantities day and night all the winter ... for fuel.' For over 200 years, fuelwood represented 'the most extensive and important use' (Emerson 1846, 14) of America's forests. Until 1890, considerably more wood went into fireplaces and stoves than the construction of houses (compare fuel and lumber categories in Fig. 9.2; Reynolds and Pierson 1942).

Tree species which were readily available and had a high fuel value made up the bulk of the fuelwood (Hoglund 1983, 182). Fuel value is directly related

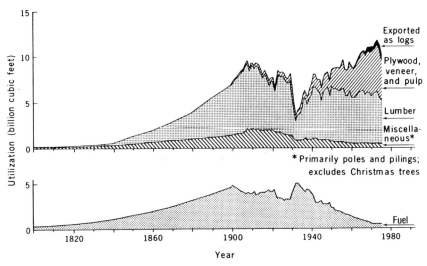

Fig. 9.2 Total utilization of United States-grown woods (in roundwood equivalent) by major form of use, 1800 to 1975. Reprinted from Clawson, M. (1979), Forests in the long sweep of American history, *Science* 204: 1168–1174, by permission of the American Association for the Advancement of Science. Copyright 1981 by the AAAS.

to the specific gravity or the density of the wood. As a general rule of thumb, a dry cord of the heavier hardwoods weighs about 2 tons and produces about as much heat as a ton of anthracite coal (Reynolds and Pierson 1942). The denser, generally slow-growing hardwoods, e.g., hickory, white oak, sugar maple, beech, red oak, and birch, yielded the most heat (Table 9.1). Hickory outdistanced the other species in terms of its fuel value and commanded the highest price on the fuelwood market (Kalm [1772] 1972, 54; Brissot de Warville [1788] 1964, 143; Michaux 1819, 1:266–267). Ease of splitting and the water content of the wood also affected the species' value. Elm and black oak, for instance, dried very imperfectly and burned poorly when placed on the fireplace. Conifers were generally avoided because of the large amount of soot and smoke they produced (Reynolds and Pierson 1942).

Woodlots generally occupied the marginal agricultural areas, i.e., poorly drained sites or the areas that were too steep or too rough and stony for cultivation (Pease and Niles 1819, 121; Schmidt 1945, 73; Marks and Smith 1989). By default, they were often managed haphazardly as a renewable resource with a long and unpredictable rotation period. Fortunately regeneration from sprouts and the formation of coppicewoods was particularly pronounced in the oak and chestnut woodlands of southern New England and the Mid-Atlantic states. As the observant Timothy Dwight ([1821] 1969, 1:75) noted, 'All these

Table 9.1. *Comparative heat values (in millions of BTUs per air-dry cord)
and ease of splitting of various species of American woods*

Species	BTU per cord	Ease of splitting
Shagbark hickory	24.6	medium
White oak	22.7	hard
Beech	21.8	hard
Sugar maple	21.3	medium
Red oak	21.3	hard
Yellow birch	21.3	medium
White ash	20.0	easy
Red maple	18.6	medium
Pitch pine	18.5	easy
Black cherry	18.5	medium
American elm	17.2	hard
Chestnut	15.6	easy
Hemlock	15.0	easy
White pine	13.3	easy
Basswood	12.6	easy
Bigtooth aspen	12.5	easy

Sources: USDA Office of Forest Investigations (1919); Panshin *et al.* (1962); Moss (1973); Beattie, Thompson, and Levine (1983).

forests renew themselves ... When a field of wood is, in the language of our farmers, cut clean, i.e., when every tree is cut down, so far as any progress is made, vigorous shoots sprout from every stump; and, having their nourishment supplied by the roots of the former tree, grow with a thrift and rapidity never seen in stems derived from the seed. Good grounds will thus yield a growth amply sufficient for fuel once in fourteen years.'

Due to the rising scarcity of fuelwood early in the nineteenth century, farmers and agricultural writers became increasingly preoccupied with the appropriate care and management of the woodlot – the length of the rotation period and the best means of securing regeneration (Welles 1823; Drown and Drown 1824, 253; Griffith 1824). Responses from a questionnaire distributed by Emerson (1846, 24–28) in Massachusetts in 1838 indicate that most woods renewed themselves in 24 years. The more rapidly growing gray birch could profitably be cut at 10 to 20 years, maple, ash, and birch at 20 to 25 years, and oak at 20 to 33 years. Most writers agreed, however, that pasturing was the greatest threat to regeneration and that cattle should be kept out of recently cut woods (Deane 1797, 125; Welles 1823; Drown and Drown 1824, 253).

America's urban areas were particularly susceptible to an imbalance in the fuelwood supply–demand system. On the East Coast, deforestation and a

reduction of the local wood supply often accompanied an expanding population and a demand for more wood (Dickinson 1813, 7). The 'common scarcitie
of woode and tymber' was a complaint which followed the Puritans across the
Atlantic. The first governor of Massachusetts, John Winthrop, noted that
Boston was 'almost readye to breake up for want of wood' during the winter of
1637–38 (Rutman 1965, 6, 35). The problem was not a general lack of wood,
but rather a lack of economically accessible wood in the more densely populated areas. Transportation costs for a rather bulky article like wood were often
exorbitant (Quercus 1833). Johann David Schoepf ([1788] 1968, 1:38), a
German doctor and forester, summarized the situation succinctly, 'So far there
is indeed no lack of wood, except in particular localities or for particular purposes. Only in towns is the price high, and for the reason that the charge for
cutting and hauling is four or five times the value of the wood on the stump.' In
1806 wood cost $1.25 a cord inland in Maine, $2.50 a cord on the coast, and
$6 to $8 a cord when transported to Boston (Michaux 1819, 1:266). By the
early nineteenth century, fuelwood was scarce in the more populated areas of
the East Coast (Dickinson 1813, 7; Lowell 1819; Gray 1831), the long-inhab-
ited and deforested islands of Nantucket and Martha's Vineyard
(Massachusetts Historical Society 1815a, 1815b) and the earliest settled
regions of the Midwest (Hamilton County Agricultural Society 1830, x).

The fragmentary information available suggests that the amount of wood consumed in urban areas was in the tens of thousands of cords (Table 9.2). By
assuming a yield of 20 cords per acre for a 20 to 40 year old stand of coppice
hardwoods and 40 cords per acre for an old-growth stand of hardwoods (Winer
1955, 155), one can convert the consumption to an area basis. Philadelphia's
consumption of 140 000 cords in 1826–27, for instance, represented the accumulated increment and the harvest of approximately 11 square miles of woods.

Readily accessible wood constituted the city's 'fuelshed' or 'woodshed'
(Fig. 9.3). The high cost of transporting wood overland meant that the fuelshed
was generally limited to a circle about the city center with a radius of 5 to 20
miles (Dwight 1811, 16; Pease and Niles 1819, 121; Carroll 1970, 454).
Larger towns located on rivers or the coast had access to considerably larger
supplies of fuelwood and generally imported the vast majority of their wood
by water. Eighty-three percent of Boston's wood in 1825, for instance, came
from Maine (Russell 1976, 384), while New York City exploited the Long
Island Sound region (Field [1819] 1892, 75; Albion 1939, 124–125), the
Palisades area along the Hudson River (Collins 1956, 22), and New Jersey
(Muntz 1959, 131). Philadelphia's fuelshed included the upper reaches of the
Schuylkill and the Delaware Rivers and southern New Jersey (Muntz 1959,
131; Lemon [1972] 1976, 199). Michael Williams' (1980) analysis of cord-

Table 9.2. *Consumption of fuelwood in selected urban areas in the seventeenth, eighteenth and early nineteenth centuries*

City (date)	Amount consumed (no. cords)	Sources
Boston (1638)	20 000–30 000	Carroll 1970, 421
Boston[a] (1825)	120 000	Cole 1970
New Haven (1806)	7 500	Dwight 1811, 16
New York City (1761)	20 000	Bridenbaugh 1968, 233
Philadelphia (1815)	210 000	Powell 1978, 60
Philadelphia (1826–1827)	140 150	Schurr and Netschert, 1960, 50–51

[a] Includes Charlestown and Cambridge.

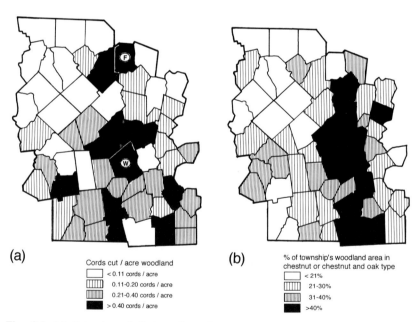

(a)

Cords cut / acre woodland
☐ < 0.11 cords / acre
▦ 0.11-0.20 cords / acre
▨ 0.21-0.40 cords / acre
■ > 0.40 cords / acre

(b)

% of township's woodland area in chestnut or chestnut and oak type
☐ < 21%
▦ 21-30%
▨ 31-40%
■ >40%

Fig. 9.3 (a) Intensity of fuelwood cutting by township in Worcester County, Massachusetts, in 1885 and (b) prevalence of chestnut or chestnut and oak forest types in 1916. Letters indicate locations of major urban areas: W = Worcester, F = Fitchburg. Information from Wright (1887) and Cook (1917).

wood sales reported in the 1840 census of the United States reveals the massive size of some of the urban fuelsheds of the East Coast.

In spite of the large size of many fuelsheds and the ease of transporting fuel by water, urban areas generally witnessed a rise in the price of wood late in the eighteenth century and early in the nineteenth century. From 1780 to 1806, the price of fuelwood doubled, reaching a high of $40 per cord on one occasion in New York City (Michaux 1819, 1:265). Both Kalm (Dahllöf 1966) and Michaux (1819, 1:269) noted that firewood was as expensive in America's cities as it was in Europe's urban areas. The value of woodlots within the fuelshed appreciated considerably (Bradbury 1817, 325; Holditch 1818, 46; Collins [1830] 1971, 93) and rich urbanites purchased woods or sprout lots in the outlying countryside (Collins 1956, 23). Paradoxically, the land of the wood rich had become the land of the wood poor. Michaux (1819, 1:269) implied that much of the difficulty could be traced to the poor preservation and management of America's woods.

In light of the above figures, it is not surprising that many notables like Noah Webster (1817) felt that America had to alter her energy policy. His review of the fuelwood crisis highlighted two solutions to the problem: 'We must either reduce the annual consumption within the limits of the annual growth, or that time will arrive when we must search the earth for fuel...' The short-term answer lay in energy conservation or the more efficient utilization of existing supplies of wood. As much as nine-tenths of the heat generated in large colonial fireplaces escaped up the chimney (Reynolds and Pierson 1942; Muntz 1959, 98; US Department of Energy 1980). The introduction of cast-iron stoves initiated a new era of energy efficiency and fuelwood conservation. Because iron stoves reradiated much of their heat to the surrounding room (Shelton and Shapiro 1976, 45), they generated the same amount of heat as a fireplace on one-quarter to one-fifth of the fuel (Bull 1830; Fletcher 1950, 388; US Department of Energy 1980). Although Benjamin Franklin invented the fuel-efficient Franklin stove or fireplace in 1742 (Franklin [1744] 1960), technical difficulties, the expense of the stove, and the cost of chopping up the fuel prohibited its widespread adoption until the 1820s (Anonymous 1867). By the 1840s fireplaces were considered old-fashioned (Hoglund 1962).

The introduction of a substitute fuel provided another solution to the fuelwood problem. Anthracite, the major source of coal available east of the Appalachians, had a number of advantages. It contained more energy on both a weight and a bulk basis than wood. It lasted a long time. Coal fires burned free of smoke and required relatively little attention (Silliman 1826; Schurr and Netschert 1960, 51). Its adoption, however, awaited the construction of an extensive canal system linking the anthracite deposits of northeastern

Pennsylvania with the Atlantic seaboard (Powell 1978, 3). Coal interests created the canals and canals made the coal competitive in the fuel market (Blackmer 1982). By 1830 and 1840 coal-burning stoves had made serious inroads into the space-heating (fuel-burning) market in New York City and Philadelphia (Hoglund 1962). In rural areas, the substitution of coal for wood was a more gradual process. Sargent's (1884) map in the Tenth Census showing the type of fuel used across the United States indicates that wood was still the dominant fuel in northern New England, most of upstate New York, and all of the Midwest outside of eastern Ohio, northern Illinois, and parts of Iowa.

The increasing use of coal and the shift from fireplaces to stoves had a demonstrable impact on the fuelwood situation. Although it is difficult to obtain hard data, reliable estimates suggest a significant decrease in the per capita consumption of fuelwood throughout the nineteenth century (Reynolds and Pierson 1942). The 30+ cords of wood used per house in southern New England during the colonial period had declined to 13 to 14 cords by 1846 (Emerson 1846, 15) and was down to less than 7 cords in many towns by 1888 (Blake 1888, 77). For a limited period of time, population growth offset the decline in per capita consumption. Total fuelwood consumption across the Northeast and the Midwest peaked at about 90 million cords per year in the 1870s and declined gradually thereafter (Reynolds and Pierson 1942). Although coal displaced wood as the major source of fuel in the 1880s (Fig. 9.1), over 45 million cords of wood were still consumed per year as late as 1910 to 1919 (Reynolds and Pierson 1942).

Wood in the transportation and iron industries

Wood also figured prominently in the early stages of the transportation revolution of the nineteenth century. Robert Fulton pioneered the use of the steamboat in 1807. By 1820 steamboats were plying the Mississippi River, the Great Lakes, and the East Coast. Wood was one of the cheaper and the more abundant fuels during the early days of the steamboat industry. At midcentury the larger steamboats consumed 50 to 75 cords a day (Hunter [1949] 1969, 266) or 529 cords for the 2700 mile roundtrip journey between Louisville and New Orleans (Schob 1977). Railroads arrived on the scene in 1826 (Fletcher 1950, 268). The large consumption of wood necessitated frequent stops for refueling (Hunter [1949] 1969, 264). Locomotives were somewhat more conservative than steamboats in their use of fuel. One report on railroads published in 1850 (Slade 1850, 22) indicated that 3 cords of wood were required for a trip of 74 miles. Farmers located along railroad lines and wood hawks on the banks of major rivers found that they possessed a new 'cash' crop in the form of cordwood (Hunter [1949] 1969, 265; Fletcher 1950, 270; Schob 1977). One Midwesterner estimated that a farmer situated along the Mississippi River or the Ohio River could clear $250 per acre by cutting, hauling, and selling wood to steamboats (Hall 1837, 144–145).

Estimates of the total amount of wood devoured by wood-burning locomotives and steamboats are rather crude. Sargent's 1884 *Report on the Forests of North America* provides the first really reliable breakdown on the use of fuelwood for various purposes across the United States (Table 9.3). Railroads and steamboats together accounted for nearly three million cords of wood, less than 2% of all the fuelwood consumed in 1879. Even at the peak of their fuelwood consumption period around 1860, railroads and steamboats combined probably used less than nine million cords a year or approximately 5 to 7% of the wood consumed in 1860 (Schurr and Netschert 1960, 52). Due to the large amount of heat it produced on either a volume or a weight basis, coal was an attractive alternative to wood. As production increased and prices declined, coal increasingly dominated the fuel market. By 1880 it was the dominant fuel on both steamboats and railroads throughout the Northeast and the Midwest (Hunter [1949] 1969, 267–269; White 1981).

The forest, for the most part, was relatively immune to the effects of the emerging transportation systems of the nineteenth century. When fuel wood demands were confined to certain species or areas, however, the impact could be substantial. Prior to the shift to anthracite in the 1840s, easily ignited pitch pine was the preferred fuel of steamboats along the East Coast (Silliman 1831; Muntz 1959, 101). In the 1820s and 1830s the increasing demand for pitch pine pushed up the value of southern New Jersey's pinelands to all time highs (Anonymous 1829; Gordon 1834, 2). Many writers expressed concern about the ultimate fate of the cutover pinelands and the apparent shift from pine to oak (Anonymous 1829; Silliman 1831).

Steamboats navigating the Great Lakes often concentrated their refueling activities on islands with good harbors, while steamboats on rivers drew most of their fuelwood from the land adjacent to the river. As a result, large segments of land along the Mississippi and Ohio Rivers (Williams 1980) and islands like South Manitou Island in Lake Michigan and South Bass Island in Lake Erie were deforested or heavily cutover at a very early date (Hudgins 1943; Vent 1973, 32, 41). Paradoxically, the biggest effect of introducing wood-burning locomotives into the eastern United States was an outcome few would have anticipated. Wood-burning locomotives with their 'storm of fiery snow' (White 1981), soon became a major cause of fires in America's woods (Sargent 1884, 489). As one historian (White 1981) expressed it, railroads may have burned 'more wood outside than inside the locomotive's firebox.'

Table 9.3. *Wood used as fuel for various purposes in 1879*

Use	Thousands of cords	Percentage of total fuelwood use
Domestic use[a] (heating, etc.)	140 655	95.2
Transportation (railroads)	1 972	1.3
Steamboats	788	0.5
Mining and production of metals[a]	628	0.4
Manufacture of iron[a]	1 901	1.3
Manufacture of brick and tile	1 158	0.8
Manufacture of salt	540	0.4
Manufacture of wood	158	0.1
Totals	147 800	100.0

[a] Includes wood used in the production of charcoal, with a conversion factor of 36.6 bushels charcoal per cord wood (Hough 1882).
Source: Sargent (1884, 489).

Due to its universal nature and its abundance, wood also figured prominently in the development of a number of important industries in the eighteenth and nineteenth centuries (Williams 1989, 146). It was utilized extensively (Table 9.3) in the manufacture of such disparate items as iron, salt, glass, lime, and bricks (Kalm [1772] 1972, 54; Schoepf [1788] 1968, 2:2; Campbell [1793] 1937, 212–213; Winer 1955, 153; Coolidge 1963, 432; Russell 1976, 384). Iron production was once one of America's largest industries and, as such, it deserves a more detailed discussion of its relation to America's forests. Iron oxides such as magnetite, hematite, and limonite (bog ore) were widely distributed in metasedimentary and igneous rocks and swamps and low-lying areas throughout the Northeast and the Midwest. Iron production involved the reduction of the iron oxide to an alloy of iron and carbon better known as pig iron. Blast furnaces supplied the high temperatures necessary for the conversion process. At temperatures of 2600 to 3000°F (1425 to 1650°C) the oxygen in the iron oxide combined with carbon monoxide from a carbon source to produce pig iron and carbon dioxide. Much of the excess carbon was removed from the pig iron in a forge to produce a more malleable form of iron known as bar iron. Charcoal was the ideal fuel or carbon source. It produced the intense heat required to melt the ore and it represented an almost pure, i.e., sulfur and phosphorus free, source of carbon (Lewis 1983).

Charcoal had one major drawback as a fuel. Its production required a significant amount of labor, skill, and time. Coaling wood in large earthen kilns or meilers in a low-oxygen environment removed the more volatile elements, i.e., water and various gases, from the wood, leaving a carbon-enriched residue (Hicock 1974). The 100 to 400 bushels of charcoal required per ton of pig iron (Table 9.4) kept a veritable army of woodcutters, colliers, and teamsters occupied in the woods. They often represented well over 50% of the workers on the large iron operation or 'plantation' of the eighteenth and nineteenth centuries (Walker 1966, 238).

America's 'infinite store of wood' attracted the attention of a number of European entrepreneurs at a very early date (Hariot [1588] 1903; Penn [1685] 1912). The English arboriculturist John Evelyn ([1664] 1729, 251) even recommended moving England's iron mills to New England, where they could proceed to devour the New World's woods. As Evelyn noted, 'Twere better to purchase all our Iron out of America, than thus to exhaust our woods at home ...' The late eighteenth century shift to a cheaper fuel, i.e., coke made from bituminous coal, spared England's woods and led to a dramatic expansion of the English iron industry. By 1806 only 11 out of a total of 173 pig iron furnaces in England were still using charcoal (Temin 1964, 14–15; Hammersley 1973). Americans were much slower to abandon the use of charcoal as a blast furnace fuel (Williams 1989, 338). As late as 1847, three-quarters of all the pig iron produced in the United States was still made with charcoal (Temin 1964, 20) and in the Upper Great Lakes region the charcoal iron industry continued down to the twentieth century (Hatcher 1950, 202–207). Although the long term persistence of the charcoal iron industry in the United States has often been tied to the sheer abundance of wood (Bining [1938] 1979, 61), a number of more complex factors contributed to its longevity.

To a large degree, the early iron industry was dependent on its geography. Due to the primitive nature of the transportation network, anthracite was the only coal available east of the Allegheny Mountains in the eighteenth and early nineteenth centuries. The use of anthracite awaited the introduction of the hot blast furnace in the 1820s and the 1830s (Temin 1964, 58–61). Bituminous or soft coal was the dominant coal west of the Allegheny Mountains. The difficulty of discovering soft coal deposits suitable for smelting, however, inhibited the adoption of a coal or coke-based technology west of the Alleghenys (Bining [1938] 1979, 61; Temin 1964, 76–77).

Charcoal pig iron also held its own against the cheaper coal or coke-based pig iron due to its superior quality. Impurities, e.g., sulfur, and phosphorus, and a higher silicon content made the coke iron weaker, harder to work with, and less likely to keep a fine cutting edge than the charcoal iron (Schallenberg

Table 9.4. *Wood use, output, and efficiency of charcoal iron operations*

Year	Name, location	Furnace type (cold or hot blast)	Output iron (tons per year)	Efficiency (bushels (bu) charcoal or cords wood required per ton pig iron)	Acres cut per year	Size of operation (acres)	Sources
1650	Saugus, Mass.	cold	144	265 bu			Hartley 1957, 163, 174
1773	Hasenclever Works, Ringwood, N.J.	cold	700	288 bu			Hasenclever 1773, 67, 81
1783	Udree Furnace, Reading, Pa.	cold	200–300	400 bu (11 cords)	1 acre per day	10000	Schoepf [1788] 1968, 1: 198
1783	Warwick, Hopewell, and Cornwall Furnaces, Pa.	cold	900 each	233 bu	240[a]	1800[a]–9700[b]	Hermelin 1931, 48, 59–60, 72; Bining [1938] 1979, 21, 61, 63–68
1837–1849	Hopewell Furnace, Pa.	cold	1000	4.7 cords		3900–8000	Walker 1966, 63, 121, 140
1850–1870	Buena Vista, Conn.	cold?		250 bu	300–600		Winer 1955, 154–155
1869	Pine Grove Furnace, Ohio	hot	3102	131 bu (3.56 cords)	300		Lord 1884
1869	Pioneer Furnace, Mich.	?	9500	5.5 cords	1500		Hatcher 1950, 192
1900	Gladstone U.P. Mich.	hot?	48000		1200–1600		Schallenberg 1981

1903	Average for U.P. Mich. furnaces	hot	20000+	100 bu (2.25 cord)	1000	Mather 1903; Schallenberg and Ault 1977
1919	Large New England and New York furnaces	?	5000–8000	126–140 bu		Brown 1919, 245

Averages for various periods

1750–1800	100–400	200–400 bu	50	
1850	725–1000	150–250 bu	150	
1900	20000	80–100 bu	1200–1600	

[a] Warwick Furnace.
[b] Hopewell and Cornwall Furnaces.
Sources for averages: Mather (1903); Schallenberg and Ault (1977); Schallenberg (1981) and main table above.

1975, 1981; Williams 1989, 148). Up until the 1890s, large quantities of high-grade charcoal iron went into a number of specialty items like railroad car wheels and axles. The development of high-quality open-hearth steel eventually eliminated the demand for charcoal iron (Schallenberg 1975). The charcoal iron industry made its last stand in the Upper Great Lakes region. Large quantities of rich, low-priced iron ore in Michigan's Upper Peninsula permitted the development of a massive charcoal iron industry which utilized fuelwood more efficiently. The adoption of charcoal kilns and retorts increased the yield of charcoal per cord of wood (Table 9.4), while the use of larger blast furnaces reduced the amount of charcoal required per ton of iron (Schallenberg and Ault 1977). Labor associated with the production of charcoal was always an expensive item in the charcoal iron industry (Walker 1966, 62–63; Williams 1989, 149–150). Cutting the amount of wood and charcoal required kept the charcoal iron industry competitive with the coke iron industry.

Concern about the charcoal iron industry's exploitation of the woods was as unwarranted in the United States in the nineteenth century as it was in England in the seventeenth century. Reynolds and Pierson (1942) estimated that charcoal represented less than 1% of all the fuelwood burned from 1800 to 1930. Certainly Sargent's 1879 figures (Table 9.3) suggest that, even at its peak, the charcoal iron industry accounted for a relatively small percentage of the fuelwood consumed across the United States.

Locally the impact of the iron industry was a different matter. Blast furnaces consumed large quantities of fuel. Approximately 100 acres (40 ha) of woods had to be cutover each year to keep the typical blast furnace of the eighteenth century in operation. By the late nineteenth century large firms like the Chateaugay Ore and Iron Company and the J. and J. Rodgers Iron Company in northern New York were cutting 1000 to 2000 acres (400 to 800 ha) annually from their 80 000 to 100 000 acre (32 000 to 40 000 ha) holdings (New York Forest Commission 1886, 34). Similar sized cuts characterized the larger blast furnaces of Michigan's Upper Peninsula in 1900 (Table 9.4). The poorer cutover land reverted to forests and was managed under a coppice system. Regeneration could take anywhere from 15 to 50 years depending upon the species involved and the quality of the site (Hough 1882, 60–68). Assuming an average regeneration period of 25 years (Hough 1882, 60–68; Hermelin 1931, 47; Stout 1933) and multiplying this value by the area harvested annually (Table 9.4), one can determine the total amount of land required for the sustained operation of an iron plantation. The 2500 acre estimate for the eighteenth century is close to the reported size of many colonial iron plantations (Bining [1938] 1979, 20–21). Figure 9.4 provides an idea of the scale and the magnitude of iron plantation operations in the famed Hanging Rock iron

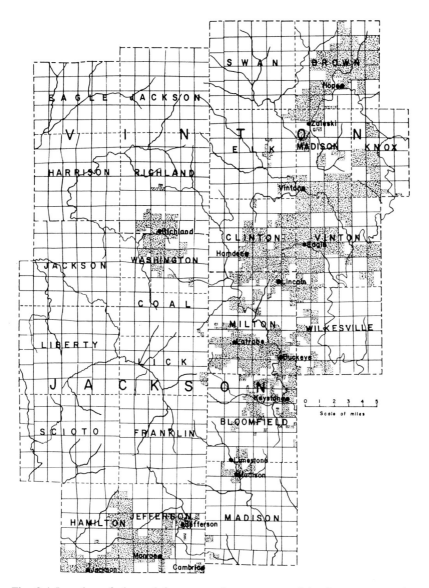

Fig. 9.4 Location of charcoal furnaces and acreage owned by furnace companies (shaded areas) around 1875, Vinton and Jackson Counties, Ohio. Reprinted from Beatley (1959), courtesy of the Ohio Biological Survey.

region of southern Ohio in the nineteenth century. Charcoal iron operations reached their peak in the late nineteenth century when firms like the Cleveland Cliffs Iron Company acquired 750 000 acres (300 000 ha) in Michigan (Hatcher 1950, 219). Large blast furnaces (Table 9.4) converted the Upper Peninsula into a woodlot for the efficient conversion of charcoal and iron ore into iron (Schallenberg 1975).

On the better land where farming accompanied the charcoal iron industry, the cutover land was often converted to pasture and tillage (Schoepf [1788] 1968, 1:37; Beatley 1959, 56). Cattle and charcoal cutting represented a lethal combination for coppice management. Grazing by cattle inhibited the growth of new sprouts and seedlings in the Hanging Rock region of Ohio and contributed to some of the highest rates of deforestation known in the state. Jackson and Lawrence Counties, for instance, lost an average of 2.1% of their woodland area each year from 1853 to 1880, a value well in excess of the 1.3% rate for the state as a whole (Leue 1886, 16, 171–172, 200–201). Fortunately, much of the land utilized by the charcoal iron industry was marginal from an agricultural standpoint. One crude estimate suggested that approximately 10 000 acres (4000 ha) or 25% of the land cutover for charcoal throughout the United States in 1879 was permanently converted to agricultural land (US Association of Charcoal Iron Workers 1880).

A decrease in the amount of wood available locally figured prominently in the demise of many a blast furnace (Schoepf [1788] 1968, 1:36–37; Keeler 1933; Walker 1966, 135). The cost of hauling a bulky item like charcoal over rugged terrain was a significant factor in the success or the failure of any furnace (Hermelin 1931, 48–49; Keeler 1933; Walker 1966, 238–239; Kury 1974). Until 1870 most of the charcoal was produced within 2 to 5 miles of the furnace (Temin 1964, 83). For much of the nineteenth century hauling costs for greater distances were simply prohibitive (Keeler 1933). It was not a shortage of charcoal per se but a shortage of economically accessible charcoal which forced the closure of many iron operations.

Impact of coppicing on woodlands

Frequent cutting for fuelwood kept many of the woods along the densely populated eastern seaboard in an immature state. Timothy Dwight ([1821] 1969, 1:74) noted that by the start of the nineteenth century 'almost all the original forests of [southern New England had] long since been cut down.' Most had been felled repeatedly and were composed of small trees (Dwight [1821] 1969, 1:74–75). Even as late as 1885, when coppicing was on the decline, over 70% of Massachusetts' forests were of 30 years' growth or less (Wright 1887, 759).

It is difficult to determine the impact of past harvesting practices on the composition of the forest. Although coppicing was often employed in the past to generate fuel for the charcoal iron industry and for domestic heating, coppicing is rarely practiced today. We have no modern analogues. The historical literature, however, contains a number of anecdotal comments on the effects of coppicing. Coppicing was formerly considered a valuable silvicultural tool and was widely discussed in the early forestry literature of the twentieth century.

There is a strong consensus in the literature that repeated cutting at short intervals favored the sprouters (Frothingham 1912; Nichols 1913; Bromley 1935; Winer 1955; Smith 1976). This was particularly true of the heavily cutover 'sprout hardwood' region of southern New England, the southern Hudson River Valley, and northern New Jersey (Graves 1911; Braun [1950] 1967, 251–252). Drawing upon carbohydrate reserves stored in the root system, the sprouts grew rapidly, soon shading out those species which depended upon slow-growing seedlings for their regeneration. Sprouts of chestnut had the highest growth rate, followed by red, black, and white oak respectively (Mattoon 1909; Hawley and Hawes 1912, 60–62; Leffelmen and Hawley 1925). Chestnut was especially interesting in this regard because it was one species that was particularly suited to the coppice system of management (Hawley and Smith 1954). Unlike many species, chestnut also retained its ability to sprout in the larger size-class stems (Spaeth 1928). Many investigators believe that the rapidly growing chestnut increased its representation in the forest after every cutting (Hawes 1909; Frothingham 1912; Hawley and Hawes 1912, 61; Winer 1955, 146, 187–188; Muntz 1959, 17; Wacker 1964). Some (Rothrock 1894b) even declared that chestnut was about the only species which regenerated as fast as it was removed under the intensive wood-utilization practices of the nineteenth century. A moderate amount of historical evidence exists for chestnut's increase in the nineteenth century. In 1800 the Connecticut Academy of Arts and Sciences addressed a questionnaire on the geography, natural history, and industries of Connecticut to all of the towns in the state. One of the questions dealt with the original growth of timber in the town and the change in species composition following cutting (Dwight 1811). A number of the respondents noted an increase in the amount of chestnut in the uplands following cutting (Field [1819] 1892; Nott 1949; Prindle 1961). David Field's ([1819] 1892) report was typical of many: 'The chestnut, smooth-walnut [probably a hickory], and white oak sprout abundantly from the roots, as well as come up from seed, and grow on high and rough grounds, as well as on those which are suitable for tillage. Hence there is a happy increase of these valuable trees over others in the country.'

A comparison of chestnut's status in the early colonial survey records and more recent preblight surveys also suggests an increase in chestnut's abundance. Chestnut represented anywhere from 4 to 15% of the trees reported in the few scattered early land survey records of several towns in northwestern Connecticut (Winer 1955). A forest survey of the same area, Litchfield County, in 1908 revealed that chestnut was 'the most important species of the county,' forming about 60% of the mixed hardwood stands of the region (Hawes 1909). Chestnut's increase was attributed to the fact the county had been repeatedly cutover for charcoal and other wood products (Hawes 1909). Chestnut fared well throughout southern New England and the remaining portions of the sprout hardwoods region. Several foresters (Hawes 1906a; Frothingham 1912) reported that chestnut constituted fully one-half of the standing timber of the state of Connecticut at the turn of the century. Chestnut likewise dominated the heavily cutover urban fuelsheds of Worcester County, Massachusetts (Fig. 9.3). Chestnut represented 4 to 15% of the trees reported in the early land survey records of northern New Jersey (Russell 1981). By the early 1900s, however, chestnut was the most abundant species of the uplands of northern New Jersey (Harper 1918b).

Coppicing also had a pronounced effect on the understory layers of the forest. Although the American literature on coppicing is not as voluminous as that in England, e.g., Rackham (1980, 77–82), Peterken (1981a, 52–56), one can still utilize the comments of early naturalists like Henry David Thoreau to reconstruct the response of the ground vegetation to coppicing (Whitney and Davis 1986). In Massachusetts the earliest phases of the coppice cycle, i.e., recently cutover oak woods or land dominated by sprouting oaks, frequently supported a rather transient community of weedy, sun-loving plants. Cinquefoil and blackberry grew from seeds that had lain dormant in the forest floor. Fireweed (*Erechtites hieracifolia* and *Epilobium angustifolium*), goldenrod, and senecio started from seeds blown in from the surrounding countryside. The alternation of light and shade also encouraged the gradual rise and fall of another group of shade intolerant species. Some, like the seedlings of black cherry, flourished for a short time after the woods were cut but were soon shaded out by the rapidly growing sprouts. Other species, notably the blueberries and the huckleberries, maintained a precarious position under the closed forest canopy. Cutting the trees helped such plants to spread and eventually culminated in a dense ground cover of ericaceous shrubs 15 to 30 years after the felling (Whitney and Davis 1986).

10

Predatory agriculture

The American farmer despoils his field without the least attempt at method in the process. When it ceases to yield him sufficiently abundant crops, he simply quits it and, with his seeds and plants, betakes himself to a fresh field... [He is] guilty of the grossest vandalism in the management of [his] land.
Baron Justus von Liebig. 1859. *Letters on Modern Agriculture*, pp. 179, 188.

Waste depends. Apparent extravagance is often real economy.
Jenks Cameron. 1928. *The Development of Governmental Forest Control in the United States*, p. 117.

Critiques of American farming practices

The noted ecologist, Paul Sears (1974), once wrote, 'One cannot have a sound perspective on human history if one ignores the role that soil has played.' The use or, more frequently, the abuse of America's soil is a topic which has fascinated historians and scientists alike. From Sear's ([1935] 1959) *Deserts on the March* to historian Donald Worster's more contemporary (1979) *Dust Bowl: The Southern Plains in the 1930s,* many have censured the American farmer for his misuse of the soil. 'Earth-butchery' (Bogart 1908, 67), 'predatory agriculture' (Bidwell and Falconer [1925] 1941, 84), 'spoilation or skinning system' of agriculture (Gardner 1849; Baron Justus von Liebig 1859, 179), are all terms which have been applied to the farmer's use of the land over the past 200 years. As an 1849 article in the farm journal, the *Ohio Cultivator*, stated, 'There is no portion of the globe that is being exhausted of its fertility by injudicious cultivation, so rapidly as the Mississippi Valley ...' (Bateham 1849). To many observers, the advent of European colonization marked 'the beginning of the era of the most rapid rate of wasteful land use in the history of the world' (McDonald 1941, 1).

England was noted for its progressive agriculture in the eighteenth and early nineteenth centuries. New kinds of crops and livestock and innovative methods of cultivation commanded the respect of the world. The heavy use of manures and convertable or up and down husbandry, e.g., the alternation of grains, grasses, and legumes, maintained the fertility of England's soils and increased the productivity of the cropland. European visitors found the American system of farming inferior to that of England. Their sharpest criticisms were directed against the extensive system of cultivation characteristic of the Northeast prior to the Revolution and the Midwest well into the nineteenth century. In the extensive system of farming, farmers rotated their fields rather than their crops. Grains were frequently cultivated without the benefit of manure. When the crop yield began to decline, the cultivator shifted to new land. The worn-out fields were temporarily abandoned to weeds, brush, and trees. Occasionally the weed and rubbish-filled fields were pastured (Kalm [1772] 1972, 299; Mitchell [1775] 1939, 93). After a lapse of 5 to 15 years, during which the land recovered much of its lost fertility, the land was again brought into production (Kalm [1772] 1972, 99; Mitchell [1775] 1939, 123; Schoepf [1788] 1968, 1:130; Strickland 1801, 38; Bidwell and Falconer [1925] 1941, 86). It is estimated that at any given time as much as a third to a half of the cleared area of the farm was devoted to the long weed or brush-filled fallow (Bidwell and Falconer [1925] 1941, 102; Olson 1935). The extensive system of farming remained an enigma to those familiar with the more progressive farming techniques of England. The American cut down trees on one side of his farm while he suffered bushes to grow up on the other (Johnson 1819, 62).

Criticism centered on the fact the American farmer preferred to cultivate large fields poorly rather than a small area intensively (Drown and Drown 1824, 24–25; Livingston 1832, 338). He bought too much land (Caird 1859, 54). In his attempt to engross and cultivate large quantities of land, the American farmer did little more than scratch the surface of the soil (Carman 1934). He neglected many of the labor-intensive farming practices of the Old World. He failed to adequately manure his land, to care for his cattle, to eradicate his weeds, to utilize root crops as forage, or to alternate legumes and grasses with grains (Warren 1787; Bidwell 1916; Carman 1934). His yields of wheat were roughly a third to a half those of his English counterparts (Cooper 1794, 113–115; Stuart 1833, 265; French 1861; Rutman 1967, 52–53). A 50 acre farm in England produced more grain than a 200 acre farm in North America (Weld [1807] 1968, 1:113). At best, many felt that American farming was a primitive form of agriculture. It was a century behind England's progressive system of farming (Fearon 1819, 223). At worst, America's farmers were 'the greatest slovens in Christendom' (Mitchell [1775] 1939, 106).

Often the critics who advocated more intensive farming practices were well-placed individuals, members of the English nobility or upper squirearchy, who could afford to experiment with new methods of farming. They were not always aware of the problems that the ordinary farmer faced (Garrison 1985, 7). At times, their criticism reflected a bias against America's egalitarian class structure. One English visitor, William Strickland (1801, 52–55), for instance, attributed America's primitive system of farming to the decline of the aristocracy after the Revolution. Agriculture had become the preserve of a mass of uneducated, ignorant farmers (Herndon 1975). Contrary to Strickland's observations, however, Americans were often acquainted with recent developments in the field of agriculture. The learned New England minister and farmer Jared Eliot publicized the use of manures and legumes as early as 1760. George Washington and Thomas Jefferson were honorary members of the progressive English Board of Agriculture and corresponded regularly with its officers, Sir John Sinclair and Arthur Young (Loehr 1937). By the mid-1800s a burgeoning agricultural press kept many farmers informed of the latest agricultural practices (Danhof 1969, 56–59).

American agriculture also had its local critics. Many were gentlemen farmers interested in improving America's major industry, agriculture. They cited the same deficiencies noted by their English counterparts, e.g., insufficient use of manures, lack of crop rotation, poor cultivation, etc. (Bordley 1801; Dwight [1821] 1969, 1:76; French 1861). By buttressing their arguments against America's 'exhausting' system of agriculture with the innovative scientific theories of the day, they added a new dimension to the sustainable agriculture debate of the nineteenth century. The 1854 issue of the *Transactions of the Michigan State Agricultural Society* expressed the dominant theme of America's reformers with these words: '... history teaches that no husbandry can be long prosperous which takes everything from the soil, and gives back nothing in return ... This deterioration has been and still is going on to a rapid and alarming extent ... The produce of the soil has been from year to year diminishing in nearly all parts of this country – slowly in some, rapidly in others ... [and] the once fertile fields of the old states [are] year by year abandoned for the unexhausted soils of the broad west ...' (Hubbard 1855, 332–333).

By the mid-nineteenth century concern over soil exhaustion shifted to the West. The skinning system of agriculture practiced in the Midwest was invariably compared with the more enlightened system of agriculture characteristic of the urban East (Lapham 1833; Buel 1837; Hammond 1849). Newly available state and county crop yield statistics were marshalled to support the reformers' and the fertilizer manufacturers' claims of impending soil exhaustion (Ohio Farmer 1852; Bateham 1855; Hubbard 1855; Baron Justus von Liebig 1859, 180–181). Unfortunately, the use of statistics was fraught with a number of difficulties. The figures on crop yields are poor and scattered before 1880 (Bogue [1963] 1968, 126). Estimates of earlier yields were often inflated (Ohio Farmer 1852) while the declines attributed to soil exhaustion could just as easily have been due to pests, parasites, and climatic anomalies (Bateham 1855; Thorne 1951; Bogue [1963] 1968, 126; LeDuc 1963). Timothy Dwight ([1822] 1969, 3:210–211), for instance, believed that the introduction of the Hessian fly in 1784, not soil exhaustion, was responsible for the dramatic post-Revolutionary decline in the production of wheat in southern New England.

Criticism of America's early farming methods had at least one unforeseen result. The negative appraisals were eventually incorporated into academic folklore and textbooks (Scoville 1953). The early colonial farmers and their lineal descendants in the Midwest became ruthless despoilers whose exhausting system of agriculture impoverished the land. As one agricultural historian noted, 'it was ... corn, corn, corn forty years in succession and then move to the Far West' (Jones 1983, 53). They mined the resources of the land and then moved on to exploit the more fertile soils of the West. Their legacy was a trail of abandoned, worn-out farms, cellar holes and old stonewalls (Stilwell 1937; Jacobs 1978).

Early concepts of soil fertility

Because many reformers believed that America's farming practices culminated in soil exhaustion, it is useful to explore the concept of soil exploitation in an eighteenth and nineteenth century context. Even the scientifically inclined members of society at the time had a very inexact knowledge of soil fertility and soil restoration (Browne 1944; Bardolph 1948). Two prevalent theories of the period were the humus theory and the mineral theory. The humus theory was favored by many of the important agricultural chemists of the early nineteenth century, i.e., the German, Albrecht Thaier, the English chemist, Sir Humphry Davy, and the Dutch chemist, Gerardus Mulder, and formed the basis for the views expressed in Samuel Dana's widely read 1855 'Muck Manual' for farmers (Browne 1944). According to the humus theory, plants were wholly dependent upon humus, the insoluble portion of the vegetable matter of plants, for their nutrients (Rossiter 1975, 13–14). The humus theory was popular because it explained the decline of the soil's productive powers under continual cultivation. Most of the proponents of the humus theory looked back wistfully to the thick, rich vegetable mold of the pre-Columbian period, a vegetable mold 'fattened by the continual fall of leaves from the trees growing thereon' (Hutchinson 1760, 482). Most writers, including many modern historians, have assumed that the humus accumulated over the centuries was responsible for the initial fertility of the soil (Olson 1935). 'Seduced by the fertility of the soil on first settling,' America's farmers proceeded to rapidly exhaust the land (Mitchell [1775] 1939, 93). One realistic observer, however, noted that, 'A great deal has been said about the "vegetable mould of centuries!" – this sounds very imposing but ... it is generally from two to four inches in depth, and its fertility for the first year is wonderful, but after two or three crops its effects will altogether vanish' (Ex-settler 1835). More recent studies have demonstrated that the humus layer of most old-growth forest stands in the Northeast is only 2 to 6 inches deep (Lull 1959). 'The soil is like your woodland in England,' wrote an early Massachusetts Bay colonist, 'best at first, yet ... after five or six years, it grows barren beyond belief ...' (Hutchinson 1760, 482). The effect of the centuries-old leaf mold layer throughout the Northeast was exaggerated and short-lived.

Work by the respected German chemist, Baron Justus von Liebig, in the 1840s stressed the importance of mineral elements as determinants of the soil's fertility (Browne 1944, 262–281; Aulie 1974; Rossiter 1975). The mineral theory favored a quantitative approach to soil chemistry. The earth contained certain inorganic mineral elements which were removed from the soil by crops. According to the mineral theory of fertilizers, soil was the natural repository of mineral elements. It functioned like a storage bin or a bank account. Minerals were withdrawn from the soil in the form of grain or milk and beef sold off the farm. By analyzing the ash content of the soil and the minerals in the ashes of the crops, the farmer could determine the status of the soil's fertility and its ability to supply nutrients to crops. Applications of artificial fertilizers, produced by the agricultural chemists, could correct any deficits in the input and output of nutrients. The mineral theory was popular in the 1840s and the 1850s because it gave a certain scientific legitimacy to many of the concerns expressed by agricultural reformers. Reformers could quantify the flow of produce and mineral nutrients from the countryside to the city (Lee 1850). Liebig believed that continuous cropping without the benefit of fertilizers, represented the irrational and unscientific robbery of the soil. Liebig's theory explained the occurrence of 'exhausted' or 'worn-out' soils in the eastern United States and it fuelled the sale of commercial fertilizers. The use of artificial fertilizers promised to improve the eastern farmer's position relative to the vigorous agricultural competition of the West (Rossiter 1975, xii–xiii).

Although Liebig's mineral theory was widely publicized by commercial fertilizer manufacturers and many agricultural perodicals of the mid-nineteenth century, the agricultural chemistry fad was ultimately discredited (Bardolph 1948, 118–120). Liebig was essentially correct when he noted that plants withdraw mineral nutrients from the soil. However, he neglected a number of other important variables in the soil fertility equation, notably the fixation and the availability of nutrients in the soil, and the importance of nitrogen and the ameliorating influence of legumes and grasses (Kellogg 1941, 282; Aulie 1974). The beneficial effects of legumes were known at the time, but their mode of action was not understood.

We realize today that the soil exists in a dynamic balance between the forces of depletion, i.e., leaching, erosion, gaseous losses, and the removal of nutrients by plants and animals, and the forces of renewal, i.e., weathering, decomposition, nitrogen fixation, and meteorological, animal and plant inputs. Both the humus theory and the mineral theory focused attention on two important elements of the soil fertility equation – the significance of organic matter and the removal of nutrients by crops. At the same time, however, the reformers' single-minded preoccupation with the crop removal portion of the equation encouraged them to overlook other important elements. With a few notable exceptions, most reformers of the eighteenth and nineteenth centuries neglected the equally serious problems of soil erosion and the impact of cultivation on the soil's structure. Due to their influence, American agriculture became synonymous with a fixed cycle of events – settlement, the exploitation and ultimately the exhaustion of the soil, abandonment, and movement to the new, fertile lands to the west to repeat the cycle.

Rationale for the American system of farming

Were the concerns of the agricultural reformers justified? Did poor farming practices precipitate a chain of events which eventually led to soil exhaustion and abandonment? It would be easy to follow the well-worn trail of the agricultural improvers and simply attribute the problem to the conservatism and the shortsightedness of the American farmer. The average farmer's failure to adopt the suggestions of the reformers, however, should encourage us to search for other reasons. Many of the improvements were not adopted because they were poorly suited to local conditions (Wines 1981). Agriculture, the English visitor Patrick Shirreff ([1835] 1971, 341) pointed out, 'is affected by local circumstances.' Local circumstances went a long way towards explaining the differences in the American and the English systems of husbandry. The more discerning visitors took note of local circumstances and included them in their evaluations. The seemingly 'slovenly' American system of farming was not without its rationale. A number of factors accounted for the extensive system of husbandry practiced in America.

(1) Fertilizer was not always necessary. The well-known agricultural historian, Clarence Danhof (1969, 251), claimed that the more intensive fertility maintaining practices of the Europeans were 'neither necessary nor practical' initially in North America. Few of the soils, particularly the more fertile soils of the Midwest, required manure for the first few years of cropping (Hamilton County Agricultural Society 1830, 40; Fowler 1831, 79). Manures were often considered a hindrance on newly cleared lands because they increased the chance of rust or lodging of the grain (Johnston 1851, 1:54; Kelly 1971). Many compared the organically rich soils of the Midwest to natural ash-heaps (Caird 1859, 81), as rich as barnyard soils (Nowlin [1876] 1937, 7). They were heavily manured by nature (Kennedy 1864) and yielded abundantly for a number of years without the aid of animal manures (Stuart 1833, 2:259; Atwater 1838, 317; Thorne 1951; Bogue [1963] 1968, 145). The time required to deplete the initial fertility of the land varied from one soil to the next. Danhof (1969, 253–254) stated that most of the East's farmers experienced a significant drop in the productivity of their soils 10 to 20 years after settlement. A number of other agricultural writers and historians substantiated Danhof's claim (Hill 1840; Adams 1853; Hedrick 1933, 75; Neidhard 1951). Poor soils, i.e., coarse-textured soils with a low cation exchange capacity or a limited ability to store nutrients, 'ran out' in less than six years (Ratzel 1878, 2:245). The pitch pine plains of the Northeast and the jack pine plains of the upper Midwest fell into this category (Belknap 1813, 3:95; Roth 1903). The fertile soils of the coveted bottomlands or intervales were at the other end of the fertility spectrum. In the words of Thomas Hutchinson (1760, 484), Massachusetts' colonial governor, they were 'so often overflowed as to need no other manure, the waters in a freshet bringing down so much muck from the mountains, like the water of the Nile, as to keep the ground in good heart to bear a crop of wheat every year.' The fertility of the intervales and the bottomlands of the Connecticut, the Genesee, the Scioto, and the Mississippi Rivers was legendary, many of them producing crops continuously for 40 or more years without the aid of animal manures or fertilizers (Beck 1823, 14; Lapham 1833).

(2) American farms suffered from a lack of manure. The application of large quantities of manure could have arrested the decline of the soil's fertility. On many English farms, the production of livestock, grain, and grass was

closely integrated to produce an abundant supply of manure. The manure from the livestock in turn increased the yield of grain, grass, and root crops, which meant more forage for the overwintering livestock. In America the two activities were often separated or one activity was emphasized to the detriment of the other. Little attempt was made to increase or even properly preserve the manure that was produced (Mitchell [1775] 1939, 58). One French visitor wrote, 'the art of getting good dung is ... little known here' (La Rochefoucauld-Liancourt 1799, 1:33). As a result, the fields and the pastures frequently suffered from a lack of fertilizing elements while the cattle produced a scanty supply of milk (Eliot [1760] 1934, 28). The shortage of manure extended to the field of grassland husbandry. The idea of more manure to raise more grass, clover, and grain to feed more livestock to produce more manure was foreign to the average American farmer before the Revolution (Day 1954, 278). An emphasis on the more important cash crops, like wheat in southeastern Pennsylvania, to the exclusion of livestock also hindered a shift to a more balanced system of husbandry (Lemon [1972] 1976, 182).

Unfortunately the number of manure-producing animals was in short supply in America (Eliot [1760] 1934, 17; L'Hommedieu 1801). Most of the available evidence suggests that it required anywhere from one to three cattle to produce the manure required for an acre of cropland (Moore 1801, 55; Lemon [1972] 1976, 173–174; Bormann 1982, 96–97). The small number of cattle, generally 6 to 12 head, on the average colonial farm, (Rutherford 1867; Bidwell and Falconer [1925] 1941, 26; Lemon [1972] 1976, 173–174) permitted the manuring of at best a few acres of cropland (Warren 1787). In contrast, the typical English farmer had three times as many cattle as his American counterpart (Warren 1787). The 15 to 20 or at best 60 loads of manure produced annually on the average American farm was insignificant compared to the 800 to 1000 loads of manure collected annually by the English farmer (Warren 1787; Massachusetts Society for Promoting Agriculture 1807; Ely 1815). Ten to twenty loads of manure at 30 bushels per load were normally spread on an acre of cropland (Massachusetts Society for the Promoting Agriculture 1807). In addition, the English farmer was willing to increase his supply of manure by raising large quantities of roots crops (turnips, etc.) as forage and by stall-feeding or soiling his cattle (Bordley 1801, 119–122; Drown and Drown 1824, 172–175). During the colonial period, few Americans took the trouble to house their cattle in the winter or to tend them in the field (Kalm [1772] 1972, 59). Generally the cattle were encouraged to fend for themselves in the woods. As a result their manure was dissipated over a wide area (Eliot [1760] 1934, 58–59).

The avoidance of labor-intensive activities accounted for much of the American farmer's aversion to the use of manure. Farming practices were always evaluated in relation to their return upon the labor invested in the activity (Livingston 1832). Stall-feeding cattle, and carting and spreading manure were very laborious activities (Bidwell 1916). Even near urban areas where manure was relatively available and inexpensive, the high cost of carriage and application often prohibited its use (Shirreff 1835 [1971], 396).

(3) Given the shortage of manure and the abundance of land, extensive cultivation represented a rational economic decision (Perkins 1980, 45). There were, of course, alternatives to the heavy use of manure. Shifting cultivation or the use of a long fallow period allowed the land to regain much of its fertility. It insured the productivity of at least a part of the farmer's land. Nitrogen fixation and meterological inputs (rain, dust, etc.) built up the supply of nutrients during the long fallow period (Loomis 1978). Shifting cultivation also minimized the use of labor outside the farmer's family. Admittedly, a portion of the land would always be devoted to run-down pastures or brush fallow. Historians (Danhof 1969, 137; Henretta 1973, 15–18) have noted, however, that at best the average colonial farmer could only cultivate 10 to 20 acres of cropland. Considering the fact that the farmer could till but a fraction of the 100 or so acres of land he owned, large segments of the land in fallow do not appear to have been too burdensome. Shifting cultivation or land rotation brought another added benefit. By limiting the amount of land under tillage and thus subject to severe erosion, it minimized the loss of soil and nutrients. The tracts of regenerating forest or scrub adjoining the cultivated fields trapped most of the sediments and the nutrients in the surface runoff and the subsurface water flow before it reached the local stream channel (Peterjohn and Correll 1984; Brush 1986). Contemporary historians now agree that the long fallow was a very ecologically sound or benign system of cultivation (Miller 1986; Earle 1988; Merchant 1989, 153–159).

(4) Farming in America was constrained by a shortage of capital and labor. England was a densely populated island where land was costly, labor was inexpensive, and food prices were high. The result was a very labor-intensive form of agriculture which generated profits and attracted capital. America's position was completely different. Undercapitalization and a shortage of labor were chronic problems on many a pioneer farm where the settler went into debt to purchase the new land (French 1861). As the more discerning visitors noted, Americans were not always able to implement an intensive system of husbandry due to the high cost of labor and a limited amount of capital (Stuart 1833, 1:257–258; Erickson 1972, 47–48).

Labor and capital intensive, high farming activities based upon the use of intensive cultivation and weeding, stall-feeding, manures, root crops, and the application of expensive mineral fertilizers were simply not feasible (Bardolph 1948; Lemon [1972] 1976, 158). 'It is this consideration,' one farmer in Ohio stated, 'that induces us to prefer purchasing more lands to graze our flocks and herds upon at $10 or $20 per acre, rather than double the produce of the old homestead by under-draining, subsoiling, and manuring, at an expense of from $30 to $50 per acre. These outlays for improvements so highly recommended, and no doubt very beneficial, will of necessity be delayed in any country, till population becomes dense and lands high priced' (Summers 1853). Root crops, e.g., turnips, represented an important component of the famous Norfolk system of crop rotation in England. Utilized as a forage, turnips increased the number of livestock that could be carried over the winter and correspondingly the manure available for grain. High labor costs and a superior fodder crop in the form of corn prevented their general adoption in the United States (Bidwell and Falconer [1925] 1941, 241; Loehr 1937). Attempts to overcome the limitations of capital and labor placed a permanent imprint on America's agricultural practices. In America labor and capital were allocated to those activities which promised the greatest return. To put it bluntly, American farmers favored 'the most paying crop which [could] be grown at the least cost of labour' (Caird 1859, 27).

America's farmers were quick to adopt new techniques which reduced the input of labor. They frequently altered English tools and machines to economize on labor (Loehr 1937). Visitors to the Midwest in particular marveled at the large number of labor-saving machines employed on farms (Johnston 1851, 161; Caird 1859, 61, 75). Caird (1859, 121) noted that the number of reaping and mowing machines manufactured in the state of Ohio alone in 1857 was seven times that produced in all of England. America is still torn between the vision of a small farm well-tilled and a large farm run efficiently by machines (Bogue [1963] 1968, 147).

(5) Purchases of large quantities of land were due to the profitable return on the land and inheritance patterns. The limited amount of capital accumulated by farming was invested in more profitable enterprises. In America, few enterprises were as profitable as buying and selling land (Willis 1840, 2:43; Talleyrand 1942, 154; LeDuc 1963). There was the increase in the value of land due to settlers filling in partially occupied areas and the increase associated with forest clearance and the construction of dwellings, barns, fences, etc. Many farmers were speculators who 'regarded their land as a means of quickly making a fortune through the

rising land values which the progress of the community and their own individual improvements would give it' (Gates 1960, 399–400). As the French statesman and entrepreneur Talleyrand (1942, 154) noted, uncultivated land often tripled in value in the space of ten years while the value of cultivated land rose 5, 10, 20, and even 100-fold. It is little wonder that the purchase of more land absorbed much of the farmer's spare capital while improvements on the farm monopolized his time. Many observers (Williams 1794, 312–313; Faux [1823] 1905, 176–178; Kuhne 1860) commented that the capital accumulated in improved land was at least as important as the income generated by crops. Every stroke of the axe represented an increase in the farmer's equity and capital (Dwight [1821] 1969, 2:327). The historian, Sung Bok Kim (1978, 250–251), has termed the equity generated by these farm improvements one of the more neglected aspects of American history. Many farmers looked forward to the day when they could sell off their improved farms in the East and move to the West where they could acquire new farms at a fraction of the cost of farms in the East (Shirreff [1835] 1971, 8; Johnston 1851, 162–163; Atack and Bateman 1987, 130–144). Visitors commented that Americans were forever on the move (Griffiths 1835, 54; Bogue [1963] 1968, 27; Niemcewicz 1965, 170). Americans were a 'highly mobile people' in the nineteenth century (Allen 1977). As capital-building itinerants (Brandenburg 1958), they brought 'land into tillage in order to sell it again and not to farm it' (Tocqueville [1835] 1966, 2:157). Many could have more appropriately been termed farm-makers rather than farmers (Adams 1899).

It would be hazardous to suggest that all of the land purchases were motivated by a speculative urge or that all farmers were forever moving. Some of the large purchases of land were motivated by the farmer's desire to provide an economically viable inheritance for each of his childern (Atack and Bateman 1987, 121–125; Lemon 1987). Kinship ties could also discourage migration. The support network provided by relatives and the promise of inheriting the old family farm in the East encouraged many a farmer's son to remain in the East (Barron 1984). As a general rule, however, the geographic mobility of the American farmer was much higher than that of his British counterpart.

The English visitor, Harriet Martineau ([1837] 1966, 2:93–94), summarized the contrast between the English farmer and the American settler very succinctly: 'The Englishman clears half the quantity of land, – clears it very thoroughly; ploughs deep, sows thick, raises twice the quantity of grain on half the area of land, and points proudly to his crop. But the American has meantime, fenced, cleared, and sown more land, improved his house and stock, and kept his money in his pocket.' A few observers (Russell 1857, 30) even admitted that the American system of farming was the best system under the circumstances. English farmers would do the same if land was abundant and labor was costly (Johnston 1851, 1:104). Immigrants from England soon learned to adapt their farming methods to America's circumstances (Erickson 1972, 49).

(6) Changing circumstances eventually encouraged the adoption of many of the practices recommended by the English improvers. By the early to mid-nineteenth century, the shift to a more intensive system of farming was well under way in the East. Stimulated by the growing urban markets of the East Coast and the attendant opportunities for increased profits, farmers increasingly applied lime, gypsum, and manures to their fields and rotated their crops (Dickinson 1813, 8). The use of lime and plaster decreased the acidity of the soil, permitting the growth of a number of soil-improving legumes, notably clover (Strickland 1801, 39). The clover, in turn, increased the nitrogen supply of the soil, the number of animals the farmer could keep over winter, the manure supply and the yield of grain (Strickland 1801, 43; Fletcher 1950, 135). Clover and artificial grasses replaced the extended fallows and rubbish pastures of the eighteenth century (Bordley 1801, 29–34, 85–86; Strickland 1801, 39; Field [1819] 1892; Ellis 1946, 92–94). Red clover was America's answer to England's convertible or up-and-down husbandry (Buel 1823). The use of lime and gypsum coincided with an increased interest in the use of animal manures. Farmers devoted more time to the art of making and preserving good manures. Barns were built with scuttles on the floors of the stalls and cellars for collecting the liquid and the solid droppings of the livestock (Lincoln 1851). Manure was composted with mud from the roadsides and muck from the swamps (Hill 1842). Talk of soil exhaustion ceased as the new husbandry took hold. As the Italian visitor Luigi Castiglioni ([1790] 1983, 334) noted, 'Certain authors, judging on the basis of decreasing fertility of cleared lands in America, have supposed that in time they would be completely exhausted, so that they could no longer serve for the sustenance of human beings. Such an assertion clearly demonstrates an utter ignorance of agriculture, since it is known that any terrain, although very fertile at first, after a number of years needs rest or the help of fertilizers. This latter method will be introduced into all parts of America with the increase of population, as has already been done near Philadelphia and the most populous cities of the United States.'

Much of the impetus for the new system of husbandry was tied to the rising urban demand for food. 'We shall farm better,' asserted the agricultural report of the Eighth United States Census (Kennedy 1864, ix), 'as soon as such improvement is perceived to be profitable and necessary.' The rapidly expanding urban markets of the East made improving the farm a profitable enterprise (Craven [1926] 1965, 127). Market forces justified the adoption of a number of costly, more labor-intensive farming practices near urban areas (Dickinson 1813, 8; Collins [1830] 1971, 21; Bidwell and Falconer [1925] 1941, 200–203). Agricultural historians have documented the farmer's adaptation to urban market conditions in nineteenth century eastern Massachusetts (Gross 1982; Karr 1987; Baker and Patterson 1988) and southeastern Pennsylvania (James 1928).

Decline in the fertility of the soil?

Regardless of the economic constraints involved, most agricultural reformers in the eighteenth and nineteenth centuries believed that extensive farming eventually resulted in the exhaustion of the soil. Did 'exploitation' necessarily lead to exhaustion or a long-term decline in the productivity of the soil? To answer this question, one has to quantify, or at least objectively define, the term 'soil exhaustion.' Defining the term is not an easy task. 'No phrase is more common in agricultural literature, and none more vague and indefinite,' declared the agricultural report of the Eighth Census (Kennedy 1864, ix). The concept embraced a host of competitive and psychological factors as well as the fertility of the soil (Rossiter 1975, 207). Anecdotal evidence, however, suggests that many farmers considered their fields 'worn-out' or exhausted when their yields dropped to 6 to 10 bushels of wheat per acre. Yields of this magnitude were reported in many of the older farming areas of the East, i.e., New York, New Jersey, and Pennsylvania, late in the eighteenth century (Strickland 1801, 42; Watson 1830, 717; Rutherford 1867; Lemon [1972] 1976, 154). The yields were low compared to the 18 bushels per acre produced by Pennsylvania's better farmers with the aid of clover and gypsum (Strickland 1801, 44) or the 20 to 30 bushels per acre yield of newly cleared lands (Lemon [1972] 1976, 154). The low output of the older, established farming areas, however, probably reflected an attempt to push the extensive system to its limits, not a breakdown in the extensive system of husbandry per se. One might speculate that the extended fallow was reduced a few years in order to bring more land into production in the older, settled areas. Shorter fallow periods may have prohibited the restoration of the soil's nutrients and led to a gradual decline in the soil's fertility (Henretta 1973, 15–23).

The brisk business in second-hand or 'improved' farms in at least the first half of the nineteenth century suggests that few of the 'worn out' farms of the

East Coast were all that undesirable. 'Old lands [were] capable of renovation' and 'worn farms always [found] purchasers' (Peters 1847). Competent observers often recommended the purchase of second-hand farms over new farms (Johnson 1819, 42; Jakle 1977, 101). A few cautionary notes were expressed about the buildup of noxious weeds (Edmundson 1852) or the loss of the original vegetable mold on improved farms (Stuart 1833, 258–259). The strong market in second-hand farms in the East (Johnston 1851, 2:33), however, belies the importance of these deficiencies.

Long-term plot studies, like the Morrow plots at the Illinois Agricultural Experiment Station and a series of plots at the Ohio Agricultural Experiment Station, represent another valuable source of information on the effects of management practices on the soil's fertility. The influence of various cropping practices has been illustrated by changes in the nitrogen and the carbon content of the soil and the yield of crops in the Morrow plots and the Ohio plots. In both of the studies, continuous cropping without the addition of fertilizers reduced the organic matter and the nitrogen content of the soil to the point that the crop yield was limited by a deficiency of nitrogen (Salter and Green 1933; Salter, Lewis, and Slipher 1936; Odell *et al.* 1984). The decline in the yield was very rapid in the first ten years of continuous cropping. By the 20th year, the yield of corn had been cut in half. The rate of decline was considerably lower thereafter. The addition of lime, nitrogen, phosphorus, and potassium to the Morrow plots dramatically increased the yield of corn. Perhaps more than anything else, the long-term plot experiments demonstrated that soil exhaustion was a relative term. One could reduce the productivity of the more fertile soils of the Midwest, but it took years to do it. Even more importantly, the experiments suggested that soil exhaustion did not permanently impair the soil's fertility. The application of large quantities of fertilizers quickly restored the soil's productivity.

Although there is little evidence that exploitation, exhaustion, and decline was the inevitable fate of America's soils, continuous cropping did have its drawbacks. Cultivation reduced the organic matter returned to the soil and increased the breakdown and decomposition of the organic matter already in the soil (Albrecht 1956; Anderson and Coleman 1985). The result was a decrease in the organic matter content of the soil and a change in the soil's structure. Organic matter binds, lightens, and expands the soil. It is the major factor responsible for the very porous, granular, friable structure of the soil's surface horizons (Brady 1984, 57). By destroying the organic matter, cultivation reduced the tilth, the pore space, and the natural drainage of the soil. On the better drained soils, this may not have been much of a problem. On the heavy textured, lacustrine soils south of the Great Lakes, however, continuous cultivation and the deterioration of the soil's structure significantly lowered crop yields (Page and Willard 1946).

Accelerated soil erosion

Continuous cropping exposed the soil to another serious problem – the problem of soil erosion. Rocks and the soil are continuously being broken lose and placed in motion by physical processes. 'All land ...,' Aldo Leopold (1941) wrote, 'represents a downhill flow of nutrients from the hill to the sea.' The natural process of erosion is known as 'normal' or 'geological erosion.' By destroying the natural protective cover of the vegetation, human activities can increase the rate of erosion. Runoff is increased and the bare surface of the soil is subject to raindrop splash. The result is 'accelerated erosion' (Hudson 1981, 26–39).

Despite the attention accorded soil erosion today, recognition of its importance was slow in coming. A few perceptive farmers like Jared Eliot, John Bartram, and George Washington commented upon the occurrence of accelerated erosion during the colonial period (McDonald 1941; Meyer and Moldenhauer 1985). A general awareness of the seriousness of the problem, however, awaited the advent of the Dust Bowl days and the creation of the Soil Erosion Service and its successor, the Soil Conservation Service in the 1930s (Held and Clawson 1965, 38–63; Trimble 1985). One of the first activities of the newly established agency was an attempt to quantify the magnitude of the problem. Plots were established at a number of experimental stations across the country. The plots were carefully monitored to determine the effect of various land use practices on the loss of soil. As the 1934 to 1936 data from the Zanesville station in Ohio suggest (Table 10.1), accelerated erosion is a reality whose magnitude varies inversely with the natural protective cover of the vegetation. By tying information on the erosion rates of various management practices together with the known land use practices of the past, scientists and geographers have been able to reconstruct the erosional history of limited sections of the country (Wolman 1967; Trimble 1974; Wilson and Ryan 1988; Wilson 1989).

Erosion is only one half of the equation associated with the movement of soil. The material eroded from the upstream area or the headlands of the valley is deposited at a lower elevation. Some of the sediment, often the larger share of the material, is stored as colluvium or slopewash on the lower slopes of hills (Costa 1975). Bays, floodplains, reservoirs, and lakes are other active sites of deposition. Historical and stratigraphic studies of the sediments of these areas provide relevant examples of both the magnitude and the effects of accelerated

Table 10.1. *Rates of soil erosion associated with various land use activities.*
Data from Soil and Water Conservation Experiment Station, Zanesville,
Ohio, 1934–1936. Experimental plots located on Muskingum silt loam and
12% slope

Land use	Runoff (% rainfall)	Rate of erosion (t/ha/yr)
Woods	0.12	< 0.01
Grass	6.5	0.09
Rotated fields	16.9	25.54
Bare land (fallow)	48.8	154.61
Corn	41.9	164.02

Source: Bennett (1939, 147).

erosion. Land clearance and commercial agriculture resulted in a four-fold
increase in the deposition of sediments at several sites in the Chesapeake Bay
(Brush 1986). Sedimentation led to the abandonment of many of the early
ports of the region. Former port towns, like Joppa Town, Maryland, are now
two or more miles from navigable water (Gottschalk 1945; Fig. 10.1). The
paleolimnological record of many of North America's lakes also shows a massive influx of sediments following the conversion of forests to farms.
Inorganic sediment exports to one lake in southern Michigan increased ten-
fold following settlement and the development of a farm-based economy
(Davis 1976, Fig. 10.2). The unglaciated Upper Mississippi River hill country
of southwestern Wisconsin and northwestern Illinois experienced some of the
highest rates of erosion in the northern United States (Trimble 1985). Changes
in the channel morphology of a number of streams in the region have been
attributed to the postsettlement alteration of erosion and sedimentation patterns (Trimble 1976; Knox, 1977, 1987; Trimble and Lund 1982; Magilligan
1985). By resurveying many of the stream widths first recorded in the early
Federal Land Survey of 1832–1833, James Knox (1977) was able to demonstrate an increase in the width of many of the headwater and tributary stream
channels of the Platte River system in southwestern Wisconsin and a decrease
in the width of the main channel downstream. The wider and shallower
upstream channels were associated with bank erosion and an increase in the
bedload of the streams following settlement. The changes reflect the geomor-
phic response of the channel to the occurrence of larger and more frequent
floods since settlement (Knox 1977). The reduced width of the main channel
downstream was due to excessive overbank sedimentation and the deposition
of the finer, suspended particles downstream. At their peak in the 1920s and
the 1930s, historic rates of overbank floodplain sedimentation exceeded their

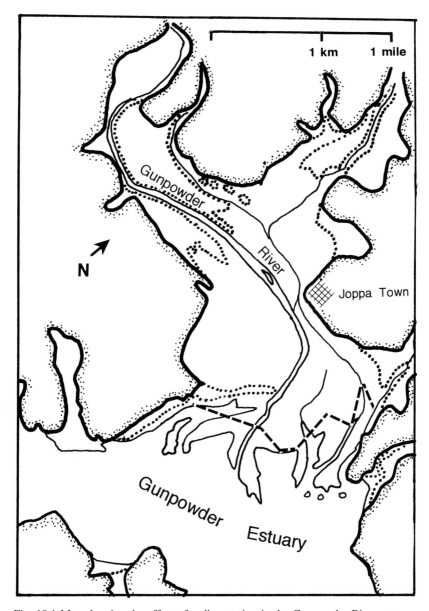

Fig. 10.1 Map showing the effect of sedimentation in the Gunpowder River estuary, Maryland, upper Chesapeake Bay. The thick solid line shows the approximate shore-line of the estuary in the early eighteenth century, the time Joppa Town was founded; the dotted line, the shoreline in 1846; the dashed line, the shoreline in 1897; and the thin solid line, the shoreline in 1944. Modified from Gottschalk (1945).

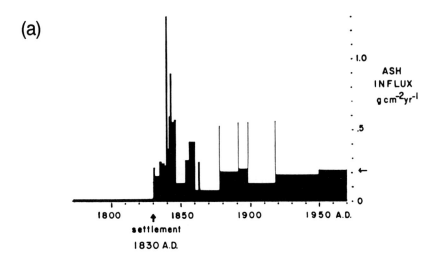

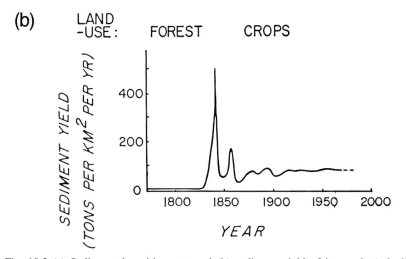

Fig. 10.2 (a) Sediment deposition rate and (b) sediment yield of inorganic (ashed) materials through time in Frains Lake, southern Michigan. Note dramatic (10 to 30-fold) increase in sediment yield after settlement in 1830 and the conversion of forest to cropland. Reprinted from Davis (1976) by permission of the Foundation for Environmental Conservation.

presettlement rates by two orders of magnitude (Knox 1987). The implementation of an active program of soil conservation over the last 50 years has significantly decreased the rate of sedimentation (Trimble 1976; Trimble and Lund 1982; Magilligan 1985; Knox 1987).

Accelerated erosion has had a measurable impact on the productivity of America's soils (Stallings 1957, 195–220; Schertz 1983). The first nationwide study of soil erosion in the 1930s indicated that approximately 50 million acres (20 million hectares) of former cropland had been ruined by cultivation. The majority of the land, however, was located in the South and the Great Plains region (Bennett 1939, 57–60). One of the more obvious problems associated with accelerated erosion is the loss of nutrients contained in the surface layer of the soil. Fertilizers are commonly applied to the soil to offset the loss of nutrients. For the past 60 years, technology has more than masked any short-term declines in the productivity of the soil due to erosion (Cardwell 1982; Schertz 1983). Assessing long-term changes in the productivity of the soil is more problematical. The deep, fertile soil of the Midwest encompasses some of the richest farmland in the United States today. Most of the level to gently rolling terrain of the region is buffered against severe erosional problems. Although they make up only a small percentage of the soils in the Midwest, soils on steep slopes and soils with a thin solum are particularly susceptible to erosion and degradation over the long run. Substantial declines in productivity have been projected for these soils in the next century if erosion is allowed to continue at its present rate (Young 1980; Pierce *et al.* 1983, 1984).

Patterns of farm abandonment and agricultural readjustment

Agriculture in America has always been a dynamic affair, constantly changing and shifting in response to new opportunities and demands. The return of large segments of New England's farmland to forests over the last 100 years was part of a broader pattern of rural 'decline' or farm reorganization which characterized much of the eastern United States (Fowler 1909). Farm abandonment started on the hill farms of New England in the mid-nineteenth century and continues today on the western margin of Appalachia and the cutover lands of the Upper Great Lakes region (Thompson 1959; Hart 1968). The amount of land in farms in New England and New York reached a peak of 44.5 million acres (18 million hectares) or 63% of the total land area in 1880 (Vaughan 1929; Black 1950, 146–149; US Senate 1957, 43–44). A rapid decline in the land in farms and the cleared land in farms set in after 1880 to 1900 (Behre 1932; Bell 1989). By 1950 the same area had lost over a third of its farmland

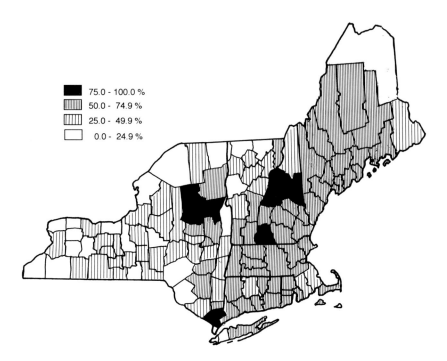

75.0 - 100.0 %
50.0 - 74.9 %
25.0 - 49.9 %
0.0 - 24.9 %

Fig. 10.3 Percent decline in acreage of agricultural land by county in New England and New York from peak of development to 1950. Data from US Census Office (1883, 127–128); US Bureau of the Census (1952, 40–45); US Senate (1957, plate 56).

(Fig. 10.3; Black 1950, 146–149; Bond, Rinkcas, and Mitchell 1954). Other areas to the west exhibited a similar pattern of farm expansion and contraction, although the sequence occurred at a later date. Ohio and Pennsylvania, for instance, lost over ten million acres of cleared farmland between 1910 and 1959 or approximately one-fifth of the total acreage of cleared farmland in the two states (Goldenweiser and Ball 1918; Hart 1968). Most of the loss was concentrated in the rugged Appalachian Plateau region of western Pennsylvania and eastern Ohio. Northern lower Michigan and southern Indiana experienced a similar though less drastic decline over the same period (Hart 1968).

It would be easy to attribute the abandoned farmland to poor management practices and worn-out soils. According to this theory, the onus falls upon the farmer who exhausted the soil and then abandoned the land when it ceased to yield a profitable income. Given the fact that soil exhaustion was a very amorphous concept and certainly one which could be corrected by careful husbandry, we are forced to turn to other causative factors. Most of the abandoned farmland was concentrated in areas which have always been at best mediocre and at worst marginal or poor for agricultural purposes. The soils were either too shallow, too wet, too dry, or too infertile for farming or the slopes were too steep or the climate too rigorous for the successful conclusion of an agricultural venture (Hartman and Black 1931; Woodworth, Abell, and Holmes 1937; Thompson 1959; Conklin 1964). New England's stony, acidic uplands, for instance, encompassed some of the poorest cropland in the nation. As one critical agricultural expert who visited New England in the nineteenth century noted, 'It is nonsense to talk of the land being exhausted, for evidently there never was anything to exhaust' (Russell 1857, 14). Hilly terrain precluded the use of labor-saving horse-drawn machinery (Massachusetts Bureau of Statistics of Labor 1891; Woodworth 1937; Barron 1984, 61). Mechanization has increasingly favored the concentration of farming activities on level land and the abandonment of the steeper terrain of the Northeast and the Midwest (Sauer 1963; Auclair 1976). The small size of New England's farms also hampered the adoption of labor-saving machinery (Baker 1928).

Many of the marginal areas were settled under a unique set of circumstances. Northern New England, for instance, was one of the more accessible frontier regions of the late eighteenth and the early nineteenth centuries. The uplands were easy to clear and yielded a low but dependable harvest. They were attractive to the semi-subsistence hill farmers of the period (Taylor 1982). The cutover region of the Upper Midwest likewise came on the market at an opportune time – at the end of an almost inexhaustible supply of free land in the West. Large land companies, speculators, railroads, and a host of state and local government agencies pushed the cutover areas of Michigan and Wisconsin (Black and Gray 1925; Hartman and Black 1931; Helgeson 1962, 25–52,114–115; Schmaltz 1983). Even under the best of conditions, farming has often been a precarious activity. On the poor, cold soils of the cutover region, it was doomed from the start. Competition and agriculture's increasingly commercial orientation soon finished many of New England's small, inefficient hill farms (Taylor 1982). The opening of the Erie Canal in 1825 and the development of an effective railroad network in the 1850s linked the Northeast with the richer, more productive farmlands of the Midwest (Bidwell and Falconer [1925] 1941, 181–182, 398–400). It encouraged a vast outmigration of individuals to the cheaper and potentially more remunerative lands of the Midwest and the eventual abandonment of the poorer areas of the Northeast. As the Yale economist William Parker (1976) noted, 'On the whole, westward movement did not wait for yields to decline in older areas. The attraction of the equal or potentially higher yields in the Middle West ... was more than enough to attract population.'

The overall decline of agriculture in the more rugged sections of New England also reflected the rise of new economic opportunities in the rapidly expanding urban areas of the East Coast. Wages and the opportunities for economic advancement were often better off the soil than on it (Whitney 1901; Behre 1932; Rossiter 1975, 6). Low farm prices and agricultural depressions speeded the abandonment of the poorer farmlands (Hartman and Black 1931; Helgeson 1962, 116). In summation, a variety of forces must be factored into the farm decline equation. New economic opportunities and the natural limitations of the land were two of the more important factors.

Proximity to urban markets and competition from the West encouraged the remaining farmers in the Northeast to shift from corn and wheat to a new, often more labor-intensive, mix of crops (Atack and Bateman 1987, 10; Hurt 1990). Farmers near large urban areas of the East Coast and the Great Lakes region found the production of fruits, vegetables, poultry, and fluid milk profitable. On marginal lands, hay was raised as forage for city horses, draught animals, and dairy cattle. The very perishable or bulky nature of these goods protected them from western competition and favored their production near urban areas (Bidwell 1921; Munyon 1978, 80–81). The farmers of New England even managed to make a profit on their milk while importing large quantities of livestock feed from the Midwest (Baker 1928). Increasing dependence on western feed grains and the loss of the horse hay market after the introduction of the automobile contributed to the decrease of the region's cleared farmland in the twentieth century (Fowler 1942).

The history of America's agriculture has always been much more than a simple case of land exploitation and westward movement. The dominant theme is one of constant adjustment to new economic conditions and forces. It was a process of trial and error which resulted in a better use of the land's resources and the farmer's capital. Poor land was abandoned to forests, particularly where the forests promised a more remunerative crop in the form of cordwood (Blake 1856; Closson and Crosby 1856). Intensive agriculture increasingly favored the level, more fertile sites (Baker 1921; Hart 1968; Auclair 1976). Crops were eventually adjusted to local climatic and edaphic conditions and market forces. Although many writers have emphasized the decline of New England's agriculture in the nineteenth century, the same period was also a time of improved farming and prosperity for farmers located close to urban markets (Massachusetts Bureau of Statistics of Labor, 1891; Baker and Paterson 1988; Bell 1989). By 1910 the major farming regions of the United States had essentially assumed their present-day distribution and outline (Parker 1982). The economic crop geography of the United States (Fig. 10.4) resembled Johann von Thünen's (a German locational theorist) model of the isolated state.

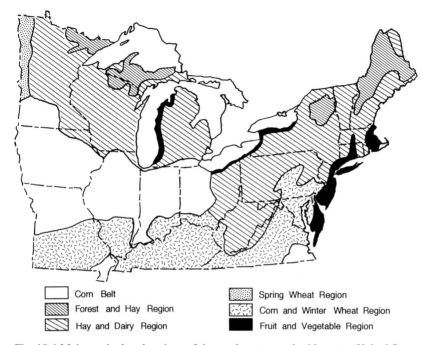

Fig. 10.4 Major agricultural regions of the northeastern and midwestern United States in 1920. Modified slightly from Meyer (1987). Note concentration of fruit and vegetable farming along urbanized East Coast.

Vegetables, fruits, poultry, and dairying, particularly fluid milk, dominated the Northeast. To the west, lay the Corn Belt of Iowa, Illinois, Indiana, and Ohio. It featured feed grains and livestock. The western extremity of the Middle West was devoted to wheat. Climate also influenced the distribution of crops. Corn favored the hot, humid summers of the middle Mississippi Valley. Wheat was planted to the west where the climate was too dry for corn, while pasture, hay, and silage were characteristic of the north where the summers were too cool for the maturation of corn (Hart 1972). Winds blowing over the Great Lakes produced a long frost-free season, excellent for the growth of fruits on the eastern edge of Lake Michigan and the southern edge of Lake Erie and Lake Ontario. The basic outlines of North America's farming regions were to remain fixed for decades. Regional specialization reflected the differing physical qualities of the land and the demand for land and agricultural commodities.

11

Grassland agriculture

The riches of England proceed from the plenty of grass, and the
poverty of the colonies from the want of that original source both
of plenty and wealth.

> John Mitchell. 1767. *The Present State of Great Britain and
> North America, with Regard to Agriculture, Population, Trade,
> and Manufactures, Impartially Considered*, p. 155.

The prairies [of North America] afford abundant pasturage and hay
for cattle, horses, and sheep. No country in the world has greater
advantages for raising live stock.

> Robert Baird. 1832. *View of the Valley of the Mississippi; or, the
> Emigrant's and Traveller's Guide to the West*, p. 206

Development of artificial grasslands

Maintaining the fertility of the soil was only one of a variety of problems the
American farmer faced. In large segments of the Northeast, obtaining adequate forage for the livestock was a major challenge. The early colonists
adhered to northwestern Europe's mixed husbandry tradition. Animal husbandry, the production of beef, butter, cheese, and milk, was combined with
the growing of grain. The meadows and the grazing lands of northwestern
Europe were just as important as the plowed fields (Sauer [1976] 1981, 37).

North America's long, cold winters necessitated a four to five months' supply of hay and fodder (Winthrop 1976). During this period of time the typical
cow consumed approximately 2 tons of hay (Colman 1838, 53; Johnston 1851,
51; Gray 1856, 6) or the produce of one to two acres of meadow or mowing
land (Rutman 1967, 51; Thomas 1979, 91). Unfortunately, North America
possessed few of the world's better forage grasses for pasture or hay (Crosby
1986, 288). Early reports of the New World's grasses were uniformly discour-

aging. Critics complained that 'the ground grazeth not so well as O[ld] E[ngland]' (Browne 1976, 227). Most of the native grasses on the uplands became coarse and harsh as they matured. Few could tolerate the combined effects of trampling and grazing (Kalm [1772] 1972, 176; Sauer 1941). Hay made from native grasses was inferior to English hay due to its high proportion of roughage to nutrients (Edwards 1948). 'Beasts [grew] lousy with feeding upon it' (Emerson 1976, 214). 'There are a great many kinds of grasses ... here,' Peter Kalm observed, 'but I have scarcely found one which deserves special attention or compares with any of our European grasses for meadow cultivation' (Larsen 1943). A scarcity of good hay plagued the earliest plantations and resulted in the 'poore starveing condition' of many of their cattle (Johnson [1654] 1910, 115; Innes 1983, 9).

New England's natural saltwater marshes and freshwater meadows were crucial to the colonists' early livestock industry. Although they were inferior to English hay, the native black grass (*Juncus gerardi*) and *Spartina patens* dominated hay of the saltwater marshes (Smith *et al.* 1989), and the sedge (*Carex* spp.) filled hay of the freshwater meadows (Lowell 1831) sustained the colonists' cattle during the long, hard winters. Spring floods and seasonally high tides supplied the fertilizing elements that kept the meadows and marshes in heart. Given the New Englander's strong attatchment to livestock, it is not surprising that most of New England's early towns were intentionally located near saltwater marshes along the coast or freshwater meadows inland (Bushman 1967, 32; Russell 1976, 55). The lower Connecticut River Valley with its extensive intervales and meadows was one of the first inland areas settled in the interior of southern New England. Many of the towns in the valley, e.g., Northfield, Greenfield, Deerfield, Hatfield, Springfield, Suffield, Enfield, Wethersfield, Longmeadow, Hampton, and Northhampton (hamp is an English term implying flat, low-lying pastureland near a river), still retain names which are indicative of their early treeless condition (Wood 1978, 53–54).

Although opinions differed as to the relative value of the different types of hay, the native saltwater and freshwater meadow hay generally had only a third to a half the value of upland or English hay (Ely 1815; Newbury and Vassalborough Agricultural Societies 1815; Nichols 1815; Dunstable Agricultural Society 1816; Colman 1838, 19). Attempts to correct the deficiency of nutritious forage species started at an early date. White clover (*Trifolium repens*) and Kentucky bluegrass (*Poa pratensis*), two of the major components of English grass, probably came ashore unintentionally with the first shipments of European stock (Russell 1976, 129). A number of towns deliberately encouraged the introduction and spread of English grass. Ipswich

and Lynn, Massachusetts, for example, temporarily granted lots to those who
were willing to sow English grass or hayseed on the land. At the end of a stipu-
lated period of time, the improved pasture reverted to the town (Weeden
[1890] 1963, 61; Perzel 1968). Many of the larger landowners of southern
New England were also actively acquiring and sowing English hayseed and
grass on their lands in the 1630s and 1640s (Bridenbaugh 1974, 31–32; Innes
1983, 9). By 1670, the General Court of Massachusetts recognized English
grass as one of the three major types of mowing land in the colony (Judd 1905,
362).

The scarcity of good forage may also have contributed to the retention of various common-field customs in New England's early towns. In many towns, the
stubble in the planting fields and the aftermath in the meadows were carefully
husbanded and opened for grazing at the appropriate time of year (Andrews
1889, 69–71; Slater 1907, 183–186; Bidwell and Falconer [1925] 1941, 22–23;
Allen 1981, 50). Even the grass along the highways adjoining the fields and
meadows was apportioned among the proprietors (Sheldon 1895, 1:266–269).
In England, the common-field system insured a more efficient use of the scarce
forage resources of the manor (Thrisk 1964 – see chapter 6). It is conceivable
that the common-field system filled a similar function in the early history of
New England's towns prior to the development of improved pastures of
English grasses. Care was also taken to see that the commons were not over-
charged with cattle. Stinting rights or 'gates' set a limit on the number of
animals an individual could graze upon the commons or the aftermath of the
meadow (Walcott 1884, 20, 68; Andrews 1889, 69–70; Slater 1907, 183–186;
Allen 1981, 50). Meadows were among the more valued pieces of real estate in
the early colonial period. They were carefully doled out to all the members of
the community. The early inhabitants of Springfield, Massachusetts, for
instance, were allotted two acres of mowing land for each head of cattle (Innes
1983, 8). Given an average yield of one ton of hay per acre (Kelsey 1968), this
would have been enough to support one cow throughout the winter.

By the later half of the eighteenth century, New England was firmly
entrenched in the livestock business. Stock raising had gained an ascendancy
over the production of grain and other costly, labor-intensive activities
(Bushman 1967, 31). Farmers had finally recognized that the cold, stony soils
of New England were better suited to pasture than tillage (Whitney 1793, 107;
Colby 1941). They were rapidly converting the forests of New England's hill
towns to pasture and mowing land. The initial flush of nutrients released by the
clearing process favored the growth of a number of the more nutritious and
nutrient-demanding European grasses (Stewart 1933; Colby 1941). Some
species like white clover appeared spontaneously in the new plantations

(Colby 1941), apparently having hitched a ride in the manure of deer and cattle (Gordon 1959). Other species, particularly the grasses, were deliberately introduced at the completion of the clearing process (Belknap 1813, 2:99–100). Cattle were pastured on the grasses of the upland hill towns and then fattened on the surplus winter-feed grain of the fertile Connecticut River Valley (Garrison 1987).

By the early nineteenth century, nonnative grasses were New England's premier crop (Dwight [1821] 1969, 1:30). They came in a variety of forms and occupied the lion's share of the farm. The Massachusetts valuation returns of 1792 indicate that 85% of the improved farm acreage of Massachusetts and Maine was in grass. English mowing or upland hay meadows had surpassed freshwater meadows and saltmarshes in importance and constituted 20% of the improved farmland. Saltwater marshes and freshwater meadows accounted for another 15% of the land while pastures occupied 50% and tillage 15% of the improved acreage (Wolcott 1832). Old World species, tolerant of mowing and grazing, dominated the artificial grasslands. Timothy (*Phleum pratense*) and red clover (*Trifolium pratense*) formed most of the hay while Kentucky bluegrass (actually a native of Eurasia) and white clover were the prevailing species of the pastures (Welles 1824; Cutler and Cutler 1888, 264; Russell 1976, 131).

The recognition that hay was also a valuable cash crop encouraged many farmers to adopt a more aggressive attitude towards its production (Colman 1838, 17, 1841, 237; Gross 1982). Both the acreage (Table 11.1) and the production of superior English upland hay expanded as swamps and meadows were increasingly ditched and drained and seeded down to clover and timothy (Hill 1842; Flint 1854). Farmers were also encouraged to manure their mowing land to replace the nutrients lost in the cut hay (Boardman 1863; Stockbridge 1873).

New England's pastures did not fare as well as her hayfields. Pastures were New England's stepchild. Often they were relegated to land that was too rocky, too steep, or too wet for tillage. Worn-out croplands were also converted to pastures when the yield of grain or hay declined. Decaying humus and the residue of the forest formed the initial nutrient reserve of the sites that were directly converted into pastures. Grasses were and are normally very effective at recycling and retaining nutrients. Over an extended period of time, however, leaching and the export of nutrients in various farm products (milk, beef, etc.) took their toll (Harlan 1956, 254–255). The result was a deficiency of one or more nutrients, e.g., calcium, potassium, and phosphorus, critical to the growth of the better grasses. Manure applications could have counteracted the loss of some of the nutrients, but the supply of manure was limited and

Table 11.1. *The changing grassland resources of Worcester County, Massachusetts, 1771–1860*

Year	Upland mowing acres	Upland mowing % of total	Freshwater mowing (acres)	Total mowing (acres)	Pasture (acres)	Acres of pasture required to support one cow
1771						~2.40
1781	40 052	48.6	42 369	82 421	104 440	–
1791	43 339	48.4	46 105	89 444	127 466	–
1801	50 536	47.2	56 428	106 964	182 978	3.28
1811	52 016	49.1	53 990	106 006	188 057	3.40
1821	62 713	51.5	59 110	121 823	229 389	4.20
1831	86 793	60.0	60 353	147 146	299 231	4.20
1841	104 398	66.2	53 390	157 788	320 578	4.84
1850	128 136	74.4	44 163	172 299	354 589	5.01
1860	134 245	78.4	37 080	171 325	338 249	–

Sources: Data is based upon the Massachusetts Valuation Returns for Worcester County 1781, 1791, 1801, 1811, 1821, 1831 in Manuscript Collection, Worcester County, at the American Antiquarian Society, Worcester, Mass.; and Valuation Returns for Worcester County 1841, 1850, 1860 at the State Archives, Boston, Mass. Information was compiled by Andrew Baker, Agricultural Historian, Old Sturbridge Village, Sturbridge, Mass. The 1771 value of acres of pasture required per cow is from Pruitt (1981, 155).

most of it was allocated to the mowing and the arable land (Warren 1787; Flint 1862, 83; Colby 1941). It is not surprising that the middle of the nineteenth century brought an increasing number of complaints about the deteriorating state of New England's pastures (Colby 1941). New England's pastures suffered from 'constant and too close cropping, without adequate returns' (Felton, Lathrop, and Lewis 1860). The result was a change in the pasture's composition. The more nutrient-demanding forage species gave way to coarser grasses and species characteristic of impoverished sites. Poverty grass (*Danthonia spicata*), five-finger (*Potentilla* sp.), brakes (*Pteridium aquilinum*), and mosses (*Polytrichum* spp.) replaced the bluegrass and clover (*Trifolium repens*) of the earlier pastures (Hildreth 1825; Cooper, Wilson, and Barron 1929; Stewart 1933; Colby 1941). Hardhack (*Spiraea tomentosa*), sweet-fern (*Comptonia peregrina*), and pines invaded many of the neglected, worn-out pastures (Flint 1862, 80–83). State tax assessors in Massachusetts were required to obtain information on the number of acres of pastureland on each farm and the number of cows the pastureland would support. The increasing number of acres required to support one cow from 1771 to 1850 in one central Massachusetts county (Table 11.1) suggests that the State Board of Agriculture's concerns in the middle of the nineteenth century were justified. As a report on the renovation of exhausted pastures noted, 'The grazing lands of the State are greatly exhausted – feeding from one-sixth to three-sixths less stock than the same fed twenty-five to forty years ago' (Felton, Lathrop, and Lewis 1860). Applications of lime and phosphorus could have increased the pastures' productivity. Unfortunately few farmers outside of the limestone regions could afford the use of lime (Colman 1839, 11; Lincoln 1851). High transportation costs probably accounted for the expensive nature of the lime. The eventual fate of most of the pastures was abandonment and the return of the forest.

Use and demise of the native grasslands

North America was not entirely without its complement of nutritious native grasses. For hundreds and thousands of years the interior plains of the Midwest had supported a luxuriant growth of grasses. Both the forest and the prairie fixed large quantities of carbon. In the forest much of the photosynthate or surplus carbon was stored in the trunks and the branches of the trees. In the prairie the majority of the photosynthate went to the roots of the grasses (Sears 1974; Foth 1984, 155–157). Large inputs of carbon from the decaying roots of the grasses and the slow decay of the resulting residue below ground built up very large pools of organic matter and nitrogen in the soil of the prairie (Brady 1984, 274–275). Differences in the nutrient cycling characteristics of grasses and trees also made the prairies richer in a number of important bases (Foth 1984, 231–232). The black-soil prairies of the Midwest encompassed some of the richest and the most productive soils in the world.

In addition to their fertility, the grasslands of the Midwest offered a number of other advantages to the enterprising settler. Although breaking the tough prairie sod and the roots of the leadplant (*Amorpha canescens*) required the assistance of professional prairie breakers and a large plow mounted on wheels (Robinson 1840; Bogue [1963] 1968, 70–72), the prairie could be brought into production rapidly. Farmers with the requisite capital thought nothing of preparing 80 to 160 acres of prairie in two to four years (Danhof 1941). The increasing demand for grain and the improved transportation network made it possible to realize a good return on one's investment (Danhof 1941). Prairie farms of the nineteenth century were a creation of the commercial market and the railroad (Parker 1982). The grasses of the prairies represented another resource of inestimable value to the settler. They formed ready-made pastures which could easily be converted into beef by the settlers' free-ranging cattle (McManis 1964, 58–59). The more nutritious and palatable grasses like big bluestem, Indian grass, switchgrass, and sloughgrass also made excellent hay (Weaver 1954, 25–34).

Prairies had their disadvantages. Prairie farmers were plagued by fever and ague and a deficiency of wood. Fever and ague were a characteristic feature of many of the wet prairies (McManis 1964, 41–44). Dry prairies were universally considered healthier (Birkbeck [1818] 1966, 69). Most attributed the fevers to a miasma arising from stagnant water or decaying vegetation (McManis 1964, 41–44). The discovery that fevers and ague were tied to malaria, mosquitoes, and stagnant water awaited the latter half of the nineteenth century. Many maintained that the scarcity of wood, particularly wood for fencing, hindered the settlement of the prairies (Bogue [1963] 1968, 74). The average farm required a surprising amount of fencing. Agricultural statistics suggest that 100 acres (40.5 ha) of farmland typically carried anywhere from 300 to 800 rods (1500–4000 m) of fencing (Dodge 1872; Primack 1969). With 14 rails to the rod (Jarchow 1949, 7) and a normal lifespan of 10 to 20 years (Danhof 1944), fences often taxed the wood supply of even the more favorably situated eastern farmer. The scarcity of wood on the prairie encouraged a number of innovative approaches to the enclosure problem. Farmers often purchased small tracts of woods in the neighboring valleys and floodplains to insure a supply of rails for their farms (Fuller 1923). Post and board fences were substituted for the traditional rail fence because they were more conservative in their use of wood. Other farmers experimented with sod fences and ditches (Hewes and Jung 1981). Osage orange (*Maclura pomifera*) was widely planted on the prairie as a hedge from 1850 to 1875 (Hewes and Jung 1981; Smith and Perino 1981). Unfortunately the living fences of osage orange required a prohibitive amount of care and they were subject to winterkill during severe winters (Primack 1969). By 1890, the invention and the production of large quantities of inexpensive barbed wire had largely solved the fencing problem on the prairies (Hayter 1939; Bogue [1963] 1968, 80–81).

The occupation of the tallgrass prairie took slightly more than half a century. It began in the 1820s around the southern and eastern borders of the Prairie Peninsula. Proximity to wood, grass, and water was the '*magnum desideratum*,' the *sine qua non* of the farmer (Flagg [1838] 1906, 302). As a result, the earliest settlements were confined to the smaller prairies or the margins of the larger prairies (Hewes 1950; Jordan 1964; Walters and Mansberger 1983), where a 'convenience of timber and fire wood, a supply of water, and land adjoining ready cleared' supplied most of the farmer's necessities (Thomas [1819] 1970, 185). The interiors of the larger prairies, like the Grand Prairie of eastern and central Illinois, were the last areas to be occupied. Distant from any navigable stream and wet and impassible during much of the year, the interior of the Grand Prairie was isolated from the outside world. Only the coming of the railroad in the 1850s brought the fertile Grand Prairie into the larger market economy of the East Coast (Gates 1934, 238–241). Thirty years later the transformation of the tall-grass prairie to the Corn Belt was essentially complete (Bogue [1963] 1968, 239).

Few ecosystems on the earth's surface have been modified as rapidly and as thoroughly as North America's mid-latitude grasslands. They were degraded and often destroyed on a number of fronts. Most of the alterations can be summarized in three phrases. They were 'plowed out,' 'grazed out,' and 'mown out.' The drier prairies were immediately converted to cropland. Observers like J. Allen (1870) noted the ease and the rapidity of the transformation. 'Since vast areas of the prairies offer no obstructions to the revolutionizing plow, the astonishing rapidity of the change in the flora that follows its march can scarcely be conceived by those who have not witnessed its actual progress. No sooner is the sod inverted than scores of species of the original and most characteristic plants almost wholly disappear; in a few years the luxuriant wild grasses, overtopped with showy flowers, varying the hue of the landscape with the advancing season, have become supplanted by the cultivated grasses and the cereals, and that constant scourge of the agriculturist, the ever intrusive weeds.' Many considered the waving fields of grain an improvement. A few viewed the changes with apprehension. The botanist, C.W. Short (1845), for instance, expressed dismay at the destruction of a prairie near Terre Haute, Indiana.

The first sight of a prairie with which we were greeted was in the neighborhood of Terre Haute on the eastern side of the Wabash, and consequently in the State of Indiana. In approaching this new and apparently thriving town, from the east, over the national road, the eye is filled with the prospect of an extensive plain entirely destitute of all timber-trees, and stretching to a great distance both above and below the town. Such a view, agreeable at all times, was peculiarly so as it opened suddenly upon us just after emerging from the heavily wooded forest through which we had traveled all day. The Terre Haute prairie, however, has been all reclaimed, or rather botanically speaking, desecrated by the hand of man, and no portion of it now remains in a state of nature. Corn, grass, small grain, and other cultivated crops now occupy the hundreds of acres which lately bloomed and blossomed with indigenous productions; and almost the only relics of these to be seen were occasionally on the road-side, or in fence-corners, a few plants of *Verbena stricta* and *Vernonia fasciculata*.

Some of the richest prairies – the wet, black-soil prairies of eastern Illinois – were often the last areas to be plowed. Many remained intact until the massive drainage operations of the late 1870s (Bogue [1963] 1968, 85).

Next to the breaking plow, overgrazing was the major factor responsible for the decline of the tallgrass prairie (Weaver 1954, 271). The open range of the wetter prairies supported some of the largest cattle kings of the early nineteenth century (Bogue [1963] 1968, 93–94; Gates 1973). Pasturage was abundant and free. Opinions vary as to the value of the prairies as pastures. America's prairie grasses were noted for their high productivity (Weaver 1954, 274), their palatability, and their feeding qualities (Oliver [1843] 1966, 22; Caird 1859, 60). Introduced, cool-season grasses, however, had the advantage of a longer feeding season (Caird 1859, 61). They renewed their growth earlier in the spring and continued their growth in the autumn when the native, warm-season grasses were dormant. More importantly, they tolerated a regime of heavy grazing and trampling. Unlike their European counterparts, the native grasses, e.g., big bluestem, Indian grass, and switchgrass, did 'not bear much eating ... where a considerable number of cattle [were] kept' (Oliver [1843] 1966, 22). Sensitivity to grazing was related to a number of morphological and physiological factors. Grazing disrupted the normal hormonal control of the growth patterns of many of the native grasses. It also seriously reduced the photosynthetic area and eliminated the meristematic or growth producing tissue of the more erect, tussock-forming native species (Branson 1953; Neiland and Curtis 1956; Dix 1959). In contrast, grazing favored the spread and the eventual domination of the short-stemmed, rhizomatious bluegrass (*Poa pratensis* and *P. compressa*) pastures (Caird 1859, 78–79). The deliberate suppression of spring fires also aided the expansion of the cool-season *Poas* (Curtis and Partch 1948; Ehrenreich and Aikman 1963). Comparisons of grazed and ungrazed virgin prairies demonstrated major changes in the indigenous forbs of the prairie. Flowering spurge (*Euphorbia corollata*), bush lespedeza (*Lespedeza capitata*), leadplant (*Amorpha canescens*), white prairie clover (*Petalostemum candidum*), purple prairie clover (*P. purpureum*), scurf pea (*Psoralea tenuiflora*), and the numerous species of blazing stars (*Liatris* spp.) were among the more prominent 'decreasers' (Drew 1947; Voigt and Weaver 1951; Kucera 1956; Dix 1959; Ehrenreich and Aikman 1963; Nyboer 1981). Unpalatable species with pubescent leaves, e.g., horseweed (*Erigeron canadensis*) and hoary vervain (*Verbena stricta*), and prostrate species, e.g., *Antennaria* spp. and *Plantago* spp., appear to have been the major beneficiaries (Drew 1947; Dix 1959; Ehrenreich and Aikman 1963).

Meadows were among the last major refuges of the prairie. Mowing was not as destructive to the native grasses as grazing. Early mowing and the deliberate removal of the coarser 'weeds' did reduce the forb component of the prairie (Drew 1947; Conard and Arthaud 1957). Mowing at frequent intervals also encouraged the invasion of timothy, red clover, and white sweet clover (*Melilotus alba*). A serious invasion of white sweet clover diminished the value of the prairie hay and often led to the breaking of the prairie (Weaver and Fitzpatrick 1934). All of these factors, plus the ease of establishing tame hay meadows of timothy and clover, reduced the importance of the prairie hay meadow. State agricultural censuses document the decline of the tallgrass prairie in Iowa. In 1895 Iowa had 1 760 000 acres (700 000 ha) of wild prairie hay (McFarland 1896, 632). By 1910 the state was down to less than 850 000 acres (344 000 ha) of wild hay and by 1940 native prairie hay had largely disappeared from Iowa (Hughes and Heath 1946), although it was still common to the west in Nebraska and South Dakota (Weaver and Flory 1934).

The destruction of North America's mid-latitude grasslands took less than a century. The prairie flora persisted for a while along public highways and in the 'corners' of old worm rail fences. Highway improvements, undiscriminating weed laws, and the advent of the wire fence eventually eliminated these holdovers from the prairie (Hilgard 1915; Shimek 1925). Less than 1.0% of Minnesota's and Missouri's prairies and only 0.02% and 0.01% of Iowa's and Illinois' prairies respectively are left today (see Table 4.3). The loss is even greater if one limits one's attention to the prairies occupying prime agricultural land. Less than 260 ha of black-soil prairies remain in Illinois out of the 6.6 million ha that once covered the state (White 1981). The prairies of Missouri and Minnesota have fared somewhat better, probably due to the fact that large segments of the remaining prairies are on agriculturally marginal sites (Wendt 1984; White 1986). Most of the remaining fragments of the tallgrass prairie in the Midwest are concentrated on railroad right of ways, old cemeteries, 'odd corners of land,' hayfields, undeveloped tracts of land held by speculators, and land that is too steep, too rocky, or too shallow for plowing. Railroad right of ways and pioneer cemeteries contain some of the best remnants. They have escaped most of the plowing and grazing, yet have been burned or mowed frequently enough to suppress the invasion of woody plants.

The loss of the prairie was a paradoxical affair which was intimately associated with the biology of the prairie's forbs and grasses. The tallgrass prairie was a very stable entity, yet it was also susceptible to human influences. Under natural conditions the prairie exhibited a high degree of stability (Weaver and Flory 1934; Weaver 1954, 118–121). Changes occurred in the species composition of the prairie but, for the most part, they were relatively minor (Anderson 1946; Weaver 1954, 118; Betz and Cole 1969). The high leaf area index (5 to 8 acres of leaves covered each acre of ground) and the dense root network of the bluestem prairie (Weaver 1954, 120) led to intense competition for light and water (Weaver and Flory 1934). Seedling establishment was a rare event, often associated with the death of mature individuals (Blake 1935; Christiansen and Landers 1966). Most of the dominant forbs produced a small number of large seeds on at least a sporadic basis. The large food reserves of the seeds favored the rapid development of a root system and ultimately the successful establishment of the seedling. Vegetative growth by means of rhizomes, roots, or stolons eventually allowed the expansion of the species under the competitive conditions of the prairie. The long lifespans (in the vicinity of 10 to 30 years) and the reproductive habits of the prairie's dominant forbs and grasses brought continuity to the prairie (Havercamp and Whitney 1983).

Plowing and grazing upset the natural equilibrium of the prairie. It was commonly believed that the forbs and grasses of the prairie would not return once the prairie was broken (Shimek 1925). In reality, the return to predisturbance conditions was painfully slow. The botanist, Bohumil Shimek (1925), for example, noted a railroad cut in a mesic prairie in Iowa that had st¹¹ not returned fully to its original condition 70 years after a disturbance in 1854. Several other investigators (Brotherson and Landers 1978; Glenn-Lewin 1980) documented the slow recovery of a segment of Iowa's 65 ha Kalsow Prairie from grazing. Heavy grazing had eliminated many of the forbs and grasses from the northwest corner of the prairie prior to its acquisition as a natural area in 1949. The cessation of grazing allowed the recovery of the degraded corner of the prairie. Twenty-eight years later, however, only the 10 to 20 m segment of the grazed prairie adjacent to the undisturbed prairie contained the normal complement of native grasses and forbs. Vegetative reproduction probably accounted for the slow spread of many of the natives, e.g., the blazing stars, the prairie phlox (*Phlox pilosa*), the gentians, and the prairie dropseed (*Sporobolus heterolepsis*), to the grazed area (Glenn-Lewin 1980). The reversion of cultivated land to prairie was an equally long, drawn-out process. A 20 year successional study of a reseeded field of little bluestem (*Schizachyrium scoparium*) and switchgrass (*Panicum virgatum*) in Kansas likewise showed very few of the forbs in the adjoining prairie had invaded the field (Fitch and Hall 1978).

The low mobility and the relatively sedentary nature of many prairie species makes them excellent indicators of the original tallgrass prairie. Gould (1941) compared the distribution of a number of prairie species in Dane County, Wisconsin, in 1936 with the location of the county's presettlement prairies as shown in the 1836 land survey maps of the area. After 100 years, compass plant (*Silphium laciniatum*) and rattlesnake master (*Eryngium yuccifolium*) were still largely confined to areas initially mapped as prairies (Fig. 11.1). A similar study of prairies in northwestern Ohio (Anderson 1971, 135–166) showed a strong correspondence between the distribution of *Asclepias sullivantii*, *Coreopsis tripteris*, *Helianthus grosseserratus*, *Monarda fistulosa*, *Pycnanthemum virginianum*, *Ratibida pinnata*, *Silphium terebinthinaceum*, and *Solidago rigida* and areas mapped as prairies in 1821. More detailed lists of indicator species have been compiled for prairies in the states of Wisconsin (Thompson 1940; Curtis and Greene 1949; Curtis 1959, 294), Ohio

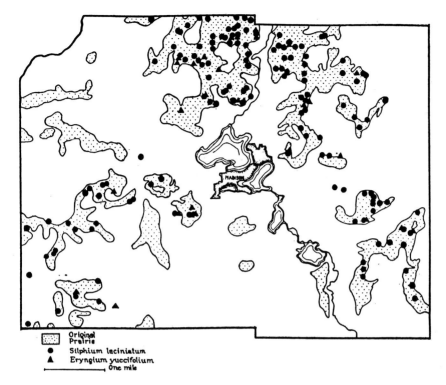

Fig. 11.1 Distribution of compass plant (*Silphium laciniatum*) and rattlesnake master (*Eryngium yuccifolium*) in Dane County, Wisconsin, in 1936 and location of prairie openings (stippled areas) in county in 1836 as shown on early surveyor's map of county. Of the 171 locations in which one or both of these species were recorded in 1936, only seven were outside of the areas originally mapped as prairie. Reprinted from Gould (1941) by permission of the Ecological Society of America.

(Gordon 1969, 58–59; Cusick and Troutman 1978), and Illinois (Kerr and White 1981).

Many individuals have lamented the loss of the prairie. Few have expressed their views on the subject as eloquently as John Weaver, the dean of America's grassland ecologists. On the last page of his book *North American Prairie*, Weaver (1954, 325) stated:

The disappearance of a major natural unit of vegetation from the face of the earth is an event worthy of causing pause and consideration by any nation. Yet so gradually has the prairie been conquered by the breaking plow, the tractor, and the overcrowded herds of man, and so intent has he been upon securing from the soil its last measure of innate fertility, that scant attention has been given to the significance of this endless grassland or the course of its destruction. Civilized man is destroying a masterpiece of nature without recording for posterity that which he has destroyed.

The prairie provides us with a background against which we may measure the success or failure of our own land use and management. ... [It] is the outcome of thousands of years of sorting of species and adaptations to soil and climate. ... prairie is much more than land covered with grass. It is a slowly evolved, highly complex organic entity, centuries old. It approaches the eternal. Once destroyed, it can never be replaced by man.

12

Forest influences

The clearing of forests, the want of permanent springs, and the existence of torrents, are three phenomena closely connected together.
Alexander von Humboldt. 1819. *Personal Narrative of Travels to the Equinoctial Regions of the New Continent ...1799–1804*

The first thing needed in trying to stop floods by tree growth is to drop all exaggeration about it.
William B. Greeley, Chief Forester, US Forest Service. 1927.
'The part of forestry in flood control.'

Few areas on the face of the earth realized as dramatic a transformation of their surface as North America experienced in the eighteenth and nineteenth centuries (Zon 1927). North America represented a natural laboratory where major modifications of the earth's surface, e.g., forest clearance and drainage, were undertaken on a vast, continental scale. Contemporary observers noted the effects of many of these chance experiments (Chinard 1945). Most felt that North America's climate and water resources had been altered – sometimes for the better, more often for the worse.

Effects of forest clearance on climate

The widespread effects of deforestation were obvious to even the less scientifically inclined members of society. Their casual observations were eventually codified into a body of information known as 'forest influences.' Few issues attracted as much speculation or generated as much controversy as the effect of deforestation on the climate. As early as 1654 Captain Edward Johnson ([1654] 1910, 84) noted that many Puritans believed deforestation had moderated New England's cold winter climate. George Perkins Marsh in a thorough review of the subject in *Man and Nature* ([1864] 1965, 122), however, expressed the opinion that many of the theories were 'inferential' and 'somewhat discordant.'

The lack of suitable instrumentation hampered the analysis of the theories. Long-term records based upon the use of thermometers and rain gauges were very scattered before the nineteenth century (Kincer 1933, Brown 1951, Ludlum 1966). Timothy Dwight ([1821] 1969, 1:41) correctly pointed out in 1821 that 'the observation on this subject has been so loose, and the records are so few and imperfect, as to leave our real knowledge of it very limited.'

Since the disputants lacked hard data to support their theories, the subject of forest influences often slipped into the realm of armchair speculation. Observers managed to construct grandiose theories on the basis of a few known facts. Limited numbers of facts were logically pyramided into full-blown theories. Witness the case of the effect of forests on precipitation patterns. Forests have long been associated with precipitation. The opinion has often been expressed that forests induce precipitation (Golding 1970). George Perkins Marsh is credited with formulating a popular theory concerning forests and precipitation (Emmons 1971). According to Marsh, forests cooled the air in their immediate vicinity. Precipitation occurred whenever a current of saturated air swept in over the cold forest. Cooling condensed the water vapor in the air and reduced the air's ability to hold water. The result was precipitation (Marsh [1864] 1965, 158). Marsh overlooked the equally logical argument that the lower temperature of the forest would reduce the frequency and the intensity of locally formed convectional rain showers (Kittredge 1948, 95). Forests have also been credited with moistening the atmosphere by means of transpiration (Zon 1927). Theoretically this should increase the precipitation in their immediate vicinity. Most scientists, however, feel that local evaporation accounts for only a small percentage of the annual precipitation of a given area (Golding 1970). Other forms of vegetation also release large quantities of water into the atmosphere. The difference in the precipitation between between a forested area and an adjacent grassland is probably minimal (Golding 1970).

Armchair speculation occasionally led to the transposition of cause and effect. Many observers, for instance, cited the close association of forests and precipitation as evidence of the beneficial effects of forests upon the climate (Kedzie 1867). Charles Sprague Sargent (1882), the director of Harvard's Arnold Arboretum, succinctly dismissed this theory when he stated 'forests do not produce rain; rain produces the forests.'

The short-term outlook of many observers also precluded an accurate assessment of long-range trends. The late eighteenth century and the early nineteenth century, for instance, witnessed a spate of accounts on North America's improved climatic conditions (Jefferson 1787, 134; Williamson 1789; Volney [1804] 1968, 221). Most alluded to the fact that the climate was more equitable. The winters were shorter and the snow was less frequent than in the past. The improved conditions were commonly attributed to the removal of the forest. Clearing, it was argued, allowed the sun's rays to heat the lower atmosphere (Williamson 1789). Milder conditions were the rule at the start of the nineteenth century, but that was only the upturn of a longer term climatic cycle (Kincer 1933; Baron *et al.* 1984). A series of cold winters could lead to quite the opposite conclusion. The learned German traveler, Johann David Schoepf (1875) noted wryly, 'The credulous Americans have long flattered themselves that, by the progress of cultivation and the destruction of the forests of the country, their climate has been rendered much milder and the severity of the winters more moderated. The past winter, however, has disappointed these premature considerations.'

The average American farmer probably drew upon his own store of experience to assess the effects of deforestation. He knew, for example, that the woods felt cooler in the summer and warmer in the winter than his own exposed fields. Noah Webster's summary of Dr Samuel Williams' early (1794) microclimatological studies in Vermont substantiated the farmer's experience. Thermometers placed in the earth in the forest and in a nearby open field showed that the field was warmer in the summer and cooler in the winter (Webster [1799] 1843, 145–148). Clearing, Webster ([1799] 1843, 146–148) concluded, only increased the winter's cold, augmented the summer's heat, and exposed the crops to more violent winds.

Noah Webster's observations were only the first in a long series of reports linking forest clearance with a deteriorating climate. The publication of George Perkins Marsh's book, *Man and Nature*, in 1864 lent additional weight to the climatic deterioration scenario. 'So far as we are able to sum up the results,' Marsh ([1864] 1965, 158) stated, 'it would appear that in countries in the temperate zone, still chiefly covered with woods, the summers would be cooler, shorter; the winters milder, drier, longer than in the same regions after the removal of the forests.' Marsh ([1864] 1965, 130–133) also emphasized the importance of trees as windbreaks – as protection from the frigid blasts of winter and the drying winds of summer. The implications of *Man and Nature* were clear. Agricultural writers soon reiterated and embellished Marsh's warnings (Watson 1866; Edge 1878). Forest clearance became synonymous with a decline in the productivity of the nation's farmlands. Scientists cited the loss of frost sensitive and disease ravaged fruit trees in Maine and Massachusetts (Sargent 1877) and the death of winter-killed wheat and clover in Michigan (Kedzie, Woodman, and Fellows 1866) as only a few of the evils attending forest clearance. The state legislature of Wisconsin even commissioned a study on the impact of deforestation. The result was Lapham, Knapp, and Crocker's (1867) comprehensive, yet at times hyperbolic, *Report on the Disastrous Effects of the Destruction of Forest Trees*. Lapham and his coworkers concluded their report with this assertion: 'clearing away the forests of Wisconsin will have a very decided effect upon the climate and productions.' They then proceeded to enumerate the evil consequences of deforestation and predicted a return to barbarism unless Americans mended their ways (Lapham, Knapp, and Crocker 1867, 24).

The validity of many of these early theories, particularly the extrapolation from micro- to macroscale conditions, is more suspect today. One reviewer of the subject, the silviculturist H. G. Wilm (1946), stated: 'No conclusive evidence has been found to demonstrate that climate, and especially precipitation, has been appreciably modified by the progress of settlement and the removal of forests.' Given the current interest in tropical or planet-wide deforestation, however, it would be difficult to fault Marsh and Lapham for following a similar line of reasoning in the nineteenth century. Recent reviews, particularly as they relate to deforestation, atmospheric carbon dioxide levels, and albedo changes have revived the forest–climate issue at the macroscale level (Thompson 1980; Jager and Barry 1990).

Deforestation and streamflow

Not all of Marsh and Lapham's contemporaries believed that forests were a major determinant of the climate. If forests had little to do with increasing the rainfall, however, most observers believed that they definitely influenced the disposition of the rain (Wood 1875; Sargent 1882). Conventional wisdom suggested that the deep, spongy mass of the forest floor absorbed the rain and regulated the flow of water to the stream. During downpours, the forest slowed the rush of water to the stream. Forests husbanded the rain, gradually releasing it to maintain the flow of springs and streams during the long, dry summer period (Emerson 1846, 4–5). Forests also diminished the chance of ground frost, the rapid melting of the snow, and the outbreak of freshets in the spring (Piper 1855–1858, 48). Gifford Pinchot (1910, 53), the first director of the US Forest Service, summarized the relationship very succinctly: 'The connection between forests and rivers is like that between father and son. No forests, no rivers.'

Much of the theory was based on information of an anecdotal nature. Colonial observers, for instance, noted the association of deforestation and low flow periods. The New England journalist Dr William Douglass (1760,

2:55) commented upon the loss of small streams as the country was cleared. Lewis Evans ([1753] 1939, 96–97), one of Pennsylvania's better known geographers, provided a more detailed account of the changes that followed settlement:

Before the Arrival of the Europeans, the whole Country was a Wood, The swamps full of Cripple & Brush; & The Ground unbroke. Our Runs dry up apace, several which formerly wou'd turn a fulling Mill, are now scarce sufficient for The Use of a Farm, the Reason of which is this, When the Country was cover'd with Woods, & Swamps with Brush, the Rain That fell was detained by These Interruptions, & so had time to insinuate into the Earth, & contribute to the Springs & Runs. But now the Country is clear'd, the Rain as fast as it falls, is hurried into the Rivers & washes away the Earth & Soil of our naked Fields, fills & Choaks the Springs, & makes Shoals & Sand-banks in our Creeks & Rivers, & hence several Creeks, mentioned by Mr. Penn to be navigable, are now no longer so.

George Perkins Marsh's review of the European literature in *Man and Nature* ([1864] 1965) lent additional weight to the argument. Though he lacked precise measurements, Marsh ([1864] 1965, 182) was convinced 'that the flow of springs and the normal volume of rivers rise and fall with the extension and the diminution of the woods where they originate and through which they run ...'

Defining the relationship between forests and streamflow was more than just an academic enterprise in the nineteenth century. Reduced streamflow had important economic consequences. It 'materially injured the manufacturing interests dependent upon hydraulic power' and it disrupted the commerce tied to the nation's rivers and canals (Hough 1878, 289). Interest in preserving the real and the fancied streamflow benefits of the forest eventually would play a key role in the development of the nation's forest reserve system (Schiff 1962; Lull and Reinhart 1972, 2–3).

By the end of the nineteenth century, the positive influence of the forest was firmly entrenched in the public mind. Surveys conducted by state agricultural societies and forestry bureaus repeatedly emphasized the forest's value in regulating the flow of streams (Lull 1963). A questionnaire distributed to over 150 long-time residents of the state of Pennsylvania in 1894 revealed the following: two-thirds of the respondents cited instances where they believed forest clearance had been responsible for a change in streamflow. Half of the respondents were aware of mills which had ceased operation or had been forced to convert to steam due to a scarcity of water. Forty-eight percent attributed the loss of a local spring to forest clearance (Rothrock and Shunk 1896, 79–109).

Not all observers adhered to the conventional wisdom that forests regulated streamflow. Engineers (Mead 1911) and meteorologists (Moore 1910), in particular, had serious reservations about the forest's ability to control floods. Hiram Chittenden (1908) of the US Army Corps of Engineers argued that forests were unable to prevent the occurrence of floods during periods of heavy and prolonged precipitation. Forests, he asserted, could even increase the severity of freshets by delaying snowmelt until the arrival of hot weather. Pronouncements by engineers, however, were always suspect because they were more inclined to favor the construction of dams and downstream flood control projects.

An appeal to scientific evidence might have resolved the streamflow–flood control controversy. Unfortunately the long-term data on forest cover, the discharge of rivers, and the occurrence of flood crests were either nonexistent or inconclusive (Hall and Maxwell 1910; Moore 1910). Comparisons of the streamflow characteristics of forested and unforested catchments were often complicated by differences in the substrate or the topographic features of the two watersheds (Vermeule 1896; Griffith 1910; Lull and Storey 1957). Scientific tests of the various forest–streamflow hypotheses awaited the more controlled watershed experiments of the twentieth century (Satterlund and Adams 1992, 43–45).

Most hydrologists today realize that forests are only one of a variety of factors that influence streamflow patterns. As Chittenden (1908) pointed out, severe floods, i.e., those occurring on the order of once every 50 to 100 years, are usually caused by intense or prolonged periods of rainfall, snowmelt, or a combination thereof (Ward 1975, 274–275). They are generally the result of direct runoff or quickflow. Quickflow is water which reaches the stream channel within a day or so of rainfall (Dunne and Leopold 1978, 257). It is partially determined by the soil-moisture storage characteristics of the watershed. Forests have the ability to intercept, detain, and retain some of the precipitation so that it doesn't reach the stream within 24 hours. Unfortunately their storage capacities are usually rather limited. Extreme precipitation events, like the maximum 100 year frequency storm can drop as much as 4 to 7 inches of precipitation on a given area in the Northeast over a 24 hour period (Dunne and Leopold 1978, 63). Four to seven inches of water is well in excess of the storage capacity of the forest floor. The humus layer in the Northeast typically retains anywhere from 0.3 to 1.5 inches of rain. Temporary storage or detention on the forest floor can account for another 0.3 to 1.5 inches of rain (Trimble and Lull 1956; Lull 1959).

The watershed's substrate, topography, and antecedent soil-moisture conditions should also be factored into the direct runoff or quickflow equation. Areas with saturated soil or a limited soil-water storage capacity, e.g., watersheds with a shallow soil mantle or a limited depth to an impervious layer, often contribute a disproportionate share of their water to direct runoff (Hewlett and Hibbert 1967; Hewlett and Nutter 1969, 102–103; Anderson, Hoover, and Reinhart 1976). Due to their frequent association with steep slopes, shallow soils, and other agriculturally marginal areas, forested basins have been the site of some of the worst floods in history (Lull and Reinhart 1972, 15–16; Lee 1980, 278–280). Flood records on the Ohio River at Pittsburgh extend back to 1762, well before there was any large-scale deforestation of the drainage basin. The floods of 1762 and 1763 were among the worst in the 175 years of observation (Moseley 1939). The floods occurred during a winter thaw accompanied by heavy rains. The soil was already saturated and had a very limited capacity to absorb more water (Trautman 1977).

Land use practices can also influence streamflow patterns, although their effects must be superimposed upon the previously mentioned factors (Hewlett and Hibbert 1967). Forests utilize large quantities of water during the growing season. Water losses from transpiration generally outweigh the small water gains that result from shade and reduced evaporation. Complete deforestation of experimental watersheds in the East has typically increased the water yield or streamflow anywhere from 20 to 40% (Lee 1980, 206–207) or 25 mm for each 10% decrease in forest cover (Bosch and Hewlett 1982). Much of the increased flow occurred during the summertime or the growing season (Riggs 1965; Dunne and Leopold 1978, 453). Reforestation of abandoned farmlands and regrowth following logging has had the opposite effect. Streamflow decreased following reforestation (Brakensiek and Amerman 1960; Harrold *et al.* 1962; Eschner and Satterlund 1966; Trimble, Weirich, and Hoag 1987). The reductions have been attributed to sublimation of the snow and an increase in the amount of water lost by interception and transpiration in the reforested areas. Reductions of water yield in the Piedmont have been greater in dry years, suggesting that trees can maintain high rates of transpiration by tapping moisture deep in the soil (Trimble, Weirich, and Hoag 1987).

Deforestation was not the only factor responsible for major changes in the hydrological cycle. Frequently it was the agricultural activity which followed deforestation, not the cutting of the forest per se, that altered the streamflow pattern. Forests and other relatively undisturbed forms of vegetation normally promote the infiltration of water. Precipitation that infiltrates the soil and slowly percolates to the groundwater is known as baseflow or delayed flow. Baseflow is important because it sustains the flow of springs and streams during dry periods.

Agricultural activities often have the effect of discouraging infiltration. Heavy grazing has frequently been cited as one of the more harmful agricultural activities (Spurr and Barnes 1980, 359). As the early Pennsylvanian naturalist John Bartram ([1760] 1934) noted, 'When ye woods was not pastured &

full of high weeds & ye ground light then ye rain sunk much more into ye earth and did not wash & tear up ye surface ...' Although the harmful effects of grazing have probably been overexaggerated (Patric and Helvey 1986), grazing in its extreme form can compact the soil and reduce the infiltration of water. The situation, however, is much more severe on cultivated land. Rain has the ability to detach small particles from the unprotected surface of the soil. The detached particles seal off the surface of the soil, eventually lowering the infiltration of water into the soil. Much of the water on cultivated land is diverted from infiltrated subsurface flow to overland flow and direct runoff (Sartz and Tolsted 1974; Sartz 1975; Sartz, Curtis, and Tolsted 1977; Sartz 1978). Water is hurried to the stream by means of overland flow as opposed to the slower subsurface route. The result is a feast and a famine situation – an increase in peak flows and an increase in low flow periods. Frequent references to disappearing springs in the nineteenth century were probably prompted by reduced infiltration and increased overland flow, although it is difficult to rule out other causative factors such as normal climatic fluctuations or overactive imaginations (Verry 1986; Satterlund and Adams 1992, 286).

John T. Curtis' (1951) study of Jordan Township in southern Wisconsin represents an intriguing attempt to tie streamflow patterns to changing land use practices. Building upon various documentary sources and an earlier study by Shriner and Copeland (1904), Curtis detailed the expansion of farmland in the township and the loss of the township's permanently flowing streams. In 1831, before it was settled, Jordan Township was 97.8% wooded and had 40.5 miles of permanently flowing streams. By 1902 it was heavily involved in the dairy industry. Its woodland coverage had been reduced to 9.4% and over ten miles of the formerly permanently flowing streams were dry during the low flow summer period (Shriner and Copeland 1904). The state's Land Economic Inventory map of 1935 indicated that the woodland area had decreased to 4.3% of the township. Stream length had been reduced another 4.1 miles, making a cumulative loss of 14.8 miles or 36.5 % of the length of the permanently flowing streams during the first 100 years of the township's history. Curtis (1956) attributed most of the loss to reduced infiltration and a decrease in subsoil water storage associated with cultivation and pasturing. Increased erosion and changes in the form of the channel may also have contributed to some of the loss (Beschta and Platts 1986). Similar decreases have been noted in the lengths of stream drainage networks in urban areas, although here most of the decrease has been attributed to paving (Dunne and Leopold 1978, 693–694).

Due to the large quantities of overland flow involved, peak flows from croplands on small watersheds can exceed those from forests by a factor of five to ten times (Lull and Reinhart 1972, 55–57). Documenting changes in the peak flow and discharge patterns of larger river basins over time is a much more complicated affair. Some of the alterations may be due to climatic causes. A technique known as double mass analysis excludes many of the changes associated with climatic factors. In double mass analysis the cumulative flow pattern of the basin in question is plotted against that of a nearby control basin or against the cumulative precipitation of the basin. Changes in the slope of the plotted line signify a change in the hydrologic relationship of the two basins or the water yield for a given amount of precipitation. E. S. Verry's (1986) comparison of flood peaks on the Upper Mississippi River at St Paul, Minnesota, and peak flows on the Red River of the North at Grand Forks, North Dakota, from 1883 to 1980 is one of the more interesting examples of the use of double mass analysis. Starting in 1908 annual peak flow on the Mississippi River increased approximately 40%. The increase coincided with the peak of cutting and the conversion of the area to farmland. Verry attributed the augumented peak flow to forest clearance, an increase in surface runoff, and an alteration of the area's snowmelt patterns. As Verry's study and other work in temperate forests suggests (Clark 1987), forest clearance can increase the peak discharge of lesser flood events, i.e., storms with a return interval of 1 to 20 years. Double mass analysis has been employed in a variety of situations to illustrate the effects of forests and other external factors on river flow patterns. Patric (1974) demonstrated a short-term increase in flow patterns in New England following the destructive hurricane of 1938 while Patric and Gould (1976) detailed a decrease in river flow patterns in Massachusetts following reforestation in the twentieth century. Their work points out the broader relationship of deforestation and streamflow patterns. Fortunately for New England, maximum deforestation in the nineteenth century and increased water flow coincided with the start of the Industrial Revolution and its water-powered factory system.

If nothing else, the above discussion should illustrate the fact that the relationship of forests and water is a very complex affair. Forests are only one of a number of factors which influence streamflow. Many early conservationists made forceful claims about the beneficial effects of forests. Although the claims often proved to be exaggerated, they did have the effect of highlighting the hydrological consequences of altering the landscape.

Wetland drainage

Forest clearance represented one of the more obvious alterations of the American landscape. There were also a number of other activities, like the major drainage operations of the nineteenth century, which were more subtle yet left their mark upon the landscape. Historians have reviewed the drainage of America's wetlands from the legal, the political, and the technological viewpoint (Bogue 1951; Weaver 1964; Herget 1978) and there are a number of excellent regional studies of the history of drainage enterprises (Hewes and Frandson 1952; Taylor 1955; Richason 1960a, 1960b; Moline 1969; Kelly 1975b; Winsor 1975). Few historians, however, have dealt with the broader ecological implications of the issue.

Wetlands delayed the settlement of large portions of the Midwest and represented a major barrier to the successful agricultural exploitation of the area (Power 1935; Kaatz 1955). Settlers and surveyors alike wrote the wetlands off as 'lost or 3rd rate lands' in the belief they would never be used for farming (Lindsey 1966, xv). Draining the wetlands of the Midwest took roughly twice as long as clearing the forests.

In the Midwest poor drainage and wet terrain often characterized the same area. Glaciation obliterated much of the area's preglacial stream system, leaving in its wake a relatively inefficient, poorly developed drainage network. Level to gently rolling terrain and a veneer of impermeable drift exacerbated the drainage situation.

Early descriptions of the till and lake plains of Michigan, Indiana, Ohio, and Illinois made frequent reference to extensive morasses (Kaatz 1955) and 'miles of low, level wet land covered with successive pools of water' (Hall 1916, 346). Swamplands covered by water more than half the summer were known as 'slashes' (Howe 1848, 98). Water which remained ponded on the surface of the land for an unseasonably long period of time caused the death of trees and probably accounted for references to 'scalded lands' in the early land surveyors' field notes (Ives 1947, 18–19). Standing water also contributed to the Midwest's reputation as 'a gigantic emporium of malaria' (Winsor 1975, 45).

Large accumulations of fallen trees and driftwood in many of the rivers of the Midwest compounded the drainage problem. The French geographer E. Desor ([1879] 1907) described several of the larger obstructions on the Manistique River in Michigan. His account, reproduced below, provides a picture of the extremely obstructed nature of the early waterways.

The rafts, which the Canadians called 'embarras,' are by no means rare in the forest, wherever the gradient of the rivers is slight. A tree uprooted by the current, and dragged along by the river catches on the side of a meander; if the current does not dislodge it, a second trunk coming along is stopped, others come along and their branches interlacing, they end by forming a barrier which increases indefinitely. There are some of these barriers which have a considerable area and are very old, since they are often found covered with bushes which have taken root upon the floating trunks.

One of the larger obstructions Desor encountered was several hundred fathoms (probably 400 to 800 m) long. The debris dam was covered by raspberries and other shrubs which grew 'as parasites' on the half rotten trunks of the trees. Large woody debris dams were apparently fairly common on the nation's pristine rivers and streams (Chamberlain 1849, 13; Kaatz 1955). By holding the water back upstream, they extended the floodplain's reach creating a unique riparian habitat full of channels, cutoffs, sloughs, and other backwater areas (Keller and Swanson 1979; Sedell and Froggatt 1984; Triska 1984).

Clearing the downed trees from North America's rivers and streams was a major undertaking which spanned several centuries. The town records of Dedham, Massachusetts, relate how the early inhabitants cleared their clogged streams and swamps in order to create the valuable Charles River meadows (Worthington 1827, 10–11). Obstructions on many of New England's streams increased the incidence of flooding and made the grass poor and the hay uncertain in the neighboring meadows (Whitney 1793, 77). Removing the debris from the nation's principal waterways became a major government works project. Thousands of hazardous 'snags' and 'sawyers,' i.e., trees caught in the river so that they sawed back and forth with the water, were removed from the Ohio River in the 1820s (Flagg [1838] 1906, 57; Parsons 1920, 25–26). The nineteenth and early twentieth century reports of the Secretary of War provide a conservative estimate of the number of snags pulled from several rivers in the Midwest. Seven thousand and seven hundred snags, for instance, were removed from 48 snag-infested miles of the Wabash River in Illinois and Indiana between 1872 and 1906 (Sedell, Everest, and Swanson 1982). Snag removal, drainage, the construction of dams, channelization, and other government sponsored improvements inexorably reduced the extent of the floodplain associated with many of the nation's rivers (Sedell and Froggatt 1984).

The construction of small open ditches and the clearing of streams dominated the early colonial phases of the drainage process (Wooten and Jones 1955). Ditching natural swamps and meadows and converting them to productive fields of English hay was part of the improving spirit of early nineteenth century New England agriculture (Hill 1842; Newhall 1847). Large-scale reclamation activites in the form of subsurface drainage projects awaited the latter half of the nineteenth century. Technological developments, rising world commodity demands, and higher agricultural prices spurred a new interest in bringing the Midwest's fertile wetlands into production after 1870 (Richards 1984).

Tile under-drainage was introduced in England in the early 1800s (Duffey *et al.* 1974, 36) and soon found its way across the Atlantic. John Johnston, a

Scottish immigrant who settled on a farm in upstate New York, is credited with the first use of clay tiles in the early 1830s (Weaver 1964). The earliest clay tiles were handmade, horseshoe-shaped affairs, without any bottom (Kaatz 1955). Initially drainage was a very costly operation in relation to the value of the land (Johnston 1851, 2:162). Few could justify the expense of draining land at $20 – $40 an acre when unimproved land sold for $3 – $10 per acre (Winsor 1975, 80–84). The mass production of improved, round, clay pipe tiles and the dramatic expansion of tile factories in the 1860s (Weaver 1964, 222), however, soon brought the price of clay tiles within the means of the average farmer (Winsor 1975, 167–172). Rising land values in the 1870s and the 1880s and the increased demand for grain also made drainage a cost-effective investment.

Both the federal and the state governments were deeply involved in reclamation activities. Congress passed the Swamp Land Acts of 1849 and 1850 with the ostensible purpose of promoting wetland reclamation. Although millions of acres of swamplands were turned over to the states, few of the wetlands were immediately reclaimed. Large-scale reclamation was impeded by the amount of cooperative planning required. It was impractical for a small farmer to under-drain his fields if the requisite surface outlets for the tile drains were nonexistent. The passage of state drainage laws and the formation of drainage districts in the latter half of the nineteenth century and the early twentieth century facilitated the spread of large-scale drainage enterprises (Bogue 1951; Herget 1978). The drainage laws provided for surface outlets to carry away the water from the tile drains while the drainage districts supplied the capital required for the construction of the expensive ditches (Moline 1969, 127; Winsor 1975, 245–246).

Once under way, the drainage of the Midwest's prairies and wetlands proceeded at a rapid pace. By 1872 the great Black Swamp of northwestern Ohio had over 5000 miles of county and township drains together with thousands of tile, plank, and sapling under-drains (Howe 1908, 2:473). The wetter portions of Illinois' Grand Prairie were largely reclaimed in the drainage boom of the 1880s and 1890s (Winsor 1975, 101–184). The wet prairies of northern Iowa and western Minnesota were the last to be reclaimed in the early 1900s (Woodward and Nagler 1929; Hewes and Frandson 1952; Moline 1969, 110).

By 1978 drainage activities in the North Central States had converted over 45 million acres (18.2 million ha) of wetlands to arable land (US Bureau of the Census 1981b). Figure 12.1 shows the heavy concentration of drainage activities in the Midwest. The figure is an estimate based on data provided by state and county Soil Conservation Service offices. The latest US Bureau of the

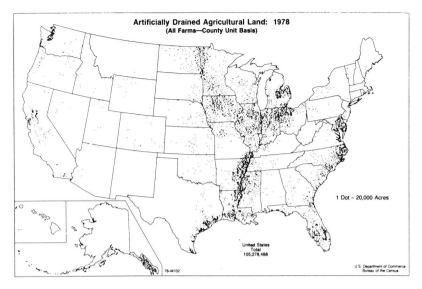

Fig. 12.1 Drained farmland in the United States, 1978. From US Bureau of the Census (1981a, 60).

Census (1981b) figures indicate that the area drained in each of the leading states in 1978 was as follows (values are expressed in millions of hectares and percentage of total surface area of state): Illinois 3.9 million ha (27%), Iowa 3.1 (22%), Indiana 2.7 (29%), Minnesota 2.5 (12%), Michigan 2.2 (15%), Ohio 2.0 (19%), and Missouri 1.7 (9%).

The drainage of the great Kankakee Swamp of northern Indiana and Illinois typifies the changing fortunes of the Midwest's wetlands. The Kankakee region at one time was 'one of the largest marsh–swamp basins in the interior of the United States' (Mitsch and Gosselink 1986, 49). Situated on a flat out-wash plain sandwiched between several moraines (Fig. 12.2), the historic Kankakee was 'a notoriously rambling and snag-infested stream, ever aban-doning old and establishing new channels, producing an intricate maze of meanders, oxbow lakes, sloughs, and bayous' (Meyer 1935). The following land surveyor's 1835 description of Township 31 North, Range 9 West is fairly typical of the questionable value accorded much of the area:

A great portion of this township is ... a marsh. There is a small portion of timber [pri-marily birch, maple, swamp ash and willow] growing along the margin of the Kankakee ... The marshes are principally covered with alder and wild rice ... In many places it is difficult to tell where the bed of the Kankakee River is placed. Such is the unfavorable aspect of the country that I cannot in justice give a more flattering charac-ter and keep within bounds of all matters pertaining to facts (Wilson 1919).

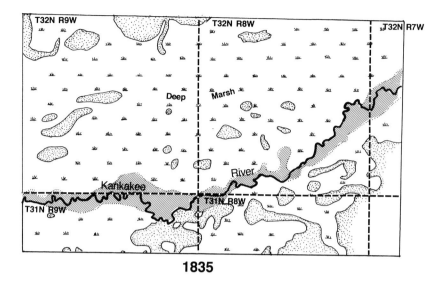

1835

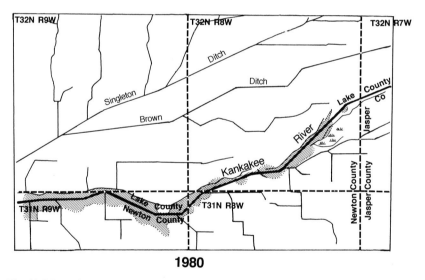

1980

Fig. 12.2 Transformation of a segment of the Kankakee Marsh of northwestern Indiana. The 1835 map is based on the presettlement GLO township plat maps of the area, National Archives, Washington, D.C. Stippled areas are upland barrens and oak woodlands. Diagonally lined areas, along the river, are swamp forests of ash, elm, and maple. Dashed lines are 6 mile by 6 mile township boundaries. The 1980 map is based on 7.5 minute series USGS topographic maps (Shelby, Ind. quadrangle and Schneider, Ind. quadrangle) of the region. Surface and subsurface drainage and the channelization of the Kankakee River have eliminated most of the marsh.

The geographer Alfred Meyer (1935) divided the history of the area into four different periods: presettlement and Indian (pre-1840), pioneer (1840–1880), recreation and ranching (1880–1910), and large-scale reclamation (1910–present). 'Fur, fowl, and fen' sustained the Indians and the earliest settlers of the Kankakee. The recreation and ranching period was based upon 'a cattle economy on the higher, drier, and artificially drained lands side by side with public shooting and trapping grounds of wild fowl and other game on the ill-drained marshes and swamps' (Meyer 1935). The Kankakee Valley Draining Company was organized in 1870–1871 with the express purpose of reclaiming the wetland areas (Gillespie 1876). Ditching accelerated dramatically after the introduction of the steam dredge in 1884. Channelization of the Kankakee River followed in 1906–1917 (Fig. 12.2). Spoil materials from the channelization and the construction of levees obliterated most of the old meanders, bayous and oxbows (Meyer 1935). Today it is difficult to realize that the extensive fields of corn, soybeans, potatoes, and other cash crops of the Kankakee region occupy land that once was a 'hideous' marsh.

In most instances, drainage was an unqualified success. Drainage promoted the breakdown of organic matter in the soil, a process that had been hindered by low levels of oxygen in the poorly drained soil. Abnormally high concentrations of organic matter made many of the Midwest's wetland soils among the most productive soils on the face of the earth. Drainage released the potential productivity of the Midwest's soils by warming the ground up earlier in the spring, advancing the cropping season, and promoting the diffusion of oxygen to the roots of the crop (Brady 1984, 529–530). In Illinois drainage increased the yield of corn 50% (Winsor 1975, 89). Land values soared as the land was drained (Winsor 1975, 91).

A few spectacular drainage failures tarnished an otherwise spotless record of success. High land values and a rising demand for agricultural commodities stimulated a rash of ill-fated drainage activities in the peatlands of the Upper Midwest during the first two decades of the twentieth century. Major reclamation projects included the drainage of parts of the peatlands of Minnesota's glacial Lake Agassiz basin and central Wisconsin's glacial Lake Wisconsin basin (Miller 1936). The state-sponsored drainage of northern Minnesota's peatlands was conducted on a massive scale. Large dredges laid out ditches a mile or so apart in a gridiron pattern following the federal surveyors' section lines (Soper 1919). Inadequate drainage, nutrient deficiencies, a lack of suitable crops, distant markets, and microclimatic conditions (early frosts, etc.) led to the failure of many of the reclamation projects (Miller 1936, 170; Catenhusen 1950; Curtis 1959, 241; Bradof 1992) and impoverished a number of counties in the process (Dana, Allison, and Cunningham 1960, 297–298).

The state of Minnesota eventually assumed the counties' debts and converted the partially drained wetland to a large game preserve (Bradof 1992). Aldo Leopold ([1949] 1968, 95–101) lamented the loss of glacial Lake Wisconsin's peatlands in his 'Marshland Elegy' and then went on to describe the 'counterepidemic of reflooding' which set in when the federal government attempted to restore the wetlands as wildlife refuges.

The drainage of the nation's wetlands had a number of inadvertent as well as premeditated consequences. The most immediate effect was the loss of wetland habitat. While a variety of factors, e.g., flood control, waste disposal, and urban expansion, were involved, agricultural development was responsible for most of the destruction of the nation's wetlands (Shaw and Fredine 1971; Tiner 1984, 31–32). The best estimates suggest that the lower 48 states lost approximately 50% of their original wetland area (Mitsch and Gosselink 1986, 39–41; Dahl 1990). Gross figures, however, obscure the fact that much of the loss was concentrated in the richer, more agriculturally oriented segments of the country. Both Illinois and Iowa in the heart of the Corn Belt lost over 85% of their prairie potholes and marshes (Table 12.1). Over 80% of Ohio, Indiana, and Michigan's rich elm and ash swamp forests were converted to agricultural activities. The loss was considerably less in the case of the poorer conifer bogs and swamps to the north (Table 12.1). Even here, however, regional differences in the extent of conversion were tied to the agricultural potential of the land. Minnesota lost only 12% of its original 2 380 000 ha of peatland, most of which was marginal from the agricultural standpoint (Center for Urban and Regional Affairs 1981). Scores of tamarack bogs and fens in southern Wisconsin, southern Michigan, northern Indiana, and northern Ohio once represented the southernmost outposts of the boreal conifer bog–swamp complex in North America. Many of southern Wisconsin's and southern Michigan's richer tamarack fens were deliberately converted to bluejoint (*Calamagrostis* sp.) and sedge meadows (Fuller 1928, 292; Frolick 1941). Peatlands occupied at least 74 000 ha or > 0.7% of Ohio's land surface area at the beginning of European settlement (Dachnowski 1912, 27). Less than 1300 ha or 2% of the area originally in peatland remains today (Andreas and Knoop 1992). The larger tamarack swamps reported by the early land surveyors covered several hundred hectares (Dachnowski 1912, 135; Aldrich 1943). By the time Dachnowski's classic study on the peat deposits of Ohio appeared in 1912, however, artificial drainage, fire, and cultivation had already eliminated a number of the bogs and fens. Fortunately Dachnowski's (1912) and Selby's (1902) studies provide us with important baseline data on tamarack's status and occurrence in Ohio at the turn of the century. Comparisons with more recent studies (Amann 1961; Herrick 1974; Andreas 1980, 1985) indicate that

Table 12.1. *Estimated loss of wetlands by state, region, and selected plant community types*

	Presettlement extent of wetlands (ha)	Extent of wetlands circa 1980s	% of wetland lost	Sources
States (with regional totals)				
Connecticut	271 000	70 000	74	
Maine	2 615 000	2 105 000	20	
Massachusetts	331 000	238 000	28	
New Hampshire	89 000	81 000	9	
Rhode Island	41 000	26 000	37	
Vermont	138 000	89 000	35	
New England	3 485 000	2 609 000	25	
Delaware	194 000	90 000	54	
Maryland	668 000	178 000	73	
New Jersey	607 000	370 000	39	
New York	1 037 000	415 000	60	Dahl 1990
Pennsylvania	456 000	202 000	56	
Middle Atlantic	2 962 000	1 255 000	58	
Illinois	3 325 000	508 000	85	
Indiana	2 267 000	304 000	87	
Iowa	1 619 000	171 000	89	
Michigan	4 534 000	2 260 000	50	
Minnesota	6 101 000	3 522 000	42	
Missouri	1 961 000	260 000	87	
Ohio	2 024 000	195 000	90	
Wisconsin	3 968 000	2 158 000	46	
Midwest	25 799 000	9 378 000	64	
Plant community type				
Northern conifer bogs and swamps	2 963 000	2 678 000	10	Klopatek *et al.* 1979
Elm–ash swamp forests	2 239 000	279 000	88	Klopatek *et al.* 1979
Atlantic white cedar swamps (Connecticut)	86 stands in 1939	39 stands in 1987	55	Laderman *et al.* 1987
Sedge (*Carex stricta–Calamagrostis canadensis*) meadows (Wisconsin)	459 000	3 000	> 99	Reuter 1986
Wetlands in prairie pothole region			50	Leitch 1981
Coastal marshes (New York and New England)	105 000 (in 1886)	50 000	52	Gosselink and Baumann 1980

over two-thirds of the 40 to 50 tamarack bogs and fens extant in Ohio in 1900–1912 have subsequently disappeared.

Drainage inevitably modified the native vegetation. Where it failed to completely destroy the natural vegetation, it at least altered the composition of the community. The wetland community remained intact although the representation of the various species shifted. Swamp forests, salt marshes, and conifer bogs were only a few of the wetland communities that were impacted by drainage. The amateur botanist, E. J. Hill (1895) reported that black ash was once very abundant in the swamps of upstate New York, 'the trees frequently outnumbering all other species combined.' Drainage eliminated the water which stood in the swamps throughout most of the year and exposed the roots of the ash to decay. The black ash gave way to elm and soft maples (Hill 1895). Dunn (1987) has documented a similar shift in the tree species composition of southeastern Wisconsin's forested wetlands. Land Office survey records indicate that black ash was the dominant species in the presettlement period. Silver maple is the most abundant species in the same area today. Drainage is also believed to have encouraged the establishment of sugar maple in the mixed swamp forest of northern Ohio's till plains (Cho and Boerner 1991).

A variety of factors, including the small size of the landholdings, mosquito plagues, and the primitive ditching technology of the eighteenth and nineteenth centuries, limited the early reclamation of New England's salt marshes (Smith *et al.* 1989). Much of the ditching of the East Coast's marshes awaited the WPA (Works Progress Administration) and the CCC (Civilian Conservation Corps) mosquito control programs of the 1930s (Nixon 1982, 52–53). Common reed grass (*Phragmites australis*) appears to have been the major beneficiary of the dredging, the ditching, the diking, and the tide gating of the Northeast's saltwater marshes. Saltmeadow grass (*Spartina patens*) – the saltmarsh hay of the colonists – and saltwater cordgrass (*S. alterniflora*) have increasingly given way to dense stands of *Phragmites* over the last 60 years (Heusser 1949; Sipple 1971; Roman, Niering, and Warren 1984).

The ill-fated history of the northern conifer bogs was determined by a number of interrelated factors. It is difficult to determine whether natural disasters or human activities were primarily responsible for the changes seen over the last 200 years. Both cutting and the larch sawfly epidemic, for instance, favored the increase of red maple and alder (*Alnus rugosa*) in northern Michigan's conifer (black spruce–tamarack–white cedar) swamps (LeBarron and Neetzel 1942). Drainage significantly increased the incidence of fires in glacial Lake Wisconsin's peatlands and converted many of the larch and spruce bogs to pure stands of aspen (Catenhusen 1950). Reflooding the same areas in the 1930s subsequently encouraged the invasion of cattail (*Typha lati-folia*) and reed (*Phragmites australis*).

It is considerably more difficult to assess the broader hydrological implications of artificial drainage. Contemporary observers believed that wetlands played a role similar to that of the forests, holding back runoff during peak periods of precipitation. According to the conventional wisdom, wetlands acted as reservoirs, impeding the delivery of water to streams. They later released the water, maintaining the flow of the streams during dry periods (Evans [1753] 1939, 96–97; Beckwith 1879, 28; Cunningham 1900). Naturally occurring, leisurely winding streams allowed the water to soak into the ground. Ditching and artificial drainage, however, hurried the water off the land (Sears 1956b), contributing to floods downstream.

Although the positive values of wetlands in mitigating flood peaks (Horwitz 1978; Novitzki 1978; Bardecki 1984) and the negative effects of drainage are widely cited in the literature, our understanding of the role of wetlands in the hydrological cycle is still limited (Carter 1986). Wetlands have frequently been compared to sponges that absorb precipitation during wet periods and slowly release the stored water during dry periods. Holding basins or tubs constitute a better analogy. By spreading the storm water over a large area and decreasing the velocity of the water, wetlands temporarily detain the runoff, releasing it over an extended period of time. The result is lower flood peaks downstream (Novitzki 1989). The flood mitigation potential of the wetland, however, depends upon the size and the location (upstream or downstream) of the wetland (Ogawa and Male 1986; Novitzki 1989). Several regression analyses have shown a negative relationship between the size of the flood peak and the percentage of the basin in lakes and wetlands (O'Brien 1987; Novitzki 1989). Novitzki (1989), for instance, demonstrated that the floodflow of streams in central Pennsylvania with 4% of their basin in wetlands was only half as large as the floodflow of streams without any basin (wetland) storage.

The effect of drainage on the wetland's flood mitigation potential is still an issue that is open to debate. One might argue, for instance, that the topography of the wetland area is more important than whether the wetland is drained or not (Bardecki 1984). Woodward and Nagler (1929) failed to find any significant differences in the streamflow patterns and the flood peaks of the Des Moines and Iowa Rivers before and after the extensive drainage activities of the region in the early twentieth century. Other studies have (Daniel 1981) and have not (McCubbin 1938) linked drainage to increased flooding. The question of the wetland's ability to slowly release water during dry periods and increase low flows has a more clear cut answer. The majority of the evidence indicates that wetlands *do not* add water to streams during low flow periods. In fact they often decrease streamflow during the summer due to the heavy use of water by wetland plants (Motts and O'Brien 1981, Ogawa and Male 1983, Novitzki 1989).

Peatlands have been studied more thoroughly than any other type of wetland in the United States, so we have a better idea of what drainage does to the flow of streams draining peatlands. Here the available evidence suggests that drainage can augment the low flow of streams 'because the lower water table limits evapotranspiration and causes slower water movement through the deeper [less permeable] peats' (Verry and Boelter 1978). The impact of drainage on peak flow varies from site to site, depending on local conditions. On the one hand, a large drainage network can contribute to a rapid rise in streamflow due to the direct channel delivery of rain and snow. Alternatively, drainage can reduce the peak flow by lowering the water table and creating additional storage space for the incoming water (Verry and Boelter 1978). The hydrology of wetlands is a relatively complex issue. Like the concept of forest influences, the reality often transcends the conventional wisdom.

13

A transported flora

Wherever [man] plants his foot, the harmonies of nature are turned to discords ... Indigenous vegetable and animal species are extirpated, and supplanted by others of foreign origin, spontaneous production is forbidden or restricted, and the face of the earth is either laid bare or covered with a new and reluctant growth of vegetable forms, and with alien tribes of animal life. These intentional changes and substitutions constitute, indeed, great revolutions.

George Perkins Marsh. [1864] 1965. *Man and Nature*, p. 36.

Given the apparent stability of many environments today, it is easy to overlook the dramatic changes which have occurred in America's flora over the last 200 to 400 years. The change was a two-step process involving (1) the destruction of the native flora and (2) the creation of new plant communities. 'Man,' Marsh ([1864] 1965, 36) noted, 'is everywhere a disturbing agent.' Clearing, cutting, draining, flooding, plowing, grazing, and picking – all took their toll on the indigenous flora. Simultaneously, the influx of a new group of species resulted in the formation of a landscape more attuned to human activities, a landscape which many have termed the cultural landscape. The following is a review of the changing floristic patterns of the Northeast and the Midwest and the rise of the cultural landscape.

Comparisons of the modern flora with earlier plant collections and floral lists provide at least a crude estimate of the changing plant geography of the region (Brown *et al.* 1987). Unfortunately, the early colonists were not inclined to discuss the flora in any detail. Although they occasionally provided lists of the economically important species, e.g., the trees, they were much more reticent about the herbaceous species. Local floras, comprehensive lists of the species of a given area, did not appear until the end of the eighteenth century and the beginning of the nineteenth century. Cutler's (1785) 'An account of some of the vegetable productions, naturally growing in ... [New England]', Muhlenberg's (1793) 'Index Florae Lancastriensis', Bigelow's (1814) *Florula Bostoniensis*, Barton's (1818) *Compendium Florae Philadelphicae*, and Darlington's (1826) *Florula Cestrica*, represent only a few of the better floras of the period. By the time they were published, much of the East Coast had already been settled for 100 to 200 years.

Loss of native species

Many of America's early naturalists and plant collectors were all too aware of the changing nature of the flora. William Bartram, for instance, wrote to his British friend, Peter Collinson, in 1764 that he frequently had difficulty relocating plants that he had seen on earlier collecting expeditions. He attributed their loss to forest clearance and grazing (Darlington [1849] 1967, 254–263). Comments about America's disappearing flora appeared sporadically throughout the plant literature of the nineteenth century (Teschemacher 1835; Kumlein 1876). Attempts to actually quantify the loss of species, however, languished until the passage of the Federal Endangered Species Act of 1973. A compilation of the existing information (Table 13.1) suggests that most states have lost anywhere from 1 to 5% of their flora.

Admittedly, some of the figures may reflect differences in the intensity of botanizing in the past and the present and differences in the definition of the term 'extirpated.' How many years have to elapse since a species was last collected, for instance, for that species to be considered extirpated? The preliminary figures on extirpation, however, also mirror real differences in the intensity of human activity in the region. Stuckey and Roberts (1977), for example, ascribed the loss of 40 of Ohio's lake, bog, fen, and marsh species to urbanization and agricultural development. Thirty of the sixty-two vascular plant species listed as extirpated in Pennsylvania are coastal plain species which have suffered from intense urbanization in the southeastern corner of the state (Rhoads 1986). Somewhat paradoxically, the return of the forest in the Northeast has also eliminated a number of species. A majority of the species lost in Massachusetts were species associated with early successional environments. Open fields, pastures, and meadows were much more common in the nineteenth century when most of the species were first recorded (Sorrie 1989). Agriculture has exacted its toll. We probably know less about the species composition of the Connecticut River's rich intervales than any other comparable area in New England due to the fact that they constituted prime agricultural land, e.g., hayfields and meadowlands, which was altered at a very early date (Hodgdon 1973). Likewise, few regions of the earth's surface have been modi-

Table 13.1. *Loss of native vascular plant species and gain of alien plant species by state. Figures are incomplete for several states*

State	Total no. plant species	Number of alien species	% aliens	Number of native species	Estimated no. species extirpated	% native species extirpated	Sources
New England							
Connecticut	2489	851	34	1638	84	5.6	Mehrhoff 1987
Maine				1500	53	3.1	Dibble et al. 1989; Silkman 1990
Massachusetts	2700	1000	37	1700	46		Sorrie 1990
Rhode Island							Enser and Caljouw 1989
Middle Atlantic							
New York	3080	1080	35	2000	59	3.0	Mitchell 1986
Pennsylvania				2100	62	3.0	Rhoads 1986
Lower Midwest							
Illinois	2800	811	29	~2000	50	2.5	Henry and Scott 1981; Sheviak 1981
Indiana	2265	350–400	18	~1900	22	1.2	Deam 1940; Bacone and Hedge 1980; Crovello, Keller, and Kartesz 1983
Iowa	1700	~350	21	1350	49	3.6	Eilers 1975; Roosa, Pusateri, and Eilers 1986
Ohio	2700	900	33	1800	84	4.7	Cooperrider 1982
Upper Midwest							
Michigan					36		Beaman et al. 1985
Minnesota	2010	392	20	1618	13	0.7	Ownbey and Morley 1991
Wisconsin	~2050	250	12	1750–1800			Read 1976; Lange 1981

fied as thoroughly as the Midwest's fertile grasslands. A number of naturalists (Kumlein 1876; Pammel 1901; Squires 1906; Herre 1940) have presented vignettes of the coming of the plow and the disappearance of the prairie flora. One respected botanist, Robert I. Cratty (cited by Hightshoe 1984), wrote of Iowa in 1919: 'So large a proportion of our state is suitable for cultivation that our native flora is being rapidly swept away, and while many of the species may survive along the roadsides, in hilly and stony locations and along the streamside, others which are local or rare must eventually disappear altogether.' As Cratty's statement suggests, most of the extirpated species in the Northeast and the Midwest have been disjuncts, species at the edge of their range (McCance and Burns 1984; Brown *et al.* 1987; Vickery *et al.* 1989), or species confined to restricted habitats, like wetlands (Rhoads 1989).

Although they are relatively scarce, studies of the changing flora at the county and the township level provide a much more detailed picture of the impact of human activities. McVaugh's (1935, 1958) study of Columbia County, New York, and Dore's (1961) analysis of Prescott, Ontario, located directly across the Saint Lawrence River from Ogdensburg, New York, suggest that the northern species were the first species to go. Many species, notably *Taxus canadensis*, *Coptis groenlandica*, *Acer spicatum*, and *Viola rotundifolia*, disappeared when the original forests were cut (McVaugh 1958, see also chapter 7). Rising soil temperature following the cutting of the forest may have been responsible for the disappearance of some of the more temperature sensitive boreal orchids (Case 1987, 18). Other species, particularly the bog species *Drosera rotundifolia*, *Ledum groenlandicum*, *Menyanthes trifoliata*, *Scheuchzeria palustris*, and *Calopogon pulchellus*, survived until their wetland habitats were flooded or silted out (Dore 1961). Situated at the meeting ground of many northern, southern, and coastal plain species, southeastern Pennsylvania's Chester County possesses a very rich flora. It was also the locale of William Darlington's early (1826) *Florula Cestrica*. More recent work (Stone 1945; Overlease 1987) on the county's flora suggests a relatively complex pattern with respect to the loss of native species, certain species being much more susceptible to extirpation than others. Of the 49 species lost over the last 150 years, 7 (14%) were species with a more southern distribution, 2 (4%) were predominantly coastal plain species, 13 (26%) were species with a more northern distribution, 7 (14%) were species with a more western distribution, 14 (28%) were species with a very localized distribution in the state, and 6 (12%) were species with a wide-ranging distribution throughout the East. Hancock and McDonough Counties, located at the edge of the grasslands and the forests of western Illinois, have been the site of several intensive floristic studies (Mead 1846; Kibbe 1952; Myers and Henry 1976). Myers and Henry (1976) reported the loss of 130 species or 16% of the native flora of the two counties since European settlement 140 years ago. Over 40% of the extirpated species were aquatic species whose sloughs and wetland habitat were destroyed by large-scale drainage and channelization projects (Kibbe 1952, 55–67; Myers and Henry 1976).

Certain groups of species, like the orchids, appear to have been particularly susceptible to human intervention. Historic records at the county level indicate a significant decline in the occurrence of several species of orchids throughout the Northeast and the Midwest (Bowles 1983; Lamont, Beitel, and Zaremba 1988). Overcollecting has probably contributed to the loss of showier orchids like *Cypripedium reginae* (Coddington and Field 1978). Exacting mycorrhizal or pollinator requirements and the loss of specific habitats to which they were tied, e.g., old-growth forests, are other factors which may have played a role in the decline of species like *Aplectrum hyemale*, *Isotria medeoloides*, *Plantanthera ciliaris*, *Triphora trianthophora*, *Corallorhiza maculata*, and *C. odontorhiza* (Case 1964; Ayensu 1975; Coddington and Field 1978; Overlease 1987). Two species of the tallgrass prairie, *Plantanthera leucophaea* and *Cypripedium candidum*, were conditioned to dormant-season fires. Fire eliminated many woody competitors and stimulated the flowering and growth of the orchids (Bowles 1983). The cessation of fires in the post-settlement period has jeopardized their existence.

While floral lists are important, they obscure the equally important issue of changes in the relative abundance of species. Changes in the relative abundance of species could alter one's overall impression of the landscape. 'Where a half century ago,' the botanist Cratty (1929) wrote, 'one might travel for miles over ... [Iowa's] prairies without seeing a single plant that was not indigenous, today the conditions are almost reversed ...' Few of Iowa's native prairie species entirely disappeared. Many which were formerly abundant, however, species like *Liatris squarrosa*, have been considerably reduced in numbers (Shimek 1925).

Aliens and weeds

The destruction of the native vegetation and the proliferation of human activities created opportunity for a new group of species. Most of the plants which stepped in to fill the ecological vacuum were species associated with disturbed habitats. Ecologists have termed these invader species which are symptomatic of a disturbed order 'weeds' (Sears [1935] 1959, 92; Baker 1965). Most native plant communities are relatively resistant to the invasion of weedy species (Rafinesque 1811; Shimek 1932; Dansereau 1957, 268–269). Disturbed environments, however, place a premium on species which can (1) germinate, grow, and reproduce under the more extreme conditions of open areas, (2) complete their life cycle at an early age, e.g., annuals, and (3) produce large numbers of offspring (Curtis 1959, 416; Baker 1965). Weeds typically possess one or more of these features.

A few of the more aggressive weeds were native species. Some like poke-weed (*Phytolacca americana*) and giant ragweed (*Ambrosia trifida*) were ini-tially associated with the disturbed habitats of riverbanks and bottomlands (Sauer 1952; Menges and Waller 1983). Others, like the goldenrods and the asters, were probably more characteristic of the permanently open habitats of the presettlement period, e.g., marshes, meadows, prairies, and cliffs, which were either too dry or too wet for the occurrence of trees (Harper 1908; Marks 1983). Forest clearance, the development of the railroads, and increasing com-munication with the open grasslands of the West favored the eastward expan-sion of a number of weedy natives, e.g., evening primrose (*Oenothera bien-nis*), squirrel-tail grass (*Hordeum jubatum*), horseweed (*Erigeron canadensis*), ragweed (*Ambrosia artemisiifolia*), black-eyed Susan (*Rudbeckia hirta*), blue vervain (*Verbena hastata*), and witch-grass (*Panicum capillare*) (Gray 1879; Halsted 1891; Pammel 1913). The proliferation of open habitats also encour-aged the expansion, the genetic intermingling, and the explosive speciation of the genus *Crataegus*, i.e., the native hawthorns (Cain 1944; Palmer 1946).

Of even greater import were the large number of alien species which flooded America's new fields, roadsides, fencerows, and cities. Some had a transitory or ephemeral existence. They were railway and highway migrants or escapees from gardens which required the continual introduction of new propagules to maintain their existence (Myers and Henry 1979). Others flourished for a brief period of time and then faded away as the customs which favored their exis-tence declined. Henbane (*Hyoscyamus niger*) is a slimy-leaved, poisonous biennial noted for its narcotic and analgesic properties. The root was formerly used as a painkiller for toothaches (McAtee 1938). Cutler (1785) noted that it was common along New England's manure-enriched roadsides and rubbish heaps in the eighteenth century. The substitution of superior drugs, better sani-tation, and the mowing of the roadsides led to a decline in its numbers in the nineteenth century. Although its seeds have a long period of viability and it periodically reappears on disturbed sites (Bigelow 1817, 1:161–162), it is currently a rather rare species in New England. Many aliens found a permanent home in the New World. A few arrived with the American Indian. The over-whelming majority, however, accompanied the great wave of human immi-grants across the Atlantic. As the historian Alfred Crosby (1972, 64) noted, the success of the Europeans 'depended on their ability to "Europeanize" the flora and fauna of the New World,' to reproduce the forage and the crop species so essential for their livestock and grain oriented economy. Europeanization included the importation of the less reputable members of Europe's flora as well as the valuable forage and crop species. Many of America's naturalists had difficulty separating the ubiquitous foreigners from the natives (Barton 1793). Quite understandably, visiting Europeans readily picked out the foreign elements of the flora. The eccentric European naturalist Constantine Rafinesque (1811) divided the known exotics at the beginning of the nineteenth century into three different categories. The first group of 40 species included the plants introduced intentionally for agricultural purposes. Ornamentals, pot herbs, and medicinal herbs were covered under the second group of 218 species, the plants introduced by gardening. It is interesting to note that some of the more obnoxious weeds of today were formerly cultivated in gardens for medicinal, e.g., ground ivy (*Glechoma hederacea*), selfheal (*Prunella vulgaris*), celandine (*Chelidonium majus*), yarrow (*Achillea millefolium*), dock (*Rumex* sp.), ox-eye daisy (*Chrysanthemum leucanthemum*), or ornamental, e.g., butter-and-eggs (*Linaria vulgaris*) and soapwort (*Saponaria officinalis*), purposes (Josselyn [1672] 1860; Gilmore 1931; Fogg, 1956, 4). Ann Leighton ([1970] 1986, 90), the American garden historian, in fact questioned the commonly held belief that 'a lot of our "escaped" wildflowers arrived accidentally in feed for cattle and packing for furniture.' She marshalled a large amount of evidence suggesting that most were deliberately planted in early colonial gardens for 'meate or medicine' (Leighton [1970] 1986). Inadvertently introduced plants or weeds constituted Rafinesque's last group of 60 species. Most of these were stowaways – species which came as seed-grain contaminants or species which hitched a ride in packing materials and livestock fodder (Schweinitz 1832; Gray 1884; Dewey 1897). Ballast from foreign cargo ships and wool wastes played an important role in the introduction of many weeds. Boats with a light cargo typically loaded their holds with rocks, gravel, and earth and then discharged the ballast when they picked up a full cargo in North America. The waste from woolen mills, i.e., the bur and seed-filled tangles cut from the wool, was frequently allowed to decay, mixed with other matter and then deposited on the ground as a manure (Fernald 1905). Combing ballast grounds and woolen mill refuse heaps for the appearance of new plants was a popular botanical pastime of the late nineteenth and early twentieth centuries (Alcott 1882; Knowlton and Deane 1923; Muhlenbach 1979).

The transformation of New England's flora has been particularly well documented (Fernald 1905) and gives one an idea of the rapidity with which the aliens were introduced. In 1672 John Josselyn reported no less than 40 species of European weeds which had 'sprung up since the English planted and kept cattle in New England.' Manasseh Cutler's (1785) account of the vegetable productions of New England featured 66 aliens, including the buttercup, 'common in moist pastures and fields,' and the white-weed (*Chrysanthemum leucanthemum*), 'very injurious to grass lands.' The number of introduced plants rose to 83 species with the publication of the first (1814) edition of Bigelow's *Florula Bostoniensis* and to 140 species with the appearance of the third (1840) edition. Fernald (1905) put the number of introduced species at more than 600 in 1905, while Seymour's (1969) *Flora of New England* includes 877 foreign species or approximately 30% of the flora of the region. By the middle of the nineteenth century, New England had become 'the garden of European weeds' (Lyell 1849, 1:53). 'Every weed of England' grew in such 'quantity and vigor' in the fields, the streets, and the gardens that one might have thought 'them intentionally cultivated' (Strickland 1971, 55–56). It was a landscape occupied by a 'man-dominated and in part ... [a] man-created' flora (Anderson 1956). New England's transformation, however, was only part of a larger change taking place throughout the Northeast and the Midwest. The 318 aliens noted in Rafinesque's aforementioned 1811 report on the exotic plants of the Middle States of North America had grown to 1098 species (20% of the vascular plant flora of the Northeast and the Midwest) in the eighth edition of *Gray's Manual of Botany* (Fernald 1950) and the end is not in sight. A review of the changing flora of the state of Illinois indicates that the rate of introduction of alien species has increased in recent years (Henry and Scott 1981).

Floras of agricultural and urban areas

Few activities altered the complexion of the landscape as thoroughly as the rise of urban ecosystems and the expansion of agroecosystems. Each developed its own specialized flora and fauna. Each in its own way represented the epitome of the cultural landscape. Their importance warrants a brief review of their development.

Agricultural areas

From the day the first hoe broke the ground to the more mechanized farming of today, agriculture has always been associated with major ecological dislocations (Jones 1974). Unfortunately, crops were not the only beneficiaries of those dislocations. As the American farmer soon learned, each region, each crop, and each farming practice had its own suite of weeds. During the eighteenth and nineteenth centuries the worn-out, old fields of the East Coast (Kalm [1772] 1972, 58–59, 99, 298–299; Lemon [1972] 1976, 170) supported a sparse cover of asters, poverty grass (*Danthonia spicata*), cinquefoil (*Potentilla canadensis*), and sorrel (*Rumex acetosella*) (Judd 1857; Darlington

1866). Fertile soils and a cavalier attitude toward the control of weeds encouraged the buildup of large weed populations in the West (Thomas 1845;
Delafield 1851). Spanish needles (*Bidens* spp.), cockleburs (*Xanthium* spp.)
and pigweeds (*Amaranthus* spp.) infested many Midwestern corn fields
(Nuttall [1821] 1905, 58; Utter 1942, 152). Some crops, like winter wheat,
favored the development of a very specialized weed flora. Because the weeds
often 'mimicked' or resembled the crop in habit, phenology, seed size, and
ecological requirements, they were extremely difficult to control (Barrett
1983). They were harvested with the wheat, distributed as a contaminant of the
grain, and resown with the wheat in the autumn (Dewey 1897). Notable examples are corn cockle (*Agrostemma githago*), darnel (*Lolium temulentum*),
chess (*Bromus secalinus*), and corn-gromwell (*Lithospermum arvense*) (Fig.
13.1). All are winter annuals from Europe which at one time infested the major
winter-wheat-growing areas of North America (Douglass 1760, 2:206;

Corn Cockle or Corn Campion.   Chess or Darnel,   Wild Mustard or Charlock.
                                The Tare of Canaan.

Fig. 13.1 Problem weeds of nineteenth century grainfields: corn cockle, chess, and wild
mustard. Reprinted from Delafield (1851).

Darlington 1847, 15; Stark 1847; Delafield 1851; Johnston 1851, 1:306). As the wheat-growing region shifted to the west and improved threshing and seed cleaning procedures took hold, corn cockle, darnel, chess, and corn-gromwell faded into obscurity (Pammel 1910; Shinners 1940; Dore 1961; Barrett 1983). Corn cockle is even threatened with extinction (Zeevaart1989). The increasing use of red clover in the nineteenth century to restore the fertility of the soil also produced its crop of weeds. Because they matured in the autumn when the clover seed was harvested and their seeds were difficult to separate from the clover, ribgrass (*Plantago lanceolata*), foxtail (*Setaria* spp.), and sorrel (*Rumex acetosella*) made red clover the most weed-filled seed in the commercial market (Dewey 1897). Contaminated clover and hayseed was probably responsible for the introduction of a number western weeds, e.g., black-eyed Susan, in New England (Harrington 1909; Gade 1991).

The increasing post-World War II use of nitrogen-based fertilizers and the recent shift to various conservation tillage systems, e.g., no-till and minimum tillage, are only the latest in a long line of management practices which have altered the weed flora (Haas and Streibig 1982; Overlease 1987). Herbicides have replaced soil cultivation as the major mechanism of weed control. Frequent tillage once kept the perennials under control and favored the annuals. Perennials which reproduce vegetatively, often at great depths in the soil, and species which are resistant to herbicides, e.g., quackgrass, Canada thistle, and dandelions, are a much more serious problem in today's conservation tillage systems (Peters 1972; Squiers 1986).

Urban areas

America has not always been an urban nation. As late as 1820, only 7% of the United States' population lived in cities and towns with a population of 2500 or more people. The coming of the Industrial Revolution in the nineteenth century fueled a dramatic shift in the population from rural to urban areas. Urban areas currently encompass over 75% of the population but only 2 to 3% of the surface area of the United States (Stearns 1978; Miller 1985, 167).

The urban environment typically embraces a variety of human activities and correspondingly contains a wealth of habitats and plant materials. Abrupt changes in soil nutrient levels, toxic materials, soil moisture, and microclimatic conditions have created a rather heterogeneous, coarse-grained urban environment (Stearns 1978; Berrang, Karnosky, and Stanton 1985; Craul 1985). Cities also form the hubs of vast transportation networks. As the ultimate destination of shipping lanes and highway networks, America's cities have accumulated species from around the world. Mulhenbach's (1979) study of the adventive flora of the railroads of St Louis, Missouri, and Shinner's (1940) analysis of the changing flora of Milwaukee, Wisconsin, from its early establishment in 1835 are two of the better examples of studies of man's ability to transport plants across continents. The strongly cosmopolitan character of the flora of America's cities was noted at a very early date (Kalm [1772] 1972, 83; Michaux [1805] 1904, 185–186). The almost ubiquitous occurrence of Jimson weed (*Datura stramonium*), a native of Asia, in many of America's cities in the eighteenth and early nineteenth centuries was probably indicative of the cities' poor refuse disposal systems. Jimson weed is a nitrophilous species which thrives on rubbish heaps (Swink and Wihelm 1979, 250). Early cities were the sites of large quantities of rotting organic matter and numerous roaming livestock. By today's standards, their flora probably approximated that of a badly maintained farmyard (Hall 1988).

A number of investigators have attempted to develop a typology of urban habitats (Stearns 1971; Brady *et al.* 1979). One of the simpler and more broadbased schemes of classification recognizes three major types of habitat: residual, ruderal, and managed (Stearns 1971; Whitney 1985). The three habitats and their plant communities can be arranged along a continuum – from the natural to the highly artificial. The residual vegetation represents one end of the spectrum. Residual vegetation is commonly associated with parks and estates on inaccessible slopes or wetlands on poorly drained sites and floodplains (Stearns 1971; Greller 1975; Whitney 1985; Hobbs 1988). Although they represent the closest approach to natural conditions, most of these sites show the influence of human activities to varying degrees. Dumping, heavy pedestrian traffic, ground fires, and the deliberate removal of the vegetation have destroyed the ground layer, the seedlings, and the saplings of many of the forests (Greller 1975; Hoehne 1981; Stalter 1981; Rudnicky and McDonnell 1989). The few herbs and shrubs that are present are frequently weedy woodland species (Carleton and Taylor 1983; Whitney 1985.) Exotic shrubs have infiltrated the more disturbed woodland sites to the extent that they have taken on a decidedly mixed character. The honeysuckles (*Lonicera japonica, L. morrowi, L. tatarica*), the buckthorns (*Rhamnus cathartica* and *R. frangula*), European highbush cranberry (*Viburnum opulus*), Japanese barberry (*Berberis thunbergii*), and privet (*Ligustrum vulgare*) are just a few of the more aggressive, bird-dispersed species of many urban areas (Barnes and Cottam 1974; Schmid 1975, 38–39; Greller, Calhoon, and Iglich 1979; Swink and Wilhelm 1979; Levenson 1981; Airola and Buchholz 1984; Overlease 1987). On the more heavily disturbed sites, the shrubs are joined by the tree of heaven (*Ailanthus altissima*) and the Norway maple (*Acer platanoides*) (Airola and Buchholz 1984).

The ruderal category includes the plant communities of waste areas – the weed patches of dumps and roadside verges, railroad yards, construction sites, industrial areas, vacant lots, sidewalks and alleys. Ruderal habitats encompass a wide variety of sites and conditions where disturbance is sustained and normal successional processes are arrested. Exotics and annuals are often over-represented in these inner city sites (Boehmer 1976, 44–48; Whitney 1985). The urban areas of eastern North America and Europe share a large portion of their flora. Many of Europe's ruderal plant communities have direct analogues in America's cities (Whitney 1985). European chenopods (*Kochia scoparia*), composites (*Lactuca* spp., *Sonchus* spp., and *Artemisia* spp.), and grasses (*Setaria* spp.) typically dominate the dry, rubbly, inner city habitats of America's urban areas (Dowden 1972; Swink and Wilhelm 1979; Whitney 1985). Dumps support various nitrophilous European species, e.g., common burdock (*Arctium minus*) and motherwort (*Leonurus cardiaca*), while the cracks in sidewalks contain a number of prostrate species, e.g., love grass (*Eragrostis pectinacea*), knotgrass (*Polygonum aviculare*), common plantain (*Plantago major*), and the moss, *Bryum argentum*, which are resistant to trampling (Whitney 1985). The equivalent communities in Europe are known as the Sisymbrietalia (ruderal communities dominated by annuals), the Artemisietalia (dry site ruderal communities dominated by perennials), and the Plantaginctalia (communities of heavily trampled sites) (Sukopp and Werner 1983; Ellenberg 1988). Ruderal communities bordering railroads and highways frequently contain a distinctive flora. Calcicoles or lime-loving species like butter-and-eggs (*Linaria vulgaris*) and small snapdragon (*Chaenorrhinum minus*) are often found on dry, rubbly, calcareous railroad ballast (Widrlechner 1983; Whitney 1985). The widespread use of deicing salts has favored the development of a number of unique halophytic communities along roadside verges in recent years. Most of the halophytes are recent introductions from alkaline habitats to the west or from salt marshes on the East Coast (Catling and McKay 1980; Reznicek 1980).

The lawn and its treed counterpart the urban savanna is the best example of a managed urban habitat (Detwyler 1972). America's fascination with the lawn has frequently been credited to the pasture oriented economy of northwestern Europe. The cool, moist oceanic climate of northwestern Europe encouraged the growth of grasses while sheep, goats, and cattle kept the grass in a finely shorn condition. William Kent and Lancelot 'Capability' Brown made the open park with its sweeping vistas of lawns and trees the epitome of the country estate in England (Detwyler 1972). Americans created a bourgeois version of the country estate. In a book entitled *The Art of Beautifying Suburban Home Grounds*, Frank J. Scott (1870) recommended cutting large greenswards into smaller slices everyone could afford. By throwing their front lawns together and planting an occasional specimen tree here and there,

Americans adapted the art of 'decorative gardening' to the 'small grounds of most suburban homes' (Leighton 1987, 249–260). Many suburban dwellers today spend an inordinate amount of time and energy maintaining their pure cultures of Kentucky bluegrass (Detwyler 1972; Falk 1976).

Although cities have occasionally been defined as places where they cut down the trees and then name the streets after them (Richardson 1977, 292), most of America's urban areas contain a large number of shade trees (Detwyler 1972; Grey and Deneke 1978, 12–13). The development of the urban forest is a fascinating story. A number of investigators (Browne 1847; Grey and Deneke 1978, 3–4; Whitney and Adams 1980) have reviewed the changing patterns of taste and style which have fashioned America's urban forest. Of particular interest is Daryl Watson's (1978) study of shade and ornamental trees in the nineteenth century. By analyzing early travelers' accounts, the agricultural and horticultural journals of the period, and the extant records of the larger nurseries, Watson was able to assemble the following picture of the introduction and the spread of the Northeast's more popular shade trees. Many towns went through a succession of tree species as the winds of fashion changed or the dominant trees succumbed to insects and pathogens. The ornamentals of the colonial period were often exotics, e.g., English elm (*Ulmus campestris*) and European linden (*Tilia vulgaris*), ordered by the wealthy from European nurseries. Planting in the early nineteenth century was heavily influenced by the development of the modern American nursery. The larger nurseries and their local representatives, the tree peddlers, aggressively promoted the sale of a limited number of 'weedy' species which were easily propagated and grew rapidly. They also catered to the public's taste at the time for exotic oriental and European trees. The Lombardy poplar (*Populus nigra* var. *italica*) and the weeping willow (*Salix babylonica*) were America's first 'fashion' trees, the first in a long line of species which included the black locust (*Robinia pseudoacacia*), the ailanthus (*Ailanthus altissima*), the Chinese mulberry (*Morus multicaulis*), and the catalpa (*Catalpa speciosa*) among others. Few of the mulberry trees, grown by those interested in establishing an indigenous silk-worm industry, survived the Northeast's harsh winters. Some ornamentals like the weeping willow were eventually relegated to cemeteries and the edge of ponds. The black locust, a species widely planted in the countryside for fence posts and in urban areas for its ornamental value, fell victim to the locust borer beetle. Others were vanquished by the pen of America's foremost landscape designer and tastemaker, Andrew Jackson Downing. Downing castigated the ailanthus for its 'treacherous,' odorous nature. He likewise assailed the Lombardy poplar for its susceptibility to caterpillar attacks and its generally filthy habits. A number of evergreens attracted public attention in the last half of the century. Many Norway spruce (*Picea abies*), Scots pines (*Pinus sylvestris*), and Austrian pines (*Pinus nigra*), particularly in rural areas in the Midwest, date back to plantings for shelterbelts during this period of time. By the early twentieth century native maples and elms were the dominant street trees of many towns (Watson 1978). The Dutch elm disease caused by the fungus *Ceratocystis ulmi* subsequently eliminated most of the elms in the 1940s and 1950s (Karnosky 1979). Maples (Norway, sugar, red, and silver) are probably the most common shade trees of residential areas today (Whitney and Adams 1980; Richards *et al.* 1984; DeGraaf 1985).

A wide variety of European and Asiatic shrubs have also been extensively planted in residential areas. Like their arboreal counterparts, shrubs have been subject to the vagaries of fashion. Some, like lilacs and forsythias, have always been popular. Others like bush-honeysuckles, mock-oranges, peegee hydrangea, deutzias, and weigelas peaked in popularity late in the nineteenth century (Scott 1870, 456). The rise of 'foundation planting' in the twentieth century brought evergreen shrubs, like yews, cedars, junipers, and rhododendrons, to the forefront of the house. 'Foundation planting' or the concept of tying the house to the grounds with evergreen shrubs is a distinctly American custom (Leighton 1987, 249) which came into vogue late in the nineteenth century when houses with high foundations, deep basements, and the recently introduced gravity warm air furnace became common (Whitney and Adams 1980).

The urban environment is largely a creation of man – a series of structures and spaces which reflect humanity's tastes and value systems. Given this connection, it is not surprising that many studies have found a close association between social class and the more decorative aspects of vegetation in residential areas (Schmid 1975; Whitney and Adams 1980). Due to its enduring nature, the woody vegetation of a given area often reflects the landscaping styles and fashions of the past. As America's urban areas expanded outward in the nineteenth and twentieth centuries, they frequently created a concentric series of different-aged residential zones or districts (Burgess 1925). It is not unusual to find a close association between the dominant shade trees of the residential district and the age of the district. The shift from the volunteer species (ailanthus, mulberries, and elms) of the inner city areas to the exotics (Norway maples, etc.) of the formerly fashionable areas, to the evergreens (white cedars and junipers) of the blue collar areas, and finally the sugar maples, dogwoods, and pin oaks of the outlying suburbs has been documented in a number of Midwestern cities (Detwyler 1972; Whitney and Adams 1980). The resulting communities and vegetational patterns are as much a product of the cultural environment as they are a part of the physical landscape.

Impact of introduced pathogens

Plant exotics like the horse chestnut and the dandelion were not the only organisms which altered North America's landscape. A number of microorganisms also managed to hitch a ride across the Atlantic. Their impact upon the native inhabitants of the New World was often substantial. Witness the smallpox, measles, and typhus epidemics which swept through populations of native Americans (Crosby 1972). Plant pathogens, likewise, were major agents of change. The fungus *Cryphonectria parasitica*, the causative agent of the chestnut blight, is one of the more frequently cited examples of an introduced pathogen which literally altered the face of North America's forests. As noted earlier, the American chestnut (*Castanea dentata*) was once a dominant or a codominant species of the oak–chestnut region of the Mid-Atlantic states and southern New England. It is difficult to determine its exact abundance in the preblight period, although fragmentary records suggest that it was common throughout the middle Appalachians. It frequently made up more than half of the stems and up to 90% of the volume of the forests of the slopes and the ridges of the Allegheny Mountains of Pennsylvania and western Maryland (Aughanbaugh 1935; Mackey and Sivec 1973; Russell 1987). Chestnut Ridge in southwestern Pennsylvania was named after the immense forests of chestnuts which clothed its sides and summit (Hildreth 1843). Chestnut was an extremely valuable as well as a common species. Hogs, turkeys, and squirrels fattened on its nuts every autumn. Settlers used its durable and easily split wood extensively for fences and poles (Hildreth 1843; Hepting 1974). The blight was apparently introduced in the New York City area at the turn of the century on nursery stock of imported Asiatic chestnuts. Despite the formation of a Chestnut Blight Commission and a valiant attempt to control the blight, the disease spread rapidly (Beattie and Diller 1954; Hepting 1974). In less than 50 years most of North America's chestnuts were dead or dying (Hepting 1974; Cech 1986).

The reorganization of the forest following the loss of a major canopy species was a complex affair. One of the more obvious effects was an increase in the representation of chestnut's preblight associates. The existing red oak and chestnut oak filled in many of the gaps in the canopy – converting the oak–chestnut forest type into a forest of mixed oak (Korstian and Stickel 1927; Aughanbaugh 1935). Larger openings, produced where chestnut formerly occupied greater than 30 to 40% of the canopy, favored an influx of the opportunistic, intolerant black cherry, red maple, and black birch (Good 1968; Mackey and Sivec 1973; Cech 1986). Chestnut exists today as little more than a shadow of its former self. Dormant buds at the base of the root collar allow chestnut to resprout after the stem is killed by the blight. Many root systems have persisted through several blight infections (Paillet 1984). The discovery of a nonlethal, i.e., a hypovirulent, strain of *Cryphonectria parasitica* and its ability to neutralize the effects of the lethal strain are encouraging signs. Scientists are also attempting to bring the American chestnut back by incorporating blight-resistant genes from the Chinese chestnut into the American chestnut by means of backcross breeding (Burnham 1988).

Chestnut is only one of a number of tree species which have suffered serious declines at the hands of an alien pathogen. Interest in reforesting cutover regions at the turn of the century led to an excessive demand for white pine planting stock. Because the demand exceeded the local supply, many organizations turned to European nurseries as a source of inexpensive planting stock. Unfortunately, the end result was the introduction of a new pathogen, the fungus *Cronartium ribicola* (Hirt 1956), and the outbreak of white pine blister rust. White pine's economic importance eventually encouraged the passage of the first federal Plant Quarantine Act. It also resulted in the implementation of the largest tree disease control program ever undertaken – the massive *Ribes* eradication program of the early 1900s. Wild currants and gooseberries (*Ribes*) are the alternate hosts of *Cronartium* (Anderson 1973; Ahlgren and Ahlgren 1984, 108). The hazard of white pine blister rust is relatively low in much of the Northeast and the southern portion of the Great Lakes region today. Throughout large segments of northern Michigan, Wisconsin, and Minnesota, however, the disease has seriously inhibited both the natural and the artifical regeneration of white pine (King 1958; Anderson 1973; Ahlgren and Ahlgren 1984, 109).

American elm and beech are two recent casualties of introduced pathogens. Although the American elm is still a dominant component of the swamp forests and the old-field communities of the Midwest, its lifespan has been dramatically reduced by *Ceratocystis ulmi*. *Ceratocystis*, the fungal agent responsible for the Dutch elm disease, was first noted in North America in Ohio in 1930 (Barnes 1976; Richardson and Cares 1976; Karnosky 1979; Parker and Leopold 1983; Whitney and Somerlot 1985). It is more difficult to assess the long-range consequences of the beech bark disease, a complex disease caused by the interaction of scale insects and fungi of the genus *Nectria*. In some areas the death of the larger beeches has resulted in dense thickets of beech sprouts (Houston 1976). Many investigators, however, feel that the long-term impact of the beech bark disease on the hardwood forests of the Northeast will be minimal (Twery and Patterson 1984; Leak 1987).

14

An impoverished fauna

Not only have most of the larger species [of mammals] greatly
decreased in numbers throughout the more thickly settled portions
of the Eastern States, but not a few have become extirpated over
regions where they were formerly abundant. This restriction of
range and numerical decrease are obviously due to man's agency.

> J. A. Allen. 1876. 'The former range of some New England
> carnivorous mammals.'

Wildlife is never destroyed ... it is simply converted from one form
to another.

> A. Leopold. 1945. 'The outlook for farm wildlife.'

Abundance of game in the presettlement period

Aldo Leopold (1931, 25) once wrote 'we are accustomed to thinking of all
game as unbelievably abundant before the advent of the white man.' Most
reviews of North America's wildlife history start with a testimonial to the
abundance of the continent's fish and game in the pre-Columbian or early settlement period (Matthiessen 1959, 13; Williamson 1987, 1). We read that the
rivers and lakes teemed with fish. The noted ornithologist Ludlow Griscom
(1949, 3), considered 'the prodigious and spectacular' supply of game birds
and mammals 'an established fact.'

Not all wildlife experts, of course, agreed with Griscom. A few rejected his
vision of an early Eden, abounding in wildlife. They suggested the idea was
more a 'popular misconception' than an established fact (Swift 1946, 9; Allen
1952). Unfortunately our understanding of the early wildlife history of the
country is at best fragmentary. References to vast numbers of wildlife frequently appear in early travel accounts and county histories. Many of these,
however, appear to be stock pieces, i.e., traditional themes repeated without

verification. Ecologists and historians reading the accounts should also be aware of the context in which they were written. The early Puritans, for instance, extolled the wealth of New England's wildlife. The Plymouth leader, Edward Winslow (1925) wrote 'For fish and fowl, we have great abundance.' 'Of heath-cocks [heath hen] and partridges [ruffed grouse],' Samuel Clarke (1670, 360) stated, 'our English kill many.' In Europe game was scarce and hunting was a royal prerogative. A kill of 6 to 12 heath-cocks or partridges in a morning (Wood [1634] 1977, 51) probably sounded like a bonanza to the commoner sort of Englishman whose hunting rights were rather restricted (Tober 1981, 4).

The trials and tribulations experienced by early settlers in their fight against bears, wolves, and other vexatious beasts are likewise given a place of prominence in many county histories. They represent a testimonial to the settler's stalwart nature and his ability to transform a wasteland into a fruitful garden. Finally it is necessary to note that wildlife was not uniformly distributed across the landscape (Kay 1979; Tober 1981, 4). Many presettlement accounts of the Midwest suggest that the largest concentrations of game, e.g., deer, turkey, elk, and buffalo, were associated with areas where the forests gave way to grasslands (Lahontan [1703] 1905, 320; Gist 1898, 133; Croghan 1904, 140; La Mothe 1904; La Salle [1905] 1968, 1:151–153).

Determining the actual number of game a given region supported is a much more complicated affair than simply categorizing the game as abundant or scarce. A few attempts have been made to estimate the numbers of various species in the presettlement period (Seton [1925] 1953; Shelford 1963, 26–29). The more sophisticated efforts have usually involved extrapolations from known densities in optimal habitats today (Alcoze 1981). Unfortunately we have a very limited knowledge of the carrying capacity of the presettlement environment, i.e., the ability of the vegetation, particularly the herb and shrub layers, to support game. The impact of predators and Indian hunting practices on pre-Columbian game populations are other issues which complicate the simple extrapolation techniques.

At first glance, the records of the early fur-trading concerns might appear to be a valid means of estimating the abundance of at least the fur-bearing mammals. A number of historians have published reports of the returns of the major fur-trading companies (Lart 1922; Johnson 1969). Unfortunately it is often difficult to determine the origin of the furs or the extent of the area harvested (Schorger 1965). The few published results of large ring hunts or communal drives suggest that eastern North America was well stocked with carnivores. The drives, which progressively confined the animals to smaller and smaller areas, were organized to rid the early settlements of the more obnoxious predators (Whittlesey 1843). The great central Pennsylvania circle drive of 1760 covered an area of over 700 square miles (1800 km^2) or most of present-day Snyder County. Two hundred hunters participated in the event, forming a 100 mile circle at the start of the hunt. Forty-one panthers, 109 wolves, 112 foxes, 114 mountain lions, 18 bears, 3 fishers, and 12 wolverines were killed (Seton [1925] 1953, 1:65). This probably represents a minimum estimate of the density of the mammals given the rugged nature of the terrain and the difficulty of shooting all of the game when the hunters were initially spread over such a large area. The celebrated Hinckley hunt of 1818 in Medina County, Ohio, probably provides a better estimate of the density of the larger mammals under presettlement conditions. Over 600 hunters converged on unsettled Hinckley Township on December 24, 1818. The total kill for the 25 square mile (65 km^2) area included 17 wolves, 21 bears, and 300 deer. Observers noted that some of the deer in the township broke through the hunters' lines and escaped (Howe 1891, 2:463–467).

Pests and staples of the pioneer economy

It has commonly been accepted that settlement initiated a period of profligate waste and a precipitous decline in the country's wildlife resources. 'The story of what the white man has done to the continent's wealth of wildlife,' wrote one ornithologist, 'is not a pleasant one' (Pough 1959). Much of the concern about the devastation of America's wildlife can be traced to a very intense period of exploitation at the end of the nineteenth century. Large quantities of fish and game were systematically extracted from the nation's forests, rivers, and grasslands to supply a growing urban market. Many early conservationists, however, believed that the market hunting era was merely the culmination of hundreds of years of exploitation and wastefulness (Reiger 1986, 70). Game had disappeared from large sections of the United States. The fate of America's remaining game species was precarious at best.

The reality was much more complex than the early conservationists suggested. Admittedly many species declined or suffered a retraction in their ranges. Simultaneously, however, civilization created new opportunities for the increase and spread of other species. Viewed in a larger context, it was more a case of exchanging one species for another. As Aldo Leopold (1945) noted, 'Wildlife is never destroyed ... it is simply converted from one form to another.' The conversion was a side effect of the transformation of America's landscape. The loss of wilderness areas, the shift from a rural, subsistence-based economy to an urban, market oriented state – all left their imprint upon the nation's wildlife.

The earliest landscape the Europeans encountered resembled a world which had disappeared in Europe centuries ago. To quote one of the early Puritan leaders, William Bradford ([1856] 1981, 70), it was 'but a hideous and desolate wilderness, full of wild beasts.' It was a world of silent forests (Belknap 1813, 3:56), populated by creatures that had long been exterminated in civilized Europe. Most of the beasts of the forest fell into one of two categories – the obnoxious and the useful. The wolf fell into the first category. It was one of the more annoying, and unfortunately more ubiquitous, inhabitants of the forest. Due to their acquired taste for free-ranging hogs and sheep (Audubon and Bachman [1854] 1974, 2:128), they soon incurred the enmity of the farmer. They were a great hindrance to the raising of sheep (Hildreth 1848, 497). The first settlers of Marietta, Ohio, were obliged to build pens to protect their hogs (Hildreth 1848, 497) while the residents of Massachusetts toyed with the idea of building a wolf-proof fence across Cape Cod to create a livestock sanctuary on the outer Cape (Tober 1981, 24). Farmers and hunters alike pushed for the enactment of bounties on wolves and other ravenous beasts (Cooper [1810] 1897, 23). Although even one wolf would have been too many for most farmers, wolves appear to have been fairly common during the early phases of the settlement process. William Wood ([1634] 1977, 46), an early promoter of New England, termed them 'the greatest inconveniency the country hath.' Their nocturnal howlings were a common occurrence. Massachusetts alone paid bounties on more than 340 wolves in 1694 (Judd 1905, 344). Bounty payments and historical records suggest that wolves were a constant threat for the first 20 to 30 years of a settlement's existence (Hildreth 1848, 497; Anonymous 1865; Hays 1871; Goodwin 1936; Genoways 1986).

Bears likewise were a nuisance in many early settlements. They destroyed cornfields and they were fond of feeding on swine they found in the forest (Cooper [1810] 1897, 24; Zeisberger 1910, 57). They were hunted to extinction in many areas for bounties, their skin, their grease, and their meat (Flint [1828] 1970, 1:93; Silver 1974, 114; Eveland 1985). Rattlesnakes were among the more feared inhabitants of the forest. Many accounts suggest that they were fairly numerous throughout Ohio and segments of the Northeast (Kirtland 1838, 189). Large numbers of rattlesnakes, for instance, occupied the rockier, more rugged portions of northern Pennsylvania (Tome [1854] 1928, 34–35; Zeisberger 1910, 70–71). Settlement and the advent of the free-ranging hog, the rattlesnake's inveterate enemy (Chamberlain 1849, 15), soon brought the rattlesnake problem under control (Hildreth 1825; Atwater 1838, 68; Hahn 1910).

The early settlers also had to contend with a number of other annoying pests. Gray squirrels were particularly fond of green Indian corn and young wheat (Audubon and Bachman [1854] 1974, 1:270). Woods, maintained for fuel and fences, provided a convenient base of operation for their raids into neighboring fields (Bradbury 1817, 290; Flint [1828] 1970, 1:102). Competitive squirrel hunts were a commonplace event in many early settlements (Seton [1925] 1953, 4:21; Trautman 1939; Schorger 1949). Ohio passed a law in 1807 requiring a specified number of squirrel scalps from every inhabitant or the payment of a fine (Trautman 1977, 6) while Pennsylvania paid three pence a head or eight thousand pounds for the destruction of 640 000 squirrels in 1749 (Audubon and Bachman [1854] 1974, 1:270).

One should not overlook the more positive contributions of North America's quadrupeds. Deer were a staple of the early pioneer economy (Trefethen 1970). Venison was 'held in the highest esteem,' while deer skins were considered an article of commerce in many sections of the country (Audubon and Bachman [1854] 1974, 2:221–222; McCabe and McCabe 1984, 60). As the term buck suggests, the buckskin soon became the equivalent of the Spanish dollar (Zeisberger 1910, 57).

Fur was one of the first products of the New World to be exported on a large-scale basis. Records of the early fur-trading industry are fragmentary at best. The records that do exist, however, indicate that large quantities of beaver pelts, the mainstay of the early fur-trading industry, were shipped to Europe. At the peak of fur-trading activity in the 1650s, New York exported 40 000 beaver pelts annually to Europe (Norton 1974, 100–101). Michillimackinac, the major British fur trading post in the Great Lakes region, posted a take of 50 938 beaver skins in 1767 (Lart 1922). Beaver insured the economic independence of the early Separatist colony at Plymouth (Maloney [1931] 1967, 16–20; Phillips 1961, 1:118–127). It was the most important element of New York's trade-based economy throughout the seventeenth century (Norton 1974, 100–101).

The fur-trading frontier preceded the timber and the agricultural frontiers. The industry rose, enjoyed a brief period of prosperity and then faded away before the forests were even explored by lumbermen for their timber (Curtis 1956). The beaver supply of the Connecticut River Valley was seriously depleted by the late 1660s (Innes 1983, 30). By 1793 few beavers were left east of the Mississippi River (Schorger 1965).

A few investigators like John T. Curtis (1956) have downplayed the beaver's ecological role in the presettlement period. However, a growing body of evidence suggests that the beaver was a major agent of landscape change. Beavers normally construct large numbers of dams on small (second to fifth order), low-gradient streams (Slough and Sadlier 1977; Naiman, Melillo, and Hobbie 1986). Densities can reach one colony per kilometer of stream in optimal habitats (Howard and Larson 1985). The dams are abandoned as the beavers deplete the available food supply, generally aspen, in the vicinity of the dam (Lawrence 1952; Bergerud and Miller 1977; Baker 1983b, 255). The total area affected by the beaver's activity was and still is often substantial (Naiman, Johnston, and Kelley 1988). The following account by Bela Hubbard (1887, 362–363), an early land surveyor in Michigan, provides a clear picture of their impact on the presettlement landscape.

To a great extent level, [the region between Lake Erie and Saginaw was] intersected by numerous water courses, which [had] but moderate flow. At the head-waters and small inlets of these streams the beaver established his colonies. Here he dammed the streams, setting back the water over the flat lands, and creating ponds in which were his habitations. Not one or two, but a series of such dams were constructed along each stream so that very extensive surfaces became thus covered permanently with the flood. The trees were killed, and the land converted into a chain of ponds and marshes ... In time these filled with muck or peat ... In a semi-circle of twelve miles around Detroit, having the river for base, and embracing about 100,000 acres fully one-fifth part consists of marshy tracts or prairies which had their origin in the work of the beaver.

Beaver ponds acted as settling basins and were an important factor in the aggradation of small stream valleys (Ruedemann and Schoonmaker 1938; Ives 1942). Due to anaerobic conditions and low decay rates, the ponds also retained large quantities of organic matter (Naiman, Melillo, and Hobbie 1986; Naiman, Johnston, and Kelley 1988). In fact, some investigators believe that many broad, flat valley floors are actually the result of the work of beavers (Ruedemann and Schoonmaker 1938; Lawrence 1954, 157).

The beaver meadow complex, a temporary phase of plant succession dominated by bluejoint grass (*Calamagrostis canadensis*) and sedges (*Carex* spp.) (Lawrence 1954, 157), was critical to the settler's early farm operation. This ready-made hay supported the settler's stock until he cleared enough ground to raise English hay (Belknap 1813, 3:118–119; Lapham 1846, 70). The better beaver meadows yielded up to 4 tons of hay per acre. Fortunate indeed was the farmer who purchased land where the industrious beaver had made a settlement (Wansey [1798] 1970, 130).

Effects of the first 100 years of settlement

Many European visitors, like Peter Kalm, were acutely aware of the changes occasioned by the arrival of the Europeans. In 1748 Kalm ([1772] 1972, 150–151) commented that the decline of many forms of wildlife was apparent to all second-generation Americans.

[During their fathers'] childhood the bays, rivers, and brooks were quite covered with all sorts of water fowl, such as wild geese, ducks, and the like. But at present there is sometimes not a single bird upon them; about sixty or seventy years ago, a single person could kill eighty ducks in a morning; but at present you frequently wait in vain for a single one ... Cranes at that time came hither by hundreds in the spring: at present there are but very few. The wild Turkeys, and the birds, which the Swedes in this country call Partridges and Hazel-hens, were in whole flocks in the woods. But at this time a person is tired with walking before he can start a single bird. The cause of this diminution is not difficult to find ... since the arrival of great crowds of Europeans, things are greatly changed: the country is well peopled, and the woods are cut down: the people increasing in this country, they have by hunting and shooting in part extirpated the birds, in part scared them away ...

The first 100 years of the settlement process often dramatically altered the nature of the faunal community. Unfortunately many of the changes on the East Coast occurred before records were kept or ornithological history began. By the time a number of competent naturalists appeared on the scene in the early 1800s, the East Coast's landscape had already been heavily modified (Griscom 1949, 54–55). To the west conditions were much more propitious for conducting an analysis of the initial changes accompanying settlement. Trained naturalists like John James Audubon ([1840] 1967) of Kentucky, Samuel P. Hildreth (1848) and Jared P. Kirtland (1850) of Ohio, Philo R. Hoy (1885) of Wisconsin and Robert Ridgway (1889, 13–16, 1915) of Illinois witnessed and commented upon the impact of settlement on the Midwest's early fish and wildlife populations.

Jared P. Kirtland, a physician by training, was one of the more knowledgeable and well-versed amateur naturalists of the nineteenth century. An early inhabitant of the Connecticut Western Reserve in northeastern Ohio and the discoverer of the Kirtland's warbler, Kirtland prepared the first published state report (1838) on the zoology of Ohio. His (1850) review of the natural history of the Western Reserve is a particularly revealing analysis of the faunal changes accompanying the first half century of settlement. 'Of the extent of these changes,' Kirtland (1850) wrote, 'few have any conception.' The full extent of these changes is summarized below, following Kirtland's (1850) outline on a point by point basis.

(1) The loss of the larger quadrupeds. The disappearance of the larger mammals soon followed upon the heels of settlement (Cooper [1810] 1897, 25; Flint [1822] 1904, 121; Macauley 1829, 449; Matthiessen 1959, 112). Kirtland (1838, 1850) noted that elk, deer, bear, wolves, panthers, lynx, wolverine, bison, and possibly moose were once common or at least had been found in the state of Ohio. Some like the elk and the bison were

eliminated at a very early date due to the ease with which they were killed and their low reproductive rates (Silver 1974, 220; Genoways 1986). Others like the wolf and the bear were simply incompatible with a live-stock-based economy. DeVos (1964) has documented the historic retreat of many of the larger quadrupeds and carnivores from the Northeast and the Midwest as civilization advanced. For all intents and purposes, most of the larger game animals had disappeared from the Northeast by 1850 (Goodwin 1936). New England's fauna had been reduced to 'a few small species of no consequence,' (Dwight [1821] 1969, 1:33), while game in the more settled parts of Pennsylvania was limited to a 'few pheasants [ruffed grouse and heath hen], partridges [bob-white], squirrels, and hares' (Schoepf [1788] 1968, 2:5).

(2) Substitution of species of open areas and forest edge for species more characteristic of the interior of the forest. Kirtland, like scores of other naturalists and sportsmen, e.g., Forester (1914), noted the changing composition of the wildlife. Massive alteration of the forest-clad landscape caused a perceptible shift in the make up of the fauna. 'The universal forest [had] been so far destroyed [on the Western Reserve], that [by 1850] only broken patches remain[ed]' (Kirtland 1850). Species associated with the 'universal forest', i.e., the species of the mature 'climax' forest, decreased in abundance. In reality few vertebrate species were limited solely to old-growth forests although the woodland caribou and the ivory-billed woodpecker may have fallen into this category (Leopold 1978). The caribou's dependence on mature conifer forests may have been related to the abundant supply of tree lichens, a source of winter food, in mature forests (Cringan 1957). A preference for wood-boring insects in large, dead snags (Pough 1949, 40–41, 50) and the occurrence of suitable nesting sites in large diameter (>24 inch d.b.h.) cavity trees (Conner 1979; Tubbs *et al.* 1987) probably accounted for the ivory-billed woodpecker's and to a lesser extent the pileated woodpecker's association with old-growth forests (Kirtland 1850). The large, hollow trees of the old-growth forest supported a diverse array of cavity-nesting birds and mammals. The colorful Carolina parakeet, for instance, was a common inhabitant of the broad, river bottom forests of the Ohio and Mississippi River Valleys. Great flocks of the raucous parakeet once nested and roosted in the large, hollow sycamore trees of the floodplains of the region. One investigator has even suggested that the extinction of the parakeet may have been due to the destruction of the hollow 'bee-trees' by honeybee hunters (McKinley 1960). The turkey, the passenger pigeon, the bear, the marten, the fisher, the bobcat, the gray squirrel, the gray fox, and the panther

were a few of the other species that benefited from the mature forest's cover and abundant supply of nuts, acorns, and other foods (Thomas *et al.* 1988).

If the disappearance of the forest resulted in the loss of forest dwellers, it also favored the multiplication of a number of other species. The advent of civilization converted the uniformity of the forest and the prairie to a much more complex, heterogeneous entity. It was a landscape of fields and woodlots interspersed with hedgerows and orchards. Wildlife managers have long extolled the virtures of such an environment. 'Wildlife,' wrote Aldo Leopold ([1933] 1986, 131), is largely a 'phenomenon of edges.' Edge species like the cottontail, the skunk, the woodchuck, the opossum, the quail (bob-white), the woodcock, and the mourning dove prospered in the newly formed landscape (Cooper [1810] 1897, 25–26; Doddridge [1824] 1912, 60; Forester 1914; DeVos 1964; Allen 1970; Burger 1978). Midwestern settlers welcomed the first appearance of the edge-inhabiting songbirds, e.g., the robins, bluebirds, thrashers, and catbirds, that had formerly graced their gardens and orchards in the East (Flint [1828] 1970, 1:105; Farnham 1846, 77; Kirtland 1850; Allen 1871). Kirtland carefully annotated many of the changes in the margins of his two-volume set of Nuttall's *Manual of Ornithology* (Christy 1936). The admixture of waste grain and weed-seed-filled fields and berry and fruit-filled edge habitats favored the increase of the smaller omnivores and grainivores (Chamberlain 1849, 15; Parsons 1920, 198).

The substitution of open country forms of wildlife for closely related forest species characterized the changing composition of the Northeast's fauna. The raven, for instance, was initially much more common than the crow south of the Great Lakes (Doddridge [1824] 1912, 58; Hubbard 1887, 299; Woodruff 1907; Schorger 1941; Andrle and Carroll 1988, 282, 286; Mayfield 1988–1989). The raven, however, was very sensitive to deforestation and the encroachment of civilization. By 1900 it had virtually disappeared from most of the region (Wheaton 1882; Harlow 1922; Schorger 1941). The crow, which preferred open country, made its appearance in the nineteenth century and increased dramatically thereafter (Hubbard 1887, 299–301: Schorger 1941). The forest-loving red-shouldered hawk once outnumbered the red-tailed hawk throughout much of the Northeast. Forest fragmentation and the drainage of its preferred wetland habitat have eliminated it from large sections of its former range. The adaptable red-tailed hawk is now the dominant diurnal raptor of the more settled agricultural regions of the Northeast (Andrle and Carroll 1988, 110, 114; Peterjohn and Rice 1991, 80–81).

Kirtland (1850) reported that the red fox, an inhabitant of open areas and semi-cultivated farmlands, was unknown in Ohio until settlement. The red fox, however, eventually supplanted the gray fox throughout the more settled regions of the Midwest and the Northeast (Leopold 1931, 217; Baker 1983b, 124). The origin of the red fox is unclear. It may have been derived from a small indigenous population or it may represent the spread of a population of red fox introduced to the East Coast from Europe about 1750 (Gottschang 1981, 124).

The fox squirrel initially was an inhabitant of the oak openings and prairie groves south of the Great Lakes. The gray squirrel occupied extensive tracts of closed forests (Kennicott 1857, 55–63). Grazing and the fragmentation of the forest favored the spread of the fox squirrel at the expense of the gray squirrel (Schorger 1949; Gottschang 1981, 73–74; Mumford and Whitaker 1982, 271–272; Baker 1983b, 217). Research suggests that the gray squirrel requires a landscape that is at least 10 to 20% wooded to exist while the fox squirrel disappears if more than 70% of the landscape is forested (Nixon, Havera, and Greenberg 1978).

Forest clearance also set the stage for another new development – an influx of species more characteristic of the grasslands to the west. The creation of artificial grasslands in areas which were formerly forests favored the range expansion of a number of campestral species. Eastward range extensions have been documented for the thirteen-lined ground squirrel, the Franklin ground squirrel, the prairie vole, the badger, the white-tailed jackrabbit, the western harvest mouse, and the coyote (DeVos 1964; Bowles 1981; Gottschang 1981, 66, 98; Mumford and Whitaker 1982, 244–246, 305–306; Baker 1983b, 190–195). The prairie horned lark, the lark sparrow, the dickcissel, the cowbird, the western meadowlark, the Brewer's blackbird, and the upland sandpiper represent avian species that participated in the eastward expansion (Brooks 1938; Thomas 1951; Smith 1965; Stepney and Power 1973; Hurley and Franks 1976; Andrle and Carroll 1988, 158, 264). Originally the cowbird or the 'buffalo bird' subsisted on insects stirred up by the great herds of bison to the west of the Mississippi. Today it occupies a similar niche on land grazed by cattle in the East (Pough 1949, 210).

(3) Loss of many freshwater fishes. Kirtland recognized that by 1850 the status of many species of fish was precarious. The sturgeon and the muskellunge had become scarce. Migratory species had been excluded from rivers with the construction of dams and many smaller species had increased following the reduction of the larger, more voracious species (Kirtland 1850). No other class of wildlife has suffered as much as the

freshwater fishes. They were 'chronic victims of civilization' (Matthiessen 1959, 270), subject to overharvesting as well as the physical and chemical alteration of their habitat (Marsh [1864] 1965, 107–108). Dredging, ditching, stream channelization, siltation, changes in the chemical characteristics of the water, the widespread use of pesticides and other toxic chemicals, fluctuating water levels, the construction of dams, the loss of spawning habitats due to the drainage of swamps and wetlands, and the introduction of a large number of exotic species (Table 14.1) – all conspired to degrade the fish fauna of many rivers and lakes (Lachner 1956; Gammon 1977; Smith 1979, xiv–xix; Menzel 1981; Trautman 1981, 13–35; Burr and Page 1986; Pearson and Pearson 1989). The magnitude of the decline of the freshwater fishes is difficult to assess although intensive studies of several agriculturally oriented watersheds in the Midwest have provided us with crude estimates of the losses. Reliable data on the species composition of the Maumee River of northwestern Ohio and the Illinois River of central Illinois dates back to the nineteenth century. Over two-thirds of the species in the Illinois River and 44% of the species in the Maumee River have either decreased in abundance or disappeared. Top carnivores and species in small headwater streams experienced the greatest declines (Trautman and Gartman 1974; Karr, Toth, and Dudley 1985). Siltation associated with intensive agricultural land use practices appears to be the major factor responsible for the decline (Trautman and Gartman 1974; Havera and Bellrose 1984). Alterations in the temperature, the flow regimes, and the organic substrates of the streams, e.g., a shift from leaf litter inputs to *in situ* algal production, have been implicated in some of the declines (Schlosser 1982; Barton, Taylor, and Biette 1985).

Changes in the fish fauna of a wide variety of lakes following settlement were equally dramatic. Lake Wingra is a shallow eutrophic lake adjacent to Madison, Wisconsin, and the University of Wisconsin. It has been the site of a number of important limnological studies over the past 100 years. Once Lake Wingra, its bordering marshes, and its diverse aquatic macrophyte communities supported 14 native species of fish including large populations of yellow perch and northern pike. Dredging, draining, and filling eliminated the shallow marshes, the spawning grounds of the northern pike. The lake was subjected to a massive series of fish introductions beginning with carp late in the nineteenth century. The carp uprooted and destroyed much of the littoral vegetation. Yellow perch and northern pike are uncommon in the lake today while two of the twenty or so introduced species, the white crappie and the yellow bass, are currently among the more abundant species in the lake (Baumann *et al.* 1974).

Table 14.1. *Loss of native vertebrates and gain of alien vertebrates by state*

State	Number of introduced species	Number of native species having regularly bred in region	Native species extirpated or extinct	% native species extirpated or extinct	Sources
Mammals					
New England	8	70	6	9	Godin 1977
Massachusetts	5	58	8	14	Bickford and Dymon 1990
Pennsylvania	2	70	8	11	Merritt 1987
Ohio	2	65	13	20	Gottschang 1981
Indiana	2	65	13	20	Mumford and Whittaker 1982
Illinois	3	67	8	12	Hoffmeister 1989
Iowa	2	68	10	15	Bowles 1981
Missouri	3	70	3	4	Schwartz and Schwartz 1981
Michigan	2	66	6	9	Baker 1983b
Minnesota	2	78	5	6	Hazard 1982
Birds					
Massachusetts	5	186	3	2	Bickford and Dymon 1990
Pennsylvania	6	~180	8	4	Brauning 1992
Ohio	6	~188	8	4	Smith *et al.* 1973; Peterjohn and Rice 1991
Indiana	6	~180	15	8	Mumford and Keller 1984
Illinois		~215	16	7	George 1971; Bowles 1981
Iowa	5	~160	15	9	Dinsmore 1981; Dinsmore *et al.* 1984
Missouri	7	184	32[a]	17	Robbins and Easterla 1992
Michigan	6	~214	5	2	Brewer, McPeek, and Adams 1991
Minnesota	5	~245[a]	8[a]	3	Green 1988
Wisconsin	7	~220	4	2	Robbins 1991

Fish				
Connecticut	24	40[b]	1	2	Whitworth, Berrien, and Keller 1968
Massachusetts	27	41[b]	1	2	Bickford and Dymon 1990
Pennsylvania	7	180	28	15	Cooper 1983
Ohio	15	154	9	6	Smith et al. 1973; Trautman 1981
Indiana	9	168	10	6	Gammon and Gerking 1966
Illinois	13	186	9	5	Smith 1979
Iowa	>9	~140	12	9	Menzel 1981
Wisconsin	11	155	9	6	Becker 1983

[a] The value for Missouri is high because it includes species which currently only accidently nest in the state as well as extinct and extirpated species. Values for Minnesota include sporadic as well as regular breeders in the breeding column and two formerly sporadic breeders in the extirpated column.

[b] Includes diadromous species.

The Great Lakes were once one of the greatest freshwater fisheries of the world. Records of commercial fishing catches dating back to the nineteenth century document the changing nature of the Great Lakes (Regier and Hartman 1973). One hundred and sixty years of environmental stress has significantly altered the composition of the fish communities. Species which once made up the bulk of the catch in Lake Erie, for instance, lake trout, lake sturgeon, lake whitefish, and lake herring, have either disappeared or are relatively scarce. Exotics like rainbow smelt, carp, and alewife presently dominate many of the fish communities of the Great Lakes region (Smith 1968; Regier and Hartman 1973; Gates, Clarke, and Harris 1983). Most of the changes have been attributed to (1) overfishing, (2) the increased export of silt and nutrients to the lakes from the surrounding farmlands and urban areas, and (3) the introduction of harmful exotics like the smelt, the sea lamprey, and the alewife (Regier and Hartman 1973; Gates, Clarke, and Harris 1983; Miller, Williams, and Williams 1989).

(4) Introduction of harmful exotics. Kirtland (1850) only touched upon the 'new species [which] are constantly finding their way among us.' As the discussion of the Great Lakes fisheries suggests, however, exotics were to have a major impact upon America's fauna as well as her commercial activities. No other class of introduced organisms wreaked as much havoc as the insects. Many of Europe's crop pests found a congenial home in North America's 'Europeanized' landscape. Aliens like the codling moth, the Hessian fly, the European cabbage butterfly, and the European corn borer eventually colonized North America's monotypic grain fields, orchards, and gardens (Osmun and Giese 1966; Burger 1978). The resulting disruption of America's agricultural endeavors was a very costly affair (Fletcher 1950, 147). The ravages of the Hessian fly, for instance, induced many of the East Coast's farmers to abandon their favorite cash crop, wheat, and turn instead to a more diversified form of agriculture (Jones 1974).

Not all of the exotics, of course, were injurious to humans. The white man's fly or the honeybee (*Apis mellifera*) and the common earthworm (*Lumbricus terrestris*) represent two of the more useful additions to America's fauna (Smith 1928; McKinley 1964; Schorger 1968; Reynolds 1973).

Effects of logging, forest fragmentation, and intensive farming

The wildlife changes following Kirtland's time represented an elaboration of the earlier mentioned processes as well as the development of new forces. The advent of large-scale commercial logging in the latter half of the nineteenth century significantly altered the Northeast's forests. The intensive exploitation of the hemlock–white pine–northern hardwood forest region, for instance, reduced the conifer component of the forests. The loss of the conifers, in turn, contributed to the decrease of many of the birds and mammals associated with the conifers (Hicks 1935; Poole 1964, 7–8). The solitary vireo, the magnolia warbler, the blackburnian warbler, and the golden-crowned kinglet bred sporadically in extensive groves of hemlock and spruce throughout the Northeast (Saunders 1936, 74, 130; Johnston 1947; Pough 1949, 126). Their numbers declined with the cutting of the hemlocks and the spruce (Forbush 1929, 2:377; Kendeigh 1946; Poole 1964, 7–8). Many of the more northern, conifer-loving warblers and kinglets eventually returned to the Allegheny Plateau as the cutover forests and the artificial conifer plantations, initiated in the widespread reforestation efforts of the 1930s, matured (Andrle and Carroll 1988, 310, 372, 380, 490; Brauning 1992, 260–261). The disappearance of the pine marten from the mature hemlock–hardwood forests of Pennsylvania has also been attributed to the commercial exploitation of the forest (Shoemaker 1919, 2:132–133).

If lumbering imperiled the existence of some species, it also created a favorable habitat for the spread of other species. Lumbering and the recurring fires which followed generated extensive areas of sproutlands and young pine barrens. Both the prairie warbler and the chestnut-sided warbler profited from the brushy sprout growth which followed the cutting of the hardwoods (Brooks 1940; Pough 1949, 173, 178). The rare Kirtland's warbler, a species which prefers young stands of jack pines, also experienced a minor population boom at the turn of the century in Michigan's cut and burned-over forests (Harwood 1981).

Many of America's larger mammals like the white-tailed deer are subclimax species which thrive in disturbed habitats (Leopold 1978). During the presettlement period deer populations were probably as low as $2/km^2$ over large sections of the mature deciduous forest (Alverson, Waller, and Solheim 1988). The regrowth of the forest following the heavy cuttings of the early twentieth century created a wealth of nutritious browse in the form of hardwood sprouts and seedlings. The increased food supply, the disappearance of many natural predators, and the passage of legislation protecting the deer prompted a dramatic upswing in the number of deer. The regrowth of the forest, however, soon put the browse beyond the reach of the deer. By 1930 deer had exceeded the carrying capacity of the forest in large sections of Pennsylvania, New York, Michigan, and Wisconsin (Leopold 1943; Leopold, Sowis, and Spencer 1947; Marquis 1975). Deer densitites in excess of 8 to 10 $deer/km^2$ suppressed the regeneration of hemlock, yew, and white cedar

(Graham 1954; Beals, Cottam, and Vogl 1960; Anderson and Loucks 1979; Frelich and Lorimer 1985) and altered the species composition and the size-class structure of the forest (Whitney 1984, 1990). Rapidly growing species, e.g., black cherry and cucumber magnolia, are poorly represented in the sapling to small tree size categories of old-growth forests on the Allegheny Plateau of northern Pennsylvania today. Most of the slow-growing hemlock which dominates these size classes originated prior to the buildup of the deer herd. Large populations of deer still threaten the regeneration of Pennsylvania's forests (Marquis 1981; Marquis and Brenneman 1981; Tilghman 1989). Some ecologists (Alverson, Waller, and Solheim 1988) even believe that deer densities as low as $4/km^2$ can extirpate the more sensitive plant species. A virgin forest that appears to be natural or free of the influence of deer today could have been profoundly affected by the ups and downs of deer populations years ago (Leopold 1938).

The end of the nineteenth century also witnessed a reorganization of America's agricultural landscape. Marginal farmland, land which was too poor, too dry, or too steep to farm, was taken out of production while the better, more profitable farmland was utilized more intensively. Both events altered the wildlife.

Farmers abandoned large segments of the hill country of northern New England and the more rugged sections of the Appalachian Plateau of New York, Pennsylvania, and eastern Ohio. Secondary succession has always been a popular area of research among ecologists. A number of animal ecologists turned to the abandoned farms of the Northeast and the Midwest to document the wildlife changes accompanying the return of the forest (Hicks 1933; Saunders 1936; Bump 1950; Beckwith 1954; Lanyon 1981). Species of the hayfields and pastures, e.g., the bobolink and the meadowlark, gave way to a heterogeneous community of thicket and shrub dwellers, e.g., the northern yellowthroat, the song sparrow, the golden-winged warbler and the chestnut-sided warbler (Andrle and Carroll 1988, 356, 370, 416). The chestnut-sided warbler appears to have been relatively rare 150 years ago. Audubon ([1840] 1967, 2:35–36) reported seeing it once. By the late nineteenth century, however, it was one of New York state's more common species (Kendeigh 1946). It was only one of a number of species like the ruffed grouse, the woodcock, and the white-tailed deer which temporarily benefited from the widespread reversion of farmlands to forests (Fisher 1933). The widespread, late twentieth century maturation of the Northeast's forests has again reduced the abundance of many of these early successional species (Brooks and Birch 1988).

The level, rich farmland of the Midwest experienced a very different pattern of development. Here the passage of time witnessed a much more intensive utilization of the land's resources. Increasingly the remaining forests were cut, the prairies cultivated, and the wetlands drained in order to bring more land into production. The diminution of the forests had a number of unforeseen consequences. The smaller size of the woodlots and the increasing ratio of edge to interior habitat significantly altered the bird species composition of the remaining woodlots. The recent decrease of a number of 'area-sensitive', forest interior species like the hooded warbler, the ovenbird, and the yellow-throated vireo on the East Coast has alarmed many ornithologists (Robbins 1979; Whitcomb *et al.* 1981; Wilcove, McLellan, and Dobson 1986; Robbins, Dawson, and Dowell 1989; Terborgh 1989, 40–44). The agriculturally oriented, largely deforested landscape of the Midwest has been heavily affected by the decline (Trautman 1940, 52–53; Whitcomb 1977). Drawing upon field notes and bird surveys extending over the last 60 years, Ambuel and Temple (1982) and Temple and Cary (1988) have documented the retreat of the more sensitive interior species from the smaller woodlots of southern Wisconsin. Ovenbirds and worm-eating warblers, two of the more area-sensitive species, are limited to the larger woodlots of the region and currently breed in fewer than 20 sites in Illinois (Robinson 1988). Their disappearance has variously been attributed to (1) the small size of the remaining woodlots (a size smaller than the home range of some bird species – Forman, Galli, and Leck 1976), (2) a decrease in overall forest cover and the inability of marginal woodlots to recruit surplus young from the larger tracts of neighboring woods (Lynch and Whigham 1984; Askins and Philbrick 1987; Freemark and Collins 1992), (3) the limited habitat heterogeneity of the smaller woodlots, and (4) the increased incidence of brood parasitism (Brittingham and Temple 1983) and nest predation (Wilcove 1985) in the edge oriented habitats of the smaller woodlots.

Recent years have witnessed the appearance of a number of excellent breeding bird atlases at the state level (Laughlin and Kibbe 1985; Andrle and Carroll 1988; Brewer, McPeek, and Adams 1991; Peterjohn and Rice 1991; Brauning 1992). Species maps, showing the distribution of a species across a grid-based map of the state, highlight the dependence of the more area-sensitive species on overall forest cover. In the Ohio atlas, for instance, the worm-eating warbler is largely confined to the heavily wooded (>50% forest cover) counties of the rugged Appalachian Plateau (Peterjohn and Rice 1991, 302–303). The black-throated blue warbler's, the blackburnian warbler's and the dark-eyed junco's distributions in the Pennsylvania atlas generally coincide with those counties that are more than 75% wooded (Brauning 1992, 314–315, 320–321, 394–395).

It is significant that the regions which have sustained the greatest songbird declines also support large populations of nest predators (blue jays and raccoons) and brood parasites (brown-headed cowbirds) (Terborgh 1989, 57).

Long-term studies of bird population changes in large forested tracts of land, notably the Great Smoky Mountains National Park, Allegany State Park in western New York, and the Hubbard Brook Experimental Forest in the White Mountains of New Hampshire, have not shown any consistent pattern of decline. Nest predation and brood parasitism rates are still very low in the Great Smoky Mountains (Wilcove 1988; Terborgh 1989, 48–49, 64–67). Most of the long-term changes in bird populations in these areas, however, appear to be related to forest maturation and changes in the structure of the vegetation (Holmes and Sherry 1988; Askins, Lynch, and Greenberg 1990; Baird 1990; Finch 1991). A number of ornithologists have attributed the decline of neotropical migrants in recent breeding bird surveys to tropical deforestation and the loss of habitat on wintering grounds (Robbins *et al.* 1989; Finch 1991).

If agricultural reorganization resulted in the increasing fragmentation of the forest, it almost entirely eliminated the tallgrass prairie as a viable habitat. Grassland species unable to adapt to artificial grasslands such as pastures and hayfields suffered a serious decline. The contrast between the historical accounts of the tallgrass prairie's avifauna and the avifauna of the same areas today is 'striking' (Ridgway 1873, 1889, 13–16; Graber and Graber 1963; Anderson 1971, 34–39; Hoffman and Sample 1988). Approximately half of the native prairie birds of Illinois (12 of 21 species) are either endangered or threatened (Bowles 1981). Formerly common species like the marsh hawk, the short-eared owl, Henslow's sparrow, the upland sandpiper, and the greater prairie chicken are now rare and often confined to larger tracts of grassland (Bowles and Thom 1981; Samson 1983). The decline of the tallgrass prairie's fauna was not limited to the vertebrates. Due to their dependence on a narrow range of host plants or nectar sources, many prairie-related insects have suffered range contractions (Opler and Krizek 1984; Panzer 1988). Millions of regal fritillary butterflies (*Speyeria idalia*) once swarmed over the tallgrass prairies of the Midwest. Today, the butterfly and its larval foodplant, the prairie violet (*Viola pedatifida*), are mainly limited to the few small remaining patches of virgin prairie (Hammond and McCorkle 1983). The regal fritillary and other butterflies like the Dakota skipper (*Hesperia dacotae*), the Powesheik skipper (*Oarisma powesheik*), and the ottoe skipper (*Hesperia ottoe*), are some of the better known species whose existence has been threatened by the loss of the tallgrass prairie (Orwig 1992).

Drainage also took its toll upon the wildlife. The loss of cattail and sedge marshes adversely affected local breeding populations of marsh wrens, least bitterns, Virginia rails, soras and common moorhens in the Northeast and the Midwest (Adams, McPeek, and Evers 1988; Andrle and Carroll 1988, 308; Brauning 1992, 126). The prairie potholes of the northern United States and

Canada have always produced a large share of the continent's dabbling and diving ducks (Allen and Leedy 1970). By the mid-1950s more than half of the prairie potholes in the United States had been drained (Louma 1985). The result was a marked decline in the number of migrating waterfowl (Ridgway 1915; Trautman 1977). The decline was exacerbated by an intense period of market hunting at the end of the nineteenth century (Trefethen 1975, 146–147).

The impact of the reorganization of America's farm economy in the twentieth century extended well beyond the loss of the occasional woodlot and wetland. It was part of a broader trend to increasing specialization and monocultures. If the earlier phases of farm development created a more diverse assemblage of wildlife habitats, the later phases systematically eliminated a number of habitats. The general purpose farm with its patchwork quilt of row crops, small grains, hayfields, pastures, orchards, small waste areas, and unkempt fencerows gave way to modern agribusiness with its capital-intensive monocultures. During economically difficult times, farmers compensated for their narrower profit margins by producing a greater volume of food, by 'planting fence row to fence row' (Edwards 1985). Berner's (1985) and Vance's (1976) analyses of the land use changes of two representative sections of farmland in the Midwest provide an indication of the increasing homogeneity of the landscape (Fig. 14.1). Graber and Graber (1963, 388) have quantita-

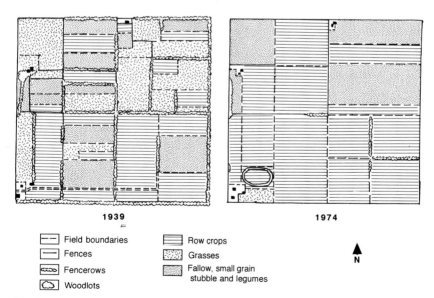

1939   1974

⊏⁻⁻⊐ Field boundaries	⊟ Row crops	
⊏⁻⊐ Fences	▨ Grasses	▲
⊏⟳⊐ Fencerows	▦ Fallow, small grain	N
⊏◊⊐ Woodlots	stubble and legumes	

Fig. 14.1 Comparative cover types and fencerow cover of a representative section (259 ha) of farmland in Jasper County, Illinois, in 1939 and 1974. Modified slightly from Vance (1976).

tively documented the disappearance of many wildlife habitats in Illinois. Aldo Leopold (1945) succinctly summarized the changes when he stated: 'The woodlot is in process of conversion to pasture; the fencerow is in process of abolition; the remaining marsh is in process of drainage; the creeks are getting so flashy that there is a tendency to channelization.' Today we might add that the pasture is in the process of conversion to row crops. All of these activities were part of a 'psychological coup de grace' that the farmer unintentionally handed the farm's wildlife under the banner of clean farming (Allen 1974, 64). The relative importance of the activities shifted through time. Their ultimate impact, however, was the same - a decrease in many forms of wildlife.

Grazing the woodlot was a continuation of the old tradition of setting cattle and hogs free to range the woods. It was particularly common during the depression era and declined thereafter. By eliminating those species which nested or foraged in the lower strata of the woods (the ovenbird, the Kentucky warbler, the towhee, the redstart, the indigo bunting, and the yellow-billed cuckoo), grazing impoverished the woodlot's fauna (Day 1930; Saunders 1936, 86–91; Dambach and Good 1940; Good and Dambach 1943; Dambach 1944).

Orchards, hedgerows, and brushy, tree-filled fencerows have long been among the farm's more productive wildlife habitats (Saunders 1936, 42–43; Petrides 1942; Graber and Graber 1963, 425–430, 438–439; Best 1983; Best and Hill 1983; Shalaway 1985). They gave a savanna-like appearance to the general purpose farm of the nineteenth century. They also provided the cover, the aerial perches, and the foraging sites required by many birds and mammals. Like other facets of the nineteenth century farm, however, they succumbed to the more intensive farming of the twentieth century. The small family orchard was a victim of the high costs of production, increasing specialization, and competition from the fruit farms of the West (Fletcher 1950, 276–282; Graber and Graber 1963, 429–430). As early as the latter half of the nineteenth century, orchards in Illinois and Ohio had been reduced to approximately 10% of their acreage at the beginning of the century (Graber and Graber 1963, 429; Sitterley 1976, 13). Brushy rail fences died with the advent of the wire fence. Eventually even the wire fences were removed as they interfered with the efficient operation and mechanization of the farm (Burger 1978). Hedges were uprooted because they reduced the yield of corn and they harbored scale insects (Leopold 1931, 65).

The impact of the increasing simplification of the farm landscape was predictable. Surveys of Illinois' breeding bird populations in 1906–1909 and in 1956–1958 indicate a major decline in many of the species normally associated with orchard and fencerow habitats, e.g., the yellow-billed cuckoo, the flicker, the red-headed woodpecker, the blue jay, the mockingbird, the brown thrasher, the eastern kingbird, the robin, the orchard oriole, the chipping sparrow, and the field sparrow (Graber and Graber 1963, 505–506).

The loss of habitat also extended to the farm's grasslands (Fig. 14.2). Grasses or grasses and legumes have long played several critical roles on the farm. They supplied the livestock with food and they replenished the soil's fertility. The typical three to five course rotation of the early to mid-nineteenth century kept at least 25% of the cropland in temporary grass or a grass and legume mixture. Many farmers currently have almost 100% of their cropland in row crops. The shift from grasses and small grains to corn and soybeans was related to a number of factors. The post-World War II availability of low-cost nitrogen fertilizers, the relative profitability of row crops versus other crops, the introduction of conservation tillage techniques (which minimize losses due to erosion), and changes in the numbers of livestock, livestock feed sources, and thus forage requirements are among the more important factors (Sitterley 1976, 12; Colvin 1985; Richmond and Nicholson 1985). In one representative 1000 ha study area in Jasper County, Illinois, grasses, including those areas harvested for hay and seed, declined from 47% of the area in 1939 to 1% of the area in 1974. Soybeans took up the slack, increasing from 9 to 69% of the study area during the same interval (Vance 1976). Species which initially profited from the clearing of the forests and the new supply of grain in the nineteenth century, species like the prairie chicken and the upland sandpiper, experienced a dramatic decline as the grasslands disappeared (Leopold 1931, 161–188; Graber and Graber 1963, 468–469; Vance 1976). Both required the

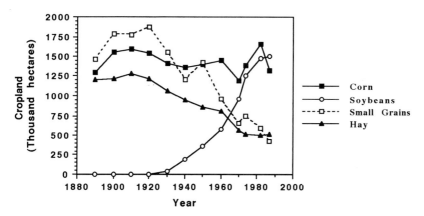

Fig. 14.2 Changes in area devoted to major crops in the state of Ohio, 1890–1987. Based on information in US Census Office (1895, 380); Sitterley (1976); US Bureau of the Census (1977, 5); US Bureau of the Census (1989, 35).

nesting and brood cover sites provided by large expanses of grasslands (Stempel and Rodgers 1961; Yeatter 1963; Drobney and Sparrowe 1977; Samson 1980; Osborne and Peterson 1984). Less severe patterns of decline have been noted more recently in a number of other grassland dependent species in the East. The bobolink, the eastern meadowlark, the barn owl, the savannah sparrow, the grasshopper sparrow, and the vesper sparrow are other species that declined with the waning of the grassland tradition (Colvin 1985; Andrle and Carroll 1988, 444–448; Bollinger 1991). More intensive management of the remaining grassland has also taken its toll on the avifauna. Earlier mowing of hayfields for silage, the shift from timothy and clover to alfalfa, and frequent conversion of hayfields to cash crops have reduced the abundance of a number of grassland species in recent years (Robbins 1991, 84–85; Bollinger and Gavin 1992). Data collected from the North American Breeding Bird Survey since 1965, in fact, suggest that birds breeding in grassland areas are at greater risk than birds breeding in forests (Bollinger 1991; Finch 1991). Some have found a temporary reprieve in the thousands af acres of reclaimed strip-mined land that has been planted to grasses and legumes in the Appalachians (Peterjohn and Rice 1992, 356; Brauning 1992, 94–95, 164–165, 370–371, 386 387).

The massive shift to row crops was not detrimental to all species. A small number of species, notably the horned lark, the killdeer, the prairie deer mouse, and the house mouse, even found the great corn desert a relatively hospitable environment. All are adaptable species which forage on insects and weed seeds in very open areas (Allen 1938; Graber and Graber 1963, 467–468, 477–478; Mumford and Whitaker, 1982, 31–34; Warburton and Klimstra 1984).

The recent rise of conservation tillage represents one bright spot in the inexorable march to simpler agroecosystems. No-till corn fields typically support a more diverse community of birds and small mammals than conventionally tilled fields. The greater structural complexity, food supply, and cover of the no-till field appears to be responsible for the higher wildlife diversity of the conservation tillage system. The Soil Conservation Service's emphasis on grassed waterways and other conservation practices over the past 50 years, and long-term government set-aside programs like the Soil Bank have also benefited many forms of wildlife (Dambach and Good 1940; Harmon and Nelson 1973). Cottontail rabbits and pheasants have flourished as federally sponsored programs have diverted large amounts of cropland to legumes and grasses (Edwards 1985). Unfortunately present trends make the continued existence of much of the farm's wildlife questionable at best (Burger 1981; Carlson 1985).

The twentieth century has generally been characterized as the age of rampant air and water pollution. Rivers have long been the receptacles of wastes – from raw domestic sewage and the refuse of slaughter houses and breweries in the past to the heavy metals, agricultural chemicals, and silt of the present. Long-term studies of the sensitive bottom-dwelling organisms of several major rivers have dramatically underscored the impact of pollutants on aquatic life. Mollusc shells preserved in streambanks and the collections of early naturalists have been particularly useful in outlining the changes which have occurred over the last 100 years (Stansbery 1961; Starrett 1971; Strayer 1980; Suloway 1981). The Scioto River below Columbus, Ohio, lost 10 of its 52 species before 1858 and another 5 species by 1961. Thirteen more species are represented by only a few living specimens or a single relict population (Stansbery 1961). The Illinois River has been the recipient of much of Chicago's wastes. At least 49 different species of mussels were recorded in the river and its adjoining bottomland lakes in 1870–1900. Twenty-five species have been extirpated over the last 100 years and the upper reaches of the river are virtually devoid of mussels (Starrett 1971).

Wildlife of urban areas

Few events tested the versatility of America's wildlife as much as the rise of the sprawling urban metropolises of the nineteenth and twentieth centuries. Fortunately a number of investigators have documented the nature of America's urban animal communities (Minton 1968; Speirs, Markle, and Tozer 1970; Geis 1974; Stearns 1975; Aldrich and Coffin 1980; Matthiae and Stearns 1981). Their work has given us a good idea of the faunal changes that accompany urbanization. Most native species found the brick, stone, and asphalt of the inner city a relatively inhospitable environment. The nighthawk managed to shift from nesting on the gravel bars of rivers to the flat gravel rooftops of the city (Armstrong 1965), but this was more an exception to the general rule. The dominant species of the inner city environment are the exotics, the commensals and pests which followed the Europeans across the Atlantic.

The outlying regions of the city – the suburbs and the residential areas – fared somewhat better and still encompass a moderately diverse fauna of native species. Raccoons and gray squirrels frequent the more wooded residential areas of many cities (Hoffmann and Gottschang 1977; VanDruff and Rowse 1986). Open expanses of trees and lawns with their concentrated supplies of food (weed seeds, insects, grubs, and worms) typically support a number of ground foraging, seed eaters and omnivores, e.g., robins, blue jays, grackles, and mourning doves (Falk 1976; DeGraaf and Wentworth 1981, 1986; Beissinger and Osborne 1982). Plantings of ornamental shrubs favor the occurrence of many fruit-eating omnivores like cardinals, catbirds, and mockingbirds (Williamson 1974). Barn swallows and tree swallows can frequently be found patrolling the open skies of newly established suburbs (DeGraaf and Wentworth 1986).

Although urban environments lost a number of native species, particularly the ground-nesting species and the forest-inhabiting insectivores (Aldrich and Coffin 1980; DeGraaf and Wentworth 1986), they also experienced an influx of aliens. America's urban areas resemble their European counterparts. The same trees, ornamental shrubs, grasses, and weeds grace lawns on both continents so it is not surprising that their faunas are also similar. Europe's birds, insects, and mammals have had a long history of accommodation with dense human settlements (Kimball and Johnson 1978). Some might even term house mice, rats, roaches, house sparrows, starlings, and pigeons obligate commensals of man (Jarvis 1979). Most exhibit 'a high degree of dependence upon human culture' (Lindroth 1957, 216). The synanthropic element is very evident in America's urban animal communities today. The Norway rat, for instance, is one of the more common mammals of many inner city districts (VanDruff and Rowse 1986). Its density often exceeds one for every 20 to 40 human inhabitants (Gottschang 1981, 108). The rock dove or domestic pigeon, a former inhabitant of Europe's coastline cliffs, adjusted admirably to the artificial cliffs and waste grain of the urban environment (Pough 1951; Murton, Thearle, and Thompson 1972). The starling also thrived in the warm, dry, snow-free perches and nesting sites of urban areas (Miller 1975).

The aliens had their drawbacks. William Brewster's (1906) and Charles Walcott's (1974) detailed studies of the changing bird life of Cambridge, Massachusetts, over the last 100 years have documented the negative impact of the house sparrow. The house sparrow first nested in the Cambridge area in 1875. By 1906 Brewster (1906, 66) remarked, 'It is probable ... that only those of us who personally remember the condition which existed before the sparrows came ... can realize to the full the disastrous and far-reaching effects which their introduction has had on our native bird population.' Within ten years, the bluebirds, the house wrens, and the tree swallows were gone. The purple finches, song sparrows, indigo buntings, and least flycatchers soon followed suit (Walcott 1974). Within 60 years of its successful 1852 introduction on the East Coast, the house sparrow was the most abundant bird species of Illinois' urban areas as well as the state as a whole (Graber and Graber 1963, 436, 488, 507).

It would be easy to minimize the changes that have occurred in America's wildlife over the last 300 years. Deer, bear, and turkey are still common, sometimes all too common. A hard look at the numbers (Table 14.1), however, belies the apparent stability of America's wildlife. Due to their high visibility, their mobility, and their economic importance, mammals were among the first species to be affected by civilized man's penetration of the continent. The words of the great biologist, Alfred Wallace (1876, 150), written in another context over 100 years ago, are equally applicable today: 'We live in a zoologically impoverished world, from which all the hugest, and fiercest, and strangest forms have recently disappeared.' Losses in most states ranged anywhere from 5 to 20% of the state's mammalian fauna. The elimination of wildlife habitat probably accounted for most of the loss (McConnell and Harmon 1976). The plow accomplished what the gun never could.

European settlement initiated a period of very rapid change in most of North America's animal and plant communities. Few plant communities were altered as extensively or suffered as great a loss as the fish and the larger mammalian communities. From an economic standpoint, the short-term costs were considerable. Note the decline of the Great Lakes' fisheries (Gates, Clarke, and Harris 1983). The long-term ecological consequences are still only imperfectly known.

15

The legislated landscape

> ... it is not as ornaments that I value the noble trees of this country; it is for their usefulness. We are stripping the forests, as if a single year would replace what we destroy. But the hour approaches, when the laws will take notice of not only the woods, but the game they contain also.
>
> Marmaduke Temple, a character in James Fenimore Cooper's novel *The Pioneers* ([1823] 1985, p. 230).

Landscapes are formed by human activities as well as natural processes. The history of the American landscape is just as much a history of the cultural forces and philosophies which shaped the land as it is a history of nature's influences. Large segments of America's landscape today are owned and managed by federal and state agencies devoted to the conservation of the nation's resources. Hundreds of parks, forest reserves, and wildlife refuges scattered across the Northeast and the Midwest make up the legislated landscape of the twentieth century. Most are creations of the last 50 to 100 years. Although America has often been depicted as a country intent upon despoiling its natural heritage for short-term material gain, the United States was one of the first countries of the world to set aside large blocks of land for conservation purposes. I do not intend to review all the social and political forces which generated the modern conservation movement. For a detailed analysis of America's changing attitude toward the use of the land, the reader should consult Widner's (1968) *Forests and Forestry in the American States: A Reference Anthology,* Nash's (1973) *Wilderness and the American Mind*, Trefethen's (1975) *An American Crusade for Wildlife*, Graham's (1978) *The Adirondack Park: A Political History*, Runte's (1979) *National Parks: The American Experience*, Dana and Fairfax's (1980) *Forest and Range Policy*, and Reiger's (1986) *American Sportsmen and the Origins of Conservation*.

Factors contributing to the exploitation of the region

The rise and maturation of the conservation movement in the late nineteenth and early twentieth centuries signaled a major change in the government's management of the public domain. Because state and federal policies at this time dramatically altered the face of the landscape, a brief discussion of some of the factors underlying the government's change of policy follows. The earliest government programs were primarily oriented towards liquidating the public domain as a means of encouraging settlement and generating revenue for the fledgling state and federal governments (Dana and Fairfax 1980, 1–32). Cheap government land, it was argued, insured the well-being of the yeoman farmer, the backbone of the new republic (Cox *et al.* 1985, 138). Regulations concerning the use of the land were virtually nonexistent once the land passed into private hands. Foreign visitors, accustomed to Europe's paternalistic attitude toward land and strict governmental control of its use, were amazed by America's lack of regulations. As Johann David Schoepf ([1788] 1968, 1:38), a German forester, observed in 1788: 'In America there is no sovereign right over forests and game, no forest service. Whoever holds new land, in whatever way, controls it as his exclusive possession, with everything on it, above it, and under it. It will not easily come about therefore that, as a strict statutory matter, farmers and landowners will be taught how to manage their forests so as to leave for their grandchildren a bit of wood over which to hang a tea kettle. Experience and necessity must here take the place of magisterial provision.'

Historians, scientists, and geographers alike have stressed the destructive nature of this laissez-faire attitude toward the use of the land (Sargeant 1882; Sears [1935] 1959; Sauer 1938, 145; Jacobs 1978; Williams 1989, 232–237, 392–399). Americans had a penchant for squandering their resources (Coan 1983). Other countries have had a similar history of exploiting their resources without concern for the future. America was unique, however, because its profligate activities were intensified by an unusual land–labor relationship and a technologically advanced civilization. Of the three classic factors of production – land, labor, and capital – land was the cheapest and the most abundant feature of the New World. There was little value in economizing on the 'land' factor of the equation (Zobler 1962). Europeans labored to save their scarce land. Americans spent their land to save their labor (Martineau [1837] 1966, 2:94). The very prodigality of the land invited waste (Brewer 1877). Free or relatively inexpensive land in the West, however, also placed a premium on the limited labor pool (Shirreff [1835] 1971, 401). Labor was the major factor in short supply in the New World (Fordham 1906, 120; Bidwell and Falconer

[1925] 1941, 59). The result was an inordinate reliance on labor-saving devices. As the economist Nathan Rosenberg (1975) noted, 'much of early American industrialization ... should be understood in terms of a technology specifically geared to the intensive exploitation of natural resources which existed in considerable abundance relative to capital and labor.'

A constant stream of inventions allowed Americans to harvest their trees, their game, and the products of their soil with a proficiency and an ease which amazed many Europeans. The axe, the gun, and the plow transformed the landscape. Unique American versions of these instruments permitted the transformation. American felling axes, rifles, and farm tools were generally considered superior to their European counterparts (Oliver [1843] 1966, 37–38; Clark 1929, 1:175, 477; Kauffman 1972, 21; Jewell 1976). The American felling axe, for instance, eventually became the standard for much of the civilized world (Bealer 1976, 22). America's first professional forester Bernhard Fernow (1895) wrote, 'If Germany has become the teacher of the world in the matter of forestry,-that is, in the rational reproduction and management of timber crops,-the lumbermen of the United States have become the most expert exploiters of the natural forest resources. Methods of cutting, hauling, handling, sawing, marketing, and all the appliances and tools employed have been developed to the highest degree, and all means have been adapted to the end which from the standpoint of private interest appears desirable, namely, largest immediate profits.' From the simplest hand tool to the more complex woodworking machinery of the late nineteenth century, America's inventive genius was hard at work creating a more labor-saving, yet resource-intensive technology (Richards 1872 [1966]; Clark 1929, 1:48; Habakkuk 1962; Rosenberg 1975; see also Table 8.1). Intense competition from newer timberland to the west and the south encouraged the adoption of technology on a massive scale (Cox *et al.* 1985, 155). The increasing scale of mill operations became apparent in the last half of the nineteenth century (Fernow 1907, 404). Early sawmills were relatively inefficient affairs with a short period of operation and a total cut of 1000 board feet per day (Clark 1929, 1:176). By the 1890s the larger band sawmills were operating throughout the year and producing 50 000 to 300 000 board feet of lumber a day (Hotchkiss 1898, 660).

The unreliability of muzzleloading pieces and muskets likewise limited the activity of the colonial hunter. Improvements in firearms in the nineteenth century significantly increased the efficiency of the more market oriented hunters. Percussion guns and wild fowling pieces like the punt gun, mounted on a shallow-drafted boat, made it possible to kill a hundred or more geese or ducks with a single shot (Trefethen 1975, 59–60).

The improved transportation network of the late nineteenth century also played a crucial role in the wholesale exploitation of the nation's resources. Large segments of the forests of the Northeast and the Midwest remained relatively unscathed until well after the Civil War. Railroads, however, allowed the lumberman to penetrate the more rugged portions of the Northeast, e.g., the Appalachians and the more isolated portions of the Midwest, e.g., areas far from any driveable streams. With the development of an effective system of refrigeration, railroads also became a major ingredient in the large-scale, commercial exploitation of the country's game (Trefethen 1975, 58). Thousands of pounds of game were shipped to the growing urban markets of the East and the Midwest on a yearly basis (Tober 1981, 77–79). The end of the nineteenth century was the 'golden era' of the market hunter (Reiger 1986, 27).

The economics of the late nineteenth century also encouraged the frenzied exploitation of the nation's resources. High labor costs, local taxes, and intense competition resulted in 'a cut and get out attitude' among lumbermen (Rothrock 1894a; Walker 1910). Neither lumbermen nor market hunters were likely to curtail the scale of their operations when their competitors were the only beneficiaries (Twining 1964). Cheap timberland to the west also made it more profitable for eastern operators to move their operations to the West than stay and reforest their old, cutover lands (Cox *et al.* 1985, 155).

Europe's landscape had been subjected to thousands of years of human activity. The effects were so pervasive and longstanding that it was difficult to distinguish the human influences from the natural influences. The American landscape was subjected to a much more abrupt change. Large segments of the forest remained relatively intact until the second half of the nineteenth century. Then technological innovations, an improved transportation network, and the advent of mass-production methods of logging swept the forests away. The change was evident to anyone who lived in the last half of the nineteenth century. Conservationists like George Perkins Marsh, Charles Sprague Sargent, the director of Harvard's Arnold Arboretum, and Joseph T. Rothrock, the father of Pennsylvania's forestry program, could write about the destruction of the Northeast's forests on a firsthand basis. Sportsmen used to an abundance of wildlife in their youth commented upon the scarcity of fish and game in their maturity (Dupree ([1957] 1986, 236; Reiger 1986, 36). The conservation movement began in the United States. An awareness of the movement's importance and its early appearance in the United States can probably be attributed to the dramatic changes which overtook the United States at the end of the century. It was an awareness that came, 'not to men living in the midst of the industrial and commercial centers of the older countrysides, but to foresters who witnessed devastation about the Great

Lakes, ... to naturalists who lived through the winning of the West' (Sauer 1956).

Many of the early conservationists spoke out against the irresponsible depletion of the nation's resources with a sense of moral outrage. It was nothing more than a case of 'wanton, barbarous, disgraceful vandalism ... a spendthrift people recklessly wasting its heritage' (Schurz 1889). The demise of the passenger pigeon and a series of destructive fires in the cutover regions of Michigan, Wisconsin, and the Adirondacks dramatized the exhaustible nature of America's resources and served as rallying points for the early conservation movement (Thompson 1963; Trefethen 1975, 65). Wanton wastefulness had blotted out game from large segments of the country (Grinnell and Reynolds 1894) and reduced the nation's forests to blackened ruins and areas of desolation (Rothrock 1915; see also Plate 15 in photographic essay).

Pragmatic arguments for conservation

Although the early conservationists were motivated by moralistic concerns, their public pronouncements took a much more pragmatic turn. They were forced to emphasize the utilitarian aspects of their arguments because practical justifications were more likely to succeed (Reiger 1986, 51, 84). Most of their arguments centered on one of three major issues: wood, water, and wildlife.

Wood

By the end of the nineteenth century, foresters like Gifford Pinchot were convinced that America faced a timber famine. Years of unrestrained cutting and exploitation had depleted the nation's timber supply. Fortunately trees were renewable resources which would last forever if they were managed scientifically on a sustained yield basis. In the eyes of Gifford Pinchot and Theodore Roosevelt conservation was synonymous with the 'wise use' of the nation's resources (Dana and Fairfax 1980, 1–2). Pinchot and Roosevelt's program of conserving the nation's resources followed the closing of the American frontier. It represented an increasing awareness on the part of historians and politicians alike that land was no longer free and abundant (Turner 1920, 292–294; Ekrich 1963, 81–99). The national priority was no longer one of clearing away the forest and exploiting the fertility of the soil but rather one of insuring the continued maintenance of the nation's resources. Roosevelt and Pinchot challenged the nation to scientifically manage its resources on a sustained yield basis (Turner 1920, 292–294). Conservation was a conscious response to a perceived scarcity (Kay 1985).

Water

The publication in 1864 of George Perkins Marsh's book *Man and Nature* alerted the public to the more positive influences of the forest. The steady flow of streams and rivers was linked to the forest. Rivers, in turn, regulated the nation's commerce. Many were convinced that the destruction of the nation's forests would cause an endless cycle of flood and drought. Marsh's watershed argument was instrumental in the creation of the Adirondack Forest Preserve in New York State in 1885 (Graham 1978, 96–106; Terrie 1981). It also played a central role in the 1911 passage of the Weeks Act which authorized the purchase of forestlands on the headwaters of navigable streams in the East. The purchase was justified on the belief that forests equalized streamflow and contributed to the navigability of rivers. The Constitution gave Congress the right to regulate interstate commerce and thus the authority to purchase forests to control the flow of water (Dodds 1983).

Wildlife

The loss of the passenger pigeon at the end of the nineteenth century epitomized the dramatic changes overtaking the American landscape. The passenger pigeon (*Ectopistes migratorius*) was once the most abundant bird species on the face of the earth. No other species ever approached it in sheer numbers (Schorger 1955, 199). Large flocks of pigeons migrated across the eastern deciduous forest, stopping to establish nesting colonies wherever a bumper crop of acorns and nuts littered the ground (Blockstein and Tordoff 1985). Estimates of the size of the breeding colonies ranged from one to two billion birds (Schorger 1955, 200–201).

Although some investigators believe that the mass nesting behavior of the pigeons shielded the young squabs from predators, a concept known as predator satiation (Blockstein and Tordoff 1985), the size of the colony also played into the hands of the market hunters. Technological developments permitted the systematic exploitation of the pigeons' breeding grounds. The telegraph kept the professional hunters informed of the pigeons' movements while the railroad carried the hunters into the nesting sites and the birds out to the big city markets. The resulting disruption sealed the pigeon's fate. The passenger pigeon suffered a precipitous decline from 1871 to 1880 (Schorger 1955, 216; Blockstein and Tordoff 1985). Few of the small remaining bands successfully fledged young. The last passenger pigeon died in a zoo in Cincinnati in 1914. 'The pigeon,' remarked Aldo Leopold ([1949] 1968, 111), 'was a biological storm ... [a] feathered tempest [which] roared up, down, and across the continent, sucking up the laden fruits of forest and prairie ... When the pigeoners subtracted from his numbers, and the pioneers chopped gaps in the continuity of his fuel, his flame guttered out with hardly a sputter or even a wisp of smoke.'

Not all of the above-mentioned arguments for the conservation of the nation's resources were scientifically justifiable. The validity of the timber scarcity and the watershed or streamflow arguments, at least in their more extreme forms, have already been called into question. Fortunately most of the arguments were accepted by the public. In the long run this acceptance produced a number of positive results.

State and federal response

Concern about the environment generated a profusion of laws and actions which eventually reorganized the American landscape (Sears 1942; Kelly 1974b). Many of the earliest attempts to improve the environment were halting or superficial. A number of state legislatures set up committees to review the status of their forests. Bounties or tax abatements were established to encourage the planting of shade trees along public highways (Graham 1978, 74). Observance of Arbor Day was legislated to call attention to the importance of trees (Fernow 1907, 408–411). State fish and game commissions embarked on a major program of artificial propagation. The artificial propagation of carp and pheasants was a quick and easy panacea for the nation's wildlife problems (Trefethen 1975, 107–109).

Federal and state governments assumed a much more active role in the regulation of the nation's supply of timber and game. The passage of the Weeks–McLean Migratory Bird Act in 1913 and later the Migratory Bird Treaty Act outlawed market hunting and granted legal protection to the nation's nongame birds (Trefethen 1975, 152–156). Fire control was the *sine qua non* of any successful forestry program at the beginning of the twentieth century. Predictably many of the newly established state forestry departments soon found themselves involved in an active program of fire prevention and control (Pyne 1983). The cessation of fires permitted the normal development and maturation of the woodlands. Large segments of the existing forests of the Northeast and the Midwest date back to the early fire suppression and control period of the 1920s and 1930s (Spencer 1983).

By the end of the nineteenth century, it became increasingly apparent that the federal and state governments would have to acquire land in order to implement their conservation programs. Only they had the time and funds necessary to convert the nation's despoiled forests to a sustained yield program and to restore the nation's wildlife. New York and Pennsylvania were two of the earliest states to embark upon an active program of land acquisition. They had different reasons for acquiring large tracts of state-owned land. Their management of the acquired land reflected these differences. New York State became known for its extensive forest preserve system. Over 280 000 ha of mountainous terrain in the Adirondacks and the Catskills formed the nucleus of New York's forest preserves. Much of the land had already been cutover and fell into the hands of the state when the owners failed to pay taxes and interest on the land. Preservationists and commercial interests in New York City believed that harvesting timber in the reserve was not compatible with the protection of the region's water supply (water from the Adirondacks fed the Hudson River and the Erie Canal). They pushed for the creation of a park to protect the region's forests from cutting and the fires which frequently followed and to maintain the flow of water to rivers and streams draining the region. The Adirondacks were recognized as a park in 1892 and two years later an amendment to the state constitution decreed that state-owned lands within the boundary of the park were 'to be forever kept as wild forest lands' (Thompson 1963; Graham 1978; Terrie 1981).

Pennsylvania's forest reserve system owes its existence to a somewhat more 'use' oriented philosophy. By the early twentieth century, the cumulative impact of the tanbark interests, loggers, fires, and erosion left much of northern Pennsylvania's forests in an unproductive, poorly stocked condition. According to some estimates, more than two million hectares or 17% of the state fell into the category of barren, unproductive forest land (Illick 1923). Concern over the state's depleted timber resources and the uncertain fate of the water supply eventually led to the acquisition of the first state-owned forest land on the headwaters of the Susquehanna and the Delaware Rivers in 1898. Much of the acquired land was cheap, abandoned, tax-delinquent acreage that had already been cut or burned-over (Rupp 1924; Clepper 1945, 1981). Pennsylvania's 800 000 ha forest system is still managed for its timber supply, its wildlife, its recreational potential, and its watershed protection functions today. Of all the states, Pennsylvania probably comes the closest to putting Gifford Pinchot's 'wise use' concept into practice (Clepper 1945; Widner 1968, 29).

Although New York and Pennsylvania's conservation programs are respectively cited as prime examples of the 'preservationist' and the 'wise use' schools of thought (Widner 1968, 29), the dichotomy is actually not that clearcut. Both states established a series of state game refuges early in the twentieth century to protect their dwindling supply of game (Dickinson 1980). The dominant idea at that time was to provide a refuge for the remaining game. Surplus game from the refuge could then restock the surrounding area. An overabundance of deer and the increasing realization that wildlife was a renewable resource that could be managed scientifically eventually prompted both New York and Pennsylvania to open their refuges to hunting (Leopold [1933] 1986, 16–21; Burroughs 1946). The preservationist viewpoint gave way to the management viewpoint as game refuges became wildlife management areas and state game lands.

New York also selected the management or 'wise use' option when it embarked upon a massive reforestation campaign in 1929. The objective was to replant the state's idle, abandoned farmland with rapidly growing conifers. The basic idea behind the program was to retire the state's marginal farmland and to put the land to more productive uses. Conifers were planted because they were easy to raise and plant, they could be grown on infertile sites, and there was a large market demand for conifers in relation to their supply at the time. The farmland purchased for the program was to be managed for timber, watershed protection, and recreation. Ultimately almost 280 000 ha of land was acquired; about half of this was reforested with spruce, pine, and larch (Hamilton, Askew, and Odell 1980).

The Lake States, i.e., Michigan, Wisconsin, and Minnesota, duplicated the early land management policies of New York and Pennsylvania. They were the recipients of millions of hectares of land from the federal government. They quickly liquidated their holdings, much of which fell into the hands of loggers, land developers, and homesteaders. By the 1920s most of the land had been cutover and it became increasingly evident that the region's agricultural potential was rather limited. Tax forfeiture and farm abandonment shifted the land back to the states' hands (Barlowe 1983). The land nobody wanted eventually formed the Lake States' forest reserves, parks, and game lands (Lee and Wooten 1958).

Although activities at the state level dominated the early conservation movement (Smith 1938; Widner 1968, 28), it was not long until the federal government entered the fray. President Harrison established the first forest reserve, the Yellowstone Park Timber Reserve, in 1891 on land owned by the federal government in Wyoming. Later acts defined the purposes of the reserves (to protect the forests, to safeguard the flow of water from the forests, and to insure the nation's timber supply) and allowed for their expansion by purchase in the East, e.g., the Weeks Act of 1911 and the Clarke–McNary Act of 1924 (Dana and Fairfax 1980, 56–64, 128). Teddy Roosevelt created the nation's first wildlife refuge on federal land in 1903 to protect several species of birds from plume hunters (Trefethen 1975, 122). It is worth emphasizing again that little of the terrain acquired by the federal government and the states could be considered prime agricultural land. The vast majority of the land was concentrated in the rugged Appalachians and the lean, cold, frostbitten lands of the Upper Great Lakes region. States like New York, Pennsylvania,

Michigan, Wisconsin, and Minnesota with 10–25% of their land in the public domain today form a marked contrast to the richer agricultural states like Illinois and Iowa with only 2% of their land in the public domain (Merz 1978; Powell and Considine 1982; Considine 1984). It was the cheaper, agriculturally marginal, often cut and burned-over land which formed the nucleus of the forest reserves and the game lands. The same land, however, eventually demonstrated that the nation's resources could be managed scientifically for a variety of purposes – for watershed protection, for wildlife, and for recreational activites as well as a continuing supply of timber.

Although the early conservation movement was dominated by utilitarian concerns, the movement also benefited from an aesthetic impulse. America possessed some of the best natural wonders of the world. Preserving America's outstanding scenery and historic sites became a matter of national pride (Runte 1979). As early as 1874, George Perkins Marsh (1874, 327) argued for the creation of a large park as 'a museum for the instruction of ... students, a garden for the recreation of the lovers of nature, and an asylum where indigenous trees ... plants ... [and] beasts may dwell and perpetuate their kind.' It was a uniquely American idea. Unfortunately the park movement languished until the early 1900s. Promoting public recreation and public health through the preservation of America's scenic wonders was a major goal of many early twentieth century civic reformers (Huth [1957] 1972, 190–191). The reformers were part of the back to nature movement or the Arcadian impulse, characteristic of America's urban middle class (Schmitt [1969] 1990). The back to nature movement, the development of the automobile, and an increasing interest in outdoor recreation generated a constituency for the parks movement. Most state and national parks in the East date back to the early 1900s (Torrey 1926).

Scientists lent their weight to the preservation movement. The preservation of unique ecological communities was a major goal of the early Ecological Society of America. One of the ESA's offshoots, the Ecologists Union, developed into the Nature Conservancy, a national nonprofit organization devoted to identifying, acquiring, and managing unique natural areas. Today its 900 plus preserve system forms 'the largest privately owned group of nature sanctuaries in the world' (Blair 1986).

By the mid-twentieth century James Fenimore Cooper's prophetic utterance, cited in the epigraph, had become a reality. The country exhibited a more regulated appearance – one might almost say it was a legislated landscape. Conservationists recognized that change due to human activities was inevitable. But the effect of human activities could be creatively managed. Aldo Leopold ([1933] 1986, 21) summarized the prevalent mood of the day when he stated: 'The hope of the future lies not in curbing the influence of human occupancy – it is already too late for that – but in creating a better understanding of the extent of that influence and a new ethic for its governance.'

16

Conclusion

... it's an interestin' study to look into things as they were so long
back, and see what wild animals, birds, fishes, and such things,
then existed; to know what of them have been pushed entirely out
of the world, and what of 'em have been left, and to understand
what changes white men, and tame life all around 'em, have
worked on 'em.

Tucker, an Adirondack guide in S. H. Hammond's (1854) book
Hills, Lakes, and Forest Streams: Or, a Tramp in the
Chateaugay Woods.'

The last 15 chapters have highlighted many of the changes accompanying the
European settlement of a small portion of the New World. Change, of course,
is inevitable. It is a feature of natural ecosystems as well as the ecosystems
modified by human activities. We cannot assume that North America's forests
and grasslands were free of disturbing influences prior to European colonization. Certainly the available evidence (chapter 4) suggests that the forests and
grasslands were periodically subject to fire, windthrows, attacks by pathogens,
and outbreaks of pests. The realization that disturbance is a natural part of the
environment and that ecosystems have enormous powers of recovery has led a
number of investigators to minimize humankind's effects (Malin [1947] 1967,
120–155). They argue that forests and grasslands have always operated in a
natural state of disharmony. 'It may be,' as Hugh Raup (1967) states, 'nothing
we, as invading Europeans, have ever done to our eastern forests ... has
exceeded in sheer catastrophic upheaval what Nature herself has done to them
repeatedly.' At the worst human disturbances simply mimic natural disturbances. These theorists contend that we should not expect any major changes
in the nature of the vegetation due to human activities.

Unfortunately, the above argument overlooks the fact that human distur-

335

bances have often been unique both in terms of the frequency and the severity of their occurrence. Repeated cuttings and forest fires at short-term intervals have profoundly altered the face of North America's forests. Witness the demise of the pine forests of the Great Lakes region and the loss of the hemlock–hardwood forests of northern Pennsylvania. The deliberate and the unintentional introduction of a number of alien species represents another disturbing influence. Most Americans today live in an environment dominated by alien plants, be it a bluegrass lawn, a vacant lot of crabgrass, or a wheat field. Of even greater import are the introduced pathogens which have selectively altered the composition of North America's forests. Admittedly records of the widespread and almost instaneous decline of a species are not unique to the postsettlement period. Palynologists (Davis 1981), for instance, have attributed the widespread decline of hemlock across the Northeast approximately 4800 year ago to the outbreak of a pathogen. What is new is the increasing incidence of their occurrence. Contrast the hemlock decline of the last 4000 years with the introduction of four new pathogens (chestnut blight, white pine blister rust, Dutch elm disease, and beech bark disease) and the decline of their host species over the last 100 years.

Ecologists once believed that natural communities were ordered to resist change, that they functioned as orderly integrated units which maintained the stability of their constitutent populations (McIntosh 1985, 70–71). Although few ecologists subscribe to the 'balance of nature' concept today (Rowe 1961), it is worth pointing out that human activities have often led to unusual increases of pest and herbivore populations. The white pine weevil (*Pissodes strobi*), for instance, is an insect which lays its eggs on pine leaders exposed to sunlight. Boards in old buildings indicate that the weevil deformed white pine trees prior to settlement (Smith 1976). Land abandonment in New England in the nineteenth century and the subsequent invasion of white pine encouraged the spread of the weevil and the development of thousands of acres of 'weeviled' old-field white pine. Wolves and other predators probably maintained deer populations at relatively low levels in the presettlement forest. Hunters have not been as successful at regulating herbivores like the deer. The result has been overbrowsing and a lack of regeneration in many forests.

Disruptions like those mentioned above fostered the belief that the human race is inevitably headed to disaster. The so-called 'doomsday' mentality (Raup 1979) can be seen in the predicted fuelwood shortage of the early nineteenth century and the streamflow controversy and abortive timber famines of the late nineteenth and early twentieth centuries. Fortunately the predicted disasters never materialized. The shift to coal and stoves with a greater fuel efficiency solved the fuelwood problem of the early nineteenth century. We now know that forests exercise little control over major flood events. Technological developments which permitted the use of lower quality trees and wood substitutes averted the timber famine of the late nineteenth and early twentieth centuries. The pessimists omitted one variable from their equations: the ingenuity of the human mind. Although it would be foolish to suggest that all our resource-related problems have a technological solution, we should never discount 'the contriving brain and the skillful hand of man' (Malin 1955). Many post-Earth Day environmental histories can be placed in the doomsday category. Although their criticisms merit consideration, their single-minded focus on human folly and the destructive exploitation of the New World's resources runs the risk of creating a biased view of history. Environmental history is as much a study of human achievements as it is a discourse on human folly (Sheail 1983).

North America today is neither a lost paradise nor a land of endless resources. Human activities have all but eliminated some of North America's ecosystems, e.g., the tallgrass prairie. Other ecosystems have proven more resilient to human activity, or have changed and taken on new values. There are obvious success stories. Careful management has restored the beaver and the wild turkey to much of their former range in the East. The worthless stands of aspen which followed the devastation of pine in the Upper Great Lakes region now fuel the Midwest's pulp and paper industry. The repeatedly cutover hemlock–hardwood region of northern Pennsylvania is currently the center of the commercial black cherry industry. The chief question today is not whether we should or should not alter nature, but whether we can manage change in a constructive fashion (Cronon 1991). The changes that white men and tame life worked on nature are more than just an 'interestin' study' or an academic question as the homespun quote at the beginning of the chapter suggests. They provide us with insight into how our actions have affected nature and how nature has responded to those actions. We cannot predict the outcome of every human action, but we can use our knowledge of environmental change in the past to create a better future – a future that respects the land and its ecological constraints.

References

Abrams, M.D. and M.L. Scott. 1989. Disturbance-mediated accelerated succession in two Michigan forest types. *Forest Science* **35**:42–49.

Abrell, D.B. and M.T. Jackson. 1977. A decade of change in an old-growth beech–maple forest in Indiana. *American Midland Naturalist* **98**:22–32.

Acrelius, I. 1876. *A History of New Sweden; or the Settlements on the River Delaware.* Translated by W.M. Reynolds. Philadelphia: Memoirs of the Historical Society of Pennsylvania. Vol. 9.

Adams, A. 1899. Agriculture in Michigan. *Publications of the Michigan Political Science Association* **3** (7):1–40.

Adams, B.F. 1853. Opening a new farm. *Transactions of the Wisconsin State Agricultural Society* **3**:134–155.

Adams, J.T. 1931. *The Epic of America.* Boston: Little, Brown and Company.

Adams, R.J., Jr., G.A. McPeek and D.C. Evers. 1988. Bird population changes in Michigan, 1966–1985. *Jack-Pine Warbler* **66**:71–86.

Agassiz, L. and J.E. Cabot. 1850. *Lake Superior: Its Physical Character, Vegetation, and Animals Compared with Those of Other and Similar Regions.* Boston: Gould, Kendall and Lincoln.

Ahlgren, C. and I. Ahlgren. 1984. *Lob-Trees in the Wilderness.* Minneapolis: University of Minnesota Press.

Ahlgren, H.L., M.L. Wall, R.J. Muckenhirn and J.M. Sund. 1946. Yields of forage from woodland pastures on sloping land in southern Wisconsin. *Journal of Forestry* **44**:709–711.

Airola, T.M. and K. Buchholz. 1984. Species structure and soil characteristics of five urban forest sites along the New Jersey palisades. *Urban Ecology* **8**:149–164.

Albert, D.A. and B.V. Barnes. 1987. Effects of clearcutting on the vegetation and soil of a sugar maple-dominated ecosystem, western Upper Michigan. *Forest Ecology and Management* **18**:283–298.

Albion, R.G. [1926]1965. *Forests and Sea Power: The Timber Problems of the Royal Navy, 1652–1862.* Reprint. Hamden, Conn.: Archon Books.

Albion, R.G. 1939. *The Rise of New York Port (1815–1860).* New York: Charles Scribners.

Albrecht, W.A. 1956. Physical, chemical, and biochemical changes in the soil community. In W.L. Thomas Jr. (ed.), *Man's Role in Changing the Face of the Earth*, 648–673. Chicago: University of Chicago Press.

Alcott, W.P. 1882. Introduced plants found in the vicinity of a wool-scouring establishment. *Bulletin of the Essex Institute* **13**:162–166.

Alcoze, T.M. 1981. Pre-settlement beaver population density in the upper Great Lakes region. Ph.D. diss. Michigan State University.

Aldrich, J.R., J.A. Bacone and M.D. Hutchison. 1981. Limestone glades of Harrison County, Indiana. *Proceedings of the Indiana Academy of Science* **91**:480–485.

Aldrich, J.R. and M.A. Homoya. 1984. Natural barrens and post oak flatwoods in Posey and Spencer Counties, Indiana. *Proceedings of the Indiana Academy of Science* **93**:291–301.

Aldrich, J.W. 1943. Biological survey of the bogs and swamps in northeastern Ohio. *American Midland Naturalist* **30**:346–402.

Aldrich, J.W. and R.W. Coffin. 1980. Breeding bird populations from forest to suburbia after thirty-seven years. *American Birds* **34**:3–7.

Allen, D.G. 1981. *In English Ways: The Movement of Societies and the Transferal of English Local Law and Custom to Massachusetts Bay in the Seventeenth Century*. Chapel Hill: University of North Carolina Press.

Allen, D.L. 1938. Ecological studies on the vertebrate fauna of a 550-acre farm in Kalamazoo County, Michigan. *Ecological Monographs* **8**:348–436.

Allen, D.L. 1952. Wildlife history and the soil. *Soil Conservation* **18**:123–126.

Allen, D.L. 1974. *Our Wildlife Legacy*. rev. ed. New York: Funk and Wagnalls.

Allen, D.L. and D.L. Leedy. 1970. Special problems of waters and watersheds. In *Land Use and Wildlife Resources*, 149–180. Washington, D.C.: National Academy of Sciences.

Allen, J.A. 1870. The flora of the prairies. *American Naturalist* **4**:577–585.

Allen, J.A. 1871. The fauna of the prairies. *American Naturalist* **5**:4–9.

Allen, J.A. 1876. The former range of some New England carnivorous mammals. *American Naturalist* **10**:708–715.

Allen, J.M. 1941. An ecological and wildlife study of fencerow communities in the Maumee Drainage System. M.S. thesis. Ohio State University.

Allen, J.P. 1977. Changes in the American propensity to migrate. *Annals of the Association of American Geographers* **67**:577–587.

Altpeter, L.S. 1937. A history of the forests of Cape Cod. Masters thesis. Harvard University.

Alverson, W.S., D.M. Waller and S.L. Solheim. 1988. Forests too deer: Edge effects in northern Wisconsin. *Conservation Biology* **2**:348–358.

Amann, J.E. 1961. A study of the vascular plants of Stark County, Ohio. M.A. thesis. Kent State University.

Ambuel, B. and S.A. Temple. 1982. Songbird populations in southern Wisconsin forests: 1954 and 1979. *Journal of Field Ornithology* **53**:149–158.

Ames, J.N. 1881. Contribution to a discussion following P.T. Schotzka's talk on the forests of the country. *Transactions of the Wisconsin State Agricultural Society* **19**:179.

Amphlett, W. 1819. *The Emigrant's Directory to the Western States of North America*. London: Longman, Hurst, Rees, Orme, and Brown.

Andersen, S.T. 1986. Palaeoecological studies of terrestrial soils. In B.E. Berglund (ed.), *Handbook of Holocene Palaeoecology and Palaeohydrology*, 165–180. New York: John Wiley and Sons.

Anderson, D.M. 1971. The floristic compositions of northwestern Ohio prairie remnants. Ph.D. diss. Bowling Green State University.

Anderson, D.W. and D.C. Coleman. 1985. The dynamics of organic matter in grassland soils. *Journal of Soil and Water Conservation* **40**:211–216.

Anderson, E. [1952]1971. *Plants, Man and Life*. Berkeley: University of California Press.

Anderson, E. 1956. Man as a maker of new plants and new plant communities. In

W.L. Thomas Jr. (ed.), *Man's Role in Changing the Face of the Earth*, 763–777. Chicago: University of Chicago Press.

Anderson, H.W., M.D. Hoover and K.G. Reinhart. 1976. *Forests and water: Effects of forest management on floods, sedimentation, and water supply.* USDA Forest Service General Technical Report, no. PSW-18. Berkeley, Calif.: Pacific Southwest Forest and Range Experiment Station.

Anderson, R.C. 1983. The eastern prairie–forest transistion – an overview. In R. Brewer (ed.), *Proceedings of the Eighth North American Prairie Conference*, 86–92. Kalamazoo: Department of Biology, Western Michigan University.

Anderson, R.C. and D.E. Adams. 1978. Species replacement patterns in central Illinois white oak forests. In P.E. Pope (ed.), *Proceedings of the 2nd Central Hardwood Forest Conference*, 284–300. West Lafayette, Ind.: Department of Forestry and Natural Resources, Purdue University.

Anderson, R.C. and M.R. Anderson. 1975. The presettlement vegetation of Williamson County, Illinois. *Castanea* **40**:345–363.

Anderson, R.C. and L.E. Brown. 1983. Comparative effects of fire on trees in a midwestern savanna and an adjacent forest. *Bulletin of the Torrey Botanical Club* **110**:87–90.

Anderson, R.C. and O.L. Loucks. 1979. White-tailed deer (*Odocoileus virginianus*) influence on the structure and composition of *Tsuga canadensis* forests. *Journal of Applied Ecology* **16**:855–861.

Anderson, R.L. 1973. *A summary of white pine blister research in the Lake States.* USDA Forest Service General Technical Report, no. NC-6. St. Paul, Minn.: North Central Forest Experiment Station.

Anderson, R.S., R.B. Davis, N.G. Miller and R. Stuckenrath. 1986. History of late- and post-glacial vegetation and disturbance around Upper South Branch Pond, northern Maine. *Canadian Journal of Botany* **64**:1977–1986.

Anderson, W.A. 1946. Development of prairie at Iowa Lakeside Laboratory. *American Midland Naturalist* **36**:431–435.

Andreas, B.K. 1980. The flora of Portage, Stark, Summit, and Wayne Counties, Ohio. Ph.D. diss. Kent State University.

Andreas, B.K. 1985. The relationship between Ohio peatland distribution and buried river valleys. *Ohio Journal of Science* **85**:116–125.

Andreas, B.K. and J.D. Knoop. 1992. 100 years of change in Ohio peatlands. *Ohio Journal of Science* **92**:130–138

Andrews, C.M. 1889. *The river towns of Connecticut: A study of Weathersfield, Hartford, and Windsor.* Johns Hopkins University Studies in Historical and Political Science, Seventh series, no. 7–9. Baltimore: Johns Hopkins University.

Andrews, H.N., Jr. 1948. The royal pines of New Hampshire. *Appalachia* **27** (2): 186–198.

Andrle, R.F. and J.R. Carroll (eds.). 1988. *The Atlas of Breeding Birds in New York State.* Ithaca, N.Y.: Cornell University Press.

Angle, P.M. 1968. *Prairie State: Impressions of Illinois, 1673–1967, by Travellers and Other Observers.* Chicago: University of Chicago Press.

Annala, A.E., J.D. DuBois and L.A. Kapustka. 1983. Prairies lost to forests: A 33-year history of two sites in Adams County, Ohio. *Ohio Journal of Science* **83**:22–27.

Anonymous. 1811. Of the Scioto Country. *The Western Intelligencer* [a Worthington, Ohio newspaper]. Vol. 1 (no. 4) (September 11, 1811): 1.

Anonymous. 1829. Pinelands of New Jersey. *The Pennsylvania Register* **4** (4):63

Anonymous. 1857. Observations on the flora of the western states. *The Cincinnatus* **1**:13–17, 80–84, 209–214.

Anonymous. 1865. The war on the wolves. *Firelands Pioneer*, o.s., **6**:25–26.

Anonymous. 1867. The history of the stove. *Scientific American*, n.s., **17**:293

Anonymous. 1882. The pine supply of the Lake Region. *The Nation* (Feb. 16, 1882) **34**: 138–139.

Apsley, D.K., D.J. Leopold and G.R. Parker. 1985. Tree species response to release from domestic livestock grazing. *Proceedings of the Indiana Academy of Science* **94**:215–226.

Armstrong, J.T. 1965. Breeding home range in the nighthawk and other birds: Its evolutionary and ecological significance. *Ecology* **46**:619–629.

Arnason, T., R.J. Hebda and T. Johns. 1981. Use of plants for food and medicine by Native Peoples of eastern Canada. *Canadian Journal of Botany* **59**:2189–2325.

Arno, S.F. and K.M. Sneck. 1977. *A method for determining fire history in coniferous forests of the mountain West*. US Forest Service General Technical Report, no. INT-42. Ogden, Utah: Intermountain Forest and Range Experiment Station.

Ashby, W.C. 1959. Limitation to growth of basswood by mineral nutrient deficiencies. *Botanical Gazette* **121**:22–28.

Ashe, T. 1808. *Travels in America, Performed in 1806, for the Purpose of Exploring the Rivers Alleghany, Monongahela, Ohio, and Mississippi*. Newburyport, Mass.: Reprinted by E.M. Blunt for William Sawyer and Company.

Askins, R.A., J.F. Lynch and R. Greenberg. 1990. Population declines in migratory birds in eastern North America. *Current Ornithology* **1**:1–57.

Askins, R.A. and M.J. Philbrick. 1987. Effect of changes in regional forest abundance on the decline and recovery of a forest bird community. *Wilson Bulletin* **99**:7–21.

Atack, J. and F. Bateman. 1987. *To Their Own Soil: Agriculture in the Antebellum North*. Ames: Iowa State University Press.

Atwater, C. 1818. Notices on the scenery, geology, mineralogy, botany, etc. of Belmont County, Ohio. *American Journal of Science and Arts* **1**:226–230.

Atwater, C. 1827. Prairies in Ohio. *Western Journal of Medical and Physical Sciences* **1**:85–92.

Atwater, C. 1838. *A History of the State of Ohio, Natural and Civil*. Cincinnati: Glezen and Shepard.

Auclair, A.N. 1976. Ecological factors in the development of intensive-management ecosystems in the Midwestern United States. *Ecology* **57**:431–444.

Auclair, A.N. and G. Cottam. 1971. Dynamics of black cherry (*Prunus serotina* Erhr.) in southern Wisconsin oak forests. *Ecological Monographs* **41**:153–177.

Audubon, J.J. [1840]1967. *The Birds of America*. 7 vols. Reprint. New York: Dover Publications.

Audubon, J.J. and J. Bachman. [1854]1974. *The Quadrupeds of North America*. 3 vols. Reprint. New York: Arno Press.

Aughanbaugh, J.E. 1935. *Replacement of the chestnut in Pennsylvania*. Bulletin, no. 54. Harrisburg: Pennsylvania Department of Forests and Waters.

Aulie, R.P. 1974. The mineral theory. *Agricultural History* **48**:369–382.

Ault, W.O. 1965. Open-field husbandry and the village community: A study of agrarian by-laws in medieval England. *Transactions of the American Philosophical Society*, n.s., **55**, part 7.

Auten, J.T. 1941. *Notes on some old-growth forests in Ohio, Indiana, and Illinois*. USDA Forest Service Technical Note, no. 49. Columbus, Ohio: Central States Forest Experiment Station.

Ayensu, E.S. 1975. Endangered and threatened orchids of the United States. *American Orchid Society Bulletin* **44**:384–394.

Backman, A.E. 1984. 1000-year record of fire–vegetation interactions in the northeastern United States: A comparison between coastal and inland regions.

M.S. thesis. University of Massachusetts.

Bacone, J.A., L.A. Casebere and M.D. Hutchison. 1982. Glades and barrens of Crawford and Perry Counties, Indiana. *Proceedings of the Indiana Academy of Science* **92**:367–373.

Bacone, J.A. and C.L. Hedge. 1980. A preliminary list of endangered and threatened vascular plants in Indiana. *Proceedings of the Indiana Academy of Science* **89**:358–371.

Baily, F. 1856. *Journal of a Tour in Unsettled Parts of North America in 1796 and 1797*. London: Baily Brothers.

Baird, R. 1832. *View of the Valley of the Mississippi; or, the Emigrant and Traveller's Guide to the West*. 2d ed. Philadelphia: H.S. Tanner.

Baird, T.H. 1990. *Changes in breeding bird populations between 1930 and 1985 in the Quaker Run Valley of Allegany State Park, New York*. New York State Museum Bulletin, no. 477. Albany: New York State Museum, University of the State of New York.

Bakeless, J. [1950]1961. *The Eyes of Discovery*. New York: Dover Publications.

Baker, A.H. and H.I. Patterson. 1988. Farmers' adaptations to markets in early-nineteenth-century Massachusetts. In P. Benes (ed.), *The Farm: The Dublin Seminar for New England Folklife: Annual Proceedings, 1986*, 95–108. Boston: Boston University Press.

Baker, A.J. 1983a. Charcoal. In R.C. Davis (ed.), *Encyclopedia of American Forest and Conservation History*, Vol. 1, 73–77. New York: Macmillan Publishing Company.

Baker, D.G., B.F. Watson and R.H. Skaggs. 1985. The Minnesota long-term temperature record. *Climatic Change* **7**:225–236.

Baker, H. 1937. Alluvial meadows: A comparative study of grazed and mown meadows. *Journal of Ecology* **25**:408–420.

Baker, H.G. 1965. Characteristics and modes of origin of weeds. In H.G. Baker and G.L. Stebbins (eds.), *The Genetics of Colonizing Species*, 147–172. New York: Academic Press.

Baker, O.E. 1921. The increasing importance of the physical conditions in determining the utilization of land for agricultural and forest production in the United States. *Annals of the Association of American Geographers* **11**:17–46.

Baker, O.E. 1928. Agricultural regions of North America. Part V – The hay and dairying belt. *Economic Geography* **4**:44–73.

Baker, R.H. 1983b. *Michigan Mammals*. East Lansing: Michigan State University Press.

Baldwin, H.I. 1977. The induced timberline of Mount Monadnock, N.H. *Bulletin of the Torrey Botanical Club* **104**:324–333.

Barber, K.E. 1976. History of vegetation. In S.B. Chapman (ed.), *Methods in Plant Ecology*, 5–83. Oxford: Blackwell Scientific Publications.

Bardecki, M.J. 1984. What value wetlands? *Journal of Soil and Water Conservation* **39**:166–169.

Bardolph, R. 1948. *Agricultural Literature and the Early Illinois Farmer*. Illinois Studies in the Social Sciences. Vol. 29, nos. 1 and 2. Urbana: University of Illinois Press.

Barker, J. 1958. *Recollections of the First Settlement in Ohio*. Edited by G.J. Blazier. Marietta, Ohio: Marietta College.

Barlowe, R. 1983. Changing land use and policies: The Lake States. In S.L. Flader (ed.), *The Great Lakes Forest: An Environmental and Social History*, 156–176. Minneapolis: University of Minnesota Press.

Barnes, B.V. 1976. Succession in deciduous swamp communities of southeastern

Michigan formerly dominated by American elm. *Canadian Journal of Botany* **54**:19–24.

Barnes, B.V. 1989. Old-growth forests of the northern Lake States: A landscape ecosystem perspective. *Natural Areas Journal* **9**:45–57.

Barnes, W.J. 1974. A history of the vegetation of Eau Claire County, Wisconsin. *Transactions of the Wisconsin Academy of Sciences, Arts and Letters* **62**:357–375.

Barnes, W.J. and G. Cottam. 1974. Some autecological studies of the *Lonicera* × *bella* complex. *Ecology* **55**:40–50.

Barnett, L. 1979. Milestones in Michigan mapping: Modern waymarks. *Michigan History* **63**:29–38.

Baron, W.R. 1982. The reconstruction of eighteenth century temperature records through the use of content analysis. *Climatic Change* **4**:385–398.

Baron, W.R. 1989. Retrieving American climate history: A bibliographic essay. *Agricultural History* **63**:7–35.

Baron, W.R. and G.A. Gordon. 1985. A reconstruction of New England climate using historical materials, 1620–1980. In C.R. Harington (ed.), *Climatic Change in Canada*, in *Syllogeus* **55**: 229–245.

Baron, W.R., G.A. Gordon, H.W. Borns Jr. and D.C. Smith. 1984. Frost-free record reconstruction for eastern Massachusetts, 1733–1980. *Journal of Climate and Applied Meterology* **23**:317–319.

Baron, W.R., D.C. Smith, H.W. Borns Jr., J. Fastook and A.E. Bridges. 1980. *Long-term series temperature and precipitation records for Maine, 1808–1978.* Bulletin, no. 771. Orono: University of Maine Life Sciences and Agricultural Experiment Station.

Barrett, J.W., C.E. Farnsworth and W. Rutherford Jr. 1962. Logging effects on regeneration and certain aspects of microclimate in northern hardwoods. *Journal of Forestry* **60**:630–639.

Barrett, J.W., E.H. Ketchledge and D.R. Satterlund. 1961. *Forestry in the Adirondacks.* Syracuse, N.Y.: State University College of Forestry at Syracuse University.

Barrett, S.C.H. 1983. Crop mimicry in weeds. *Economic Botany* **37**:255–282.

Barron, H. 1984. *Those Who Stayed Behind: Rural Society in Nineteenth-century New England.* Cambridge: Cambridge University Press.

Barton, B.S. 1793. An inquiry into the question, whether the *Apis mellifica*, or true honey-bee, is a native of America. *Transactions of the American Philosophical Society* **3**:241–261.

Barton, D.R., W.D. Taylor and R.M. Biette. 1985. Dimensions of riparian buffer strips required to maintain trout habitat in southern Ontario streams. *North American Journal of Fisheries Management* **5**:364–378.

Barton, J.D. and D.V. Schmelz. 1987. Thirty years of growth records in Donaldson's Woods. *Indiana Academy of Science Proceedings* **96**:209–214.

Barton, W.P.C. 1818. *Compendium Florae Philadelphicae: Containing a Description of the Indigenous and Naturalized Plants Found Within a Circuit of Ten Miles Around Philadelphia.* 2 vols. Philadelphia: M. Carey and Son.

Bartram, J. 1751. *Observations on the Inhabitants, Climate, Soil, Rivers, Productions, Animals, and other Matters Worthy of Notice Made by Mr. John Bartram, in his Travels from Pensilvania to Onondago, Oswego and the Lake Ontario, in Canada.* London: J. Whiston and B. White.

Bartram, J. [1760]1934. Undated letter from John Bartram to Eliot in which the former describes the soils of the middle and southern English colonies. In H.J. Carman and R.G. Tugwell (eds.), *Essays Upon Field Husbandry by Jared Eliot,*

201–206. New York: Columbia University Press.

Bateham, M.B. 1849. Exhaustion of the soil. *Ohio Cultivator* **5**:71.

Bateham, M.B. 1855. Professor Mapes and the wheat crop of Ohio. *Ohio Cultivator* **11**:322–323.

Bates, G.H. 1935. The vegetation of footpaths, sidewalks, cart-tracks and gateways. *Journal of Ecology* **23**:470–487.

Bates, G.H. 1937. The vegetation of wayside and hedgerow. *Journal of Ecology* **25**:469–481.

Baumann, P.C., J.F. Kitchell, J.J. Magnuson and T.B. Kayes. 1974. Lake Wingra, 1837–1973: A case history of human impact. *Wisconsin Academy of Sciences, Arts and Letters* **62**:57–94.

Bazzaz, F.A. and J.A.D. Parrish. 1982. Organization of grassland communities. In J.R. Estes, R.J. Tyrl and J.N. Brunken (eds.), *Grasses and Grasslands*, 233–255. Norman: University of Oklahoma Press.

Beal, W.J. 1888. The names of pine trees as known to lumbermen. In *Twenty-seventh Annual Report of the Secretary of the State Board of Agriculture for the State of Michigan*, 79. Lansing, Mich.: Thorp and Godfrey.

Beal, W.J. 1904. Some of the changes now taking place in a forest of oak openings. *Fourth Report of the Michigan Academy of Science*:107–108.

Bealer, A.W. 1976. *The Tools that Built America*. Barre, Mass.: Barre Publishing.

Beals, E.W., G. Cottam and R.J. Vogl. 1960. Influence of deer on the vegetation of the Apostle Islands, Wisconsin. *Journal of Wildlife Management* **24**:68–80.

Beaman, J.H., E.A. Bourdo, F.W. Case, S.R. Crispin, D. Henson, R.W. Pippen, A.A. Reznicek, E.G. Voss and P.W. Thompson. 1985. Endangered and threatened vascular plants in Michigan. II. Third biennial review proposed list. *Michigan Botanist* **24**:99–116.

Beardsley, L. 1852. *Reminiscences*. New York: Charles Vinten.

Beatley, J.C. 1959. *The primeval forests of a periglacial area in the Allegheny Plateau (Vinton and Jackson Counties, Ohio)*. Bulletin of the Ohio Biological Survey, n.s., vol. 1, no. 1. Columbus: Ohio State University Press.

Beattie, M., C. Thompson and L. Levine. 1983. *Working With Your Woodland: A Landowner's Guide*. Hanover, N.H.: University Press of New England.

Beattie, R.K. and J.D. Diller. 1954. Fifty years of chestnut blight. *Journal of Forestry* **52**:323–329.

Bebb, M.S. 1860. The flora of Ogle and Winnebago Counties, Illinois. *Prairie Farmer* **22**:182–183.

Beck, L. 1823. *A Gazetteer of the States of Illinois and Missouri*. Albany: Charles R. and George Webster.

Becker, G.C. 1983. *Fishes of Wisconsin*. Madison: University of Wisconsin Press.

Beckwith, H.W. 1879. *Historic Notes on the Northwest*. Chicago: H.H. Hill and Company.

Beckwith, S.L. 1954. Ecological succession on abandoned farm lands and its relationship to wildlife management. *Ecological Monographs* **24**:349–376.

Behre, C.E. 1932. Some aspects of the forest planting situation in the Northeast. *Journal of Forestry* **30**:162–168.

Behre, C.E., K.E. Barraclough, P.L. Buttrick, F.M. Callward and R.C. Hawley. 1929. Grazing in relation to forestry in New England. *Journal of Forestry* **27**:602–608.

Behre, K.E. 1981. The interpretation of anthropogenic indicators in pollen diagrams. *Pollen et Spores* **23**:225–245.

Behre, K.E. 1988. The role of man in European vegetation history. In B. Huntley and T. Webb III (eds.), *Vegetation History*, 633–672. Dordrecht: Kluwer Academic Publishers.

Beissinger, S.R. and D.R. Osborne. 1982. Effects of urbanization on avian community organization. *Condor* **84**:75–83.

Belknap, J. 1813. *The History of New Hampshire.* 3 vols. Boston: Bradford and Read.

Bell, M.M. 1989. Did New England go downhill? *Geographical Review* **79**:450–466.

Beltrami, J.C. [1828]1962. *A Pilgrimage in America.* Reprint. Chicago: Quadrangle Books.

Beltz, R.C., N.D. Cost, N.P. Kingsley and J.R. Peters. 1992. *Timber volume distribution maps for the eastern United States.* US Forest Service General Technical Report, no. WO-60. Washington, D.C.: U.S. Forest Service, Washington Office.

Belyea, H.C. 1924. A study of mortality and recovery after logging. *Journal of Forestry* **22**:768–779.

Bennett, H.H. 1939. *Soil Conservation.* New York: McGraw-Hill.

Bennett, H.S. 1937. *Life on the English Manor: A Study of Peasant Conditions, 1150–1400.* Cambridge: Cambridge University Press.

Bennett, M.K. 1955. The food economy of the New England Indians, 1605–1675. *Journal of Political Economy* **63**:369–397.

Bennett, M.K. 1970. Aspects of the pig. *Agricultural History* **44**:223–235.

Bennison, A.P. 1976. *Geological Highway Map – Northeastern Region.* Tulsa, Okla.: American Association of Petroleum Geologists.

Benson, B.L. 1976. Logs and lumber: The development of the lumber industry in Michigan's Lower Peninsula, 1837–1870. Ph.D. diss. Indiana University.

Benson, L. 1979. *Plant Classification.* 2d ed. Lexington, Mass.: D.C. Heath & Company.

Benson, M.A. 1962. *Factors influencing the occurrence of floods in a humid region of diverse terrain.* USGS Water-Supply Paper, no. 1580-B. Washington, D.C.: US Geological Survey.

Bergerud, A.T. and D.R. Miller. 1977. Population dynamics of Newfoundland beavers. *Canadian Journal of Zoology* **55**:1480–1492.

Bernabo, J.C. and T. Webb III. 1977. Changing patterns in Holocene pollen record of northeastern North America: A mapped summary. *Quaternary Research* **8**:64–96.

Berner, A. 1985. How's wildlife doing down on the farm? *Outdoor America* **50** (4): 17–19.

Berrang, P., D.F. Karnosky and B.J. Stanton. 1985. Environmental factors affecting tree health in New York City. *Journal of Arboriculture* **11**:185–189.

Beschta, R.L. and W.S. Platts. 1986. Morphological features of small streams: Significance and function. *Water Resources Bulletin* **22**:369–379.

Best, L.B. 1983. Bird use of fencerows: Implications of contemporary fencerow management practices. *Wildlife Society Bulletin* **11**:343–347.

Best, L.B. and B.J. Hill. 1983. Fencerows are for the birds. *Iowa Bird Life* **53**:16–21.

Betz, R.F. 1978. The prairies of Indiana. In D.C. Glenn-Lewin and R.Q. Landers Jr. (eds.), *Proceedings of the Fifth Midwest Prairie Conference*, 25–31. Ames: Iowa State University.

Betz, R.F. and M.H. Cole. 1969. The Peacock Prairie – a study of a virgin Illinois mesic black-soil prairie forty years after initial study. *Transactions of the Illinois Academy of Science* **62**:44–53.

Betz, R.F. and H.F. Lamp. 1992. Species composition of old settler savanna and sand prairie cemeteries in northern Illinois and northwestern Indiana. In D.D. Smith and C.A. Jacobs (eds.), *Proceedings of the Twelfth North American Prairie Conference: Recapturing a Vanishing Heritage*, 79–87. Cedar Falls: University of Northern Iowa.

Bickford, W.E. and U.J. Dymon. (eds.). 1990. *An Atlas of Massachusetts River Systems: Environmental Designs for the Future*. Amherst: Published for the Massachusetts Department of Fisheries, Wildlife and Environmental Law Enforcement by the University of Massachusetts Press.

Bidwell, P.W. 1916. Rural economy in New England at the beginnings of the nineteenth century. *Transactions of the Connecticut Academy of Arts and Sciences* **20**:241–399.

Bidwell, P.W. 1921. The agricultural revolution in New England. *American Historical Review* **26**:683–702.

Bidwell, P.W. and J.I. Falconer. [1925]1941. *History of Agriculture in the Northern United States, 1620–1860*. Carnegie Institute Publication, no. 358. Reprint. New York: Peter Smith.

Bigelow, J. 1814. *Florula Bostoniensis*. Boston: Cummings, Hilliard and Company.

Bigelow, J. 1817–1820. *American Medical Botany*. 3 vols. Boston: Cummings and Hiliard.

Bigelow, J. 1840. *Florula Bostoniensis*. 3d ed. Boston: Charles C. Little and James Brown.

Billings, W.D. 1970. *Plants, Man and the Ecosystem*. 2d ed. Belmont, Calif.: Wadsworth Publishing Company.

Billington, R.A. 1974. *Westward Expansion: A History of the American Frontier*. 4th ed. New York: Macmillan.

Bindoff, S.T. 1950. *Tudor England*. Harmondsworth, Middlesex: Penguin Books.

Bingham, M.T. 1945. *The flora of Oakland County, Michigan: A study in physiographic plant ecology*. Bulletin, no. 22. Bloomfield Hills, Mich.: Cranbrook Institute of Science.

Bining, A.C. [1938]1979. *Pennsylvania Iron Manufacture in the Eighteenth Century*. 2d ed. Harrisburg: Pennsylvania Historical and Museum Commission.

Birkbeck, M. [1818]1966. *Notes on a Journey in America, from the Coast of Virginia to the Territory of Illinois*. 4th ed. Reprint. Ann Arbor, Mich.: University Microfilms.

Birks, H.H., H.J.B. Birks, P.E. Kaland and D. Moe. (eds.). 1988. *The Cultural Landscape: Past, Present and Future*. Cambridge: Cambridge University Press.

Birks, H.J.B. 1986. Late-Quaternary biotic changes in terrestrial and lacustrine environments, with particular reference to north-west Europe. In B.E. Berglund (ed.), *Handbook of Holocene Palaeoecology and Palaeohydrology*, 3–65. New York: John Wiley and Sons.

Birks, H.J.B. and H.H. Birks. 1980. *Quaternary Paleoecology*. London: Edward Arnold.

Bishop, L.L. 1923. Pines of Hearts Content. *American Forestry* **29**:361–363.

Bishop, R.A. 1981. Iowa's wetlands. *Proceedings of the Iowa Academy of Science* **88**:11–16.

Bjorkbom, J.C. and R.G. Larson. 1977. *The Tionesta Scenic and Research Natural Areas*. USDA Forest Service General Technical Report, no. NE-31. Upper Darby, Pa.: Northeastern Forest Experiment Station.

Black, J.D. 1950. *The Rural Economy of New England: A Regional Study*. Cambridge, Mass.: Harvard University Press.

Black, J.D. and L.C. Gray. 1925. *Land settlement and colonization in the Great Lakes states*. USDA Bulletin, no. 1295. Washington, D.C.: GPO.

Blackbird, A.J. 1887. *History of the Ottawa and Chippewa Indians of Michigan; A Grammar of their Language, and Personal and Family History of the Author*. Ypsilanti, Mich.: Ypsilanti Job Printing House.

Blackmer, S.D. 1982. Fossils, fuel and the forest: The effect of coal on New

England's use of wood fuel in the 19th century. Unpublished student report. Yale University School of Forestry and Environmental Studies.

Blaine, W. 1918. An excursion through the United States and Canada during the years 1822–1823. In M.M. Quaife (ed.), *Pictures of Illinois One Hundred Years Ago*, 44–81. Chicago: R.R. Donelley and Sons.

Blair, W.D., Jr. 1986. The Nature Conservancy: Conservation through cooperation. *Journal of Forest History* **30**:37–41

Blake, A.K. 1935. Viability and germination of seeds and early life history of prairie plants. *Ecological Monographs* **5**:406–460.

Blake, I. 1856. Report on agriculture in Kensington, N.H. In *Transactions of the New Hampshire State Agricultural Society for the Year 1855*, 303–304. Concord, N.H.: Amos Hadley, State Printer.

Blake, W. 1888. *History of the Town of Hamden, Connecticut, with an Account of the Centennial Celebration, June 15th, 1886*. New Haven, Conn.: Price, Lee and Company.

Blaney, W.N. [1824]1916. Excerpts from 'An Excursion through the United States and Canada' 1822–23, by an English gentleman. In H. Lindley (ed.), *Indiana as Seen by Early Travelers: A Collection of Reprints from Books of Travel, Letters and Diaries Prior to 1830*, 276–290. Indianapolis: Indiana Historical Commission.

Blasing, T.J. and D. Duvick. 1984. Reconstruction of precipitation history in North American corn belt using tree rings. *Nature* **307**:143–144.

Blewett, M.D. and J.E. Potzger. 1950. The forest primeval of Marion and Johnson Counties, Indiana, in 1819. *Butler University Botanical Studies* **10**:40–52.

Blockstein, D.E. and H.B. Tordoff. 1985. Gone forever – a contemporary look at the extinction ot the passenger pigeon. *American Birds* **39**:845–851.

Blois, J.T. [1838]1975. *Gazetteer of the State of Michigan in Three Parts*. Reprint. New York: Arno Press.

Blowe, D. 1820. *A Geographical, Commercial, and Agricultural View of the United States of America*. Liverpool: Henry Fischer.

Boardman, S.L. 1863. Some outlines on the agriculture of Maine. In *Report of the Commissioner of Agriculture for the Year 1862*, 39–59. Washington, D.C.: GPO.

Boehmer, C.H. 1976. A phytosociological study of the voluntary urban vegetation of Racine, Wisconsin. Ph.D. diss. University of Wisconsin–Milwaukee.

Bogart, E.L. 1908. *The Economic History of the United States*. New York: Longmans, Green and Company.

Bogue, A.G. [1963]1968. *From Prairie to Cornbelt: Farming on the Illinois and Iowa Prairies in the Nineteenth Century*. Chicago: Quadrangle Books.

Bogue, M.B. 1951. The Swamp Land Act and wetland utilization in Illinois, 1850–1890. *Agricultural History* **25**:169–180.

Bollinger, E.K. 1991. Conservation of grassland birds in agricultural areas. In D.J. Decker, M.E. Krasny, G.R. Goff, C.R. Smith and D.W. Gross (eds.), *Challenges in the Conservation of Biological Resources: A Practitioner's Guide*, 279–287. Boulder, Co.: Westview Press.

Bollinger, E.K. and T.A. Gavin. 1992. Eastern bobolink populations: Ecology and conservation in an agricultural landscape. In J.M. Hagan III and D.W. Johnston (eds.), *Ecology and Conservation of Neotropical Migrant Landbirds*, 497–506. Washington, D.C.: Smithsonian Instution Press.

Bond, M.C., T.R. Rinkcas and P. Mitchell. 1954. *Changes in New York State agriculture 1850–1950 as indicated by state and federal censuses*. Agricultural Economics Paper, no. 917. Ithaca, N.Y.: Department of Agricultural Economics, New York State College of Agriculture, Cornell University.

Borchert, J.R. 1950. The climate of the central North American grasslands. *Annals of the Association of American Geographers* **40**:1–29.

Bordley, J.B. 1801. *Essays and Notes on Husbandry and Rural Affairs.* 2d ed. Philadelphia: Thomas Dobson.

Bormann, F.H. and M.F. Buell. 1964. Old-age stand of hemlock–northern hardwood forest in central Vermont. *Bulletin of the Torrey Botanical Club* **91**:451–465.

Bormann, F.H. and G.E. Likens. 1979. *Pattern and Process in a Forested Ecosystem.* New York: Springer-Verlag.

Bormann, F.H., G.E. Likens and J.M. Melillo. 1977. Nitrogen budget for an aggrading northern hardwood forest ecosystem. *Science* **196**:981–983.

Bormann, R.E. 1982. Agricultural disturbance and forest recovery at Mt. Cilley. Ph.D. diss. Yale University.

Bosch, J.M. and J.D. Hewlett. 1982. A review of catchment experiments to determine the effect of vegetation changes on water yield and evaporation. *Journal of Hydrology* **55**:3–23.

Bougher, C.K. and J.E. Winstead. 1974. A phytosociological study of a relict hardwood forest in Barren County, Kentucky. *Transactions of the Kentucky Academy of Science* **35**:44–54.

Bourdo, E.A., Jr. 1955. A validation of methods used in analyzing original forest cover. Ph.D. diss. University of Michigan.

Bourdo, E.A., Jr. 1956. A review of the General Land Office Survey and of its use in quantitative studies of former forests. *Ecology* **37**:754–768.

Bourdo, E.A., Jr. 1961. Some observations on a virgin stand of eastern white pine. *Papers of the Michigan Academy of Science, Arts and Letters* **46**:259–265.

Bourdo, E.A., Jr. 1983. The forest the settlers saw. In S.L. Flader (ed.), *The Great Lakes Forest: An Environmental and Social History*, 3–16. Minneapolis: University of Minnesota Press.

Bourne, A. 1820. On the prairies and barrens of the West. *American Journal of Science and Arts* **2**:30–34.

Bowden, M.J. 1992. The invention of American tradition. *Journal of Historical Geography* **18**:3–26.

Bowen, G.W. 1981. A quantitative analysis of forest island pattern in selected Ohio landscapes. M.S. thesis. University of Tennessee.

Bowers, D. 1969. *A List of References for the History of Agriculture in the United States: 1790–1840.* Davis: Agricultural History Center, University of California, Davis.

Bowers, D.E. and J.B. Hoehn. 1973. *A List of References for the History of Agriculture in the Midwest: 1840–1900.* Davis: Agricultural History Center, University of California, Davis.

Bowles, J.B. 1981. Iowa's mammal fauna: An era of decline. *Proceedings of the Iowa Academy of Science* **88**:38–42.

Bowles, M. and R.H. Thom. 1981. Endangered and threatened birds. In M.L. Bowles (ed.), *Endangered and Threatened Vertebrate Animals and Vascular Plants of Illinois*, 34–58. Illinois Department of Conservation and US Fish and Wildlife Service. Washington, D.C.: GPO.

Bowles, M.L., (ed.). 1981. *Endangered and Threatened Vertebrate Animals and Vascular Plants of Illinois.* Illinois Department of Conservation and US Fish and Wildlife Service. Washington, D.C.: GPO.

Bowles, M.L. 1983. The tallgrass prairie orchids *Platanthera leucophaea* (Nutt.) Lindl. and *Cypripedium candidum* Muhl. ex Willd.: Some aspects of their status, biology, and ecology and implications toward management. *Natural Areas Journal* **3** (4):14–37.

Bowman, I. 1979. The Draper site: Historical accounts of vegetation in Pickering and Markham Townships with special reference to the significance of a large, even-aged stand adjacent to the site. In B. Hayden (ed.), *Settlement patterns of the Draper and White sites: 1973 excavations.* Publication no. 6., 47–58. Burnaby, B.C.: Department of Archaeology, Simon Frazier University.

Bradbury, J. 1817. *Travels in the Interior of America in the Years 1809, 1810, and 1811.* London: Sherwood, Neeley, and Jones.

Bradbury, J.P., S.J. Tarapchak, J.C.B. Waddington and R.F. Wright. 1975. The impact of forest fire on a wilderness lake in northeastern Minnesota. *Verhandlungen der Internationale Vereinigung für Theoretische und Angewandte Limnologie* **19**:875–883.

Bradford, W. 1856. *History of Plymouth Plantation.* Boston: Published for the Massachusetts Historical Society by Little, Brown and Company.

Bradford, W. [1856]1981. *Of Plymouth Plantation, 1620–1647.* Reprint. New York: The Modern Library.

Bradford, W. and E. Winslow. [1622]1865. *Mourt's Relation or Journal of the Plantation of Plymouth.* Edited by H.M. Dexter. Boston: John Kimball Wiggin.

Bradley, C.P. 1906. Journal of Cyrus P. Bradley. *Ohio Archaeological and Historical Publications* **15**:207–270.

Bradof, K.L. 1992. Ditching of red lake peatland during the homestead era. In H.E. Wright, Jr., B.A. Coffin and N.E. Aaseng (eds.), *The Patterned Peatlands of Minnesota*, 263–284. Minneapolis: University of Minnesota Press.

Bradshaw, R.H. 1988. Spatially-precise studies of forest dynamics. In B. Huntley and T. Webb III (eds.), *Vegetation History*, 725–751. Dordrecht: Kluwer Academic Publishers.

Bradshaw, R.H.W. and T. Webb III. 1985. Relationship between contemporary pollen and vegetation data from Wisconsin and Michigan, U.S.A. *Ecology* **66**:721–737.

Brady, D.S. 1964. Relative prices in the nineteenth century. *Journal of Economic History* **24**:145–203.

Brady, N.C. 1984. *The Nature and Properties of Soils.* 9th ed. New York: Macmillan Publishing Company.

Brady, R.F., T. Tobias, P.F.J. Eagles, R. Ohrner, J. Micak, B. Veale and R.S. Dornery. 1979. A typology for the urban ecosystem and its relationship to larger biogeographical landscape units. *Urban Ecology* **4**:11–28.

Brakensiek, D.L. and C.R. Amerman. 1960. Evaluating effect of land use on stream flow. *Agricultural Engineering* **41**:158–161, 167.

Brandenburg, D.J. 1958. A French aristocrat looks at American farming: La Rochefoucauld-Liancourt's voyages dans les Etats-Unis. *Agricultural History* **32**:155–165.

Branson, F.A. 1953. Two new factors affecting resistance of grasses to grazing. *Journal of Range Management* **6**:165–171.

Bratton, S.P. 1974. The effect of the European wild boar (*Sus scrofa*) on the high-elevation vernal flora in Great Smoky Mountains National Park. *Bulletin of the Torrey Botanical Club* **101**:198–206.

Braun, E.L. [1950]1967. *Deciduous Forests of Eastern North America.* Reprint. New York: Hafner Publishing Company.

Brauning, D.W. (ed.) 1992. *Atlas of Breeding Birds in Pennsylvania.* Pittsburgh: University of Pittsburgh Press.

Bray, W.H. 1930. *The development of the vegetation of New York State.* Technical Publication, no. 29. Syracuse: New York State College of Forestry.

Breen, T.H. 1980. *Puritans and Adventures: Change and Persistence in Early America.* New York: Oxford University Press.

Brereton, J. [1602]1906. *Briefe and true relation of the discoverie of the north part of Virginia in 1602.* Reprinted in H.S. Burrage (ed.), *Early English and French Voyages, 1534–1608,* 325–340. New York: Charles Scribner's Sons.

Brewer, L.G. 1983. A study of the vegetational tension zone in Michigan using pre and postsettlement tree surveys. Unpublished manuscript.

Brewer, L.G., T.W. Hodler and H.A. Raup. 1984. Presettlement vegetation of southwestern Michigan. *The Michigan Botanist* **23**:153–156.

Brewer, R. 1960. *A brief history of ecology: Part I – Pre-nineteenth century to 1919.* Occassional Papers of the C.C. Adams Center for Ecological Studies, no. 1. Kalamazoo: Western Michigan University.

Brewer, R. 1980. A half-century of changes in the herb layer of a climax deciduous forest in Michigan. *Journal of Ecology* **68**:823–832.

Brewer, R., G.A. McPeek and R.J. Adams, Jr. (eds.) 1991. *The Atlas of Breeding Birds of Michigan.* East Lansing: Michigan State University Press.

Brewer, R. and P.G. Merritt. 1978. Wind throw and tree replacement in a climax beech-maple forest. *Oikos* **30**:149–152.

Brewer, W.H. 1874. The woodland and forest systems of the United States. Contains a map (plates 3 and 4) showing in five degrees of density the distribution of woodland within the territory of the United States together with commentary. In F.A. Walker (ed.), *A Statistical Atlas of the United States, Based on the Results of the Ninth Census.* Washington, D.C.: GPO.

Brewer, W.H. 1877. Woods and woodlands. In *Tenth Annual Report of the Secretary of the Connecticut Board of Agriculture,* 180–204. Hartford, Conn.: Case, Lockwood, and Brainard, Printers.

Brewster, W. 1906. *The birds of the Cambridge region of Massachusetts.* Memoirs of the Nuttall Ornithological Club, no. 4.

Bridenbaugh, C. 1967. *Vexed and Troubled Englishmen: 1590–1642.* London: Oxford University Press.

Bridenbaugh, C. 1968. *Cities in Revolt: Urban Life in America, 1743–1776.* New York: Alfred A. Knopf.

Bridenbaugh, C. 1974. *Fat, Mutton and Liberty of Conscience: Society in Rhode Island, 1636–1690.* Providence, R.I.: Brown University Press.

Brissot de Warville, J.P. [1788]1964. *New Travels in the United States of America.* Translated by M.S. Vamos and D. Echeverria. Edited by D. Echeverria. Cambridge, Mass.: Belknap Press of Harvard University Press.

Brittingham, M.C. and S.A. Temple. 1983. Have cowbirds caused forest songbirds to decline? *Bioscience* **33**:31–35.

Britton, N.L. 1890. A list of state and local floras of the United States and British America. *Annals of the New York Academy of Science* **5**:237–299.

Bromley, S.W. 1935. The original forest types of southern New England. *Ecological Monographs* **5**:61–89.

Bromley, S.W. 1945. An Indian relict area. *Scientific Monthly* **60**:153–154.

Brooks, M. 1938. The eastern lark sparrow in the Upper Ohio Valley. *The Cardinal* **4**:181–200.

Brooks, M. 1940. The breeding warblers of the central Allegheny Mountain region. *Wilson Bulletin* **52**:249–267.

Brooks, R.T. and T.W. Birch. 1988. Changes in New England forests and forest owners: Implications for wildlife habitat resources and management. *Transactions of the North American Wildlife and Natural Resources Conference* **53**:78–87.

Brotherson, J.D. and R.Q. Landers Jr. 1978. Recovery from severe grazing in an Iowa tall-grass prairie. In D.C. Glenn-Lewin and R.Q. Landers Jr. (eds.), *Proceedings of the Fifth Midwest Prairie Conference*, 51–56. Ames: Iowa State University.

Brown, J.H., Jr. 1960. The role of fire in altering the species composition of forests in Rhode Island. *Ecology* **41**:310–316.

Brown, M.L., J.L. Reveal, C.R. Broome and G.R. Frick. 1987. Comments on the vegetation of colonial Maryland. *Huntia* **7**:247–283.

Brown, N.C. 1917. *The hardwood distillation industry in New York*. Technical Publication, no. 5. Syracuse: New York State College of Forestry at Syracuse University.

Brown, N.C. 1919. *Forest Products: Their Manufacture and Use*. New York: John Wiley and Sons.

Brown, R.H. 1940. The first century of meteorological data in America. *Monthly Weather Review* **68**:130–133.

Brown, R.H. 1943. *Mirror for Americans: Likeness of the Eastern Seaboard, 1810*. Special Publication, no. 27. New York: American Geographical Society.

Brown, R.H. 1948. *Historical Geography of the United States*. New York: Harcourt Brace Jovanovich.

Brown, R.H. 1951. The seaboard climate in the view of 1800. *Annals of the Association of American Geographers* **61**:217–232.

Browne, C.A. 1944. *A Source Book of Agricultural Chemistry. Chronica Botanica* **8**: 1–290. Waltham, Mass.: Chronica Botanica Company.

Browne, D.J. 1832. *The Sylva Americana: or, a Description of the Forest Trees Indigenous to the United States Practically and Botanically Considered*. Boston: William Hyde and Company.

Browne, D.J. 1847. On the choice of trees and shrubs for cities and rural towns. *Transactions of the New York State Agricultural Society* **6**:376–404.

Browne, E. 1976. Edmund Browne to Sir Simonds D'Ewes, September 7, 1638. In E. Emerson (ed.), *Letters from New England: The Massachusetts Bay Colony, 1629–1638*, 224–231. Amherst: University of Massachusetts Press.

Brubaker, L.B. and E.R. Cook. 1983. Tree-ring studies of Holocene environments. In H.E. Wright Jr. (ed.), *Late-Quaternary Environments of the United States*. Vol. 2. *The Holocene*, 222–235. Minneapolis: University of Minnesota Press.

Bruchey, S. 1965. *The Roots of American Economic Growth, 1607–1861*. New York: Harper and Row.

Brush, G.S. 1986. Geology and paleoecology of Chesapeake Bay: A long-term monitoring tool for management. *Journal of the Washington Academy of Sciences* **76**:146–160.

Bryant, A. 1871. *Forest Trees, For Shelter, Ornament and Profit*. New York: Henry T. Williams.

Buck, S. and E.H. Buck. 1939. *The Planting of Civilization in Western Pennsylvania*. Pittsburgh: University of Pittsburgh Press.

Budd, T. [1685]1966. *Good Order Established in Pennsylvania and New Jersey*. Ann Arbor, Mich.: University Microfilms.

Buel, J. 1823. The improvement of our meadow and pasture lands, and the various grasses applicable to these objects. *New England Farmer* **2**:161–163, 174–175.

Buel, J. 1837. The contrast between the husbandry of new and old settled districts. *The Cultivator* **4**:93.

Buell, M.F., H.F. Buell and J.A. Small. 1954. Fire in the history of Mettler's woods. *Bulletin of the Torrey Botanical Club* **81**:253–255.

Buell, M.F. and J.E. Cantlon. 1953. Effects of prescribed burning on ground cover in the New Jersey pine region. *Ecology* **34**:520–528.

Bull, M. 1830. Experiments to determine the comparative quantities of heat evolved in the combustion of the principal varieties of wood and coal used in the United

States ... *Transactions of the American Philosophical Society*, n.s., **3**:1–63.

Bump, G. 1950. *Wildlife habitat changes in the Connecticut Hill Game Management Area: Their effect on certain species of wildlife over a twenty-year period.* Memoir, no. 289. Ithaca: New York [Cornell] Agricultural Experiment Staion.

Burden, E.T., J.H. McAndrews and G. Norris. 1986. Palynology of Indian and European forest clearance and farming in lake sediment cores from Awenda Provincial Park. *Canadian Journal of Earth Science* **23**:43–54.

Burger, G. 1981. Where has all the farm game gone? *Outdoor America* **46** (6):5–8.

Burger, G.V. 1978. Agriculture and wildlife. In H.P. Brokaw (ed.), *Wildlife in America: Contributions to an Understanding of American Wildlife and its Conservation. U.S. Council on Environmental Quality*, 89–107. Washington, D.C.: GPO.

Burges, G. 1965. A *Journal of a Surveying Trip into Western Pennsylvania under Andrew Ellicott in the Year 1795, when the Towns of Erie, Warren, Franklin, and Waterford were Laid Out.* Mt. Pleasant, Mich.: John Cumming.

Burgess, E.W. 1925. The growth of the city: An introduction to a research project. In R.E. Park, E.W. Burgess and R.D. McKenzie (eds.), *The City*, 47–62. Chicago: University of Chicago Press.

Burgess, R.L. and D.M. Sharpe. 1981. Introduction. In R.L. Burgess and D.M. Sharpe (eds.), *Forest Island Dynamics in Man-Dominated Landscapes*, 1–5. New York: Springer-Verlag.

Burgis, W.A. 1977. Late Wisconsin history of northeastern lower Michigan. Ph.D. diss. University of Michigan.

Burnham, C.F., M.J. Ferree and F.E. Cunningham. 1947. *The scrub oak forests of the anthracite region.* USDA Forest Service, Northeastern Forest Experiment Station, Station Paper, no. 4. Philadelphia: Northeastern Forest Experiment Station.

Burnham, C.R. 1988. The restoration of the American chestnut. *American Scientist* **76**:478–487.

Burr, B.M. and L.M. Page. 1986. Zoogeography of fishes of the lower Ohio–upper Mississippi basin. In C.H. Hocutt and E.O. Wiley (eds.), *The Zoogeography of North American Freshwater Fishes*, 287–324. New York: John Wiley and Sons.

Burroughs, R.D. 1946. Game refuges and public hunting grounds in Michigan. *Journal of Wildlife Management* **10**:285–296.

Bushman, R.L. 1967. *From Puritan to Yankee: Character and the Social Order in Connecticut, 1690–1765.* Cambridge, Mass.: Harvard University Press.

Butler, A.F. 1947–1949. Rediscovering Michigan's prairies. *Michigan History* **31**:267–286, **32**:15–36, **33**:117–130.

Butterfield, R.L. 1958. The great days of maple sugar. *New York History* **39**:151–164.

Buttrick, P.L. 1912. The effect of forest fires on trees and reproduction in southern New England. *Forestry Quarterly* 10:195–207.

Buttrick, P.L. 1916. The red spruce. *American Forestry* **22**:705–711.

Byrne, R. and J.H. McAndrews. 1975. Pre-Columbian purslane (*Portulaca oleracea* L.) in the New World. *Nature* **253**:726–727.

Cain, S.A. 1935. Studies on virgin hardwood forest. III. Warren Woods, a beech–maple climax forest in Berrien County, Michigan. *Ecology* **16**:500–513.

Cain, S.A. 1944. *Foundations of Plant Geography.* New York: Harper and Brothers.

Caird, J. 1859. *Prairie Farming in America.* New York: D. Appleton and Company.

Caldwell, J.A. 1897. *Caldwell's Atlas of Wayne County, Ohio.* Mount Vernon, Ohio: Atlas Publishing Company.

Calkin, P.E. 1969. Strand lines and chronology of the glacial Great Lakes in northwestern New York. *Ohio Journal of Science* **70**:78–96.

Callender, C. 1978. Shawnee. In B.G. Trigger (ed.), *Handbook of North American Indians*. Vol. 15. *Northeast*, 622–635. Washington, D.C.: Smithsonian Institution.

Cameron, J. 1928. *The Development of Governmental Forest Control in the United States*. Baltimore: The Johns Hopkins Press.

Cameron, M.R., III and J.E. Winstead. 1978. Structure and composition of a climax mixed mesophytic forest system in Laurel County, Kentucky. *Transactions of the Kentucky Academy of Science* **39**:1–11.

Campbell, J.T. 1886. Track of a cyclone which passed over western Indiana more than three hundred years ago. *American Naturalist* **20**:348–355.

Campbell, P. [1793]1937. *Travels in the Interior Inhabited Parts of North America in the Years 1791 and 1792*. Edited by H.H. Langton. Toronto: Champlain Society.

Candee, R.M. 1970. Merchant and millwright: The water powered sawmills of the Piscataqua. *Old Time New England* **60**:131–149.

Canham, C.D. 1988. Growth and canopy architecture of shade-tolerant trees: Response to canopy gaps. *Ecology* **69**:786–795.

Canham, C.D. and O.L. Loucks. 1984. Catastrophic windthrow in the presettlement forests of Wisconsin. *Ecology* **65**:803–809.

Carboneau, L.E. 1986. Old-growth forest stands in New Hampshire. M.S. thesis. University of New Hampshire.

Cardwell, V.B. 1982. Fifty years of Minnesota corn production: Sources of yield increase. *Agronomy Journal* **74**:984–990.

Carleton, T.J. and S.J. Taylor. 1983. The structure and composition of a wooded urban ravine system. *Canadian Journal of Botany* **61**:1392–1401.

Carlson, C.A. 1985. Wildlife and agriculture: Can they coexist? *Journal of Soil and Water Conservation* **40**:263–266.

Carlton, W.R. 1939. New England masts and the King's navy. *New England Quarterly* **12**:4–18.

Carlyle, J.C. 1986. Nitrogen cycling in forested ecosystems. *Forestry Abstracts* **47**:307–336.

Carman, H.J. 1934. English views on Middle Western agriculture, 1850–1870. *Agricultural History* **8**:3–19.

Carman, H.J. (ed.). [1775]1939. *American Husbandry*. Reprint. New York: Columbia University Press.

Carrier, L. 1923. *The Beginnings of Agriculture in America*. New York: McGraw-Hill.

Carroll, C.F. 1970. The forest civilization of New England: Timber, trade, and society in the age of wood, 1600–1688. Ph.D. diss. Brown University.

Carroll, C.F. 1973. *The Timber Economy of Puritan New England*. Providence, R.I.: Brown University Press.

Carroll, C.F. 1975. The forest society of New England. In B. Hindle (ed.), *America's Wooden Age: Aspects of its Early Technology*, 13–36. Tarrytown, N.Y.: Sleepy Hollow Restorations.

Carter, G.F. 1950. Ecology–geography–ethnobotany. *Scientific Monthly* **70**:73–80.

Carter, V. 1986. An overview of the hydrologic concerns related to wetlands in the United States. *Canadian Journal of Botany* **64**:364–374.

Carvell, K.L. and E.H. Tyron. 1961. The effect of environmental factors on the abundance of oak regeneration beneath mature oak stands. *Forest Science* **7**:98–105.

Carver, J. 1778. *Travels Through the Interior Parts of North America in the Years 1766, 1767, and 1768*. London: Printed for the author and sold by J. Waller.

Case, F.W., Jr. 1964. *Orchids in the Great Lakes Region*. Bulletin no. 48. Bloomfield Hills, Mich.: Cranbrook Institute of Science.

Case, F.W., Jr. 1987. *Orchids of the Western Great Lakes Region.* rev. ed. Bulletin no. 48. Bloomfield Hills, Mich.: Cranbrook Institute of Science.

Castiglioni, L. [1790]1983. *Luigi Castiglioni's Viaggio: Travels in the United States of North America 1785–87.* Translated by A. Pace. Syracuse, N.Y.: Syracuse University Press.

Catchpole, A.J.W. and D.W. Moodie. 1978. Archives and the environmental scientist. *Archivaria* **6**:113–136.

Catenhusen, J. 1950. Secondary successions on the peat lands of glacial Lake Wisconsin. *Transactions of the Wisconsin Academy of Sciences, Arts and Letters* **40**:29–48.

Catling, P.M. and S.M. McKay. 1980. Halophytic plants in southern Ontario. *Canadian Field-Naturalist* **94**:248–258.

Caton, J.D. 1876. *Origin of the prairies.* Fergus Historical Series, no. 3: 31–55. Chicago: Fergus Printing Company.

Cawley, E.T. 1960. Phytosociological study of the effect of grazing on southern Wisconsin woodlots. Ph.D. diss. University of Wisconsin, Madison.

Cech, F.C. 1986. American chestnut (*Castanea dentata*) – replacement species and current status. In S.K. Majumdar, F.J. Brenner and A.F. Rhoads (eds.), *Endangered and Threatened Species Programs in Pennsylvania and Other States: Causes, Issues and Management,* 145–155. Easton: Pennsylvania Academy of Science.

Ceci, L. 1975. Fish fertilizer: A native North American practice? *Science* **188**:26–30.

Center for Urban and Regional Affairs. 1981. *Thematic maps: Presettlement wetlands of Minnesota and available wetlands for bioenergy purposes.* Minneapolis: University of Minnesota.

Chamberlain, E. 1849. *The Indiana Gazetteer or Topographical Dictionary of the State of Indiana.* 3d ed. Indianapolis, Ind.: E. Chamberlain.

Champlain, S., de. [1905]1968. Discovery of the coast of the Almouchiquois as far as the forty-second degree of latitude and details of this voyage. In G.P. Winship (ed.), *Sailors' Narratives of Voyages along the New England Coast 1524–1624,* 64–97. Reprint. New York: Burt Franklin.

Chapman, A.G. 1944. Original forests. In O.D. Diller (ed.), *Ohio's forest resources,* Forestry Publication no. 76, 73–84. Wooster: Ohio Agricultural Experiment Station.

Chapman, J., P.A. Delcourt, P.A. Cridlebaugh, A.B. Shea and H.R. Delcourt. 1982. Man–land interaction: 10,000 years of American Indian impact on native ecosystems in the lower Little Tennessee River Valley, eastern Tennessee. *Southeastern Archaeology* **1**:115–121.

Chapman, J., R.B. Stewart and R.A. Yarnell. 1974. Archaeological evidence for PreColumbian introduction of *Portulaca oleracea* and *Mollugo verticillata* into eastern North America. *Economic Botany* **28**:411–412.

Charlevoix, P., de. [1761]1966. *Journal of a Voyage to North-America.* 2 vols. Reprint. Ann Arbor, Mich.: University Microfilms.

Chastellux, F.J., marquis de. [1786]1963. *Travels in North America in the Years 1780, 1781, and 1782.* Translated by H.C. Rice, Jr. 2 vols. Reprint. Chapel Hill: University of North Carolina Press.

Cheney, W. 1971. William Cheney (1787–1875): The life of a Vermont woodsman and farmer. Edited by R.C. Skillin. *Vermont History* **39** (1):43–50.

Cheyney, E.G. 1916. The development of the lumber industry in Minnesota. *Journal of Geography* **14**:189–195.

Cheyney, E.G. 1942. *American Silvics and Silviculture.* Minneapolis: University of Minnesota Press.

Chinard, G. 1945. The American Philosophical Society and the early history of forestry in America. *Proceedings of the American Philosophical Society* **89**:444–488.

Chittenden, A.K. 1904. Forest conditions of northern New Hampshire. In *Biennial Report of the [New Hampshire] Forestry Commission for the Years 1903–1904*, 1–131. Concord, N.H.: Rumford Printing Company.

Chittenden, H.M. 1908. Forests and reservoirs in their relation to stream flow with particular reference to navigable rivers. *Proceedings of the American Society of Civil Engineers* **34**:924–997.

Cho, D.S. and R.E. Boerner. 1991. Structure, dynamics, and composition of Sears Woods and Carmean Woods State Nature Preserves, north-central Ohio. *Castanea* **56**:77–89.

Christensen, N.L. 1989. Landscape history and ecological change. *Journal of Forest History* **33**:116–124.

Christiansen, P.A. and R.Q. Landers. 1966. Notes on prairie species in Iowa. I. Germination and establishment of several species. *Iowa Academy of Science* **73**:51–73.

Christy, B.H. 1936. Kirtland marginalia. *Cardinal* **4**:77–89.

Clapp, R.T. 1938. The effects of the hurricane upon New England forests. *Journal of Forestry* **36**:1177–1181.

Clark, C. 1987. Deforestation and floods. *Environmental Conservation* **14**:67–69.

Clark, C.E. 1970. *The Eastern Frontier: The Settlement of Northern New England*. New York: Alfred A. Knopf.

Clark, J.S. 1988. Stratigraphic charcoal analysis on petrographic thin sections: Application to fire history in northwestern Minnesota. *Quaternary Research* **30**:81–91.

Clark, J.S. 1990. Fire and climate change during the last 750 years in northwestern Minnesota. *Ecological Monographs* **60**:135–159.

Clark, V.S. 1929. *History of Manufactures in the United States, 1607–1913*. 3 vols. New York: McGraw-Hill for the Carnegie Institution of Washington.

Clarke, J. and G.F. Finnegan. 1984. Colonial survey records and the vegetation of Essex County, Ontario. *Journal of Historical Geography* **10**:119–138.

Clarke, S. 1670. *A True and Faithful Account of the Four Chiefest Plantations of the English in America*. London: Robert Clavel, Thomas Passenger, etc.

Clawson, M. 1979. Forests in the long sweep of American history. *Science* **204**:1168–1174.

Clawson, M. and C.L. Stewart. 1965. *Land Use Information: A Critical Survey of U.S. Statistics Including Possibilities for Greater Uniformity*. Washington, D.C.: Resources for the Future.

Clements, F.E. 1920. *Plant Indicators: The Relation of Plant Communities to Process and Practice*. Publication, no. 290. Washington, D.C.: Carnegie Institution of Washington.

Clements, F.E. 1936. Nature and the structure of the climax. *Journal of Ecology* **24**:252–284.

Clepper, H. 1945. Rise of the forest conservation movement in Pennsylvania. *Pennsylvania History* **12**:200–216.

Clepper, H. 1981. Forest conservation in Pennsylvania: The pioneer period, from Rothrock to Pinchot. *Pennsylvania History* **48**:41–50.

Clepper, H.E. 1934. *Hemlock: The state tree of Pennsylvania*. Bulletin, no. 52. Harrisburg: Pennsylvania Department of Forests and Waters.

Clewley, F.A. [1910]1976. *Colonial Precedents of Our National Land System as it Existed in 1800*. Reprint. Philadelphia: Porcupine Press.

Cline, A.C. and S.H. Spurr. 1942. *The virgin upland forest of central New England: A study of old growth stands in the Pisgah Mountain section of southwestern New Hampshire.* Harvard Forest Bulletin, no. 21. Petersham, Mass.: Harvard Forest.

Closson, A.B. and T.R. Crosby. 1856. Report on agriculture in Hanover, N.H. In *Transactions of the New Hampshire State Agricultural Society for the Year 1855*, 279–288. Concord, N.H.: Amos Hadley, State Printer.

Coad, O.S. 1972. *New Jersey in Travellers' Accounts, 1524–1971.* Metuchen, N.J.: Scarecrow Press.

Coan, E. 1983. James Graham Cooper: Pioneer naturalist and forest conservationist. *Journal of Forest History* **27**:126–129.

Cobb, S.S. 1958. Trends in forest fire occurrence and area burned in Pennsylvania. *Pennsylvania Forests* **38** (2):28–29.

Coddington, J.A. and K.G. Field. 1978. *Rare and endangered vascular plant species in Massachusetts.* Newton Corner, Mass.: The New England Botanical Club in cooperation with the US Fish and Wildlife Service.

Cogbill, C.V. 1985. Dynamics of the boreal forests of the Laurentian Highlands, Canada. *Canadian Journal of Forest Research* **15**:252–261.

Colby, W.G. 1941. *Pasture culture in Massachusetts.* Bulletin, no. 380. Amherst: Massachusetts Agricultural Experiment Station, Massachusetts State College.

Colden, C. 1851. Observations on the situation, soil, climate, water communications, boundaries, etc. of the province of New York, 1738. In E.B. O'Callaghan (ed.), *Documentary History of the State of New York.* Vol. 4, 169–179. Albany: Charles Van Benthuysen.

Cole, A.H. 1970. The mystery of fuel wood marketing in the United States. *Business History Review* **44**:339–359.

Cole, D.W. and M. Rapp. 1981. Elemental cycling in forest ecosystems. In D.E. Reichle (ed.), *Dynamic Properties of Forest Ecosystems*, 341–409. Cambridge: Cambridge University Press.

Cole, G.L. 1984. *Travels in America, from the Voyages of Discovery to the Present, An Annotated Bibliography of Travel Articles in Periodicals, 1955–1980.* Norman: University of Oklahoma Press.

Collin, N. 1793. An essay on those inquiries in natural philosophy, which at present are most beneficial to the United States of North America. *Transactions of the American Philosophical Society* **3**:iii–xxvii.

Collins, S. 1956. The biotic communities of Greenbrook Sanctuary. Ph.D. diss. Rutgers University. Also published by Palisades Nature Association, Englewood Cliffs, N.J.

Collins, S.H. [1830]1971. *The Emigrant's Guide to and Description of the United States of America.* 4th ed. Reprint. Englewood, N.J.: Jerome S. Ozer.

Collot, V. 1909. A journey in North America. *Transactions of the Illinois State Historical Society* for the year 1908:269–298.

Colman, H. 1838. *First Report of the Agriculture of Massachusetts: County of Essex.* Boston: Dutton and Wentworth, State Printers.

Colman, H. 1839. *Second Report of the Agriculture of Massachusetts: County of Berkshire.* Boston: Dutton and Wentworth, State Printers.

Colman, H. 1841. *Fourth Report of the Agriculture of Massachusetts: Counties of Franklin and Middlesex.* Boston: Dutton and Wentworth, State Printers.

Colvin, B.A. 1985. Common barn-owl population decline in Ohio and the relationship to agricultural trends. *Journal of Field Ornithology* **56**:224–235.

Commissioners on the Boundary Line between the State of New York and the State of Pennsylvania. 1886. *Report of the Regents' Boundary Commission upon the New York and Pennsylvania Boundary.* Albany, N.Y.: Weed, Parsons and Company,

Legislative Printers.

Conard, E.C. and V.H. Arthaud. 1957. *Effect of time of cutting on yield and botanical composition of prairie hay in southeastern Nebraska*. Research Bulletin, no. 184. Lincoln: Agricultural Experiment Station, College of Agriculture, University of Nebraska.

Conklin, H.E. 1964. The dynamics of land use in New York State. *The [New York State] Conservationist* **18** (5):2–3.

Conner, R.N. 1979. Minimum standards and forest wildlife management. *Wildlife Society Bulletin* **7**:293–296.

Considine, T., Jr. 1984. *An analysis of New York's timber resources*. USDA Forest Service Resource Bulletin, no. NE-80. Broomall, Pa.: Northeastern Forest Experiment Station.

Considine, T., Jr. and T. Frieswyk. 1982. *Forest statistics for New York, 1980*. USDA Forest Service Resource Bulletin, no. NE-71. Broomall, Pa.: Northeastern Forest Experiment Station.

Conway, E. 1940. *Forest resources of Wayne County, Ohio*. Forestry Publication, no. 65. Wooster: Ohio WPA and Ohio Agricultural Experiment Station.

Conzen, M.P. 1969. Spatial data from nineteenth century manuscript censuses: A technique for rural settlement and land use analysis. *Professional Geographer* **21**:337–343.

Conzen, M.P. 1984. III. Landownership maps and county altases. *Agricultural History* **58**:118–122.

Cook, D.B., R.H. Smith and E.L. Stone. 1952. The natural distribution of red pine in New York. *Ecology* **33**:500–512.

Cook, E.R. and G.C. Jacoby. 1977. Tree-ring–drought relationships in the Hudson Valley, New York. *Science* **198**:399–401.

Cook, E.R. and G.C. Jacoby. 1983. Potomic River streamflow since 1730 as reconstructed by tree rings. *Journal of Climate and Applied Meteorology* **22**:1659–1672.

Cook, F. 1887. *Journals of the Military Expedition of Major General John Sullivan Against the Six Nations of Indians in 1779 with Records of Centennial Celebrations*. Auburn, N.Y.: Knapp, Peck, and Thomson.

Cook, H.O. 1917. *The forests of Worcester County: The results of a forest survey of the fifty-nine towns in the county and a study of their lumber industry*. Boston, Mass.: Wright and Potter, State Printers.

Cook, S.F. 1973. The significance of disease in the extinction of the New England Indians. *Human Biology* **45**:485–508.

Cook, S.F. 1976. *The Indian population of New England in the seventeenth century*. Publications in Anthropology, no. 12:1–91. Berkeley: University of California.

Coolidge, P.T. 1963. *History of the Maine Woods*. Bangor, Maine: Furbush-Roberts Printing Company.

Coones, P. 1985. One landscape or many?: A geographical perspective. *Landscape History* **7**:5–12.

Cooper, E.L. 1983. *Fishes of Pennsylvania and the Northeastern United States*. University Park: Pennsylvania State University Press.

Cooper, H.P., J.K. Wilson and J.H. Barron. 1929. Ecological factors determining the pasture flora in the northeastern United States. *Journal of the American Society of Agronomy* **21**:607–627.

Cooper, J.F. [1823]1985. *The Pioneers*. Reprinted in *The Leatherstocking Tales*. Vol. 1. New York: Literary Classics of the United States, Inc.

Cooper, J.F. 1860. *The Oak Openings: or, the Bee-hunter*. New York: W.A. Townsend and Company.

Cooper, T. 1794. *Some Information Respecting America, Collected by Thomas Cooper, Late of Manchester.* 2d ed. London: J. Johnson.

Cooper, W. 1792. A letter on the manufacture of maple sugar. *Transactions of the New York State Society for the Promotion of Agriculture, Arts and Manufactures* **1**:83–87.

Cooper, W. [1810]1897. *A Guide in the Wilderness or the History of the First Settlements in the Western Counties of New York with Useful Instructions to Future Settlers.* Reprint. Rochester, N.Y.: G.P. Humphrey.

Cooper, W.S. 1928. Sixteen years of successional change upon Isle Royale, Lake Superior. *Ecology* **9**:1–5.

Cooperrider, T.S. (ed.) 1982. *Endangered and threatened plants of Ohio.* Biological Notes, no. 16. Columbus: Ohio Biological Survey.

Cooter, W.S. 1978. Ecological dimensions of medieval agrarian systems. *Agricultural History* **52**:458–477.

Cope, T.M. 1936. Observations on the vertebrate ecology of some Pennsylvania virgin forests. Ph.D. diss. Cornell University.

Costa, J.E. 1975. Effects of agriculture on erosion and sedimentation in the Piedmont Province, Maryland. *Geological Society of America Bulletin* **86**:1281–1286.

Cottam, G. 1949. The phytosociology of an oak woods in southwestern Wisconsin. *Ecology* **30**:271–287.

Cottam, G. and J.T. Curtis. 1949. A method for making rapid surveys of woodlands by means of pairs of randomly selected trees. *Ecology* **30**:101–104.

Cox, D.L., R.M. Miller and J.A. Hostetler. 1972. Succession in and composition of a central Illinois prairie grove. *Transactions of the Illinois State Academy of Science* **65**:33–41.

Cox, T.R. 1983. Logging technology and tools. In R.C. Davis (ed.), *Encyclopedia of American Forest and Conservation History.* Vol. 1, 347–354. New York: Macmillan Publishing Company.

Cox, T.R., R.S. Maxwell, P.D. Thomas and J.J. Malone. 1985. *This Well-Wooded Land: Americans and Their Forests from Colonial Times to the Present.* Lincoln: University of Nebraska Press.

Coxe, T. 1794. *A View of the United States of America, in a Series of Papers Written at Various Times between the Years 1787 and 1794.* Philadelphia: William Hall and Wrigley and Berriman.

Coxe, T. 1814. *A Statement of the Arts and Manufactures of the United States of America, for the Year 1810: Digested and Prepared by Tench Coxe, Esq. of Philadelphia.* Philadelphia: A. Cornman.

Coyne, F.E. 1940. *The Development of the Cooperage Industry in the United States 1620–1940.* Chicago: Lumber Buyers Publishing Company.

Crabtree, P.J. 1983. Seeds and subsistence in the Northeast: The paleoethnobotany of the Delaware Park and Van Voorhiss farm sites. *Man in the Northeast* **26**:75–79.

Crankshaw, W.B., S.A. Quadir and A.A. Lindsey. 1965. Edaphic control of tree species in presettlement Indiana. *Ecology* **46**:688–698.

Cratty, R.I. 1929. The immigrant flora of Iowa. *Iowa State College Journal of Science* **3**:247–269.

Craul, P.J. 1985. A description of urban soils and their desired characteristics. *Journal of Arboriculture* **11**:330–339.

Craven, A.O. [1926]1965. *Soil Exhaustion as a Factor in the Agricultural History of Virginia and Maryland, 1606–1860.* Reprint. Gloucester, Mass.: Peter Smith.

Crèvecoeur, J.H., St. John de. 1925. *Sketches of Eighteenth Century America., or More Letters from an American Farmer.* Edited by H.L. Bourdin, R.H. Gabriel and S.T. Williams. New Haven, Conn.: Yale University Press.

Crèvecoeur, J.H., St. John de. 1964. *Journey into Northern Pennsylvania and the State of New York.* Translated by C.S. Bostelmann. Ann Arbor: University of Michigan Press.

Cringan, A.T. 1957. History, food habits and range requirements of the woodland caribou of continental North America. *Transactions of the North American Wildlife Conference* **22**:485–501.

Croghan, G. 1904. *Journals of George Croghan (1750–1765).* Reprinted in R.G. Thwaites (ed.), *Early Western Travels, 1748–1846.* Vol. 1, 45–173 Cleveland, Ohio: Arthur H. Clark.

Cronon, W. 1983. *Changes in the Land: Indians, Colonists, and the Ecology of New England.* New York: Hill and Wang.

Cronon, W. 1991. Landscape and home: Environmental traditions in Wisconsin. *Wisconsin Magazine of History* **74**:83–105.

Crosby, A.W., Jr.1972. *The Columbian Exchange: Biological and Cultural Consequences of 1492.* Westport, Conn.: Greenwood Press.

Crosby, A.W., Jr. 1986. *Ecological Imperialism: The Biological Expansion of Europe, 900–1900.* Cambridge: Cambridge University Press.

Crovello, T.J., C.A. Keller and J.T. Kartesz. 1983. *The Vascular Plants of Indiana: A Computer Based Checklist.* Notre Dame, Ind.: University of Notre Dame Press.

Crow, T.R. 1978. Biomass and production in three contiguous forests in northern Wisconsin. *Ecology* **59**:265–273.

Crowl, G.S. 1937. A vegetation survey of Ross County. M.S. thesis. Ohio State University.

Cunningham, J.E. 1900. Some observations of Ohio woodlands. *The Forester* **6**:103–104.

Curtis, D.S. 1852. *Western Portraiture and Emigrants Guide.* New York: J.H. Colton.

Curtis, J.T. 1951. Hardwood woodlot cover and its conservation. In N.H. Hoveland (ed.), Report to the people of Wisconsin on cover destruction, habitat improvement and watershed problems of the state in 1950. *Wisconsin Conservation Bulletin* **16** (2):11–15.

Curtis, J.T. 1956. The modification of mid-latitude grasslands and forests by man. In W.L. Thomas Jr. (ed.), *Man's Role in Changing the Face of the Earth*, 721–736. Chicago: University of Chicago Press.

Curtis, J.T. 1959. *The Vegetation of Wisconsin: An Ordination of Plant Communities.* Madison: University of Wisconsin Press.

Curtis, J.T. and H.C. Greene. 1949. A study of relic Wisconsin prairies by the species-presence method. *Ecology* **30**:83–92.

Curtis, J.T. and M.L. Partch. 1948. Effects of fire on the competition between bluegrass and certain prairie plants. *American Midland Naturalist* **39**:437–443.

Cusick, A.W. and R.K. Troutman. 1978. *The prairie survey project: A summary of data to date.* Information Circular, no. 10. Columbus, Ohio: Ohio Biological Survey.

Cutler, M. 1785. An account of some of the vegetable productions, naturally growing in this part of America, botanically arranged. *Memoirs of the American Academy of Arts and Sciences* **1**:396–493.

Cutler, M. [1787]1888. An explanation of the map of federal lands, etc. Reprinted in W.P. Cutler and J.P. Cutler (eds.), *Life, Journals and Correspondence of Reverend Manasseh Cutler, L.L.D.* Vol. 2, 393–406. Cincinnati, Ohio: R. Clarke and Company.

Cutler, W.P. and J.P. Cutler. (eds.) 1888. *Life, Journals and Correspondence of Reverend Manasseh Cutler, L.L.D.* Vol. 2. Cincinnati: R. Clarke and Company.

Cwynar, L.C. 1978. Recent history of fire and vegetation from laminated sediments of

Greenleaf Lake, Algonquin Park, Ontario. *Canadian Journal of Botany* **56**:10–21.

Dablon, C. 1900. Relation of the discovery of many countries situated to the south of New France, made in 1673. In R.G. Thwaites (ed.), *The Jesuit Relations and Allied Documents: Travels and Explorations of the Jesuit Missionaries in New France, 1610–1791.*Vol. 58, 93–109. Cleveland, Ohio: Burrows Brothers.

Dachnowski, A. 1912. *Peat deposits of Ohio: Their origin, formation, and uses.* Bulletin of the Geological Survey of Ohio, 4th ser., no. 16. Columbus, Ohio.

Dahl, T.E. 1990. *Wetland losses in the United States 1780's to 1980's.* Washington, D.C.: US Department of the Interior, Fish and Wildlife Service.

Dahllöf, T. 1966. Pehr Kalm's concern about forests in America, Sweden and Finland two centuries ago. *Swedish Pioneer Historical Quarterly* **17**:123–145.

Dambach, C.A. 1944. A ten-year ecological study of adjoining grazed and ungrazed woodlands in northeastern Ohio. *Ecological Monographs* **14**:257–270.

Dambach, C.A. 1948. *A study of the ecology and economic value of crop field borders.* Ohio State Graduate School Studies. Biological Science ser., no. 2. Columbus: Ohio State University Press.

Dambach, C.A. and E.E. Good. 1940. The effect of certain land use practices on populations of breeding birds in southwestern Ohio. *Journal of Wildlife Management* **4**:63–76.

Dana, E. 1819. *Geographical Sketches on the Western Country: Designed for Emigrants and Settlers.* Cincinnati: Looker, Reynolds and Company.

Dana, S.T. 1909. *Paper birch in the Northeast.* USDA Forest Service Circular, no. 163. Washington, D.C.: USDA Forest Service.

Dana, S.T. 1939. Fire over the Lake States. *American Forests* **45**:170–172, 234.

Dana, S.T., J.H. Allison and R.N. Cunningham. 1960. *Minnesota Lands: Ownership, Use, and Management of Forest and Related Lands.* Washington, D.C.: American Forestry Association.

Dana, S.T. and S.K. Fairfax. 1980. *Forest and Range Policy: Its Development in the United States.* 2d ed. New York: McGraw-Hill.

Danhof, C.H. 1941. Farm making costs and the safety valve. *Journal of Political Economy* **49**:317–359.

Danhof, C.H. 1944. The fencing problem in the eighteen fifties. *Agricultural History* **19**:168–186.

Danhof, C.H. 1969. *Change in Agriculture: The Northern United States, 1820–1870.* Cambridge, Mass.: Harvard University Press.

Daniel, C.C., III. 1981. Hydrology, geology, and soils of pocosins: A comparison of natural and altered systems. In C.J. Richardson (ed.), *Pocosin Wetlands: An Integrated Analysis of Coastal Plain Freshwater Bogs in North Carolina,* 69–108. Stroudsburg, Pa.: Hutchinson Ross Publishing Company.

Daniel, T.W., J.A. Helms and F.S. Baker. 1979. *Principles of Silviculture.* 2d ed. New York: McGraw-Hill.

Daniels, E. 1988. The specter of the deadly woodlands. *Timeline* **5** (5):45–54.

Dansereau, P. 1957. *Biogeography: An Ecological Perspective.* New York: Ronald Press.

Darby, H.C. 1951. The clearing of the English woodlands. *Geography* **36**:71–83.

Darby, H.C. 1956. The clearing of the woodland in Europe. In W.L. Thomas Jr. (ed.), *Man's Role in Changing the Face of the Earth,* 183–216. Chicago: University of Chicago Press.

Darlington, H.T. 1945. *Taxonomic and ecological work on the higher plants of Michigan.* Technical Bulletin, no. 201. East Lansing: Michigan Agricultural Experiment Station.

Darlington, W. 1826. *Florula Cestrica*. West Chester, Pa.: S. Siegfried.

Darlington, W. 1847. *An Enumeration and Description of Useful Plants and Weeds, which Merit Notice, or Require the Attention of American Agriculturists.* Philadelphia: J.W. Moore.

Darlington, W. [1849]1967. *Memorials of John Bartram and Humphrey Marshall.* Reprint. New York: Hafner Publishing Company.

Darlington, W. 1866. Weeds of American agriculture. In *Report of the Commissioner of Agriculture for the Year 1865*, 509–519. Washington, D.C.: GPO.

Daubenmire, R.F. 1936. The 'Big Woods' of Minnesota: Its structure, and relation to climate, fire, and soils. *Ecological Monographs* **6**:233–268.

Davis, A.M. 1977a. The prairie-deciduous forest ecotone in the Upper Middle West. *Annals of the Association of American Geographers* **67**:204–213.

Davis, I.G. 1933. Agricultural production in New England. In J.K. Wright (ed.), *New England's Prospect: 1933*, 118–167. New York: American Geographical Society.

Davis, M.B. 1965. Phytogeography and palynology of northeastern United States. In H.E. Wright Jr. and D.G. Frey (eds.), *The Quaternary of the United States*, 377–401. Princeton, N.J.: Princeton University Press.

Davis, M.B. 1976. Erosion rates and land-use history in southern Michigan. *Environmental Conservation* **3**:139–148.

Davis, M.B. 1981. Outbreaks of forest pathogens in Quaternary history. In *Proceedings of the IV International Palynological Conference, Lucknow (1976–77)*. Vol. 3, 216–227.

Davis, M.B. 1985. History of the vegetation on the Mirror Lake watershed. In G.E. Likens (ed.), *An Ecosystem Approach to Aquatic Ecology: Mirror Lake and its Environment*, 53–65. New York: Springer-Verlag.

Davis, R.B. 1974. Stratigraphical effects of tubificids in profundal lake sediments. *Limnology and Oceanography* **19**:466–488.

Davis, R.C. 1977b. *North American Forest History: A Guide to Archives and Manuscripts in the United States and Canada*. Santa Barbara, Calif.: Clio Books.

Day, C.A. 1954. *A History of Maine Agriculture, 1604–1860*. University of Maine Studies, no. 68. Orono: University of Maine Press.

Day, G.M. 1953. The Indian as an ecological factor in the Northeastern forest. *Ecology* **34**:329–346.

Day, M.A. 1899–1900. The local floras of New England. *Rhodora* **1**:111–142, 158, 174–178,194–196, 208–211, **2**: 254–257.

Day, R.K. 1930. Grazing out the birds. *American Forests* **36**:555–557, 594.

Day, R.K. 1934. *Reduce woodland grazing by increasing pastures*. Station Note, no. 12. Columbus, Ohio: USDA Forest Service Central States Forest Experiment Station.

Day, R.K. and D. Den Uyl. 1932. *Studies in Indiana farmwoods I. The natural regeneration of farmwoods following the exclusion of livestock*. Bulletin, no. 368. West Lafayette, Ind.: Purdue University Agricultural Experiment Station in cooperation with the Central States Forest Experiment Station.

De Mars, B.G. and J.R. Runkle. 1992. Groundlayer vegetation ordination and site-factor analysis of the Wright State University woods (Greene County, Ohio). *Ohio Journal of Science* **92**: 98–106.

Deam, C.C. 1940. *Flora of Indiana*. Indianapolis: Indiana Department of Conservation.

Deane, S. 1797. *The New England Farmer, or, Georgical Dictionary*. 2d ed. Worcester, Mass.: Isiah Thomas.

DeCoster, L.A. 1983. Maine forests. In R.C. Davis (ed.), *Encyclopedia of American*

Forest and Conservation History. Vol. 2, 402–404. New York: Macmillan Publishing Company.

Defebaugh, J.E. 1906–1907. *History of the Lumber Industry of America*. 2 vols. Chicago: American Lumberman.

DeGraaf, R.M. 1985. Residential forest structure in urban and suburban environments: Some wildlife implications in New England. *Journal of Arboriculture* **11**:236–241.

DeGraaf, R.M. and J.M. Wentworth. 1981. Urban bird communities and habitats in New England. *Transactions of the North American Wildlife and Natural Resources Conference* **46**:396–413.

DeGraaf, R.M. and J.M. Wentworth. 1986. Avian guild structure and habitat associations in suburban bird communities. *Urban Ecology* **9**:399–412.

Delabarre, E.B. and H.H. Wilder. 1920. Indian corn-hills in Massachusetts. *American Anthropologist*, n.s., **22**:203–225.

Delafield, J. 1851. A general view and agricultural survey of the county of Seneca. *Transactions of the New York State Agricultural Society* **10**:436–516.

Delcourt, H.R. and P.A. Delcourt. 1977. Presettlement magnolia–beech climax of the Gulf coastal plain: Quantitative evidence from the Apalachicola River Bluffs, north-central Florida. *Ecology* **58**:1085–1093.

Delcourt, P.A., H.R. Delcourt, P.A. Cridlebaugh and J. Chapman. 1986. Holocene ethnobotanical and paleoecological record of human impact on vegetation in the Little Tennessee River Valley, Tennessee. *Quaternary Research* **25**:330–349.

Delcourt, P.A., H.R. Delcourt and T.Webb III. 1984. *Atlas of mapped distributions of dominance and modern pollen as percentages for important tree taxa of eastern North America*. Contribution Series, no. 14. Dallas: American Association of Stratigraphic Palynologists.

Den Uyl, D. 1955. Indiana's old growth forests. *Proceedings of the Indiana Academy of Science* **63**:73–79.

Den Uyl, D. 1961. *Natural tree reproduction in mixed hardwood stands*. Research Bulletin, no. 728. West Lafayette, Ind.: Purdue University Agricultural Experiment Station.

Den Uyl, D., O.D. Diller and R.K. Day. 1938. *The development of natural regeneration in previously grazed farmwoods*. Bulletin, no. 431. West Lafayette, Ind.: Purdue University Agricultural Experiment Station in cooperation with the Central States Forest Experiment Station.

Denevan, W.M. 1992. The pristine myth: The landscape of the Americas in 1492. *Annals of the Association of American Geographers* **82**:369–385.

Dennis, D.D. and T.W. Birch. 1982. *Forest statistics for Ohio, 1979*. USDA Forest Service Resource Bulletin, no. NE-68. Broomall, Pa.: Northeastern Forest Experiment Station.

Denny, C.S. 1982. *Geomorphology of New England*. US Geological Survey Professional Paper, no. 1208. Washington, D.C.: US Geological Survey.

Denny, C.S. and W.H. Lyford. 1963. *Surficial geology and soils of the Elmira–Williamsport region, New York and Pennsylvania*. US Geological Survey Professional Paper, no. 379. Washington, D.C.: US Geological Survey.

Denton, D. [1670]1966. *A Brief Description of New York*. March of America facsimile series no. 26. Ann Arbor, Mich.: University Microfilms.

Desor, E. [1879]1907. Sections from 'La Foret Vierge'. In C.A. Davis (ed.), *'Peat: Essays on its origin, uses and distribution in Michigan'* in *Report of the State Board of Geological Survey of Michigan for the Year 1906*, cited on pages 118–119. Lansing, Mich.: Wynkoop Hallenbeck Crawford Company, State Printer.

Detwyler, T.R. 1966. Forest vegetation, environment, and process in the Ontonagon area, Michigan. Ph.D. diss. Johns Hopkins University.

Detwyler, T.R. 1972. Vegetation of the city. In T.E. Detwyler and M.G. Marcus (eds.), *Urbanization and Environment*, 230–259. Belmont, Calif.: Duxbury Press.

DeVos, A. 1964. Range changes of mammals in the Great Lakes region. *American Midland Naturalist* **71**:210–231.

DeVries, D.P. [1655]1857. Voyages from Holland to America, A.D. 1632 to 1644. Translated by H.C. Murphy. *Collections of the New York Historical Society*, 2d ser., **3** (1):1–136.

Dewey, L.H. 1897. Migration of weeds. In *USDA Yearbook of Agriculture, 1896*, 263–286. Washington, D.C.: GPO.

Dexter, H.M. 1865. Notes accompanying text. In H.M. Dexter (ed.), *Mourt's Relation or Journal of the Plantation at Plymouth*, 306–311. Boston: John Kimball Wiggin.

Dexter, R.W. 1981. Early description of the natural environment of Ohio (1788): science or propaganda? *Environmental Review* **5**:76–78.

Dibble, A.C., C.S. Campbell, H.R. Tyler Jr. and B. Vickery. 1989. Maine's official list of endangered and threatened plants. *Rhodora* **91**:244–269.

Dick-Peddie, W.A. 1955. Presettlement forest types in Iowa. Ph.D. diss. Iowa State University.

Dicken, S.N. 1935. The Kentucky barrens. *Bulletin of the Geographical Society of Philadelphia* **43**:42–51.

Dickens, C. [1842]189? *American Notes and Pictures From Italy*. Reprint. Chicago: M.A. Donohue and Company.

Dickinson, N.R. 1980. State land: wildlife management area: for everybody. *The [New York] Conservationist* **34** (1):10–14.

Dickinson, R. 1813. *A Geographical and Statistical View of Massachusetts Proper*. Greenfield, Mass.: Deno and Phelps.

Diebold, C.H. 1941. Effect of fire and logging upon the depth of the forest floor in the Adirondack region. *Proceedings of the Soil Science Society of America* **6**:409–413.

Dietz, E.F. 1956. Phosphorus accumulation in soil of an Indian habitation site. *American Antiquity* **22**:405–409.

Dietz, M.A. 1947. A review of the estimates of the sawtimber stand in the United States, 1880–1946. *Journal of Forestry* **45**:865–874.

Diller, O.D. 1932. The vegetation of Logan County, Ohio. M.S. thesis. Ohio State University.

Diller, O.D. 1935. *The effect of woodland grazing on certain site factors in the oak–hickory type*. Station Note, no. 24. Columbus, Ohio: USDA Forest Service Central States Forest Experiment Station.

Diller, O.D. 1937. The forage cover in heavily grazed farm woods of northern Indiana. *Journal of the American Society of Agronomy* **29**:924–933.

Dineen, R. 1975. *Geology and land uses in the pine bush, Albany County, New York*. Circular, no. 47. Albany: New York State Museum and Science Service.

Dinsdale, E.M. 1963. The lumber industry of northern New York: A geographical examination of its history and technology. Ph.D. diss. Syracuse University.

Dinsdale, E.M. 1965. Spatial patterns of technological change: The lumber industry of northern New York. *Economic Geography* **41**:258–265.

Dinsmore, J.J. 1981. Iowa's avifauna: Changes in the past and prospects for the future. *Proceedings of the Iowa Academy of Science* **88**:28–37.

Dinsmore, J.J., T.H. Kent, D. Koenig, P.C. Petersen and D.M. Roosa. 1984. *Iowa Birds*. Ames: Iowa State University Press.

Dix, R.L. 1957. Sugar maple in forest succession at Washington, D.C. *Ecology* **38**:663–665.

Dix, R.L. 1959. The influence of grazing on the thin-soil prairies of Wisconsin. *Ecology* **40**:36–49.

Dobbins, R.A. 1937. Vegetation of the northern 'Virginia Military Lands' of Ohio. Ph.D. diss. Ohio State University.

Doddridge, J. [1824]1912. *Notes on the Settlement and Indian Wars of the Western Parts of Virginia and Pennsylvania from 1763 to 1783.* Pittsburgh, Pa.: John S. Ritenour and W.T. Lindsey.

Dodds, G.B. 1983. Streamflow controversy. In R.C. Davis (ed.), *Encyclopedia of American Forest and Conservation History.* Vol. 2, 625–627. New York: Macmillan Publishing Company.

Dodds, J.S., J.P. McKean, L.O. Stewart and G.F. Tigges. 1943. *Original Instructions Governing Public Land Surveys of Iowa: A Guide to Their Use in Resurveys of Public Lands.* Ames: Iowa Engineering Society.

Dodge, J.R. 1872. Statistics of fences in the United States. In *Report of the Commissioner of Agriculture for the Year 1871*, 497–512. Washington, D.C.: GPO.

Dodge, S.L. 1987. Presettlement forest of south-central Michigan. *Michigan Botanist* **26**:139–152.

Dodge, S.L. 1989. Forest transistions and buried glacial outwash within the beech–maple region of Michigan, U.S.A. *Geografiska Annaler* **71A**:137–144.

Dodge, S.L. and J.R. Harman. 1985. Woodlot composition and successional trends in south-central lower Michigan. *Michigan Botanist* **24**:43–54.

Donahue, R.L. 1935. A forest soil study of the University of Michigan biological tract. *Papers of the Michigan Academy of Science, Arts and Letters* **21**:269–279.

Donahue, W.H. 1954. Some plant communities in the anthracite region of northeastern Pennsylvania. *American Midland Naturalist* **51**:203–231.

Donselman, E.O. 1975. A chronological comparison of the vegetation of Vigo County, Indiana, presettlement (1814) versus contemporary (1974). Masters thesis. Indiana State University.

Dopp, M. 1913. Geographical influences in the development of Wisconsin. *Bulletin of the American Geographical Society* **45**:736–749.

Dore, W.G. 1961. A centennial floristic census of Prescott, Ontario. *Transactions of the Royal Canadian Institute* **33** (2):49–115.

Dorney, C.H. and J.R. Dorney. 1989. An unusual oak savanna in northeastern Wisconsin: The effect of Indian-caused fire. *American Midland Naturalist* **122**:103–113.

Dorney, J. and F. Stearns. 1980. Land use changes in southeastern Wisconsin: The landscape pattern project. *University of Wisconsin–Milwaukee Field Station Bulletin* **13**:8–14.

Dorney, J.R. 1981. The impact of native Americans on presettlement vegetation in southeastern Wisconsin. *Transactions of the Wisconsin Academy of Sciences, Arts and Letters* **69**:26–36.

Dorney, J.R. 1983. Increase A. Lapham's pioneer observations and maps of land forms and natural disturbances. *Transactions of the Wisconsin Academy of Sciences, Arts and Letters* **71**:25–30.

Douglass, W. 1760. *A Summary, Historical and Political of the First Planting, Progressive Improvements, and Present State of the British Settlements in North-America.* 2 vols.London: R. and J. Dodsley.

Dowden, A.O. 1972. Weed hunting in Manhattan. *Garden Journal* **22**:134–138.

Downs, R.B. 1987. *Images of America: Travelers from Abroad in the New World.*

Urbana: University of Illinois Press.

Drew, W.B. 1947. Floristic composition of grazed and ungrazed prairie vegetation. *Ecology* **28**:26–41.

Driver, H.E. and W.C. Massey. 1957. Comparative studies of North American Indians. *Transactions of the American Philosophical Society*, n.s., **47** (2): 165–449.

Drobney, R.D. and R.D. Sparrowe. 1977. Land use relationships and movements of greater prairie chickens in Missouri. *Transactions of the Missouri Academy of Science* **10–11**:146–160.

Drown, W. and S. Drown 1824. *Compendium of Agriculture, or the Farmer's Guide in the Most Essential Parts of Husbandry and Gardening*. Providence, R.I.: Field and Maxcy.

Druckerman, B. 1926. An ecological survey of Pennsylvania with particular reference to its limestone soils. *Bulletin of the Geographical Society of Philadelphia* **24**:135–150.

Dubos, R. 1980. *The Wooing of Earth*. New York: Charles Scribners' Sons.

Duffey, E., M.G. Morris, J. Sheail, L.K. Ward, D.A. Wells and T.C.E. Wells. 1974. *Grassland Ecology and Wildlife Management*. London: Chapman and Hall.

Dunbar, W.F. and G.S. May. 1980. *Michigan: A History of the Wolverine State*. rev. ed. Grand Rapids, Mich.: W.B. Eerdmans Publishing Company.

Dunn, C.P. 1987. Post-settlement changes in tree composition of southeastern Wisconsin forested wetlands. *Michigan Botanist* **26**:43–51.

Dunn, C.P., D.M. Sharpe, G.R. Guntenspergen, F. Stearns and Z. Yang. 1991. Methods for analyzing temporal changes in landscape pattern. In M.G. Turner and R.H. Gardner (eds.), *Quantitative Methods in Landscape Ecology: The Analysis and Interpretation of Landscape Heterogeneity*, 173–198. New York: Springer-Verlag.

Dunn, G.E. and B.I. Miller. 1960. *Atlantic Hurricanes*. Baton Rouge: Louisiana State University Press.

Dunne, T. and L.B. Leopold. 1978. *Water in Environmental Planning*. San Francisco: W.H. Freeman and Company.

Dunstable Agricultural Society. 1816. Response of Dunstable Agricultural Society to inquiries addressed to farmers. *Massachusetts Agricultural Repository and Journal* **4**:45–53.

Dunwiddie, P.W. 1989. Forest and heath: The shaping of the vegetation on Nantucket Island. *Journal of Forest History* **33**:126–133.

Dunwiddie, P.W. 1990. Postglacial vegetation history of coastal islands in southeastern New England. *National Geographic Research* **6** (2):178–195.

Dunwiddie, P.W. 1992. *Changing Landscapes: A Pictorial Field Guide to a Century of Change on Nantucket*. New Bedford, Mass.: Nantucket Conservation Foundation, the Nantucket Historical Association, and the Massachusetts Audubon Society.

Dupree, A.H. [1957]1986. *Science in the Federal Government: a History of Policies and Activities*. Baltimore: Johns Hopkins University Press.

Dwight, T. 1811. *A Statistical Account of the City of New Haven*. Vol. 1, no. 1 of *A Statistical Account of the Towns and Parishes in Connecticut*. New Haven: Connecticut Academy of Arts and Sciences.

Dwight, T. [1821–1822]1969. *Travels in New England and New York*. 4 vols. Edited by B.M. Solomon. Cambridge, Mass.: Harvard University Press.

Dzwonko, Z. and S. Loster. 1992. Species richness and seed dispersal to secondary woods in southern Poland. *Journal of Biogeography* **19**:195–204.

Earle, C. 1988. The myth of the southern soil miner: Macrohistory, agricultural innovation, and environmental change. In D. Worster (ed.), *The Ends of the*

Earth: Perspectives on Modern Environmental History, 175–210. Cambridge: Cambridge University Press.

East, W.G. 1965. *The Geography Behind History*. New York: W.W. Norton and Company.

Ebinger, J.E. 1986. Presettlement vegetation of Douglas County, Illinois. *Erigenia* **7**:15–22.

Ebinger, J.E. 1987. Presettlement vegetation of Coles County, Illinois. *Transactions of the Illinois State Academy of Science* **80**:15–24.

Edge, T.J. 1878. The forests of our state: Their value and their influence upon streams, temperature, climate and rain-fall. In *First Annual Report of the Pennsylvania Board of Agriculture*, 61–77. Harrisburg, Pa.: Lane S. Hart.

Edmundson, W.G. 1852. Prairie farming – breaking the sod. *The Cultivator* **9**:67.

Edwards, E.E. 1939. Agricultural records; their nature and value for research. *Agricultural History* **13**:1–12.

Edwards, E.E. 1948. The settlement of grasslands. In *Grass, USDA Yearbook of Agriculture, 1948*, 16–25. Washington, D.C.: GPO.

Edwards, K.J. 1979. Palynological and temporal inference in the context of prehistory, with specieal reference to the evidence from lake and peat deposits. *Journal of Archaeological Science* **6**:255–270.

Edwards, W.R. 1985. *Man, agriculture, and wildlife habitat – a perspective*. Management Notes, no. 5. Champaign: Illinois Natural History Survey.

Egerton, F.N. 1985. The history of ecology: Achievements and opportunities, part two. *Journal of the History of Biology* **18**:1–12.

Eggler, W.A. 1938. The maple–basswood forest type in Washburn County, Wisconsin. *Ecology* **19**:243–263.

Egler, F.E. 1940. Berkshire Plateau vegetation. *Ecological Monographs* **10**:145–192.

Egler, F.E. 1959. A cartographic guide to selected regional vegetation literature: where plant communities have been described. Part I. Northeastern United States. *Sarracenia* **1**:1–50.

Egnal, M. 1975. Economic development of the thirteen continental colonies, 1720 to 1775. *William and Mary Quarterly*, 3d ser., **32**:191–222.

Ehrenberg, R.E. 1975. Bibliography to resources on historical geography in the National Archives. In R.E. Ehrenberg (ed.), *Pattern and Process: Research in Historical Geography*, 315–350. Washington, D.C.: Howard University Press.

Ehrenreich, J.H. and J.M. Aikman. 1963. An ecological study of the effect of certain management practices on native prairie in Iowa. *Ecological Monographs* **33**:113–130.

Eilers, L.J. 1975. History of studies on the Iowa vascular flora. *Proceedings of the Iowa Academy of Science* **82**:59–64.

Ekirch, A.A., Jr. 1963. *Man and Nature in America*. New York: Columbia University Press.

Eliot, J. [1760]1934. *Essays upon Field-husbandry in New-England*. Edited by H.J. Carman and R.G. Tugwell. New York: Columbia University Press.

Ellarson, R.S. 1949. The vegetation of Dane County, Wisconsin in 1835. *Transactions of the Wisconsin Academy of Sciences, Arts and Letters* **39**:21–45.

Ellenberg, H. 1988. *Vegetation Ecology of Central Europe*. Translated by G.K. Strutt. 4th ed. Cambridge: Cambridge University Press.

Ellicott, J. 1795. Instructions pointing out the methods of classing the different kinds of land. In Description of lands in East Alleghany by assistants of J. Ellicott and instructions for these people. Manuscript item no. 593. Holland Land Company Papers, 1789–1869 (Municipal Archives of Amsterdam). Holland Land Company Project. State University of New York at Freedonia.

Elliott, J.C. 1953. Composition of upland second growth hardwood stands in the tension zone of Michigan as affected by soils and man. *Ecological Monographs* **23**:271–288.

Ellis, D.M. 1946. *Landlords and Farmers in the Hudson–Mohawk Region 1790–1850.* Ithaca, N.Y.: Cornell University Press.

Ellis, F. 1879. *History of Cattaraugus County, New York.* Philadelphia: L.H. Everts.

Ellsworth, L.F. 1975. *Craft to National Industry in the Nineteenth Century: A Case Study of the Transformation of the New York State Tanning Industry.* New York: Arno Press.

Ely, J. 1815. Response to inquiries of Massachusetts Society for Promoting Agriculture. *Massachusetts Agricultural Repository and Journal* **3**:55–67.

Emerson, E. (ed.) 1976. *Letters from New England: The Massachusetts Bay Colony, 1629–1638.* Amherst: University of Massachusetts Press.

Emerson, G.B. 1846. *Report on the Trees and Shrubs Growing Naturally in the Forests of Massachusetts.* Boston: Dutton and Wentworth, State Printers.

Emerson, R.W. [1836]1950. 'Nature' in *The Selected Writings of Ralph Waldo Emerson.* Edited by B. Atkinson. New York: Random House.

Emmons, D.M. 1971. Theories of increased rainfall and the timber culture act of 1873. *Forest History* **15** (3):6–14.

Engelmann, H. 1863. Remarks on the causes producing the different characters of vegetation known as prairies, flats and barrens in southern Illinois, with special reference to observations made in Perry and Jackson Counties. *American Journal of Science and Arts*, 2d ser., **36**:384–396.

Engelmann, H.A. 1865. On the fruit soils of Illinois. *Transactions of the Illinois State Agricultural Society* **5**:938–947.

Englebright, S. 1980. Long Island's secret wilderness. *The [New York] Conservationist* **34** (4):23–29.

Engstrom, D.R., E.B. Swain and J.C. Kingston. 1985. A palaeolimnological record of human disturbance from Harvey's Lake, Vermont: Geochemistry, pigments and diatoms. *Freshwater Biology* **15**:261–288.

Engstrom, D.R. and H.E. Wright Jr. 1984. Chemical stratigraphy of lake sediments as a record of environmental change. In E.Y. Haworth and J.W.G. Lund (eds.), *Lake Sediments and Environmental History*, 11–67. Leicester: Leicester University Press.

Enser, R.W. and C.A. Caljouw. 1989. Plant conservation concerns in Rhode Island – A reappraisal. *Rhodora* **91**:121–130.

Erickson, E. 1972. *Invisible Immigrants: The Adaptation of English and Scottish Immigrants in Nineteenth-century America.* Coral Gables, Fla.: University of Miami Press.

Ernst, F. 1904. Travels in Illinois in 1819. In *Transactions of the Illinois State Historical Society for the Year 1903*, 150–165.

Ernst, J.W. [1958]1979. *With Compass and Chain: Federal Land Surveyors in the Old Northwest, 1785–1816.* New York: Arno Press.

Eschner, A.R. and D.R. Satterlund. 1966. Forest protection and streamflow from an Adirondack watershed. *Water Resources Research* **2**:765–783.

Etter, A.G. 1953. Wildwood: A study in historical ecology. *Annals of the Missouri Botanical Garden* **40**:227–253.

Evans, E.B. 1971. The National Archives and Records Service and its research resources – a select bibliography. *Prologue* **3**:88–112.

Evans, G. 1852. A general view and agricultural survey of the county of Madison. *Transactions of the New York State Agricultural Society* **11**:659–777.

Evans, L. [1753]1939. A brief account of Pennsylvania. In L.H. Gipson (ed.), *Lewis*

Evans, 87–137. Philadelphia: Historical Society of Pennsylvania.

Evans, P.D. 1924. *The Holland Land Company*. Buffalo, N.Y.: Buffalo Historical Society.

Eveland, T. 1985. Of white men and wildlife. *Pennsylvania Game News* **56** (2): 20–24.

Evelyn, J. [1664]1729. *Silva: or, a Discourse of Forest-Trees*. 5th ed. London: Printed for J. Walthoe, J. Knapton, D. Midwinter, A. Bettesworth, J. Tonson. W. Innys, R. Robinson, J. Wilford, J. Osborn and T. Longman, B. Motte, A. Ward.

Ex-Settler. 1835. *Canada in the Years 1832–33, and 34, Containing Important Information and Instructions to Persons Intending to Emigrate Thither in 1835*. London: Richard Groombridge.

Eyre, F.H. and W.M. Zillgitt. 1953. *Partial cuttings in northern hardwoods of the Lake States: Twenty-year experimental results*. USDA Technical Bulletin, no. 1076. Washington, D.C.: USDA.

Faegri, K. 1988. Preface. In H.H. Birks, H.J.B. Birks, P.E. Kaland and D. Moe (eds.), *The Cultural Landscape: Past, Present and Future*, 1–4. Cambridge: Cambridge University Press.

Fahey, T.J. and W.A. Reiners. 1981. Fire in the forests of Maine and New Hampshire. *Bulletin of the Torrey Botanical Club* **108**:362–373.

Fahl, R.J. 1977. *North American Forest and Conservation History: A Bibliography*. Santa Barbara, Calif.: Clio Press. Published under contract with the Forest History Society.

Falk, J.H. 1976. Energetics of a suburban lawn ecosystem. *Ecology* **57**:141–150.

Farnham, E.W. 1846. *Life in Prairie Land*. New York: Harper and Brothers.

Farrand, W.R. 1982. *Quaternary geology of Michigan* (map). Lansing: Michigan Department of Natural Resources, Geological Survey Division.

Fassett, N.C. 1944. Vegetation of the Brule Basin, past and present. *Transactions of the Wisconsin Academy of Sciences, Arts and Letters* **36**:33–56.

Faux, W. [1823]1905. *Faux's Memorable Days in America, 1819–1820*. Reprinted in R.G. Thwaites (ed.), *Early Western Travels, 1748–1846*. Vol. 9, part 1, 33–305. Cleveland, Ohio: Arthur H. Clark Company.

Fearon, H.B. 1819. *Sketches of America, a Narrative of a Journey of Five Thousand Miles through the Eastern and Western States of America*. 3d ed. London: Longman, Hurst, Rees, Orme and Brown.

Featherstonhaugh, G.W. [1847]1962 . *A Canoe Voyage up the Minnay Soter*. 2 vols. Reprint. St. Paul: Minnesota Historical Society Press.

Federal Committee on Research Natural Areas. 1968. *A Directory of Research Natural Areas on Federal Lands of the United States of America*. Washington, D.C.: Superintendent of Documents.

Felton, O.C., P. Lathrop and W.G. Lewis. 1860. Report on the renovation of exhausted pastures. In *Seventh Annual Report of the Secretary of the Massachusetts Board of Agriculture*, 22–29. Boston: William White, State Printer.

Fenneman, N.M. 1931. Map of physical conditions of the United States. In *Physiography of Western United States*. New York: McGraw-Hill Book Company.

Fenneman, N.M. 1938. *Physiography of Eastern United States*. New York: McGraw-Hill Book Company.

Fenton, A.D. 1978a. The physical environment. In R.E. Nelson (ed.), *Illinois: Land and Life in the Prairie State*, 21–107. Dubuque, Iowa: Kendall/Hunt Publishing Company (published for the Illinois Geographical Society).

Fenton, W.N. 1978b. Northern Iroquois culture patterns. In B.G. Trigger (ed.),

Handbook of North American Indians. Vol. 15. *Northeast,* 296–321.
  Washington, D.C.: Smithsonian Institution.
Ferguson, R.H. 1958. *The timber resources of Pennsylvania.* Upper Darby, Pa.:
  Northeastern Forest Experiment Station, USDA Forest Service.
Ferguson, R.H. and N.P. Kingsley. 1972. *The timber resources of Maine.* USDA
  Forest Service Resource Bulletin, no. NE-26. Upper Darby, Pa.: Northeastern
  Forest Experiment Station.
Ferguson, R.H. and C.E. Mayer. 1970. *The timber resources of New York.* USDA
  Forest Service Resource Bulletin, no. NE-20. Broomall, Pa.: Northeastern Forest
  Experiment Station.
Fernald, M.L. 1905. Some recently introduced weeds. In *Transactions of the
  Massachusetts Horticultural Society for the Year 1905* (part 1), 11–22.
Fernald, M.L. 1950. *Gray's Manual of Botany.* 8th ed. New York: Van Nostrand.
Fernow, B.E. 1895. American lumber. In C.M. Depew (ed.), *One Hundred Years of
  American Commerce, 1795–1895.* Vol. 1, 196–203. New York: D.O. Haynes and
  Company.
Fernow, B.E. 1899. *Report upon the Forestry Investigations of the United States
  Department of Agriculture, 1877–1898.* 55th Cong., 3d sess., House Doc. 181.
Fernow, B.E. 1907. *A Brief History of Forestry in Europe and the United States and
  Other Countries.* Toronto: University of Toronto Press.
Ferris, J.E. 1980. The fire and logging history of Voyageur's National Park. M.S.F.
  thesis. Michigan Technological University.
Fessenden, T.G. 1835. *The Complete Farmer and Rural Economist.* 2d ed. Boston:
  Russell, Odiorne and Company.
Fetherston, K. 1987. Computer cartographic study of hurricane damage on the
  Harvard Forest. M.F.S. thesis. Harvard University.
Field, D.D. [1819]1892. *A Statistical Account of the County of Middlesex in
  Connecticut.* Reprint. Haddam, Conn.: J.T. Kelsey.
Finch, D.M. 1991. *Population ecology, habitat requirements, and conservation of
  neotropical migratory birds.* US Forest Service General Technical Report, no.
  RM-205. Ft. Collins, Co.: Rocky Mountain Forest and Range Experiment
  Station.
Findell, V.E., R.E. Pfeifer, A.G. Horn and C.H. Tubbs. 1960. *Michigan's forest
  resources.* USDA Forest Service Lake States Forest Experiment Station Paper,
  no. 82. St. Paul: Lake States Forest Experiment Station.
Finlayson, W.D. and R. Byrne. 1975. Investigations of Iroquoian settlement and
  subsistence patterns at Crawford Lake, Ontario: A preliminary report. *Ontario
  Archaeology* no. **25**:31–36.
Finley, J.B. [1857]1971. *Life Among the Indians or Personal Reminiscences and
  Historical Incidents Illustrative of Indian Life and Character.* Reprint. Edited by
  D.W. Clark. Freeport, N.Y.: Books For Libraries Press.
Finley, R.W. 1951. The original vegetation cover of Wisconsin. Ph.D. diss. University
  of Wisconsin.
Finley, R.W. 1976. *Original vegetation cover of Wisconsin* (map). St. Paul, Minn.: US
  Forest Service, North Central Forest Experiment Station.
Fisher, R.T. 1918. Second-growth white pine as related to the former uses of the land.
  Journal of Forestry **16**:253–254.
Fisher, R.T. 1921. *The management of the Harvard Forest 1909–19.* Harvard Forest
  Bulletin, no. 1. Petersham, Mass.: Harvard Forest.
Fisher, R.T. 1933. New England's forests: Biological factors. In J.K. Wright (ed.),
  New England's Prospect, 1933. Special Publication no. 16, 213–223. New York:
  American Geographical Society.

Fitch, H.S. and E.R. Hall. 1978. *A 20-year record of succession on reseeded fields of tallgrass prairie on the Rockefeller Experimental Tract.* Special Publication, no. 4. Lawrence: University of Kansas Publications, Museum of Natural History.

Fithian, P.V. 1934. *P.V. Fithian: Journal 1775–1776: Written on the Virginia and Pennsylvania Frontier and in the Army around New York.* Edited by R.G. Albion and L. Dodson. Princeton, N.J.: Princeton University Press.

Flagg, E. [1838]1906. *The Far West: Or a Tour Beyond the Mountains.* Reprinted in R.G. Thwaites (ed.), *Early Western Travels, 1748–1846.* Vol. 26. Cleveland, Ohio: Arthur H. Clark Company.

Flagg, W. 1872. *The Woods and By-ways of New England.* Boston: J.R. Osgood and Company.

Fleischer, H.O. 1983. Plywood and veneer industries. In R.C. Davis (ed.), *Encyclopedia of American Forest and Conservation History.* Vol. 2, 536–540. New York: Macmillan Publishing Company.

Fleischman, J. 1985. The lost forest: In search of Ohio primeval. *Ohio Magazine* **7** (10):18–27.

Fleischmann, C.L. 1849. *Der Nordamerikanische Landwirth: Ein Handbuch für Ansiedler in den Vereinigten Staaten.* Frankfurt am Main: G.F. Heyer.

Fletcher, S.W. 1950. *Pennsylvania Agriculture and Country Life 1640–1840.* Harrisburg: Pennsylvania Historical and Museum Commission.

Flinn, M.W. 1959. Timber and the advance of technology: A reconsideration. *Annals of Science* **15**:109–120.

Flint, C.L. 1854. Reclaimed lands. In *First Annual Report of the Secretary of the Massachusetts Board of Agriculture*, 66–68. Boston: Dutton and Wentworth, State Printers.

Flint, C.L. 1862. *Ninth Annual Report of the Secretary of the Massachusetts Board of Agriculture.* Boston: Wright and Potter, State Printers.

Flint, J. [1822]1904. *Letters from America.* Reprinted in R.G. Thwaites (ed.), *Early Western Travels, 1748–1846.* Vol. 9. Cleveland, Ohio: Arthur H. Clark.

Flint, R.F. 1930. *The glacial geology of Connecticut.* Bulletin, no. 47. Hartford: Connecticut Geological and Natural History Survey.

Flint, R.F. 1971. *Glacial and Quaternary Geology.* New York: John Wiley and Sons.

Flint, T. [1828]1970. *A Condensed Geography and History of the Western States of the Mississippi Valley.* 2 vols. Gainesville, Fla.: Scholars Facsimiles and Reprints.

Flora, S.P. 1973. *Tornadoes of the United States.* rev. ed. Norman: University of Oklahoma Press.

Fobes, C.B. 1948. Historic forest fires in Maine. *Economic Geography* **24**:269–273.

Fobes, C.B. 1953. Barren mountain tops in Maine and New Hampshire. *Appalachia* **19**:315–322.

Fogg, J.M., Jr. 1956. *Weeds of Lawn and Garden: A Handbook for Eastern Temperate North America.* Philadelphia: University of Pennsylvania Press.

Fogle, D.P., C. Mahan and C. Weeks. 1987. *Clues to American Gardens.* Washington, D.C.: Starrhill Press.

Foot, L. 1836. Remarks on Indian summers. *American Journal of Science and Arts* **30**:8–13.

Forbush, E.H. 1925–1929. *Birds of Massachusetts and Other New England States.* 3 vols. Norwood, Mass.: Printed for the Massachusetts Department of Agriculture by Norwood Press.

Forcier, L.K. 1975. Reproductive strategies and the co-occurrence of climax tree species. *Science* **189**:808–810.

Fordham, E.P. 1906. *Personal Narrative of Travels in Virginia, Maryland,*

Pennsylvania, Ohio, Indiana, Kentucky; and of a Residence in the Illinois Territory: 1817–1818. Edited by F.A. Ogg. Cleveland, Ohio: Arthur H. Clark.

Forester, F. 1914. Frank Forester foresaw game destruction. *Forest and Stream* **22**:83–84, 90.

Forman, B.M. 1970. Mill sawing in seventeenth-century Massachusetts. *Old Time New England* **60**:110–130.

Forman, R.T.T. and J. Baudry. 1984. Hedgerows and hedgerow networks in landscape ecology. *Environmental Management* **8**:495–510.

Forman, R.T.T. and R.E.J. Boerner. 1981. Fire frequency and the New Jersey Pine Barrens. *Bulletin of the Torrey Botanical Club* **108**:34–50.

Forman, R.T.T., A.E. Galli and C.F. Leck. 1976. Forest size and avian diversity in New Jersey woodlots with some land use implications. *Oecologia* **26**:1–8.

Forman, R.T.T. and M. Godron. 1986. *Landscape Ecology.* New York: John Wiley and Sons.

Forman, R.T.T. and E.W.B. Russell. 1983. Evaluation of historical data in ecology. *Bulletin of the Ecological Society of America* **64**:5–7.

Forsyth, J.L. 1959. *The beach ridges of northern Ohio.* Information Circular, no. 25. Columbus: Ohio Department of Natural Resources, Division of Geological Survey.

Forsyth, J.L. 1970. A geologist looks at the natural vegetation map of Ohio. *Ohio Journal of Science* **42**:220–236.

Foster, D.R. 1988a. Disturbance history, community organization and vegetation dynamics of the old-growth Pisgah Forest, south-western New Hampshire, U.S.A. *Journal of Ecology* **76**:105–134.

Foster, D.R. 1988b. Species and stand response to catastrophic wind in central New England, U.S.A. *Journal of Ecology* **76**:135–151.

Foster, J.R. and W.A. Reiners. 1983. Vegetation patterns in a virgin subalpine forest at Crawford Notch, White Mountains, New Hampshire. *Bulletin of the Torrey Botanical Club* **110**:141–153.

Foth, H.D. 1984. *Fundamentals of Soil Science.* 7th ed. New York: John Wiley and Sons.

Fowler, F.H. 1909. Abandoned farms. In L.H. Bailey (ed.), *Cyclopedia of American Agriculture.* Vol. 4, 102–106. New York: Macmillan.

Fowler, H.C. 1942. *The competitive position of dairying in southern New England.* USDA Technical Bulletin, no. 812. Washington, D.C.: GPO.

Fowler, J. 1831. *Journal of a Tour in the State of New York.* London: Whittaker, Treacher, and Arnot.

Fox, C. 1856. Michigan – historical and statistical. *Transactions of the Michigan State Agricultural Society* **7**:283–304.

Fox, W.F. 1902. *History of the lumber industry in the state of New York.* USDA Bureau of Forrestry Bulletin, no. 34. Washington, D.C.: GPO.

Franklin, B. [1744]1960. An account of the new-invented Pennsylvania fire-place. In L.W. Labaree (ed.), *The Papers of Benjamin Franklin.* Vol. 2, 419–445. New Haven, Conn.: Yale University Press.

Franklin, T.B. 1953. *British Grasslands: From the Earliest Times to the Present Day.* London: Faber and Faber.

Freemark, K. and B. Collins. 1992, Landscape ecology of birds breeding in temperate forest fragments. In J.M. Hagan III and D.W. Johnston (eds.) *Ecology and Conservation of Neotropical Migrant Landbirds,* 443–454. Washington D.C.: Smithsonian Institution Press.

Freidel, F. (ed.). 1974. *Harvard Guide to American History.* rev. ed. Cambridge, Mass.: Harvard University Press.

Frelich, L.E. and C.G. Lorimer. 1985. Current and predicted long-term effects of deer browsing in hemlock forests in Michigan, U.S.A. *Biological Conservation* **34**:99–120.

Frelich, L.E. and C.G. Lorimer. 1991. Natural disturbance regimes in hemlock–hardwood forests of the Upper Great Lakes region. *Ecological Monographs* **61**:145–164.

French, H.F. 1861. Observations on English husbandry. *Agricultural Report of the Commissioner of Patents for the Year 1860*, 140–165. Washington, D.C.: GPO.

French, J.C. 1922. Clarion River was famous rafting stream of Keystone. In J.H. Walker (ed.), *Rafting Days in Pennsylvania*, 58–82. Altoona, Pa.: Times-Tribune Company.

Fries, R.F. 1951. *Empire in Pine: The Story of Lumbering in Wisconsin, 1830–1900*. Madison: State Historical Society of Wisconsin.

Frissell, S.S., Jr. 1973. The importance of fire as a natural ecological factor in Itasca State Park, Minnesota. *Quaternary Research* **3**:397–407.

Fritts, H.C. 1976. *Tree Rings and Climate*. New York: Academic Press.

Fritzell, P.A. 1983. Changing conceptions of the Great Lakes forest: Jacques Cartier to Sigurd Olson. In S.L. Fladder (ed.), *The Great Lakes Forest: An Environmental and Social History*, 274–294. Minneapolis: University of Minnesota Press.

Frolick, A.L. 1941. Vegetation on the peat lands of Dane County, Wisconsin. *Ecological Monographs* **11**:117–140.

Frothingham, E.H. 1912. *Second-growth hardwoods in Connecticut*. USDA Forest Service Bulletin, no. 96. Washington, D.C.: GPO.

Frothingham, E.H. 1915. *The northern hardwood forest: Its composition, growth and management*. USDA Bulletin, no. 285. Washington, D.C.: USDA.

Fujita, T.T. 1981. *Proposed characterization of tornadoes and hurricanes by area and intensity*. Satellite and Meso-meteorology Research Project Research Paper, no. 91. Chicago: Department of Geophysical Sciences, University of Chicago.

Fuller, G.D. 1923. An edaphic limit to forests in the prairie region of Illinois. *Ecology* **4**:135–140.

Fuller, G.N. (ed.) 1928. *Geological Reports of Douglass Houghton: First State Geologist of Michigan 1837–1845*. Lansing: Michigan Historical Commission.

Fulling, E.H. 1956. Botanical aspects of the paper-pulp and tanning industries in the United States – an economic and historical survey. *American Journal of Botany* **43**:621–634.

Fussell, G.E. 1964. The grasses and grassland cultivation of Britain. *Journal of the British Grassland Society* **19**:212–217.

Gade, D.W. 1991. Weeds in Vermont as tokens of socioeconomic change. *Geographical Review* **81**:153–169.

Gajewski, K. 1987. Environmental history of Caribou Bog, Penobscot County, Maine. *Le Naturaliste Canadien* **114**:133–140.

Gajewski, K., A.M. Swain and G.M. Peterson. 1987. Late Holocene pollen stratigraphy in four northeastern United States lakes. *Geographie Physique et Quaternaire* **41**:377–386.

Gammon, J.R. 1977. The status of Indiana streams and fish from 1800 to 1980. *Proceedings of the Indiana Academy of Science* **86**:209–216.

Gammon, J.R. and S.D. Gerking. 1966. The fishes. In A.A. Lindsey (ed.), *Natural Features of Indiana*, 401–425. Indianapolis: Indiana Academy of Science.

Gardner, D.E. 1849. Progress of agriculture in Ohio. *The Cultivator*, n.s., **6**:28.

Garrison, J.R. 1985. Surviving strategies: In commercialization of life in rural Massachusetts, 1790–1860. Ph.D. diss. University of Pennsylvania.

Garrison, J.R. 1987. Farm dynamics and regional exchange: The Connecticut Valley beef trade, 1670–1850. *Agricultural History* **61**:11–17.

Garrison, O.E. 1881. The upper Mississippi region. In *Ninth Annual Report of the Geological and Natural History Survey of Minnesota*, 175–224. St. Peter: J.K. Moore, State Printer.

Gates, D.M., C.H.D. Clarke and J.T. Harris. 1983. Wildlife in a changing environment. In S.L. Flader (ed.), *The Great Lakes Forest: An Environmental and Social History*, 52–80. Minneapolis: University of Minnesota Press.

Gates, P.W. 1934. *The Illinois Central Railroad and Its Colonization Work*. Cambridge, Mass.: Harvard University Press.

Gates, P.W. 1960. *The Farmer's Age: Agriculture, 1815–1860*. New York: Holt, Rinehart, and Winston.

Gates, P.W. 1969. Agricultural change in New York state, 1850–1890. *New York History* **50**:115–141.

Gates, P.W. 1972. Problems of agricultural history, 1790–1840. *Agricultural History* **46**:33–58.

Gates, P.W. 1973. *Landlords and Tenants on the Prairie Frontier. Studies in American Land Policy*. Ithaca, N.Y.: Cornell University Press.

Geis, A.D. 1974. Effects of urbanization and type of urban development on bird populations. In J.H. Noyes and D.R. Progulske (eds.), *Wildlife in an Urbanizing Environment*, 97–105. Massachusetts Cooperative Extension Service Monograph, Planning and Resource Development Series, no. 28. Amherst: University of Massachusetts.

Geller, L.D. 1974. *Pilgrims in Eden: Conservation Policies at New Plymouth*. Wakefield, Mass.: Pride Publications.

Genoways, H.H. 1986. Causes for species of large animals to become threatened or endangered. In S.K. Majumdar, F.J. Brenner and A.F. Rhoads (eds.), *Endangered and Threatened Species Programs in Pennsylvania and Other States: Causes, Issues and Management*, 234–251. Easton: Pennsylvania Academy of Science.

George, W.G. 1971. Vanished and endangered birds of Illinois: A new 'black list' and 'red list'. *Illinois Audubon Society Bulletin* **158**:2–11.

Gerhard, F. 1857. *Illinois As It Is*. Chicago: Keen and Lee.

Gibbens, R.P. and H.F. Heady. 1964. *The influence of modern man on the vegetation of Yosemite Valley*. Manual, no. 36. California Agricultural Experiment Station.

Gibbons, J. 1983. The travel notes of Joseph Gibbons, 1804. Edited by J.E. Walker. *Ohio History* **92**:96–146.

Gilbert, G.E. and V.L. Riemenschneider. 1980. Vegetative structure of an essentially undisturbed beech–maple ecosystem in central Ohio. *Ohio Journal of Science* **80**:129–133.

Gillespie, G.L. 1876. Examination for a route for a canal from Lake Michigan to the Wabash River, Indiana. In *Report of the Chief of Engineers*. 44th US Congress, 2d sess., House Exec. Doc. 1, part 2 (1744), 454–463.

Gilmore, M.R. 1930. Dispersal by Indians a factor in the extension of discontinuous distribution of certain species of native plants. *Papers of the Michigan Academy of Sciences, Arts, and Letters* **13**:89–94.

Gilmore, M.R. 1931. Plant vagrants in America. *Papers of the Michigan Academy of Sciences, Arts and Letters* **15**:65–79.

Gist, C. 1898. *Colonel Christopher Gist's Journal of a Tour Through Ohio and Kentucky in 1751, with Notes and Sketch*. Edited by J.S. Johnston. Filson Club Publication no. 13, 85–185. Louisville, Ky.

Glacken, C.J. [1967]1976. *Traces on the Rhodian Shore: Nature and Culture in Western Thought from Ancient Times to the End of the Eighteenth Century.*

Berkeley: University of California Press.

Gleason, H.A. 1909. Some unsolved problems of the prairies. *Bulletin of the Torrey Botanical Club* **36**:265–271.

Gleason, H.A. 1912. An isolated prairie grove and its phytogeographical significance. *Botanical Gazette* **53**:38–49.

Gleason, H.A. 1917. A prairie near Ann Arbor, Michigan. *Rhodora* **19**:163–165.

Gleason, H.A. 1922. The vegetational history of the Middle West. *Annals of the Association of American Geographers* **12**:39–85.

Gleason, H.A. 1923. Botanical observations in northern Michigan. *Journal of the New York Botanical Garden* **24**:273–280.

Glenn-Lewin, D.C. 1980. The individualistic nature of plant community development. *Vegetatio* **43**:141–146.

Goder, H.A. 1955. A phytosociological study of *Tsuga canadensis* at the termination of its range in Wisconsin. Ph.D. thesis. University of Wisconsin.

Goder, H.A. 1957. The presettlement vegetation of Racine County, Wisconsin. *Transactions of the Wisconsin Academy of Sciences, Arts, and Letters* **45**:169–176.

Godfrey, E.K. 1882. *The Island of Nantucket: What It Was and What It Is.* Boston: Lee and Shepard.

Godin, A.J. 1977. *Wild Mammals of New England.* Baltimore: Johns Hopkins University Press.

Godwin, H. 1975. History of the natural forests of Britain: Establishment, dominance and destruction. *Philosophical Transactions of the Royal Society of London*, ser. B, **271**:47–67.

Goff, F.G. and D. West. 1975. Canopy–understory interaction effects on forest population structure. *Forest Science* **21**:98–108.

Goff, F.G. and P.H. Zedler. 1968. Structural gradient analysis of upland forests in the western Great Lakes area. *Ecological Monographs* **38**:65–86.

Goldenweiser, E.A. and J.S. Ball. 1918. *Pasture land on farms in the United States.* USDA Bulletin, no. 626. Washington, D.C.: USDA.

Golding, D.L. 1970. The effects of forests on precipitation. *Forestry Chronicle* **46**:397–402.

Goldsmith, R. 1982. Recessional moraines and ice retreat in southeastern Connecticut. In G.J. Larson and B.D. Stone (eds.), *Late Wisconsin Glaciation of New England*, 61–76. Dubuque, Iowa: Kendall-Hunt.

Goldthwait, J.W., L. Goldthwait and R.P. Goldthwait. 1951. *The Geology of New Hampshire. Part I. Surficial Geology.* Concord: New Hampshire Department of Resources and Economic Development.

Goldthwait, R.P., G.W. White and J.L. Forsyth. 1961. *Glacial map of Ohio.* USGS Miscellaneous Geological Investigations Map, no. I-316. Washington, D.C.: US Geological Survey.

Good, E.E. and C.A. Dambach. 1943. Effect of land use practices on breeding bird populations in Ohio. *Journal of Wildlife Management* **7**:291–297.

Good, N.F. 1968. A study of natural replacement of chestnut in six stands in the Highlands of New Jersey. *Bulletin of the Torrey Botanical Club* **95**:240–253.

Goodlett, J.C. 1954. *Vegetation adjacent to the border of the Wisconsin drift in Potter County, Pennsylvania.* Harvard Forest Bulletin, no. 25. Petersham, Mass.: Harvard Forest.

Goodrich, B. 1954. *Ridgefield in 1800.* Publication no. 25. The Acorn Club of Connecticut. Hartford, Conn.: Case, Lockwood and Brainard.

Goodwin, G.G. 1936. Big game animals in the northeastern United States. *Journal of Mammalogy* **17**:48–50.

Gordon, J.M. 1959. The Michigan land rush in 1836. Edited by D.H. Gordon and G.S. May. *Michigan History* **43**:1–42, 129–149, 257–293, 433–478.

Gordon, N. 1986. The Harvard Forest Models: Is that the way it really was? Paper presented at the April 26, 1986 meeting of the New England Historical Association, American Antiquarian Society, Worcester, Mass.

Gordon, R.B. 1937. The botanical survey of the Allegany State Park. In New York State Museum Handbook, no. 17, 23–88. Albany: The University of the State of New York.

Gordon, R.B. 1940. *The primeval forest types of southwestern New York*. New York State Museum Bulletin, no. 321. Albany: University of the State of New York.

Gordon, R.B. 1966. *The natural vegetation of Ohio at the time of the earliest land surveys* (map). Ohio Biological Survey. Columbus: Ohio State University.

Gordon, R.B. 1969. *The natural vegetation of Ohio in pioneer days*. Bulletin of the Ohio Biological Survey, n.s., vol. 3, no. 2. Columbus: Ohio State University.

Gordon, T.F. 1832. *A Gazetteer of the State of Pennsylvania*. Philadelphia: T. Belknap.

Gordon, T.F. 1834. *A Gazetteer of the State of New Jersey*. Philadelphia: Daniel Trenton.

Gore, J.A. and W.A. Patterson Jr. 1986. Mass of downed wood in northern hardwood forests in New Hampshire: Potential effects of forest management. *Canadian Journal of Forest Research* **16**:335–339.

Gosselink, J.G. and R.J. Baumann. 1980. Wetland inventories: Wetland loss along the United States coast. *Zeitschrift für Geomorphologie* N.F. Suppl. **34**:173–187.

Gottschalk, L.C. 1945. Effects of soil erosion on navigation in Upper Chesapeake Bay. *Geographical Review* **35**:219–238.

Gottschang, J.L. 1981. *A Guide to the Mammals of Ohio*. Columbus: Ohio State University Press.

Goudie, A. 1981. *The Human Impact: Man's Role in Environmental Change*. Cambridge, Mass.: MIT Press.

Gould, F.W. 1941. Plant indicators of original prairies. *Ecology* **22**:427–429.

Graber, R.R. and J.W. Graber. 1963. A comparative study of bird populations in Illinois, 1906–1909 and 1956–1958. *Illinois Natural History Survey Bulletin* **28**: 383–528.

Graham, F., Jr. 1978. *The Adirondack Park: A Political History*. New York: Alfred A. Knopf.

Graham, S.A. 1954. Changes in northern Michigan forests from browsing by deer. *Transactions of the North American Wildlife Conference* **19**:526–533.

Graham, S.A., R.P. Harrison and C.E. Westell Jr. 1963. *Aspens: Phoenix Trees of the Great Lakes Region*. Ann Arbor: University of Michigan Press.

Graves, H.S. 1911. The management of second-growth sprout forests. In *USDA Yearbook of Agriculture, 1910*, 157–168. Washington, D.C.: GPO.

Gray, A. 1878. Forest geography and archaeology. *American Journal of Science and Arts*, 3d ser., **16**:85–94, 183–196.

Gray, A. 1879. The pertinacity and predominance of weeds. *American Journal of Science and Arts* **118**:161–167.

Gray, A. 1884. Characteristics of the North American flora: An address to the botanists of the British Association for the Advancement of Science at Montreal. *American Journal of Science*, 3d ser., **28**:323–340.

Gray, J.C. 1831. An address delivered before the Massachusetts Society for Promoting Agriculture at the Brighton cattle show, October 20, 1850. *Massachusetts Agricultural Journal* **10**:209–222.

Gray, J.C. 1856. Remarks on New England agriculture. In *Essays: Agricultural and*

Literary, 1–73. Boston: Little Brown and Company.

Greeley, W.B. 1909. Reduction of timber supply through abandonment or clearing of forest lands. In H. Gannett (ed.), *Report of the National Conservation Commission.* 60th Congress, 2d sess., Senate Doc. 676. Vol. 2, 633–644.

Greeley, W.B. 1925. The relation of geography to timber supply. *Economic Geography* **1**:1–14.

Greeley, W.B. 1927. The part of forestry in flood control. *Forest Worker* **3** (5):6–8.

Greeley, W.B., E.H. Clapp, H.A. Smith, R. Zon, W.N. Sparhawk, W. Shepard and J. Kittredge Jr. 1923. Timber: Mine or crop? In *USDA Yearbook of Agriculture, 1922*, 83–180. Washington, D.C.: GPO.

Green, J.C. 1988. Endangered birds, introduction. In B. Coffin and L. Pfannmuller (eds.), *Minnesota's Endangered Flora and Fauna*, 253–255. Minneapolis: Published for the Department of Natural Resources, State of Minnesota, by the University of Minnesota Press.

Greene, H.C. and J.T. Curtis. 1955. *A bibliography of Wisconsin vegetation.* Publications in Botany, no. 1. Milwaukee: Milwaukee Public Museum.

Greene, J.C. 1984. *American Science in the Age of Jefferson.* Ames: Iowa State University Press.

Greenhalgh, W. 1853. Wentworth Greenhalgh's journal of a tour to the Indians of western New York. In E.B. O'Callaghan and B. Fernow (ed.), *Documents Relative to the Colonial History of the State of New York.* Vol. 3, 250–252. Albany: Weed and Parsons.

Greig, J. 1982. Past and present lime woods of Europe. *British Archaeological Reports*, international series, **146**:23–55.

Greller, A.M. 1972. Observations on the forests of northern Queens County, Long Island, from colonial times to the present. *Bulletin of the Torrey Botanical Club* **99**:202–206.

Greller, A.M. 1975. Persisting natural vegetation in northern Queens County, New York, with proposals for its conservation. *Environmental Conservation* **2**:61–69.

Greller, A.M., R.E. Calhoon and E. Iglich. 1979. The upland, oak-dominated community of Forest Park, Queens County, New York. *Bulletin of the Torrey Botanical Club* **106**:135–139.

Greven, P.J., Jr. 1970. *Four Generations: Population, Land, and Family in Colonial Andover, Massachusetts.* Ithaca, N.Y.: Cornell University Press.

Grey, G.W. and F.J. Deneke. 1978. *Urban Forestry.* New York: John Wiley and Sons.

Griffith, E.M. 1910. The intimate relation of forest cover to stream flow. In *Report of the State Forester of Wisconsin for 1909–1910*, 66–78. Madison, Wis.

Griffith, T.W. 1824. Plantation of timber. *New England Farmer* **2**:11.

Griffiths, D., Jr. 1835. *Two Years' Residence in the New Settlements of Ohio, North America: With Directions to Emigrants* London: Westley and Davis.

Grigal, D.F. and L.F. Ohmann. 1975. Classification, description and dynamics of upland plant communities within a Minnesota wilderness area. *Ecological Monographs* **45**:389–407.

Griggs, R.F. 1914. *Botanical survey of the Sugar Grove region.* Bulletin of the Ohio Biological Survey, vol. 1, no. 4. Columbus: The Ohio State Universtiy.

Grigson, C. 1982. Porridge and pannage: Pig husbandry in Neolithic England. *British Archaeological Reports*, international series, **146**:297–314.

Grim, R.E. 1982. *Historical Geography of the United States: A Guide to Information Sources.* Detroit: Gale Research Company.

Grimm, E.C. 1981. An ecological and paleoecological study of the vegetation in the Big Woods region of Minnesota. Ph.D. diss. University of Minnesota.

Grimm, E.C. 1984. Fire and other factors controlling the Big Woods vegetation of

Minnesota in the mid-nineteenth century. *Ecological Monographs* **54**:291–311.
Grimm, E.C. 1988. Data analysis and display. In B. Huntley and T. Webb III (eds.), *Vegetation History*, 43–76. Dordrecht: Kluwer Academic Publishers.
Grinnell, G.B. and C.B. Reynolds. 1894. A plank. *Forest and Stream* **42**:89 (February 3, 1894 issue).
Griscom, L. 1949. *The Birds of Concord*. Cambridge, Mass.: Harvard University Press.
Gross, R.A. 1982. Culture and cultivation: Agriculture and society in Thoreau's Concord. *American History* **69**:42–61.
Guest, B.R. and G.P. Stevens. 1967. The utilization of woodlots in Dekalb County, Illinois: A case study of forest use in an area of intensive agriculture. *Bulletin of the Illinois Geographical Society* **9** (2):46–52.
Guillet, E.C. 1963. *The Pioneer Farmer and Backwoodsman*. Vol. 1. Toronto: University of Toronto Press.
Guntenspergen, G. 1983. The minimum size for nature preserves: Evidence from southeastern Wisconsin forests. *Natural Areas Journal* **3** (4):38–46.
Gysel, L.W. 1944. The forest resources of Auglaize County, Ohio. *Ohio Journal of Science* **44**:103–122.
Haas, H. and J.C. Streibig. 1982. Changing patterns of weed distribution as a result of herbicide use and other agronomic factors. In H.M. LeBaron and J. Gressel (eds.), *Herbicide Resistance in Plants*, 57–79. New York: John Wiley and Sons.
Habakkuk, H.J. 1962. *American and British Technology in the Nineteenth Century: The Search for Labour-Saving Inventions*. Cambridge: Cambridge University Press.
Haggett, P. 1979. *Geography: A Modern Synthesis*. 3d ed. Hagerstown, Md.: Harper and Row.
Hahn, J.T. and M.H. Hansen. 1985. *Data bases for forest inventory in the North–Central Region*. USDA Forest Service General Technical Report, no. NC-101. St. Paul, Minn.: North Central Forest Experiment Station.
Hahn, W.L. 1910. An analytical study of faunal changes in Indiana. *American Midland Naturalist* **1**:145–157, 171–186.
Haines, D.A. 1977. *Where to find weather and climatic data for forest research studies and management planning*. USDA Forest Service General Technical Report, no. NC-27. St. Paul, Minn.: North Central Forest Experiment Station.
Hair, D. 1958. *Historical forestry statistics of the United States*. USDA Forest Service Statistical Bulletin, no. 228. Washington, D.C.: US Forest Service.
Hale, H.M. 1906. *Wood used for distillation in 1905*. USDA Forest Service Circular, no. 50. Washington, D.C.: USDA.
Hall, A.R. 1988. Problems of reconstructing past urban floras and vegetation. In M. Jones (ed.), *Archaeology and the Flora of the British Isles: Human Influence on the Evolution of Plant Communities*, 93–95. Oxford: Oxford University Committee for Archaeology Monograph, no. 14.
Hall, B.R. 1916. *The New Purchase or, Seven and a Half Years in the Far West*. Princeton, N.J.: Princeton University Press.
Hall, J. 1837. *Statistics of the West*. Cincinnati: J.A. James and Company.
Hall, W.L. and H. Maxwell. 1910. *Surface conditions and streamflow*. USDA Forest Service Circular, no. 176. Washington, D.C.: GPO.
Halsted, B.D. 1891. The migration of weeds. *Proceedings of the American Association for the Advancement of Science* **39**:304–312.
Hamburg, S.P. 1984. Organic matter and nitrogen accumulation during 70 years of old-field succession in central New Hampshire. Ph.D. diss. Yale University.
Hamburg, S.P. and R.L. Sanford Jr. 1986. Disturbance, *Homo sapiens*, and ecology.

Bulletin of the Ecological Society of America **62**:169–171.

Hamilton County Agricultural Society. 1830. *The Western Agriculturist, and Practical Farmer's Guide*. Cincinnati: Robinson and Fairbank.

Hamilton, L., B. Askew and A. Odell. 1980. *Forest history in New York*. New York State forest resources assessment: Technical Report, no. 1. Albany: New York State Department of Environmental Conservation.

Hammersley, G. 1957. The crown woods and their exploitation in the sixteenth and seventeenth centuries. *Bulletin of the Institute of Historical Research* **30**:136–161.

Hammersley, G. 1973. The charcoal iron industry and its fall, 1540–1750. *Economic History Review,* 2d ser., **26**:593–613.

Hammond, J.R. 1849. Farming in Missouri, etc. *The Cultivator*, n.s., **6**:302–303.

Hammond, P.C. and D.V. McCorkle. 1983. The decline and extinction of *Speyeria* populations resultling from human environmental disturbances (Nymphalidae: Argynninae). *Journal of Research on the Lepidoptera* **22**:217–224.

Hammond, S.H. 1854. *Hills, Lakes, and Forest Streams: Or, a Tramp in the Chateaugay Woods*. New York: J.C. Derby.

Hanson, P.C. 1981. The presettlement vegetation of the plain of glacial Lake Chicago in Cook County, Illinois. In R.L. Stuckey and K.J. Reese (eds.), *The Prairie Peninsula – In the 'shadow' of Transeau: Proceedings of the Sixth North American Prairie Conference*. Biological Notes no. 15, 159–164. Columbus: Ohio Biological Survey.

Harding, P.T. and F. Rose. 1986. *Pasture-woodlands in Lowland Britain: A Review of their Importance for Wildlife Conservation*. Monks Wood, Abbots Ripton: Institute of Terrestrial Ecology, Natural Environment Research Council.

Haring, H.A. 1931. *Our Catskill Mountains*. New York: G.P. Putnam's Sons.

Hariot, T. [1588]1903. *A Briefe and True Report of the New Found Land of Virginia*. Facsimile of 1st ed. New York: Dodd, Mead and Company.

Harlan, J.R. 1956. *Theory and Dynamics of Grassland Agriculture*. Princeton, N.J.: D. Van Nostrand Company.

Harlow, R.C. 1922. The breeding habits of the northern raven in Pennsylvania. *Auk* **39**:399–410.

Harlow, W.H., E.S. Harrar and F.M. White. 1979. *Textbook of Dendrology*. 6th ed. New York: McGraw-Hill Book Company.

Harman, J.R. and M.D. Nutter. 1973. Soil and forest pattern in northern lower Michigan. *East Lakes Geographer* **8**:1–12.

Harmon, K.W. and W.M. Nelson. 1973. Wildlife and soil considerations in land retirement programs. *Wildlife Society Bulletin* **1**:28–38.

Harmon, M., J.F. Franklin, F.J. Swanson, P. Sollins, S.V. Gregory, J.D. Lattin, N.H. Anderson, S.P. Cline, N.G. Aumen, J.R. Sedell, G.W. Lienkaemper, K. Cromack Jr. and K.W. Cummins. 1986. Ecology of coarse woody debris in temperate ecosystems. *Advances in Ecological Research* **15**:133–302.

Harper, R.M. 1908. Some native weeds and their probable origin. *Bulletin of the Torrey Botanical Club* **35**:347–360.

Harper, R.M. 1918a. Changes in the forest area of New England in three centuries. *Journal of Forestry* **16**:442–452.

Harper, R.M. 1918b. A sketch of the forest geography of New Jersey. *Bulletin of the Geographical Society of Philadelphia* **16** (1):107–125.

Harrington, G.T. 1909. *Grass and clover seed trade in Vermont 1907–1909*. Vermont Agricultural Experiment Station Bulletin, no. 146. Burlington: Vermont Agricultural Experiment Station.

Harrison, R.W. 1954. Public land records of the federal government. *Mississippi*

Valley Historical Review **41**:277–288.

Harrold, L.L., D.L. Brakensiek, J.L. McGuinness, C.R. Amerman and F.R. Dreibelbis. 1962. *Influence of land use and treatment on the hydrology of small watersheds at Coshocton, Ohio, 1938–57.* USDA Technical Bulletin, no. 1256. Washington, D.C.: USDA.

Harshberger, J.W. 1911. *Phytogeographic Survey of North America.* New York: Stechert and Company.

Hart, A.A. 1983. Woodworking machines. In R.C. Davis (ed.), *Encyclopedia of American Forest and Conservation History.* Vol. 2, 724–728. New York: Macmillan Publishing Company.

Hart, A.C. 1963. Spruce–fir silviculture in northern New England. *Proceedings of the Society of American Foresters,* **1963**:107–110.

Hart, J.F. 1968. Loss and abandonment of cleared farm land in the eastern United States. *Annals of the Association of American Geographers* **58**:417–440.

Hart, J.F. 1972. The Middle West. *Annals of the Association of American Geographers* **62**:258–282.

Hartesveldt, R.T. 1951. Forest-tree distribution in Jackson County, Michigan, according to original land survey records. M.S. thesis. University of Michigan.

Hartley, E.N. 1957. *Ironworks on the Saugus.* Norman: University of Oklahoma Press.

Hartman, W.A. and J.D. Black. 1931. *Economic aspects of land settlement in the cut-over region of the Great Lakes States.* USDA Circular, no. 160. Washington, D.C.: GPO.

Harvey, C.L. 1979. *Agriculture of the American Indian: a select bibliography.* Bibliographies and Literature of Agriculture, no. 4. Washington: Economics, Statistics, and Cooperatives Service, USDA.

Harvey, G. [1841]1925. *Harvey's Scenes of the Primeval Forests of America at the Four Periods of the Year.* Originally published in London by G. Harvey. Reprinted by W. Abbott in *The Magazine of History with Notes and Queries* **27** (3):138–147.

Harwood, M. 1981. Kirtland's warbler – a born loser? *Audubon* **83** (3):98–111.

Hasenclever, P. 1773. *The Remarkable Case of Peter Hasenclever, Merchant; Formerly One of the Proprietors of the Iron Works, Pot-ash Manufactory, etc. Established, and Successfully Carried on under his Direction, in the Provinces of New York, and New Jersey, in North America, till November 1776 ...* London.

Hastings, J. and R. Turner. 1965. *The Changing Mile.* Tucson: University of Arizona Press.

Hatcher, H. 1950. *A Century of Iron and Men.* Indianapolis, Ind.: The Bobbs-Merrill Company.

Havera, S.P. and F.C. Bellrose. 1984. The Illinois River: A lesson to be learned. *Wetlands* **4**:29–41.

Havercamp, J. and G.G. Whitney. 1983. The life history characteristics of three ecologically distinct groups of forbs associated with the tallgrass prairie. *American Midland Naturalist* **109**:105–119.

Hawes, A.F. 1906a. *Chestnut in Connecticut and the improvement of the woodlot.* Connecticut Agricultural Experiment Station Bulletin, no. 154. (Forestry publication no. 2). New Haven: Connecticut Agricultural Experiment Station.

Hawes, A.F. 1906b. The forests of Connecticut. *Connecticut Magazine* **10**:260–270.

Hawes, A.F. 1909. *Forest survey of Litchfield County, Connecticut.* Connecticut Agricultural Experiment Station Bulletin, no. 162 (Forestry publication no. 5). New Haven: Connecticut Agricultural Experiment Station.

Hawes, A.F. 1923. New England forests in retrospect. *Journal of Forestry*

21:209–224.

Hawes, A.F. 1933. *The present condition of Connecticut forests, A neglected resource*. Hartford: Connecticut State Forester.

Hawksworth, D.L. and D.J. Hill. 1984. *The Lichen-Forming Fungi*. London: Blackie and Son.

Hawley, R.C. 1924. Early development of white and red pine plantations. *Journal of Forestry* **22**:275–281.

Hawley, R.C. 1933. Forest fires in the Poconos. *Forest Leaves* **23**:157–159.

Hawley, R.C. and A.F. Hawes. 1912. *Forestry in New England: A Handbook of Eastern Forest Management*. 1st ed. New York: John Wiley and Sons.

Hawley, R.C. and D.M. Smith. 1954. *The Practice of Silviculture*. 6th ed. New York: John Wiley and Sons.

Hays, W.J. 1871. Notes on the range of some of the animals in America at the time of the arrival of the white men. *American Naturalist* **5**:387–392.

Hayter, E.W. 1939. Barbed wire fencing – a prairie invention. *Agricultural History* **13**:189–207.

Hazard, E.B. 1982. *The Mammals of Minnesota*. Minneapolis: The University of Minnesota Press.

Heckewelder, J. 1888. Narrative of John Heckewelder's journey to the Wabash in 1792. *Pennsylvania Magazine of History and Biography* **11**:466–475, **12**: 34–54, 165–184.

Heckewelder, J. 1958. *Thirty Thousand Miles with John Heckewelder*. Edited by P.A. Wallace. Pittsburgh: University of Pittsburgh Press.

Hedrick, U.P. 1933. *A History of Agriculture in the State of New York*. New York: J.B. Lyon for the New York State Agricultural Society.

Hedrick, U.P. 1948. *The Land of the Crooked Tree*. New York: Oxford University Press.

Heerwagen, A.J. 1971. *A selected bibliography of natural plant communities in 11 Midwestern states*. Miscellaneous Publication, no. 1205. Washington, D.C.: USDA Soil Conservation Service.

Hehr, D.W. 1970. A comparative study of the composition of the pre-settlement vegetation and the characteristic geologic substrates of the Oak Openings and surrounding area in northwestern Ohio. M.A. thesis. Bowling Green State University.

Heidenreich, C. 1971. *Huronia: A History and Geography of the Huron Indians, 1600–1650*. Toronto: McClelland and Stewart.

Heidenreich, C. 1978. Huron. In B. Trigger (ed.), *Handbook of North American Indians*. Vol. 15. *Northeast,* 368–388. Washington, D.C.: Smithsonian Institution.

Heilbron, B.C. 1931. Minnesota as seen by travellers: A New Yorker in the great West. *Minnesota History* 12:43–64.

Heinselman, M.L. 1973. Fire in the virgin forests of the Boundary Waters Canoe Area, Minnesota. *Quaternary Research* **3**:329–382.

Heinselman, M.L. 1975. *Interpretation of Francis J. Marschner's map of the original vegetation of Minnesota*. St. Paul, Minn.: US Forest Service, North Central Forest Experiment Station.

Heizer, R.F. 1955. Primitive man as an ecologic factor. *Kroeber Anthropological Society Papers* **13**:1–31.

Held, M.E. and J.E. Winstead. 1975. Basal area and climax status in mesic forest systems. *Annals of Botany* **39**:1147–1148.

Held, R.B. and M. Clawson. 1965. *Soil Conservation in Perspective*. Baltimore: Published for Resources for the Future by the Johns Hopkins Press.

Helgeson, A.C. 1962. *Farms in the Cutover: Agricultural Settlement in Northern Wisconsin*. Madison: The State Historical Society of Wisconsin for the Department of History, University of Wisconsin.

Henderson, N.R. and J.N. Long. 1984. A comparison of stand structure and fire history in two black oak woodlands in northwestern Indiana. *Botanical Gazette* **145**:222–228.

Hennepin, L. [1698]1903. *A New Discovery of a Vast Country in America*. 2 vols. Edited by R.G. Thwaites. Chicago: A.C. McClurg and Company.

Henretta, J.A. 1973. *The Evolution of American Society, 1700–1815: An Interdisciplinary Analysis*. Lexington, Mass.: D.C. Heath and Company.

Henry, J.D. and J.M.A. Swan. 1974. Reconstructing forest history from live and dead plant material – an approach to the study of forest succession in southwest New Hampshire. *Ecology* **55**:772–783.

Henry, R.D. and A.R. Scott. 1981. Time of introduction of the alien component of the spontaneous Illinois vascular flora. *American Midland Naturalist* **106**:318–324.

Hepting, G.H. 1974. Death of the American chestnut. *Journal of Forest History* **18**:61–67.

Hergert, H.L. 1983. Tannins. In R.C. Davis (ed.), *Encyclopedia of American Forest and Conservation History*. Vol. 2, 631–632. New York: Macmillan Publishing Company.

Herget, J.E. 1978. Taming the environment: The drainage district in Illinois. *Journal of the Illinois State Historical Society* **71**:107–118.

Hermelin, S.G. 1931. *Report about the Mines in the United States of America, 1783*. Translated by A. Johnson. Philadelphia: The John Morton Memorial Museum.

Herndon, G.M. 1975. Agriculture in America in the 1790s: An Englishman's view. *Agricultural History* **49**:505–516.

Herre, A.W. 1940. An early Illinois prairie. *American Botanist* **46**:39–44.

Herrick, J.A. 1974. *The natural areas project [of Ohio], a summary of data to date*. Information Circular, no. 1. Columbus: Ohio Biological Survey.

Hett, J.M. and O.L. Loucks. 1968. Application of life-table analyses to tree seedlings in Quetico Provincial Park, Ontario. *Forestry Chronicle* **44**:29–32.

Heuser, C.J. 1949. History of an estuarine bog at Secaucus, New Jersey. *Bulletin of the Torrey Botanical Club* **70**:385–406.

Hewes, L. 1950. Some features of early woodland and prairie settlement in a central Iowa county. *Annals of the Association of American Geographers* **40**:40–57.

Hewes, L. 1951. The northern wet prairie of the United States: Nature, sources of information, and extent. *Annals of the Association of American Geographers* **41**:307–323.

Hewes, L. 1953. Drained land in the United States in the light of the Drainage Census. *Professional Geographer* **5** (6):6–12.

Hewes, L. and P.E. Frandson. 1952. Occupying the wet prairie: The role of artificial drainage in Story County, Iowa. *Annals of the Association of American Geographers* **42**:24–50.

Hewes, L. and C.L. Jung. 1981. Early fencing on the Middle Western prairie. *Annals of the Association of American Geographers* **71**:177–201.

Hewlett, J.D. and A.R. Hibbert. 1967. Factors affecting the response of small watersheds to precipitation in humid areas. In W.E. Sopper and H.W. Lull (eds.), *Forest Hydrology*, 275–290. New York: Pergamon Press.

Hewlett, J.D. and W.L. Nutter. 1969. *An Outline of Forest Hydrology*. Athens: University of Georgia Press.

Hickerson, H. 1965. The Virginia deer and intertribal buffer zones in the Upper Mississippi Valley. In A. Leeds and A.P. Vayda (eds.), *Man, Culture, and*

Animals: The Role of Animals in Human Ecological Adjustments. Publication no. 78, 43–65. Washington, D.C.: American Association for the Advancement of Science.

Hicks, L.E. 1933. The breeding birds of Ashtabula County, Ohio. *Wilson Bulletin* **45**:168–195.

Hicks, L.E. 1935. Small birds are not decreasing! *Bird-Lore* **37**:303–309.

Hicock, H.W. 1974. The making of charcoal: Man's oldest chemical industry. *Connecticut Woodlands* **39** (2):11–15.

Higgeson, F.H. [1630]1806. New England's plantation. *Massachusetts Historical Society Collections,* 1st ser., **1**:117–124.

Hightshoe, G.L. 1984. Computer assisted program for forest preservation/ conservation/restoration: Upper Midwest region. *Landscape Journal* **3**:45–60.

Hildreth, S.P. 1825. Notes on certain parts of the state of Ohio. *American Journal of Science and Arts* **10**:152–162, 319–331.

Hildreth, S.P. 1843. Early emigration, or, the journal of some emigrant families 'across the mountains,' from New England to Muskingum, in 1788. *American Pioneer* **2**:112–134.

Hildreth, S.P. 1848. *Pioneer History: Being an Account of the First Examinations of the Ohio Valley, and the Early Settlement of the Northwest Territory.* Cincinnati: H.W. Derby and Company.

Hilgard, E.W. 1914. *Soils: Their Formation, Properties, Composition, and Relations to Climate and Plant Growth in the Humid and Arid Regions.* New York: Macmillan Company.

Hilgard, E.W. 1915. Botanical features of the prairies of Illinois in ante-railroad days. Manuscript. Hilgard Family Papers, Illinois Historical Survey, University of Illinois at Urbana-Champaign.

Hill, D.B. 1985. Forest fragmentation and its implications in central New York. *Forest Ecology and Management* **12**:113–128.

Hill, E.J. 1895. Notes on western New York woodlands. *Garden and Forest* **8**:342–343, 382–383.

Hill, I. 1840. Address delivered before the Lyceum at Candia, N.H., February 19, and the Lyceum at Hill, N.H., March 2, 1840. *Farmer's Monthly Visitor* **2**:34–39.

Hill, J.M. 1842. Worcester County, Massachusetts. *Farmer's Monthly Visitor* **4**:49.

Hirt, R.R. 1956. Fifty years of white pine blister rust in the Northeast. *Journal of Forestry* **54**:435–438.

Hitchcock, C.H. 1874. Remarks upon the distribution of animals and plants. In C.H. Hitchcock (ed.), *The Geology of New Hampshire. Part I. Physical Geography,* 559–589. Concord, N.H.: E.A. Jenks, State Printer.

Hix, D.M. and B.V. Barnes. 1984. Effects of clear-cutting on the vegetation and soil of an eastern hemlock dominated ecosystem, western Upper Michigan. *Canadian Journal of Forest Research* **14**:914–923.

Hobbs, E. 1988. Using ordination to analyze the composition and structure of urban forest islands. *Forest Ecology and Management* **23**:139–158.

Hobbs, H.C. and J.E. Goebel. 1982. *Geologic map of Minnesota. Quaternary geology.* Map S-1. St. Paul: University of Minnesota.

Hochschild, H.K. 1962. *Lumberjacks and Rivermen in the Central Adirondacks 1850–1950.* Blue Mountain Lake, N.Y.: Adirondack Museum.

Hodgdon, A.R. 1973. Endangered plants of New Hampshire. *Forest Notes* no. 173 (spring 1973):2–6.

Hoehne, L.M. 1981. The groundlayer vegetation of forest islands in an urban–suburban matrix. In R.L. Burgess and D.M. Sharpe (eds.), *Forest Island Dynamics in Man-Dominated Landscapes,* 41–54. New York: Springer-Verlag.

Hoffman, C.F. [1835]1966. *A Winter in the West by a New Yorker.* March of America Facsimile series no. 75. 2 vols. Ann Arbor, Mich.: University Microfilms.

Hoffman, R.M. and D. Sample. 1988. Birds of wet-mesic and wet prairies in Wisconsin. *Passenger Pigeon* **50**:143–152.

Hoffmann, C.O. and J.L. Gottschang. 1977. Numbers, distribution, and movements of a raccoon population in a suburban residential community. *Journal of Mammalogy* **58**:623–636.

Hoffmeister, D.F. 1989. *Mammals of Illinois.* Urbana: University of Illinois Press.

Hoglund, A.W. 1962. Forest conservation and stove inventors – 1789–1850. *Forest History* **5** (4):2–8.

Hoglund, A.W. 1983. Firewood. In R.C. Davis (ed.), *Encyclopedia of American Forest and Conservation History.* Vol. 1, 182–185. New York: Macmillan Publishing Company.

Holditch, R. 1818. *The Emigrant's Guide to the United States of America.* London: W. Hone.

Hole, F.D. 1975. Some relationships between forest vegetation and podzol B horizons in soils of Menominee tribal lands, Wisconsin, U.S.A. *Soviet Soil Science* **7**:714–723.

Holmes, R.T. and T.W. Sherry. 1988 Assessing population trends of New Hampshire forest birds: Local vs. regional patterns. *Auk* **105**:756–768.

Holmes, V.R., T.T. Cable and V. Brack Jr. 1986. Avifauna as indicators of habitat quality in some wetlands of northern Indiana. *Proceedings of the Indiana Academy of Science* **95**:523–528.

Holyoke, E.A. 1793. An estimate of the excess of heat and cold of the American atmosphere. *Memoirs of the American Academy of Arts and Sciences* **2** (part 1):65–92.

Homans, G.C. [1941]1975. *English Villagers of the Thirteenth Century.* New York: W.W. Norton and Co.

Hooke, J.M. and R.J.P. Kain. 1982. *Historical Change in the Physical Environment.* London: Butterworth Scientific.

Horwitz, E.L. 1978. *Our nation's wetlands: An interagency task force report.* Coordinated by the Council on Environmental Quality. Washington, D.C.: GPO.

Hoskins, W.G. 1968. History of common land and common rights. *Report of the Royal Commission on Common Land, 1955–58,* Cmnd. 462, Appendix II, 149–166. London: HMSO.

Hosmer, R.S. and E.S. Bruce. 1901. *A forest working plan for township 40, Totten and Crossfield Purchase, Hamilton County, New York State Forest Preserve.* USDA Division of Forestry Bulletin, no. 30. Washington, D.C.: GPO.

Hotchkiss, G.W. 1898. *History of the Lumber and Forest Industry of the Northwest.* Chicago: George W. Hotchkiss and Company.

Hough, A.F. 1936. A climax forest community on East Tionesta Creek in northwestern Pennsylvania. *Ecology* **17**:9–28.

Hough, A.F. 1955. The long-lasting effects of forest fires on the Allegheny Plateau. *Pennsylvania Forests* **45**:36.

Hough, A.F. and R.D. Forbes. 1943. The ecology and silvics of forests in the High Plateaus of Pennsylvania. *Ecological Monographs* **13**:299–320.

Hough, F.B. 1857. *Census of the State of New York for 1855.* Albany, N.Y.: Charles Van Benthuysen.

Hough, F.B. 1878. *Report upon Forestry.* Vol. 1. Washington, D.C.: GPO.

Hough, F.B. 1882. *Report on Forestry.* Vol. 3. Washington, D.C.: GPO.

Hough, F.B. 1884. The decrease of woodlands in Ohio. In N.H. Egleston (ed.), *Report on Forestry.* Vol. 4, 174–180. Washington, D.C.: GPO.

Houghton, D. 1958. Journal, letters, and reports of Dr. Douglass Houghton. In P.P. Mason (ed.), *Schoolcraft's Expedition to Lake Itasca: The Discovery of the Source of the Mississippi*, 242-305. East Lansing: Michigan State University Press.

Houghton, G.C. 1902. Leather, tanned, curried, and finished. *Twelfth Census of the United States*. Vol. 9. *Manufactures*. Part III. *Special Reports on Selected Industries*, 701–738. Washington, D.C.: United States Census Office.

House, H.D. 1941–1942. *Bibliography of the botany of New York State, 1751–1940. Parts 1 and 2*. New York State Museum Bulletins, no. 328–329. Albany: University of the State of New York.

Houston, D.R. 1976. Beech bark disease: The aftermath forests are structured for a new outbreak. *Journal of Forestry* **73**:660–663.

Howard, R.J. and J.S. Larson. 1985. A stream habitat classification system for beaver. *Journal of Wildlife Management* **49**:19–25.

Howe, H. 1848. *Historical Collections of Ohio*. Cincinnati: Bradley and Anthony.

Howe, H. 1891. *Historical Collections of Ohio*. 3 vols. Columbus, Ohio: Henry Howe and Son.

Howe, H. 1908. *Historical Collections of Ohio*. 2 vols. Cincinnati: C.J. Krehbiel and Company.

Howe, K.M. 1974. Tornado path sizes. *Journal of Applied Meteorology* **13**:343–347.

Howell, D.L. and C.L. Kucera. 1956. Composition of presettlement forests in three counties of Missouri. *Bulletin of the Torrey Botanical Club* **83**:207–217.

Hoy, P.R. 1885. Man's influence on the avifauna of southeastern Wisconsin. *Proceedings of the Natural History Society of Wisconsin* (March 1885):4–9.

Hubach, R.R. 1961. *Early Midwestern Travel Narratives: An Annotated Bibliography, 1634–1850*. Detroit: Wayne State University Press.

Hubbard, B. 1847a. Michigan as an agricultural state. No. II. *The Cultivator*, n.s., **4**:270.

Hubbard, B. 1847b. Michigan as an agricultural state. No. III. *The Cultivator*, n.s., **4**:300–301.

Hubbard, B. 1855. Address delivered before the Michigan State Agricultural Society at its sixth annual fair, held at Detroit, September 1854. *Transactions of the Michigan State Agricultural Society* **6**:309–336.

Hubbard, B. 1881. A Michigan geological expedition in 1837. *Michigan Pioneer and Historical Collections* **3**:189–201.

Hubbard, B. 1887. *Memorial of a Half-century* . New York: G.P. Putnam's Sons.

Hubbard, B. 1928. Report of B. Hubbard, Assistant Geologist, Detroit, January 12, 1840. In G.N. Fuller (ed.), *Geological Reports of Douglass Houghton: First State Geologist of Michigan, 1837–1845*, 439–473. Lansing: The Michigan Historical Commission.

Huden, J.C. 1962. *Indian place names of New England*. Contribution from the Museum of the American Indian. HEYE Foundation. Vol. 18. New York: HEYE Foundation.

Hudgins, B. 1943. The South Bass Island community (Put-in-Bay). *Economic Geography* **19**:16–36.

Hudgins, B. 1961. *Michigan: Geographic Backgrounds in the Development of the Commonwealth*. 4th ed. Ann Arbor, Mich.: Edwards Brothers.

Hudson, N. 1981. *Soil Conservation*. 2d ed. Ithaca, N.Y.: Cornell University Press.

Huey, P.R. 1975. History of the pine bush from 1624 to 1815, Albany County, New York. In R. Dineen (ed.), *Geology and land uses in the Pine Bush, Albany County, New York*. Circular 47, 7–8. Albany: New York State Museum and Science Service.

Hughes, H.D. and M.E. Heath. 1946. Forage crops that feed livestock and save the soil. In *A Century of Farming in Iowa, 1846–1946*, 54–65. Ames: The Iowa State College Press.

Hughes, J.D. 1977. Forest Indians: The holy occupation. *Environmental Review* **2**:2–13.

Hughes, J.D. 1983. *American Indian Ecology*. El Paso: Texas Western Press.

Humboldt, A., von. 1819. *Personal Narrative of Travels to the Equinoctial Regions of the New Continent…1799–1804*. Translated by H. M. Williams. 7 vols. London: Longman, Hurst, Rees, Orme and Brown.

Hunt, C.B. 1974. *Natural Regions of the United States and Canada*. San Francisco: W.H. Freeman and Company.

Hunter, L.C. [1949]1969. *Steamboats on the Western Rivers: An Economic and Technological History*. Reprint. New York: Octagon Books.

Hurley, R.J. and E.C. Franks. 1976. Changes in the breeding ranges of two grassland birds. *Auk* **93**:108–115.

Hurt, R.D. 1990. Northern agriculture after the Civil War, 1865–1900. In L. Ferleger (ed.), *Agriculture and National Development: Views on the Nineteenth Century*, 53–74. Ames: Iowa State University Press.

Hushen, T.W., R.E. Kapp, R.D. Bogue and J.T. Worthington. 1966. Presettlement forest patterns in Montcalm County, Michigan. *Michigan Botanist* **5**:192–211.

Hutchins, T. 1778. *A Topographical Description of Virginia, Pennsylvania, Maryland, and North Carolina*. London: Printed for author and sold by J. Almon.

Hutchins, T. 1878. Western Pennsylvania in 1760. *Pennsylvania Magazine of History and Biography* **2**:149–153.

Hutchinson, T. 1760. *The History of the Colony of Massachusetts Bay*. 2d ed. London: M. Richardson.

Hutchison, M. 1988. A guide to understanding, interpreting, and using the public land survey field notes in Illinois. *Natural Areas Journal* **8**:245–255.

Huth, H. [1957]1972. *Nature and the American: Three Centuries of Changing Attitudes*. Lincoln: University of Nebraska Press.

Hutslar, D.A. 1971. The log architecture of Ohio. *Ohio History* **80**:171–271.

Illick, J.S. 1923. *The forest situation in Pennsylvania*. Bulletin, no. 30. Harrisburg: Pennsylvania Department of Forestry.

Imlay, G. 1797. *A Topographical Description of the Western Territory of North America*. 3d ed. London: J. Debrett.

Imlay, G. [1797]1849. The Genesee Country (from Imlay's Topographical Description of the Western Territory of North America). In B. O'Callaghan (ed.), *Documentary History of New York*. Vol. 2, 1111–1125. Albany, N.Y.: Weed and Parsons.

Ineson, F.A. and M.J. Ferree. 1948. *The anthracite forest region – a problem area*. USDA Miscellaneous Publication, no. 648. Washington, D.C.: USDA.

Innes, S. 1983. *Labor in a New Land: Economy and Society in Seventeenth-Century Springfield*. Princeton, N.J.: Princeton University Press.

Ireland, L.C. 1982. *Wildlands and Woodlots: The Story of New England's Forests*. Hanover, N.H.: University Press of New England.

Iverson, L.R. 1988. Land-use changes in Illinois, USA: The influence of landscape attributes on current and historic land-use. *Landscape Ecology* **2**:45–61.

Iverson, L.R. and P.G. Risser. 1987. Analyzing long-term changes in vegetation with geographic information system and remote sensing data. *Advances in Space Research* **7**:183–194.

Ives, L.J., Jr. 1947. The natural vegetation of Lorain County, Ohio. M.A. thesis. Oberlin College.

Ives, R.L. 1942. The beaver-meadow complex. *Journal of Geomorphology* 5:191–203.

Jack, E. and R. Conners. 1883. The white pine. *American Journal of Forestry* 1:276–280.

Jackson, J.B. 1972. *American Space: The Centennial Years 1865–1876.* New York: W.W. Norton and Company.

Jackson, J.B. 1984. *Discovering the Vernacular Landscape.* New Haven, Conn.: Yale University Press.

Jackson, M.T. and P.R. Allen. 1969. Detailed studies of old-growth forests in Versailles State Park, Indiana. *Proceedings of the Indiana Academy of Science* 78:210–230.

Jackson, S.T. 1990. Pollen source area and representation in small lakes of the northeastern United States. *Review of Palaeobotany and Palynology* 63:53–76.

Jacobs, W. 1978. The great despoilation: Environmental themes in American frontier history. *Pacific Historical Review* 47:1–26.

Jacobs, W. 1980. Indians as ecologists and other environmental themes in American frontier history. In C. Vecsey and R.W. Venables (eds.), *American Indian Environments: Ecological Issues in Native American History*, 46–64. Syracuse, N.Y.: Syracuse University Press.

Jacobson, G.L., Jr. and R.H.W. Bradshaw. 1981. The selection of sites for paleovegetational studies. *Quaternary Research* 16:80–96.

Jacobson, G.L., Jr. and E.C. Grimm. 1986. A numerical analysis of Holocene forest and prairie vegetation in central Minnesota. *Ecology* 67:958–966.

Jacobson, G.L., Jr., T. Webb III and E.C. Grimm. 1987. Patterns and rates of vegetation change during the deglaciation of eastern North America. In W.F. Ruddiman and H.E. Wright Jr. (eds.), *North America and Adjacent Oceans during the Last Deglaciation.* Vol. K-3 of the *Geology of North America*, 277–288. Boulder, Colorado: Geological Society of North America.

Jacobson, H.A., J.B. Petersen and D.E. Putnam. 1988. Evidence of pre-Columbian *Brassica* in the northeastern United States. *Rhodora* 90:355–362.

Jacquart, E.M., T.V. Armentano and A.L. Spingarn. 1992. Spatial and temporal tree responses to water stress in an old-growth deciduous forest. *American Midland Naturalist* 127:158–171.

Jager, J. and R.G. Barry. 1990. Climate. In B.L. Turner II, W.C. Clark, R.W. Kates, J.F. Richards, J.T. Matthews and W.B. Meyer (eds.), *The Earth as Transformed by Human Action: Changes in the Biosphere over the Past 300 Years*, 335–351. Cambridge: Cambridge University Press.

Jahns, R.H. and M.E. Willard. 1942. Late Pleistocene and recent deposits in the Connecticut Valley, Massachusetts. *American Journal of Science* 240:161–287.

Jakle, J.A. 1967. Salt and the initial settlement of the Ohio Valley. Ph.D. diss. Indiana University.

Jakle, J.A. 1977. *Images of the Ohio Valley: A Historical Geography of Travel, 1740 to 1860.* New York: Oxford University Press.

Jakle, J.A. 1980. *Past landscapes: A bibliography for historic preservationists.* rev. ed. Monticello, Ill.: Vance Bibliographies.

James, H.F. 1928. The agricultural industry of southeastern Pennsylvania. VI. Historical introduction. *Bulletin of the Geographical Society of Philadelphia* 26:208–229.

James, N.D.G. 1981. *A History of English Forestry.* Oxford: Basil Blackwell.

Janke, R.A., D. McKaig and R. Raymond. 1978. Comparison of presettlement and modern upland boreal forests on Isle Royale National Park. *Forest Science* 24:115–121.

Jarchow, M.E. 1949. *The Earth Brought Forth: A History of Minnesota Agriculture to 1885*. St. Paul: Minnesota Historical Society.

Jarvis, P.J. 1979. The ecology of plant and animal introduction. *Progress in Physical Geography* **3**:185–214.

Jedry, C.M. 1979. *The World of John Cleaveland: Family and Community in Eighteenth-century New England*. New York: W.W. Norton and Company.

Jefferson, T. 1787. *Notes on the State of Virginia*. London: Stockdale.

Jenkins, M.T. 1941. Influence of climate and weather on growth of corn. In *Climate and Man, USDA Yearbook of Agriculture 1941*, 308–320. Washington, D.C.: GPO.

Jennings, F. 1975. *The Invasion of America: Indians, Colonialism, and the Cant of Conquest*. Chapel Hill: University of North Carolina Press.

Jennings, F. 1978. Susquehannock. In B.G. Trigger (ed.), *Handbook of North American Indians*. Vol. 15. *Northeast*, 362–367. Washington, D.C.: Smithsonian Institution.

Jennings, O. 1958. Comments on Pennsylvania's primeval forests. Cited on page 67 in *Penn's Woods West* by E.L. Peterson. Pittsburgh: University of Pittsburgh Press.

Jenny, H. 1941. *Factors of Soil Formation: A System of Quantitative Pedology*. New York: McGraw-Hill Book Company.

Jensen, V.S. 1943. Suggestions for the management of northern hardwood stands in the Northeast. *Journal of Forestry* **41**:180–185.

Jewell, C.A. 1976. The impact of America on English agriculture. *Agricultural History* **50**:125–136.

Jewett, A.S. 1889. *Town Records of Manchester [Massachusetts]*. Salem, Mass.: Salem Press.

Johnson, C.B. 1819. *Letters from the British Settlement in Pennsylvania*. Philadelphia: H. Hall.

Johnson, C.D. and D.B. King. 1976. *Wetland use in Wisconsin: historical perspective and present picture*. Madison: Division of Environmental Standards, Water Quality Planning Section, Wisconsin Department of Natural Resources.

Johnson, D.R. 1969. Returns of the American Fur Company, 1835–1839. *Journal of Mammalogy* **50**:836–839.

Johnson, E. [1654]1910. *Johnson's Wonder Working Providence, 1628–1651*. Edited by J.F. Jameson. New York: Charles Scribner's Sons.

Johnson, F.L. and D.T. Bell. 1975. Size-class structure of three streamside forests. *American Journal of Botany* **62**:81–85.

Johnson, F.L. and P.G. Risser. 1975. A quantitative comparison between an oak forest and an oak savannah in central Oklahoma. *Southwestern Naturalist* **20**:75–84.

Johnson, H.B. 1976. *Order Upon the Land: The U.S. Rectangular Land Survey and the Upper Mississippi Country*. New York: Oxford University Press.

Johnson, N.B. 1952. The American Indian as conservationist. *Chronicles of Oklahoma* **30**:333–340.

Johnson, S. 1805. *A Dictionary of the English Language*. Philadelphia: Jacob Johnson and Company.

Johnston, J.F.W. 1851. *Notes on North America: Agricultural, Economical, and Social*. 2 vols. Edinburgh: W. Blackwood and Sons.

Johnston, V.R. 1947. Breeding birds of the forest edge in Illinois. *Condor* **49**:45–53.

Jones, A.D. 1838. *Illinois and the West*. Boston: Weeks, Jordan and Company.

Jones, B. 1935. Was Nantucket ever forested? *Proceedings of the Nantucket Historical Association* **41**:19–26.

Jones, C.L. and R.D. Kapp. 1972. Relationship of Bay County, Michigan presettlement forest patterns to Indian cultures. *Michigan Academician* **5**:17–28.

Jones, E.L. 1974. Creative disruptions in American agriculture. *Agricultural History* **48**:510–528.

Jones, R.L. 1983. *History of Agriculture in Ohio to 1880*. Kent, Ohio: Kent State University Press.

Jordan, T.G. 1964. Between the forest and the prairie. *Agricultural History* **38**:205–216.

Josselyn, J. [1672]1860. *New England's Rarities Discovered*. Edited by E. Tuckerman. Reprinted in *Transactions and Collections of the American Antiquarian Society* **4**:105–238.

Josselyn, J. [1675] 1833. *An Account of Two Voyages to New England*. Reprinted in *Massachusetts Historical Society Collections*, 3d ser., **3**:211–354.

Judd, S. 1857. Notes from Maine. *New England Farmer* **9**:395.

Judd, S. 1905. *History of Hadley Including the Early History of Hatfield, South Hadley, Amherst and Granby*. 2d ed. Springfield, Mass.: H.R. Huntting and Company.

Kaatz, M.R. 1955. The Black Swamp: A study in historical geography. *Annals of the Association of American Geographers* **45**:1–35.

Kalm, P. [1772]1972. *Travels into North America*. Translated by J.R. Forster. Barre, Mass.: The Imprint Society.

Kaplan, L. 1973. Ethnobotany of the Upper Creek archeological site, southern Illinois. Abstract. *American Journal of Botany* (supplement) **60** (4):39.

Karnosky, D.F. 1979. Dutch elm disease: A review of the history, environmental implications, control, and research needs. *Environmental Conservation* **6**:311–322.

Karr, J.R., L.A. Toth and D.R. Dudley. 1985. Fish communities of Midwestern rivers: A history of degradation. *Bioscience* **35**:90–95.

Karr, R.D. 1987. The transformation of agriculture in Brookline, 1770–1885. *Historical Journal of Massachusetts* **15**:33–49.

Kauffman, H.J. 1972. *American Axes: A Survey of their Development and their Makers*. Brattleboro, Vt.: Stephen Greene Press Publishing.

Kawashima, Y. 1992. Forest conservation policy in early New England. *Historical Journal of Massachusetts* **20** (1):1–15.

Kawashima, Y. and R. Tone. 1983. Environmental policy in early America: A survey of colonial statutes. *Journal of Forest History* **27**:168–179.

Kay, J. 1979. Wisconsin Indian hunting patterns, 1634–1836. *Annals of the Association of American Geographers* **69**:402–418.

Kay, J. 1985. Preconditions of natural resource conservation. *Agricultural History* **59**:124–135.

Kedzie, R.C. 1867. The influence of forest trees on agriculture. In *Sixth Annual Report of the Secretary of the State Board of Agriculture of the State of Michigan*, 465–483. Lansing, Mich.: J.A. Kerr and Company.

Kedzie, R.C., J.J. Woodman and D.H. Fellows. 1866. Report of the committee on the injurious destruction of forest trees. In *Fifth Annual Report of the Secretary of the State Board of Agriculture of the State of Michigan*, Appendix, 1–31. Lansing, Mich.: J.A. Kerr and Company.

Keeler, V.D. 1933. An economic history of the Jackson County iron industry. *Ohio Archaeological and Historical Society Publications* **42**:132–238.

Keith, J.H. 1983. Presettlement barrens of Harrison and Washington Counties, Indiana. In C.L. Kucera (ed.), *Proceedings of the Seventh North American Prairie Conference*, 17–25. Springfield: Southwest Missouri State University.

Keller, E.A. and F.J. Swanson. 1979. Effect of large organic material on channel form and fluvial processes. *Earth Surface Processes* **4**:361–380.

Kellog, C.E. 1941. Climate and soil. In *Climate and Man, Yearbook of Agriculture, 1941*, 265–291. Washington, D.C.: GPO.

Kellog, R.S. 1906. *The lumber cut of the United States in 1905*. Circular, no. 52. Washington, D.C.: USDA Forest Service.

Kellog, R.S. 1909. *The timber supply of the United States*. Ciruclar, no. 166. Washington, D.C.: USDA Forest Service.

Kelly, D.L., J.T. Schaefer, R.P. McNulty and C.A. Dowswell III. 1978. An augmented tornado climatology. *Monthly Weather Review* **106**:1172–1183.

Kelly, K. 1970. The evaluation of land for wheat cultivation in early nineteenth century Ontario. *Ontario History* **62**:57–64.

Kelly, K. 1971. Wheat farming in Simcoe County in the mid-nineteenth century. *Canadian Geographer* **15**:95–111.

Kelly, K. 1974a. Practical knowledge of physical geography in southern Ontario during the nineteenth century. In A. Falconer, B.D. Fahey and R.D. Thompson (eds.), *Physical Geography: The Canadian Context*, 10–18. Toronto: McGraw-Hill Ryerson.

Kelly, K. 1974b. Damaged and efficient landscapes in rural and southern Ontario 1880–1900. *Ontario History* **66**:1–14.

Kelly, K. 1975a. The impact of nineteenth century agricultural settlement on the land. In J.D. Wood (ed.), *Perspectives on Landscape and Settlement in Nineteenth Century Ontario*, 64–77. Toronto: McClelland and Stewart.

Kelly, K. 1975b. The artificial drainage of land in nineteenth-century southern Ontario. *Canadian Geographer* **19**:279–298.

Kelsey, D.P. 1968. Farm crops, 1790–1840. Unpublished research report. Sturbridge, Mass.: Old Sturbridge Village.

Kelty, M.J. 1984. The development and productivity of hemlock–hardwood forests in southern New England. Ph.D. diss. Yale University.

Kelty, M.J. 1986. Development patterns in two hemlock–hardwood stands in southern New England. *Canadian Journal of Forest Research* **16**:885–891.

Kendeigh, S.C. 1946. Breeding birds of the beech–maple–hemlock community. *Ecology* **27**:226–245.

Kennedy, J.C.G. 1864. Introduction – Agriculture in the United States. In *Agriculture of the U.S. in 1860: The 8th Census*, viii–x. Washington, D.C.: GPO.

Kennicott, R. 1857. The quadrupeds of Illinois. In *Agricultural Report of the Commissioner of Patents for the Year 1856*, 52–110. Washington, D.C.: A.D.P. Nicholson.

Kenoyer, L.A. 1930. Ecological notes on Kalamazoo County, Michigan based on the original land survey. *Papers of the Michigan Academy of Science, Arts, and Letters* **11**:211–217.

Kerr, K. and J. White. 1981. A volunteer-supported effort to find and preserve prairie and savanna remnants in Illinois cemeteries. In R.L. Stuckey and K.J. Reese (eds.), *The Prairie Peninsula – In the 'Shadow' of Transeau: Proceedings of the Sixth North American Prairie Conference*. Biological Notes no. 15, 181–183. Columbus: Ohio Biological Survey.

Kerridge, E. 1968. *The Agricultural Revolution*. New York: Augustus M. Kelley.

Kerridge, E. 1973. *The Farmers of Old England*. Totowa, N.J.: Rowan and Littlefield.

Ketchledge, E.H. 1965. Changes in the forests of New York. *The [New York] Conservationist* **19** (2):29–34.

Kibbe, A.L. 1952. *A Botanical Study and Survey of a Typical Midwestern County (Hancock County, Illinois)*. Carthage, Ill.: Published by the author.

Kiefer, W.E. 1969. *Rush County, Indiana: A study in rural settlement geography*. Geographic Monograph Series, Vol. 2. Bloomington: Department of Geography,

Indiana University.

Kilburn, P.D. 1958. Historical development and structure of the aspen, jack pine and oak vegetation types on sandy soils in northern lower Michigan. Ph.D. diss. University of Michigan.

Kilburn, P.D. 1959. The forest–prairie ecotone in northeastern Illinois. *American Midland Naturalist* **62**:206–217.

Kim, S.B. 1978. *Landlord and Tenant in Colonial New York: Manorial Society, 1664–1775*. Chapel Hill: University of North Carolina Press.

Kimball, T.L. and R.E. Johnson. 1978. The richness of American wildlife. In H.P. Brokaw (ed.), *Wildlife and America*, 3–17. Council on Environmental Quality, Washington, D.C.: GPO.

Kimenker, J. 1983. The Concord farmer: An economic history. In D.H. Fischer (ed.), *Concord: The Social History of a New England Town, 1750–1850*, 139–197. Waltham, Mass.: Brandeis University.

Kincer, J.B. 1933. Is our climate changing? A study of long-time temperature trends. *Monthly Weather Review* **61**:251–259.

Kincer, J.B. 1941. Climate and weather data for the United States. In *Climate and Man: USDA Yearbook of Agriculture, 1941*, 685–699. Washington, D.C.: GPO.

Kinch, M.P. 1983. Forest and conservation publications. In R.C. Davis (ed.), *Encyclopedia of American Forest and Conservation History*, Vol. 1, 192–196. New York: Macmillan Publishing Company.

King, D.B. 1958. *Incidence of white pine blister rust infection*. USDA Forest Service Lake States Forest Experiment Station Paper, no. 64. St. Paul, Minn.: Lake States Forest Experiment Station.

King, F.B. and J.B. Johnson. 1977. Presettlement forest composition of the central Sangamon River basin, Illinois. *Transactions of the Illinois State Academy of Science* **70**:153–163.

King, G. [1696] 1936. Natural and political observations and conclusions upon the state and condition of England. In G.E. Barnett (ed.), *Two Tracts by Gregory King*, 9–56. Baltimore: Johns Hopkins Press.

King, J.E., W.E. Klippel and R. Duffield. 1975. Pollen preservation and archaeology in eastern North America. *American Antiquity* **40**:180–190.

Kirtland, J.P. 1838. Report on the zoology of Ohio. In *Second Annual Report of the Geological Survey of the State of Ohio*, 157–200. Columbus, Ohio: Samuel Medary, State Printer.

Kirtland, J.P. 1850. Fragments of natural history. *Family Visitor [Cleveland, Ohio]* **1** (1):1.

Kittredge, J. 1948. *Forest Influences*. New York: McGraw-Hill.

Kittredge, J. and A.K. Chittenden. 1929. *Oak forests of northern Michigan*. Special Bulletin, no. 90. East Lansing: Agricultural Experiment Station, Michigan State College.

Kleinmaier, J. 1973. Fire ravaged forests for years before yielding to control. *Wisconsin Then and Now* **19** (7):2–5, 8.

Kline, V.M. and G. Cottam. 1979. Vegetation response to climate and fire in the Driftless Area of Wisconsin. *Ecology* **60**:861–868.

Klopatek, J.M., R.J. Olson, C.J. Emerson and J.C. Jones. 1979. Land use conflicts with natural vegetation in the United States. *Environmental Conservation* **6**:191–200.

Knowlton, C.H. and W. Deane. 1923. Reports on the flora of the Boston district,-38. *Rhodora* **25**:25–31.

Knox, J.C. 1977. Human impacts on Wisconsin stream channels. *Annals of the Association of American Geographers* **67**:323–342.

Knox, J.C. 1987. Historical valley floor sedimentation in the Upper Mississippi Valley. *Annals of the Association of American Geographers* **77**:224–244.

Komarek, E.V., Sr. 1965. Fire ecology – grasslands and man. In *Proceedings of the Fourth Annual Tall Timbers Fire Ecology Conference*, 169–220.

Komarek, E.V. 1983. Fire as an anthropogenic factor in vegetation ecology. In W. Holzner, M.J.A. Werger and I. Ikusiwa (eds.), *Man's Impact on Vegetation*, 77–82. Boston: Dr. W. Junk Publishers.

Korling, T. and R.O. Petty. 1977. *Wild Plants in Flower.* Vol. 3. *Eastern Deciduous Forest.* rev. ed. Toledo, Ohio: Seidel, Farris and Clark.

Korstian, C.F. and P.W. Stickel. 1927. The natural replacement of blight-killed chestnut in the hardwood forests of the Northeast. *Journal of Agricultural Research* **34**:631–648.

Kramer, P.J. and T.T. Kozlowski. 1979. *Physiology of Woody Plants.* New York: Academic Press.

Kreps, T.J. 1930. Vicissitudes of the American potash industry. *Journal of Economic and Business History* **3**:630–660.

Kroeber, A.L. 1939. *Cultural and natural areas of native North America.* Publications in American Archaeology and Ethnology, no. 38. Berkeley: University of California.

Kucera, C.L. 1956. Grazing effects on composition of virgin prairie in north-central Missouri. *Ecology* **37**:389–391.

Kucera, C.L. 1961. *The Grasses of Missouri.* University of Missouri Studies, vol. 35. Columbia: University of Missouri Press.

Kucera, C.L. and S.C. Martin. 1957. Vegetation and soil relationships in the glade region of the southwestern Missouri Ozarks. *Ecology* **38**:285–291.

Kucera, C.L. and R.E. McDermott. 1955. Sugar maple–basswood studies in the forest–prairie transition of central Missouri. *American Midland Naturalist* **54**:495–503.

Küchler, A.W. 1964. *The potential natural vegetation of the conterminous United States.* Special Publication, no. 36. New York: American Geographical Society.

Küchler, A.W. and J. McCormick. [1965]1971. *Vegetation Maps of North America.* Reprint of University of Kansas Publication, Library Series, no. 21. Naarden: Anton W. VanBekhoven.

Kudish, M. 1971. Vegetational history of the Catskill high peaks. Ph.D. diss. Syracuse University.

Kuhne, F. 1860. History and review of the condition of agriculture in Ohio. In *14th Annual Report of the Ohio State Board of Agriculture*, 450–581. Columbus, Ohio: Richard Nevins, State Printer.

Kumlein, T. 1876. On the rapid disappearance of Wisconsin wild flowers: A contrast of the present with thirty years ago. *Transactions of the Wisconsin Academy of Sciences, Arts, and Letters* **3**:56–57.

Kury, T.W. 1974. Iron and settlement: The New York–New Jersey highlands in the eighteenth century. *Geoscience and Man* **5**:7–23.

L'Hommedieu, E. 1801. Observations on manures. *Transactions of the New York Society for the Promotion of Agriculture, Arts, and Manufactures* **1** (2d ed rev.):231–239.

La Mothe, M. de 1904. Description of the river of Detroit by M. de la Mothe, the commandant there. *Michigan State Historical Society Historical Collections* **33**:111–112.

La Rochefoucauld-Liancourt, F., duc de. 1799. *Travels through the United States of North America and the Country of the Iroquois and Upper Canada in the Years 1795, 1796, and 1797.* 2 vols. London: R. Phillips.

La Salle, R.R.C., Sieur de. [1905]1968. *The Journeys of Réné Robert Cavelier Sieur de La Salle.* Edited by I.J. Cox. Vol. 1. Austin, Texas: The Pemberton Press.

Lachner, E.A. 1956. The changing fish fauna of the upper Ohio basin. In C.A. Tyron Jr. and M.A. Shapiro (eds.), *Man and the Waters of the Upper Ohio Basin.* Special Publication no. 1, 64–78. Pittsburgh, Pa.: Pymatuning Laboratory of Field Biology, University of Pittsburgh.

Laderman, A.D., F.C. Golet, B.A. Sorrie and H.L. Woolsey. 1987. Atlantic white cedar in the glaciated Northeast. In A.D. Laderman (ed.), *Atlantic White Cedar Wetlands*, 19–31. Boulder, Colo.: Westview Press.

Lafer, N.G. and W.A. Wistendahl. 1970. Tree composition of Dysart Woods, Belmont County, Ohio. *Castanea* **35**:302–308.

Lahontan, Baron de. [1703]1905. *New Voyages to North-America.* Edited by R.G. Thwaites. Vol. 1. Chicago: A.C. McClurg.

Lamont, E.E., J.M. Beitel and R.E. Zaremba. 1988. Current status of orchids on Long Island, New York. *Bulletin of the Torrey Botanical Club* **115**:113–121.

Lane, C. 1980. The development of pastures and meadows during the sixteenth and seventeenth centuries. *Agricultural History Review* **28**:18–30.

Lang, G.E. and R.T.T. Forman. 1978. Detrital dynamics in a mature oak forest: Hutcheson Memorial Forest, New Jersey. *Ecology* **59**:580–595.

Lange, K.I. 1981. An historic look at weeds in Wisconsin particularly Sauk and Columbia Counties. *Bulletin of the Botanical Club of Wisconsin* **12** (3):4–8.

Lanman, C. 1871. *The Red Book of Michigan: A Civil, Military, and Biographical History.* Detroit: E.B. Smith and Company.

Lanyon, W.E. 1981. Breeding birds and old field succession on fallow Long Island farmland. *Bulletin of the American Museum of Natural History* **168** (1):1–60.

Lapham, I.A. 1833. Agriculture in Ohio. *Genesee Farmer* **3**:330.

Lapham, I.A. 1846. *Wisconsin: Its Geography and Topography, History, Geology, and Mineralogy: Together with Brief Sketches of its Antiques, Natural History, Soil, Productions, Population, and Government.* 2d ed. Milwaukee: I.A. Hopkins.

Lapham, I.A., J.G. Knapp and H. Crocker. 1867. *Report on the Disasterous Effects of the Destruction of Forest Trees, now Going on so Rapidly in the State of Wisconsin.* Madison, Wis.: Atwood and Rublee, State Printers.

Larsen, E.L. 1943. Pehr Kalm's observations on the natural history and climate of Pennsylvania. *Agricultural History* **17**:172–174.

Larson, A.M. 1949. *History of the White Pine Industry in Minnesota.* Minneapolis: University of Minnesota Press.

Lart, C.E. 1922. Fur-trade returns. *Canadian Historical Review* **3**:351–358.

Lathrop, B.F. 1948. History from the census returns. *Southwestern Historical Quarterly* **51**:293–312.

Latrobe, C.J. [1836]1970. *The Rambler in North America.* 2 vols. 2d ed. Reprint. New York: Johnson Reprint Corporation.

Lawrence, W.H. 1952. Evidence of the age of beaver ponds. *Journal of Wildlife Management* **16**:69–79.

Lawrence, W.H. 1954. Michigan beaver populations as influenced by fire and logging. Ph.D. diss. University of Michigan.

Leach, D.E. 1958. *Flintlock and Tomahawk: New England in King Philip's War.* New York: Macmillan.

Leaf, A.L. 1958. Effect of grazing on fertility of farm woodlot soils in southern Wisconsin. *Journal of Forestry* **56**:138–139.

Leak, W.B. 1964. An expression of diameter distribution for unbalanced, uneven-aged stands and forests. *Forest Science* **10**:39–50.

Leak, W.B. 1973. *Species and structure of a virgin northern hardwood stand in New Hampshire.* USDA Forest Service Research Note, no. NE-181. Upper Darby, Pa.: Northeastern Forest Experiment Station.

Leak, W.B. 1987. Fifty years of compositional change in deciduous and coniferous forest types in New Hampshire. *Canadian Journal of Forest Research* **17**:388–393.

Leak, W.B. and R.W. Wilson Jr. 1958. *Regeneration after cutting of old-growth northern hardwoods in New Hampshire.* US Forest Service Northeastern Forest Experiment Station Paper, no. 103. Upper Darby, Pa.: Northeastern Forest Experiment Station.

LeBarron, R.K. and J.R. Neetzel. 1942. Drainage of forested swamps. *Ecology* **23**:457–465.

LeDuc, T. 1963. Public policy, private investment, and land use in American agriculture, 1825–1875. *Agricultural History* **37**:3–9.

Lee, A.T.M. and H.H. Wooten. 1958. The management of state lands. In *Land, USDA Yearbook of Agriculture, 1958,* 72–86. Washington, D.C.: GPO.

Lee, D. 1850. A general view of American agriculture. In *Report of the Commissioner of Patents for the Year 1849. Part II. Agricuture,* 22–37.

Lee, R. 1980. *Forest Hydrology.* New York: Columbia University Press.

Leffelmen, L.J. and R.C. Hawley. 1925. *Studies of Connecticut hardwoods: The treatment of advance growth arising as a result of thinnings and shelterwood cuttings.* Yale University School of Forestry Bulletin, no. 15. New Haven, Conn.: Yale University School of Forestry.

Leighton, A. [1970]1986. *Early American Gardens: 'For Meate or Medicine'.* Amherst: University of Massachusetts Press.

Leighton, A. 1987. *American Gardens of the Nineteenth Century: 'For Comfort and Affluence'.* Amherst: University of Massachusetts Press.

Leitch, J.A. 1981. *The wetlands and drainage controversy – revisited.* Minnesota Agricultural Economist, no. 626. St. Paul: University of Minnesota.

Leitner, L.A. and M.T. Jackson. 1981. Presettlement forests of the unglaciated portion of southern Illinois. *American Midland Naturalist* **105**:290–304.

Lemon, J.T. [1972]1976. *The Best Poor Man's Country: A Geographical Study of Early Southeastern Pennsylvania.* New York: W.W. Norton and Company.

Lemon, J.T. 1987. Agriculture and society in early America. *Agricultural History Review* **35**:76–94.

Leopold, A. 1931. *Report on a Game Survey of the North Central States.* Madison Wis.: Sporting Arms and Ammunition Manufactures' Institute.

Leopold, A. [1933]1986. *Game Management.* Reprint. Madison: University of Wisconsin Press.

Leopold, A. 1938. *Report on Huron Mountain Club.* Big Bay, Mich.: Huron Mountain Club.

Leopold, A. 1941. Lakes in relation to terrestrial life patterns. In J.G. Needham (ed.), *A Symposium on Hydrology,* 17–22. Madison: University of Wisconsin Press.

Leopold, A. 1943. Deer irruptions. *Wisconsin Conservation Bulletin* **8**:3–11.

Leopold, A. 1945. The outlook for farm wildlife. *Transactions of the North American Wildlife Conference* **10**:165–168.

Leopold, A. [1949]1968. *A Sand County Almanac and Sketches Here and There.* New York: Oxford University Press.

Leopold, A., L.K. Sowis and D.L. Spencer. 1947. A survey of overpopulated deer ranges in the United States. *Journal of Wildlife Management* **11**:162–177.

Leopold, A.S. 1978. Wildlife and forest practice. In H.P. Brokaw (ed.), *Wildlife in America: Contributions to an Understanding of American Wildlife and its*

Conservation. U.S. Council on Environmental Quality, 108–120. Washington,
    D.C.: GPO.

Leopold, L.B. 1973. River channel change with time – an example. *Bulletin of the
    Geological Society of America* **84**:1845–1860.

Lesquereux, L. 1865. On the origin and formation of prairies. *American Journal of
    Science and Arts,* 2d ser., **39**:317–327.

Leue, A. 1886. The Forestal Relation of Ohio. *First Annual Report of the Ohio State
    Forestry Bureau.* Columbus, Ohio: Westbote Company, State Printers.

Levenson, J.B. 1976. Forested woodlots as biogeographic islands in an
    urban–agricultural matrix. Ph.D. diss. University of Wisconsin–Milwaukee.

Levenson, J.B. 1981. Woodlots as biogeographic islands in southeastern Wisconsin.
    In R.L. Burgess and D.M. Sharpe (eds.), *Forest Island Dynamics in Man-
    Dominated Landscapes,* 13–39. New York: Springer-Verlag.

Levett, C. [1628]1893. *A Voyage into New England.* Reprinted in J.P. Baxter (ed.),
    Christopher Levett of York: The Pioneer Colonist in Casco Bay. Vol. 5. Portland,
    Maine: Gorges Society.

Lewis, W.D. 1983. Ironmaking in early America. In Division of Publications,
    National Park Service, USDI (ed.), *Hopewell Furnace.* National Park Handbook,
    no. 124, 6–21. Washington, D.C.: GPO.

Liebig, Baron Justus von, 1859. *Letters on Modern Agriculture.* Edited by J. Blyth.
    London: Walton and Maberly.

Liegel, C. 1982. The pre-European settlement vegetation of the Aldo Leopold
    Memorial Reserve. *Transactions of the Wisconsin Academy of Sciences, Arts and
    Letters* **70**:13–26.

Lifitau, P. 1724. *Moeurs, Coutumes et Religions des Sauvages Americans.* Paris.

Lincklaen, J. 1897. *Travels in the Years 1791 and 1792 in Pennsylvania, New York
    and Vermont.* New York: G.P. Putnam's Sons.

Lincoln, B. 1814. Remarks on the cultivation of the oak. *Collections of the
    Massachusetts Historical Society,* 2d ser., **1**:187–194.

Lincoln, J.W. 1851. Farming in Worcester, Massachusetts. In *Report of the
    Commissioner of Patents for the Year 1850.* Part II. *Agriculture,* 268–277.
    Washington: Printer to the House of Representatives.

Lindestrom, P. [1925]1979. *Geographia Americae with an Account of the Delaware
    Indians Based on Surveys and Notes Made in 1654–1656.* Translated by A.
    Johnson. Reprint of 1925 Swedish Colonial Society of America edition. New
    York: Arno Press.

Lindroth, C.H. 1957. *The Faunal Connections between Europe and North America.*
    New York: John Wiley and Sons.

Lindsey, A.A. 1955. Testing the line-strip method against full tallies in diverse forest
    types. *Ecology* **36**:485–495.

Lindsey, A.A. 1961. Vegetation of the drainage-aeration classes of northern Indiana
    soils in 1830. *Ecology* **42**:432–436.

Lindsey, A.A. 1962. Analysis of an original forest of the lower Wabash floodplain and
    upland. *Proceedings of the Indiana Academy of Science* **72**:282–287.

Lindsey, A.A. 1966. The Indiana of 1816. In A.A. Lindsey (ed.), *Natural Features of
    Indiana,* x–xxix. Indianapolis: Indiana Academy of Science.

Lindsey, A.A., W.B. Crankshaw and S.A. Quadir. 1965. Soil relations and distribution
    map of the vegetation of presettlement Indiana. *Botanical Gazette* **126**:155–163.

Lindsey, A.A., D.V. Schmelz and S.A. Nichols. 1969. *Natural Areas in Indiana and
    their Preservation.* West Lafayette: Indiana Natural Areas Survey, Purdue
    University.

Lineback, J.A., N.K. Bleuer, D.M. Mickelson, W.R. Farrand, R.P. Goldthwait, G.M.

Richmond and D.S. Fullerton. 1983. *Quaternary geologic map of the Chicago 4 × 6 quadrangle, United States.* US Geological Survey Miscellaneous Investigation Series Map, no. I-1420 (NK-16). Washington, D.C.: US Geological Survey.

Little, E.L., Jr. 1979. *Checklist of United States trees (native and naturalized).* USDA Agricultural Handbook, no. 541. Washington, D.C.: USDA Forest Service.

Little, S. 1946. *The effects of forest fires on the stand history of New Jersey's pine region.* US Forest Service Northeastern Forest Experiment Station Forest Management Paper, no. 3. Philadelphia: Northeastern Forest Experiment Station.

Livingston, C.H. 1832. American agriculture. In D. Brewster (ed.), *New Edinburgh Encyclopedia.* Vol. 1, 332–341. Philadelphia: J. and E. Parker.

Lockridge, K.A. 1968. Land, population and the evolution of New England society, 1630–1790. *Past and Present* **39**:62–80.

Loeb, R.E. 1987. Pre-European settlement forest composition in east New Jersey and southeastern New York. *American Midland Naturalist* **118**:414–423.

Loehr, R.C. 1937. The influence of English agriculture on American agriculture, 1775–1825. *Agricultural History* **11**:3–15.

Longfellow, H.W. [1847]1893. Evangeline. In H.W. Longfellow (ed.), *The Complete Poetical Works of Henry Wadsworth Longfellow*, 70–98. Boston: Houghton, Mifflin and Company.

Loomis, L. 1855. Letter [on girdling trees] from Mr. Loomis. *Michigan Farmer* **13**:365.

Loomis, R.S. 1978. Ecological dimensions of medieval agrarian systems: An ecologist responds. *Agricultural History* **52**:478–487.

Loope, W.L. 1991. Interrelationships of fire history, land use history, and landscape pattern within Pictured Rocks National Lakeshore, Michigan. *Canadian Field-Naturalist* **105**:18–28.

Lorain, J. 1814. Observations upon the agriculture and roads of the new settlements in Pennsylvania, with hints for improvement. *Memoirs of the Philadelphia Society for Promoting Agriculture* **3**:98–111.

Lorain, J. 1825. *Nature and Reason Harmonized in the Practice of Husbandry.* Philadelphia: H.C. Carey and I. Lea.

Lord, N.W. 1884. Iron manufacture in Ohio. In *Report of the Ohio Geological Survey.* Vol. 5, 438–554. Columbus, Ohio: Westbote Company.

Lorimer, C.G. 1977. The presettlement forest and natural disturbance cycle of northeastern Maine. *Ecology* **58**:139–148.

Lorimer, C.G. 1980. The use of land survey records in estimating presettlement fire frequency. In M.A. Stokes and J.H. Dieterich (tech. coordinators), *Proceedings of the Fire History Workshop, Oct. 20–24, 1980, Tucson*, pages 57–62. USDA Forest Service General Technical Report, no. RM-81. Fort Collins, Colo.: Rocky Mountain Forest and Range Experiment Station.

Lorimer, C.G. 1985a. Methodological considerations in the analysis of forest disturbance history. *Canadian Journal of Forest Research* **15**:200–213.

Lorimer, C.G. 1985b. The role of fire in the perpetuation of oak forests. In J.E. Johnson (ed.), *Proceedings, Challenges in Oak Management and Utilization*, 8–25. Madison: Cooperative Extension Service, University of Wisconsin.

Lorimer, C.G. 1989. Relative effects of small and large disturbances on temperate hardwood forest structure. *Ecology* **70**:565–576.

Lorimer, C.G. and L.E. Frelich. 1989. A methodology for estimating canopy disturbance frequency and intensity in temperate forests. *Canadian Journal of Forest Research* **19**:651–663.

Lorimer, C.G. and W.R. Gough. 1988. Frequency of drought and severe fire weather in north-eastern Wisconsin. *Journal of Environmental Management* **26**:203–219.

Losensky, B.J., III. 1961. The Great Plains of central Pennsylvania. M.S. thesis. Pennsylvania State University.

Loskiel, G.H. 1794. *History of the Mission of the United Brethren among Indians in North America.* Translated by C.I. LaTrobe. 3 parts. London: Printed for the Brethren's Society for the Furtherance of the Gospel.

Louma, J.R. 1985. Nursery on the northern plains. *Nature Conservancy News* **35**:8–12.

Love, J.B. 1970. The colonial surveyor in Pennsylvania. Ph.D. diss. University of Pennsylvania.

Lovejoy, P.S. 1921. The effects of forest fires upon the soil of the North Lake States. In *Twenty-second Annual Report of the Michigan Academy of Science*, 9–20.

Lowell, J. 1819. Remarks on the gradual diminution of the forests of Massachusetts, and the importance of an early attention to some effectual remedy. *Massachusetts Agricultural Repository* **5**:32–61.

Lowell, J. 1831. Letter from Hon. John Lowell. *Massachusetts Agricultural Journal* **10**:303–309.

Lowenthal, D. 1953. George Perkins Marsh and the American geographical tradition. *Geographical Review* **43**:207–213.

Lower, A.R.M. 1938. *A History of the Lumber Trade Between Canada and the United States.* Toronto: Ryerson Press.

Ludlum, D.M. 1963. *Early American Hurricanes 1492–1870.* Boston: American Meteorological Society.

Ludlum, D.M. 1966. *Early American Winters 1604–1870.* Boston: American Meteorological Society.

Ludlum, D.M. 1970. *Early American Tornadoes 1586–1870.* Boston: American Meteorological Society.

Lull, H.W. 1959. Humus depth in the Northeast. *Journal of Forestry* **57**:905–909.

Lull, H.W. 1963. Forest influences research by questionnaire. *Journal of Forestry* **61**:778–782.

Lull, H.W. and K.G. Reinhart. 1972. *Forests and floods in the eastern United States.* USDA Forest Service Research Paper, no. NE-226. Upper Darby, Pa.: Northeastern Forest Experiment Station.

Lull, H.W. and H.C. Storey. 1957. Factors influencing streamflow from two watersheds in northeastern Pennsylvania. *Journal of Forestry* **55**:198–200.

Lurie, E. 1953. Some manuscript resources in the history of nineteenth century American natural science. *Isis* **44**:363–370.

Lutz, H.J. 1930a. Original forest composition in northwestern Pennsylvania as indicated by early land survey notes. *Journal of Forestry* **28**:1098–1103.

Lutz, H.J. 1930b. The vegetation of Hearts Content, a virgin forest in northwestern Pennsylvania. *Ecology* **11**:1–29.

Lutz, H.J. 1930c. Effect of cattle grazing on vegetation of a virgin forest in northwestern Pennsylvania. *Journal of Agricultural Research* **41**:561–570.

Lutz, H.J. 1931. Have forest fires always occurred? *Forest Leaves* **23**:36–37.

Lutz, H.J. 1934. *Ecological relations in the pitch pine plains of southern New Jersey.* Yale University School of Forestry Bulletin, no. 38. New Haven, Conn.: Yale University School of Forestry.

Lutz, H.J. and A.L. McComb. 1935. Origin of white pine in virgin forest stands of northwestern Pennsylvania as indicated by stem and basal branch features. *Ecology* **16**:252–256.

Lyell, C. 1849. *A Second Visit to the United States of North America.* 2 vols. New York: Harper and Brothers.

Lynch, J.F. and D.F. Whigham. 1984. Effects of forest fragmentation on breeding bird communities in Maryland, U.S.A. *Biological Conservation* **28**:287–324.

Macauley, J. 1829. *The Natural, Statistical and Civil History of the State of New York.* 3 vols. Albany, N.Y.: Gould and Banks and William Gould and Company.

MacConnell, W.P. 1975. *Remote sensing 20 years of change in Massachusetts, 1951/52 – 1971/72.* Bulletin, no. 630. Amherst: Massachusetts Agricultural Experiment Station.

MacConnell, W.P. and W. Niedzwiedz. 1974. *Remote sensing 20 years of change in Worcester County, Massachusetts, 1951–1971.* Bulletin, no. 625. Amherst: Massachusetts Agricultural Experiment Station.

Mackey, H.E., Jr. and N. Sivec. 1973. The present composition of a former oak-chestnut forest of the Allegheny mountains of western Pennsylvania. *Ecology* **54**:915–919.

MacMillan, P.C. 1981. Log decomposition in Donaldson's Woods, Spring Mill State Park, Indiana. *American Midland Naturalist* **106**:335–344.

Macy, O. [1880]1972. *The History of Nantucket.* 2d ed. Reprint. Clifton: Augustus M. Kelley.

Madison, J. 1833. Woodlots. From President Madison's address before the Albemarle (Virginia) Agricultural Society, 1819. *Genesee Farmer and Gardener's Journal* **3**:111.

Magilligan, F.J. 1985. Historical floodplain sedimentation in the Galena River Basin, Wisconsin and Illinois. *Annals of the Association of American Geographers* **75**:583–594.

Maissurow, D.K. 1935. Fire as a necessary factor in the perpetuation of white pine. *Journal of Forestry* 33:373-378.

Malin, J.C. [1947]1967. *The Grassland of North America: Prolegomena to Its History.* Reprint with addenda and postscript. Gloucester, Mass.: Peter Smith.

Malin, J.C. 1950. Ecology and history. *Scientific Monthly* **70**:295–298.

Malin, J.C. 1953. Soil, animal, and plant relations of the grassland, historically reconsidered. *Scientific Monthly* **75**:207–220.

Malin, J.C. 1955. *The Contriving Brain and the Skillful Hand in the United States.* Lawrence, Kansas: Published by the author.

Malone, J.J. 1964. *Pine Trees and Politics: The Naval Stores and Forest Policy in Colonial New England, 1691–1775.* Seattle: University of Washington Press.

Maloney, F.X. [1931]1967. *The Fur Trade in New England, 1620–1676.* Reprint. Hamden, Conn.: Archon Books.

Mannion, A.M. 1989. Palaeoecological evidence for environmental change during the last 200 years. I. Biological data. *Progress in Physical Geography* **13**:23–46.

Marbut, C.F. 1935. Soils of the United States. *USDA Atlas of American Agriculture,* part 3, Washington, D.C.: GPO.

Marks, J.B. 1942. Land use and plant succession in Coon Valley, Wisconsin. *Ecological Monographs* **12**:114–133.

Marks, P.L. 1983. On the origin of the field plants of the northeastern United States. *American Naturalist* **122**:210–228.

Marks, P.L., S. Gardescu and F.K. Seischab. 1992. *Late eighteenth century vegetation of central and western New York State on the basis of original land surveys.* New York State Museum Bulletin, no. 484. Albany: New York State Museum, University of the State of New York.

Marks, P.L. and B.E. Smith. 1989. Changes in the landscape: A 200-year history of forest clearing in Tompkins County. *New York's Food and Life Sciences Quarterly* **19** (2):11–14.

Marquis, D.A. 1972. Effect of forest clearcutting on ecological balances. In R.D.

Nyland (ed.), *A Perspective on Clearcutting in a Changing World, Proceedings 1972 Winter Meeting of the New York Section of the Society of American Foresters, February 23–25, 1972, Syracuse, New York.* Applied Forestry Research Institute, Misc. Report no. 4, 47–59. Syracuse: State University of New York, College of Environmental Science and Forestry.

Marquis, D.A. 1975. *The Allegheny hardwood forests of Pennsylvania.* USDA Forest Service General Technical Report, no. NE-15. Broomall, Pa.: Northeastern Forest Experiment Station.

Marquis, D.A. 1981. *Effect of deer browsing on timber production in Allegheny hardwood forests of northwestern Pennsylvania.* USDA Forest Service Research Paper, no. NE-308. Broomall, Pa.: Northeastern Forest Experiment Station.

Marquis, D.A. and R. Brenneman. 1981. *The impact of deer on forest vegetation in Pennsylvania.* US Forest Service General Technical Report, no. NE-65. Broomall, Pa.: Northeastern Forest Experiment Station.

Marschner, F.J. 1959. *Land use and its patterns in the United States.* Agricultural Handbook, no. 153. Washington, D.C.: USDA.

Marschner, F.J. 1974. *The original vegetation of Minnesota* (map). St. Paul, Minn.: US Forest Service, North Central Forest Experiment Station.

Marschner, F.J. and A.D. Perejda. 1946. *Original forests of Michigan* (map). Detroit: Wayne State University Press.

Marsh, G.P. [1848]1973. Address delivered before the Agricultural Society of Rutland County. Reprinted in B.G. Rosenkrantz and W.A. Koelsch (eds.), *American Habitat: A Historical Perspective,* 340–364. New York: Collier Macmillan.

Marsh, G.P. [1864]1965. *Man and Nature; or, Physical Geography as Modified by Human Action.* Edited by D. Lowenthal. Cambridge, Mass.: Harvard University Press.

Marsh, G.P. 1874. *The Earth as Modified by Human Nature: A New Edition of Man and Nature.* New York: Scribner, Armstrong and Company.

Marshall, J.T. 1845. *The Farmer's and Emigrant's Handbook: Being a Full and Complete Guide for the Farmer and the Emigrant.* 2d ed. New York: D. Appleton and Company.

Martin, C. 1974. The European impact on the culture of a northeastern Algonquian tribe: An ecological interpretation. *William and Mary Quarterly,* 3d ser., **31**:3–26.

Martin, C.W. 1977. *Distribution of tree species in an undisturbed northern hardwood–spruce–fir forest, the Bowl, N.H.* USDA Forest Service Research Note, no. NE-244. Upper Darby, Pa.: Northeastern Forest Experiment Station.

Martin, W.H. 1975. The Lilly Cornet Woods: A stable mixed mesophytic forest in Kentucky. *Botanical Gazette* **136**:171–183.

Martineau, H. [1837]1966. *Society in America.* 2 vols. Reprint. New York: AMS Press.

Mason, R.J. 1981. *Great Lakes Archaeology.* New York: Academic Press.

Massachusetts Bureau of Statistics of Labor. 1891. Abandoned farms in Massachusetts. In *Twenty-first Annual Report of the Massachusetts Bureau of Statistics of Labor,* 177–257. Boston: Wright and Potter, State Printers.

Massachusetts Historical Society. 1815a. Notes on Nantucket. *Massachusetts Historical Society Collections,* 2d ser., **3**:19–38.

Massachusetts Historical Society. 1815b. A description of Duke's County. *Massachusetts Historical Society Collections,* 2d ser., **3**:38–94.

Massachusetts Society for Promoting Agriculture. 1807. Questions, proposed by the Massachusetts Society for Promoting Agriculture and a summary of the replies which have been hitherto received by the Society. In *Papers; Consisting of*

Communications Made to the Massachusetts Society for Promoting Agriculture, and Extracts, 19–47. Boston: Adams and Rhoades.

Mast, J.H. 1957. John Pearson's description of Lancaster and Columbia in 1801. *Journal of the Lancaster County Historical Society* **61**:49–61.

Mather, W.G. 1903. Charcoal iron industry of the Upper Peninsula of Michigan. *Proceedings of the Lake Superior Mining Institute* **9**:63–88.

Matthiae, P.E. and F. Stearns. 1981. Mammals in forest islands in southeastern Wisconsin. In R.L. Burgess and D.M. Sharpe (eds.), *Forest Island Dynamics in Man-Dominated Landscapes*, 55–66. New York: Springer-Verlag.

Matthiessen, P. 1959. *Wildlife in America*. New York: Viking Press.

Mattoon, W.R. 1909. The origin and early development of chestnut sprouts. *Forestry Quarterly* **7**:34–47.

Maude, J. 1826. *Visit to the Falls of Niagara in 1800*. London: Longman, Rees, Orme, Brown and Green.

Maximilian, A.P., Prince of Wied. 1843. *Travels in the Interior of North America*. Translated by H.E. Lloyd. London: Ackerman and Company.

Maxwell, H. 1910. The use and abuse of the forests by the Virginia Indians. *William and Mary College Quarterly Historical Magazine* **19**:33–103.

Maxwell, H. 1912. *Wood-using Industries of Michigan*. Produced by the Michigan Public Domain and State Land Office in cooperation with the US Forest Service. Lansing, Mich.: Wynkoop Hallenbeck Crawford Company, State Printers.

Maxwell, H. 1915. The story of white pine. *American Forestry* **21**:34–46.

Maybee, R.H. [1960]1976. *Michigan's white pine era, 1840–1900*. John M. Muson History Fund Publication, Pamphlet, no. 1. Lansing: Michigan History Division, Michigan Department of State.

Mayfield, H.F. 1988–1989. Changes in bird life at the western end of Lake Erie (three parts). *American Birds* **42**:393–398, 1259–1264, **43**:46–49.

Mayr, H. 1890a. *Die Waldungen von Nordamerika*. München: M. Rieger.

Mayr, H. 1890b. The general condition of North American forests. *Garden and Forest* **3**:445–447, 457–458.

McAndrews, J.H. 1976. Fossil history of man's impact on the Canadian flora: An example from southern Ontario. *Canadian Botanical Association Bulletin* **9** (1):1–6.

McAndrews, J.H. 1988. Human disturbance of North American forests and grasslands: The fossil record. In B. Huntley and T. Webb III (eds.), *Vegetation History*, 673–697. Dordrecht: Kluwer Academic Publishers.

McAtee, W.L. (ed.) 1938. Journal of Benjamin Smith Barton on a visit to Virginia, 1802. *Castanea* **3**:85–117.

McCabe, R.E. and T.R. McCabe. 1984. Of slings and arrows: An historical perspective. In L.K. Halls (ed.), *White-tailed Deer: Ecology and Management*, 19–72. Harrisburg, Pa.: Stackpole Books.

McCance, R.M., Jr. and J.F. Burns. 1984. *Ohio endangered and threatened vascular plants: Abstracts of state-listed taxa*. Columbus: Division of Natural Areas and Preserves, Ohio Department of Natural Resources.

McCarthy, E.F. and H.C. Belyea. 1920. *Yellow birch and its relation to the Adirondack forest*. Technical Publication, no. 12. Syracuse: The New York State College of Forestry at Syracuse.

McChesney, P. 1974. Hedgerows in the Hopkins Forest. Unpublished report for Biology 305. Williams College, Williamstown, Mass.

McClain, W.E. 1983. Photodocumentation of the loss of hill prairie within Pere Marquette State Park, Jersey County, Illinois. *Transactions of the Illinois State Academy of Science* **76**:343–346.

McClain, W.E. and J.E. Ebinger. 1968. Woody vegetation of Baber Woods, Edgar County, Illinois. *American Midland Naturalist* **79**:419–428.

McClure, D. 1811. *Memoirs of the Rev. Eleazar Wheelock, D.D., Founder and President of Dartmouth College and Moor's Charity School.* Newburyport, Mass.: Edward Little and Company.

McClure, D. 1899. *Diary of David McClure, Doctor of Divinity, 1748–1820.* Edited by F.B. Dexter. New York: Knickerbocker Press.

McComb, A.L. and W.E. Loomis. 1944. Subclimax prairie. *Bulletin of the Torrey Botanical Club* **71**:46–76.

McConnell, C.A. and K.W. Harmon. 1976. Agricultural effects on wildlife in America: A brief history. In *Critical Conservation Choices: A Bicentennial Look. Proceedings 31st Annual Meeting Soil Conservation Society of America*, 35–44.

McCubbin, G.A. 1938. Agricultural drainage in southwestern Ontario. *Engineering Journal* **21**:66–70.

McCune, B., C.L. Cloonan and T.V. Armentano. 1988. Tree mortality and vegetation dynamics in Hemmer Woods, Indiana. *American Midland Naturalist* **120**:416–431.

McCune, B. and E. Menges. 1986. Quality of historical data on Midwestern old-growth forests. *American Midland Naturalist* **116**:163–172.

McDonald, A. 1941. *Early American soil conservationists.* USDA Miscellaneous Publication, no. 449. Washington, D.C.: USDA.

McDonnell, M.J. and E.W. Stiles. 1983. The structural complexity of old field vegetation and the recruitment of bird-dispersed plant species. *Oecologia* **56**:109–116.

McFarland, W.M. 1896. *Census of Iowa for the Year 1895.* Des Moines, Iowa: F.R. Conway, State Printer.

McInteer, B.B. 1946. A change from grassland to forest vegetation in the 'Big Barrens' of Kentucky. *American Midland Naturalist* **36**:276–282.

McInteer, B.B. 1952. Original vegetation of the Blue Grass Region of Kentucky. *Castanea* **17**:153–157.

McIntosh, R.P. 1962. The forest cover of the Catskill Mountain region, New York, as indicated by land survey records. *American Midland Naturalist* **68**:409–423.

McIntosh, R.P. 1972. Forests of the Catskill Mountains, New York. *Ecological Monographs* **42**:143–161.

McIntosh, R.P. 1985. *The Background of Ecology: Concept and Theory.* New York: Cambridge University Press.

McIntyre, A.C. 1932. The scrub oak type in Pennsylvania. *Forest Leaves* **23**:74–77.

McKinley, D.L. 1960. The Carolina parakeet in pioneer Missouri. *Wilson Bulletin* **72**:274–287.

McKinley, D.L. 1964. The white man's fly on the frontier. *Missouri Historical Review* **58**:442–451.

McManis, D.R. 1964. *The initial evaluation and utilization of the Illinois prairies, 1815–1840.* Research Paper, no. 94. Chicago: Department of Geography, The University of Chicago.

McMartin, B. 1992. *Hides, Hemlocks and Adirondack History: How the Tanning Industry Influenced the Region's Growth.* Utica, N.Y.: North Country Books.

McMaster, W.C. 1941. *Forest resources of Portage County, Ohio.* Ohio Forest Survey Report, no. 9. Wooster: Ohio WPA in cooperation with the Central States Forest Experiment Station and the Ohio Agricultural Experiment Station.

McMillan, R.B. 1976. The Pomme de Terre study locality: Its setting. In W.R. Wood and R.B. McMillan (eds.), *Prehistoric Man and His Environments: A Case Study in the Ozark Highland*, 13–46. New York: Academic Press.

McMullan, J.T., R. Morgan and R.B. Murray. 1976. *Energy Resources and Supply*. New York: John Wiley and Sons.

McVaugh, R. 1935. Recent changes in the composition of a local flora. *Bulletin of the Torrey Botanical Club* **62**:479–489.

McVaugh, R. 1958. *Flora of the Columbia County area, New York*. Bulletin, no. 360. Albany: New York State Museum and Science Service.

Mead, D.W. 1911. The flow of streams and the factors that modify it, with special reference to Wisconsin conditions. *Bulletin of the University of Wisconsin*, no. 425. *Engineering Series* vol. **6** (5):175–366.

Mead, S.B. 1846. Catalogue of the plants growing spontaneously in the State of Illinois, the principal part near Augusta, Hancock County. *Prairie Farmer* **6**:35–36, 60, 93, 119–122.

Mehrhoff, L.J. 1987. A tabular summary of the vascular flora of Connecticut. *Connecticut Geological and Natural History Survey Natural History Notes* **2** (1):7–8.

Meine, C. 1988. *Aldo Leopold: His Life and Work*. Madison: University of Wisconsin Press.

Meinig, D.W. (ed.) 1979. *The Interpretation of Ordinary Landscapes: Geographical Essays*. New York: Oxford University Press.

Meisel, M. 1924–1926. *Bibliography of American Natural History: The Pioneer Century, 1769–1865*. 2 vols. New York: Premier Publishing Company.

Mellars, P. 1976. Fire ecology, animal populations and man: A study of some ecological relationships in prehistory. *Proceedings of the Prehistoric Society* **42**:15–45.

Menges, E.S. and D.M. Waller. 1983. Plant strategies in relation to elevation and light in floodplain herbs. *American Naturalist* **122**:454–473.

Menzel, B.W. 1981. Iowa's waters and fishes: A century and a half of change. *Proceedings of the Iowa Academy of Science* **88**:17–23.

Merchant, C. 1989. *Ecological Revolutions: Nature, Gender, and Science in New England*. Chapel Hill: University of North Carolina Press.

Merk, F. 1916. *Economic History of Wisconsin During the Civil War Decade*. Madison: State Historical Society of Wisconsin.

Merk, J.W. 1951. Tree species distribution on the basis of the original land survey of Washtenaw County, Michigan. M.S. thesis. University of Michigan.

Merritt, C. 1979. An overview of oak regeneration problems. In H.A. Holt and B.C. Fischer (eds.), *Proceedings of the 1979 John S. Wright Forestry Conference, Purdue University: Regenerating Oaks in Upland Hardwood Forests*, 1–10. West Lafayette, Ind.: Purdue University Publications.

Merritt, J.F. 1987. *Guide to the Mammals of Pennsylvania*. Pittsburgh: University of Pittsburgh Press.

Merz, R.W. (compiler) 1978. *Forest atlas of the Midwest*. St. Paul: USDA North Central and Northeastern Forest Experiment Stations and College of Forestry, Universtiy of Minnesota.

Merz, R.W. 1981. *A history of the Central States Forest Experiment Station, 1927–1965*. Minneapolis, Minn.: USDA Forest Service North Central Forest Experiment Station.

Meyer, A.H. 1935. The Kankakee 'marsh' of northern Indiana and Illinois. *Papers of the Michigan Academy of Sciences, Arts, and Letters* **21**:359–396.

Meyer, A.H. 1956. Circulation and settlement patterns of the Calumet region of northwest Indiana and northeast Illinois (the second stage of occupance – pioneer settler and subsistence economy, 1830–1850). *Annals of the Association of American Geographers* **46**:312–356.

Meyer, D.R. 1987. The national integration of regional economies, 1860–1920. In R.D. Mitchell and P.A. Groves (eds.), *North America: The Historical Geography of a Changing Continent*, 321–346. London: Hutchinson.

Meyer, L.D. and W.C. Moldenhauer. 1985. Soil erosion by water: The research experience. *Agricultural History* **59**:192–204.

Miceli, J.C., G.L. Rolfe, D.R. Pelz and J.M. Edgington. 1977. Brownfield Woods, Illinois: Woody vegetation and changes since 1960. *American Midland Naturalist* **98**:469–476.

Michaux, A. 1889. Portions of the journal of Andre Michaux, botanist, written during his travels in the United States and Canada, 1785 to 1796. *Proceedings of the American Philosophical Society* **26**:1–145.

Michaux, F.A. [1805]1904. *Travels to the West of the Alleghany Mountains in the States of Ohio, Kentucky, and Tennessea.* Reprinted in R.G. Thwaites (ed.), *Early Western Travels, 1748–1846.* Vol. 3, 105–306. Cleveland, Ohio: Arthur H. Clark.

Michaux, F.A. 1818–1819. *The North American Sylva, or a Description of the Forest Trees, of the United States, Canada and Nova Scotia.* 3 vols. Philadelphia: Thomas Dobson-Solomon Conrad.

Michigan Department of Conservation. 1951–1960. *Sixteenth to Twentieth Biennial Reports of the Department of Conservation of the State of Michigan.* Lansing, Mich.: Allied Printing.

Michigan Department of Natural Resources. 1982. *Michigan's Wetlands.* Lansing: Michigan Department of Natural Resources.

Mickelson, D.M., L. Clayton, D.S. Fullerton and H.W. Borns Jr. 1983. The late Wisconsin glacial record of the Laurentide ice sheet in the United States. In S.C. Porter (ed.), *Late-Quaternary Environments of the United States.* Vol. 1. *The Late Pleistocene*, 3–37. Minneapolis: University of Minnesota Press.

Middleton, J. and G. Merriam. 1983. Distribution of woodland species in farmland woods. *Journal of Applied Ecology* **20**:625–644.

Miller, E.M. 1932. *Bibliography of Ohio botany.* Bulletin, no. 27. Columbus: Ohio Biological Survey.

Miller, E.R. 1927. A century of temperature in Wisconsin. *Transactions of the Wisconsin Academy of Science* **22**:165–177.

Miller, G.J. 1936. Reclaimation of wet and overflow lands. In A.E. Perkins and J.R. Whitaker (eds.), *Our Natural Resources and Their Conservation*, 160–176. New York: John Wiley and Sons.

Miller, G.T., Jr. 1985. *Living in the Environment: An Introduction to Environmental Science.* Belmont, Calif.: Wadsworth Publishing Company.

Miller, H. 1980. Potash from wood ashes: Frontier technology in Canada and the United States. *Technology and Culture* **21**:187–208.

Miller, H.M. 1986. Transforming a 'splendid and delightsome land': Colonists and ecological change in the Chesapeake 1607–1820. *Journal of Washington Academy of Sciences* **76**:173–187.

Miller, J.W. 1975. Much ado about starlings. *Natural History* **84** (7):38–45.

Miller, R.B. 1923. First report on a forestry survey of Illinois. *Illinois Natural History Survey Bulletin* **14**:291–377.

Miller, R.R., J.D. Williams and J.E. Williams. 1989. Extinctions of North American fishes during the past century. *Fisheries* **14**:22–38.

Milliken, R., Jr. 1983. *Forests for the Trees: A History of the Baskahegan Company.* Privately printed.

Millington, B.R. 1930. Glacial topography and agriculture in central Massachusetts. *Economic Geography* **6**:408–415.

Minton, S.A., Jr. 1968. The fate of amphibians and reptiles in a suburban area.

Journal of Herpetology **2**:113–116.

Mitchell, J. 1748. On the preparation and uses of the various kinds of potash. *Philosophical Transactions of the Royal Society of London* **45**:572–583.

Mitchell, J. 1767. *The Present State of Great Britain and North America, with Regard to Agriculture, Population, Trade, and Manufactures, Impartially Considered.* London: T. Becket and P.A. de Hondt.

Mitchell, J. ? [1775]1939. *American Husbandry.* Edited by J. Carman. New York: Columbia University Press.

Mitchell, J.A. and D. Robson. 1950. *Forest fires and forest fire control in Michigan.* Lansing: Michigan Department of Conservation and USDA Forest Service.

Mitchell, R.S. 1986. *A check list of New York State plants.* Bulletin, no. 458. Albany: New York State Museum.

Mitchill, S.L. 1807. *The Picture of New York; or the Traveller's Guide through the Commercial Metropolis of the United States.* New York: I. Riley and Company.

Mitsch, W.J. and J.G. Gosselink. 1986. *Wetlands.* New York: Van Nostrand Reinhold Company.

Mittleberger, G. [1756]1898. *Gottleib Mittelberger's Journey to Pennsylvania in the Year 1750 and Return to Germany in the Year 1754.* Translated by C.T. Eber. Philadelphia: J.J. McVey.

Mladenoff, D.J. and E.A. Howell. 1980. Vegetation change on the Gogebic Iron Range (Iron County, Wisconsin) from the 1860s to the present. *Transactions of the Wisconsin Academy of Sciences, Arts and Letters* **68**:74–89.

Moline, R.T. 1969. The modification of wet prairie in southern Minnesota. Ph.D. diss. University of Minnesota.

Monk, C.D. 1961. Past and present influences on reproduction in the William L. Hutcheson Memorial Forest, New Jersey. *Bulletin of the Torrey Botanical Club* **88**:167–175.

Montanus, A. [1671]1851. *Description of New Netherland.* Reprinted in E.B. O'Callaghan (ed.), *The Documentary History of the State of New York.* Vol. 4, 113–131, Albany, N.Y.: C. van Benthuysen.

Mooney, H.A., T.M. Bonnicksen, N.L. Christensen, J.E. Lotan and W.A. Reiners. (eds.) 1981. *Proceedings of the Conference: Fire Regimes and Ecosystem Properties.* USDA Forest Service General Technical Report, no. WO-26. Washington, D.C.: US Forest Service, Washington Office.

Moore, C.T. 1972. Man and fire in the central North American grassland 1535–1890: A documentary historical geography. Ph.D. diss. University of California, Los Angeles.

Moore, P.D. 1975. Origin of blanket mires. *Nature* **256**:267–269.

Moore, P.D. 1977. Ancient distribution of lime trees in Britain. *Nature* **268**:13–14.

Moore, P.D. 1986a. Prehistoric ecology: Clues from the pollen record. *Nature* **319**:361-362.

Moore, P.D. 1986b. Paleoecology: Unravelling human effects. *Nature* **321**:204.

Moore, T. 1801. *The Great Error of American Agriculture Exposed: And Hints for Improvement Suggested.* Baltimore: Printed by Bonsal and Niles for the author.

Moore, W.L. 1910. *A report on the influence of forests on climate and floods.* Report presented to US House of Representative's Commitee on Agriculture. Washington, D.C.: GPO.

Moran, R.C. 1978. Presettlement vegetation of Lake County, Illinois. In D.C. Glen-Lewin and R.Q. Landers Jr. (eds.), *Proceedings of the Fifth Midwest Prairie Conference*, 12–18. Ames: Iowa State University.

Moran, R.C. 1980. Presettlement (1830) vegetation of DeKalb, Kane and DuPage Counties, Illinois. M.S. thesis. Southern Illinois University.

More, T. 1961. Thomas More's first letter to William Sherard from New England, accompanying a box of specimens herein catalogued with observations on the people and colony of Massachusetts Bay. Dated at Boston, 27 October, 1722. In G.F. Frick and R.P. Stearns (eds.), *Mark Catesby: The Colonial Audubon*, 120–124. Urbana: University of Illinois Press.

Morey, H.G. 1936. A comparison of two virgin forests in northwestern Pennsylvania. *Ecology* **17**:43–55.

Morgan, L.H. [1901]1954. *League of the Ho-do-no-san-nee or Iroquois.* 2 vols. Reprint of H.M. Lloyd edition. New York: Burt Franklin.

Morris, W.W. 1785. Description of soil and timber in a part of the western land. Dec. 27, 1785. Manuscript. In Papers of the Continental Congress, 1774–1789. Letters of Joseph Carleton and Thomas Hutchins, 1779–1788 and papers relating to military affairs. Microcopy no. 247, roll 74, item no. 60, pages 229–236. Washington, D.C.: National Archives.

Morse, J. 1792. *The American Geography: or a View of the Present Situation of the United States of America.* 2d ed. London: John Stockdale.

Morton, T. [1632]1967. *New English Canaan, or New Cannan: Containing an Abstract of New England.* Reprinted in C.F. Adams, Jr. (ed.), *New English Canaan of Thomas Morton.* Prince Society Publications. Vol. 14. New York: Burt Franklin reprint.

Moseley, E.L. 1930. Some plants that were probably brought to northern Ohio from the west by Indians. *Papers of the Michigan Academy of Sciences, Arts, and Letters* **13**:169–172.

Moseley, E.L. 1939. Long time forecasts of Ohio River floods. *Ohio Journal of Science* **39**:220–231.

Moss, A.E. 1973. Chestnut and its demise in Connecticut. *Connecticut Woodlands* **38** (1):7–13.

Motts, W.S. and A.L. O'Brien. 1981. *Geology and hydrology of wetlands in Massachusetts.* Publication, no. 123. Amherst: Water Resources Research Center, University of Massachusetts.

Mroz, G.D., M.R. Gale, M.F. Jurgensen, D.J. Frederick and A. Clark III. 1985. Composition, structure, and aboveground biomass of two old-growth northern hardwood stands in Upper Michigan. *Canadian Journal of Forest Research* **15**:78–82.

Mudrak, F. 1978. Equilibrium dynamics of oak islands in southeastern Wisconsin. M.S. thesis. University of Wisconsin–Milwaukee.

Muhlenbach, V. 1979. Contributions to the synanthropic (adventive) flora of the railroads in St. Louis, Missouri, USA. *Annals of the Missouri Botanical Garden* **66**:1–108.

Muhlenberg, H. 1793. Index Florae Lancastriensis. *Transactions of the American Philosophical Society* **3**:157–184.

Muir, J. 1897. The American forest. *Atlantic Monthly* **80**:145–157.

Muir, J. 1916. *The Story of my Boyhood and Youth.* Boston: Houghton Mifflin Company.

Muller, E.H. 1963. *Geology of Chautauqua County, New York. Part II. Pleistocene.* Bulletin, no. 392. Albany: New York State Museum and Science Service.

Muller, R.N. and Y. Liu. 1991. Coarse woody debris in an old-growth deciduous forest on the Cumberland Plateau, southeastern Kentucky. *Canadian Journal of Forest Research* **21**:1567–1572.

Multhauf, R.P. 1981. Potash. In B. Hindle (ed.), *Material Culture of the Wooden Age*, 227–240. Tarrytown, N.Y.: Sleepy Hollow Press.

Mumford, R.E. and C.E. Keller. 1984. *The Birds of Indiana.* Bloomington: Indiana

University Press.

Mumford, R.E. and J.O. Whittaker Jr. 1982. *Mammals of Indiana.* Bloomington: Indiana University Press.

Munger, D.B. 1991. *Pennsylvania Land Records: A History and Guide for Research.* Wilmington, Del.: Scholarly Resources, Inc.

Munns, E.N. 1940. *A selected bibliography of North American forestry.* 2 vols. USDA Miscellaneous Publication, no. 364. Washington, D.C.: GPO.

Munro, R. [1804]1849. A description of the Genesee Country, in the State of New-York. In E.B. O'Callaghan (ed.), *The Documentary History of the State of New York.* Vol. 2, 1171–1185. Albany, N.Y.: Weed, Parsons and Company.

Munroe, C.E. and T. Michatard. 1902. Wood distillation. *Twelfth Census of the United States.* Vol. 10. *Manufactures,* Part IV. *Chemicals,* 555–560. Washington, D.C.: US Census Office.

Muntz, A.P. 1959. The changing geography of the New Jersey woodlands, 1600–1900. Ph.D. diss. University of Wisconsin–Madison.

Munyon, P.G. 1978. *A Reassessment of New England Agriculture in the Last Thirty Years of the Nineteenth Century: New Hampshire, a Case Study.* New York: Arno Press.

Murton, R.K., R.J.P. Thearle and J. Thompson. 1972. Ecological studies of the feral pigeon *Columba livia* I. Population breeding biology and method of control. *Journal of Applied Ecology* **9**:835–874.

Mutch, R.W. 1970. Wildland fires and ecosystems – a hypothesis. *Ecology* **51**:1046–1051.

Myers, R.L. and P.A. Peroni. 1983. Approaches to determining aboriginal fire use and its impact on vegetation. *Bulletin of the Ecological Society of America* **64**:217–218.

Myers, R.M. and R.D. Henry. 1976. Some changes that have occurred in the indigenous flora of two adjoining west-central Illinois Counties (Hancock and McDonough) during the last 140 years. *Transactions of the Illinois State Academy of Science* **69**:19–36.

Myers, R.M. and R.D. Henry. 1979. Changes in the alien flora on two west-central Illinois counties during the past 140 years. *American Midland Naturalist* **101**:226–230.

Naiman, R.J., C.A. Johnston and J.C. Kelley. 1988. Alteration of North American streams by beaver. *Bioscience* **38**:753–762.

Naiman, R.J., J.M. Melillo and J.E. Hobbie. 1986. Ecosystem alteration of boreal forest streams by beaver (*Castor canadensis*). *Ecology* **67**:1254–1269.

Nash, R. 1970. The state of environmental history. In H.J. Bass (ed.), *The State of American History,* 249–260. Chicago: Quadrangle Books.

Nash, R. (ed.) 1972. *Environment and Americans: The Problem of Priorities.* New York: Holt, Rinehart and Winston.

Nash, R. 1973. *Wilderness and the American Mind.* rev. ed. New Haven, Conn.: Yale University Press.

National Inventory of Documentary Sources in the United States. 1983–. Teaneck, N.J.: Chadwyck-Healey.

Nef, J.U. 1932. *The Rise of the British Coal Industry.* 2 vols. London: Routledge and Kegan Paul.

Neidhard, K. 1951. Karl Neidhard's Reise nach Michigan. Ed. by R.B. Brown. Translated by F. Braun. *Michigan History* **35**:32–84.

Neiland, B.M. and J.T. Curtis. 1956. Differential responses to clipping of six prairie grasses in Wisconsin. *Ecology* **37**:355–365.

Nelson, P. and D. Ladd. 1983. Preliminary report on the identification, distribution and classification of Missouri glades. In C.L. Kucera (ed.), *Proceedings of the Seventh North American Prairie Conference*, 59–76. Springfield: Southwest Missouri State University.

NETSA. 1943. *Report of the U.S. Forest Service programs resulting from the New England hurricane of September 21, 1938*. Boston: Northeastern Timber Salvage Administration.

Neumann, C.J., G.W. Cry, E.L. Caso and B.R. Jarvinen. 1981. *Tropical cyclones of the North Atlantic Ocean, 1871–1980*. Ashville, N.C.: USDC National Oceanic and Atmospheric Administration.

Nevel, R.L., Jr., P.R. Lammert and R.H. Widmann. 1985. *Maine timber industries – a periodic assessment of timber output*. USDA Forest Service Resource Bulletin, no. NE-83. Broomall, Pa.: Northeastern Forest Experiment Station.

New York Forest Commission. 1886. Iron manufacturing companies. In *First Annual Report of the Forest Commission of the State of New York*, 33–35. Albany, N.Y.: The Argus Company.

New York [State] Secretary of State. 1836. *Census of the State of New York for 1835*. Albany, N.Y.: Croswell, Van Benthuysen and Burt.

New York [State] Secretary of State. 1846. *Census of the State of New York for 1845*. Albany, N.Y.: Carroll and Cook.

Newberry, J.S. 1860. *Catalogue of the Flowering Plants and Ferns of Ohio*. Columbus, Ohio: R. Nevins, Printer.

Newbury and Vassalborough Agricultural Societies. 1815. Response to queries addressed to farmers. *Massachusetts Agricultural Repository and Journal* **3**:259–271.

Newhall, J. 1847. Meadow and swamp lands. In J.G. Palfrey, *Abstract from the Returns of Agricultural Societies in Massachusetts, for the Year 1846*, 27–28. Boston: Dutton and Wentworth, State Printers.

Newman, J.A., Jr. and J.E. Ebinger. 1985. Woody vegetation of Baber Woods: Composition and change since 1965. In J.D. Dawson and K.A. Majerus (eds.), *Proceedings of the Fifth Central Hardwood Forest Conference*, 178–180. Urbana-Champaign: Department of Forestry, University of Illinois.

Nichols, A. 1815. Response of Danvers Agricultural Society to inquiries addressed to farmers. *Massachusetts Agricultural Repository and Journal* **3**:338–349.

Nichols, G.E. 1913. The vegetation of Connecticut. II. Virgin forests. *Torreya* **13**:199–215.

Nichols, G.E. 1935. The hemlock–white pine–northern hardwood region of eastern North America. *Ecology* **16**:403–422.

Nicollet, J.N. 1976. *Joseph N. Nicollet on the Plains and Prairies: The Expeditions of 1838–39 with Journals, Letters, and Notes on the Dakota Indians*. Edited and translated by E.C. Bray and M.C. Bray. St. Paul: Minnesota Historical Society.

Niemcewicz, J.U. 1965. *Under Vine and Fig Tree: Travels through America in 1797–1799, 1805 with Some Further Account of Life in New Jersey*. Translated by M.J.E. Budka. Elizabeth, N.J.: Grassmann Publishing Company.

Niering, W.A. 1981. The role of fire management in altering ecosystems. In H.A. Mooney, T.M. Bonnicksen, N.L. Christensen, J.E. Lotan and W.A. Reiners (eds.), *Proceedings of the Conference: Fire Regimes and Ecosystem Properties*. USDA Forest Service Technical Report WO-26, 489-510. Washington, D.C.: USDA Forest Service.

Niering, W.A. and F.E. Egler. 1981. *Vegetation of the Babcock Property, Greenwich, Connecticut*. Greenwich, Conn.: Greenwich Conservation Commission.

Niering, W.A. and R.H. Goodwin. 1962. Ecological studies in the Connecticut Arboretum natural area I. Introduction and a survey of vegetation types. *Ecology*

43:41–54.

Nisbet, J. 1906. The history of the forest of Dean, in Gloucestershire. *English Historical Review* **21**:445–459.

Nixon, C.M., S.P. Havera and R.E. Greenberg. 1978. *Distribution and abundance of the gray squirrel in Illinois*. Biological Notes, no. 105. Urbana: Illinois Natural History Survey.

Nixon, S.W. 1982. *The ecology of New England high salt marshes: A community profile*. US Fish and Wildlife Service, Division of Biological Services. FWS/OBS-81/55. Washington, D.C.: GPO.

Noble, A.G. and A.J. Korsok. 1975. *Ohio – an American heartland*. Bulletin, no. 65. Columbus: Ohio Department of Natural Resources, Division of Geological Survey.

Noble, M.G., L.K. DeBoer, K.L. Johnson, B.A. Coffin, L.G. Fellows and N.A. Christensen. 1977. Quantitative relationships among some *Pinus banksiana–Picea mariana* forests subjected to wildfire and postlogging treatments. *Canadian Journal of Forest Research* **7**:368–377.

Norden, J. 1618. *The Surveyor's Dialogue*. 3d ed. London: Printed by T. Snodham.

Norris, F.H. 1948. Primary forest types of Highland County, Ohio. Ph.D. diss. Ohio State University.

Norton, T.E. 1974. *The Fur Trade in Colonial New York*. Madison: University of Wisconsin Press.

Nott, S. 1949. *Franklin in 1800*. Publication no. 20. The Acorn Club of Connecticut. Hartford, Conn.: Case, Lockwood and Brainard.

Novak, B. 1980. *Nature and Culture: American Landscape and Painting 1825–1875*. New York: Oxford University Press.

Novitzki, R.P. 1978. Hydrologic characteristics of Wisconsin's wetlands and their influence on floods, stream flow, and sediment. In P.E. Greeson, J.R. Clark and J.E. Clark (eds.), *Wetland Functions and Values: The State of Our Understanding*, 377–388. Minneapolis, Minn.: American Water Resources Association.

Novitzki, R.P. 1989. Wetland hydrology. In S.K. Majumdar, R.R. Brooks, F.J. Brenner and R.W. Tiner Jr. (eds.), *Wetlands Ecology and Conservation: Emphasis in Pennsylvania*, 47–64. Easton: Pennsylvania Academy of Science.

Nowacki, G.J. and P.A. Trianosky. 1993. Literature on old-growth forests of eastern North America. *Natural Areas Journal* **13**:87–107.

Nowlin, W. [1876]1937. *The Bark Covered House or, Back in the Woods Again*. Edited by M.M. Quaife. Chicago: Lakeside Press, R.R. Donnelley and Sons.

Nuttall, T. [1821]1905. *Nuttall's Travels Into the Arkansa Territory, 1819*. Reprinted in R.G. Thwaites (ed.), *Early Western Travels, 1748–1846*. Vol. 13. Cleveland, Ohio: Arthur H. Clark Company.

Nuttall, T. 1951. Nuttall's travels into the Old Northwest: An unpublished 1810 diary. Edited by J. Graustein. *Chronica Botanica* **14**:1–88.

Nuzzo, V.A. 1986. Extent and status of Midwest oak savanna: Presettlement and 1985. *Natural Areas Journal* **6** (2):6–36.

Nÿboer, R.W. 1981. Grazing as a factor in the decline of Illinois hill prairies. In R.L. Stuckey and K.J. Reese (eds.), *The Prairie Peninsula – In the 'Shadow' of Transeau: Proceedings of the Sixth North American Prairie Conference*. Biological Notes no 15, 209–211. Columbus: Ohio Biological Survey.

Nyland, R.D., W.C. Zipperer and D.B. Hill. 1986. The development of forest islands in exurban central New York state. *Landscape and Urban Planning* **13**:111–123.

O'Brien, A.L. 1987. Hydrology and the construction of a mitigating wetland. In J.S. Larson and C. Neill (eds.), *Mitigating freshwater wetland alterations in the* glaciated northeastern United States: An assessment of the science base. Publication, no. 87-1, 82-100. Amherst: The Environmental Institute of the University of Massachusetts.

O'Reilly, H. 1838. *Sketches of Rochester; with Incidental Notices of Western New-York.* Rochester: William Alling.

O'Sullivan, P.E. 1983. Annually-laminated lake sediments and the study of Quaternary environmental changes – a review. *Quaternary Science Reviews* **1**:245–313.

Odell, R.T., S.W. Melsted and W.M. Walker. 1984. Changes in organic carbon and nitrogen of Morrow plot soils under different treatments, 1904–1973. *Soil Science* **137**:160–171.

Office of Forest Investigations. 1919. *The use of wood for fuel.* Bulletin, no. 753. Washington, D.C.: USDA Forest Service.

Ogawa, H. and J.W. Male. 1983. *The flood mitigation potential of inland wetlands.* Bulletin, no. 138. Amherst: Water Resources Research Center, University of Massachusetts.

Ogawa, H. and J.W. Male. 1986. Simulating the flood mitigation role of wetlands. *Journal of Water Resources Planning and Management* **112**:114–128.

Ogden, J.G., III. 1961. Forest history of Martha's Vineyard, Massachusetts. I. Modern and pre-colonial forests. *American Midland Naturalist* **66**:417–430.

Ogden, J.G., III. 1965. Early forests of Delaware County, Ohio. *Ohio Journal of Science* **65**:29–36.

Ohio Farmer. 1852. Professor Mapes and the wheat crop of Ohio. *Ohio Cultivator* **8**:340.

Old Seventy. 1840. Clearing land. *Western Farmer* **1**:231–232.

Oldale, R.N. 1982. Pleistocene stratigraphy of Nantucket, Martha's Vineyard, the Elizabeth Islands, and Cape Cod. In G.J. Larson and B.D. Stone (eds.), *Late Wisconsin Glaciation of New England*, 1–34. Dubuque, Iowa: Kendall-Hunt.

Olenderski, K. 1985. The tornadoes of '85. *Pennsylvania Forests* **75** (4):10–11.

Oliver, C.D. and E.P. Stephens. 1977. Reconstruction of a mixed species forest in central New England. *Ecology* **58**:562–572.

Oliver, W. 1843 [1966]. *Eight Months in Illinois: With Information to Emigrants.* March of America facsimile series no. 81. Ann Arbor, Mich.: University Microfilms.

Olson, A.L. 1935. *Agricultural Economy and the Population in Eighteenth-Century Connecticut.* Tercentenary Commission of the State of Connecticut. New Haven: Yale University Press.

Olson, D.F. and S.G. Boyce. 1971. Factors affecting acorn production and germination and early growth of seedlings and seedling sprouts. *Oak Symposium Proceedings*, 44–89. Upper Darby, Pa.: USDA Forest Service, Northeastern Forest Experiment Station.

Olson, G.W. 1968. New York's soil use history. *New York's Food and Life Sciences* **1** (2):8–10.

Olson, S.H. 1971. *The Depletion Myth: A History of Railroad Use of Timber.* Cambridge, Mass.: Harvard University Press.

Olwig, K.R. 1980. Historical geography and the society/nature 'problematic': the perspective of J.F. Schouw, G.P. Marsh and E. Redus. *Journal of Historical Geography* **6**:29–45.

Onthank, A.H. 1917. *The Tanning Industry.* Basic Industry Library, Robert Morris Club. Detroit: National Association of Credit Men.

Oosting, H.J. and W.D. Billings. 1951. A comparison of virgin spruce–fir forest in the northern and southern Appalachian systems. *Ecology* **32**:84–103.

Oosting, H.J. and J.F. Reed. 1944. Ecological composition of pulpwood forests in northwestern Maine. *American Midland Naturalist* **31**:182–210.

Opie, J. 1983. Environmental history: Pitfalls and opportunities. *Environmental Review* **7**:8–16.

Opler, P.A. and G.O. Krizek. 1984. *Butterflies East of the Great Plains: An Illustrated Natural History*. Baltimore: Johns Hopkins University Press.

Orwig, T. 1992. Loess Hills prairies as butterfly survivia: Opportunities and challenges. In D.D. Smith and C.A. Jacobs (eds.), *Proceedings of the Twelfth North American Prairie Conference: Recapturing a Vanishing Heritage*, 131–135. Cedar Falls: University of Northern Iowa.

Orwin, C.S. and C.S. Orwin. 1967. *The Open Fields*. 3d ed. Oxford: Clarendon Press.

Osborne, D.R. and A.T. Peterson. 1984. Decline of the upland sandpiper (*Bartramia longicauda*) in Ohio: An endangered species. *Ohio Journal of Science* **84**:8–10.

Osmun, J.V. and R.L. Giese. 1966. Insect pests of forests, farm and home. In A.A. Lindsey (ed.), *Natural Features of Indiana*, 362–389. Indianapolis: Indiana Academy of Science.

Overlease, W.R. 1987. 150 years of vegetation change in Chester County, Pennsylvania. *Bartonia* **53**:1–12.

Overlease, W.R. and E.D. Overlease. 1976. A study of spring herbaceous ground cover as an indicator of site conditions in mesic northern hardwoods, Benzie County, northwestern Michigan. *Proceedings of the Pennsylvania Academy of Science* **50**:173–178.

Overpeck, J.T. 1985. A pollen study of a late Quaternary peat bog, south-central Adirondack Mountains, New York. *Geological Society of America Bulletin* **96**:145–154.

Ownbey, G.B. and T. Morley. 1991. *Vascular Plants of Minnesota: A Checklist and Atlas*. Minneapolis: University of Minnesota Press.

Packard, S. 1988a. Rediscovering the tallgrass savanna of Illinois. In A. Davis and G. Stanford (eds.), *The Prairie: Roots of Our Culture; Foundation of Our Economy: Proceedings of the Tenth North American Prairie Conference*. Dallas: Native Prairie Association of Texas.

Packard, S. 1988b. Just a few oddball species: Restoration and the rediscovery of the tallgrass savanna. *Restoration and Management Notes* **6** (1):13–20.

Page, J.B. and C.J. Willard. 1946. Cropping system and soil properties. *Proceedings of the Soil Science Society of America* **11**:81–88.

Paillet, F.L. 1984. Growth-form and ecology of American chestnut sprout clones in northeastern Massachusetts. *Bulletin of the Torrey Botanical Club* **111**:316–328.

Pallardy, S.G., T.A. Nigh and H.E. Garrett. 1988. Changes in forest composition in central Missouri: 1968–1982. *American Midland Naturalist* **120**:380–390.

Palmer, E.J. 1946. *Crataegus* in the northeastern and central United States and adjacent Canada. *Brittonia* **5**:471–490.

Pammel, L.H. 1901. Rare plants and their disappearance. *The Plant World* **4**:151–152.

Pammel, L.H. 1910. The problem of weeds in the West. *Proceedings of the Iowa Academy of Science* **17**:34–46.

Pammel, L.H. 1913. Weed migration. In *The Weed Flora of Iowa* (Bulletin no. 4 of the Iowa Geological Survey), 685–769. Des Moines, Iowa: Robert Henderson, State Printer.

Panshin, A.J., E.S. Harrar, J.S. Bethel and W.J. Baker. 1962. *Forest Products: Their Sources, Production, and Utilization*. New York: McGraw-Hill.

Panzer, R. 1988. Managing prairie remnants for insect conservation. *Natural Areas Journal* **8**:83–90.

Pappas, L.G., K. Toews and R. Fischer. 1982. Loss of trees in Nemaha County,

Nebraska since 1856 due to agricultural expansion. *Transactions of the Nebraska Academy of Sciences* **10**:7–11.

Parker, A.C. 1910. *Iroquois uses of maize and other food plants*. Bulletin, no. 144. Albany: New York State Museum.

Parker, G.R. 1989. Old-growth forests of the central hardwood region. *Natural Areas Journal* **9**:5–11.

Parker, G.R. and D.J. Leopold. 1983. Replacement of *Ulmus americana* in a mature east-central Indiana woods. *Bulletin of the Torrey Botanical Club* **110**:482–488.

Parker, G.R., D.J. Leopold and J.K. Eichenberger. 1985. Tree dynamics in an old-growth deciduous forest. *Forest Ecology and Management* **11**:31–57.

Parker, W.N. 1976. On a certain parallelism in form between two historical processes of productivity growth. *Agricultural History* **50**:101–115.

Parker, W.N. 1982. The American farmer. In J. Blum (ed.), *Our Forgotten Past*, 181–196. London: Thames and Hudson.

Parkman, F. [1865–1892]1983. *France and England in North America.* 2 vols. Reprint. New York: Literary Classics of the United States, Inc.

Parmenter, R.B. 1929. The forests of Middlesex County: The results of a forest survey of fifty-four towns and cities in the county. Unpublished report. Boston: Division of Forestry, Massachusetts Department of Conservation.

Parsons, J. 1920. *A Tour Through Indiana in 1840.* New York: Robert M. McBride and Company.

Patric, J.H. 1974. River flow increases in central New England after the hurricane of 1938. *Journal of Forestry* **72**:21–25.

Patric, J.H. and E.M. Gould. 1976. Shifting land use and the effects on river flow in Massachusetts. *Journal of the American Water Works Association* **68**:41–45.

Patric, J.H. and J.D. Helvey. 1986. *Some effects of grazing on soil and water in the eastern forest.* USDA Forest Service General Technical Report, no. NE-115. Broomall, Pa.: Northeastern Forest Experiment Station.

Patterson, W.A., III and A.E. Backman. 1988. Fire and disease history of forests. In B. Huntley and T. Webb III (eds.), *Vegetation History*, 603–632. Dordrecht: Kluwer Academic Publishers.

Patterson, W.A., III, K.J. Edwards and D.J. Maguire. 1987. Microscopic charcoal as fossil indicators of fire. *Quaternary Science Reviews* **6**:3–23.

Patterson, W.A., III and K.E. Sassaman. 1988. Indian fires in the prehistory of New England. In G.P. Nichols (ed.), *Holocene Human Ecology in Northeastern North America*, 107–135. New York: Plenum Publishing Company.

Patterson, W.A., III, K.E. Saunders, L.J. Horton and M.K. Foley. 1985. Fire management options for coastal New England forests: Acadia National Park and Cape Cod National Seashore. In *Proceedings Fire Symposium and Workshop on Wilderness Fire, Missoula, MT, November 15–18, 1983*, 360–365. USDA Forest Service General Technical Report, no. INT-182. Ogden, Utah: Intermountain Research Station.

Pattison, W.D. 1956. Use of the U.S. public land survey plats and notes as descriptive sources. *Professional Geographer* **8** (1):10–14.

Pattison, W.D. [1957]1970. *Beginnings of the American Rectangular Land Survey System, 1784–1800.* Columbus: Ohio Historical Society.

Paull, R.K. and R.A. Paull. 1977. *Geology of Wisconsin and Upper Michigan Including Parts of Adjacent States.* Dubuque, Iowa: Kendall-Hunt.

Pearson, W.D. and B.J. Pearson. 1989. Fishes of the Ohio River. *Ohio Journal of Science* **89**:181–187.

Pease, J.C. and J.M. Niles. 1819. *A Gazetteer of the States of Connecticut and Rhode Island.* Hartford, Conn.: W.S. Marsh.

Peck, J. 1837. *A Gazetteer of Illinois*. 2d ed. Philadelphia: Grigg and Elliot.

Pelz, D.R. and G.L. Rolfe. 1977. Stand structure and composition of a natural mixed hardwood forest. *Transactions of the Illinois State Academy of Science* **69**:446–454.

Penn, W. [1683]1912. Letter from William Penn to the Committee of the Free Society of Traders, 1683. Reprinted in A.C. Myers (ed.), *Narratives of Early Pennsylvania, West New Jersey and Delaware, 1630–1707*, 224–244. New York: Charles Scribner's Sons.

Penn, W. [1685]1912. A further account of the province of Pennsylvania and its improvements, for the satisfaction of those that are adventurers, and enclined to be so. In A.C. Myers (ed.), *Narratives of Early Pennsylvania, West New Jersey and Delaware: 1630–1707*, 259–278. New York: Charles Scribner's Sons.

Pennington, W. 1979. The origins of pollen in lake sediments: An enclosed lake compared with one receiving inflow streams. *New Phytologist* **83**:189–213.

Perkins, E.J. 1980. *The Economy of Colonial America*. New York: Columbia University Press.

Perry, L. 1987. *Illinois component of the National Wetlands Inventory*. Illinois Natural History Survey Reports, no. 264. Champaign.: Illinois Natural History Survey.

Perzel, E.S. 1968. Landholding in Ipswich. *Essex Institute Historical Collections* **104**:303–328.

Peterjohn, B.G. and D.C. Rice. 1991. *The Ohio Breeding Bird Atlas*. Columbus: Ohio Department of Natural Resources.

Peterjohn, W.T. and D.L. Correll. 1984. Nutrient dynamics in an agricultural watershed: Observations on the role of a riparian forest. *Ecology* **65**:1466–1475.

Peterken, G.F. 1974. A method for assessing woodland flora for conservation using indicator species. *Biological Conservation* **6**:239–245.

Peterken, G.F. 1981a. *Woodland Conservation and Management*. London: Chapman and Hall.

Peterken, G.F. 1981b. Wood anemone in central Lincolnshire: An ancient woodland indicator? *Transactions of the Lincolnshire Naturalists Union* **20** (2):78–82.

Peterken, G.F. and M. Game. 1981. Historical factors affecting the distribution of *Mercurialis perennis* in central Lincolnshire. *Journal of Ecology* **69**:781–796.

Peters, B.C. 1970. No trees on the prairie: Persistence of error in landscape terminology. *Michigan History* **54**:19–28.

Peters, B.C. 1972. Oak openings or barrens: Landscape evaluation on the Michigan frontier. *Proceedings of the Association of American Geographers* **4**:84–86.

Peters, B.C. 1978. Michigan's oak openings: Pioneer perceptions of a vegetative landscape. *Journal of Forest History* **22**:18–23.

Peters, J.R. and T.M. Bowers. 1977. *Forest statistics for Rhode Island*. USDA Forest Service Resource Bulletin, no. NE-49. Broomall, Pa.: Northeastern Forest Experiment Station.

Peters, R. 1808. Departure of southern pine timber, a proof of the tendency in nature to a change of products on the same soil. *Memoirs of the Philadelphia Society for Promoting Agriculture* **1**:27–39.

Peters, R. 1847. Letter to George Washington, 1793. In F. Knight (ed.), *Letters on Agriculture from his Excellency George Washington, President of the United States, to Arthur Young and Sir John Sinclair*, 104–112. Washington, D.C.: Published by the editor.

Peters, R.A. 1972. Control of weeds in no-till crops. In *Proceedings of the No-tillage Systems Symposium Held at Ohio State University in February 1972*, 132–135. Sponsored by Ohio State University, Ohio Agricultural Research and Development Center and Chevron Chemical Company.

Petrides, G.A. 1942. Relation of hedgerows in winter to wildlife in central New York. *Journal of Wildlife Management* **6**:261–280.

Petty, R.O. and A.A. Lindsey. 1961. Hoot Woods, a remnant of virgin timber, Owen County, Indiana. *Proceedings of the Indiana Academy of Science* **71**:320–328.

Phillips, P.C. 1961. *The Fur Trade.* 2 vols. Norman: University of Oklahoma Press.

Pickering, J. 1832. *Inquiries of an Emigrant; Being the Narrative of an English Farmer from the Year 1824 to 1830; During Which Period he Travelled the United States and Canada.* London: Effingham Wilson.

Pierce, F.J., R.H. Dowdy, W.E. Larson and W.A.P. Graham. 1984. Soil productivity in the Corn Belt: An assessment of erosion's long-term effects. *Journal of Soil and Water Conservation* **39**:131–136.

Pierce, F.J., W.E. Larson, R.H. Dowdy and W.A.P. Graham. 1983. Productivity of soils: Assessing long-term changes due to erosion. *Journal of Soil and Water Conservation* **38**:39–44.

Pierce, J. 1826. Notice of the Peninsula of Michigan, in relation to its topography, scenery, agriculture, population, resources, etc. *American Journal of Science and Arts* **10**:304–319.

Pinchot, G. 1910. *The Fight for Conservation.* New York: Doubleday, Page and Company.

Pinchot, G. 1919. Forest devastation: A national danger and a plan to meet it. *Journal of Forestry* **17**:911–945.

Pinchot, G. 1937. How conservation began in the United States. *Agricultural History* **11**:255–265.

Pinchot, G. and H.S. Graves. 1896. *The White Pine: A Study with Tables of Volume and Yield.* New York: The Century Company.

Piper, R.U. 1855–1858. *The Trees of America.* Boston: William White, Printer to the Commonwealth.

Plantagenet, B. [1648]1898. *A Description of the Province of New Albion.* American Colonial Tracts Monthly, vol. 2, no. 6. Rochester, N.Y.: G.P. Humphrey.

Plummer, G.L. 1975. 18th century forests in Georgia. *Bulletin of the Georgia Academy of Science* **33**:1–19.

Pollard, E., M.D. Hooper and N.W. Moore. 1974. *Hedges.* London: Collins.

Pond, J. 1976. Letter of John [?] Pond to William Pond. In E. Emerson (ed.), *Letters from New England: The Massachusetts Bay Colony, 1629–1638,* 64–66. Amherst: University of Massachusetts Press.

Poole, E.L. 1964. *Pennsylvania Birds: An Annotated List.* Narbeth, Pa.: Published for Delaware Valley Ornithological Club by Livingston Publishing Company.

Porter, W.A. 1880. A sketch of the life of General Andrew Porter. *Pennsylvania Magazine of History and Biography* **4**:261–300.

Potzger, J.E. 1948. A pollen study in the tension zone of lower Michigan. *Butler University Botanical Studies* **8**:161–177.

Potzger, J.E. and R.C. Friesner. 1934. Some comparisons between virgin forest and adjacent areas of secondary succession. *Butler University Botanical Studies* **3**:85–98.

Potzger, J.E. and C.O. Keller. 1952. The beech line in northwestern Indiana. *Butler University Botanical Studies* **10**:108–113.

Potzger, J.E. and M.E. Potzger. 1950. Composition of the forest primeval from Hendricks County southward to Lawrence County, Indiana. *Proceedings of the Indiana Academy of Science* **60**:109–113.

Potzger, J.E., M.E. Potzger and J. McCormick. 1956. The forest primeval of Indiana as recorded in original U.S. land surveys and an evaluation of previous interpretations of Indiana vegetation. *Butler University Botanical Studies*

13:95–111.

Pough, R.H. 1949. *Audubon Land Bird Guide*. Garden City, NY: Doubleday and Company.

Pough, R.H. 1951. *Audubon Water Bird Guide: Water, Game, and Large Land Birds*. Garden City, N.Y.: Doubleday and Company.

Pough, R.H. 1959. Introduction to P. Matthiessen's *Wildlife in America*. New York: Viking Press.

Powell, B.W. 1981. Carbonized seed remains from prehistoric village sites in Connecticut. *Man in the Northeast* **21**:75–85.

Powell, D.S. 1985. *Forest composition of Maine: An analysis using number of trees*. USDA Forest Service Resource Bulletin, no. NE-85. Broomall, Pa.: Northeastern Forest Experiment Station.

Powell, D.S. and T.J. Considine Jr. 1982. *An analysis of Pennsylvania's forest resources*. USDA Forest Service Resource Bulletin, no. NE-69. Broomall, Pa.: Northeastern Forest Experiment Station.

Powell, D.S. and D.R. Dickson. 1984. *Forest statistics for Maine, 1971 and 1982*. USDA Forest Service Resource Bulletin, no. NE-81. Broomall, Pa.: Northeastern Forest Experiment Station.

Powell, E.P. 1914. *Hedges, Windbreaks, Shelters and Live Fences*. New York: Orange Judd Company.

Powell, H.B. 1978. *Philadelphia's First Fuel Crisis: Jacob Cist and the Developing Market for Pennsylvania Anthracite*. University Park: Pennsylvania State University Press.

Powell, S.C. 1963. *Puritan Village: The Formation of a New England Town*. Middletown, Conn.: Wesleyan University Press.

Power, R.L. 1935. Wet lands and the Hoosier stereotype. *Mississippi Valley Historical Review* **22**:33–48.

Pownall, T. [1776]1949. *A Topographical Description of the Dominions of the United States of America*. Edited by L. Mulkearn. Pittsburgh: University of Pittsburgh Press.

Pratt, P.P. 1976. *Archaeology of the Oneida Indians*. Man in the Northeast. Occasional Publications in Northeastern Anthropology, no. 1. George's Mills, N.H.

Prentice, I.C. 1986. Forest-composition calibration of pollen data. In B.E. Berglund (ed.), *Handbook of Holocene Palaeoecology and Palaeohydrology*, 799–816. New York: John Wiley and Sons.

Prentice, I.C. 1988. Records of vegetation in time and space: The principles of pollen analysis. In B. Huntley and T. Webb III (eds.), *Vegetation History*, 17–42. Dordrecht: Kluwer Academic Publishers.

Priest, W. 1802. *Travels in the United States of America; Commencing in the Year 1793, and Ending in 1797*. London: J. Johnson.

Primack, M.L. 1969. Farm fencing in the nineteenth century. *Journal of Economic History* **29**:287–291.

Prindle, C. 1961. *Watertown in 1801*. In Publication no. 28, 27–32. The Acorn Club of Connecticut. Hartford, Conn.: Case, Lockwood and Brainard.

Pring, M. [1625]1906. *A Voyage Set Out from the Citie of Bristoll, 1603*. Reprinted in H.S. Burrage (ed.), *Early English and French Voyages, 1534–1608*, 341–352. New York: Charles Scribner's Sons.

Pringle, C.G. 1884. Report on the principal lumber producing regions of the state [of Pennsylvania]. In C.S. Sargent (ed.), *Report on the Forests of North American (Exclusive of Mexico)*. Vol. 9 of the *Tenth Census of the United States*, 507–510. Washington, D.C.: GPO.

Prucha, F.P. 1987. *Handbook for Research in American History: A Guide to Bibliographies and Other Reference Works*. Lincoln: University of Nebraska Press.

Pruitt, B.H. (ed.). 1978. *The Massachusetts Tax Valuation List of 1771*. Boston: G.K. Hall.

Pruitt, B.H. 1981. Agriculture and society in the towns of Massachusetts, 1771: A statistical analysis. Ph.D. diss. Boston University.

Pruitt, B.H. 1984. Self-sufficiency and the agricultural economy of eighteenth century Massachusetts. *William and Mary Quarterly*, 3d ser., **41**:333–364.

Putnam, H.C. 1882. Forest fires. *American Journal of Forestry* **1**:27–30.

Pyne, S. 1982. *Fire in America: A Cultural History of Wildland and Rural Fire*. Princeton, N.J.: Princeton University Press.

Pyne, S.J. 1983. Fire control. In R.C. Davis (ed.), *Encyclopedia of American Forest and Conservation History*. Vol. 1, 173–178. New York: Macmillan Publishing Company.

Quercus. 1833. Fuel. *Genesee Farmer and Gardener's Journal* **3**:30.

Quick, B.E. 1923. A comparative study of the distribution of the climax association in southern Michigan. *Papers of the Michigan Academy of Science, Arts and Letters* **3**:211–243.

Rackham, O. 1976. *Trees and Woodland in the British Landscape*. London: J.M. Dent and Sons.

Rackham, O. 1977. Hedgerow trees: Their history, conservation, and renewal. *Arboriculture Journal* **3**:169–177.

Rackham, O. 1980. *Ancient Woodland: Its History, Vegetation and Uses in England*. London: Edward Arnold.

Rackham, O. 1985. Ancient woodland and hedges in England. In S.R.J. Woodell (ed.), *The English Landscape: Past, Present and Future*, 68–105. Oxford: Oxford University Press.

Rackham, O. 1986. *History of the Countryside*. London: J.M. Dent and Sons.

Rafinesque, C.S. 1811. An essay on the exotic plants, mostly European, which have been naturalized, and now grow spontaneously in the Middle States of North America. *Medical Repository* **2**:330–345.

Rakestraw, L. 1972. Conservation historiography: An assessment. *Pacific Historical Review* **4**:271–288.

Ranney, J.W., M.C. Bruner and J.B. Levenson. 1981. The importance of edge in the structure and dynamics of forest islands. In R.L. Burgess and D.M. Sharpe (eds.), *Forest Island Dynamics in Man-Dominated Landscapes*, 67–95. New York: Springer-Verlag.

Ratzel, F. 1878. *Die Vereingten Staaten von Nord-Amerika*. 2 vols. München: R. Oldenbourg.

Raup, H.M. 1937. Recent changes in climate and vegetation in southern New England and adjacent New York. *Journal of the Arnold Arboretum* **18**:79–117.

Raup, H.M. 1957. Vegetational adjustment to the instability of the site. *Proceedings of the 6th Technical Meeting of the International Union for the Conservation of Nature and Natural Resources, Edinburgh 1956*, 36–48.

Raup, H.M. 1964. Some problems in ecological theory and their relation to conservation. *Journal of Ecology* 52 (supplement):19–28.

Raup, H.M. 1967. American forest biology. *Journal of Forestry* **65**:800–803.

Raup, H.M. 1979. Beware the conventional wisdom. *Western Wildlands* **5** (3):2–9.

Raup, H.M. and R.E. Carlson. 1941. *The history of land use in the Harvard Forest*. Harvard Forest Bulletin, no. 20. Petersham, Mass.: Harvard Forest.

Raymo, C. and M.E. Raymo. 1989. *Written in Stone: A Geological and Natural*

History of the Northeastern United States. Chester, Conn.: Globe Pequot Press.

Read, R.H. 1976. *Endangered and threatened vascular plants in Wisconsin.* Technical Bulletin, no. 92. Madison: Scientific Areas Preservation Council, Wisconsin Department of Natural Resources.

Recknagel, A.B. 1923. *The Forests of New York State.* New York: Macmillan Company.

Rector, W.G. 1953. *Log Transportation in the Lake States Lumber Industry, 1840–1918: The Movement of Logs and its Relationship to Land Settlement, Waterway Development, Railroad Construction, Lumber Production, and Prices.* Glendale, Calif.: Arthur H. Clark.

Rector, W.G. 1983. Log transportation. In R.C. Davis (ed.), *Encyclopedia of American Forest and Conservation History.* Vol. 1, 354–362. New York: Macmillan Publishing Company.

Redfield, J.H. 1886. On the flora of Martha's Vineyard and Nantucket. *Proceedings of the Academy of Natural Sciences of Philadelphia for 1885*:378–379.

Reffalt, W.C. 1985. A nationwide survey: Wetlands in extremis. *Wilderness* **49** (171):28–41.

Regier, H.A. and W.L. Hartman. 1973. Lake Erie's fish community: 150 years of cultural stresses. *Science* **180**:1248–1255.

Rehder, A. 1911–1918. *The Bradley Bibliography: A Guide to the Literature of the Woody Plants of the World Published before the Beginning of the Twentieth Century.* 5 vols. Arnold Arboretum Publication, no. 3. Cambridge, Mass.: Riverside Press.

Reiger, J.F. 1986. *American Sportsmen and the Origins of Conservation.* rev. ed. Norman: University of Oklahoma Press.

Reihmer, V.A. 1939. The composition of prairie vegetation in Illinois. *Transactions of the Illinois State Academy of Science* **32**:87–88.

Reiners, N.M. and W.A. Reiners. 1965. Natural harvesting of trees. *William L. Hutcheson Memorial Forest Bulletin* 2:9–17.

Reuter, D.D. 1986. Sedge meadows of the upper Midwest: A stewardship summary. *Natural Areas Journal* 6 (4):27–34.

Reynolds, J. 1887. *The Pioneer History of Illinois.* 2d ed. Chicago: Fergus Printing Company.

Reynolds, J.E. 1938. *In French Creek Valley.* Meadville, Pa.: Tribune Publishing Company.

Reynolds, J.W. 1973. Earthworm (Annelida: Oligochaeta) ecology and systematics. In D.L. Dindal (ed.), *Proceedings of the First Soil Microcommunities Conference*, USAEC, Office of Information Services. CONF-711076, 95–120. Springfield, Va.: National Technical Information Service, USDC.

Reynolds, R.V. and A.H. Pierson. 1923. *Lumber cut of the United States, 1870–1920.* USDA Bulletin, no. 1119. Washington, D.C.: USDA.

Reynolds, R.V. and A.H. Pierson. 1925. Tracking the sawmill westward: The story of the lumber industry in the United States as unfolded by its trail across the continent. *American Forests* **31**:643–648, 686.

Reynolds, R.V. and A.H. Pierson. 1940. *Forest product statistics of the northeastern states.* USDA Statistical Bulletin, no. 70. Washington, D.C.: GPO.

Reynolds, R.V. and A.H. Pierson. 1942. *Fuelwood used in the United States 1630–1930.* USDA Circular, no. 641. Washington, D.C.: GPO.

Reznicek, A. 1980. Halophytes along a Michigan roadside with comments on the occurrence of halophytes in Michigan. *Michigan Botanist* **19**:23–30.

Rhoads, A.F. 1986. Rare plants of eastern Pennsylvania. In S.K. Majumdar, F.J. Brenner and A.F. Rhoads (eds.), *Endangered and Threatened Species Programs in Pennsylvania and Other States: Causes, Issues, and Management*, 103–110. Easton: Pennsylvania Academy of Science.

Rhoads, A.F. 1989. Endangered and threatened plants of Pennsylvania wetlands. In S.K. Majumdar, R.P. Brooks, F.J. Brenner and R.W. Tiner Jr. (eds.), *Wetlands Ecology and Conservation: Emphasis in Pennsylvania*, 139–146. Easton: Pennsylvania Academy of Science.

Rice, M.A. 1946. *Trees and Shrubs of Nantucket*. Ann Arbor, Mich.: Edwards Brothers.

Richards, J. [1872]1966. Selections from 'A Treatise on the Construction and Operation of Woodworking Machines'. *Forest History* **9**:16–23.

Richards, J.F. 1984. Documenting environmental history: Global patterns of land conversion. *Environment* **26** (9):6–13, 34–38.

Richards, N.A., J.R. Malletle, R.J. Simpson and E.A. Macie. 1984. Residential greenspace and vegetation in a mature city: Syracuse, New York. *Urban Ecology* **8**:99–125.

Richardson, C.J. and C.W. Cares. 1976. An analysis of elm (*Ulmus americana*) mortality in a second-growth hardwood forest in southeastern Michigan. *Canadian Journal of Botany* **54**:1120–1125.

Richardson, H.W., *et al.* 1903–1910. *York Deeds*. 18 vols. Bethel, Maine.

Richardson, J.L. 1977. *Dimensions of Ecology*. Baltimore, Maryland: Williams and Wilkins Company.

Richason, B.F. 1960a. The nature, extent, and drainage of the wet lands of northern Indiana, with special reference to Cass County. Ph.D. diss. University of Nebraska.

Richason, B.F. 1960b. Wetland transformation in the Wisconsin Drift area of Indiana. *Proceedings of the Indiana Academy of Science* **96**:290–299.

Richmond, G.M. and D.S. Fullerton. 1983a. *Quaternary geologic map of the Chicago 4° × 6° quadrangle*. USGS Miscellaneous Investigations Series, no. map I-1420 (NK-16). Washington, D.C.: US Geological Survey.

Richmond, G.M. and D.S. Fullerton. 1983b. *Quaternary geologic map of the Minneapolis 4° × 6° quadrangle, United States*. USGS Miscellaneous Investigations Series, no. map I-1420 (NL-15). Washington, D.C.: US Geological Survey.

Richmond, G.M. and D.S. Fullerton. 1984. *Quaternary geologic map of the Lake Superior 4° × 6° quadrangle, United States and Canada*. USGS Miscellaneous Investigations Series, no. map I-1420 (NL-16). Washington, D.C.: US Geological Survey.

Richmond, M.E. and A.G. Nicholson. 1985. *New York's farming history: Implications for wildlife abundance and habitat*. Conservation Circular vol. 23, no. 1. Ithaca: New York State College of Agriculture and Life Sciences.

Ridgway, R. 1872. Notes on the vegetation of the lower Wabash Valley. *American Naturalist* **6**:658–665.

Ridgway, R. 1873. The prairie birds of southern Illinois. *American Naturalist* **7**:197–203.

Ridgway, R. 1889. *The Ornithology of Illinois. Part I. Descriptive Catalogue*. Illinois State Laboratory of Natural History. Springfield, Ill.: H.W. Rokker.

Ridgway, R. 1915. Bird-life in southern Illinois. IV. Changes which have taken place in half a century. *Bird-Lore* **17** (3):191–198.

Riggs, H.C. 1965. *Effect of land use on low flow of streams in Rappahanock County, Virginia*. USGS Professional Paper 525C, pp. C196–C198. Washington, D.C.: US Geological Survey.

Righter, J.C., Jr. 1898. The lumbering industry of the West Branch of the

Susquehanna. In *Third Annual Report of the Pennsylvania Department of Agriculture. Part II, Division of Forestry*, 254–289. Harrisburg, Pa.: William Stanley Ray, State Printer.

Riley, G.A. 1935. A history of tanning in the state of Maine. M.A. thesis. University of Maine.

Risser, P.G. 1984. *Bibliography of Illinois vegetation*. Biological Notes, no. 121. Champaign: Illinois Natural History Survey.

Ritchie, W.A. and R.E. Funk. 1973. *Aboriginal settlement patterns in the Northeast*. Memoir, no. 20. Albany: New York State Museum and Science Service.

Robbins, C.S. 1979. Effect of forest fragmentation on bird populations. In R.M. DeGraaf and K.E. Evans (eds.), *Management of North Central and Northeastern Forests for Nongame Birds*. US Forest Service General Technical Report NC-51, 198–212. St. Paul, Minn.: North Central Forest Experiment Station.

Robbins, C.S., D.K. Dawson and B.A. Dowell. 1989. Habitat area requirements of breeding forest birds of the Middle Atlantic States. *Wildlife Monographs* **103**:1–34.

Robbins, C.S., J.R. Sauer, R. Greenberg and S. Droege. 1989. Population declines in North American birds that migrate to the Neotropics. *Proceedings of the National Academy of Sciences* **86**:7658–7662.

Robbins, M.B. and D.A. Easterla. 1992. *Birds of Missouri: Their Distribution and Abundance*. Columbia: University of Missouri Press.

Robbins, S.D., Jr. 1991. *Wisconsin Birdlife: Population and Distribution – Past and Present*. Madison: University of Wisconsin Press.

Roberts, M.L. and R.L. Stuckey. 1974. *Bibliography of theses and dissertations on Ohio floristics and vegetation in Ohio colleges and universitites*. Information Circular, no. 7. Columbus: Ohio Biological Survey.

Roberts, N. 1989. *The Holocene: An Environmental History*. New York: Basil Blackwell.

Roberts, W.I., III. 1972. American potash manufacture before the American Revolution. *Proceedings of the American Philosophical Society* **116**:383–395.

Roberts, W.I., III. 1983. Potash and pearlash. In R.C. Davis (ed.), *Encyclopedia of American Forest and Conservation History*. Vol. 2, 544–545. New York: Macmillan Publishing Company.

Robinson, S. [1835]1936. Description of northwestern Indiana. In H.A. Kellar (ed.), *Solon Robinson: Pioneer and Agriculturalist, Selected Writings, 1825–1845*. *Indiana Historical Collections* **21**:51–64.

Robinson, S. 1840. Burning prairies, etc. [Albany] *Cultivator* **7**:33.

Robinson, S.K. 1988. Reappraisal of the costs and benefits of habitat heterogeneity for nongame wildlife. *Transactions of the North American Wildlife and Natural Resources Conference* **53**:145–155.

Rodgers, C.S. and R.C. Anderson. 1979. Presettlement vegetation of two prairie peninsula counties. *Botanical Gazette* **140**:232–240.

Rogers, D.J. 1959. *Some effects of fire in southern Wisconsin woodlots*. Forestry Research Note, no. 51. Madison: University of Wisconsin.

Rohe, R.E. 1984. The Upper Great Lakes lumber era. *Inland Seas* **40** (1):16–29.

Rohr, F.W. and J.E. Potzger. 1950. Forest and prairie in three northwestern Indiana counties. *Butler University Botanical Studies* **10**:61–70.

Rohrbough, M.J. 1968. *The Land Office Business: The Settlement and Administration of American Public Land, 1789–1837*. New York: Oxford University Press.

Roman, C.T., W.A. Niering and R.S. Warren. 1984. Salt marsh vegetation change in response to tidal restoration. *Environmental Management* **8**:141–150.

Roman, J.R. 1980. Vegetation–environment relationships in virgin middle elevation forests in the Adirondack Mountains, New York. Ph.D. diss. Syracuse University.

Roosa, D.M., W.P. Pusateri and L.J. Eilers. 1986. *Distribution of endangered and threatened Iowa plants*. Special Report, no. 6. Des Moines, Iowa: [Iowa] State Preserves Advisory Board.

Root, C.A. 1941. *Forest resources of Shelby County, Ohio*. Ohio Forest Survey Report, no. 6. Wooster: Ohio WPA in cooperation with the Central States Forest Experiment Station and the Ohio Agricultural Experiment Station.

Rose, F. 1976. Lichenological indicators of environmental continuity in woodlands. In D.H. Brown, D.L. Hawksworth and R.H. Bailey (eds.), *Progress and Problems in Lichenology*, 279–307. New York: Academic Press.

Rose, F. and P.W. James. 1974. Regional studies on the British lichen flora I. The corticolous and lignicolous species of the New Forest, Hampshire. *Lichenologist* **6**:1–72.

Rose, F. and P. Wolseley. 1984. Nettlecombe Park – its history and its epiphytic lichens: An attempt at correlation. *Field Studies* **6**:117–148.

Rose, R.H. 1821. An address delivered before the Agricultural Society of Susquehanna County, at its organization, December 6, 1820. *American Farmer* **3**:101–104.

Rose, W.M. 1984. Biomass, net primary production and successional dynamics of a virgin white pine (*Pinus strobus*) stand in northern Michigan. Ph.D. diss. Michigan State University.

Rosenberg, N. 1975. America's rise to woodworking leadership. In B. Hindle (ed.), *America's Wooden Age: Aspects of its Early Technology*, 36–62. Tarrytown, N.Y.: Sleepy Hollow Press.

Rosier, J. [1605]1887. *Rosier's Relation of Waymouth's Voyage to the Coast of Maine, 1605*. Edited by H.S. Burrage. Portland, Maine: Printed for the Gorges Society.

Ross, M.I. 1950. *Pinus virginiana* in the forest primeval of five southern Indiana counties. *Bulter University Botanical Studies* **10**:80–90.

Rossiter, M. 1975. *The Emergence of Agricultural Science: Justin Liebig and the Americans, 1840–1880*. New Haven, Conn.: Yale University Press.

Rostlund, E. 1957. The evidence for the use of fish as fertilizer in aboriginal North America. *Journal of Geography* **56**:222–228.

Roth, F. 1898a. *On the forestry conditions of northern Wisconsin*. Bulletin, no. 1. Madison: Wisconsin Geological and Natural History Survey.

Roth, F. 1898b. *Forestry conditions and interests of Wisconsin*. USDA Division of Forestry Bulletin, no. 16. Washington, D.C.: GPO.

Roth, F. 1903. The jack pine plains of Michigan. In *Report of the Michigan Forestry Commission for the Year 1902*, 34–37. Lansing, Mich.: Robert Smith Printing Company, State Printer.

Rothrock, J.T. 1894a. Forests of Pennsylvania. *Proceedings of the American Philosophical Society* **33**:114–133.

Rothrock, J.T. 1894b. The forestry problem in Pennsylvania. *Proceedings of the American Forestry Association* **10**:71–78.

Rothrock, J.T. 1915. *Areas of Desolation in Pennsylvania*. Philadelphia: Herbert and Welsh.

Rothrock, J.T. and W.F. Shunk. 1896. Report of the Pennsylvania Forestry Commission appointed by act of legislature approved May 23, 1893. In *Annual Report of the Pennsylvania Department of Agriculture for 1895. Part II. Division of Forestry*. Harrisburg, Pa.: Clarence M. Bush, State Printer.

Rowe, J.S. 1961. Critique of some vegetational concepts as applied to forests of northwestern Alberta. *Canadian Journal of Botany* **39**:1007–1017.

Rudnicky, J.L. and M.J. McDonnell. 1989. Forty-eight years of canopy change in a hardwood–hemlock forest in New York City. *Bulletin of the Torrey Botanical Club* **116**:52–64.

Ruedemann, R. and W.J. Schoonmaker. 1938. Beaver dams as geologic agents. *Science* **88**:523–525.

Ruhe, R.V. 1983. Depositional environment of late Wisconsin loess in the midcontinental United States. In S.C. Porter (ed.), *Late Quaternary Environments of the United States*. Vol. 1. *The Late Pleistocene*, 130–137. Minneapolis: University of Minnesota Press.

Runkle, J.R. 1982. Patterns of disturbance in some old-growth mesic forests of eastern North America. *Ecology* **63**:1533–1546.

Runkle, J.R. 1990. Gap dynamics in an Ohio *Acer–Fagus* forest and speculations on the geography of disturbance. *Canadian Journal of Forest Research* **20**:632–641.

Runkle, J.R., J.L. Vankat and G.W. Snyder. 1984. Vegetation and the role of treefall gaps in Hueston Woods State Nature Preserve. In G.W. Willeke (ed.), *Hueston Woods State Park and Nature Preserve, Proceedings of a Symposium, April 16–18, 1982*, 1–21. Oxford, Ohio: Institute of Environmental Sciences, Miami University.

Runkle, S.T. and D.M. Roosa. 1989. *Wildflowers of the Tallgrass Prairie: The Upper Midwest*. Ames: Iowa State University Press.

Runte, A. 1979. *National Parks: The American Experience*. Lincoln: University of Nebraska Press.

Rupp, A.E. 1924. History of land purchase in Pennsylvania. *Journal of Forestry* **22**:490–497.

Rupp, I.D. 1836. *The Geographical Catechism of Pennsylvania and the Western States*. Harrisburg, Pa.: J. Winebrenner.

Rush, B. 1793. An account of the sugar maple-tree of the United States, and of the methods of obtaining sugar from it, together with observations upon the advantages both public and private of the sugar. *Transactions of the American Philosophical Society* **3**:64–78.

Russell, E.W.B. 1979. Vegetational change in northern New Jersey since 1500 A.D.: A palynological, vegetational and historical synthesis. Ph.D. diss. Rutgers University.

Russell, E.W.B. 1981. Vegetation of northern New Jersey before European settlement. *American Midland Naturalist* **105**:1–12.

Russell, E.W.B. 1983. Indian-set fires in the forests of the northeastern United States. *Ecology* **64**:78–88.

Russell, E.W.B. 1987. Pre-blight distribution of *Castanea dentata* (Marsh.) Borkh. *Bulletin of the Torrey Botanical Club* **114**:183–190.

Russell, E.W.B. and R.T. Forman. 1984. Indian burning, the unlikely hypothesis. *Bulletin of the Ecological Society of America* **65**:281–282.

Russell, H.S. 1976. *A Long, Deep Furrow: Three Centuries of Farming in New England*. Hanover, N.H.: University Press of New England.

Russell, R. 1857. *North America: Its Agriculture and Climate*. Edinburgh: Adam and Charles Black.

Rutherford, J. 1867. Notes on the state of New Jersey. *Proceedings of the New Jersey Historical Society*, 2d ser., **1**:78–89.

Rutman, D.B. 1965. *Winthrop's Boston: Portrait of a Puritan Town, 1630–1649*. New York: W.W. Norton and Company.

Rutman, D.B. 1967. *Husbandmen of Plymouth: Farms and Villages in the Old Colony, 1620–1692*. Boston: Beacon Press.

Saarnisto, M. 1988. Time-scales and dating. In B. Huntley and T. Webb III (eds.), *Vegetation History*, 77–112. Dordrecht: Kluwer Academic Publishers.

Sagard-Theodat, G. 1939. *Father Gabriel Sagard: The Long Journey to the Country of the Hurons [1632]*. Edited by G.M. Wrong. Toronto: The Champlain Society.

Sale, K. 1990. *The Conquest of Paradise: Christopher Columbus and the Columbian Legacy*. New York: Alfred A. Knopf.

Salmon, S.C. 1941. Climate and small grains. *Climate and Man, USDA Yearbook of Agriculture, 1941*, 321–342. Washington, D.C.: GPO.

Salter, R.M. and T.C. Green. 1933. Factors affecting the accumulation and loss of nitrogen and organic carbon in cropped soils. *Journal of the American Society of Agronomy* 25:622–630.

Salter, R.M., R.D. Lewis and J.A. Slipher. 1936. *Our heritage – the soil*. Bulletin, no. 175. Columbus: Agricultural Extension Service, Ohio State University.

Sampson, H.S. 1921. An ecological survey of the prairie vegetation of Illinois. *Bulletin of the Illinois Natural History Survey* 13:523–577.

Samson, F.B. 1980. Island biogeography and the conservation of nongame birds. *Transactions of the North American Wildlife and Natural Resources Conference* 45:245–251.

Samson, F.B.1983. Island biogeography and the conservation of prairie birds. In C.L. Kucera (ed.), *Proceedings of the Seventh North American Prairie Conference*, 293–299. Springfield: Southwest Missouri State University.

Sandberg, L. 1983. The response of forest industries to a changing environment. In S.L. Flader (ed.), *The Great Lakes Forest: An Environmental and Social History*, 194–204. Minneapolis: University of Minnesota Press.

Sargent, C.S. 1877. Benefits of forests and screens. *Transactions of the Wisconsin State Horticultural Society* 7:187–195.

Sargent, C.S. 1882. The protection of forests. *North American Review* 135:386–401.

Sargent, C.S. 1884. *Report on the Forests of North America (Exclusive of Mexico)*. Vol. 9 of the *Tenth Census of the United States (1880)*. Washington, D.C.: GPO.

Sargent, C.S. 1885. *Report of the Forestry Commission Appointed by the Comptroller Pursuant to Chapter 551, Laws of 1884 [Sargent Report on the Forests of the Adirondacks]*. New York State Assembly Document no. 36. Albany, N.Y.: Weed, Parsons and Company.

Sartz, R.S. 1975. Controlling runoff in the driftless area. *Journal of Soil and Water Conservation* 30:92–93.

Sartz, R.S. 1978. *Thirty years of soil and water research by the Forest Service in Wisconsin's driftless area – a history and annotated bibliography*. USDA Forest Service General Technical Report, no. NC-44. St. Paul, Minn.: North Central Forest Experiment Station.

Sartz, R.S., W.R. Curtis and D.N. Tolsted. 1977. Hydrology of small watersheds in Wisconsin's driftless area. *Water Resources Research* 13:524–530.

Sartz, R.S. and D.N. Tolsted. 1974. Effect of grazing on runoff from two small watersheds in southwestern Wisconsin. *Water Resources Research* 10:354–356.

Saterson, K.A. 1977. A vegetational history of Williamstown. Unpublished Senior thesis, Biology Department. Williams College.

Satterlund, D.R. and P.W. Adams. 1992. *Wildland Watershed Management*. 2d ed. New York: John Wiley and Sons.

Sauer, C.O. 1920. *The geography of the Ozark Highlands of Missouri*. Geographic Society of Chicago Bulletin, no. 7. Chicago: University of Chicago Press.

Sauer, C.O. 1938. Theme of plant and animal destruction in economic history. *Journal of Farm Economics* 20:765–775.

Sauer, C.O. 1941. The settlement of the humid East. In *Climate and Man, USDA*

Yearbook of Agriculture, 1941, 157–166. Washington, D.C.: GPO.

Sauer, C.O. 1947. Early relations of man to plants. *Geographical Review* **37**:9–25.

Sauer, C.O. 1956. The agency of man on earth. In W.L. Thomas Jr. (ed.), *Man's Role in Changing the Face of the Earth*. Vol. 1, 49–69. Chicago: University of Chicago Press.

Sauer, C.O. 1963. Status and change in the rural Midwest in retrospect. *Mitteilungen der Osterreichischen Geographischen Gesellschaft* **105** (3):357–365.

Sauer, C.O. [1976]1981. European backgrounds of American agricultural settlement. In C.O. Sauer (ed.), *Selected Essays 1963–1975*, 16–44. Berkeley, Calif.: Turtle Island Foundation (published for the Netzahaulcoyotl Historical Society).

Sauer, J.D. 1952. A geography of pokeweed. *Annals of the Missouri Botanical Garden* **39**:113–125.

Saunders, A.A. 1936. *Ecology of the birds of Quaker Run Valley, Allegany State Park, New York*. Handbook, no. 16. Albany: New York State Museum.

Schaetzl, R.J. and L.R. Follmer. 1990. Longevity of treethrow microtopography: Implications for mass wasting. *Geomorphology* **3**:113–123.

Schaetzl, R.J., D.L. Johnson, S.F. Burns and T.W. Small. 1989. Tree uprooting: Review of terminology, process, and environmental implications. *Canadian Journal of Forest Research* **19**:1–11.

Schaff, M. 1905. *Etna and Kirkersville*. Cambridge, Mass.: Riverside Press.

Schallenberg, R.H. 1975. Evolution, adaptation and survival: The very slow death of the American charcoal iron industry. *Annals of Science* **32**:341–358.

Schallenberg, R.H. 1981. Charcoal iron: The coal mines of the forest. In B. Hindle (ed.), *Material Culture of the Wooden Age*, 271–299. Tarrytown, N.Y.: Sleepy Hollow Press.

Schallenberg, R.H. and D.A. Ault. 1977. Raw materials supply and technological change in the American charcoal industry. *Technology and Culture* **18**:436–466.

Schertz, D.L. 1983. The basis for soil loss tolerances. *Journal of Soil and Water Conservation* **38**:10–14.

Schiff, A.L. 1962. *Fire and Water: Scientific Heresy in the Forest Service*. Cambridge, Mass.: Harvard University Press.

Schlebecker, J.T. 1969. *A Bibliography of Books and Pamphlets on the History of Agriculture in the United States from 1607 to 1967*. Santa Barbara, Calif.: Clio Press.

Schlebecker, J.T. 1975. *Whereby We Thrive: A History of American Farming, 1607–1972*. Ames: Iowa State University Press.

Schlereth, T.J. 1980. Vegetation as historical data: A historian's use of plants and natural material culture evidence. In T.J. Schlereth (ed.), *Artifacts and the American Past*, 147–159. Nashville, Tenn.: American Association for State and Local History.

Schlosser, I.J. 1982. Trophic structure, reproductive success, and growth rate of fishes in a natural and modified headwater stream. *Canadian Journal of Fisheries and Aquatic Sciences* **39**:968–978.

Schmaltz, N.J. 1983. The land nobody wanted: The dilemma of Michigan's cutover lands. *Michigan History* **67** (1):32–40.

Schmelz, D.V., J.D. Barton and A.A. Lindsey. 1975. Donaldson's Woods: Two decades of change. *Proceedings of the Indiana Academy of Science* **84**:234–243.

Schmelz, D.V. and A.A. Lindsey. 1965. Size-class structure of old-growth forests in Indiana. *Forest Science* **11**:258–264.

Schmid, J.A. 1975. *Urban vegetation: A review and Chicago case study*. Research Paper, no. 161. Chicago: Department of Geography, The University of Chicago.

Schmidt, H.G. 1945. *Rural Hunterdon: An Agricultural History*. New Brunswick,

N.J.: Rutgers University Press.

Schmidt, O.A. 1962. Lumbering in Pennsylvania. *Northeastern Logger* **10** (11):16, 17, 64–66.

Schmitt, P.J. [1969]1990. *Back to Nature: The Arcadian Myth in Urban America.* Baltimore: Johns Hopkins University Press.

Schneider, A.F. 1966. Physiography [of Indiana]. In A.A. Lindsey (ed.), *Natural Features of Indiana,* 40–56. Indianapolis: Indiana Academy of Science.

Schob, D.E. 1977. Woodhawks and cordwood: Steamboat fuel on the Ohio and Mississippi Rivers, 1820–1860. *Journal of Forest History* **21**:124–132.

Schoepf, J.D. [1788]1968. *Travels in the Confederation (1783–1784).* Translated and edited by A.J. Morrison. 2 vols. Reprint. New York: Burt Franklin.

Schoepf, J.D. 1875. *The Climate and Diseases of America.* Translated by J.R. Chadwick. Boston: Houghton and Company.

Scholtz, H.F. 1930. How long does hardwood slash remain a fire menace. *Journal of Forestry* **28**:568.

Schorger, A.W. 1941. The crow and the raven in early Wisconsin. *Wilson Bulletin* **53**:103–106.

Schorger, A.W. 1949. Squirrels in early Wisconsin. *Transactions of the Wisconsin Academy of Sciences, Arts and Letters* **39**:195–247.

Schorger, A.W. 1955. *The Passenger Pigeon: Its Natural History and Extinction.* Madison: University of Wisconsin Press.

Schorger, A.W. 1965. The beaver in early Wisconsin. *Transactions of the Wisconsin Academy of Sciences, Arts and Letters* **54**:147–178.

Schorger, A.W. 1968. The wild honeybee in Wisconsin. *Transactions of the Wisconsin Academy of Sciences, Arts and Letters* **56**:49–64.

Schroeder, M.J. and C.C. Buck. 1970. *Fire weather.* USDA Forest Service Agricultlural Handbook, no. 360. Washington, D.C.: USDA Forest Service.

Schroeder, W.A. 1983. *Presettlement prairie of Missouri.* Natural History Series, Publication, no. 2. Jefferson City: Missouri Department of Conservation.

Schurr, S.H. and B.C. Netschert. 1960. *Energy in the American Economy, 1850–1975: An Economic Study of its History and Prospects.* Baltimore: Published for Resources for the Future by the Johns Hopkins Press.

Schurz, C. 1889. *Need of a rational forest policy in the United States; Address delivered before the American Forestry Association.* Philadelphia: Printed for the American Forestry Association by Spangler and Davis.

Schwartz, C.W. and E.R. Schwartz. 1981. *The Wild Mammals of Missouri.* rev. ed. Columbia: University of Missouri.

Schwartz, M.W. 1989. Predicting tree frequencies from pollen frequency: An attempt to validate the R value method. *New Phytologist* **112**:129–143.

Schwegman, J. 1983. Illinois prairie: Then and now. Reprinted from the January 17, 1983 issue of *Outdoor Highlights* by the State of Illinois.

Schweinitz, L.D., von. 1832. Remarks on the plants of Europe which have become naturalized in a more or less degree, in the United States. *Annals of the Lyceum of Natural History of New York* **3**:148–155.

Schweinitz, L.D., von. 1927. The journey of Lewis David von Schweinitz to Goshen, Bartholomew County in 1831. Translated by A. Gerber. *Indiana Historical Society Publications* **8** (5):205–285.

Scott, F.J. 1870. *The Art of Beautifying Suburban Home Grounds.* New York: D. Appleton and Company.

Scott, J.L. [1843]1960. *A Journal of a Missionary Tour through Iowa, Wisconsin, and Michigan.* March of America Facsimile Series no. 80. Ann Arbor, Mich.: University Microfilms.

Scoville, W.C. 1953. Did colonial farmers 'waste' our land? *Southern Economic Journal* **20**:178–181.

Sears, P.B. 1926. The natural vegetation of Ohio II. The prairies. *Ohio Journal of Science* **26**:128–146.

Sears, P.B. [1935]1959. *Deserts on the March*. 3d ed. Norman: University of Oklahoma Press.

Sears, P.B. 1942. History of conservation in Ohio. In C. Whittke (ed.), *The History of the State of Ohio*. Vol. 6. *Ohio in the Twentieth Century: 1900–1938*, 219–240. Columbus: Ohio State Archaeological and Historical Society.

Sears, P.B. 1947. Man and nature in modern Ohio. *Ohio State Archaeological and Historical Quarterly* **56**:144–153.

Sears, P.B. 1956a. Some notes on the ecology of ecologists. *Scientific Monthly* **83**:21–27.

Sears, P.B. 1956b. Science and natural resources. *American Scientist* **44**:331–346.

Sears, P.B. 1974. Soil. In R.O. Utgard and G.D. McKenzie (eds.), *Man's Finite Earth*, 287–295. Minneapolis, Minn.: Burgess Publishing Company.

Sears, P.B. 1981. Peninsula or archipelago. In R.L. Stuckey and K.J. Reese (eds.), *The Prairie Peninsula – In the 'Shadow' of Transeau: Proceedings of the Sixth North American Prairie Conference*. Biological Notes no. 15, 2–3. Columbus: Ohio Biological Survey.

Seaver, F.J. 1918. *Historical Sketches of Franklin County and its Several Towns with Many Short Biographies*. Albany, N.Y.: J.B. Lyon Company.

Sedell, J.R., F.H. Everest and F.J. Swanson. 1982. Fish habitat and streamside management: Past and present. In H.C. Brown (ed.), *Proceedings of the Technical Session on Effects of Forest Practices on Fish and Wildlife Production, 1981 September 19, Orlando, Fla.*, 41–52. Washington, D.C.: Society of American Foresters.

Sedell, J.R. and J.L. Froggatt. 1984. Importance of streamside forests to large rivers: The isolation of the Willamette River, Oregon, USA, from its floodplain by snagging and streamside forest removal. *Verhandlungen Internationale Vereinigung für Theoretische und Angewandte Limnologie* **22**:1828–1834.

Seischab, F.K. 1990. Presettlement forests of the Phelps and Gorham Purchase in western New York. *Bulletin of the Torrey Botanical Club* **117**:27–38.

Selby, A.D. 1902. Preliminary list of tamarack bogs in Ohio. In *Tenth Annual Report of the Ohio State Academy of Science*, 75–77.

Selva, S.B. 1988. The lichens of northern Maine's old-growth forests. *American Journal of Botany* **75** (6 – part 2, abstracts):9.

Seton, E.T. [1925]1953. *Lives of Game Animals*. 4 vols. Boston: Charles T. Branford.

Seymour, F.C. 1969. *The Flora of New England*. Rutland, Vt.: Charles E. Tuttle Company.

Shalaway, S.D. 1985. Fencerow management for nesting birds in Michigan. *Wildlife Society Bulletin* **13**:302–306.

Shaler, N.S. 1891. *Nature and Man in America*. New York: C. Scribner's Sons.

Shaler, N.S. 1896. Environment and man in New England. *North American Review* **162**:726–739.

Shanks, R.E. 1938. The original vegetation of a part of the lake-plain of northwestern Ohio: Wood and Henry Counties. Ph.D. diss. Ohio State University.

Shanks, R.E. 1953. Forest composition and species association in the beech–maple forest region of western Ohio. *Ecology* **34**:455–466.

Sharp, L. 1975. Timber, science, and economic reform in the seventeenth century. *Forestry* **48** (1):51–86.

Sharp, P.F. 1949. The war of substitutes: The reaction of the forest industries to the competition of wood substitutes. *Agricultural History* **23**:274–279.

Sharpe, D.M., G.R. Guntenspergen, C.P. Dunn, L.A. Leitner and F. Stearns. 1987. Vegetation dynamics in a southern Wisconsin agricultural landscape. In M.G. Turner (ed.), *Landscape Heterogeneity and Disturbance*, New York: Springer-Verlag.

Sharpe, D.M., F. Stearns, L.A. Leitner and J.R. Dorney. 1986. Fate of natural vegetation during urban development of rural landscapes in southeastern Wisconsin. *Urban Ecology* **9**:267–287.

Shaw, S.P. and C.G. Fredine. 1971. *Wetlands of the United States: Their extent and their value to waterfowl and other wildlife.* USDI Fish and Wildlife Service Circular, no. 39. Washington, D.C.: GPO.

Sheail, J. 1980. *Historical Ecology: The Documentary Evidence.* Cambridge: Institute of Terrestrial Ecology.

Sheail, J. 1983. The historical perspective. In A. Warren and F.B. Goldsmith (eds.), *Conservation in Perspective*, 315–328. New York: John Wiley and Sons.

Sheldon, G. 1895. *A History of Deerfield, Massachusetts.* 2 vols. Deerfield, Mass.: Pocumtuck Valley Memorial Association.

Shelford, V.E. 1963. *The Ecology of North America.* Urbana: University of Illinois Press.

Shelton, J. and A.B. Shapiro. 1976. *The Woodburners Encyclopedia.* Waitsfield: Vermont Crossroads Press.

Sheviak, C.J. 1981. Endangered and threatened plants. In M.L. Bowles (ed.), *Endangered and Threatened Vertebrate Animals and Vascular Plants of Illinois.* Illinois Department of Conservation and US Fish and Wildlife Service, 70–179. Washington, D.C.: GPO.

Shimek, B. 1911. The pioneer and the forest. *Proceedings of the Mississippi Valley Historical Association* **3**:96–105.

Shimek, B. 1925. The persistence of the prairie. *University of Iowa Studies in Natural History* **11** (5):3–24.

Shimek, B. 1932. The relation between the migrant and native flora of the prairie region. *University of Iowa Studies in Natural History* **14** (2):10–16.

Shinners, L.H. 1940. The vegetation of the Milwaukee region. Ph.D. diss. University of Wisconsin–Madison.

Shirreff, P. [1835]1971. *A Tour through North America, together with a Comprehensive View of the Canadas and United States, as Adapted for Agricultural Emigration.* New York: Benjamin Blom.

Shoemaker, H. 1914. *Black Forest Souvenirs.* Reading, Pa.: Bright-Faust Printing Company.

Shoemaker, H.W. 1919. *Extinct Pennsylvania Animals.* 2 vols. Altoona, Pa.: Altoona Tribune Company.

Short, C.W. 1845. Observations on the botany of Illinois, more especially in reference to the autumnal flora of the prairies. *Western Journal of Medicine and Surgery*, n.s., **3**:185–198.

Shriner, F.A. and E.B. Copeland. 1904. Deforestation and creek flow about Monroe, Wisconsin. *Botanical Gazette* **37**:139–143.

Shupe, L.M. 1930. The original vegetation of Pickaway County, Ohio. M.S. thesis. Ohio State University.

Shurtleff, N.B. (ed.) 1853–1854. *Records of the Governor and Company of Massachusetts Bay in New England, 1628–1686.* 5 vols. Boston: William White.

Siccama, T.G. 1971. Presettlement and present forest vegetation in northern Vermont with special reference to Chittenden County. *American Midland Naturalist* **85**:153–172.

Silkman, R.H. 1990. Endangered plants. In *Maine Critical Areas Program Newsletter (April 1990)*.

Silliman, B. 1826. Anthracite coal of Pennsylvania, etc.: Remarks upon its properties and economical uses. *American Journal of Science and Arts* **10**:331–351.

Silliman, B. 1831. Fuel for steam boilers. *American Journal of Science and Arts* **20**:133–136.

Silver, H. 1974. *A history of New Hampshire game and furbearers*. Survey Report, no. 6. Concord: New Hampshire Fish and Game Department.

Simard, A.J. and R.W. Blank. 1982. Fire history of a Michigan jack pine forest. *Michigan Academician* **15**:59–71.

Simmons, I.G. 1988. The earliest cultural landscapes of England. *Environmental Review* **12**:105–116.

Sinclair, N.R., L.L. Getz and F.S. Bock. 1967. Influence of stone walls on the local distribution of small mammals. *University of Connecticut, Occasional Papers, Biological Sciences Series* vol. **1**:43–62.

Sipple, W.S. 1971. The past and present flora and vegetation of the Hackensack Meadows. *Bartonia* **41**:4–56.

Sitterley, J.H. 1976. *Land use in Ohio, 1900–1970: How and why it has changed*. Research Bulletin, no. 1084. Wooster: Ohio Agricultural Research and Development Center.

Skinner, B.J. and S.C. Porter. 1987. *Physical Geology*. New York: John Wiley and Sons.

Slade, J. 1850. *Report on Fuel Used in Locomotives on the Boston and Maine Railroad*. Boston: Stacy, Richardson and Company.

Slater, G. 1907. *The English Peasantry and the Enclosure of Common Fields*. London: Archibald Constable and Company.

Slough, B.G. and R.M.F.S. Sadlier. 1977. A land capability classification system for beaver (*Castor canadensis* Kuhl.). *Canadian Journal of Zoology* **55**:1324–1335.

Smith, D.C. 1970. *History of Papermaking in the United States (1691–1969)*. New York: Lockwood Publishing Company.

Smith, D.C. 1972. *A History of Lumbering in Maine 1861–1960*. University of Maine Studies, no. 93. Orono: University of Maine Press.

Smith, D.C. 1988. Maine's changing landscape to 1820. In C.E. Clark, J.S. Leamont and K. Bowden (eds.), *Maine in the Early Republic: From Revolution to Statehood*, 13–25. Hanover, N.H.: University Press of New England.

Smith, D.C., H.W. Borns, W.R. Baron and A. Bridges. 1981. Climatic stress and Maine agriculture, 1785–1885. In T.M.L. Wigley, M.J. Ingram and G. Farmer (eds.), *Climate and History: Studies on Past Climates and Their Impact on Man*, 450–464. Cambridge: Cambridge University Press.

Smith, D.C., V. Konrad, H. Koulouris, E. Hawes and H.W. Borns Jr. 1989. Salt marshes as a factor in the agriculture of northeastern North America. *Agricultural History* **63**:270–294.

Smith, D.D. 1981. Iowa prairie - an endangered ecosystem. *Proceedings of the Iowa Academy of Science* **88**:7–10.

Smith, D.M. 1946. Storm damage in New England forests. M.F.S. thesis. Yale University.

Smith, D.M. 1976. Changes in eastern forests since 1600 and possible effects. In J.F. Anderson and H.K. Kaya (eds.), *Perspectives in Forest Entomology*, 3–20. New York: Academic Press.

Smith, D.M. 1986. *The Practice of Silviculture*. 8th ed. New York: John Wiley and Sons.

Smith, F. 1928. An account of changes in the earthworm fauna of Illinois and a description of one new species. *Illinois Natural History Survey Bulletin* **17**:347–362.

Smith, H.A. 1938. The early forestry movement in the United States. *Agricultural History* **12**:326–346.

Smith, H.G., R.K. Burnard, E.E. Good and J.M. Keener. 1973. Rare and endangered vertebrates of Ohio. *Ohio Journal of Science* **73**:257–271.

Smith, J. [1616]1963. A description of New England. In P. Force (ed.), *Tracts and Other Papers Relating Principally to the Origin, Settlement, and Progress of the Colonies in North America, from the Discovery of the Country to the Year 1776.* Vol. 2, 1–34. Gloucester, Mass.: Peter Smith reprint.

Smith, J. [1631] 1833. Advertisements: or the path-way to experience to erect a plantation. *Massachusetts Historical Society Collections*, 3d ser., **3**:1–53.

Smith, J. [1799]1907. *An Account of the Remarkable Occurrences in the Life and Travels of Col. James Smith.* Cincinnati: Robert Clarke Company.

Smith, J.L. and J.V. Perino. 1981. Osage orange (*Maclura pomifera*): History and economic uses. *Economic Botany* **35**:24–41.

Smith, P.W. 1965. Recent adjustments in animal ranges. In H.E. Wright Jr. and D.G. Frey (eds.), *The Quaternary of the United States*, 633–642. Princeton, N.J.: Princeton University Press.

Smith, P.W. 1979. *The Fishes of Illinois.* Urbana: University of Illinois Press.

Smith, R. 1906. *A Tour of Four Great Rivers: The Hudson, Mohawk, Susquehanna and Delaware in 1769 being the Journal of Richard Smith of Burlington, New Jersey.* Edited by F.W. Halsey. New York: Charles Scribner's Sons.

Smith, R.H. 1954. Primeval forest of New York State (map). In R.H. Smith (ed.), *A History of Game Ranges in New York State.* Final Report, Pittman Robertson Project W-23-R, New York State Conservation Department, Division of Game. Albany: New York State Conservation Department.

Smith, S. [1765]1877. *The History of the Colony of Nova-Caesaria, or New Jersey.* 2d ed. Trenton, N.J: William S. Sharp.

Smith, S.H. 1968. Species succession and fishery exploitation in the Great Lakes. *Journal Fisheries Research Board of Canada* **25**:667–693.

Smith, T.L. 1989. An overview of old-growth forests in Pennsylvania. *Natural Areas Journal* **9**:40–44.

Smyth, J.F.D. [1784]1968. *A Tour of the United States of America.* 2 vols. Reprint. New York: Arno Press.

Snow, A.G., Jr. 1964. Maple sugaring and research. *Journal of Forestry* **62**:83–88.

Snow, D.R. 1980. *The Archaeology of New England.* New York: Academic Press.

Soper, E.K. 1919. *The peat deposits of Minnesota.* Bulletin, no. 16. Minneapolis: Minnesota Geological Survey. Published at the University of Minnesota.

Sorrie, B.A. 1989. Massachusetts flora: A review of current distribution and conservation of rare species. *Rhodora* **9**:116–120.

Sorrie, B.A. 1990. The state of the ark. *[Massachusetts Audubon Society] Sanctuary* **29** (7):8–10.

Spaeth, J.N. 1928. *Twenty years of growth of a sprout hardwood forest in New York: A study of the effects of intermediate and reproduction cuttings.* Cornell University Agricultural Experiment Station Bulletin, no. 465. Ithaca, N.Y.: Cornell University Agricultural Experiment Station.

Spalding, V.M. and B.E. Fernow. 1899. *The White Pine (Pinus strobus Linneaus).* USDA Division of Forestry Bulletin, no. 22. Washington, D.C.: GPO.

Sparhawk, W.N. and W.D. Brush. 1929. *The economic aspects of forest destruction in northern Michigan.* USDA Technical Bulletin, no. 92. Washington, D.C.: GPO.

Speirs, J.M., G. Markle and R.G. Tozer. 1970. Populations of birds in urban habitats,

Ontario County, 1969. *Ontario Field Biologist* **24**:1–12.

Spencer, J.S., Jr. 1983. *Michigan's fourth forest inventory: Area.* USDA Forest Service Resource Bulletin , no. NC-68. St. Paul, Minn.: North Central Forest Experiment Station.

Spurr, S.H. 1954. The forests of Itasca in the nineteenth century as related to fire. *Ecology* **35**:21–25.

Spurr, S.H. 1956. Forest associations in the Harvard Forest. *Ecological Monographs* **26**:245–262.

Spurr, S.H. and B.V. Barnes. 1980. *Forest Ecology.* 3d ed. New York: John Wiley and Sons.

Spurr, S.H. and A.C. Cline. 1942. Ecological forestry in central New England. *Journal of Forestry* **40**:418–420.

Squiers, E. 1986. The relationship between weed community development and tillage type in Grant County, Indiana. In *Program of the IV International Congress of Ecology and 71st Annual Meeting of the Ecological Society of America, Syracuse, N.Y., Aug. 10–16, 1986,* 320.

Squires, W.A. 1906. The passing of the prairie flora. *The Plant World* **9**:162–164.

Stallings, J.H. 1957. *Soil Conservation.* Englewood Cliffs, N.J.: Prentice-Hall.

Stalter, R. 1981. A thirty-nine year history of the arborescent vegetation of Alley Pond Park, Queens County, New York. *Bulletin of the Torrey Botanical Club* **108**:485–487.

Stansbery, D.H. 1961. A century of change in the naiad population. In *American Malacological Union Annual Reports for* 1961, 20–22.

Stark, C.M. 1847. Pigeon weed, or red root. *Transactions of the New York State Agricultural Society* **6**:435–439.

Starr, F. 1865. American forests: Their destruction and preservation. In *Report of the Commissioner of Agriculture for the Year 1865,* 210–234. Washington, D.C.: GPO.

Starrett, W.C. 1971. A survey of the mussels (Unionacea) of the Illinois River: A polluted stream. *Illinois Natural History Survey Bulletin* **30** (5):268–403.

Stearns, F.W. 1949. Ninety years change in a northern hardwood forest in Wisconsin. *Ecology* **30**:350–358.

Stearns, F.W. 1951. The composition of the sugar maple–hemlock–yellow birch association in northern Wisconsin. *Ecology* **32**:245–263.

Stearns, F.W. 1971. Urban botany – an essay on survival. *University of Wisconsin – Milwaukee Field Stations Bulletin* **4** (1):1–6.

Stearns, F.W. 1974. The use of the American General Land Office survey in syndynamical vegetation analysis. In R. Knapp (ed.), *Handbook of Vegetation Science. Part VIII. Vegetation Dynamics,* 73–80. The Hague: Dr. W. Junk.

Stearns, F.W. 1975. Urban wildlife - wildlife habitat and implications for man. In *Science for Better Environment, Proceedings of the International Congress on the Urban Environment,* 243–249.

Stearns, F.W. 1978. Urban ecology - opportunity or tar pit. *Bulletin of the Ecological Society of America* **59** (1):7–9.

Stearns, F.W. and G. Guntenspergen. 1987. Maps of presettlement forests of the Lake States and major forest types of the Lake States. In W. Shands (ed.), *The Lake States Forests – A Resources Renaissance,* Washington D.C.: The Conservation Foundation.

Stearns, R.P. 1970. *Science in the British Colonies of America.* Urbana, Ill.: University of Illinois Press.

Steavenson, H.A., H.E. Gearhart and R.C. Curtis. 1943. Living fences and supplies of fence posts. *Journal of Wildlife Management* **7**:257–261.

Steer, H.B. 1948. *Lumber production in the United States, 1799–1946*. USDA Miscellaneous Publication, no. 669. Washington, D.C.: GPO.

Steinbrenner, E.C. 1951. Effect of grazing on floristic composition and soil properties of farm woodlands in southern Wisconsin. *Journal of Forestry* **49**:906–910.

Stempel, M.E. and S. Rodgers Jr. 1961. History of prairie chickens in Iowa. *Proceedings of the Iowa Academy of Science* **68**:314–322.

Stephens, E.P. 1955. The historical–developmental method of determining forest trends. Ph.D. diss. Harvard University.

Stephens, E.P. 1956. The uprooting of trees: A forest process. *Proceedings of the Soil Science Society of America* **20**:113–116.

Stephens, G. and P.E. Waggoner. 1980. *A half century of natural transitions in mixed hardwood forests*. Bulletin, no. 783. New Haven, Conn.: Connecticut Agricultural Experiment Station.

Stephens, W.B. 1991. *Sources for U.S. History: Nineteenth Century Communities*. Cambridge: Cambridge University Press.

Stephenson, N.L. 1987. Use of tree aggregations in forest ecology and management. *Environmental Management* **11**:1–5.

Stephenson, R.W. 1967. *Landownership Maps: A Checklist of Nineteenth Century United States County Maps in the Library of Congress*. Washington, D.C.: Library of Congress.

Stepney, P.H.R. and D.M. Power. 1973. Analysis of the eastward breeding expansion of Brewer's blackbird plus general aspects of avian expansion. *Wilson Bulletin* **85**:452–463.

Stewart, D.P. and P. MacClintock. 1969. *The surficial geology and Pleistocene history of Vermont*. Bulletin, no. 31. Montpelier, Vt.: Vermont Geological Survey.

Stewart, G.R. 1933. A study of soil changes associated with the transition from fertile hardwood forest land to pasture types of decreasing fertility. *Ecological Monographs* **3**:107–131.

Stewart, L.O. 1935. *Public Land Surveys: History, Instructions, Methods*. Ames, Iowa: Collegiate Press.

Stewart, O.C. 1951. Burning and natural vegetation in the United States. *Geographical Review* **41**:317–320.

Stewart, O.C. 1956. Fire as the first great force employed by man. In W.L. Thomas Jr. (ed.), *Man's Role in Changing the Face of the Earth*, 115–133. Chicago: University of Chicago Press.

Stewart, O.C. 1963. Barriers to understanding the influence of use of fire by aborigines on vegetation. In *Proceedings of the Second Tall Timbers Fire Ecology Conference*, 117–126.

Stickel, P.W. and R.C. Hawley. 1924. The grazing of cattle and horses in pine plantations. *Journal of Forestry* **22**:846–860.

Stilgoe, J. 1976. Documents in landscape history. *Journal of Architectural Education* **30** (1):15–18.

Stillwell, L.D. 1937. Migration from Vermont. *Proceedings of the Vermont Historical Society* **5**:63–245.

Stockbridge, L. 1873. Lecture by Professor Stockbridge. In *Twentieth Annual Report of the Secretary of the Massachusetts Board of Agriculture*, 196–215. Boston: Wright and Potter, State Printers.

Stoltman, J.B. and D.A. Baerreis. 1983. The evolution of human ecosystems in the eastern United States. In S.C. Porter (ed.), *Late Quaternary Environments of the United States*. Vol. 1. *The Late Pleistocene*, 252–268. Minneapolis: University of Minnesota Press.

Stone, B.D. 1982. The Massachusetts state surficial geologic map. In O.C. Farquahar (ed.), *Geotechnology in Massachusetts*, 11–27. Amherst: Graduate School of the University of Massachusetts.

Stone, E.L. 1975. Windthrow influences on spatial heterogeneity in a forest soil. *Mitteilungen Eidgenössische Anstalt für das forstliche Versuchswisen* **51**:77–87.

Stone, H. 1945. *A Flora of Chester County, Pennsylvania.* 2 vols. Philadelphia: Pennsylvania Academy of Natural Sciences of Philadelphia.

Stout, A.B. 1946. The bur oak openings in southern Wisconsin. *Transactions of the Wisconsin Academy of Science, Arts, and Letters* **36**:141–161.

Stout, W. 1933. The charcoal iron industry of the Hanging Rock Iron district – its influence on the early development of the Ohio Valley. *Ohio Archaeological and Historical Society Publications* **42**:72–104.

Strayer, D. 1980. The freshwater mussels (Bivalvia: Unionidae) of the Clinton River, Michigan, with comments on man's impact on the fauna, 1870–1978. *The Nautilis* **94**:142–149.

Strickland, W. 1801. *Observations on the Agriculture of the United States of America.* London: W. Bulmer and Company.

Strickland, W. 1971. *Journal of a Tour in the United States of America, 1794–1795.* Edited by J.E. Strickland. New York: New York Historical Society.

Stroessner, W.J. and J.R. Habeck. 1966. The presettlement vegetation of Iowa County, Wisconsin. *Transactions of the Wisconsin Academy of Sciences, Arts and Letters* **55**:167–180.

Stuart, J. 1833. *Three Years in North America.* 2 vols. London: Whittaker and Company.

Stuckey, R.L. 1981. Origin and development of the concept of the Prairie Peninsula. In R.L. Stuckey and K.J. Reese (eds.), *The Prairie Peninsula – In the 'Shadow' of Transeau: Proceedings of the Sixth North American Prairie Conference.* Biological Notes no. 15, 4–23. Columbus: Ohio Biological Survey.

Stuckey, R.L. and M.L. Roberts. 1977. Rare and endangered aquatic vascular plants of Ohio: An annotated list of the imperiled species. *Sida* **7**:24–41.

Sukopp, H. and P. Werner. 1983. Urban environments and vegetation. In W. Holzner, M.J.A. Werger and I. Ikusima (eds.), *Man's Impact on Vegetation*, 247–260. Boston: Dr. W. Junk Publishers.

Suloway, L. 1981. The Unionid (Mollusca: Bivalvia) fauna of the Kankakee River in Illinois. *American Midland Naturalist* **105**:233–239.

Summers, B. 1853. Response to circular. In *Report of the Commissioner of Patents for the Year 1852*, 245–249. Washington, D.C.: Printer to the House of Representatives.

Svenson, H.K. 1936. The early vegetation of Long Island. *Brooklyn Botanic Garden Record* **25**:207–227.

Swain, A.M. 1973. A history of fire and vegetation in northeastern Minnesota as recorded in lake sediments. *Quaternary Research* **3**:383–396.

Swain, A.M. 1978. Environmental changes during the past 2000 years in north-central Wisconsin: Analysis of pollen, charcoal, and seeds from varved lake sediments. *Quaternary Research* **10**:55–68.

Swain, A.M. 1980. Landscape patterns and forest history in the Boundary Waters Canoe Area, Minnesota: A pollen study from Hug Lake. *Ecology* **61**:747–754.

Swan, F.B., Jr. 1970. Post-fire response of four plant communities in south-central New York State. *Ecology* **51**:1074–1082.

Swift, E. 1946. *A history of Wisconsin deer.* Publication, no. 323. Madison: Wisconsin Conservation Department.

Swink, F. and G. Wilhelm. 1979. *Plants of the Chicago Region.* rev. ed. Lisle, Ill.: The Morton Arboretum.

Taber, T.T., III. 1971. *Logging Railroad Era of Lumbering in Pennsylvania.* Vol. 5. *The Goodyears: An Empire in the Hemlocks.* Williamsport, Pa.: Lycoming Printing Company.

Taber, T.T., III. 1972. *Logging Railroad Era of Lumbering in Pennsylvania.* Vol. 4. *Sunset along Susquehanna Waters.* Williamsport, Pa.: Lycoming Printing Company.

Taber, T.T., III. 1974. *Logging Railroad Era of Lumbering in Pennsylvania.* Vol. 10. *Tanbark, Alcohol, and Lumber.* Williamsport, Pa.: Lycoming Printing Company.

Taber, T.T., III. 1975. *Logging Railroad Era of Lumbering in Pennsylvania.* Vol. 7. *Sawmills Among the Derricks.* Williamsport, Pa.: Lycoming Printing Company.

Talleyrand, C.M., de. 1942. *Talleyrand in America as a Financial Promoter 1794–96: Unpublished Letters and Memoirs.* Vol. 2. Translated and edited by H. Huth and W. J. Pugh. Washington, D.C.: GPO.

Tans, W. 1976. *The presettlement vegetation of Columbia County, Wisconsin in the 1830's.* Technical Bulletin, no. 90. Madison: Wisconsin Department of Natural Resources.

Tansley, A.G. 1953. *The British Islands and their Vegetation.* Cambridge: Cambridge University Press.

Tansley, A.G. and M.C.F. Proctor. 1968. *Britain's Green Mantle: Past, Present and Future.* London: George Allen and Unwin.

Taylor, C.E. and R.E. Spurr. 1973. *Aerial photographs in the National Archives.* Special List, no. 25. Washington, D.C.: National Archives and Records Service, General Services Administration.

Taylor, J.W. 1955. Ditch, tile, and levee: The significance of wetlands and their drainage to the Wabash lowlands of Indiana. Ph.D. diss. Indiana University.

Taylor, N. 1923. The vegetation of Long Island. Part I. The vegetation of Montauk: A study of grassland and forest. *Brooklyn Botanical Garden Memoirs* **2**:1–107.

Taylor, W.L. 1982. The nineteenth century hill town: Images and reality. *Historical New Hampshire* **37**:283–309.

Teas, T.S. 1916. Journal of a tour to Fort Wayne and the adjacent country, in the year 1821. In H. Lindley (ed.), *Indiana as Seen by Early Travelers. Indiana Historical Collections,* 246–255. Indianapolis: Indiana Historical Commission.

Telford, C.J. 1927. Third report on a forest survey of Illinois. *Bulletin of the Illinois State Natural History Survey* **16**:1–102.

Temin, P. 1964. *Iron and Steel in Nineteenth-Century America: An Economic Inquiry.* Cambridge, Mass.: MIT Press.

Temple, J.H. [1889]1905. *History of the Town of Palmer, Massachusetts, Early Known as the Elbow Tract: Including Records of the Plantation, District and Town 1716–1889.* Palmer, Mass.: Published by the Town of Palmer.

Temple, S.A. and J.R. Cary. 1988. Modeling dynamics of habitat-interior bird populations in fragmented landscapes. *Conservation Biology* **2**:340–347.

Terborgh, J. 1989. *Where Have All the Birds Gone? Essays on the Biology and Conservation of Birds that Migrate to the American Tropics.* Princeton, N.J.: Princeton University Press.

Terrie, P.G. 1981. Adirondack Forest Preserve: The irony of forever wild. *New York History* **62**:261–288.

Teschemacher, J.E. 1835. On the preservation and cultivation of the indigenous plants of North America. *American Gardener's Magazine* **1**:12–13.

Tessendorf, K.C. 1972. How the Midwest was won. *Natural History* **81** (2):22, 24, 26.

Thirsk, J. 1957. *English Peasant Farming.* London: Routledge and Kegan Paul.

Thirsk, J. 1964. The common fields. *Past and Present* **29**:3–25.

Thirsk, J. (ed.) 1967. *The Agrarian History of England and Wales.* Vol. IV.

1500–1640. Cambridge: Cambridge University Press.

Thirsk, J. 1984. Patterns of agriculture in seventeenth-century England. In D.D. Hall and D.G. Allen (eds.), *Seventeenth–Century New England, Collections of the Colonial Society of Massachusetts* **63**:39–54.

Thom, H.C.S. 1963. Toronado probabilities. *Monthly Weather Review* **91**:730–736.

Thomas, D. [1819]1970. *Travels Through the Western Country in the Summer of 1816*. Reprint. Darien, Conn.: Hafner Publishing Company.

Thomas, E.S. 1951. Distribution of Ohio animals. *Ohio Journal of Science* **51**:153–167.

Thomas, J.J. 1845. On the rotation of crops. *Ohio Cultivator* **1**:130–132.

Thomas, J.W., L.F. Ruggiero, R.W. Mannan, J.W. Schoen and R.A. Lancia. 1988. Management and conservation of old-growth forests in the United States. *Wildlife Society Bulletin* **16**:252–262.

Thomas, P.A. 1976. Contrastive subsistence strategies and land use as factors for understanding Indian–white relations in New England. *Ethnohistory* **23**:1–18.

Thomas, P.A. 1979. In the maelstrom of change: The Indian trade and cultural process in the middle Connecticut River Valley: 1635–1665. Ph.D. diss. University of Massachusetts.

Thompson, D.Q. and R.H. Smith. 1971. The forest primeval in the Northeast – a great myth. In *Proceedings of the Tenth Annual Tall Timbers Fire Ecology Conference*, 255–265.

Thompson, J.N. 1981. Elaiosomes and fleshy fruits: Phenology and selection pressures for ant-dispersed seeds. *American Naturalist* **117**: 104–108.

Thompson, K. 1980. Forests and climate change in America: Some early thoughts. *Climatic Change* **3**:47–64.

Thompson, M.J. 1959. *85 years of farming in the northern coniferous areas of Minnesota, Wisconsin, and Michigan*. Miscellaneous Report, no. 35. St. Paul, Minnesota: Agricultural Experiment Station, University of Minnesota.

Thompson, R.C. 1963. Politics in the wilderness: New York's Adirondack Forest Preserve. *Forest History* **6** (4):14–23.

Thompson, W.B. 1982. Recession of the late Wisconsin ice sheet in coastal Maine. In G.J. Larson and B.D. Stone (eds.), *Late Wisconsin Glaciation of New England*, 211–228. Dubuque, Iowa: Kendall-Hunt.

Thompson, W.B. and H.W. Borns Jr. 1985. *Surficial geologic map of Maine*. Augusta: Maine Geological Survey, Department of Conservation.

Thompson, Z. 1842. *History of Vermont, Natural, Civil, and Statistical*. Burlington, Vt.: Chauncey Goodrich.

Thomson, J.W. 1940. Relic prairie areas in central Wisconsin. *Ecological Monographs* **10**:686–717.

Thor, E. and G.M. Nichols. 1974. Some effects of fires on litter, soil, and hardwood regeneration. In *Proceedings of the Thirteenth Annual Tall Timbers Fire Ecology Conference*, 317–329.

Thoreau, H.D. [1862]1980. Walking. In R. Sattelmeyer (ed.), *The Natural History Essays*, 93–136. Salt Lake City, Utah: Peregrine Smith.

Thoreau, H.D. [1864]1972. *The Maine Woods*. Edited by J.J. Moldenhauer. Princeton, N.J.: Princeton University Press.

Thoreau, H.D. 1914. *Cape Cod*. Boston: Houghton Mifflin.

Thorley, A. 1981. Pollen analytical evidence relating to the vegetation history of the Chalk. *Journal of Biogeography* **8**:93–106.

Thorne, M. 1951. 'Book farming' in Iowa. *Iowa Journal of History* **49**:117–142.

Thwaites, F.T. 1956. *Wisconsin glacial deposits map*. Madison: Wisconsin Geological and Natural History Survey.

Tiffin, E. 1834. Letter 'Edward Tiffin to Josiah Meigs,' 30 November 1815. *American State Papers: Public Lands.* Vol. 3, 164–165. Washington, D.C.: Gales and Seaton.

Tilghman, N. 1989. Impacts of white-tailed deer on forest regeneration in northwestern Pennsylvania. *Journal of Wildlife Management* **53**:524–532.

Tiner, R.W. 1984. *Wetlands of the United States: Current status and recent trends. US Fish and Wildlife Service, National Wetlands Inventory.* Washington, D.C.: GPO.

Tober, J.A. 1981. *Who Owns the Wildlife: The Political Economy of Conservation in Nineteenth Century America.* Westport, Conn.: Greenwood Press.

Tocqueville, A., de. [1835]1966. *Democracy in America.* Translated by H. Reeves and F. Bowen. Edited by P. Bradley. 2 vols. New York: Alfred A. Knopf.

Tocqueville, A., de. [1960]1971. *Journey to America.* Edited by J.P. Mayer. Translated by G. Lawrence. Garden City, N.Y.: Anchor Books, Doubleday and Company.

Todd, C.L. 1962. Some nineteenth century European travellers in New York State. *New York History* **43**:336–370.

Tome, P. [1854]1928. *Pioneer Life; or, Thirty Years a Hunter, being Scenes and Adventures in the Life of Philip Tome.* Harrisburg, Pa.: Aurand Press.

Tonti, E.A. 1941. *Forest resources of Madison County, Ohio.* Ohio Forest Survey Report, no. 12. Wooster, Ohio: Ohio WPA in cooperation with the Central States Forest Experiment Station and the Ohio Agricultural Experiment Station.

Torbert, E. 1935. Evolution of land utilization in Lebanon, New Hampshire. *Geographical Review* **25**:209–230.

Torrey, R.H. 1926. *State Parks and Recreational Uses of State Forests in the United States.* Washington, D.C.: The National Conference on State Parks.

Towle, E.R. 1886. Farming, past and present. In *Ninth Vermont Agricultural Report by the State Board of Agriculture for the Years 1885–86,* 157–165. Montpelier, Vt.: Watchmans State Journal Press.

Trail, C.P. [1846]1929. *The Backwoods of Canada.* Reprint. Toronto: McClelland and Stewart.

Transeau, E.N. 1935. The Prairie Peninsula. *Ecology* **16**:423–437.

Trautman, M.B. 1939. The numerical status of some mammals throughout historic time in the vicinity of Buckeye Lake, Ohio. *Ohio Journal of Science* **39**:133–143.

Trautman, M.B. 1940. *The birds of Buckeye Lake, Ohio.* Museum of Zoology, University of Michigan, Miscellaneous Publication, no. 44. Ann Arbor: University of Michigan Press.

Trautman, M.B. 1977. *The Ohio country from 1750 to 1977 – A naturalist's view.* Biological Notes, no. 10. Columbus: Ohio Biological Survey.

Trautman, M.B. 1981. *The Fishes of Ohio.* rev. ed. Columbus: Ohio State University Press.

Trautman, M.B. and D.K. Gartman. 1974. Re-evaluation of the effects of man-made modifications on Gordon Creek between 1887 and 1973 and especially as regards its fish fauna. *Ohio Journal of Science* **74**:162–173.

Trefethen, J.B. 1970. The return of the white-tailed deer. *American Heritage* **21** (2):97–103.

Trefethen, J.B. 1975. *An American Crusade for Wildlife.* Alexandria, Va.: Boone and Crockett Club.

Trefethen, J.B. 1976. *The American Landscape, 1776–1976: Two Centuries of Change.* Washington, D.C.: The Wildlife Management Institute.

Trewartha, G.T. 1941. Climate and settlement of the subhumid lands. *Climate and Man, USDA Yearbook of Agriculture, 1941,* 167–176. Washington, D.C.: GPO.

Trewartha, G.T. and L.H. Horn. 1980. *An Introduction to Climate*. 5th ed. New York: McGraw-Hill.

Trimble, G.R., Jr. and H.W. Lull. 1956. *The role of forest humus in watershed management in New England*. USDA Forest Service Northeastern Forest Experiment Station Paper, no. 85. Upper Darby, Pa.: Northeastern Forest Experiment Station.

Trimble, S.W. 1974. *Man-induced Soil Erosion in the Southern Piedmont, 1700–1970*. Ankeny, Iowa: Soil Conservation Society of America.

Trimble, S.W. 1976. Sedimentation in Coon Creek Valley, Wisconsin. In *Proceedings, Third Federal Inter-Agency Sedimentation Conference*, section 5, 100–112. Washington, D.C.: Water Resources Council.

Trimble, S.W. 1985. Perspectives on the history of soil erosion control in the eastern United States. *Agricultural History* **59**:162–180.

Trimble, S.W. and R.U. Cooke. 1991. Historical sources for geomorphological research in the United States. *Professional Geographer* **43** (2):212–228.

Trimble, S.W. and S.W. Lund. 1982. *Soil conservation and the reduction of erosion and sedimentation in the Coon Creek Basin, Wisconsin*. USGS Paper, no. 1234. Washington, D.C.: US Geological Survey.

Trimble, S.W., F.H. Weirich and B.L. Hoag. 1987. Reforestation and the reduction of water yield on the southern Piedmont since circa 1940. *Water Resources Research* **23**:425–437.

Triska, F.J. 1984. Role of wood debris in modifying channel geomorphology and riparian areas of a large lowland river under pristine conditions: A historic case study. *Verhandlungen Internationale Vereinigung für Theoretische und Angewandte Limnologie* **22**:1876–1892.

Trumbull, B. [1818]1898. *A Complete History of Connecticut from the Emigration of its First Planters, from England, in the Year 1630, to the Year 1764; and to the Close of the Indian Wars*. New London, Conn.: H.D. Utley.

Tubbs, C.H., R.M. DeGraaf, M. Yamasaki and W.M. Healy. 1987. *Guide to wildlife tree management in New England northern hardwoods*. USDA Forest Service General Technical Report, no. NE-118. Broomall, Pa.: Northeastern Forest Experiment Station.

Tubbs, C.R. 1986. *The New Forest* . London: Collins (New Naturalist).

Tudor, H. 1834. *Narrative of a Tour in North America*. 2 vols. London: James Duncan.

Turner, F.J. [1893]1961. The significance of the frontier in American history. In R.A. Billington (ed.), *Frontier and Section: Selected Essays of Frederick Jackson Turner*, 11–27. Englewood Cliffs, N.J.: Prentice-Hall.

Turner, F.J. 1920. *The Frontier in American History*. New York: Holt.

Turner, J. 1962. The *Tilia* decline: An anthropogenic interpretation. *New Phytologist* **61**:328–341.

Turner, J. and S.M. Peglar. 1988. Temporally-precise studies of vegetation history. In B. Huntley and T. Webb Jr. (eds.), *Vegetation History*, 753–777. Dordrecht: Kluwer Academic Press.

Twery, M.J. and W.A. Patterson, III. 1984. Variations in beech bark disease and its effects on species composition and structure of northern hardwood stands in central New England. *Canadian Journal of Forest Research* **14**:565–574.

Twining, C.E. 1964. Plunder and progress: The lumber industry in perspective. *Wisconsin Magazine of History* **47** (2):116–124.

Tyrrell, L. and T. Crow. 1989. Old-growth in the Lake States: What is it? Why is it important? *Bulletin of the Botanical Club of Wisconsin* **21** (2–4):37–40.

US Association of Charcoal Iron Workers. 1880. The denudation of our forests.

Journal of the United States Association of Charcoal Iron Workers 1:33–38.

US Bureau of the Census. 1932. *Fifteenth Census of the United States: 1930. Agriculture.* Farms and farm property. In Vol. 4, 43–48. Washington, D.C.: GPO.

US Bureau of the Census. 1952. *Census of Agriculture: 1950.* Vol. 1, part 2. *Counties and State Economic Areas.* Washington, D.C.: GPO.

US Bureau of the Census. 1977. *1974 Census of Agriculture.* Vol. 1, *Geographic Area Series*, Part 35. *Ohio State and County Data.* Washington, D.C.: GPO.

US Bureau of the Census. 1981a. *1978 Census of Agriculture.* Vol. 5, *Special Reports.* Part 1, *Graphic Summary.* Washington, D.C.: GPO.

US Bureau of the Census. 1981b. *1978 Census of Agriculture.* Vol. 5, *Special Reports.* Part 5, *Drainage of Agricultural Lands.* Washington, D.C.: GPO.

US Bureau of the Census. 1984. *1982 Census of Agriculture.* State data. In Vol. 1, part 51, 134–144. Washington, D.C.: GPO.

US Bureau of the Census. 1989. *1987 Census of Agriculture.* Vol. 1, *Geographic Area Series*, Part 35. *Ohio State and County Data.* Washington, D.C.: GPO.

US Census Office. Department of the Interior. 1872a. *A Compendium of the Ninth Census.* Washington, D.C.: GPO.

US Census Office. Department of the Interior. 1872b. *Ninth Census.* Vol. 3. *The Statistics of the Wealth and Industry of the United States.* Washington, D.C.: GPO.

US Census Office. Department of the Interior. 1883. *Tenth Census of the U.S.: 1880.* Vol. 3. *Agriculture.* Washington, D.C.: GPO.

US Census Office. Department of the Interior. 1895. *Eleventh Census of the U.S.: 1890.* Vol. 5. *Statistics of Agriculture.* Washington, D.C.: GPO.

US Congress. 1860. Quantity and quality of unsold lands (communicated to the Senate of the United States, December 9, 1828). In *American State Papers: Public Lands.* Vol. 5, 538–581. Washington, D.C.: Gales and Seaton.

US Department of Energy. 1980. *Heating with Wood.* Washington, D.C.: GPO.

US Department of the Interior – Heritage Conservation and Recreation Service. 1980. National registry of natural landmarks. *Federal Register* **45** (232):79698–79723.

US Forest Service. 1920. *Timber depletion, lumber prices, lumber exports, and concentration of timber ownership.* Report on Senate Resolution 311 (the Caper Report). Washington, D.C.: GPO.

US Senate. 1957. *Land and water resources of the New England–New York region.* 85th Cong., 1st sess., S. Doc. 14.

USDA Forest Service. 1950–1971. *Wildfire Statistics, until 1968 called Forest Fire Statistics.* Published annually by the Division of Cooperative Forest Fire Control. Washington, D.C.: US Forest Service.

USDA Forest Service. 1954. *Forest statistics for New York. Forest District No. 4.* Forest Statistics Series, New York, no. 5. Upper Darby, Pa.: Northeastern Forest Experiment Station.

USDA Office of Forest Investigations. 1919. *The use of wood for fuel.* USDA Bulletin, no. 753. Washington, D.C.: GPO.

Utter, W.T. 1942. *The Frontier State, 1803–1825.* Vol. 2 of *History of the State of Ohio.* Edited by C.F. Wittke. Columbus: Ohio State Archaeological and Historical Society.

Vail, R.W.G. 1949. *The Voice of the Old Frontier.* New York: Thomas Yoseloff.

Vale, T.R. and G.R. Vale. 1983. *U.S. 40 Today: Thirty Years of Landscape Change in America.* Madison: University of Wisconsin Press.

Van der Donck, A. [1656]1968. *A Description of the New Netherlands.* Edited by T.F. O'Donnell. Syracuse, N.Y.: Syracuse University Press.

Vance, D.R. 1976. Changes in land use and wildlife populations in southeastern

Illinois. *Wildlife Society Bulletin* **4**:11–15.

VanDruff, L.W. and R.N. Rowse. 1986. Habitat association of mammals in Syracuse, New York. *Urban Ecology* **9**:413–434.

Vaughan, L.M. 1929. *Abandoned farm areas in New York*. Bulletin, no. 490. Ithaca, N.Y.: Cornell University Agricultural Experiment Station.

Veatch, J.O. 1927. The dry prairies of Michigan. *Papers of the Michigan Academy of Science, Arts and Letters* **8**:269–278.

Vecsey, C. 1980. American Indian environmental religions. In C. Vecsey and R.W. Venables (eds.), *American Indian Environments: Ecological Issues in Native American History*, 1–37. Syracuse, N.Y.: Syracuse University Press.

Vent, M.H. 1973. *South Manitou Island: From Pioneer Community to National Park*. New York: Produced for the Eastern National Parks and Monument Association by the Publishing Center for Cultural Resources.

Vermeule, C.C. 1896. Wood-lands and water-flow in New Jersey. *Proceedings of the American Forestry Association* **11**:130–137.

Vermeule, C.C. 1900. The forests of New Jersey. In *Annual Report of the State Geologist [of New Jersey] for the Year 1899*, 13–172. Trenton, N.J.: MacCrellish and Quigley, State Printers.

Verrazano, G. [1905]1968. Narragansett Bay. In G.P. Winship (ed.), *Sailors' Narratives of Voyages along the New England Coast 1524–1624*, 1–23. Reprint. New York: Burt Franklin.

Verry, E.S. 1986. Forest harvesting and water: The lake states experience. *Water Resources Bulletin* **22**:1039–1047.

Verry, E.S. and D.H. Boelter. 1978. Peatland hydrology. In P.E. Greeson, J.R. Clark and J.E. Clark (eds.), *Wetlands Functions and Values: The State of Our Understanding*, 389–402. Minneapolis, Minn.: American Water Resources Association.

Vestal, A.G. 1936. Barrens vegetation in Illinois. *Transactions of the Illinois State Academy of Science* **29**:79–80.

Vestal, A.G. 1939. Why the Illinois settlers chose forest lands. *Transactions* of the *Illinois State Academy of Science* **32**:85–87.

Vestal, A.G. and M.F. Heermans. 1945. Size requirements for reference areas in mixed forest. *Ecology* **26**:122–134.

Vickery, B., C.S. Campbell, L.M.E. Eastman and H.R. Tyler Jr. 1989. Progress in rare plant conservation in Maine. *Rhodora* **91**:95–102.

Vivier, L. 1900. Letter from Father Vivier of the Society of Jesus to a Father of the same Society. In R.G. Thwaites (ed.), *The Jesuit Relations and Allied Documents. Travels and Explorations of the Jesuit Missionaries in New France 1610–1791*. Vol. 69, 200–229. Cleveland, Ohio: The Burrows Brothers Company.

Vogl, R.J. 1964. Vegetational history of Crex Meadows, a prairie savanna in northwestern Wisconsin. *American Midland Naturalist* **72**:157–175.

Voigt, J.W. and J.E. Weaver. 1951. Range condition classes of native Midwestern pasture: An ecological analysis. *Ecological Monographs* **21**:39–60.

Volney, C.F. [1804]1968. *A View of the Soil and Climate of the United States of America*. Reprint. New York: Hafner Publishing Company.

Voss, E. 1972. One natural area – past and present. *Michigan Botanist* **11**:140–142.

Wacker, P.O. 1964. Man and the American chestnut. *Annals of the Association of American Geographers* **54**:440–441.

Walcott, C.F. 1974. Changes in bird life in Cambridge, Massachusetts from 1860 to 1964. *Auk* **91**:151–160.

Walcott, C.H. 1884. *Concord in the Colonial Period*. Boston: Estes and Lauriat.

Wales, B.A. 1972. Vegetation analysis of north and south edges in a mature oak–hickory forest. *Ecological Monographs* **42**:451–471.

Walker, J.E. 1966. *Hopewell Village: A Social and Economic History of an Iron-Making Community.* Philadelphia: University of Pennsylvania Press.

Walker, T.B. 1910. Conservation of the future lumber supply. *Bulletin of the Minnesota Academy of Science* **4**:347–355.

Wallace, A.L. 1876. *The Geographical Distribution of Animals.* Vol. 1. London: Macmillan.

Wallace, P.A.W. and W.A. Hunter. 1981. *Indians in Pennsylvania.* 2d rev. ed. Harrisburg: Pennsylvania Historical and Museum Commission.

Wallach, B. 1980. Logging in Maine's empty quarter. *Annals of the Association of American Geographers* **70**:542–552.

Walsh, G.E. 1896. Hemlock for the tanneries. *Garden and Forest* **9**:222–223.

Walters, W.D., Jr. and F. Mansberger. 1983. Initial field location in Illinois. *Agricultural History* **57**:289–296.

Wang, D. 1984. Fire and nutrient dynamics in a pine–oak forest ecosystem in the New Jersey pine barrens. Ph.D. diss. Yale University.

Wansey, H. [1798]1970. *Henry Wansey and his American Journal.* Edited by D.J. Jeremy. Philadelphia: American Philosophical Society.

Warburton, D.B. and W.D. Klimstra. 1984. Wildlife use of no-till and conventionally tilled corn fields. *Journal of Soil and Water Conservation* **39**:327–330.

Ward, D. 1912. *The Autobiography of David Ward.* New York: Privately printed.

Ward, R.C. 1975. *Principles of Hydrology.* New York: McGraw-Hill.

Ward, R.T. 1956a. Vegetational change in a southern Wisconsin township. *Iowa Academy of Science* **63**:321–326.

Ward, R.T. 1956b. The beech forests of Wisconsin – changes in forest composition and the nature of the beech border. *Ecology* **37**:407–419.

Warden, D.B. 1819. *A Statistical, Political, and Historical Account of the United States of North America: From the Period of Their First Colonization to the Present Day.* 3 vols. Edinburgh: Archibald Constable and Company.

Warner, D.J. 1932. Trees on old boundaries. *Wooden Nutmeg* **8** (2):2.

Warren, J. 1787. Observations on agriculture – its advantages – and the causes that have in America prevented improvements in husbandry. *American Museum* **2**:344–348.

Washington, G. 1925. *The Diaries of George Washington 1748–1799. Vol. I (1748–1770).* Edited by J.C. Fitzpatrick. Boston: Houghton Mifflin.

Watson, D.G. 1978. Shade and ornamental trees in the nineteenth century northeastern United States. Ph.D. diss. University of Illinois at Urbana-Champaign.

Watson, J.F. 1830. *Annals of Philadelphia and Pennsylvania in the Olden Times.* Philadelphia: U. Hunt.

Watson, W.C. 1866. Forests – their influence, uses and reproduction. *Transactions of the New York State Agricultural Society* **25**:288–303.

Weaver, G.T. and W.C. Ashby. 1971. Composition and structure of an old-growth forest remnant in unglaciated southwestern Illinois. *American Midland Naturalist* **86**:46–56.

Weaver, J.E. 1954. *North American Prairie.* Lincoln, Neb.: Johnsen Publishing Company.

Weaver, J.E. and F.E. Clements. 1929. *Plant Ecology.* New York: McGraw-Hill.

Weaver, J.E. and T.J. Fitzpatrick. 1934. The prairie. *Ecological Monographs* **4**:109–295.

Weaver, J.E. and E.L. Flory. 1934. Stability of climax prairie and some environmental changes resulting from breaking. *Ecology* **15**:333–347.

Weaver, M.M. 1964. *History of Tile Drainage in America Prior to 1900*. Waterloo, N.Y.: M.M. Weaver.

Webb, T., III. 1973. A comparison of modern and presettlement pollen from southern Michigan (U.S.A.). *Review of Palaeobotany and Palynology* **16**:137–156.

Webb, T., III. 1974. Corresponding patterns of pollen and vegetation in lower Michigan: A comparison of quantitative data. *Ecology* **55**:17–28.

Webb, W.P. 1931. *The Great Plains*. Boston: Ginn.

Webster, N. [1799]1843. Dissertation on the supposed change of temperature in modern winters. In N. Webster (ed.), *A Collection of Papers on Political, Literary, and Moral Subjects*, 119–162. New York: Webster and Clark.

Webster, N. 1817. Domestic economy. *Connecticut Courant* [a Hartford, Conn. newspaper]. Vol. 53, no. 2726 (April 22, 1817):1.

Weeden, W.B. [1890]1963. *Economic and Social History of New England, 1620–1789*. Reprint. New York: Hillary House Publishers.

Weld, I. [1807]1968. *Travels Through the States of North America*. 2 vols. Reprint. New York: Johnson Reprint Company.

Welles, J. 1823. Letter from the Honorable John Welles, to the Corresponding Secretary, on forest trees. *New England Farmer* **1**:329–330.

Welles, J. 1824. Hon. Mr. Welles on grasses. *New England Farmer* **2**:252–253.

Welles, J. 1831. Woodland and forest trees. *Massachusetts Agricultural Journal* **10**:293–301.

Wells, C.G., R.E. Campbell, L.F. DeBano, C.E. Lewis, R.L. Fredriksen, E.C. Franklin, R.C. Froelich and P.H. Dunn. 1979. *Effects of fire on soil: A state-of-knowledge review*. USDA Forest Service General Technical Report, no. WO-7. Washington, D.C.: GPO.

Wells, R.W. 1819. On the origin of prairies. *American Journal of Science and Arts* **1**:331–337.

Wendt, K.M. 1984. *A Guide to Minnesota Prairies*. St. Paul: Natural Heritage Program, Minnesota Department of Natural Resources.

Wentworth, E.N. 1948. *America's Sheep Trails*. Ames: Iowa State College Press.

Westveld, M. 1930. *Suggestions for the management of spruce stands in the Northeast*. USDA Circular, no. 134. Washington, D.C.: USDA.

Westveld, M. 1931. *Reproduction on pulpwood lands in the Northeast*. USDA Technical Bulletin, no. 223. Washington, D.C.: USDA.

Westveld, M. 1953. Ecology and silviculture of the spruce–fir forests of eastern North America. *Journal of Forestry* **51**:422–431.

Westveld, M., R.I. Ashman, H.I. Baldwin, R.P. Holdsworth, R.S. Johnson, J.H. Lambert, H.J. Lutz, L. Swain and M. Standish. 1956. Natural forest vegetation zones of New England. *Journal of Forestry* **54**:332–338.

Wheaton, J.M. 1882. Report on the birds of Ohio. In *Report of the Geological Survey of Ohio*. Vol. 4. *Zoology and Botany*, 187–612. Columbus, Ohio: Nevins and Myers, State Printers.

Whitcomb, R.F. 1977. Island biogeography and 'habitat islands' of eastern forest. *American Birds* **31**:3–5.

Whitcomb, R.F., C.S. Robbins, J.F. Lynch, B.L. Whitcomb, M.K. Klimkiewicz and D. Bystrak. 1981. Effects of forest fragmentation on avifauna of eastern deciduous forests. In R.L. Burgess and D.M. Sharpe (eds.), *Forest Island Dynamics in Man-Dominated Landscapes*, 125–206. New York: Springer-Verlag.

White, C.A. 1984a. *A History of the Rectangular Survey System*. Washington, D.C.: US Department of the Interior, Bureau of Land Management.

White, J. 1981. A survey of Illinois prairies. In R.L. Stuckey and K.J. Reese (eds.),

The Prairie Peninsula – In the 'Shadow' of Transeau: Proceedings of the Sixth North American Prairie Conference. Biological Notes no. 15, 172. Columbus: Ohio Biological Survey.

White, J. 1986. Why bother to protect prairies along railroads. In G.K. Clambey and R.H. Pemble (eds.), *The Prairie – Past, Present, and Future: Proceedings of the Ninth North American Prairie Conference*, 172–173. Fargo: TriCollege University Center for Environmental Studies, North Dakota State University.

White, J. and M.H. Madany. 1981. Classification of prairie communities in Illinois. In R.L. Stuckey and K.J. Reese (eds.), *The Prairie Peninsula – In the 'Shadow' of Transeau: Proceedings of the Sixth North American Prairie Conference.* Biological Notes no. 15, *169–171*, Columbus: Ohio Biological Survey.

White, J.H., Jr. 1981. Railroads: Wood to burn. In B. Hindle (ed.), *Material Culture of the Wooden Age*, 184–224. Tarrytown, N.Y.: Sleepy Hollow Press.

White, P.L. 1979. *Beekmantown, New York: Forest Frontier to Farm Community.* Austin, Texas: University of Texas Press.

White, R. 1984b. Native Americans and the environment. In W.R. Swagerty (ed.), *Scholars and the Indian Experience*, 179–204. Bloomington: Indiana University Press.

White, R. 1985. American environmental history: the development of a new historical field. *Pacific Historical Review* **54**:297–335.

Whitford, P.B. 1970. Edaphic factors in the prairie–forest border in Wisconsin. In P. Schramm (ed.), *Proceedings of a Symposium on Prairie and Prairie Restoration.* Special Publication no. 3, 18–19. Galesburg, Ill.: Knox College Biological Field Station.

Whitford, P.B. 1976. Resprouting capacity of oak roots: A ten-year experiment. *Michigan Botanist* **15**:89–92.

Whitford, P.B. and K. Whitford. 1971. Savanna in central Wisconsin. *Vegetatio* **23**:77–87.

Whitney, G.G. 1982. Vegetation–site relationships in the presettlement forests of northeastern Ohio. *Botanical Gazette* **143**:225–237.

Whitney, G.G. 1984. Fifty years of change in the arboreal vegetation of Heart's Content, an old growth hemlock–white pine–northern hardwood stand. *Ecology* **65**:403–408.

Whitney, G.G. 1985. A quantitative analysis of the flora and plant communities of a representative Midwestern U.S. town. *Urban Ecology* **9**:143–160.

Whitney, G.G. 1986. Relation of Michigan's presettlement pine forests to substrate and disturbance history. *Ecology* **67**:1548–1559.

Whitney, G.G. 1987. An ecological history of the Great Lakes forest of Michigan. *Journal of Ecology* **75**:667–684.

Whitney, G.G. 1990. The history and status of the hemlock–hardwood forests of the Allegheny Plateau. *Journal of Ecology* **78**:443–458.

Whitney, G.G. and S.D. Adams. 1980. Man as a maker of new plant communities. *Journal of Applied Ecology* **17**:431–448.

Whitney, G.G. and W.C. Davis. 1986. From primitive woods to cultivated woodlots: Thoreau and the forest history of Concord, Massachusetts. *Journal of Forest History* **30**:70–81.

Whitney, G.G. and D.R. Foster. 1988. Overstory composition and age as determinants of the understory flora of woods of central New England. *Journal of Ecology* **76**:867–876.

Whitney, G.G. and R.E. Moeller. 1982. An analysis of the vegetation of Mt. Cardigan, New Hampshire: A rocky, subalpine New England summit. *Bulletin of the Torrey Botanical Club* **109**:177–188.

Whitney, G.G. and J.R. Runkle. 1981. Edge versus age effects in the development of a beech–maple forest. *Oikos* **37**:377–381.

Whitney, G.G. and W.J. Somerlot. 1985. A case study of woodland continuity and change in the American Midwest. *Biological Conservation* **31**:265–287.

Whitney, G.G. and J.R. Steiger. 1985. Site-factor determinants of the presettlement prairie–forest border areas of north-central Ohio. *Botanical Gazette* **146**:421–430.

Whitney, J.D. 1876. Plain, prairie and forest. *American Naturalist* **10**:577–588, 656–667.

Whitney, M. 1901. *Exhaustion and abandonment of soils.* USDA Report, no. 70. Washington, D.C.: GPO.

Whitney, P. 1793. *History of the County of Worcester.* Worcester, Mass.: Isaiah Thomas.

Whittaker, R.H. and P.L. Marks. 1975. Methods of assessing terrestrial productivity. In H. Lieth and R.H. Whittaker (eds.), *Primary Productivity of the Biosphere*, 55–118. New York: Springer-Verlag.

Whittlesey, C. 1843. Drives. *American Pioneer* **2** (2):54–57.

Whitworth, W.R., P.L. Berrien and W.T. Keller. 1968. *Freshwater fishes of Connecticut.* State Geological and Natural History Survey of Connecticut Bulletin, no. 101. Hardford: Connecticut Department of Agriculture and Natural Resources.

Wible, R.C. 1951. The anthracite region – a challenge in conservation. *Pennsylvania Forests* **36**:69–70, 85.

Widner, R.R. (ed.) 1968. *Forests and Forestry in the American States: A Reference Anthology.* Washington, D.C.: National Association of State Foresters.

Widrlechner, M.P. 1983. Historical and phenological observations on the spread of *Chaenorrhinum minus* across North America. *Canadian Journal of Botany* **61**:179–187.

Wilcove, D.S. 1985. Nest predation in forest birds and the decline of migratory songbirds. *Ecology* **66**:1211–1214.

Wilcove, D.S. 1988. Changes in the avifauna of the Great Smoky Mountains: 1947–1983. *Wilson Bulletin* **100**:256–271.

Wilcove, D.S., C.H. McLellan and A.P. Dobson. 1986. Habitat fragmentation in the temperate zone. In M.E. Soule (ed.), *Conservation Biology: The Science of Scarcity and Diversity*, 237–256. Sunderland, Mass.: Sinauer Associates.

Wilde, S.A. 1964. Changes in soil productivity induced by pine plantations. *Soil Science* **97**:276–278.

Wilhelm, S.A. 1953. History of the lumber industry of the Upper Allegheny River Basin during the nineteenth century. Ph.D. diss. Unversity of Pittsburgh.

Wilkins, A.H. 1978. *Ten Million Acres of Timber: The Remarkable Story of Forest Protection in the Maine Forestry District (1909–1972).* Woolwich, Maine: TBW Books.

Williams, A.B. 1949. *The native forests of Cuyahoga County, Ohio.* Holden Arboretum Bulletin, no. 1 and Scientific Publications of the Cleveland Museum of Natural History, vol. 9. Cleveland, Ohio.

Williams, D.L. 1981. Reconstruction of Prairie Peninsula vegetation and its characteristics from descriptions before 1860. In R.L. Stuckey and K.J. Reese (eds.), *The Prairie Peninsula – In the 'Shadow' of Transeau: Proceedings of the Sixth North American Prairie Conference.* Biological Notes no. 15, 83–86. Columbus: Ohio Biological Survey.

Williams, J. 1843. Our cabin; or, life in the woods. *American Pioneer* **2** (10):434–459.

Williams, M. 1980. Products of the forest: Mapping the census of 1840. *Journal of*

Forest History **24**:4–23.

Williams, M. 1982. Clearing the United States forests: The pivotal years, 1818–1860. *Journal of Historical Geography* **8**:12–28.

Williams, M. 1983. Pioneer farm life and forest use. In R.C. Davis (ed.), *Encyclopedia of American Forest and Conservation History.* Vol. 2, 529–534. New York: Macmillan Publishing Company.

Williams, M. 1984. Predicting from inventories: A timely issue. *Journal of Forest History* **28**:92–98.

Williams, M. 1989. *Americans and their Forests: A Historical Geography.* Cambridge: Cambridge University Press.

Williams, R. [1643]1810. A key into the language of the Indians of New England. *Massachusetts Historical Society Collections* **3**:203–238.

Williams, R. 1963. *The Complete Writings of Roger Williams.* 7 vols. New York: Russell and Russell.

Williams, S. 1794. *The Natural and Civil History of Vermont.* Walpole, N.H.: Isiah Thomas and David Carlisle.

Williams, S. 1809. *Natural and Civil History of Vermont.* 2d ed. 2 vols. Burlington, Vt.: Samuel Mills.

Williamson, H. 1789. An attempt to account for the change of climate, which has been observed in the Middle Colonies in North-America. *Transactions of the American Philosophical Society* **1**:336–345.

Williamson, L.L. 1987. Evolution of a landmark law. In H. Kallman (ed.), *Restoring America's Wildlife: 1937–1987.* USDI Fish and Wildlife Service, 1–13. Washington, D.C.: GPO.

Williamson, R.D. 1974. Birds in Washington, D.C. In J.H. Noyes and D.R. Progulske (eds.), *Wildlife in an Urbanizing Environment,* 131–135. Massachusetts Cooperative Extension Service Monograph, Planning and Resource Development Series, no. 28. Amherst: University of Massachusetts.

Willis, G. 1840. *American Husbandry; Being a Series of Essays on Agriculture.* 2 vols. New York: Harper and Brothers.

Willis, G.L. and M.S. Coffman. 1975. *Composition, structure, and dynamics of climax stands of eastern hemlock and sugar maple on the Huron Mountains, Michigan.* Technical Bulletin, no. 13. L'Anse, Mich.: Ford Forestry Center.

Willman, H.B. and J.C. Frye. 1970. *Pleistocene stratigraphy of Illinois.* Bulletin, no. 94. Urbana: Illinois State Geological Survey.

Willoughby, C.C. 1906. Houses and gardens of the New England Indians. *American Anthropologist* n.s. **8**:115–132.

Wilm, H.G. 1946. The status of watershed management concepts. *Journal of Forestry* **44**:968–971.

Wilson, G.R. 1919. Early Indiana trails and surveys. *Indiana Historical Society Publications* **6**:347–457.

Wilson, J.P. 1989. Soil erosion from agricultural land in the Lake Simcoe–Couchiching basin, 1800–1981. *Canadian Journal of Soil Science* **69**:137–151.

Wilson, J.P. and C.M. Ryan. 1988. Landscape change in the Lake Simcoe–Couchiching basin, 1800–1983. *Canadian Geographer* **32**:206–222.

Wilson, J.S. 1868. *Report of the Commissioner of the General Land Office for the Year 1868.* Washington, D.C.: GPO.

Winer, H. 1955. History of the Great Mountain Forest, Litchfield County, Connecticut. Ph.D. diss. Yale University.

Wines, R.A. 1981. The nineteenth-century agricultural transition in an eastern Long Island community. *Agricultural History* **55**:50–63.

Winkler, M.G. 1985. A 12,000-year history of vegetation and climate for Cape Cod, Massachusetts. *Quaternary Research* **23**:301–312.

Winslow, E. [1624]1844. *Good News from New England.* Reprinted in A. Young (ed.), *Chronicles of the Pilgrim Fathers,* 267–375. Boston: C.C. Little and J. Brown.

Winslow, E. 1925. Letter to England, 1621. In *America: A Library of Original Sources.* Vol. 2. Chicago: Veterans of Foreign Wars.

Winsor, R.A. 1975. Artificial drainage of east central Illinois 1820–1920. Ph.D. diss. University of Illinois.

Winter, T.C. and H.E. Wright Jr. 1977. Paleohyrologic phenomena recorded by lake sediments. *EOS* **58**:188–196.

Winthrop, J. [1866]1896. *Winthrop's conclusions for the plantation in New England.* Old South Leaflets. General series, vol. 2, no. 50. Boston: Directors of the Old South Work.

Winthrop, J. 1929. Common greuances groaninge for reformation. In *Winthrop Papers.* Vol. 1, 295–299. Boston: Massachusetts Historical Society.

Winthrop, J. 1976. John Winthrop to Sir Nathaniel Rich, May 22, 1634. In E. Emerson (ed.), *Letters from New England: The Massachusetts Bay Colony, 1629–1638,* 115–118. Amherst: University of Massachusetts Press.

Winthrop, J., Jr. [1756]1968. Of the manner of making tar and pitch in New England. In T. Birch (ed.), *The History of the Royal Society of London for Improving of Natural Knowledge from its First Rise.* Facsimile of the London edition of 1756–57. Vol. 1, 99–102. New York: Johnson Reprint Corporation.

Winthrop, J., Jr. 1863. Letter to John Winthrop, Sr. (April 7, 1636). *Massachusetts Historical Society Collections,* 4th ser., **6**:514.

Winthrop, J., Jr. 1882. Letter from John Winthrop, Jr. to Henry Oldenburgh, July 25, 1668. In the 'Winthrop Papers'. *Massachusetts Historical Society Collections,* 5th ser., **8**:121–125.

Wirt, G.H. 1936. *Lessons in forest protection.* Bulletin, no. 35 (5th ed.). Harrisburg: Pennsylvania Department of Forests and Waters.

Witthoft, J. 1953. The American Indian-hunter. *Pennsylvania Game News* **24** (2):12–16.

Wolcott, O., Jr. 1832. Report of plan to collect direct taxes from states. *American State Papers: Finance.* Vol. 1, 414–465. Washington, D.C.: Gales and Seaton.

Wolman, M.G. 1967. A cycle of sedimentation and erosion in urban river channels. *Geografiska Annaler* **49A**:385–395.

Wommack, K. 1986. Nature Conservancy buys old-growth Maine forest. *Northern Logger and Timber Processor* **35** (2):23–24.

Wood, J.S. 1978. The origin of the New England village. Ph.D. diss. Pennsylvania State University.

Wood, J.W. 1880. Clearing off timberland. *Transactions of the Wisconsin State Agricultural Society* **18**:136–144.

Wood, R.G. 1935. *A History of Lumbering in Maine, 1820–1861.* University of Maine Studies, 2d ser., no. 33. Orono: Maine University Press.

Wood, S. 1828. *A Sketch of the First Settlement of the Several Towns on Long Island; With their Political Condition, to the End of the American Revolution.* Brooklyn, N.Y.: Allen Spooner.

Wood, T. 1875. Should the farmers of America oppose further the destruction of our forests? *Transactions of the Pennsylvania State Agricultural Society* **10**:153–155.

Wood, W. [1634]1977. *New England's Prospect.* Edited by A.T. Vaughan. Amherst: University of Massachusetts Press.

Wood, W.R. 1976. Vegetation reconstruction and climatic episodes. *American*

Antiquity **41**:206–208.

Woodruff, F.M. 1907. *The birds of the Chicago area*. Natural History Survey. Bulletin, no. 6. Chicago: Chicago Academy of Sciences.

Woods, B. 1984. Ants disperse seed of herb species in a restored maple forest (Wisconsin). *Restoration and Mangement Notes* 2(1):29–30.

Woods, J. [1822]1968. *Two Years Residence on the English Prairie of Illinois*. Edited by P.M. Angle. Reprint. Chicago: R.R. Donnelley and Sons.

Woods, K.D. 1974. Reciprocal replacement and the maintenance of codominance in a beech–maple forest. *Oikos* **33**:31–39.

Woodward, S.M. and F.A. Nagler. 1929. The effect of agricultural drainage upon flood run-off. *Transactions of the American Society of Civil Engineers* **93**:821–839.

Woodworth, H.C. 1937. A century of adjustments in a New Hampshire back area. *Agricultural History* **11**:223–237.

Woodworth, H.C., M.F. Abell and J.C. Holmes. 1937. *Land utilization in New Hampshire*. Bulletin, no. 298. Durham: New Hampshire Agricultural Experiment Station.

Woollett, M.L. and D. Sigler. 1928. Revegetation of beech–maple areas in the Douglas Lake Region. *Torreya* **28**:21–28.

Wooten, H.H. and L.A. Jones. 1955. The history of our drainage enterprises. In *Water, USDA Yearbook of Agriculture, 1955*, 478–491. Washington, D.C.: GPO.

Worster, D. 1979. *Dust Bowl: The Southern Plains in the 1930s*. New York: Oxford University Press.

Worster, D. 1988. Appendix: Doing environmental history. In D. Worster (ed.), *The Ends of the Earth: Perspectives on Modern Environmental History*, 289–307. Cambridge: Cambridge University Press.

Worthington, E. 1827. *The History of Dedham, from the Beginning of its Settlement in September, 1635 to May 1827*. Boston: Dutton and Wentworth.

Wright, C.D. 1887. *The Census of Massachusetts: 1885*. Vol. 3. *Agricultural Products and Property*. Boston: Wright and Potter Printing Company, State Printers.

Wright, H.E., Jr. 1974. Landscape development, forest fires, and wilderness management. *Science* **186**:487–495.

Wyckoff, W. 1981. Assessing land quality in western New York: The township surveys of 1797–1799. *Surveying and Mapping* **41**:315–325.

Yarnell, R.A. 1964. *Aboriginal relationships between culture and plant life in the Upper Great Lakes region*. Anthropological Paper, no. 23. Ann Arbor: Museum of Anthropology, University of Michigan.

Yarnell, R.A. 1976. Early plant husbandry in eastern North America. In C.E. Cleland (ed.), *Cultural Change and Continuity: Essays in Honor of Jame Bennett Griffin*, 265–273. New York: Academic Press.

Yeatter, R.E. 1963. Population responses of prairie chickens to land-use changes in Illinois. *Journal of Wildlife Management* **27**:739–757.

Young, G. 1952. Tree distribution in St. Clair and Macomb Counties, Michigan. Masters thesis. University of Michigan.

Young, K.K. 1980. The impact of erosion on the productivity of soils in the United States. In M. DeBoodt and D. Gabriels (eds.), *Assessment of Erosion*, 295–303. New York: John Wiley and Sons.

Youngquist, W.G. and H. Fleischer. 1977. *Wood in American Life, 1776–2076*. Madison, Wis.: Forest Products Research Society.

Zasada, Z.A. 1952. *Reproduction on cut-over swamplands in the Upper Peninsula of Michigan*. USDA Forest Service Lake States Forest Experiment Station Paper, no. 27. St. Paul, Minn.: Lake States Forest Experiment Station.

Zawacki, A.A., G. Hausfater and J.T. Meyers. 1969. *Early vegetation of the lower Illinois Valley: A study of the distribution of floral resources with reference to prehistoric cultural–ecological adaptations*. Illinois State Museum, Reports of Investigations, no. 17. Springfield: Illinois State Museum.

Zeevaart, J.A.D. 1989. *Agrostemma githago*. In A.H. Halevy (ed.), *Handbook of Flowering*. Vol. 6, 15–21. Boca Raton, Fla.: CRC Press.

Zeide, B. 1981. Method of mound dating. *Forest Science* **27**:39–41.

Zeisberger, D. 1910. David Zeisberger's history of the northern American Indians. Edited by A B. Hulbert and W.N. Schwarze. *Ohio Archaeological and Historical Society Publications* **19**:1–173.

Zicker, W.A. 1955. An analysis of Jefferson County vegetation using surveyors' records and present day data. M.S. thesis. University of Wisconsin.

Zobler, L. 1962. An economic-historical view of natural resource use and conservation. *Economic Geography* **38**:189–194.

Zon, R. 1914. *Balsam fir*. USDA Bulletin, no. 55. Washington, D.C.: US Department of Agriculture.

Zon, R. 1927. *Forests and water in the light of scientific investigation*. Reprinted with revised bibliography, 1927, from Appendix V of the Final Report of the National Waterways Commission, 1912. Washington, D.C.: GPO.

Zon, R. 1928. *Timber growing and logging practice in the Lake States*. USDA Bulletin, no. 1496. Washington, D.C.: US Department of Agriculture.

Zon, R. and H.F. Scholz. 1929. *How fast do northern hardwoods grow?* Research Bulletin, no. 88. Madison: Wisconsin Agricultural Experiment Station of the University of Wisconsin.

Index

444